THE INTELLECTUAL PROPERTY OF NATIONS

Drawing on macro-historical sociological theories, this book traces the development of intellectual property as a new type of legal property in the modern nation-state system. In its current form, intellectual property is considered part of an infrastructure of state power that incentivizes innovation, creativity, and scientific development, all engines of economic growth. To show how this infrastructure of power emerged, Laura Ford follows macro-historical social theorists, including Michael Mann and Max Weber, back to antiquity, revealing that legal instruments very similar to modern intellectual property have existed for a long time and have also been deployed for similar purposes. Using comparative and historical evidence, this groundbreaking work reflects on the role of intellectual property in our contemporary political communities and societies; on the close relationship between law and religion; and on the extent to which law's obliging force depends on ancient, written traditions.

Laura R. Ford is Assistant Professor of Sociology at Bard College. Professor Ford is a former attorney turned sociologist, specializing in historical sociology and the sociological theory of Max Weber.

The Intellectual Property of Nations

SOCIOLOGICAL AND HISTORICAL PERSPECTIVES ON A MODERN LEGAL INSTITUTION

LAURA R. FORD
Bard College

CAMBRIDGE
UNIVERSITY PRESS

CAMBRIDGE
UNIVERSITY PRESS

University Printing House, Cambridge CB2 8BS, United Kingdom

One Liberty Plaza, 20th Floor, New York, NY 10006, USA

477 Williamstown Road, Port Melbourne, VIC 3207, Australia

314–321, 3rd Floor, Plot 3, Splendor Forum, Jasola District Centre, New Delhi – 110025, India

79 Anson Road, #06–04/06, Singapore 079906

Cambridge University Press is part of the University of Cambridge.

It furthers the University's mission by disseminating knowledge in the pursuit of education, learning, and research at the highest international levels of excellence.

www.cambridge.org
Information on this title: www.cambridge.org/9781107198975
DOI: 10.1017/9781108182935

First published 2021

A catalogue record for this publication is available from the British Library.

ISBN 978-1-107-19897-5 Hardback
ISBN 978-1-316-64848-3 Paperback

Contents

Preface and Acknowledgments

This book represents nearly two decades of study and discussion, building on learning gleaned from generous senior colleagues as a junior attorney, fresh out of law school, to academic study of intellectual property law and sociology, then onward to doctoral and postdoctoral study, with the benefit to learning that comes from teaching. I have accumulated many debts along the way, most of which will regretfully remain unacknowledged.

My first debt is to my parents, without whom, in all senses, this book would not be. I cannot adequately express my gratitude for all the support (material and spiritual) that they have given, and this book is dedicated to them. To my father, Robert Orland Ford, who dedicated time out of an intensely busy schedule to read and comment on nearly the entire draft manuscript, and to the memory of my mother, Blanche Elizabeth Ford, who exemplified a deep commitment to compassion and justice, a beautiful person, inside and out. I wish I could have known and loved her better.

My next debt is to the University of Washington Law School's LL.M. program in intellectual property law and policy, and to my professors Bob Gomulkiewicz, Dan Laster, Sean O'Connor, and Toshiko Takenaka. Early foundations for this book were laid in my sociology dissertation work at Cornell University, and I thank my sociology faculty advisers and committee members, especially Mabel Berezin, Steve Morgan, and Richard Swedberg. For guidance in the final stages of transforming my dissertation into a book, I am grateful to the Baldy Center for Law and Social Policy, where I was fortunate to be placed in a postdoctoral fellowship between 2014 and 2016. Thank you to the Baldy Center, and especially to Errol Meidinger, for hosting a book manuscript workshop in April 2019, and thank you to Mark Bartholomew, Philip Gorski, and Damon Mayrl for taking the time to read my long manuscript and offering wise and helpful comments. Thank you also to the other participants in that workshop, who generously gave their time in reading and commenting on the draft manuscript.

Bard College colleagues and students have read and offered comments on various chapters. I am especially grateful to Rob Cioffi, Gregory ("Duff") Morton, and to the many Bard students who have challenged and deepened my thinking. I hope this book will speak to them, and to their generation.

I owe a debt of gratitude to Dr. Péter Mezei, Associate Professor of Law in the Faculty of Law, University of Szeged. Over the summer of 2020, as I was finishing the book, Dr. Mezei read every chapter, providing helpful (and encouraging) feedback. While I have not been able to address all aspects of Dr. Mezei's comments, I do hope that he will see the fruits of his labors in the final product.

Chapters 7–9 draw on material that was originally published in the *Journal of the Patent and Trademark Office Society*, Volume 97, No. 2, and I gratefully acknowledge that original opportunity to publish my arguments about the prerogative-based roots of modern patent law.

Finally, I am so grateful to my editor at Cambridge, Matt Gallaway, for extraordinary patience and kindness, as I have worked my way, painstakingly, toward completion.

Introduction

I first learned about intellectual property in law school. The conversation comes back to me quite vividly. I was speaking with a friend who was taking a course in patent law. She had studied engineering in college, and therefore had the requisite technical background for a career in patent law. She introduced me to the legal conception of patents as a type of property. I vaguely knew about copyrights, trademarks, and patents but had never considered them *as property*. The notion that such abstract things could be property was completely fascinating, but I set the interest aside and continued along my own path, which I hoped would take me to a career in human rights law.

What I found instead was a career in state and local government law, specifically the law that governs fiscal, economic, and financial affairs of municipal governments. I came to see governmental organizations – like counties, cities, and states – in a whole new way, as economically rooted communities that are formed in specific historical contexts to accomplish social and political goals, some of which are so complex, controversial, and challenging that they need specialized attention and leadership. And I learned something about the long historical path along which these kinds of economically rooted, political communities – I will call them *governing communities* – have been traveling, a path that I believe can help to shed light on the way our governing communities of today might work.

This is a book about intellectual property, and about a long historical trajectory of governing communities. I believe they are two sides of the same coin.

Property depends on governing communities. Without organized groups of people who work together to protect property rights, at most we would have temporary possession of things. With organized political communities that endure over time, which recognize and defend legal definitions of property, we can have rights to property that persist even when we grant temporary possession to others, and even after we die. Once property rights are legally defined to enable property to continue across generations, and that definition is upheld within an enduring, organized community, we have property ownership in the fullest sense that we recognize (and perhaps tend to take for granted) today.[1]

As I see it, intellectual property is the latest in a long string of developments linking property to governing communities across time. In the economic sociology of Max Weber, I have found a theoretical framework that makes this make sense. Trained as both a lawyer and an economic historian, Weber had a breadth of historical vision that encompassed communities and societies from antiquity to modernity, east to west. And he had a theory of property that I think is true.[2]

For Weber, things become property because they are first enclosed, appropriated, and protected by a group. By taking something over (e.g., a piece of land), creating boundaries against outsiders, and protecting those boundaries, a group controls and essentially monopolizes the thing. And, when we see groups and things with the breadth of vision that Weber had, we see that almost anything can be monopolized by a group: not only land and money, but also rights to wear certain kinds of clothes, rights to eat particular kinds of food, rights to worship particular gods, and rights to use knowledge in particular kinds of ways. Once a group has appropriated and monopolized a thing, whatever it may be, the group can define rights of access and use within the group, and it can privilege certain members of the group by giving them exclusive access and use. The group can even go so far as to say that privileged persons have rights to freely exchange the appropriated things, and to pass them down to their descendants by a formal declaration of intention (a "will"). According to Weber's theory of property, we have full-fledged ownership (*Eigentum*) at this point – the point at which property rights are freely transferable and are passed across generations through inheritance.[3]

A concrete example of this type of group-based appropriation, one that played an important role in the emergence of intellectual property, is the guild. Guilds are social organizations (communities) that govern craftsmanship of various kinds, ranging across history from artisans in ancient Greece to printers in early modern London. Typically, in order to exercise a particular type of craft – for example, the

[1] This is essentially a summary of Max Weber's sociological theory of property, a theory that Weber developed in the earliest parts of his encyclopedic project in economic sociology, which was published after his death as *Economy and Society* (*Wirtschaft und Gesellschaft*). Weber retained and refined this theory of property in the chapters of *Economy and Society*, which he completed right before his death in 1920. Max Weber, *Economy and Society*, edited by Guenther Roth and Claus Wittich, 2d ed. (Berkeley: University of California Press, 2013), 43–6, 339–48. See also Richard Swedberg, *Max Weber and the Idea of Economic Sociology* (Princeton: Princeton University Press, 1998), 39–45.

[2] Weber, *Economy and Society*, 43–6, 339–48; Swedberg, *Max Weber and the Idea*, 39–45 and passim.

[3] Weber, *Economy and Society*, 43–6, 339–48; Swedberg, *Max Weber and the Idea*, 39–45. I see close analogues to this way of theorizing property in the new institutionalist theories of Yoram Barzel, Douglass North, and Elinor Ostrom. See, for example, Yoram Barzel, *Economic Analysis of Property Rights*, 2d ed. (New York: Cambridge University Press, 1997); Douglass C. North, *Structure and Change in Economic History* (New York: W. W. Norton, 1981); Elinor Ostrom, *Governing the Commons* (Cambridge, UK: Cambridge University Press, 1990). I also see close connections to recent, neo-Aristotelian legal theories of property. See, for example, Gregory S. Alexander, *Property and Human Flourishing* (Oxford: Oxford University Press, 2018).

craft of printing – a person would have to be admitted into the local guild. If the person was not a member of the guild, he could not exercise the craft, and guilds have often had powerful ways of enforcing their rules, for example, the power to search houses and destroy machinery (like a printing press) that, according to the guild's rules, should only be used within the guild. The guild, in other words, monopolized the craft and controlled access to the craft. The guild also controlled the exercise of the craft, ideally ensuring that all persons admitted to the guild were provided with a minimal level of work and maintaining an overall level of quality in the guild's products. Guild officers distributed work, policed the quality of finished products, and often provided forms of insurance and pensions for dependent family members. From the perspective of Max Weber's theory of property, a guild is a governing community that appropriates and monopolizes a craft, which often means monopolizing both art and technology. In fact, as we will see, intellectual property emerged when the monopoly of a printers' guild – called the Stationers Company – was being taken over by an English and nationalizing state.[4]

The nation-state, as I see it, is a specific type of governing community and monopolizing/appropriating group, in Weber's sense. It is at once a cultural community, a political community, a military community, and an economic community, one that insists on being the primary appropriator within a defined territory, and that therefore seeks to control the existence of other governing communities (like cities and guilds) within the defined territory. As Weber famously argued, the nation-state fundamentally asserts a monopoly in the exercise of violent force within a defined territory. As the primary appropriator and monopolizer of violent enforcement in the modern world, the nation-state is the social condition that makes intellectual property possible, the sine qua non ("without which not") as lawyers sometimes say. What is it, though, about the nation-state that brings intellectual property into existence? This book is my effort to answer that question. The answer has everything to do with the historical trajectory of the nation-state, as a governing community, and as a monopolizing/appropriating group.[5]

4 For a general introduction to the role of guilds in the economic history of early modern Europe, see S. R. Epstein and Maarten Prak (eds.), *Guilds, Innovation and the European Economy*, 1400–1800 (New York: Cambridge University Press, 2008). For legal historical approaches to the role of guilds in the emergence of intellectual property, see, for example, Lyman Ray Patterson, *Copyright in Historical Perspective* (Nashville: Vanderbilt University Press, 1968); Ted Sichelman & Sean O'Connor, "Patents as Promoters of Competition: The Guild Origins of Patent Law in the Venetian Republic," *San Diego Law Review* 49: 1267–82 (2012). For Weber on guilds (and cities) as monopolizers and appropriators, see *Economy and Society*, 45–6, 339–48; Max Weber, *General Economic History*, translated by Frank H. Knight (Mineola, New York: Dover Publications, 2003), 115 ff. On the complexities of national identity in the British Isles, see Krishan Kumar, *The Making of English National Identity* (Cambridge, UK: Cambridge University Press, 2003).When we are speaking of a "United Kingdom of Great Britain," I am focusing on the period after 1707.

5 Weber, *Economy and Society*, 385–98, 901–40. I have incorporated Michael Mann's four ideal types of social power – ideological/cultural, economic, military, and political – into this discussion. As discussed later, I anchor aspects of my analysis throughout this book in Mann's theoretical framework, but I do so in the service of elaborating the more basic conception of nation-states as governing

To borrow from Hannah Arendt, I see the nation-state as a *project*, as a future into which we have politically willed ourselves. It is the latest in a very long series of efforts to build enduring, peaceful, and prosperous governing communities. It was designed to a very great extent by legal thinkers who drew on what they considered to be centuries of accumulated wisdom about how to build human communities and govern them justly. The US Constitutional Convention of 1787 is emblematic of the nation-state project, both in its transcendent hopes and in its devastating moral compromises. Intellectual property was built into the Constitution that Convention produced, and into the larger project of will that Convention entailed.[6]

The nation-state project, as I see it, places hope in accumulation of national wealth for future prosperity. It is a project of national, economic investment. Innovation in science, art, literature, and technology is seen as the key upon which a vision of economic growth and future prosperity depends. Intellectual property – the temporary ownership (by individuals or corporate groups) of innovative technologies and original creations – is seen as the great enabler of innovation and wealth creation. According to the prevailing economic theory of *public goods*, which is rooted in long historical experience, people will innovate and create more if they believe they can own, at least for a limited time, that which they originate. We moderns hope and believe that innovation and creativity are good for our national future, and so we authorize a temporary property – a temporary monopoly, backed ultimately by the nation-state's very real threat of violence – in innovation and creation in order to incentivize the things that we value. Nation-states have been built to be generators of innovation, for purposes of wealth-accumulation, and intellectual property is a legal engine that runs the generator (to borrow and adapt a metaphor from Abraham Lincoln).[7]

communities. I return to the language of governing communities in Chapter 12, and in the Conclusion to the book.

6 On projects of the will, see Hannah Arendt, *The Life of the Mind* (San Diego: Harcourt, Inc., 1977–78). On the legal-rational state as the creation of legal thinkers ("jurists"), see Max Weber, "The Social Psychology of World Religions," in H. H. Gerth and C. Wright Mills, *From Max Weber: Essays in Sociology* (New York: Oxford University Press, 1946), 299. I describe the way in which intellectual property was built into the US Constitution in Chapter 9. The short summary is that Article I, Section 8, Clause 8, of the Constitution empowered Congress to enact legislation that would grant time-limited property rights to authors and inventors.

7 I describe the economic theory of public goods that gives substantive legitimacy to modern intellectual property in Chapter 1. The belief that innovation is a key driver of economic growth is very widely shared not only by economists but also by policy-makers, as seen, for example, in a policy brief from the Organisation for Economic Cooperation and Development. OECD Policy Brief, "Science, Technology and Innovation in the New Economy," September 2000, available at www.oecd.org/science/sci-tech/1918259.pdf (accessed April 19, 2018). For Abraham Lincoln on intellectual property as a legal engine, see Chapter 1 and "Second Lecture on Discoveries and Inventions," first delivered February 11, 1859, in *Collected Works of Abraham Lincoln*, Volume 3, edited by Roy P. Basler (Brunswick, NJ: Rutgers University Press, 1953), 357–63, available at https://quod.lib.umich.edu/l/lincoln/lincoln3 (accessed September 8, 2017).

But, just as mechanical engines were designed from centuries of learning about physical forces, legal engines like intellectual property require centuries of learning to develop. As it turns out, governing communities have been in the business of incentivizing desirable activities for a long time, and they have done so using legal instruments that look a lot like intellectual property. Intellectual property, after all, is basically a privilege that is granted to the member of a group, because that member has done something that is valuable to the group. But it is a privilege that comes in the form of property, and this means that it comes with all the deep semantic (meaningful) resonances – together with very real political powers – that property has in western culture and political life. To understand those resonances, and therefore to understand why intellectual property is such a powerful legal engine, we have to reach deeply into a complex and multifaceted cultural tradition that has been powerfully formative for large parts of the world, including Europe, north Africa, western Asia, and the Americas: a cultural tradition formed from a synthesis of Roman and Biblical law.[8]

Many of our ideas about property – ideas that have provided the foundations for modern intellectual property – come ultimately from Rome. More precisely, those ideas come from Roman legal thinkers – I will follow Max Weber in calling them *jurists* – many of whom were not from, and may never have even seen, the city of Rome. These jurists took legal notions that were relatively common-sensical in the Mediterranean world of antiquity and refined them. Between the first and sixth centuries of our era, Roman jurists built an elaborate legal edifice, one that included abstract and systematized ideas about property and legal obligation. Ironically, although the Roman empire endured for a longer time in the east, Roman legal ideas sank in deeper in the west. Roman legal thinking became part of the western cultural DNA, so to speak, and developed together with governing communities. The crucial source of continuity between ancient Rome and the modern nation-state was the western church, which, according to medieval jurists, lives by Roman law.[9]

[8] On the importance of cultural synthesis between Biblical and Roman law for Western legal traditions, see Walter Ullmann, *Law and Politics in the Middle Ages: An Introduction to the Sources of Medieval Political Ideas* (London: Sources of History Limited, 1975).

[9] Max Weber articulated his conception of jurists as the bearers of a particular type of legal culture in his foundational essay on the economic sociology and history of law, now referred to in English as "The Developmental Conditions of the Law." The best English-language edition of this text is Max Rheinstein (ed.), *Max Weber on Law in Economy and Society* (New York: Simon and Schuster, 1967). The text is part of Weber's collected contributions to an *Encyclopedia of Social Economics*, which were published after his death as *Economy and Society*. Weber, *Economy and Society*, 641–900. For the famous description of the Roman Catholic Church as living according to Roman law, see the Laws of the Ripuarian Franks 61.1, in *Laws of the Salian and Ripuarian Franks*, translated by Theodore John Rivers (New York: AMS Press, 1986), 195. For helping me to locate the source of this common phrase, and for recognition that it is often misquoted, I am indebted to Michael Edward Moore, *A Sacred Kingdom: Bishops and the Rise of the Frankish Kingship, 300–850* (Washington, D.C.: Catholic University Press, 2011), 84.

And, with the western church – a governing community that, until the Reformation, was formally ruled by priests and bishops – we encounter an overtly religious source of our ideas about property: the Bible. For it is more correct to say that the western church has lived by Roman and Biblical law together. The synthesis of these two cultural traditions – Roman and Biblical law – has been complex and contested, and it has meant, for different times and peoples, radically different things with respect to community governance and property. One early Christian attitude toward property, articulated in *The Acts of the Apostles*, looks like something that would, at first glance, please the disciples of Karl Marx. But there are also attitudes of deep conservatism with respect to property, both in the Christian New Testament and in the books of the Hebrew Bible that Christians have called, with varying levels of respect, the Old Testament.[10]

Property is, in fact, a fundamental part of the promise to Abraham that prominent authors of the Christian scriptures spiritualized and reinterpreted as a universal promise of hope for all the nations of the world. This means that complex and contested ideas of property are built into a religious narrative that is, in different ways, significant for all the Abrahamic faith traditions – Judaism, Christianity, and Islam, in all their many varieties – one that I think helps to account for the cultural and political power of property in our societies today.[11]

In Abrahamic scriptural religion, as interpreted by Christians, property and law are built into a religious narrative about the way that history moves humanity into an eschatological future, a hoped-for time and place in which humans will come home to their ultimate and final governing community, one in which we will enjoy true prosperity and well-being. This eschatological future – a community of hope – is fundamental, I believe, to the basic logic – albeit one that is mostly hidden and taken for granted – by which intellectual property works today, offering as it does a vision of national prosperity that is part of the nation-state project, and that is connected to a culturally powerful narrative about property. Intellectual property, in other words, is a legal institution that taps into deep cultural well-springs, a semantic link between national hopes for the future and a participation in well-being that is interpretively connected with property.[12]

During the European "Middle Ages" – a dynamic and complex period stretching from Roman late antiquity to the early modern ages of Renaissance, Reformation,

10 Christian communitarian property: Acts 2:44–45, 4:31–5:11. Deep conservatism with respect to property in the Christian New Testament: Philemon; Titus 2:9–10. Deep conservatism with respect to property in the Hebrew Bible: Deuteronomy 19:14; Proverbs 22:28.

11 Genesis 15; Romans 4. On the spiritualization and universalization of the promises to Abraham, as seen in the writings of Paul and the author of Luke-Acts, see Luke Timothy Johnson, *Sacra Pagina: The Acts of the Apostles* (Collegeville, Minnesota: The Liturgical Press, 1992), 58. On the narrative significance of property and possession in the *Gospel of Luke* and the *Acts of the Apostles*, see Luke Timothy Johnson, *The Literary Function of Possession in Luke-Acts* (Missoula: Scholars Press, 1977).

12 *Cf.* Laura R. Ford, "Intellectual Property and Industrialization: Legalizing Hope in Economic Growth," *Theory and Society* 46:57–93 (2017).

and Enlightenment – Roman law and Biblical law were, together, interpreted anew, and new types of legal scholarship developed from a renewed study of Roman legal texts. At the same time, new types of governing community were built. Gradual breaks with patterns of community governance from late antiquity and the early Middle Ages were made, as communal movements channeled revolutionary social forces, implementing legal independence for Europe's cities, triggering the foundation of European universities, and repeatedly seeking to reform the church, culminating in division of the European church into national churches. Out of this messy and violent process, the modern nation-state came into existence. And running underneath the whole series of developments was a continuous experience in legal practice, an experience in the granting of legal privileges, which are meant to enable activities that are valued by the leaders of the governing community. Through this historical experience, a new and very this-worldly salvation logic was developed, a logic linking national wealth with property in novel products of the human mind.[13]

This book is an effort to tell the story about how intellectual property, as we know it, was formed from older privilege-granting practices. To borrow a phrase from two leading sociological theorists of today – Dan Hirschman and Isaac Reed – the story I will tell is a "social formation story," a story about how our modern nation-state project was formed from a combination of elements, and about how intellectual property was built into that project. It is, first and foremost, a story about the contribution of legal thinking and practice to this project. It is also, to my way of thinking, a story of great beauty and great tragedy. It involves a vision and a hope for law and legal communities that are intellectually beautiful, and it involves the tragedy of human fallibility, moral compromises, and unintended consequence, the gap between ideal and reality in law that no one yet has figured out how to close.[14]

Intellectual property, like law and the nation-state project, is lovely and brutal. It is very human, and this means that it involves the quest for meaning, freedom, and belonging that drives our tragic, human history.[15]

I will return to these tragic elements in the conclusion to this book, but to briefly preface now: the tragic aspect of intellectual property, as with all types of property, is

[13] On "this-worldly" salvation logics, see Max Weber, "Introduction to the Economic Ethics of the World Religions," in Sam Whimster (ed. & trans.), *The Essential Weber: A Reader* (Abingdon: Routledge, 2004); Max Weber, "Intermediate Reflection on the Economic Ethics of the World Religions," in Whimster, *Essential Weber*, 215–44; Weber, *Economy & Society*, 399–401, 526–29, 541–51, 576–79, 611–34. For a systematic integration of all the complex strands of Weberian sociology, focusing particularly on ethical attitudes toward the world engendered by religious traditions, see Wolfgang Schluchter, *Rationalism, Religion, and Domination*, translated by Neil Solomon (Berkeley: University of California Press, 1989). For understanding of the role played by secularization in our new and this-worldly salvation logic, I am indebted to Charles Taylor, *A Secular Age* (Cambridge, MA: Harvard University Press, 2007).

[14] On social formation stories, see Daniel Hirschman and Isaac Ariail Reed, "Formation Stories and Causality in Sociology," *Sociological Theory* 32(4): 259–82 (2014).

[15] Orlando Patterson, *Freedom in the Making of Western Culture* (New York: Basic Books, 1991).

seen most clearly in the historical fact that it is, paradoxically, both exclusive and inclusive. Intellectual property's very existence depends on the social fact that groups, like the nation-state, draw boundaries between insiders and outsiders, citizens and noncitizens. And, once intellectual property is recognized in some form, boundaries are drawn within the community, as well, enabling exclusivity on the part of the person or group that is privileged with ownership rights. This is the exclusive side of intellectual property, and it can mean excluding people from things that they desperately need, like life-saving medicines. But there is also an inclusive side. For intellectual property owners, and for those who hope to be intellectual property owners, property rights mean that they are members of a group that protects and includes them, recognizing the value of their creative contributions and liberating them to exercise a protected agency with respect to their innovative works. Property, freedom, and belonging are very closely linked, both in the cultural and semantic resonances that we connect with ideas of property and in the historical processes by which our nation-state project has been formed and has spread around the world.[16]

All this becomes especially evident in the history of intellectual property law, because intellectual property has emerged so recently, comparatively speaking. In telling a social formation story about how we have brought intellectual property into the world, I am also trying to say something more general about how property works in our modern world. In the ways we create property, we include some and exclude others. We use law to draw formalistic boundaries, and we orient ourselves to law – both secular and religious law – in our understandings about how this is legal, just, and reasonable. These are important social and political lessons, I believe, that we can learn from close attention to the lengthy historical development of intellectual property law.

METHODOLOGY AND STRUCTURE

Readers should be forewarned that this book is primarily a work of historically rooted theorizing, an effort to synthesize disparate historical sources across a vast sweep of time and space, elucidating a meaningful pattern. Recollection of the ancient semantic associations with *theoria* can be both useful and revealing in this context. As Andrea Wilson Nightingale reminds us, *theoria* was originally a political custom and cultural practice, one that involved journeying for the sake of learning. For example, a citizen from an ancient Greek city-state (polis) might be sent to another polis as a kind of ambassador, observing the foreign polis's religious festivals and rituals, bringing back a firsthand witness to what was seen. Similarly, travel to an

16 I am grateful to Philip Gorski for helping me to see how to articulate this tragic dimension of property ownership. The simultaneity of inclusion and exclusion with property is also highlighted by Hannah Arendt. Hannah Arendt, *The Human Condition*, 2d ed. (Chicago: University of Chicago Press, 1998), 58–73, 217.

internationally recognized oracle (e.g., the oracle at Delphi), to solicit a divine communication, would be an example of *theoria*.[17]

At its deepest historical root, then, the Greek-derived *theoria* evokes the learning that comes through a journey outside of an everyday social context, in the witnessing of a religious spectacle. In the Greek world of many poleis and many religious spectacles, *theoria* became a customary institution (*nomimos*), one closely connected with practical wisdom in governing political communities, and with ancient arts of diplomacy. With the entry of Platonic philosophy onto the world stage, however, *theoria* was transformed into something new: a vision of abstract truth and ultimate reality, one that nonetheless remained quite religious, in its own way.[18]

Sociologists – and social "science" writ large – owe more to Platonic philosophy than we like to admit. However, for contemporary sociologists, *theory* usually means something quite specific that seems to have no connection whatsoever with religion. Many sociologists, although by no means all, would want to say that theories offer a conceptual apparatus for causal explanation of social phenomena and/or events – social things that exist and/or occur. To theorize from this perspective would be to causally explain a social phenomenon at a highly generalized level. Theories are judged and compared on the basis of their explanatory capacity, that is, the degree to which they offer concepts of social action and causal processes that validly and reliably account for recurrent features of the social world, such as racial inequality, state formation, or inner-city poverty. In the ways that sociologists distinguish themselves from other scholars of the social world, particularly historians, sociological theory is often described as being more abstract and general. Unlike historians, who study events in a localized, spatiotemporal setting, sociologists offer general theories about the social world, theories that transcend localized, spatiotemporal settings.[19]

Historical narratives, from this prevailing perspective, are the very opposite thing from theory. Historical narratives describe particular events, whereas theories invoke general concepts and processes in offering an analytical explanation about general

17 Andrea Wilson Nightingale, *Spectacles of Truth in Classical Greek Philosophy: Theoria in Its Cultural Context* (Cambridge, UK: Cambridge University Press, 2004), ll. 78–140, 536–895; also Robert N. Bellah, "The Heritage of the Axial Age: Resource or Burden?," in *The Axial Age and Its Consequences*, edited by Robert N. Bellah and Hans Joas (Cambridge, MA: Belknap Press, 2012), 447–66.

18 Nightingale, *Spectacles*, Chapters 1–3. On the religious character of Platonic philosophy, as seen particularly in the connections between piety, holiness, and justice, and more generally in Plato's doctrine of the "forms," see John M. Rist, *Plato's Moral Realism: The Discovery of the Presuppositions of Ethics* (Washington, D.C.: The Catholic University of America, 2012), 43–8 and ff.

19 On the Platonic roots of social theory, see Alvin W. Gouldner, *Enter Plato: Classical Greece and the Origins of Social Theory* (New York: Basic Books, 1965). For an argument that contemporary US sociology involves a sacred, spiritual project with close connections to religion, see Christian Smith, *The Sacred Project of American Sociology* (Oxford: Oxford University Press, 2014). Max Weber offered a classic statement of the distinction between sociology and history as a distinction between levels of generality in explanation. Weber, *Economy and Society*, 19–22.

features of the social world. To tell a story is to do what is for most sociologists the very antithesis of theorizing.

I disagree. And I am not alone in doing so. In both classical and contemporary sociology, there are strong advocates for the value of narratives in sociological explanations. Indeed, according to one prominent contemporary sociologist, narratives are pervasive in contemporary sociological explanations, albeit at a meta-conceptual level that is often unrecognized.[20]

A defining, central feature of literary narratives is a plotline. Unlike analytical narratives that generalize to some form of "x causes y under condition(s) c," literary plots offer a thread of connections between characters in particular settings, tied together in the end. Plots often have a central turning point and a *denouement* that resolves an escalating tension, showing how all the parts are connected. Plots can reveal an important causal sequence, one that may stretch out for a very long time and be unlikely to be repeated. Plots are explanatory in the sense that they help us to understand how and why something happened in the way that it did. In the case of a sociological narrative, a plotline will ideally help us to understand how some important feature of the social world has come to work in the way that it does. And, perhaps, in the journey through the plotline, like a Platonic theorizer, we come to see our world anew.[21]

What I conceive myself to be doing in this book stands somewhere between the Platonic conception and the older meaning of *theoria* that Plato redeployed. I do not claim a unitary vision of truth and ultimate reality, or an all-encompassing explanation. I am simply trying to bear truthful witness to things that I have seen along a very long path of searching in legal and historical sources. I try to synthesize what I have learned into a coherent narrative, that is, a plotline, and this involves comparisons, both within and across time. My methodology, therefore, according to the categories of contemporary sociology, is historical and comparative.

Due partly to the scale at which I am seeking to see – a scale that stretches from antiquity to modernity – I rely heavily on historical sociologists, legal historians, and other historical theorists who have provided foundational narratives of macro-historical change. In many ways the ultimate methodological question in this type of project, I believe, is about reliability and interpretation. How do we identify reliable sources and interpret them in such a way that our narratives speak truthfully (if also very limitedly) about infinitely complex social realities that nonetheless seem

20 Andrew Abbott, "Process and Temporality in Sociology: The Idea of Outcome in U.S. Sociology," in George Steinmetz (ed.), *The Politics of Method in the Human Sciences* (Durham: Duke University Press, 2005). Within contemporary sociology, Margaret Somers has been a vigorous advocate for narrative methods. See Margaret R. Somers, "Narrativity, Narrative Identity, and Social Action: Rethinking English Working-Class Identity Formation," *Social Science History* 16(4): 591–630 (1992); Margaret R. Somers, "Symposium on Historical Sociology and Rational Choice Theory: 'We're No Angels': Realism, Rational Choice, and Relationality in Social Science," *American Journal of Sociology* 104(3): 722–84 (1998).

21 On the importance of plotlines for narrative methods in sociology, see Somers, "Narrativity," 599–603.

to exhibit an identifiable pattern, one that can be described with reliance on a plotline?

In this book, I work with legal and historical texts, both primary and secondary, and I rely on historical sociologists like Emile Durkheim, Michael Mann, and Max Weber to help me make sense of what I find in those texts. Intuitions about meaning and historical patterns, tested through iterated processes of reading, discussion, rereading, and comparison – these are the basic methods deployed to arrive at the conclusions presented in this book. This is fundamentally a theoretical process, one aiming at a coherent way of seeing that is well supported by historical evidence. Or, to use Michael Mann's more colorful language, it is a journey of raiding and pillaging: reading widely and greedily, moving constantly between historical sources and theoretical ideas, struggling to synthesize and theorize the patterns that seem to appear.[22]

In this book, I treat intellectual property as a legal institution, and I investigate this legal institution by focusing mainly on two types of legal texts: (1) practical legal documents, which I theorize (borrowing and adapting from the medievalist Geoffrey Koziol) as *instruments of legal power*, including royal edicts and diplomas, charters, letters patent, and (later) contracts and treaties; and (2) legal treatises, which I theorize as *jurisprudential narratives* – cultural narratives that tell a legal and moral story about where we have been and where we are going. Once statutes and case law become legal sources, by the early modern period, I include them in my analysis, but I focus primarily on the historical process by which they became legal sources, and on the type of legal power that they came to have. Part of this legal power derives, I think, from the way that statutes and case law have been integrated into jurisprudential narratives in our modern world.[23]

Case law and statutory law as we conceive of them today are both relatively modern types of law. In many ways, they are the effect rather than the cause of the legal changes that I seek to describe in this book. Cases and statutes are vitally important for understanding modern intellectual property law, as it works today, but in tracing the emergence of intellectual property as a new type of legal institution, I am trying to tell a much older type of legal story. In this older type of legal story, legal institutions depend on everyday legal practices, on the one hand, and on meaningful narratives that tell stories about what law is, how it works, and how it is to be interpreted, on the other hand. Documentary legal sources of both types –

22 Michael Mann, *The Sources of Social Power, Vol. 2, The Rise of Classes and Nation-States, 1760–1914*, 2d ed. (New York: Cambridge University Press, 2012), vii-x.

23 On theorizing, particularly the role of naming in theorizing, see Richard Swedberg, *The Art of Social Theory* (Princeton: Princeton University Press, 2014), 56–8; also "From Theory to Theorizing," in *Theorizing in Social Science: The Context of Discovery* (Stanford: Stanford University Press, 2014), 1–28. Geoffrey Koziol, *The Politics of Memory and Identity in Carolingian Royal Diplomas: The West Frankish Kingdom (840–987)* (Turnhout, Belgium: Brepols Publishers, 2012). On cultural narratives as moral narratives, see Christian Smith, *Moral, Believing Animals: Human Personhood and Culture* (Oxford: Oxford University Press, 2003).

written on animal skins or papyrus reeds – have been around for much longer than books (or electronic databases) of case law and statutes.

The overarching narrative (or "plot") of this book is structured as a ring. I begin in the present, introducing the reader to modern forms of intellectual property, as they function in the pervasive, everyday social realities of McDonald's and Facebook. I then take the reader on a journey deep into the past, showing through a series of interconnected narratives and case studies how different aspects of the modern legal institution were woven together. I finally return, at the end of the book, to present-day realities, hoping to leave the reader with a deeper understanding of intellectual property, as a modern legal institution, both in its ancient roots and in its present-day social effects. With a ring structure, as the anthropologist Mary Douglas has shown, the apex of the argument – the turning point moment – is in the middle.[24]

In this book, the turning point moment comes in Chapter 7, in what has often been called a "feudal age" of law in England. This was a surprise to me, born of a lengthy process of revision from my doctoral dissertation. In Chapter 7, I argue that the feudal age of English and European law – with its zenith roughly marked by King John's feudal homage to Pope Innocent III in 1213, followed only two years later by *Magna Carta* and the Fourth Lateran Council – was a fundamental turning point in the process of transformation from medieval privileges to modern intellectual property. The key to this transformation was a covenantal (and deeply Biblical) conception of law, which was understood to underpin solemn, reciprocal promises, and therefore to enable the formation of social bonds.

Through solemn vows and oaths – like those taken by a feudal vassal to his lord, or by a knight dedicating himself to a crusading order – social bonds were created and increasingly guaranteed by the combined strength of secular and ecclesiastical rulers. In England, this covenantal conception of law helped to solidify the prerogative powers of the king, linking those powers to an extending social and material organization, or "base." At the same time, this covenantal conception of law could be deployed to set limits on the king's prerogative powers, anchoring both prerogative powers *and their limits* in the notion of a sacred and reciprocal set of social bonds between the king and his people. The royal prerogative would become the foundation for British intellectual property, and the social bonds connected to it would become the foundation of a British national state.

From the transformative, feudal age, we move forward to the Reformation, in which the covenantal conception of law, among so many other things, was reformed. We witness the use of statutory law to expropriate the English church, thereby

[24] On extended case studies and ethnographically inspired visits into historical pasts, see Michael Burawoy, *The Extended Case Method: Four Countries, Four Decades, Four Great Transformations, and One Theoretical Tradition* (Berkeley: University of California Press, 2009). On Ring Structures, see Mary Douglas, *Thinking in Circles: An Essay on Ring Composition* (New Haven: Yale University Press, 2007).

facilitating the constitution of a new type of governing community, one that would be increasingly differentiated from the church in serving overlapping functions: the nation-state. Chapters 7–8 cover a very long and seminal period in the development of English common law and can therefore only scratch the surface of important legal developments. The basic takeaway point, however, is that the Protestant Reformation in England, initiated very largely by statutory law issued from the powerful Tudor King, Henry VIII, was just as much a revolution in law and legal institutions as in religion. The key point is that statutory law, as it operated in the English Reformation, could not have functioned in the way that it did but for the feudal age's covenantal conception of law, which was nonetheless radically recast in a nationalizing form, first through royally centralized feudalism and then in the process of Reformation.[25]

For the emergence of intellectual property in England, what was especially important about the Protestant Reformation was its dramatic enhancement of the king's prerogative powers, its massive expropriation of church property that widened and solidified a political class of property-owning elites, and its institutionalization of a role for Parliament as a guardian of proprietary, political, and natural rights. Each of these was a necessary condition for the developments that came together in the emergence of modern intellectual property in Britain.

Chapter 9 zeroes in on two legal judgments, coming in close succession, which explicitly recognized intellectual property as a new type of legal property in Britain – one in 1769 by the highest court of English common law (the Court of King's Bench) and the other in 1774 by the highest court in the land (the House of Lords). The focus in these decisions was particularly on copyrights, as these were the rights being claimed by the Stationers Company, a London guild existing from the time of the early Tudors.[26]

Under corporate charters granted first by Mary (acting jointly with her husband, King Philip of Spain) and then confirmed by Elizabeth I, the Stationers Company had been given a national monopoly in printing. While this was probably conceived by the queens and their advisers as a way to control printing, the Stationers had come to recognize the enormous economic value of their monopoly, and to conceive the *rights to copy* as *rights to property*. Their claims were first made during the seventeenth-century English revolutions associated with intensifications in Protestant religious commitments and were first recognized by the Long Parliament governing

[25] On the Reformation as a legal revolution, see particularly Harold J. Berman, *Law and Revolution II: The Impact of the Protestant Reformations on the Western Legal Tradition* (Cambridge, MA: Belknap Press, 2003); John Witte, Jr., *The Reformation of Rights: Law, Religion, and Human Rights in Early Modern Calvinism* (New York: Cambridge University Press, 2007). For an introduction to the scholarship on law and religion in the Christian West, see John Witte, Jr. and Frank S. Alexander, *Christianity and Law: An Introduction* (New York: Cambridge University Press, 2008).

[26] *Millar* v. *Taylor*, 98 Eng. Rep. 201 (King's Bench 1769); *Donaldson* v. *Becket*, 98 Eng. Rep. 257, 1 Eng. Rep. 837; William Cobbett's *Parliamentary History of England, Vol.* 17 (London: T.C. Hansard, 1813), 953–1003.

under Oliver Cromwell's armies. The jurist Edward Coke was ubiquitous in English government during the early part of this period, helping to draft the Statute of Monopolies, which is the foundation of modern patent law among England's colonial heirs, including the United States. With the Glorious Revolution in 1688–89, English Protestant commitments were stabilized into a constitutional settlement for British monarchy. Queen Anne's reign was a direct result of this settlement, and it was during her rule that England's first copyright statute was enacted. This statute was the focus of argument in the two legal cases, coming toward the end of the eighteenth century, definitively recognizing the emergence of intellectual property.[27]

A central argument of this book, in other words, is that the Protestant Reformation was a vital condition for the emergence of intellectual property, as we see it operating in our everyday lives today. The important qualification to this, though, involves the recognition that the historical and political movement we call the Reformation was really only one stage in a much longer process, one involving formalization in law and an effort to reform human communities in accordance with a heavenly legal standard. In order to see the significance of this formalization process, it is necessary to look at law and legal history from a different angle, one that attends to the close relations between law and religion, stretching all the way into our modern age, and stretching backward to the Roman empire.

Following a ring (or *chiasmus*) structure, Chapters 2–6 lead up to a crucial, cultural shift in legal formalization, one that is marked by feudalism's covenantal conception of law, which, through ongoing efforts at reform, became a transformed foundation for modern legal institutions like intellectual property. Aspects of this transformation are narrated in Chapters 7–8, and Chapters 9–12 lead away from the apex moment, drawing us into our own modern moment, when Facebook holds the social power to divide and conquer our world. A key to this modern legal transformation, I believe, involves an adaptation of Roman legal traditions, enabling increasing levels of social power to be wielded impersonally through instruments of legal power. A central conviction of this book is that we cannot understand Facebook's power if we do not understand these historically new levels of social power, wielded impersonally through intellectual property.

Seen in the light of the historical and theoretical perspective offered here, Facebook is an indicator of the extent to which our networked social and political communities – what the contemporary techno-sociologist Zeynep Tufekci calls a "networked public sphere" – are constituted by instruments of legal power.

[27] For foundational discussions of the Stationers Company and its role in the emergence of modern intellectual property law, see Cyprian Blagden, *The Stationers Company: A History, 1403–1959* (London: George Allen & Unwin, 1960), 31–33, 63–177; Ronan Deazley, *On the Origin of the Right to Copy: Charting the Movement of Copyright Law in Eighteenth-Century Britain (1695–1775)* (Oxford: Hart Publishing, 2004); Mark Rose, *Authors and Owners: The Invention of Copyright* (Cambridge, MA: Harvard University Press, 1993); Patterson, *Copyright*, 28–179.

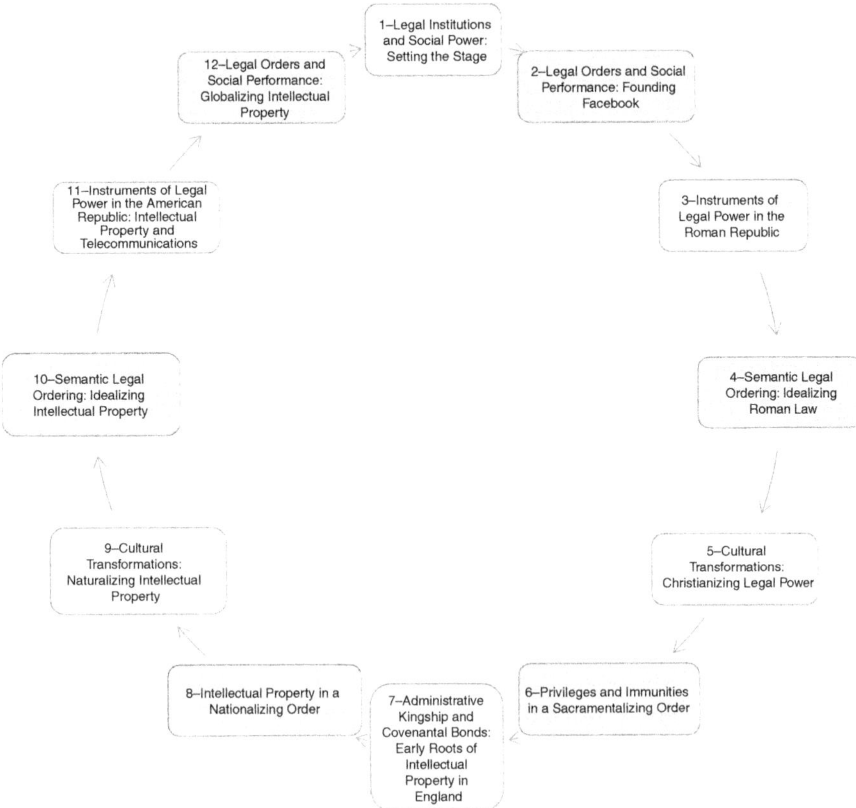

FIGURE I – Narrative Structure of Chapters

Intellectual property has been of central importance in protecting and facilitating the telecommunications infrastructure upon which Facebook depends, and in constituting Facebook itself. Chapters 9–12 develop an argument about how intellectual property was built into the legal infrastructure of the modern nation-state system, and about how that system has facilitated the development of a new type of governing community, one involving new kinds of possibility and danger in a networked and globalized public sphere. I conclude by querying the implications of this development for our contemporary political and communal life.[28]

In structuring this story about the emergence of intellectual property as a ring, represented in Figure I, I want to highlight an underlying continuity, while I am narrating a series of social transformations. In keeping with this underlying continuity, there is a very important sense, I think, in which we return to our beginnings, when we try to understand how we have arrived at the end of our social story – and by

[28] Zeynep Tufekci, *Twitter and Tear Gas: The Power and Fragility of Networked Protest* (New Haven: Yale University Press, 2017).

end I mean the social power structures of our present day. Ring structures of composition can take us on a journey, highlighting comparative parallels in transformations, aiming to bring us back to the place we started, knowing it better, and knowing it changed.

> *And the end of all our exploring will be to arrive where we started, and know the place for the first time.*[29]

AUDIENCE AND DISCIPLINARY CONTEXT

My hope for this book is that it will speak broadly. I have written with my Bard College students concretely in mind, partly because I want to invite undergraduate students into a sociological and political debate about the historical development of intellectual property law, and partly because I see my students as characterizing the broader audience I hope to engage: thoughtful people who would like to learn more about how legal institutions like patents, copyrights, and trademarks have become part of our globalized, social world, and who are willing to take the time to be reflective about how this development fits into a broader story. My intention is that the book be useful in interdisciplinary, undergraduate courses dealing with law, society, and state formation. I would also be very glad if the book could be informative, and even useful, for citizens and policy-makers.

As an interdisciplinary work, the scholarly audience for this book is both mixed and open-ended.

For sociologists, I hope that the book will do two things: (1) offer a narrative account for the emergence of intellectual property, as a legal institution, thereby contributing to a sociology of intellectual property law, and (2) help in building a case for the causal impacts of law in state formation. Law, in my opinion, has not really received its due in contemporary sociological theories of state formation, and I hope that this book can contribute to a fuller account of the myriad influences of law in processes of state formation, in close cooperation with religion.[30]

For legal scholars, especially of intellectual property law, I anticipate that the historical narrative offered in this book will be provocative, partly because it goes

[29] T. S. Eliot, *The Four Quartets*: "Little Gidding" (Orlando: Harcourt, Inc., 1971), 59.

[30] On the need for a sociology of intellectual property, see Teppo Felin, "Sociology of Intellectual Property?" Orgtheory.net, Wordpress.org (March 2, 2012); Richard Swedberg, *Principles of Economic Sociology* (Princeton: Princeton University Press, 2003), 204–5. Sociologists have certainly written about various aspects of intellectual property, but there has not yet been an effort to provide an account of intellectual property's emergence, as a new type of legal property. For exemplary articles, see Nitsan Chorev, "Changing Global Norms through Reactive Diffusion: The Case of Intellectual Property Protection of AIDS Drugs," *American Sociological Review* 77(5): 831–53 (2012); Leonhard Dobusch & Sigrid Quack, "Framing Standards, Mobilizing Users: Copyright versus Fair Use in Transnational Regulation," *Review of International Political Economy* 20(1): 52–88; Mark Suchman, "Invention and Ritual: Notes on the Interrelation of Magic and Intellectual Property in Preliterate societies," *Columbia Law Review* 89: 1264–94 (1989).

back much further than many histories of intellectual property do. There is also a provocation in the fact that the book speaks directly to debates about the role of religion in law, which polemics within legal scholarship have recently highlighted with specific reference to intellectual property law.

The influential US scholar of intellectual property law Mark Lemley has accused his fellow scholars of being "religious" in their fidelity to intellectual property rights, despite empirical evidence running contrary to their beliefs about the necessity for such rights in stimulating innovation. Lemley evidently intends that his argument will work as an insult to startle scholars into a deeper engagement with empirical evidence. However, in explicating the deep relationship between religion and law, with application to the emergence of intellectual property, I suggest that Lemley is surely right, and that we should not be surprised to see religious aspects in scholarly commitments to intellectual property law. The deep normativity of law, in western culture, has always been closely intertwined with religious faith. Only in the late twentieth century did it become possible to forget this fact, or to treat it as a dead relic of the past.[31]

The close linkage that I draw between law and religion in this book will make many people uncomfortable. At times it has made me very uncomfortable. But a narrative account like the one that I offer in this book provides strong support for this linkage. It does not resolve questions about the relationship that law and religion should have today, but it helps us to understand the religious qualities that law still bears in our societies. If we continue to see meaningful, good, and hopeful things in our laws, including our intellectual property laws, our religious histories help to explain this fact. Conversely, when we are angered by the deep injustices that persist in our laws or by the tendencies toward cruelty and imperialism that we sometimes see in our modern nation-states, our religious histories supply semantic resources that can help us to give a meaningful and edifying form to that anger.[32]

RELATION TO EXISTING LITERATURES

This book is unique in offering a combination of sociological and legal perspectives on the emergence of intellectual property, as a new type of legal property. Because I trace the history of intellectual property, approaching it from a sociological and legal perspective, this book is complementary to several overlapping areas of scholarly literature.

1. ***Economic Histories of Intellectual Property*** Economists and economic historians have shown a great deal of interest in the relationship between intellectual

[31] Mark Lemley, "Faith-based Intellectual Property," *UCLA Law Review* 62: 1328–46 (2015). I am grateful to Mark Bartholomew for bringing this article to my attention.

[32] On the semantic resources of religious traditions, see Jürgen Habermas et al., *An Awareness of What Is Missing: Faith and Reason in a Post-Secular Age*, translated by Ciaran Cronin (Cambridge, UK: Polity Press, 2010).

property and industrialization. Although I do not engage extensively with them, the account that I offer does aim at refining the timeline for intellectual property's emergence that they often assume. Economists have tended to equate the emergence of intellectual property with the English Statute of Monopolies (1624). However, as we will see, that statute did not treat patents as property, or even as rights. It merely placed limits on the powers of the English monarch to grant monopolistic privileges. To the extent that economic considerations of the emergence of intellectual property focus on the Statute of Monopolies, then, I believe they are premised on legal inaccuracy. Greater subtlety and care are needed to decide when, and how, intellectual property in its fully modern form emerged.[33]

Summarizing the literature in 2010, Christine MacLeod and Alessandro Nuvolari noted that conflict and debate remain among economists about the precise nature of the relationship between intellectual property (particularly patents) and industrialization. There is nevertheless a stubborn correlation in time and space between the emergence of intellectual property and industrialization, which makes the existence of some type of relationship likely. The question, as MacLeod and Nuvolari make clear, is really about the precise nature of the relationship.[34]

This book is complementary to this literature, because I am seeking to offer a greater level of sociological and legal depth in narrating the story of intellectual property's emergence, which I think will be relevant to these economic debates.

2. ***Legal, Cultural, and Political Histories of Intellectual Property*** Legal historians have also addressed the emergence of intellectual property; I draw freely and gratefully on their work. The legal histories, however, have tended to be quite narrow. Often they focus on one type of intellectual property or one particular country. As legal histories, moreover, they typically do not attempt to examine the broader social patterns involved in the emergence of intellectual property. This broader perspective is what differentiates a sociological approach from a historical approach, and I hope to show with this book how a broader perspective can deepen our understanding of intellectual property. In doing so, I draw extensively on the

[33] Christine MacLeod and Alessandro Nuvolari, *Patents and Industrialization: An Historical Overview of the British Case, 1624–1907*, A Report to the Strategic Advisory Board for Intellectual Property Policy (UK Intellectual Property Office, 2010), available at https://papers.ssrn.com/sol3/papers.cfm?abstract_id=2019844 (accessed August 5, 2019), 4–6; Joel Mokyr, "Intellectual Property Rights, the Industrial Revolution, and the Beginnings of Modern Economic Growth," *American Economic Review* 99(2): 349–55 (2009); Douglass C. North, *Structure and Change in Economic History* (New York: Norton, 1981), 164–66; Douglass C. North and Barry R. Weingast, "Constitutions and Commitment: The Evolution of Institutions Governing Public Choice in Seventeenth-Century England," *Journal of Economic History* 49(4): 803–32; compare Christine MacLeod, *Inventing the Industrial Revolution: The English Patent System, 1660–1800* (Cambridge, UK: Cambridge University Press, 1988). For important and influential work on the economic history in the United States, see B. Zorina Khan, *The Democratization of Invention: Patents and Copyrights in American Economic Development, 1790–1920* (New York: Cambridge University Press, 2005).

[34] MacLeod and Nuvolari, *Patents and Industrialization*, 28–30.

work of intellectual and political historians, such as Pamela Long, who have blazed the trail in considering the development of intellectual property as part of a broader, cultural and political story.[35]

3. ***Sociological Accounts of Modernization and State Formation*** Sociologists have long been interested in industrialization and modernization. Indeed, the social and economic transformations of modernity have been a central, even defining, focus for sociology. However, sociologists have not focused on the role(s) of intellectual property in these changes.[36]

Sociologists have, in fact, until quite recently, shown very little interest in intellectual property. Today this is changing, but the limited sociological literature on intellectual property focuses almost exclusively on its contemporary forms, and on contemporary contestation over its legitimacy. There are basically no direct sociological treatments of the emergence of intellectual property, as a new type of legal property.[37]

35 Examples of legal histories from which I have learned a great deal include the following: Bruce W. Bugbee, *Genesis of American Patent and Copyright Law* (Washington, D.C.: Public Affairs Press, 1967); Ronan Deazley, *On the Origin of the Right to Copy: Charting the Movement of Copyright Law in Eighteenth-Century Britain (1695–1775)* (Oxford: Hart Publishing, 2004); Harold G. Fox, *Monopolies and Patents: A Study of the History and Future of the Patent Monopoly* (Toronto: University of Toronto Press, 1947); Lyman Ray Patterson, *Copyright in Historical Perspective* (Nashville: Vanderbilt University Press, 1968); Brad Sherman and Lionel Bently, *The Making of Modern Intellectual Property Law* (New York: Cambridge University Press, 1999). For important exemplars in the cultural history of intellectual property, see Elizabeth Armstrong, *Before Copyright: The French Book-Privilege System, 1498–1526* (New York: Cambridge University Press, 1990); Carolyn C. Cooper (ed.), "Patents and Invention," a special issue of *Technology and Culture* 32(4): 837–1168 (1991); Pamela O. Long, *Openness, Secrecy, Authorship: Technical Arts and the Culture of Knowledge from Antiquity to the Renaissance* (Baltimore: Johns Hopkins University Press, 2001); Mark Rose, *Authors and Owners: The Invention of Copyright* (Cambridge, MA: Harvard University Press, 1993). For older legal histories, written with a focus on political and industrial developments, see William Hyde Price, *The English Patents of Monopoly* (Boston: Houghton, Mifflin and Co., 1906); Frank I. Schechter, *The Historical Foundations of the Law Relating to Trade-Mark Law* (New York: Columbia University Press, 1925).

36 Sociological treatments of industrialization and economic modernization: Raymond Aron, *18 Lectures on Industrial Society* (London: Weidenfeld and Nicolson, 1968); Daniel Bell, *The Coming of Post-Industrial Society: A Venture in Social Forecasting* (New York: Basic Books, 1999); Frank Dobbin, *Forging Industrial Policy: The United States, Britain, and France in the Railway Age* (New York: Cambridge University Press, 1994); Krishan Kumar, *Prophecy and Progress: The Sociology of Industrial and Post-Industrial Society* (London: Penguin Books, 1978).

37 For sociology's minimal interest in intellectual property, see Swedberg, *Principles of Economic Sociology*, 204–5. For sociological accounts of contemporary intellectual property, focusing on contestations over legitimacy, see Nitsan Chorev, "Changing Global Norms through Reactive Diffusion: The Case of Intellectual Property Protection of AIDS Drugs," *American Sociological Review* 77: 831–53 (2012); Leonhard Dobusch and Sigrid Quack, "Framing Standards, Mobilizing Users: Copyright versus Fair Use in Transnational Regulation," *Review of International Political Economy* 20(1): 52–88 (2013). Sociological scholars of institutions and organizations have also drawn attention to intellectual property: Mark Suchman, "Dealmakers and Counselors: Law Firms as Intermediaries in the Development of Silicon Valley," in Martin Kenney (ed.), *Understanding Silicon Valley: The Anatomy of an Entrepreneurial Region* (Stanford: Stanford Business Books, 2000), 71–97; Elizabeth Popp Berman, "The Materiality of Patent Law: Explaining the Passage of the Bayh-Dole Act of 1980," in Trevor Pinch and Richard Swedberg (eds.), *Living in a Material World: Economic Sociology Meets Science & Technology Studies* (Cambridge, MA: MIT Press, 2008), 191–213.

Economic sociologists are, however, interested in the "Knowledge Revolution," and they have drawn on patent data in exploring this Revolution. Although sociologists tend to be suspicious of formal law, and accordingly of arguments that posit a causal force to formal legal doctrine, they have done pathbreaking work in showing how economic changes depend on social changes. There is also general acceptance within economic sociology that social-relational changes depend on cultural and institutional forces.[38]

This book, accordingly, seeks to fill a significant gap in the sociological literature, while also building on the existing strengths of the literature, especially in the "new economic sociology." In addition, the book helps to lay a foundation for bringing sociology into an important debate about the relationship between intellectual property and industrialization. This general effort, to bring sociological perspectives to bear on debates within economic theory, is part of the core mission of the new economic sociology.[39]

4. ***Relational Contracting in Law and Society Literatures*** Similar to sociologists, scholars affiliated with the interdisciplinary "law and society" movement have often expressed skepticism about the real significance of formal legal doctrines and procedures. One particularly influential line of discussion has focused on contract law, aiming to show how contracts "in action" look very different from the doctrinal contract law "in books" that is taught to law students. More positively, this line of literature has focused attention on the ways in which contracts contribute to, and form part of, social relationships, especially relationships within and between business organizations. With its resolutely empirical focus, this scholarship has focused attention on the ways in which contractual

[38] Economic sociologists who focus on the Knowledge Revolution: Walter W. Powell and Kaisa Snellman, "The Knowledge Economy," *Annual Review of Sociology* 30: 199–220 (2004); Walter W. Powell and Jason Owen-Smith, "Universities and the Market for Intellectual Property in the Life Sciences," *Journal of Policy Analysis and Management* 17(2): 253–77 (1998); also Robert K. Merton, "Fluctuations in the Rate of Industrial Invention," *The Quarterly Journal of Economics* 49(3): 454–74 (1935). Sociological suspicion of formal law: Arthur L. Stinchcombe, *When Formality Works: Authority and Abstraction in Law and Organizations* (Chicago: University of Chicago Press, 2001), 1. Sociological work demonstrating the interdependence of economic and social relations: Ronald S. Burt, *Brokerage and Closure: An Introduction to Social Capital* (Oxford: Oxford University Press, 2005); Bruce G. Carruthers, *City of Capital: Politics and Markets in the English Financial Revolution* (Princeton: Princeton University Press, 1996); Bruce G. Carruthers and Laura Ariovich, "The Sociology of Property Rights," *Annual Review of Sociology* 30: 23–46 (2004); Mark Granovetter, "Economic Action and Social Structure: The Problem of Embeddedness," *American Journal of Sociology* 91(3): 481–510 (1985); Greta Krippner, *Capitalizing on Crisis: The Political Origins of the Rise of Finance* (Cambridge, MA: Harvard University Press, 2011); Brian Uzzi, "Embeddedness in the Making of Financial Capital: How Social Relations and Networks Benefit Firms Seeking Financing," *American Sociological Review* 64(4): 481–505 (1999); Brian Uzzi, "The Sources and Consequences of Embeddedness for the Economic Performance of Organizations: The Network Effect," *American Sociological Review* 61(4): 674–698 (1996). Sociological work demonstrating the dependence of economic changes on institutional changes: Greta Krippner & Anthony S. Alvarez, "Embeddedness and the Intellectual Projects of Economic Sociology," *Annual Review of Sociology* 33: 219–40 (2007); Greta Krippner et al., "Polanyi Symposium: A Conversation on Embeddedness," *Socio-Economic Review* 2: 109–35 (2004).

[39] Bringing sociological perspectives to bear on economic debates: Swedberg, *Principles*, 32–52.

business relations constitute forms of social ordering that challenge our easy distinctions between the public and private spheres of social life, between "state" and "civil society."[40]

Law and society literatures highlighting the relationality of contracts, together with their artifactual and performative qualities, can be readily synthesized with Geoffrey Koziol's conception of royal diplomas as "instruments of power." What is common to these perspectives is a way of viewing legal documents, like contracts and medieval charters, as a constitutive part of social relationships. In complex ways that have changed dramatically over time, legal documents like charters, diplomas, letters patent, contracts, and treaties have helped to enact and memorialize social relationships. This means that their importance for social relationships is not limited to their legal enforcement (or lack thereof) – although enforcement is doubtless important – but is also enacted, performative, and meaningfully memorializing. Important empirical questions exist about when legal documents play which kinds of role in contributing to social relationships. But the basic point is that they can contribute, in a constitutive way, to the existence and maintenance of social relationships.[41]

What I am proposing, in other words, is that we broaden our conception of relational contracting beyond business contracts, to include writs, charters, and letters patent between kings and their subjects. All these types of legal instrument enact, perform, and memorialize social relationships, contributing to the social bonds linking public and private spheres together in long, complex processes of state formation. From this perspective, the emergence of intellectual property becomes part of a broader story about how instruments of legal power have developed, both socially *and* doctrinally, and about how those developments have become patterned in the formation of modern legal institutions.

5. ***Cultural and Comparative Sociology*** This book links contemporary cultural perspectives on the economy with new developments in comparative sociology. From cultural sociology, I draw on fundamental insights about the roles that worldview, evaluative ethos, and conceptual categories play in markets and economic life. Reaching back to the Weberian inspirations for much of this scholarship within sociology, I foreground moral obligation, in both its phenomenological and its deontological aspects – in other words, I combine

40 For an introduction to the "law and society" movement and its avowedly "realistic" approaches to law, see Kitty Calavita, *Invitation to Law & Society: An Introduction to the Study of Real Law*, 2d ed. (Chicago: University of Chicago Press, 2016). For an introduction to the law and society literature on contracts, including a reprint of the agenda-setting article by Stewart Macauley, see Jean Braucher, John Kidwell, and William C. Whitford, *Revisiting the Contracts Scholarship of Stewart Macauley: On the Empirical and the Lyrical* (Oxford: Hart Publishing, 2013).

41 On the dramatic historical changes in contract law, viewed from a sociological perspective, see Richard Biernacki, "Cultural Coherence in Early Modern England: The Invention of Contract," *American Journal of Cultural Sociology* 14(2): 277–99 (2014). On the artifactual and constitutive qualities of contracts, see Mark C. Suchman, "The Contract as Social Artifact," *Law & Society Review* 37(1): 91–142 (2003).

a focus on the social *experiences* of obligation with questions about how those experiences are *intentionally theorized* as duties. At the same time, as a participant in a working group on comparative methods, I bring to this book a renewed sense of excitement and methodological reflection about the possibilities for macro-historical, comparative sociology. Linking these two developments is an important part of the contribution I am trying to make, one that will, I hope, enable the book to speak in an innovative way to the contemporary discipline of sociology.[42]

This book conveys my firm conviction that intellectual property is an important part of the story of modernity. That conviction is rooted in, and supported by, contemporary developments in cultural and comparative sociology, just as it is also rooted in the macro-historical narratives of classical sociology. That conviction is also rooted in, and supported by, contemporary lines of scholarship in economic history, legal history, and scholarship connected with the law and society movement.

I am engaging with multiple lines of developed literature while also trying to speak in a way that is accessible to a broad audience. Doubtless, this is a Herculean task, but it seems to me to be worth the effort and the risk.

MAPPING THE JOURNEY

This is a complex book, and this means – as several generous commenters on early drafts have stressed – that it needs a map. What follows is a thematic summary of contents, which aims at providing such a map, and to which the reader may wish to return, if at times, despite all best efforts, it becomes difficult to see the forest amidst the trees.

Chapter 1 seeks to provide the reader with an introduction to contemporary intellectual property law, to the pervasiveness of intellectual property in our everyday lives, and with a theoretical framework that will guide discussion throughout the book. The chapter opens with a visual metaphor – from geology and plate tectonics – for thinking about the foundational role of legal institutions in contemporary society. The metaphor is meant to convey the notion that something can be both fundamental and relatively invisible, in the sense that we do not readily see how it is shaping our everyday lives. The related metaphor of earthquakes is meant to convey the power that legal changes can have to transform our everyday lives. The primary legal changes that I have in mind are changes in property structures, and in the organization of obligation in governing communities.

42 Between 2015 and 2017, I was privileged to participate in a working group on comparative methods in sociology, organized and led by Damon Mayrl and Nick Wilson. This extended, small-group discussion was supported by Philip Gorski, with philosophical contributions from Tim Rutzou and funding from the John Templeton Foundation. Fellow discussants included Stefan Bargheer, Carly Knight, Dan Lainer-Vos, Josh Pacewicz, Xuefei Ren, and Xiaohong Xu.

Chapter 1 then offers an introduction to the world of intellectual property law, as seen in a McDonald's restaurant. The goal is to enable readers to see very concretely just how pervasive intellectual property is in our everyday lives, and to provide an intuition about how intellectual property works to provide a foundation for the basic business model of the McDonald's Corporation: franchising. By granting permission to use its intellectual property – its trademarks, copyrights, patents, and trade secrets – McDonald's enables franchisees to independently operate their restaurants as part of the broader McDonald's "family," while also exerting control over the way the restaurants are run, thereby maintaining the value of the brand. Once this strategy of conditional control is grasped, we can see how property is about much more than just exclusion: it is also a vehicle for exercising control within cooperative relationships, and this can make it an agent of social power, even while it depends upon social power.

Chapter 1 introduces a basic theoretical conception of law as an obliging force, which binds us together in governing communities, and thereby enables property of various types to exist. The chapter also sketches a stylized historical narrative, drawn from Max Weber's developmental sociology of law, about how intellectual property emerged, as a new type of legal property. The stylized narrative envisions three basic "layers" to the modern institution of intellectual property, which roughly correspond to three different paradigms for the obliging force of law: empirical formality, semantic formality, and substantive rationality. The historical development and weaving together of these three "layers" in the obliging force of law thus becomes an overarching narrative (or meta-narrative) of the book. The elements of the meta-narrative are as follows:

At the core of intellectual property, as a legal institution, is an empirical formality of legal documents. This is the oldest layer, characterized by a formality in which the experiential attributes of documents (e.g., impression with a special seal, or the use of particular words) determine whether a legal instrument is valid and binding. In a legal culture where empirical formality reigns supreme, legal documents exert social power because they are empirically valid, and they make a difference to social patterns in virtue of their empirical validity. There is a material quality to this empirical formality that is worth stressing, and that invites connections to theoretical work on the forms of causal agency that material objects can exercise in the social world.[43]

But just as important is the next layer, which surrounds the empirical formality of legal documents with a conceptual framework of meanings about what property is, and how it is acquired. When formal logic is applied to this conceptual framework of meanings, such that the framework is systematized, we have a formal rationality of a different kind, what I am calling semantic formality – formality of conceptual and logical meaning. Semantic formality of this type began to appear in republican and

[43] Dan Lainer-Vos, *Sinews of the Nation: Constructing Irish and Zionist Bonds in the United States* (Cambridge, UK: Polity Press, 2013); Bruno Latour, *Reassembling the Social* (Oxford: Oxford University Press, 2007).

imperial Roman law, and it was culturally transformed in the Christianization of the Roman empire. Added to the empirical formality of legal documents, semantic formality provides a conceptual and logical grounding, greatly enhancing the binding force of law, and enabling that binding force to be intentionally directed and defined, in accordance with cultural commitments and aspirations.[44]

The conceptual and logical grounding of semantic formality, however, is justifying and rationalizing in virtue of logical coherence and consistency, together with a background in Roman and Biblical legal conceptions, *not* in virtue of positive consequences for a polity, society, or economy. The third layer that is added, over the course of time, to the institution of intellectual property – or rather, to its early precursors – is a substantive justification about why it is good for society to privilege certain kinds of activities. The substantive rationality that ultimately comes to underpin intellectual property is a theory about how it is beneficial to our political community to encourage certain kinds of inventive and creative activities.

A meta-narrative of this book is one in which these three layers – empirical formality, semantic formality, and substantive rationality – in the binding force of law became entwined together, thereby contributing to a series of wide-ranging transformations in the institutionalized patterns of society. While the emergence of intellectual property is the guiding focus, that focus is also contextualized as part of a much broader range of social and institutional transformations.

Chapter 2 establishes a more analytical basis for our meta-narrative in a present-day context, highlighting the importance of intellectual property – particularly patents – for the foundation of Facebook. The chapter emphasizes the weaving together of formality and substantive rationality in contemporary patents, which are theorized as *instruments of legal power*. By showing how patents were important in the founding of Facebook, the chapter emphasizes the role that instruments of legal power – like patents – can play in linking people together into social groups, classes, and networks. This is explained and elaborated through the theoretical language of Michael Mann, and especially his ideal-typical analyses of social power.

Patents and intellectual property – as I theorize them in this book, drawing on Mann – deploy collective social power to formally recognize and enforce *zones of exclusivity*. A zone of exclusivity is a verbally defined space within which an individual or group is empowered to act exclusively, to design what happens within the space, and to collect any revenues that may flow from action within the space. With a modern patent, the exclusive zone is a verbally defined area of technological innovation, for example, a new way of creating a social network through computer software. A patent enables a company like Facebook to act and collect revenues within the defined area of technology, to be the exclusive economic provider of

[44] Laura R. Ford, "Dharma and Natural Law: Max Weber's Comparison of Hindu and (Occidental) Christian Traditions," *Max Weber Studies* 17(2): 160–95 (2017).

a specific type of social networking services. This has the potential to make Facebook very socially powerful, but this potential exists because it is first empowered by the nation-state, which legally grants it under very specific and highly formal legal conditions. The patent, in short, acts as an instrument of legal power, and the goal of Chapter 2 is to elaborate the social conditions and effects of patents as instruments of legal power.

Having seen how instruments of legal power can work to channel social power in a present-day context, we are prepared to look together into the past, to see how the present-day entwining of formal and substantive rationalities in law have come to work together as they do, to bind our communities together in the ways that they do, and to support property structures in the ways that they do.

Chapter 3 transports us to Hellenistic Rome, and to the issuance of a legal privilege from the Senate of Rome to the polis of Delphi. This chapter shows how empirical formality enabled ancient legal documents to work as instruments of legal power. In seeing how Rome deployed instruments of legal power – legal privileges that performatively created and memorialized patronage relationships with subordinated peoples – to forge an empire, we see how instruments of legal power were used to create governing communities and zones of exclusivity in Mediterranean antiquity. We also see how the zones of exclusivity granted to ancient city-states like Delphi are analogous to the zones of exclusivity granted to modern corporations like Facebook, in the form of intellectual property.

Chapter 4 focuses on the transformative period of Roman history in which the republic collapsed and the empire emerged. The famous historical personalities of Caesar and Cicero are sketched to contrast two prevailing methods of acquiring social power in ancient Rome: (1) charismatic leadership of soldiers, as exemplified by Caesar, and (2) rhetorical persuasion in accordance with formalistic rules, as exemplified by Cicero. In one published speech by Cicero, we see very close counterparts to intellectual property in ancient Rome: a situation in which a foreign-born poet has been granted Roman citizenship as a privilege in order to reward his poetic services to the state, described metaphorically as a kind of property. We then see how this basic pattern of granting privileges in order to incentivize valued behaviors was systematically utilized by Roman emperors, as they sought to transform the institutional structures of the republic into an institutional structure over which they exercised more autocratic levels of control. Through grants of citizenship privileges to foreign soldiers, and through senatorial privileges to Roman families, the emperors were able to establish social bonds of gratitude and obligation that enhanced their own powers, relative to other powerful Roman men.

Instruments of legal power, in other words – legal privileges, often conveyed by letters, granting citizenship and elite status – were an important vehicle for creating the obligational structure of the Roman empire. With the rise of jurists, who were themselves privileged through the formal grant of an exclusive "right of responding" to legal inquiries, Roman law was increasingly developed into a more elaborate, semantically formal conceptual system. Within this conceptual system, jurists recognized important forerunners to intellectual property, in legal methods for acquiring property that had previously belonged to no one (*res nullius*). Many centuries later, these would become the foundation for natural law doctrines that underpin modern intellectual property law.

The metaphor of an earthquake is useful for understanding the social drama that attended the institutional transformation of Rome from republic to empire. The metaphor is also useful for understanding the cultural transformation taken up in Chapter 5: the Christianization of the Roman empire. Chapter 5 traces the development of Christianity within the empire, opening with a dramatic legal moment – issuance of the imperial decree *Cunctos Populos* in AD 380 – in which Christian religion was institutionalized as the official law (*lex*) of the empire. We will examine the close counterparts to intellectual property that existed in the Roman law of late antiquity. With Christianization, however, we will also see how semantic formalities and substantive rationalities in Roman law were culturally transformed. Empirical formalities from Roman law persisted, but these were sacramentalized in accordance with Christian understandings. Instruments of legal power from the Roman empire were carried forward, and the transformations in semantic formality and substantive rationality that took place with Christianization would mean that these instruments of legal power could be deployed in newly intentional ways.

For Michael Mann, the Christian west of the early Middle Ages was a world in which ideology became transcendent, which is to say that ideology became a powerful source of social ties and organization that operated both *extensively* – over a wide geographic area – and *intensively*, as a source of social power mobilizing high levels of personal commitment, even to the point of self-sacrifice. Mann does not focus on the Christianization of law, but we can extend his analysis to think about what it means for the transformation of formal and substantive rationalities of law, underpinning early counterparts to intellectual property in the Roman empire.

For Mann, Christianity became powerful partly because it exercised a broad ideological appeal. Mann's explanation for this ideological appeal rests in the argument that Christianity injected a new level of voluntarism into social identity. The sheer success of the empire in enhancing literacy and enabling large numbers of people to experience sufficient leisure to ask existential questions had generated crises of social identity, to which Christianity offered an increasingly popular response. According to Christian religious doctrines, communal obligations and social identity involve something voluntary – something having to do with will and choice – rather than ascription on the basis of birth or blood. A new level of voluntarism, injected through Christianity, would have a gradually transformative effect on the formal and substantive rationalities in law, which the church carried forward.

As I discuss further in Chapters 1 and 2, I prefer to use the theoretical concept of culture, rather than ideology. Nonetheless, I think there is something important to be learned from Mann's basic story about how Christianity injected new levels of voluntarism into social life, thereby inaugurating a new set of transformative social possibilities. Beginning in Chapter 5, and then continuing through the remainder of the book, I discuss these transformative possibilities, as these are realized within law, using a language of "legality" that draws on Max Weber's legal sociology.

In Chapters 6–8, we will see the realization of this new set of transformative social possibilities in Christian (and post-Christian) legality. In Chapter 6, we will see instruments of legal power being deployed to create new types of intentional legal communities, including legal communities that foster invention and creativity, and that recognize new types of legal property. The chapter opens with a law that many have considered to be the world's first patent law – a statute enacted by the city of Venice, promising a particular type of privilege to an inventor of a useful device. The chapter then situates this statute in the context of dramatic cultural and economic transformations in the early and high Middle Ages. The chapter paints with a broad brush, seeking to show how the voluntarism of Christianized legal frameworks enabled the creation of three new types of governing community, which were important to the emergence of intellectual property: medieval cities, universities, and nations. Closely connected with the formation of these new types of governing communities was the rise of an organized, literate laity, which became ever more vocal.

In Chapter 7, vital foundations for the organizing framework of the modern nation-state will be laid in post-Conquest England. Feudalism, as institutionalized in the royal prerogative, was essential. In order to see how, we will investigate the historical factors that made England distinctive, in this period of time, both in the intensity of its feudal structures and in the strength of its royal, prerogative powers. The story, in brief, involves a historical combination of Anglo-Saxon legal legacies and the imposition of kingly rule, which came with the Norman Conquest of 1066. For the next century, northern French and Anglo-Saxon legal traditions and practices coalesced into a regime involving new levels of social power. Roman law, Biblical law, canon law, and very early English common law each played vital roles in this coalescence, with new levels of economic growth fueled by new types of legal privileges, some of which even facilitated new inventions, like the windmill. We briefly flash forward to the time of William Blackstone (1723-80) to see his creative refashioning of these legal traditions in providing a conceptual foundation for modern intellectual property law.

Chapter 8 whisks us through the English Reformation, tracing the rise of Parliament and the early roots of nationalization in English law. Early corporate monopolies, together with forms of property ownership that look very similar to modern freehold, appear in towns and guilds of the high Middle Ages. Idealistic notions that there is a "community of the realm" are briefly ascendant in the baronial revolt of the mid-thirteenth century, and these will be remembered later as part of a much deeper and wider revolt that was organized through the king and the Parliament in the English Reformation.

National consciousness was starting to appear in the British Isles, with close connection to an increasingly self-conscious and powerful state. A Roman law reception, seen especially in legal treatises, brought a degree of semantic formality into English common law, recognizing the king's prerogative powers in granting franchises and defining legal concepts connected with the acquisition of property. Stretching across the great divide of the Black Death, and the radical social changes this pandemic wrought, the chapter concludes with the Henrician Reformation, considering especially its implications for the royal prerogative, the supremacy of statutory law, and national religion. Of particular significance for the substantive rationalities built into modern intellectual property law is the recognition, seen in advice given by a jurist (John Fortescue) to his king, that royal privileging practices can be part of the intentional design for a powerful kingdom, playing a role in broader strategies to secure national loyalty through the enrichment of common citizens.

In Chapter 9, intellectual property will emerge in its modern form, enabled by a cultural transformation extending from Britain to the United States, a transformation that parallels, in significant respects, the Christianization of imperial Rome. In this cultural transformation, traditions of Roman law were rediscovered as a naturalistic foundation for sociability and national economic life. The commodification of human creativity and inventive discovery made sense, within this cultural context, as a justified response to natural, but extraordinary, powers of human creativity, and became part of a broader strategy for national empowerment, particularly in the US. I center initial attention on the cases of *Millar* v. *Taylor* (King's Bench 1769) and *Donaldson* v. *Becket* (House of Lords 1774), recognizing these as the first cases in which the status of intellectual property was fully considered, under English common law. Focusing especially on Lord Mansfield's arguments in *Millar*, I argue that intellectual property emerged as part of a broader process of legal nationalization facilitated by belief in natural legality that I anchor in the scholarship of John Locke and liberal Christianity. Through the faith-based confidence in this new order of natural legality, elements of the crown prerogative were transformed into the property of English subjects. I then shift to the New World context of the United States, tracing the ways in which the American revolutionaries embedded a legal foundation for intellectual property law into their constitutional text. With the American appropriation, intellectual property became part of the constitutional design for a quintessentially modern nation-state, and for a globalizing, nation-state system. Through this constitutional design, natural legality is proclaimed as a new national faith, and economic growth fueled by novelty in science and technology becomes a new basis for national hopes.

In Chapter 10, we see how this natural legality was radicalized in the French Revolution. It was in the French Revolutionary period, not surprisingly, that the national foundation for intellectual property was articulated most clearly. But the articulation was paradoxical, because it was combined with an equally radical and clear proclamation that rights to intellectual property are inherent, natural rights. Intellectual property was both natural and national, in the French Revolution, both a creature of national will and a transcendent, human right connected closely to the personality of the creative genius. In the early stages of the Revolution, French jurists and clerics played an important role in laying new foundations for a national state that protects intellectual property. But as radicalism intensified, ending in Napoleanic dictatorship, a more conservative Civil Code was drafted, one that returned to the classical conceptions of property acquisition in imperial Roman law. Concepts and principles of intellectual property law remained vital, ironically, through French case law (jurisprudence), and were eventually given a more secure, statutory foundation in the mid-nineteenth century.

In the German-speaking lands of the Holy Roman Empire, meanwhile, an even more conservative adherence to principles of status-based ("estate") society prevented anything like modern intellectual property law from emerging, although limited analogues were recognized in a Prussian code of the late eighteenth and early nineteenth century. Liberal reforms were beginning to break up the old order, however. Tracing alternative designs for intellectual property-related institutions in French and German processes of state formation, I argue that, in the end, both sets of state-building experience reinforce the extent to which intellectual property, in its modern form, depends on a national state and on a quasi-religious faith in legality, a faith that was intentionally internalized and politically radicalized in the Lutheran and Calvinist Reformations.

In Chapter 11, we return to the American context in order to see how intellectual property develops from within a nationalizing state during the nineteenth century. Encountering another irony here, we see the extent to which America's national legal foundations were inter-national and Roman. In writers of early US legal treatises, we see an overt embrace of Roman law as a foundation for the commercial law of the new nation. We see the implications of this in the will theory of contracts and in franchising arrangements that lay the foundations for a telecommunications network, at first for telegraphs and later for telephones. Contracts become a new instrument of legal power, one that can facilitate intentional strategy in the consolidation and deployment of unprecedented levels of social power, rooted in the zones of exclusivity enabled by intellectual property. In the Bell Telephone System, we will see this consolidated social power at its apex. In the regulatory reactions to this level of social power, we see an early foundation for empowerment of the American administrative state.

In Chapter 12, we will focus on the international extension of modern intellectual property, highlighting America's place in a regime of intellectual property that today is global. We will trace the foundations for this global order in international treaty frameworks, focusing on the legal parallels between treaties and contracts, as instruments of legal power. We will briefly sketch certain twentieth-century developments in US intellectual property law, highlighting the juristic "solicitude" that is shown to intellectual property in US lawmaking and international diplomacy. In the wake of World War II, the United States has used its position of global economic power to solidify commitments to intellectual property in a legal framework for trade relations that constitutes a supernational organization, the World Trade Organization, encouraging global convergence in intellectual property law. New dangers and challenges are facing us today, in this globalized legal order, with the rise of artificial intelligence, and with patent claims extending very deeply into the social dimensions of human life, through computer-implemented inventions.

Despite its integration into a trans-national, organizing order, intellectual property continues to be regarded as a guarantor of national prosperity, a basic foundation for consumption-driven membership in the national community. The attendant hopes and fears for national status and prosperity to which this contributes are seen through a moment in the "smartphone wars," intellectual property litigation on a grand scale, pitting an American company (Apple) against a South Korean company (Samsung). The disturbing forms of economic nationalism revealed in this dispute set the stage for reflection in the conclusion, which reiterates main lines of argument and seeks to facilitate discussion about the place of intellectual property in our political communities today.

Intellectual property is both new and old. It is new in the extent of its legal formality, in the way that it works through a nation-state system, and in its privileging of novelty. As a legal form, however, it has ancient roots. This book is premised on the conviction that we need to see both the old and the new in order to understand the position that intellectual property holds in the obliging forces and structural patterns of our modern world.

And so we begin.

1

Legal Institutions and Social Power

Setting the Stage

Every once in a while, the earth beneath our feet shakes and trembles, reminding us that below the hard, cool surfaces upon which we walk and build our lives, there is seething, boiling magma. The earth is not solid and cool, but liquid and hot. Underneath deep layers of ocean, soil, and rock, there are tectonic plates floating on boiling fluidity. When these plates rub against each other, or press down underneath each other, both earth and ocean tremble and roll.[1]

Modern legal institutions like property and contracts are a bit like this. Most of the time they rest solidly beneath us, enabling us to live our daily lives without thinking too much about them. But every once in a while they start to tremble and shake, and sometimes they even break apart into something new. Social forces and tensions within them gradually build, and our everyday lives start to rattle and roll. Suddenly we wake up and realize that very basic aspects of our everyday activity depend on foundations that have been mostly hidden and taken for granted. Only when these roil and transform do we become aware of our wide-ranging dependence on them.[2]

But the social world of legal institutions is in one way very different from the natural world of geology. Unlike tectonic plates, legal institutions have been made by human beings. Our English word *institution* comes from a Latin word, *institutio*, which basically means something that is established or laid down. There is a common root of meaning in the Latin verb *stare, to stand,* from which we derive our English word *state.* Institutions and states stand like solid things, but only because *we* build, stabilize, and maintain them. That *we*, though, is a many and

[1] For more on the science of plate tectonics, see the US Geological Survey publication *This Dynamic Earth: The Story of Plate Tectonics*, originally printed in 1996 and available electronically at https://pubs.usgs.gov/gip/dynamic/ (accessed February 4, 2018).

[2] Sociologists and social theorists will hear echoes of Karl Marx and Friedrich Engels here: "All that is solid melts into air, all that is holy is profaned, and man is at last compelled to face with sober senses, his real conditions of life, and his relations with his kind." *Manifesto of the Communist Party*, in *The Marx-Engels Reader*, 2nd ed., edited by Robert C. Tucker (New York: W. W. Norton, 1978), 476. While I am in many ways critical of the Marxist tradition, particularly for its impacts on sociological thinking about law, I am also indebted to that tradition, especially for its insistence on the extent to which property relations underpin our everyday social existence.

varied we. No single person or group of persons is in control. Legal institutions are bigger and stronger than us, and this is why they can start to appear so big and strong that they seem like the solid ground beneath our feet, something that we can walk and build our lives upon, without needing to think too much about them. But then they shake and roll again, reminding us that deep beneath a cool and solid surface, there is hot, boiling fluidity.[3]

This is a book about one specific legal institution, which we call *intellectual property*. This is a type of legal property that today includes patents, copyrights, trademarks, and trade secrets, together with related kinds of *knowledge-based, intangible* property. The book is driven by a very basic, and very big, set of questions. Where did intellectual property come from? And, since intellectual property could only come into the world because we made it so, how, when, and why did we do that?[4]

Fundamentally, this is a book about the ways that legal institutions, like intellectual property, have solidified upon deeper, hotter, and fluid social energies. I will talk about these social energies as social powers, drawing at times on the ambitious sociological and historical scholarship of Michael Mann, and supplementing him with the classical sociological thought of Max Weber and Emile Durkheim. I will argue that changes in legal institutions, like those we see in the emergence of intellectual property, are like earthquakes. They tell us something important about seething, social energies that are boiling up underneath us, and they transform our lives.[5]

[3] For an interdisciplinary and helpful introduction to the contemporary study of institutions in the social sciences, see W. Richard Scott, *Institutions and Organizations: Ideas, Interests, and Identities*, 4th ed. (Los Angeles: Sage, 2014). For an influential overview of the "new institutionalism" in sociology, applied to the study of organizations, see Walter W. Powell and Paul J. DiMaggio (eds.), *The New Institutionalism in Organizational Analysis* (Chicago: University of Chicago Press, 1991). For the English etymologies, see C. T. Onions (ed.), *The Oxford Dictionary of Etymology* (Oxford: Oxford University Press, 1966), 478, 864–5. For classic discussions of Cicero, see *The Republic* (*De Re Publica*, Loeb Classical Library), 1.26, 2.1 (Cambridge, MA: Harvard University Press, 1928), 65–7, 111–13.

[4] While I mainly focus on patents and copyrights throughout the book, I also occasionally extend the discussion to trademarks and trade secrets. In a US context, patents and copyrights have a certain primacy in virtue of their explicit enablement under the US Constitution's "Intellectual Property Clause" (US Constitution, Article 1, Section 1, Clause 8). Within the Anglo-American legal tradition, moreover, copyrights and patents have the oldest explicit recognition as legal property, a development I trace in Chapters 8 and 9. Trademarks and trade secrets have acquired their status as legal property more recently, and to some extent as a derivation from the older status held by patents and copyrights. See, for example, Oliver Wendell Holmes' remarks in *E.I. Du Pont de Nemours Powder Co. v. Masland*, 244 US 100, 102 (1917) ("The word 'property' as applied to trademarks and trade secrets is an unanalyzed expression of certain secondary consequences of the primary fact that the law makes some rudimentary requirements of good faith. Whether the plaintiffs have any valuable secret or not the defendant knows the facts, whatever they are, through a special confidence that he accepted. The property may be denied, but the confidence cannot be.").

[5] I draw primarily on Mann's four-volume series *The Sources of Social Power*, which I refer to as *Sources* followed by an accompanying volume number, throughout the book. These are as follows: (1) Michael Mann, *The Sources of Social Power, Vol. I, A History of Power from the Beginning to AD 1760*, 2nd ed. (New York: Cambridge University Press, 2012); (2) Michael Mann, *The Sources of Social Power, Vol. II, The Rise of Classes and Nation-States, 1760–1914*, 2nd ed. (New York: Cambridge University Press, 2012); (3) Michael Mann, *The Sources of Social Power, Vol. III, Global Empires and*

This book is about a series of social earthquakes that led to the emergence of intellectual property, as we know it today. But because intellectual property, as a modern legal institution, is one of those taken-for-granted foundations upon which we walk and build our lives, we must first take the time to recognize it, and render it visible. I will undertake this project in legal recognition in various ways throughout this book, but I will begin the project by taking you to your local McDonald's restaurant.[6]

1.1 SEEING THE INTELLECTUAL PROPERTY IN YOUR EVERYDAY LIFE

Intellectual property is everywhere at McDonald's, but to see it, you need to know where to look. The next time you order food from a McDonald's restaurant, you might look closely at the menu, or at your drinking cup. If you do, you will probably notice some peculiar symbols: ®, ©, TM, or maybe even SM. These symbols point to intellectual property ownership and claims. The first symbol indicates a registered trademark, the second a registered copyright, and the last two indicate that intellectual property – in the form of trademarks or service marks – is being *claimed*, but the claims have not been formally affirmed by the US government.[7]

Revolution, 1890–1945 (New York: Cambridge University Press, 2012); (4) Michael Mann, *The Sources of Social Power, Vol. IV, Globalizations, 1945–2011* (New York: Cambridge University Press, 2013). I also draw on the helpful analyses of Mann's theoretical framework in John A. Hall and Ralph Schroeder (eds.), *An Anatomy of Power: The Social Theory of Michael Mann* (Cambridge, UK: Cambridge University Press, 2006). Mann's "organizational materialism" is limited in its theorizing of "ideology" and culture, and this is partly why I think it is important to supplement him with a return to the classical theorists of culture, law, and religion – Weber and Durkheim – whose sensitivity and insight in these areas remains unsurpassed, in my view. Hannah Arendt also provides important supplementary insights, particularly into "the life of the mind," culture, national states, and the stabilizing effect of promises in social life. On Hannah Arendt's tension-ridden relationship to sociology, see Peter Baehr, *Hannah Arendt, Totalitarianism, and the Social Sciences* (Stanford: Stanford University Press, 2010); Philip Walsh, *Arendt Contra Sociology: Theory, Society and Its Science* (London and New York: Routledge, 2016).

6 The sociologist George Ritzer has helpfully drawn attention to McDonald's restaurant, showing how it may be seen as a contemporary and very visible indicator of a broader social development that he calls McDonaldization: "the process by which the principles of the fast-food restaurant are coming to dominate more and more sectors of American society as well as of the rest of the world." George Ritzer, *The McDonaldization of Society*, 8th ed. (Los Angeles: Sage, 2015), 1–2. For Ritzer, McDonald's exemplifies an ever-intensifying process at work in our globalizing societies, one that involves ongoing technological and organizational revolutions emphasizing efficiency, calculability, predictability, and control. Because of its global visibility and ubiquity, McDonald's helps Ritzer to illustrate a widespread social phenomenon that is difficult to see, but one that he argues is nonetheless having very real effects in our everyday lives.

7 For a brief introduction to the symbols of trademark claiming and registration, see the US Patent and Trademark Office (USPTO) information booklet "Protecting Your Trademark: Enhancing Your Rights through Federal Registration: Basic Facts about Trademarks," at www.uspto.gov/sites/default/files/documents/BasicFacts.pdf (accessed April 25, 2019), 11. For a brief introduction to the registration of copyright claims, see the US Copyright Office Circular 1, Copyright Basics, at www.copyright.gov/circs/circ01.pdf (accessed April 25, 2019), 4–5.

For the McDonald's Corporation, customer *goodwill* associated with the McDonald's brand is a vital asset. This asset is constituted as legally protected property through trademark law, which protects consumers' mental associations among (1) the McDonald's Corporation, (2) its branding symbols (e.g., slogans and logos, like the golden arches), and (3) the goods and services that McDonald's sells (e.g., the "Big Mac"). Use of these branding symbols without McDonald's Corporation's permission is called trademark *infringement* and is legally viewed as a violation of property rights.[8]

Under US law, as well as under many other legal systems, property receives special legal protections. Some courts go so far as to say that property is "sacred." Even if they do not use this language, however, courts provide a special category of *sanctions* – often called *equitable remedies* or *injunctions* – where property rights are concerned. (It is relevant to note that the word *sanction* comes from the Latin word for something sacred – *sanctio*.) This makes property the most powerful type of private right that a person can possess under the US legal system, more powerful than contract rights, which are also an important category of private rights.[9]

8 Evidence for the importance of goodwill to the McDonald's Corporation is readily found in McDonald's annual report to its shareholders. McDonald's Corporation, *Form 10-K, Annual Report Pursuant to Section 13 or 15(d) of the Securities Exchange Act of 1934, Year ended December 31, 2018* (filed February 22, 2019) (hereafter "McDonald's 2018 Annual Report"). Goodwill is separately listed as a long-lived asset in McDonald's financial statements, and as of December 31, 2018, it was valued at approximately $2.3 billion, or approximately 7.1 percent of total assets. *McDonald's 2018 Annual Report*, Consolidated Balance Sheet, 34. For discussions of the importance of intellectual property, particularly trademarks, to McDonald's, see, for example, Part I, Item 1c ("Narrative Description of Business"): "The Company owns or is licensed to use valuable intellectual property including trademarks, service marks, patents, copyrights, trade secrets and other proprietary information. The Company considers the trademarks 'McDonald's' and 'The Golden Arches Logo' to be of material importance to its business." *McDonald's 2018 Annual Report*, 2. McDonald's Annual Reports may be downloaded from the US Securities and Exchange Commission's web-based EDGAR database, www.sec.gov/edgar, an invaluable resource for such reports, which are required pursuant to the US securities law framework established in the wake of the Great Depression. See US Securities and Exchange Commission, *What We Do*, at www.sec.gov/Article/whatwedo.html (accessed April 25, 2019).

9 For references to property as "sacred," see, for example, *Kalom* v. *Brady*, 872 So. 2d 741, 743 (Miss. Ct. App. 2004) ("This State has always held the right to use and control one's property as sacred."); *Sharpless* v. *Mayor of Philadelphia*, 21 Pa. 147, 166 (Pa. 1853) ("Our constitution makes property as sacred as life."). Equitable remedies, such as injunctions – which either temporarily or permanently prohibit a defendant from taking a particular action, like selling a particular product – are seen as being more coercive, because a court is actually commanding future behavior directly, rather than simply requiring the payment of money "damages" to compensate for a wrong that has already occurred. For an accessible and historically informed discussion of equitable remedies under US law, see Lawrence M. Friedman, *American Law: An Introduction*, 2nd ed. (New York: W. W. Norton, 1998), 88–90, with more in-depth treatment in Lawrence M. Friedman, *A History of American Law*, 3rd ed. (New York: Simon & Schuster, 2005), ll. 366–99, 841–64, 2863–97, 8556–64. For an introduction to the use of equitable remedies in intellectual property litigation, provided by the authors of a leading legal textbook, see Mark A. Lemley, Peter S. Menell, and Robert P. Merges, *Intellectual Property in the New Technological Age: 2018, Vol. I, Perspectives, Trade Secrets and Patents* (Clause 8 Publishing, 2018), 139–41, 432–38.

The leading US Supreme Court case on the issue of injunctions in intellectual property litigation is *eBay* v. *MercExchange*, 547 US 388 (2006), which held that traditional principles of equity, involving

We can see some important practical aspects of trademark law, as a type of property law, at work in the 1988 film *Coming to America*, which stars Eddie Murphy and Arsenio Hall. In this film, Prince Akeem Joffer (Eddie Murphy's character) seeks a job at a *McDowell's* restaurant. The scenes involving the fictional McDowell's restaurant offer classic (and funny) illustrations of trademark infringement. At one point in the film, the owner of the restaurant is even seen reading from a McDonald's Operation Manual. He makes references to a "misunderstanding" with McDonald's and seeks to persuade Eddie Murphy and Arsenio Hall that his "golden arcs," along with his menu items, are different from their McDonald's counterparts.[10]

In real life, such a restaurant owner would certainly have reason for concern. His symbolic marks, while not identical to those of McDonald's, are so similar that they can easily be shown by a competent attorney to be infringing: they trespass on McDonald's property because they are likely to confuse a potential consumer about the source of her food products. *Likelihood of confusion* is the basic legal standard for showing trademark infringement, and in this case, it would involve showing that a consumer might think they are ordering food from McDonald's, when in reality the consumer is ordering food from McDowell's. Whether or not a consumer would actually be confused, however, McDonald's can also argue that it has a famous mark, the value of which would likely be *diluted* by McDowell's use of similar marks.[11]

The restaurant owner in *Coming to America* (Cleo McDowell) would doubtless receive threatening letters from McDonald's lawyers, warning him to *cease and desist* from infringing on McDonald's trademarks. If he should be so foolhardy as to continue infringing on McDonald's marks, lawsuits would quickly follow, and a court might even go so far as to issue those special remedies for violations of

a prudential weighing of four factors, must be applied in the decision to grant or deny a permanent injunction in patent litigation. Although *eBay* narrowly applies to permanent injunctions in the context of patent litigation, the reasoning has been recognized to apply more broadly to temporary injunctions, and in the contexts of trademark and copyright litigation. See *Herb Reed Enterprises v. Florida Entertainment Management*, 736 F.3d 1239 (9th Cir. 2013) (applying *eBay* principles to a determination concerning the propriety of a temporary injunction in trademark litigation); Mark A. Lemley, Peter S. Menell, and Robert P. Merges, *Intellectual Property in the New Technological Age: 2018, Vol. II: Copyrights, Trademarks, and State IP Protections* (Clause 8 Publishing, 2018), 1104–9; cf. *Spansion v. Int'l Trade Comm'n*, 629 F.3d 1331 (Fed. Cir. 2010) (holding that traditional principles of equity, including the four-factor balancing test elaborated in *eBay*, do not apply in the context of patent litigation before the International Trade Commission).

10 Eddie Murphy et al., *Coming to America*, directed by John Landis (Hollywood: Paramount Pictures, 1988), DVD. Many thanks to Robert Simpson, of Simpson & Simpson PLLC, a Buffalo, New York–based intellectual property law firm, for drawing my attention to the trademark-related aspects of this film.

11 For discussion of "likelihood of confusion," as the basic standard for trademark infringement, together with a brief discussion of "dilution," as a parallel basis for infringement, see Lemley, Menell, and Merges, *Intellectual Property*, Vol. II, 986–1041. For discussion of policy-based purposes of trademark law, namely protecting "the integrity of the marketplace," see Lemley, Menell, and Merges, *Intellectual Property*, Vol. I, 26–9.

property rights, which are called *injunctions*. Upon McDonald's almost certain victory, Cleo McDowell would be permanently prohibited from continuing to use his infringing marks, and he would probably have to pay a large compensation – monetary *damages* – for trademark infringement and trademark dilution.[12]

Trademarks are everywhere at McDonald's. They not only cover McDonald's core branding symbols (the golden arches, Ronald McDonald, etc.) but also any new goods and services that McDonald's develops. For example, in 2014–15 McDonald's launched a new "Create Your Taste" service, which enabled people to build their own food and drink items from basic ingredients. This service had its own logo: a black and white circle, surrounding a white chef's hat, with the words "Est. 2014" nostalgically portrayed below. Both the slogan and the logo were registered as trade/service marks to McDonald's Corporation, although they have since been abandoned as the "Create Your Taste" service has proved unpopular in the United States.[13]

McDonald's has a valuable brand, and it knows it must be vigilant in protecting the property boundaries that surround that brand. These property boundaries, to repeat, come from trademark law. The strong legal protection of these property boundaries is what helps McDonald's to transform its crucial asset – its brand – into the foundation for a profitable business model: *franchising*.[14]

Through its franchising arrangements, the McDonald's Corporation gives permission – in a contract called a *license* – to an individual restaurant owner, who is allowed to use McDonald's Corporation's intellectual property, in exchange for rental payments and submission to corporate control over many aspects of the business. In 2018, approximately 93 percent of McDonald's restaurants were operating as independent franchises. The fact that so much uniformity is nonetheless seen in McDonald's restaurants is largely attributable to the controls that the parent

12 For critical discussion of cease and desist letters in self-policing of trademark infringement, see Leah Chan Grinvald, "Policing the Cease and Desist Letter," *University of San Francisco Law Review* 49 (2015): 409–63, available at Social Science Research Network: http://ssrn.com/abstract=2515455 (accessed August 7, 2017).

13 US Trademark Serial Number 86437451 (filed October 28, 2014, abandoned January 2, 2017) (Create Your Taste Est. 2014); US Trademark Serial Number 86431619 (filed October 22, 2014, abandoned January 9, 2017) (Create Your Taste). For news about McDonald's Corporation's abandonment of the Create Your Taste Service in the United States, see Hayley Peterson and Hollis Johnson, "McDonald's Just Pulled the Plug on Its Biggest Menu Change in Years," *Business Insider*, November 3, 2016, www.businessinsider.com/mcdonalds-ends-create-your-taste-2016–11. US trademarks are searchable from the USPTO website, through the Trademark Electronic Search System (TESS), at www.uspto.gov/trademark (accessed April 26, 2019).

14 *McDonald's 2018 Annual Report*, Part I, Item 1b ("Narrative description of business"), 1: "The Company operates and franchises McDonald's restaurants . . . ."; for further discussion of the role played by trademark rights in franchising, see Lemley, Menell, and Merges, *Intellectual Property*, Vol. II, 997–8. For a historical treatment of franchising in the United States, see Thomas S. Dicke, *Franchising in America: The Development of a Business Method, 1840–1980* (Chapel Hill: University of North Carolina Press, 1992).

corporation can exercise over its franchisees, through the licensing of intellectual property.[15]

Trademark and contract law together, in other words, provide a legal foundation for profit collection and centralized control of the food-service activity in a particular McDonald's restaurant. By licensing its valuable trademarks to individual franchisees, the McDonald's Corporation secures a revenue stream for its shareholders, and is able to impose organizational controls that help to ensure that consumers receive a reasonably high-quality, standardized product. Only through this control is McDonald's able to maintain the value of its brand.[16]

Trademarks, however, are not the only form of intellectual property that the McDonald's Corporation owns and licenses to its franchisees. McDonald's also owns several patents, for example, US Patent No. 6,053,359 on an Automated Beverage System. This patent covers systems for preparing and delivering beverages, in particular the soft drink dispensing machines that McDonald's employees use. *It also covers the steps that McDonald's employees take in dispensing those beverages.*[17]

Patents provide property protection to inventions that are new, nonobvious, useful, and fully described in a patent application. There are limitations on the types of things that patents can cover. Human beings, abstract ideas, laws of nature, and physical phenomena are not patent-eligible. Genetically modified animals and plants, however, are patent-eligible, as are sequences of human DNA that have been artificially altered in a laboratory for research or medical purposes. If the patent claims are drafted carefully, software and business methods are patent-eligible, as are internet-based social networks.[18]

It might surprise you to know that patents cover not only machines but also methods of doing business, software, and internet-based social networking. This is a relatively new development in patent law, and one that has been controversial. In 2010, the US Supreme Court came very close to deciding that business methods are not patent-eligible, but a thin majority of the Court decided that complete

15 *McDonald's 2018 Annual Report*, at Part I, Item 1b ("Narrative description of business"), 1–2. The company's stated goal is to be "approximately 95% franchised over the long term." Ibid., 1.

16 Ibid., 1–2. "The success of our business depends on our continued ability to use our existing trademarks and service marks in order to increase brand awareness and further develop our branded products in both domestic and international markets. We rely on a combination of trademarks, copyrights, service marks, trade secrets, patents, and other intellectual property rights to protect our brand and branded products." Ibid., 8.

17 US Patent No. 6,053,359 (issued April 25, 2000). US patents are searchable through the USPTO website, at www.uspto.gov/patents-application-process/search-patents (accessed July 1, 2019). Google also has a dedicated website for patent searches, which offers full-text US patents going back to 1790, as well as patents for a number of worldwide patent offices, at https://patents.google.com/ (accessed July 1, 2019).

18 For a leading textbook discussion of patent eligibility, see Lemley, Menell, and Merges, *Intellectual Property*, Vol. I, 161–2, 275–316; for historical and sociological discussion of social networking patents, see Laura R. Ford, "Patenting the Social: Alice, Abstraction, and Functionalism in Software Patent Claims," *Cardozo Public Law, Policy & Ethics Journal* 14 (2016): 259–342, available at https://papers.ssrn.com/sol3/papers.cfm?abstract_id=2802750 (accessed July 1, 2019).

prohibition on the patenting of business methods would go too far and might have unintended consequences on innovation. While recognizing that business method patents raise particular concerns, and may deserve special scrutiny by courts and patent examiners, the Court refused to completely exclude business methods from patentability. In 2014, the Court affirmed that software and internet-based networking systems are also patent-eligible, while driving home the point that these patents must not be too abstract and broad.[19]

Having a patent on its Automated Beverage System gives McDonald's a property right that extends to everything that comes within the boundaries laid out by the patent claims. Through its business method patent claims, the McDonald's Corporation owns *a method of organizing human activity*. This is language that both the Supreme Court and the US Court of Appeals for the Federal Circuit have used in describing business method patents.[20]

What is the significance of owning a method of organizing human activity?

At a minimum, the significance is economic control: without first seeking and paying for McDonald's permission, no one else can legally use this particular sequence of steps in making or selling products or services in the United States. If McDonald's learns that one of its competitors is using its patented sequence of steps in beverage-dispensing services, it can sue that competitor for patent infringement. If successful in the lawsuit, McDonald's would receive money damages, and probably those special remedies available for property owners – injunctions – that go further and make commands about future behavior.[21]

Is a level of social control involved here as well? Legally speaking, McDonald's Corporation owns the sequence of steps that its employees take, many times every day, in dispensing beverages. Does this mean that McDonald's Corporation owns a dimension of its employees themselves? Many people, and probably most patent lawyers, would emphatically say no. Sociologists might answer this question

19 *Bilski* v. *Kappos*, 561 US 593 (2010); *Alice Corp.* v. *CLS Bank Int'l*, 134 S. Ct. 2350 (2014). For further discussion of these cases, see Ford, "Patenting the Social," 296–304; Lemley, Menell, and Merges, *Intellectual Property*, Vol. I, 275–316.

20 35 U.S.C. § 261 (2018) ("Subject to the provisions of this title, patents shall have the attributes of personal property."); US Patent No. 6,053,359 (issued April 25, 2000). As discussed further below, patent claims are verbal descriptions of the invention, which are laid out in very careful language at the end of a patent application. Each claim of the Automated Beverage System patent, for example, describes a particular aspect of the invention that McDonald's is claiming as its property. In this particular patent, there are 59 claims, a large number. As the patent owner, McDonald's has the legal right to prevent anyone else from making, using, or selling anything that comes within the boundaries of this written description. Whether something does come within the boundaries of this written description is, of course, a matter of interpretation and legal argumentation. On business method patents as covering methods of organizing human activity, see *Alice Corporation* v. *CLS Bank Int'l*, 134 S. Ct. 2347, 2356 (June 2014); *Bilski* v. *Kappos*, 561 US 593, 617, 628 (2010) (Stevens, J., concurring); In re Bilski, 545 F.3d 943, 970 (Fed. Cir. 2008) (Dyk, J., concurring).

21 For further discussion of patent infringement and patent litigation, see Lemley, Menell, and Merges, *Intellectual Property*, Vol. I, 367–457. For the sake of simplicity, I am solely addressing the US implications of a US patent here.

differently, however, and this is just one of many reasons why a sociological perspective on intellectual property is important.

In addition to patents and trademarks, McDonald's owns copyrights. Copyrights cover forms of creative expression that have been fixed in a tangible medium. Examples of copyrightable materials include written texts, sculptures, paintings, sound recordings, computer programming code, and the appearance of a webpage. Between 1978 and 2017, McDonald's Corporation registered over 150 copyrights. In 1978, for example, McDonald's registered a copyright for a Ronald McDonald giant story coloring book. In 2000 and 2002, McDonald's registered copyrights in its website, McDonalds.com. And, in 2009, McDonald's registered a copyright in a song written by a woman named Patricia Sowell Harris, called "None of Us Is as Good as All of Us."[22]

Normally, copyrights belong initially to the author of a creative work, unless and until the author licenses or assigns the copyright to someone else. However, there is an exception to this rule, which applied to Patricia Sowell Harris. When someone is hired to create a work, or uses employer time and resources in creating a work, the work may legally be considered to be *made for hire*. In the case of a work that is made for hire, the copyright belongs to the employer, not the employee, even though the employee is the author of the work. Patricia Sowell Harris' song was a work for hire and was registered as McDonald's Corporation's copyright.[23]

The McDonald's Corporation also owns trade secrets and discloses this in its Annual Report. However, because they are secrets, McDonald's does not tell us what they are. Trade secret law has historically been mostly state-based law that varies somewhat from state to state, and that covers things ranging from industrial espionage to violation of a contractual obligation not to disclose information. Trade secrets that are valuable to the McDonald's Corporation might include recipes for special sauces and managerial techniques that are communicated secretly to franchisees. If a franchisee were to share such secrets with a competitor, this could hurt McDonald's financially. If the franchisee had a legal duty to keep the information secret, then the release of the information would probably constitute a *misappropriation* of a trade secret, and the franchisee could be required to pay

22 For a brief introduction to US copyright law, see US Copyright Office Circular 1, Copyright Basics, at www.copyright.gov/circs/circ01.pdf (accessed June 26, 2019). For a more extensive introduction, see Lemley, Menell, and Merges, *Intellectual Property*, Vol. II, 489–856. The US Copyright Office maintains a web-based search portal for copyright registrations, available at www.copyright.gov/ (accessed June 28, 2019). A search for registered copyrights under the name McDonald's Corporation, conducted on September 3, 2017, returned 167 results. Ronald McDonald giant story coloring book, registered November 16, 1978, Doc. #V1695P229; McDonald's.com website splash page, registered February 11, 2003, Reg. # VA0001169622; McDonalds.com website splash page no. 2, registered February 11, 2003, Reg. # VA0001169621; None of Us Is as Good as All of Us by Patricia Sowell Harris, registered January 19, 2010, Reg. # TX0007130582.

23 None of Us Is as Good as All of Us by Patricia Sowell Harris, registered January 19, 2010, Reg. # TX0007130582. For a textbook discussion of works made for hire, see Lemley, Menell, and Merges, *Intellectual Property*, Vol. 2, 587–98.

money damages to McDonald's Corporation. The franchisee could also, possibly, be charged with a federal crime.[24]

In its franchise contracts, McDonald's Corporation doubtless licenses all these forms of intellectual property – patents, copyrights, trademarks, and trade secrets – to individual McDonald's restaurants. As a condition for granting permission to use its patented systems and methods, trademarked slogans and images, copyrighted music and texts, and secret recipes, McDonald's demands that its franchisees submit to strict oversight and control over every detail of food service delivery, employee training, and customer service. Because its brand is ultimately its greatest resource, McDonald's must ensure that rotten food and slovenly employees do not detract from that brand. In its effort to ensure this, McDonald's Corporation implements strict quality controls that aim to provide a uniform product across its many restaurants around the world.[25]

Intellectual property, to repeat, is everywhere at McDonald's, and is central to its basic business model. Through the example of McDonald's, we can also see the extent to which intellectual property is pervasive in our everyday lives, albeit at a level that we do not normally see.

1.2 THE PROPERTY OF NATIONS

Intellectual property is new, relatively speaking. Some scholars have argued that it is ancient, even eternal, or that it dates back to the Roman empire. Other scholars have argued that the origins of intellectual property are to be found in Venetian laws of the late fifteenth century, which provided a statutory right to new inventions deemed useful to the Venetian republic. Many scholars today locate the origins of intellectual property in England's Statute of Monopolies (1624), which carved out an exception for "new inventions" to a general prohibition on patent-based monopolies. Scholars have also noticed precursors to intellectual property in the seventeenth-century Dutch republic, where the jurist Hugo Grotius seems to have recognized a legal validity in the contractual transfer of patents, something like an early form of licensing.[26]

24 *McDonald's 2018 Annual Report*, 2, 8. For a textbook discussion of trade secret law, highlighting the increasing federal government role in protecting trade secrets, see Lemley, Menell, and Merges, *Intellectual Property*, Vol. 1, 36, 42–146. Legislation expanding the federal government's role in policing the misappropriation of trade secrets: Economic Espionage Act of 1996, codified at 18 U.S.C. § 1831 ff; Defend Trade Secrets Act of 2016, Pub. L. 114–153, amending 18 U.S.C. §§ 1836 and 1839 (enacted May 11, 2016).

25 *McDonald's 2018 Annual Report*, 1–10.

26 For arguments about the antiquity of intellectual property, see William M. Landes and Richard A. Posner, *The Economic Structure of Intellectual Property Law* (Cambridge, MA: Harvard University Press, 2003), 1 ("Intellectual property as we are defining it is ancient in origin"); Justin Hughes, "The Philosophy of Intellectual Property," *Georgetown Law Journal* 77.2 (1988): 287–366, 291("ancient Roman laws afforded a form of copyright protection to authors"); Edmund Gabbay, "All the King's Horses: Irreparable Harm in Trade Secret Litigation," *Fordham Law Review* 52.5 (1984): 804–27, 808

In this book, I will be arguing that intellectual property emerged in the eighteenth century as part of the modern nation-state. It was only in the last quarter of the eighteenth century that patents and copyrights were legally and explicitly recognized as a type of property that could be owned, in *almost* the same way that other types of property are owned. This development was recorded in two famous legal cases, which involved a dispute between English and Scottish booksellers. As we will see, these cases were in many ways testing the extent of legal union between England and Scotland.[27]

This dispute between English and Scottish booksellers was finally resolved by the House of Lords, acting as a final court of appeal. Due to peculiarities in the way the House of Lords functioned at that time, we do not have an officially published explanation of the court's reasoning in the way that we would today. This means that a great amount of confusion and controversy still surrounds this very important decision. What we can say with relative certainty, however, is the following: just before the US Revolutionary War, copyrights were recognized by Great Britain's highest court as a type of legal property, which could be owned by individuals with many of the same powers and rights held by owners of other types of legal property. However, this new type of legal property was different from other types of legal property in that the legal bond between the owner and his property was strictly limited in time. The legal bond of ownership would only endure for a period fixed by statutory law. Like patents for new inventions, which were recognized at this time as being legally analogous to copyrights, this was a type of property that existed for times and for purposes established by Parliament.[28]

("protection of rights in secret information originated in Roman law"); F. D. Prager, "The Early Growth and Influence of Intellectual Property," *Journal of the Patent Office Society* 34.2 (1952): 106–140, 106 (the idea of intellectual property is "ancient and eternal"). For a vigorous critique of scholarly assertions that intellectual property-related ideas originated in Roman law, see Alan Watson, "Trade Secrets and Roman Law: The Myth Exploded," *Tulane European and Civil Law Forum* 11 (1996): 19–29. For arguments about Venetian and English origins of patent law, see Giulio Mandich, "Venetian Origins of Inventors' Rights," *Journal of the Patent Office Society* 42.6 (1960): 378–82; Frank D. Prager, "A History of Intellectual Property from 1545 to 1787," *Journal of the Patent Office Society* 26.11 (1944): 711–60; *cf.* Ted Sichelman and Sean O'Connor, "Patents as Promoters of Competition: The Guild Origins of Patent Law in the Venetian Republic," *San Diego Law Review* 49 (2012): 1267–82. Technically, what Grotius seems to have recognized was an assignment, rather than a license, but the point is that contractual transfers were being recognized. The assignment itself was effectuated by a notarial deed. *The Opinions of Grotius as contained in the Hollandsche Consultatien en Advijsen*, collated, translated, and annotated by D. P. de Bruyn (London: Stevens and Haynes, 1894), 115–16; see *also* G. Doorman, *Patents for Inventions in the Netherlands during the 16th, 17th and 18th Centuries, Abridged English Version*, translated by John Meijer (The Hague: Martinus Nijhoff, 1942), 22.

27 *Millar* v. *Taylor*, 4 Burrow 2303, 98 Eng. Rep. 201 (1769); *Donaldson* v. *Becket*, II Brown 129; 1 Eng. Rep. 837 (1774).

28 There is an extensive literature on the foundations of intellectual property in eighteenth-century Britain, focusing especially on copyright law. For recent discussions, see Ronan Deazley, *On the Origin of the Right to Copy: Charting the Movement of Copyright Law in Eighteenth Century Britain (1695–1775)* (Oxford: Hart Publishing, 2004); Laura R. Ford, "Prerogative, Nationalized: The Social Formation of Intellectual Property," *Journal of the Patent and Trademark Office Society* 97.2 (2015):

Intellectual property emerged during a time when Britain was locked in a fierce struggle with France over economic and political control. In the United States, intellectual property emerged as independence from Britain was being legally established, a time when the fledgling United States felt themselves to be locked in a life-and-death struggle for economic and political survival. Shortly afterward, intellectual property emerged in France as part of its national revolution, which was shaped in part by military, political, and economic struggle with Prussia and Austria, as well as Britain. And, in Prussia, intellectual property would emerge through the forging of a German national union, an effort that was shaped by the struggle to survive militarily and economically. In each case, we will see a recognition that intellectual property provides important economic benefits to the nation-state in its competitive struggle with other nation-states. Intellectual property, I will argue, was legally recognized to provide economic benefits to the nation-state in its competition with other nation-states.

Intellectual property is in many ways an economic tool of nation-states, and it has been recognized as such since the eighteenth century. The creation of intellectual property, however, involved the adaptation of older legal forms that had also been used as tools for economic benefit while conveying culturally significant ideals of property ownership. The concept of a patent, as we will see, was nothing new in Europe, either in the eighteenth century or the seventeenth. English kings, like their French counterparts, had been granting economic privileges (often called "franchises" – literally meaning *freedoms*) through formal, open letters ("letters patent") since before the Norman Conquest (1066). These *letters patent* had also been granted to provide benefits to the kingdom, some (but not all) of which were economic, for example, to incentivize the development of local markets or protect international traders who were bringing revenues into the kingdom through their commercial activities. The granting of letters patent was also seen as involving property, but here the property belonged to the king not the king's subjects.[29]

Two things made intellectual property of the eighteenth century different. First, it was granted by a bureaucratizing governmental structure (the "King-in-Parliament") rather than the king personally. Many of the king's powers were now being exercised by Parliament, and by administrators who were answerable to Parliament, in accordance with statutory laws. Second, it was granted *as formally defined property* – not as a freely revocable privilege, dependent on close, personal relationships – to officially

270–306; H. Thomás Gómez-Arostegui, "Copyright at Common Law in 1774," *Connecticut Law Review* 47.1 (2014): 3–57. For further discussion, see Chapters 8 and 9.

29 Formally, *letters patent* only existed from the time of King John (r. 1199–1216) and his son, Henry III (r. 1216–1272). However, letters patent developed out of older forms that scholars call *writs* and *charters*, and it was these older forms that were used by John's predecessors, extending back well before the Norman Conquest. Scholars who study the development of legal forms in early European history often refer to this whole family of letter-based legal texts under the heading of *diplomatics*. For an introduction to medieval diplomatics, see Leonard E. Boyle, "Diplomatics," in *Medieval Studies: An Introduction*, edited by James M. Powell (Syracuse: Syracuse University Press, 1976), 69–101. English letters patent are discussed further in Chapters 7–8.

recognized members of the political organization, that is, to citizens and legal residents. It was granted as formal property to citizens and legal residents, *not so much to benefit them individually, as to benefit the organizing community (the nation-state) itself*. But it was recognized that allowing individuals (and corporations) to hold this formal property, as their own property, for a limited time, would harness creative and inventive powers that might not otherwise be awakened. Temporary individual ownership was a means to a national end. As Abraham Lincoln would put it later, intellectual property added the "fuel of interest" to the fire of genius.[30]

Intellectual property, as we will see, was created as part of the process by which a nation-state system was created. It emerged first in England and Great Britain, but then quickly spread to the United States, France, and slightly later to Germany. New nation-states that entered the arena in which the first nation-states competed and cooperated would also be compelled to include protections for intellectual property in their national legal systems, and that is the case today.

Seeing how intellectual property functions as part of a globalized, nation-state system, however, only gives us the final act in a lengthy and complex drama. We still need to understand *how* it was created. As sociologists and philosophers have recognized, describing a functional relationship (e.g., the heart functions to pump blood, or punishment of crime functions to reinforce social cohesion) does not take us all the way to an explanatory account. We need to go further and deeper to see how the functional relationship came into existence. How were hearts first formed, for example, and how did certain actions come to be defined as crimes? To answer questions like this, we need to identify the causal forces and powers, as well as preexisting social patterns, that came together in the formation of intellectual property.[31]

1.3 LEGAL POWER, SOCIAL POWER, AND CAUSALITY

Getting at social causes, however, is very difficult, especially when the focus is on legal institutions.

30 Abraham Lincoln, "Second Lecture on Discoveries and Inventions," first delivered February 11, 1859, in *Collected Works of Abraham Lincoln*, Vol. 3, edited by Roy P. Basler (Brunswick, N.J.: Rutgers University Press, 1953), 357–63, available at https://quod.lib.umich.edu/l/lincoln/lincoln3 (accessed July 1, 2019).

31 For a concise discussion of the problems with functionalist explanations in sociology, see Jon Elster, "Marxism, Functionalism, and Game Theory," in *Structures of Capital: The Social Organization of the Economy*, edited by Sharon Zukin and Paul DiMaggio (Cambridge, UK: Cambridge University Press, 1990), 87–118. For a brief narrative of recent developments away from functionalist explanations in sociology, see Ford, "Patenting the Social," 317–19. Close parallels may be found in the effort to avoid teleology (interpreting the past through the lenses of an inevitable and progressive future) in historical narratives. See, for example, Chris Wickham, *The Inheritance of Rome: A History of Europe from 400–1000* (New York: Penguin Group, 2009), 1–9. For a discussion of this problem by Max Weber, in his early methodological writings, see Max Weber, *Collected Methodological Writings*, edited by Hans Henrik Bruun and Sam Whimster, translated by Hans Henrik Bruun (London: Routledge, 2012), 20–21.

Debates have been raging for a long time within sociology about how and whether some social things do (or do not) *cause* other social things to be the way that they are. Even within philosophy, the concept of a cause is very controversial. In our everyday talk we discuss cause–effect relationships all the time, but when we really think deeply about what it means to say that something causes another thing to be the way that it is, the notion of causality starts to become elusive and mysterious.[32]

Do causes work like billiard balls, knocking into each other and pushing each other around? Do causes combine and work together in orderly ways, forming new causal compounds with emergent properties, something like the way in which chemical elements (H & O) combine to form compound substances with distinct properties (H_2O)? If, in the real world, we suspect that any given effect must actually come about through a number of distinct causes working together, can we ever isolate the effect of a single cause? Would it be informative even if we could? Must a cause be both necessary and sufficient to produce a given effect, meaning that (1) without that cause the effect would not have occurred, and (2) with the cause the effect *must* occur, without exception? What about the fact that we only ever actually observe causes and effects in regular sequences, but we cannot actually observe the "mechanisms" or processes that lead from cause to effect? In the early twentieth century, one famous philosopher – Bertrand Russell – argued that we should get rid of the notion of causality altogether, because it is too metaphysical (i.e., too close to religion) for us to think about it rationally.[33]

[32] More than any other philosopher, David Hume (1711–1776) problematized causality for the modern (and postmodern) age. Hume fatally undermined the security of inductive inference, showing that the most we can establish through our experience of regular cause–effect relations – no matter how many data points we might gather – is regularity of experience. According to Hume, we are habituated to experiencing things in regular cause–effect sequences, but that regularity of experience does not allow us to infer anything like logical or real necessity in the sequences themselves. David Hume, *A Treatise of Human Nature*, edited by Ernest C. Mossner (London: Penguin Books, 1985), 49–63, 117–225; David Hume, *An Enquiry Concerning Human Understanding*, 2d ed., edited by Eric Steinberg (Indianapolis: Hackett Publishing, 1993), 1–53).

Hume famously awakened the German philosopher Immanuel Kant from his "dogmatic slumber," and generated a variety of additional philosophical responses, nearly all of which involved rejection of the idea that causality involves intrinsic causal powers possessed by people and things. Immanuel Kant, "Prolegomena to Any Future Metaphysics that Will Be Able to Come Forward as Science," in Henry Allison and Peter Heath (eds.), *Theoretical Philosophy after 1781* (Cambridge, UK: Cambridge University Press, 2002), 57 [4:260]; see also Eric Watkins, *Kant and the Metaphysics of Causality* (Cambridge, UK: Cambridge University Press, 2005). Hume's philosophical legacy for the metaphysics of causality is very helpfully discussed, with reference to implications for sociology, by Ruth Groff, *Ontology Revisited: Metaphysics in Social and Political Philosophy* (New York and London: Routledge, 2013); see also Ruth Groff (ed.), *Revitalizing Causality: Realism about Causality in Philosophy and Social Science* (New York and London: Routledge, 2008).

[33] The billiard-ball metaphor for thinking about causality is famously Humean. Hume, *Enquiry Concerning Human Understanding* Section IV, 15–20. For contemporary philosophical discussions of the terrain, see especially Nancy Cartwright, *Hunting Causes and Using Them* (2007) (Cambridge, UK: Cambridge University Press, 2007); J. L. Mackie, *The Cement of the Universe: A Study of Causation* (Oxford: Clarendon Press, 1980); James Woodward, *Making Things Happen: A Theory of Causal Explanation* (Oxford: Oxford University Press, 2005). For Bertrand Russell's dismissal of

This matters for the way that we think about law and legal institutions. Academics in sociology and kindred disciplines are deeply ambivalent about whether law can cause anything in the social world to be the way that it is. On the one hand, for example, many of the important criticisms of mass incarceration in the United States presume that law has dramatic causal impacts: bad laws are causing too many people to be sent to prison, for terms that are too long, and are, moreover, having racially unequal effects that politically disenfranchise black Americans in particular, people of color more broadly, and people of all colors who live in heavily policed, poverty-stricken centers of post-industrial North America (and beyond). Law is presumed to be causally powerful in this type of account. Law is making the social world conform to certain patterns, and those patterns are not good.[34]

On the other hand, there is a long tradition within academic sociology of discounting the idea that law has causal powers. This can be seen most clearly in early Marxist theory. Even though sociologists rarely identify themselves as Marxists these days, the theory has deep and lingering effects in the ways that sociologists think and talk about legal institutions. The Marxist theory of law views law as a system of *ideology* – a set of ideas that reflect and reinforce the economic interests of a dominant (capitalist) class. According to the earliest and clearest articulations of

causality as metaphysical, see "On the Notion of Cause," *Proceedings of the Aristotelian Society* 13.1 (1912–13): 1–26.

In contemporary American sociology, issues of causality are again receiving attention, from both quantitatively oriented scholars of inequality – who draw primarily on philosophical foundations in American pragmatism – and scholars identifying with Critical Realism, a school of meta-theoretical reflection that focuses attention on questions of social ontology, that is, the nature of social reality. Both developments are avowedly realist, albeit with differing conceptions of realism. Stephen L. Morgan and Christopher Winship, *Counterfactuals and Causal Inference: Methods and Principles for Social Research*, 2d ed. (New York: Cambridge University Press, 2015); Philip Gorski, "What Is Critical Realism? And Why Should You Care?," *Contemporary Sociology* 42.5 (2013): 658–70. A third philosophical "school" of realism is found in contemporary analytical sociology. Peter Hedström, *Dissecting the Social: On the Principles of Analytical Sociology* (Cambridge, UK: Cambridge University Press, 2005); Gorski, "What Is Critical Realism?," 659. An ambivalent variant of realism, formulated in disagreement with critical realism and with the methodological individualism of analytical sociology, may be seen in the "relational realism" of Margaret Somers and Charles Tilly. See John Krinsky and Ann Mische, "Formations and Formalisms: Charles Tilly and the Paradox of the Actor," *Annual Review of Sociology* 39 (2013): 1–26; Margaret Somers, "Symposium on Historical Sociology and Rational Choice Theory 'We're No Angels': Realism, Rational Choice, and Relationality in Social Science," *American Journal of Sociology* 104.3 (1998): 722–84.

34 Jeff Manza and Christopher Uggen, *Locked Out: Felon Disenfranchisement and American Democracy* (Oxford: Oxford University Press, 2006); Becky Pettit, *Invisible Men: Mass Incarceration and the Myth of Black Progress* (New York: Russell Sage Foundation, 2012); Bruce Western, *Punishment and Inequality in America* (New York: Russell Sage Foundation, 2006). For a broader argument about impacts in post-industrial cities, see Loic Wacquant, *Punishing the Poor: The Neoliberal Government of Social Insecurity* (Durham and London: Duke University Press, 2009). Michelle Alexander, a legal scholar, has drawn public attention to this line of scholarship, with her argument that mass incarceration is producing a new type of legal caste structure. Michelle Alexander, *The New Jim Crow: Mass Incarceration in the Age of Colorblindness*, Revised Edition (New York: The New Press, 2012). For a sympathetic, sociological review of Alexander's argument, see James Kilgore, "Mass Incarceration: Examining and Moving Beyond the New Jim Crow," *Critical Sociology* 41.2 (2015): 283–95.

the theory, *ideas* of law (what lawyers might call *legal doctrine*) themselves have no power. They are merely a symbolic manifestation of the economic dynamics involving classes that are the real causal forces, moving and forming the social world to be the way that it is. In Marxist language, economic interests and structures are "the motor of history," a metaphor that draws on images of machinery to evoke our intuitions about how causes work. Law and religion, on the other hand, are an ideational "superstructure" – a powerless (and illusory) scaffolding that *reflects* (and at most *reinforces*) rather than *affects*.[35]

Leading sociological theories about how modern states have been formed, and about how they have come undone in revolutionary social processes, still echo the Marxist assertion that legal doctrine is not a causal factor, with real powers of its own to affect the social world. Indeed, the Marxist legacy has been so strong that sociologists have had to work quite hard to make the case that states themselves actually matter, as political organizations worth studying. The slogan for these sociologists, many of whom have been sympathetic with Marxist theory, has been to "Bring the State Back In." After the state was "brought back in" to sociological theory, during the 1980s and 1990s, religion had to be brought back in. Philip Gorski's 2003 book *The Disciplinary Revolution* has been important in this effort, highlighting a blind spot in relation to the powerful (albeit variable) role that religion has played in contributing to social order and discipline in modern, western, state formation. Max Weber, of course, gave a foundational articulation of this argument in his classic text *The Protestant Ethic and the Spirit of Capitalism* (1904/5 and 1920). In Gorski's view, however, Marxist theoretical legacies in contemporary sociology have contributed to the repression of understanding about the causal role played by religion in nation-state formation. An analogous argument can be made about law and legal doctrine.[36]

35 A relatively clear articulation of the Marxist dismissal of law as an independent causal force in history may be found in *The German Ideology*: "Morality, religion, metaphysics, all the rest of ideology and their corresponding forms of consciousness no longer retain the semblance of independence. They have no history, no development; but men, developing their material production and their material intercourse, alter, along with this their real existence .... It must not be forgotten that law has just as little an independent history as religion." (*Marx-Engels Reader*, 154–55, 188); see also *Communist Manifesto*, 487. The "motor of history" metaphor is identifiably Marxist, but seems to have come from interpretations of Marx rather than from Marx himself. Marx does describe revolution as a driving force of history in *The German Ideology* (Marx-Engels Reader, 164). Maureen Cain and Alan Hunt offer a thoughtful and nuanced plea for correcting simplistic dismissals of law as ideology, from within the Marxist tradition, in *Marx and Engels on Law* (London: Academic Press, 1979).

36 For an overview of recent sociological literature on state formation, see Philip S. Gorski, *The Disciplinary Revolution: Calvinism and the Rise of the State in Early Modern Europe* (Chicago: University of Chicago Press, 2003), 3–10. The standard-setting account of revolutions in contemporary American sociology is Theda Skocpol's *States and Social Revolutions: A Comparative Analysis of France, Russia, and China* (Cambridge, UK: Cambridge University Press, 1979). For acknowledgment that historical sociology of the late twentieth century, including the efforts to "bring the state back in," were carried out on "largely Marxist terrain," see Julia Adams, Elisabeth S. Clemens, and Ann Shola Orloff, "Introduction: Social Theory, Modernity, and the Three Waves of Historical

But sociologists are not the only ones who are ambivalent about whether, and how, law has causal impacts in the social world. Legal scholars are also ambivalent. On the one hand, legal academics and practicing lawyers often proceed on the assumption that law affects the social world, contributing significantly to changes in the social world. There would be very little point in arguing about law, after all, if it actually makes no difference; and arguing about law is what legal scholars and practitioners do. Some scholars have gone so far as to argue that law is *autonomous*, a discipline that operates according to an independent logic and that exercises causal powers independently from other social causes. On the other side, some legal scholars have argued that law is merely a reflexive response to psychological and social forces. In the language of one iconoclastic legal scholar, what a judge had for lunch may be a more powerful determinant of a decision he will make from the bench than the actual doctrines (or ideas) of the law he is supposed to interpret and apply.[37]

These may seem like abstruse and academic debates, and no doubt they are partly that. But I believe these debates really matter for the ways that we think about law and legal institutions, not only in the halls of the ivory tower, but also in the streets of social conflict and cooperation. There are many sociologists and legal scholars who are trying to find a middle ground, where law can be seen and discussed as exercising real causal powers, not all of which are necessarily coercive and oppressive, but where law is also understood as part and parcel of the social world. In this book,

Sociology," in *Remaking Modernity: Politics, History, and Sociology*, edited by Julia Adams, Elisabeth S. Clemens, and Ann Shola Orloff (Durham: Duke University Press, 2005); see also Mann, *Sources Vol. 4*, 8. A recent edition of Weber's classic argument about the impacts of Calvinist doctrine and pastoral practice on the spirit of modern, rational capitalism may be found in Richard Swedberg (ed.), *The Protestant Ethic and the Spirit of Capitalism* (New York: W. W. Norton, 2009), 3–152. For Philip Gorski's argument about the impacts of Marxist theory on the sociology of religion, see "The Return of the Repressed: Religion and the Political Unconsciousness of Historical Sociology," in Adams, Clemens, and Orloff, *Remaking Modernity*, 161–89.

37 There is a challenge of interpretive translation here. The issues that sociologists of law tend to discuss under the categorical heading of "autonomy" are often discussed by legal scholars of jurisprudence under the heading "internal/external," or "limited domain." Roger Cotterrell provides essential help in translating between these two highly specialized academic discourses in his book *The Politics of Jurisprudence: A Critical Introduction to Legal Philosophy*, 2d ed. (Oxford: Oxford University Press, 2003). Within Anglo-American legal scholarship, the iconoclastic reductionism has come, not so much from Marxism as from legal realism, in which Freudian critique and pragmatist empiricism may have been more significant. See Robert Jerome Glennon, *The Iconoclast as Legal Reformer: Jerome Frank's Impact on American Law* (Ithaca: Cornell University Press, 1985), 49–50; John Henry Schlegel, *American Legal Realism and Empirical Social Science* (Chapel Hill: University of North Carolina Press, 1995). What a judge had for lunch: Jerome Frank, *Courts on Trial: Myth and Reality in American Justice* (Princeton: Princeton University Press, 1949), 161–2. Frank's narrow point here is that a sleepy judge may miss an important element of testimony in trial proceedings, but the broader critical thrust of legal realism focuses especially on legal doctrine. See Jerome Frank, *Law and the Modern Mind* (New Brunswick, N.J.: Transaction Publishers, 2009). Frank is often (mis) quoted as saying that law depends on "what a judge had for breakfast," and I am grateful to Mark DeAngelis' "Legal Studies Classroom" blog for helping me to find the *Courts on Trial* passage: http://legalstudiesclassroom.blogspot.com/2013/10/legal-realism-law-depends-on-what-judge.html (accessed Jan. 23, 2019).

I seek to join and contribute to that effort to find a theoretical and ideological middle ground. Theory, after all, is ideology (and culture), too.[38]

This book proceeds from the foundational presumption that law can and does exercise causal powers, but it does not do so autonomously. Law is part of the social world, but, strikingly similar to – and, indeed, historically entwined with – scriptural religion, law has a distinctive, and very long, cultural history, which has helped to make it work the way that it does today. Like scriptural religion, law is an interpretive, hermeneutic discipline – a discipline that seeks meaning from texts, some of which are very old. *Law must have meaning to exercise its distinctive, causal powers.* Fundamentally, I will argue, law exercises its distinctive causal powers by harnessing our human, social capacities for *meaningful obligation*. Obligation is seen in our committed and cooperative social activities, and in the communities – like families, guilds, cities, and states – that these social activities form. *Law is a meaningful, obliging social force, one that works through social activities and relationships*, which is to say, through human persons who act in relation to one another and, in so doing, invest their activities with meanings involving complex combinations of practical reason, judgment, and emotion.[39]

1.4 SEMANTIC LEGAL ORDERING: LEGAL CULTURE AND INSTITUTIONS

The concept of legal obligation will be crucial to everything that follows, so we should take a moment to focus on the word *obligation* itself. According to cultural traditions of Roman law, as well as etymological dictionaries, the word *obligation* evokes concepts of tying and bonding. *Ligare* is a Latin verbal infinitive meaning to

38 Among sociologists of law, see Roger Cotterrell, *Politics of Jurisprudence* and *Living Law: Studies in Legal and Social Theory* (London and New York: Routledge, 2016); Terrence C. Halliday and Bruce G. Carruthers, "The Recursivity of Law: Global Norm Making and National Law Making in the Globalization of Corporate Insolvency Regimes," *American Journal of Sociology* 112.4 (2007): 1135–1202; Terrence C. Halliday and Bruce G. Carruthers, *Bankrupt: Global Lawmaking and Systemic Financial Crisis* (Stanford: Stanford University Press, 2009). Among legal scholars, see Frederick Schauer, *The Force of Law* (Cambridge, MA: Harvard University Press, 2015). On problems in distinguishing theory from ideology within the Marxist tradition of sociology of law, see Roger Cotterrell, *Law's Community: Legal Theory in Sociological Perspective* (Oxford: Oxford University Press, 1995), 7–14; on academic theories as forms of ideology, see Alvin W. Gouldner, *The Dialectic of Ideology and Technology* (New York: Oxford University Press, 1976).

39 I use the phrase "scriptural religion" to indicate that I have in mind not all possible religions but rather a specific subset of religions that draw on a notion of *scripture*, or sacred, normative, written texts that must be interpreted in order to ascertain divine nature or intention, and thereby to discern how to live well. Prominent historical examples include Hinduism, the Abrahamic faith traditions (Judaism, Christianity, and Islam), and, to some extent, Platonic philosophy. I am emphasizing the combination of practical reason and emotion, in keeping with contemporary insights into cognition and emotion from sociology and social psychology. See, for example, Chelsea Helion and David Pizarro, "Beyond Dual-Processes: The Interplay of Reason and Emotion in Moral Judgment," in *Springer Handbook for Neuroethics*, edited by Neil Levy & Jens Clausen (Dordrecht: Springer, 2015), 109–25.

tie, or to bind. Conceptually – following this old-fashioned train of reasoning according to the historical meaning of words – to impose a legal obligation is to impose a legal tie or bond. To say that law is a meaningful, obliging social force, then, is to say that law is a bonding and binding force – it exercises its distinctive causal powers through "bindingness" and constraint, through moving us do things for and with each other, perhaps to sacrifice some of our desires and interests for each other, because of a conceptual and normative sense that we should. In so doing, it helps to bond us together in enduring social communities – for example, through marriage, a business partnership, or joint ownership of property – and thereby enables a range of social activities, but it also contributes to social limitations, including bounded definitions about who does, and who does not, belong to a community.[40]

The deep powers of law, I believe, may be seen in social bonding and boundary-drawing processes. Law is about drawing boundaries with *formalizing words*, and these words are powerful because they act on our social experience of obligation. In working through formalizing words, law works through meanings (*semantics*), and, at a metaphoric level, it can be seen as a catalyzing or "crystalizing" agent in the formation and maintenance of social bonds. Law helps to tie us together in social relationships and communities, and, in doing so, it also contributes to our definition of insiders and outsiders, those to whom we point as belonging and not belonging to our communities and associations. As a formalistic, semantic agent of social bonding and boundary-drawing, law works as a fundamental causal force in contributing to the basic *structures* – enduring social patterns – of our governing communities. I will use the phrase *semantic legal ordering* to try to capture this interrelated set of intuitions and metaphors about how law helps to form – to shape, mold, and configure – our social world.[41]

[40] Cultural traditions of Roman Law: *Justinian's Institutes*, translated by Peter Birks and Grant McLeod, with the Latin text of Paul Krueger 3.13 (Ithaca: Cornell University Press, 1987), 105 (35): "An obligation (*obligatio*) is a legal tie which binds us to the necessity of making some performance in accordance with the laws of our state (*iuris vinculum*)." This echoes Cicero in the Republic/Commonwealth (1.49) and the Laws (2.41). Cicero, *De Re Publica, De Legibus*, Loeb Classical Library 213 (Harvard: Harvard University Press, 2000). For the latest scholarship and a new translation of Cicero's *Republic* and *The Laws*, I am relying on James E. G. Zetzel, *Cicero on the Commonwealth and on the Laws* (Cambridge, UK: Cambridge University Press, 2017). The "old-fashioned train of reasoning according to the meaning of words" is etymology. For the etymology of obligation, see Onions (ed.), *Oxford Dictionary of English Etymology*, 620.

[41] This way of conceiving law is deeply Durkheimian, and Roger Cotterrell has pointed to ways in which these Durkheimian theoretical roots can be fruitfully updated, developed, and deployed for socio-logical perspective on law today. Roger Cotterrell, *Emile Durkheim: Law in a Moral Domain* (Stanford: Stanford University Press, 1999); also Cotterrell, *Law's Community*, 178–203; Steven Lukes and Andrew Scull (eds.), *Durkheim and the Law*, 2d ed. (London, Palgrave Macmillan, 2013). This way of conceiving law also draws on contemporary sociological theories of culture. See Michèle Lamont and Virág Molnár, "The Study of Boundaries in the Social Sciences," *Annual Review of Sociology* 28: 167–95 (2002); also Michèle Lamont and Mario Luis Small, "How Culture Matters: Enriching Our Understanding of Poverty," in *The Colors of Poverty: Why Racial and*

A key point that I will make is that law works through meanings with old roots; we need to understand those roots to understand law's contemporary meanings and binding powers. I will rely on a concept of *legal traditions* to show how the old roots are connected to the contemporary meanings, and to explicate the notion that meanings can *endure*, even while they change. The meanings endure, I think, because they persist through legal practices of reference, which are passed down through processes of education and training, in which old legal documents are both considered to be and are treated as being binding, in the sense that our present-day understanding of what some legal word, phrase, or concept means must somehow remain coherent with a meaning that is interpreted from an older legal document. *To summarize, the thesis of semantic legal ordering is a thesis about how enduring legal meanings, received through legal traditions, exercise causal power in forming and solidifying our patterns of social activity and social relationships.*[42]

To put it simply, legal meanings make us feel bound, and in making us feel bound, they sometimes cause us to act differently than we otherwise would have. This counterfactual conception of causality is what I have in mind when I say that law exercises causal powers. Law *makes a difference*, meaning that (1) without its unique causal powers operating in the background, the social world would probably look different, and (2) with its unique causal powers operating in the background, there is an increased likelihood that social relationships of particular kinds will be formed and will persist. Legal meanings can induce us to act differently in social relationships, *to enact and perform our perceived obligations*, and those legal

Ethnic Disparities Persist, edited by Ann Chih Lin and David R. Harris (New York: Russell Sage Foundation, 2008), 76–102.

Among the oldest cultural roots of law as a binding agent may be seen in oath-taking rituals, which solemnize formal legal moments, and are meant to bind people to one another. An enduring example in our contemporary world is the vow of marriage. A historian of ancient Rome, Gary Forsythe has drawn on the metaphor of *catalysis* in conceptualizing the role of Greek and Phoenician colonial influences in the emergence of Rome's early city-state (*civitas*) structure. *A Critical History of Early Rome: From Prehistory to the Punic War* (Berkeley: University of California Press, 2005), 92. The language of crystallization, as a metaphor of social emergence, is ubiquitous in Michael Mann, for example, and in some of his interlocutors. For example, Mann, *Sources, Vol.* 2, x; Wickham, *Inheritance of Rome*, 10, 59, 111, 145, 148–68, 277–311. Important sociological insights into the role of formality in contributing to law's causal powers may be found in Arthur L. Stinchcombe, *When Formality Works: Authority and Abstraction in Law and Organizations* (Chicago: University of Chicago Press, 2001), 2–5, 43.

42 For a Weberian exposition of the ways in which value-rational judgment and imagination give coherence to meaningful, normative traditions across long stretches of time, thereby contributing to macro-historical, civilizational trajectories, see Saïd Amir Arjomand, "Rationalization, the Constitution of Meaning, and Institutional Development," in *The Dialogical Turn: New Roles for Sociology in the Postdisciplinary Age*, Essays in Honor of Donald N. Levine, edited by Charles Camic and Hans Joas (Lanham: Rowman & Littlefield Publishers, 2004), 247–69. For a recent, sociological theory of tradition, "a culture that is self-conscious of its past," see Philip Gorski, *American Covenant: A History of Civil Religion from the Puritans to the Present* (Princeton: Princeton University Press, 2017), 3–6, 30–36.

meanings can therefore give both structural form and meaning to our social relationships.[43]

To put this in Michael Mann's semi-Marxist language, the thesis of semantic legal ordering is a thesis about legal ideology. But I prefer to describe the thesis of semantic legal ordering using the language of culture. My thesis is that legal culture matters at a real, causal level in the formation and maintenance of social relationships, including the relationships that make property ownership possible. Where we see property ownership structures, legal culture, I believe, is helping to make those possible. Very importantly, however, it is doing so in large part because of historical legal traditions that give the culture its meaning and power. Karl Marx was dead wrong about at least one thing: law does have a history, and it is mostly because of that history that law is powerful.[44]

This is abstract and polemical, but I offer this sketch to give you an initial sense about where I am coming from in writing this book. The basic assertion that law can and does exercise causal powers in the world, such that it affects the social world and contributes to making the social world that we experience, stands behind everything that follows. I will nonetheless endeavor throughout the book to defend the assertion, and to give it meaning and content in relation to the basic questions that I am asking: when, how, and why did we bring the legal institution of intellectual property into the world, and, now that we have brought it into the world, what effects is it having in our world?

1.5 BUILDING AND TRANSFORMING AN INFRASTRUCTURE OF ENCOURAGEMENT

In modern intellectual property, as we see it working in McDonald's, three types of legal tradition come together: (1) an ancient and much-adapted tradition of formal legal documents, (2) a slightly less ancient set of formal legal concepts defining

[43] This conception of law's causal powers draws on my understanding of "adequate causality," as that concept was elaborated by Max Weber, and explicated more recently by H. L. A. Hart and Tony Honoré. Bruun & Whimster (eds.), *Weber's Collected Methodological Writings*, 169–84; H. L. A. Hart and Tony Honoré, *Causation in the Law*, 2d ed. (Oxford: Oxford University Press, 1985), 431–36, 465–97. The reader who is attuned to Max Weber's sociology will note that I use the word "performance" here to indicate a type of social action that is oriented toward an order, which I specify as an order of obligation. Max Weber, *Economy and Society*, edited by Guenther Roth and Claus Wittich, 2d ed. (Berkeley: University of California Press, 2013), 31–33; also Max Weber, "Introduction to the Economic Ethics of the World Religions," translated by Sam Whimster, in Sam Whimster (ed.), *The Essential Weber* (Abingdon: Routledge, 2004), 65. For contextualizing discussion of *Economy and Society*, tracing its textual development and intellectual influences, see Wolfgang Schluchter, *Rationalism, Religion, and Domination: A Weberian Perspective*, translated by Neil Solomon (Berkeley: University of California Press, 1989), 433–72; Richard Swedberg, *Max Weber and the Idea of Economic Sociology* (Princeton: Princeton University Press, 1998), 173–206.

[44] Michael Mann discusses legal ideology in Volume 2 of the *Sources of Social Power*, while he acknowledges his neglect of law in Volume 1. Mann, *Sources*, Vol. 1, xiii; Mann, *Sources*, Vol. 2, 38, 57, 66, 78, 145–6, 155–62, 175, 179–97.

property, and (3) an economic and political theory about the beneficial consequences that flow to the nation-state from granting privileges (or "franchises"), like intellectual property. I will show how these three types of legal tradition became combined, such that they support the modern legal institution that we know today as intellectual property. This is a social formation story, a story about how legal traditions developed together, such that they could have a combined legal impact, thereby contributing to the modern social patterns that we see in the institution of intellectual property.[45]

Speaking metaphorically, and drawing on Max Weber's developmental sociology of law, there are three basic layers to the modern institution of intellectual property. The first layer involves what Weber described as a somewhat primitive type of formal rationality in law: *empirical formality*. We will see this type of formality in legal documents, like medieval charters, where details about how the instrument is drafted affect its validity. We can also see it in certain types of legal procedure, where a specific step in a legal process affects the validity of the legal process. This is an empirical formality, because what matters is something that is evident to physical experience (*empeiria*): something we can see, touch, taste, smell, or hear. The legal document might need to be stamped with a special seal to be valid and binding, for example, or a set of words might need to be said in precisely the correct order to initiate or prosecute a lawsuit. In excavating the historical layers of intellectual property, as a legal institution, and in going to the deepest layer, we will be focusing on the formality of legal documents. At the ancient core of intellectual property, I will argue, is a legal tradition involving empirical formalities in legal instruments.[46]

45 On social formation stories, see Daniel Hirschman and Isaac Ariail Reed, "Formation Stories and Causality in Sociology," *Sociological Theory* 32.4: 259–82.

46 For Weber's two types of formal rationality in law, see Laura R. Ford, "Dharma and Natural Law: Max Weber's Comparison of Hindu and (Occidental) Christian Legal Traditions," *Max Weber Studies* 17.2 (2017): 160–95, esp. 173–5; *cf.* Hubert Treiber, "'Elective Affinities' between Weber's Sociology of Religion and Sociology of Law," *Theory & Society* 14.6 (1985): 809–61; Hubert Treiber, "Max Weber and Eugen Ehrlich: On the Janus-headed Construction of Weber's Ideal Type in the Sociology of Law," *Max Weber Studies* 8.2 (2008): 225–46. Max Weber's developmental sociology of law is laid out in a partially finalized manuscript, written sometime around 1913–15, as part of his editorial and authorial work for a grand project to prepare a Handbook of Social-Economics; parts of this only are what we have today as *Economy and Society*. Weber, *Economy & Society*, 641–900.

The text of Weber's writings on law for *Economy and Society* has recently been edited by Werner Gephart and Siegfried Hermes for the *Max Weber Gesamtausgabe*, the definitive, critical, German editions of Weber's complete works. Max Weber, *Wirtschaft und Gesellschaft. Die Wirtschaft und die gesellschaftlichen Ordnungen und Mächte. Nachlaß. Teilband 3: Recht. Max Weber Gesamtausgabe I:22–3* (Tübingen: J. C. B. Mohr (Paul Siebeck), 2010). Werner Gephart's *Introduction* has been translated into English by Johannes Nanz as *Law, Culture, and Society: Max Weber's Comparative Cultural Sociology of Law* (Vittorio Klostermann, Franfurt am Main, 2015). The general introduction to the *Gesamtausgabe* by its initial primary editors has been translated into English and published in the journal *Max Weber Studies*. Horst Baier, M. Rainer Lepsius, Wolfgang J. Mommsen, and Wolfgang Schluchter, "Overview of the Text of *Economy and Society* by the Editors of the *Max Weber Gesamtausgabe*," translated by Austin Harrington, *Max Weber Studies* 1.1: 104–14 (2000).

In my opinion, the best available English-language version of Weber's writings on law for *Economy and Society* is the now out-of-print edition, annotated by Max Rheinstein, a German-Jewish legal

Slightly less old, but also quite old, is a legal tradition of logical formality in the meanings of legal concepts, including concepts of property, but also extending to concepts of contract, obligation, and social status (including citizenship). The conceit of this legal tradition, which is associated particularly with Roman law, is that law can be made into a system of meanings, one that is logically coherent, and even beautiful to imaginatively behold in that logical coherence. The Romans seem to have developed their distinctive legal culture under the influence of Hellenistic culture and Greek philosophy, but they ran with it, and they left it as a deep and vital legacy for the modern world. Because the Roman state, even at its most powerful, did not penetrate as regularly and deeply into the everyday social lives of its citizens (compared to a modern nation-state), the Roman legal culture of *semantic formality* in law had limited social impacts in antiquity. However, the cultural tradition was rediscovered, reinvigorated, and redeployed in the European Middle Ages, when a more powerful state was being developed, and it was from this later medieval foundation that modern theories of property and obligation were built. With these modern theories, property became something that is universal, uniform, and powerfully motivating. To use Michael Mann's semi-Marxist language again, property was *commoditized*, with the help of semantic formality in law, and it was this commoditized form of property that was essential for modern intellectual property (and modern capitalism) to develop. The commodification of property connected to semantic formality in law, I will argue, involves a culturally specific configuration of social obligation, one that defines and therefore *limits* obligation in ways that are important for modern intellectual property and capitalism.[47]

The third layer of legal tradition – a tradition carrying economic and political theories about beneficial consequences that flow from a grant of intellectual property – is also quite old, as we will see, and it is one that has gone under many names. To use Max Weber's language, this is a legal tradition involving *substantive rationality*, a rationality explaining how legal protection of intellectual property has beneficial consequences that extend beyond the legal system itself. This is a cultural framework defining beneficial consequences for political communities, together with an instrumentalist theory about how people can be encouraged to act

scholar who had the opportunity to hear Weber lecture, who moved to the United States to escape the Holocaust, and who contributed significantly to historical and comparative legal scholarship in the United States. Max Rheinstein (ed.), *Max Weber on Law in Economy and Society*, translated by Edward Shils and Max Rheinstein (New York: Simon & Schuster, 1967); see also Kyle Graham, "The Refugee Jurist and American Law Schools, 1933–1941," *American Journal of Comparative Law* 50 (2002): 777–818, esp. 794–96; Reinhard Zimmerman, "Was Heimat hieß, nun heißt es Hölle," in *Jurists Uprooted: German-speaking Émigré Lawyers in Twentieth-century Britain*, edited by Jack Beatson and Reinhard Zimmerman (Oxford: Oxford University Press, 2004), 1–71, esp. 29 n.1, 51.

47 On semantic formality in law, see Ford, *Dharma and Natural Law*, 173–5, and the sources cited there; see also Swedberg, *Max Weber and the Idea*, 89–107. For a recent and extensive treatment of Max Weber's sociology of law, focusing partly on his development of formal rationality in law as an ideal type, see Michel Coutu, *Max Weber's Interpretive Sociology of Law* (Oxford: Routledge, 2018), 87–113. On the commoditization of property, see Mann, *Sources, Vol. 1*, 397–99, 493.

in such a way that their political communities are benefitted. Today the theory is formulated using the economic language of *public goods* – things that we need or want in society, like inventions, artistic works, and public parks, things that capitalistic markets do not provide in sufficient amounts. During the Middle Ages, an analogous theory could be articulated using the language of privileges and immunities. This was a feudal adaptation of Roman patronage, which already in Cicero's time – as we will see in Chapter 4 – was being theorized to develop an argument about how the encouragement of literary works (and, to some extent, even industrial production) can be beneficial to the state.[48]

The story that I tell in this book is one about how these three legal traditions became entwined, adapted alongside one another, in the broader story of modern state formation. Borrowing from Michael Mann, I conceptualize intellectual property as an *infrastructure of state power*, an element of the state (or governing community) that bridges public and private spheres of life in the modern world, as do so many infrastructures of state power.[49]

To see what is distinctive about intellectual property, as an infrastructure of state power, it is helpful to recall the Greek rhetorical tradition of *paraenesis* – encouragement, or exhortation. Intellectual property is an infrastructure of state power that *encourages* creative and inventive activities, thereby benefitting the state in enabling innovation, advancing knowledge, and promoting economic growth. The belief that grants of privilege like those involved in intellectual property have beneficial consequences for the state is surprisingly old, but the state powers through which this *paraenesis* operates have reached radically new levels in the modern world.[50]

Intellectual property, to reiterate, is a legal institution (or, really, a set of legal institutions) that *encourages* – that acts on people's hopes for the future, including their desires to be rewarded for doing something that is distinctive, important, and

48 For a helpful elaboration of substantive rationalities involved in early medieval privileges and immunities, particularly those involving tax exemption and jurisdiction, see Alexander Callander Murray, "Merovingian Immunity Revisited," *History Compass* 8.8 (2010): 913–28, esp. 916–17, 919–20, 922; also Alexander Callander Murray, "Immunity, Nobility, and the *Edict of Paris*," *Speculum* 69 (1994): 18–39. Michael Mann discusses tensions between formal and substantive rationalities in theorizing the ways that ideology has been powerful in the rise of the modern nation-state. Mann, *Sources Vol. 2*, 39–40.

49 Mann, *Sources Vol. 1*, 169–70; 440–45, 477–83; Mann, *Sources Vol. 2*, 59–63.

50 The theme of "encouragement" (*paraenesis*), or moral exhortation, was significant in the ancient Greek tradition of historiography, based apparently on practices of generals leading armies in the field, and developed in the scholarship and practice of ancient rhetoric. Simon Hornblower, *A Commentary on Thucydides, Vol. II: Books IV-V.24* (Oxford: Clarendon Press, 1996), 81–93; Simon Hornblower, *A Commentary on Thucydides, Vol. III: Books 5.25–8.109* (Oxford: Clarendon Press, 2008), 183–5, 472–4; Isocrates, "To Demonicus," in *Isocrates I*, translated by David C. Mirhady and Yun Lee Too (Austin, Texas: University of Texas Press, 2000). Recent scholarship on early Christianity has focused on the important role played by rhetorical conventions, including *paraenesis*, for example, in the letters of Paul. Abraham J. Malherbe, *Moral Exhortation, A Greco-Roman Sourcebook* (Philadelphia: Westminster Press, 1986), 121–29; Wayne A. Meeks, *The Origins of Christian Morality: The First Two Centuries* (New Haven: Yale University Press, 1993), 76–84.

morally good. In other words, intellectual property acts on people's experience of moral obligation. It has these impacts in society because it is an infrastructure of state power, an entwining of formal and substantive legal rationalities that is articulated in formal legal texts and legal doctrines, communicated through media and legal professionals, and popularized in various ways, including through social media.[51]

To borrow from Roger Cotterrell, law operates through intellectual property as "institutionalized doctrine," as a set of institutionalized legal teachings or instructions. Intellectual property law is a type of institutionalized doctrine that teaches in a specific kind of way, encouraging particular kinds of activity and hopes for the future, dramatically impacting and configuring our political communities in doing so. Enforcement and sanctions are important for understanding how law has social effects, as both Max Weber and Emile Durkheim (and many others both before and since) have emphasized. But with a legal institution like intellectual property, we also need to see how law can act more subtly, through acting on people's hopes and on their experience of moral obligation. When law acts on people's experience of moral obligation, it acts on them at a very deep level, at the level of the human motivational quest for a well-lived life, for a life that means something.[52]

A basic change that we will see is in the way that law encourages. Very roughly, for the first millennium of our era, law acted mainly through personal relationships involving discretion. Borrowing from the medievalist Geoffrey Koziol, I explicate this relational action of law by focusing on the social impacts of *instruments of legal power*. In connection with medieval state formation and scholastic jurisprudence, however, law was transformed, and became statutory. Instruments of legal power, like charters and letters patent, were transformed as the institutionalized doctrines of law began to teach differently – more abstractly and impersonally, and in a more clearly defined way.[53]

The legal institution that we know today as intellectual property was built through a long process involving nation-state formation and semantic legal ordering. Through this process, formalistic legal traditions were joined to a specific narrative about how and why invention and artistic creation are good for the state, as a political community, together with a set of conceptions about how to encourage inventive and creative activities. Strands of legal tradition stretching back to Roman antiquity were woven together through interpretive, hermeneutic processes and linked to broader processes of state formation. A powerful, nation-state system was created, and intellectual property was built into that system. The result was a social,

[51] I am drawing here on Michael Mann's discussion of the organizational infrastructures of ideology in the modern nation-state. Mann, *Sources* Vol. 2, 35–42.

[52] Roger Cotterrell, *Law, Culture, and Society: Legal Ideas in the Mirror of Social Theory* (Aldershot, England: Ashgate Publishing, 2006); also Cotterrell, *Law's Community*, 23–40.

[53] Geoffrey Koziol, *The Politics of Memory and Identity in Carolingian Royal Diplomas: The West Frankish Kingdom (840–987)* (Turnhout, Belgium: Brepols Publishers, 2012).

economic, and political world – our world – that both depends upon and is repeatedly destabilized through constant innovation.

In order to explicate the earliest layers of this long, developmental process, it is necessary to first see the role that formal legal documents – Geoffrey Koziol's instruments of legal power – play in modern intellectual property law. This is an aspect of modern legal institutions that tends to remain hidden, unless we focus on revealing it. To do so, I will draw your attention to the role of patents in the founding of one of our most recent and destabilizing of societies: the society of Facebook.

2

Legal Orders and Social Performance

Founding Facebook

Imagine that you are a sophomore at Harvard, majoring in computer science and psychology. You have come up with a great new idea: a social networking website for college students. Working from your dorm room with a few friends, you write the computer code and register a website.[1]

The year is 2004, and you are Mark Zuckerberg. During your summer break you head west to Silicon Valley, land of internet start-ups and Goldrush memories. By July you have a corporation in Delaware. By September you have a major investor. But, as the venture capitalists start noticing, they advise you to secure your intellectual property rights. Crucially, you need patents, and you need to look out for existing patents. You are told, in fact, that someone already has a patent that is broad enough to cover Thefacebook.com, which is the name you are giving to your expanding, college-based social network.[2]

Why does intellectual property – especially patents – matter so much to your potential investors? Because an existing patent might keep you out of the social networking business altogether, or make it so expensive for you to enter the business that it will be hard for you to make a profit. You are entering an arena of fierce competition, an arena in which others have spectacularly failed. Patents give you (or your competitors) the legal protection of property over a narrowly defined, new technology. They last for only about seventeen years, but for that length of time they create a *zone of exclusivity*, a line beyond which a competitor cannot legally pass. If a competitor should attempt to cross the line of your patented technology during the seventeen-year period, you can invoke the power of the state against him.[3]

[1] George Beahm, *The Boy Billionaire: Mark Zuckerberg in His Own Words* (Chicago: Agate Publishing, 2012); David Kirkpatrick, *The Facebook Effect* (New York: Simon & Schuster, 2010).

[2] Beahm, *Boy Billionaire*, 24 (highlighting the Goldrush memories); Kirkpatrick, *Facebook Effect*, 19–128; Nicholas Carlson, "How Mark Zuckerberg Booted His Co-Founder Out of the Company," *Business Insider*, May 15, 2012; Nicholas Carlson, "At Last – The Full Story of How Facebook Was Founded," *Business Insider*, March 5, 2010; Tomio Geron, "The Untold Story of Two Early Facebook Investors," *Forbes*, February 1, 2012.

[3] Patents typically endure for 20 years from the date the inventor first files for patent protection. 35 U.S. C. §154(a)(2). Since patents are never immediately granted but must first be tested by the US Patent

Patents, in short, are instruments of legal power. Your capacity to wield these instruments of legal power will make people more willing to take you seriously and lend you money. You intend to dominate the world, and this you cannot do without money.[4]

To see how patents work as instruments of legal power in our contemporary world, we will look at one. But first a quick note about why we are now focusing on patents rather than on other types of intellectual property, such as copyrights or trademarks. One reason is that patents are very old. Indeed, they are arguably the oldest type of intellectual property. Other types of intellectual property – especially copyrights, but also trademarks and trade secrets – have developed alongside them. Patents are also the most powerful type of intellectual property, which is a reason they are not allowed to last for very long. During the period of patent validity, no one else is allowed to make, use, or sell anything that comes within the zone of exclusivity defined by the patent, unless they have the patent owner's explicit legal permission. In seeking to understand how patents work, and where they came from, we will be going a long way toward a broader understanding about how intellectual property works, and where it came from.[5]

Patents played a vital role in the foundation of Facebook, both as a company and as a social network that approximately 1.66 billion people use to interact with each other every day. Patents, in short, are part of the legal foundation of Facebook. Other parts of that legal foundation include contractual relationships with lenders, employees, and suppliers of equipment, as well as other forms of tangible and intangible property, like the buildings in which Facebook employees work, and the trademarks that protect the Facebook brand. Very importantly, there is also the corporate status that makes Facebook, as a company, a legal person, capable of incurring obligations and owning property under its own name.[6]

and Trademark Office to make sure they meet the legal requirements for patent eligibility, a process that on average takes about 2.5 years, issued patents will endure for something close to 17.5 years.

4 I am borrowing and adapting the concept of "instruments of power" from Geoffrey Koziol, *The Politics of Memory and Identity in Carolingian Royal Diplomas: The West Frankish Kingdom (840–987)* (Turnhout, Belgium: Brepols Publishers, 2012). Intention to dominate: Kirkpatrick, *Facebook Effect*, 50–1.

5 To be more precise, according to statute, a US patent will grant the patentee a right to exclude all others from making, using, and selling the invention throughout the United States, or from importing the invention into the United States. If the patent covers a process, then the exclusionary right extends to all products made, used, sold, or imported using that process. 35 U.S.C. §154(a)(1). The patent rights, in other words, are explicitly territorial and exclusionary. Unlike copyrights, patents exclude any independently created technology that comes within the patent boundaries, even where that technology was created without intentional copying or reverse engineering. This added strength of patent rights, relative to copyrights, is emphasized in the guidelines for intellectual property licensing, issued jointly by the US Department of Justice and the Federal Trade Commission. See *Antitrust Guidelines for the Licensing of Intellectual Property*, issued by the US Department of Justice and the Federal Trade Commission (January 12, 2017), available at www.justice.gov/atr/IPguidelines/download (accessed July 5, 2019), 1.

6 In its reports to shareholders, Facebook provides estimates of daily active users (DAUs). As of December 2019, the reported number of DAUs was 1.66 billion, a figure that can be contextualized as roughly 21.5 percent of the global population estimate (1.66/7.7 billion). Facebook Corporation,

We all recognize that Facebook is socially powerful. What I am saying is that legal institutions help to make Facebook powerful, providing a legal foundation upon which Facebook has been built. Patents are one type of legal institution – a type that I am calling an instrument of legal power – that gives Facebook legal power. To see this, though, we need to think like geologists, digging through layers of social power. A patent is legally powerful, but this is because it mobilizes deep social powers. Those deep social powers are seen in social bonds and communities that exist because of our human capacities for meaningful obligation, and for binding ourselves together into organized, social groups.

The key point is that law – because of its powers to support and direct meaningful obligation – contributes to this social power. Law helps to configure and reinforce the social obligation that is mobilized by instruments of legal power, like patents. Law, in short, is part of an *order of obligation* that mobilizes social action and performance through relational institutions like intellectual property. Instruments of legal power are a material means through which an order of obligation is mobilized, and in this sense they are a type of social action, one that has meaning, stabilizing power, and institutional form in reference to an order of obligation, which includes both law and religion. This chapter will unpack and develop these abstract ideas. To begin with, we will look at an early Facebook patent, seeking to understand how it works as an instrument of legal power.

2.1 PATENTS AS PROPERTY FROM A NATIONAL GOVERNMENT

We can focus on one of Facebook's earliest patents – a patent covering software technology for the News Feed. This, as Facebook users know, is a scrolling feed of information on a Facebook user's homepage. Here, for example, is where you learn about your friends' new pets and babies, their latest hobbies, and their political opinions. Software designed to dynamically generate part of that information feed was patented by Facebook in 2010, although the company continues to update the software.[7]

Patents are public documents, and they are readily available, especially in our internet age. To find the Facebook News Feed patent, go to your internet search engine and enter "US patent 7669123." To read the patent, open it as a pdf document and focus first on the top-left side. You'll see that it says **United States Patent** in large, boldface type. On the top right is the patent number, **US7,669,123**, also in large, bold type. This number uniquely and sequentially identifies the patent. With

Form 10-K, Annual Report Pursuant to Section 13 or 15(d) of the Securities Exchange Act of 1934, Annual Period ended December 31, 2019 (filed January 30, 2020).

[7] US Patent No. 7,669,123 (issued February 23, 2010). In 2013, Facebook announced that it would maintain a blog to post information about periodic updates to the News Feed: https://newsroom.fb.com/news/2013/08/announcing-news-feed-fyi-a-series-of-blogs-on-news-feed-ranking (accessed July 3, 2019).

Facebook's News Feed patent, we have reached 7,669,123 patents issued by the US government since 1836.[8]

Just below **United States Patent** on the left-hand side, we see the name(s) of the inventors: Zuckerberg et al. For this patent, Mark Zuckerberg has seven named coinventors. Their names are listed later in full, but there is symbolic significance in placing the first inventor's name at the very top of the patent. The person named here is endowed with a heightened prestige, as is the government that honors him by naming him in this public document.[9]

Typically, however, as we can also see from the News Feed patent, a corporation is the actual owner. Just below the named inventors on the left-hand side of the patent, we see that Facebook, Inc. is the assignee. This tells us that Mark Zuckerberg and his coinventors have legally transferred their ownership to the Facebook corporation.[10]

Just by looking at the first page of a patent, then, we can learn a lot about what patents are. They are a grant from a national government to an inventor, and often (ultimately) to a corporation. But what do they grant? Patents grant time-limited property protections for new technology. Recently the US Supreme Court defined patents as *public franchises*, a type of public right given by the government to the patentee, as a legal reward for providing useful services to the state, in the form of invention and innovation. In the case of a social network like Facebook, the new technology is typically computer programming, that is, software. For our Facebook News Feed patent, a new software design configures a massive network of computers to display continuous feeds of information about other social network users.[11]

The drawings and specifications of the patent describe this proprietary technology. The description is very precisely honed, because it was contested with the US Patent Office in a process called *prosecution*. Prosecution is an administrative process by which the government tests a patent application to see if a patent should be granted. This is a legal sequence of arguments between patent attorneys – some employed by the government and some by the inventor. Facebook's News Feed patent was filed with the US Patent Office on August 11, 2006, but it was not issued

8 This walk-through in reading a patent borrows a great deal from a very helpful (and now out-of-print) textbook on patent law for engineers and scientists. Howard B. Rockman, *Intellectual Property Law for Engineers and Scientists* (Hoboken: John Wiley & Sons, 2004), 35–45. In 1836, the United States enacted a wholesale revision to the existing patent law, initiating an examination procedure for patents. 5 Stat. 117 (July 4, 1836). The first patent issued under the new legal framework was for traction wheels under a locomotive engine, to "prevent the evil" of sliding wheels in conditions of snow and ice, issued to John Ruggles on July 13, 1836. US Patent No. 1 (issued July 13, 1836).

9 US patent law requires listing of the actual inventor(s) in the patent application. 35 U.S.C. § 115(a).

10 With this patent, the assignment of ownership went into effect from the moment the patent was issued. With other patents, the assignment comes later and is separately registered with the US Patent and Trademark Office (from hereon, I will abbreviate as US Patent Office). 35 U.S.C. § 261.

11 Patents as public franchises: *Oil States Energy Services* v. *Greene's Energy Group*, 138 S. Ct. 1365 (2018). In January 2019, the US Court of Federal Claims interpreted this case as reinforcing the principle that patents are not property in the strong sense required to justify a claim under the US Constitution's Fifth Amendment Takings Clause. *Christy, Inc.* v. *US*, 141 F. Cl. 641 (Fed. Cl. 2019).

until February 23, 2010. During this 3.5-year period, Facebook's patent lawyers argued with US patent lawyers (called *examiners*) about whether the patent should be issued, and about how it should be described. The outcome of that argument is the patent that we see, a patent that ends with twenty-five *claims*.[12]

And here we come to the heart of a patent. Because, of course, the important question is: what counts as a patented News Feed? Where exactly are the boundaries that Facebook's competitors shall not pass? The patent claims, which are the focus of the prosecution process, define the new technology and delineate the boundaries of the patent property. By analogy to a line that is drawn around landed property, which might connect stones, trees, and rivers that we can physically touch and see, patent claims define verbal boundaries for *intangible property* – property that we cannot physically touch and see. With patents we can touch and see only a particular *embodiment* (or manifestation) of the property, not the object of property itself. Other potential embodiments (or manifestations) are also covered – anything that comes under the verbal description of the patent claims. At the time a patent is claimed and issued, we do not really know what that is yet. Only time and argumentation will tell which future inventions come under the terms of the verbal description. The patent claims, which tell us through a system of signs (language) what this property is, are therefore the most important part of the patent.[13]

2.2 ZONES OF EXCLUSIVITY AND INSTRUMENTS OF LEGAL POWER

Patents draw boundaries with words, and these words matter. To see how, start by imagining that you want to exclude people from something, say an apartment or dorm room. Can you do this by yourself? The obvious answer is no. You need people to help you. You can form a gang to keep people out by force, terrifying them into staying away. Or you can put a sign on your door telling people to stay out. If people follow the words on your sign, they will be excluding themselves, but, in doing so, they will be doing what you want, namely, staying out of your room. With the words on your sign, you will have accomplished your exclusion through the cooperative social action of others, who impose an obligation on

[12] US Patent No. 7,669,123 (issued February 23, 2010).

[13] For further discussion of patent claims, see *Renishaw PLC* v. *Marposs Societa per Azioni*, 158 F.3d 1243 (Fed. Cir. 1998) (discussing use of written specification to construe the meaning of claims); In re Vamco Machine and Tool, Inc., 752 F.2d 1564, 1577 n.5 (Fed. Cir. 1985) ("The function of claims is (a) to point out what the invention is in such a way as to distinguish it from what was previously known, i.e., from the prior art; and (b) to define the scope of protection afforded by the patent. In both of these aspects, claims are not technical descriptions of the disclosed inventions but are legal documents like the descriptions of lands by metes and bounds in a deed which define the area conveyed but do not describe the land." (emphasis in original)).

themselves, limiting themselves and perhaps sacrificing their own desires, in respecting your orders.[14]

Notice how, in this example, your capacity to harness the cooperative social action of others with words on a page is just as powerful as a gang. Indeed, it is even more powerful because less effort is expended to achieve it. Rather than a group of people threatening violence, whose coordination creates a whole new set of challenges, the power comes from a combination of words on a page, and from the fact that people care enough about what the words say to be willing to change what they do. *Harnessing people's capacity to impose obligations upon themselves* (i.e., *to intentionally obey an order*) *is one of the most powerful social forces that exist.* Of course, we always need to understand *why* an order is obeyed, and Max Weber's sociological categories become useful precisely here.[15]

For now, though, we can say that, if a zone of exclusivity (i.e., property) exists in social reality, it exists because of cooperative social action – people acting and interacting together in some way that is collectively organized and coordinated. According to the example that I have posed, which involves an individual person initiating a process of social exclusion, the coordinating organization is either that of a gang or it is a combination of words and self-imposed, self-excluding action. Distilling the motivations involved in my examples of obedience, we can say that they are either raw fear or deferential respect.

In actual reality, though, the process of exclusion is almost never this extreme. Before you ever put up your sign or form your gang, there are many people who are

[14] One extreme type of self-imposed obligation comes close to what the philosopher Immanuel Kant meant by autonomy. In the *Metaphysics of Morals*, Kant worked out conditions and principles for an ideal system of law, one that preserves autonomy for all, starting with a conception of moral personhood as involving free, rational beings who conform to laws that they impose on themselves. "The Metaphysics of Morals, Part I, Metaphysical First Principles of the Doctrine of Right," in Mary J. Gregor (ed. & trans.), *Immanuel Kant, Practical Philosophy* (Cambridge, UK: Cambridge University Press, 1996), 378. See also Paul Guyer, *Kant on Freedom, Law, and Happiness* (Cambridge, UK: Cambridge University Press, 2000), 129–71; J. B. Schneewind, *The Invention of Autonomy: A History of Modern Moral Philosophy* (Cambridge, UK: Cambridge University Press, 1998). In somewhat different ways, Max Weber and Emile Durkheim built heavily on Kant in formulating their foundations for legal sociology, focusing more on the empirical social processes by which obligations are compelled, either through internal motivations or external, social pressures. For contemporary extension of the Kantian foundation, which builds also on Weber and Durkheim, see Jürgen Habermas, *Between Facts and Norms: Contributions to a Discourse Theory of Law and Democracy*, translated by William Rehg (Cambridge, MA: MIT Press, 1996). Although the notion of self-imposed obligation is significant in the Kantian philosophy of law, and in contemporary sociological theories building on Max Weber and Emile Durkheim, it is also important to note that the concept is much older. Something like this notion is implicated in Plato's theory about the importance of the prologue ("prelude," proem) to a set of laws. *The Laws of Plato*, translated by Thomas L. Pangle (Chicago: University of Chicago Press, 1988), 720a–724a (Book IV).

[15] I am partly borrowing here from Philip Gorski's argument about what made Calvinist religious doctrines so powerful in processes of early modern state formation – the ways in which doctrines helped to mobilize self-discipline and mutual policing within nationally bounded, religious communities. Philip S. Gorski, *The Disciplinary Revolution: Calvinism and the Rise of the State in Early Modern Europe* (Chicago: University of Chicago Press, 2003), 17–38 and passim.

already excluding themselves from your apartment or dorm room. In many cases, they will be doing so for reasons that have nothing to do with your sign (or gang). But, for those people who might be tempted to enter your room, the reason that they do not do so will be, in the extreme, either because they are afraid of being punished or because they are affirmatively obliging themselves to respect the meanings conveyed through words on your sign. In reality, it is usually a bit of both – the social powers harnessed by law partake of both the armed gang and the people who respectfully adhere to obligations from words. There is a common source of social power underlying both, however, and this is the power of meaningful and reciprocal obligation.[16]

When we think about social power, we often emphasize coercion and domination – making other people do what we want them to do, even when they want to do the exact opposite thing. However, a mid-twentieth-century sociologist, Talcott Parsons, emphasized another important aspect, which Michael Mann has borrowed to develop a wide-ranging, historical theory of social power for our contemporary world.[17]

For both Talcott Parsons and Michael Mann, it is important to distinguish *distributive power* – power that a person exercises over another – from *collective power*, which involves *consolidated powers from coordinated activity*. As we all know, many people working effectively together can accomplish more than one person working alone. Ironically, this may be true even when people are struggling against each other. Sometimes even competitive struggles may work out into a pattern of collective action that involves consolidated social power. This, after all, is how many economists think about competitive markets, which have the magical power to set prices, according to economic theory.[18]

For Michael Mann, social power involves networks of social interaction – many people interacting, over time, to form patterns of organized social relationships. These are organized social bonds, or simply *organizations*. Sometimes, to use language from Max Weber, these organizations are *communities*, because the people participating in them believe that they *belong together* in some way. Other times, however, the organizations are formed for limited, utilitarian purposes, and there is little (if any) sense among those participating that they "belong together" in

16 Recognition of habituated motivations in social action (*habitus*), as a preeminent source of social-relational patterns, is shared by Max Weber and Pierre Bourdieu. Pierre Bourdieu, *Outline of a Theory of Practice*, translated by Richard Nice (Cambridge, UK: Cambridge University Press, 1977); Max Weber, "Introduction to the Economic Ethics of the World Religions," translated by Sam Whimster, in Sam Whimster (ed.), *The Essential Weber* (Abingdon: Routledge, 2004), 66–8, 74; Max Weber, *Economy and Society*, edited by Guenther Roth and Claus Wittich, 2d ed. (Berkeley: University of California Press, 2013), 22–6.

17 Talcott Parsons, *Structure and Process in Modern Societies* (New York: The Free Press, 1960), 199–225; Mann, *Sources, Vol. 1*, 6. Max Weber, for example, drew a careful distinction between power (*Macht*) – making someone do something against their own will – and rulership or lordship (*Herrschaft*, often translated as domination), which involves voluntary – intentional and willed – obedience to commands. Weber, *Economy & Society*, 53–4, 212–16.

18 Mann, *Sources, Vol. 1*, 6; Parsons, *Structure and Process*, 219–21.

a meaningful way. However, they are committed to the goals of the organization – for example, earning an economic profit, or empowering workers and racial minorities – and so, for that reason, they are committed to each other. Either way, an organization exists, and, because of the power of the social bonds that are coordinated, a zone of exclusivity potentially comes into existence. Zones of exclusivity exist, in other words, because of organized social bonds, which are organized through the commitments and meaningfully obligated performances that order them. Law, I am arguing, contributes to these social relationships, because it is itself a meaningful, obliging force.[19]

To give some vibrancy and metaphoric life to this set of intuitions, think of an analogy to nuclear power. Nuclear bombs are the most powerful weapon that human beings have managed yet to invent. The force holding bonded protons and neutrons together within the nucleus of an atom is so massive that, when unleashed, it becomes – to quote J. Robert Oppenheimer quoting the *Baghavad Gita* – the destroyer of worlds. I am arguing that the social powers enabling zones of exclusivity to exist are a bit like that. Zones of exclusivity, like those we see with intellectual property, exist because of massive social power, and this massive social power comes, ultimately, from the powers of human commitment and obligation that organize and enable enduring social relationships.[20]

As a formal instrument of legal power, a patent is something like the words on the page of your sign telling people to stay out of your room. It has the power that it does partly because something with more than a few points of comparison with an organized gang (which we call a *nation-state*) stands behind it, and partly because it conveys meaningful content in words through a material means (the internet). Instruments of legal power harness and mobilize the social powers of law as a meaningful, obliging force, and they do so fundamentally through semantic powers, the powers of meaning and language to elicit, mobilize, and configure human social relationships of commitment, obligation, and respectful obedience.

Through instruments of legal power, like patents, people enact, perform, and memorialize relationships of obligation. To see this, though, we need to deepen our theory of property, to see how property involves powers not simply to exclude others, but also to impose additional obligations.

2.3 PROPERTY AS OBLIGING POWER IN COOPERATIVE RELATIONSHIPS

Intellectual property is not simply about exclusion. It also involves what Max Weber called "powers of control and disposal," which the legal scholar Larissa Katz has more recently described as the authority to "set the agenda for a resource." Within

19 Mann, *Sources, Vol. I*, 1–33, 52; Weber, *Economy & Society*, 40–56.

20 For a recent, historical treatment of the famous Oppenheimer quote, see James A. Hijiya, "The 'Gita' of J. Robert Oppenheimer," *Proceedings of the American Philosophical Society* 144.2 (2000): 123.

the zone of exclusivity defined by a property boundary, the property owner has a unique level of freedom (a "public franchise," in the recent language of the US Supreme Court) to decide what should happen, and to thereby (indirectly) impose obligations on anyone who wishes to step inside the boundary.[21]

To see this, we can start with the example of landed property. Think of a case in which two plots of land with houses on them stand right next to one another. The two houses share a common sidewalk that passes between them to their respective backyards. In order for one of the homeowners to get to her backyard, she must walk across this common sidewalk, but technically the sidewalk is on the property of the other homeowner. To walk across the common sidewalk, the first homeowner must obtain permission from the second homeowner. In granting this permission, if the second homeowner so wishes, he can impose obligations on the first homeowner. She is free to refuse, but if she does, she will lose the right to walk across his land. To fully enjoy her property, she must obey his orders.

This, as we saw in the case of McDonald's restaurant, is how intellectual property licensing arrangements work. If a person wishes to operate a McDonald's restaurant as a franchisee, they may acquire some rights to use intellectual property, but in exchange they must agree to submit themselves to a wide-ranging set of obligations that, from the McDonald's Corporation's perspective, aim to ensure uniformity of food service across McDonald's restaurants worldwide. This submission to these wide-ranging obligations is a condition for using McDonald's patents, copyrights, trademarks, and trade secrets. The McDonald's Corporation does not have the power to directly issue orders to its franchisees, in the way that a sovereign government does, but McDonald's does have the power to make the use of its property conditional on voluntary submission to licensing obligations by franchisees.

Notice that the power to set the agenda for a resource, where that resource is a computer-based social network like Facebook, is effectively the power to set the agenda for social relationships. Facebook's property resource, which is claimed directly in its patents – like the News Feed patent that we have been studying – involves the formation and maintenance of social relationships through a combination of personal computers and telecommunications infrastructures, that is, the internet. Facebook's patent claims, which define the zone of exclusivity constituting its intellectual property, are written to cover various aspects of the "management of interaction" between people. This language comes from the US Patent and Trademark Office, which has recently defined a new class of social networking patents. Since February 2010, there has existed a growing group of patents where the property defined by the patent involves a "computerized

[21] Weber, *Economy & Society*, 67–8; Larissa Katz, "Exclusion and Exclusivity in Property Law," *University of Toronto Law Journal* 58 (2008): 275–315; *Oil States Energy Services* v. *Greene's Energy Group*, 138 S. Ct. 1365 (2018).

arrangement for the management of interaction between individuals or entities who are connected by one or more common relations or interests."[22]

In the case of social networking patents, then, the power to set the agenda for a property resource approaches the power to directly impose obligations on "subject users." This power to impose obligations on subjects is traditionally the power of a sovereign government. Analogies and affinities between sovereignty and property ownership have long been noted, but those affinities become especially close in the case of social networking patents, like Facebook's News Feed patent. The submission to this power is voluntary, however, and the power is often imposed through technical controls – limitations built into the software programming that runs the social network – rather than through the verbal issuance of commands.[23]

Property, to return to Larissa Katz's language, involves agenda-setting powers – powers to impose conditional obligations – for every activity that comes within the zone of exclusivity defined by the property boundaries. In the case of nonphysical (intangible) property, like intellectual property, the boundaries are verbal and conceptual. We cannot see or touch the boundaries, but we can understand them through conceptual language articulated in the patent.[24]

As Larissa Katz notes, it is rarely the case that a property owner solely wishes to exclude. Often she is more interested in agenda-setting powers than in exclusion per se, but she wants her agenda-setting powers to be exclusive, or at least superior. Think of the example of the homeowner who wishes to lease her home to someone else. Here she is using her home to generate income, and this use requires a cooperative social relationship between the homeowner and her lessees. Her powers of exclusivity, as a property owner, are being exerted to set the agenda for her resource, and to earn an income in doing so, but this use of her property involves an enduring, social bond between the lessor and the lessee.[25]

With intellectual property, like patents, exclusion is an important part of the goal, but it is rarely the entire goal. Patents are typically very narrow, so narrow that they cover only the tiniest sliver of a new technology, like a social network or a smartphone. Social networks and smartphones embody hundreds of thousands of patents, as well as copyrights, trademarks, and trade secrets. In order to market and sell social networks and smartphones, it was necessary for many high-technology companies to enter into complex licensing arrangements with one another. A very high degree of cooperation and aggregated obligation, in other

[22] United States Patent Classification (USPC) System, Class 705, Subclass 319, description available at www.uspto.gov/web/patents/classification/selectnumwithtitle.htm (accessed February 10, 2019); see also US Dept. of Commerce: Patent and Trademark Office, Classification Order 1892 (February 2, 2010), available at www.uspto.gov/sites/default/files/patents/resources/classification/orders/1892.pdf (accessed February 10, 2019).

[23] For further elaboration of this argument, see Ford, *Patenting the Social*, 284–96.

[24] Katz, "Exclusion and Exclusivity," 289, 293–5.

[25] Ibid., 296–315.

words, actually underlies the high-technology products that we buy in contemporary commercial markets.[26]

2.4 SOCIAL POWER AND VENTURE CAPITAL

Intellectual property, then, becomes possible through multiple layers of social power. There is, first, the social power that enables the property to exist at all. Powers of exclusion depend on causally prior social powers that come from cooperation and coordinated social obligation. *Behind every zone of exclusivity (or "property right") is a social organization, which is enabling that zone of exclusivity to exist, by virtue of the cooperative social action that the organization coordinates.* But secondly, there is the social power that comes with property ownership, the power to set the agenda for a resource and to conditionally impose obligations. In setting the agenda for a resource, new cooperative relationships are often created, and new levels of social power become possible. There is therefore a recursive structure – a cyclical process with feedback loops – in the relationship between intellectual property and social power. Intellectual property depends on social power, but it also facilitates the wielding of social power.[27]

Through his focus on the sources of social power, Michael Mann can help us to explicate these layers of social power. Mann distinguishes four sources of social power: ideological, economic, military, and political (IEMP is the abbreviation he uses to encapsulate all four). These are *sources* of social power, because they link people together into social relationships, networks, and groups, and it is these social bonds linking people together that make for consolidated, social power. Each source, however, links people together in a distinctive way, which Mann (following Max Weber) calls an *ideal type*. The basic point is that these sources never operate independently from each other. In the real world that we live in, ideological (cultural), economic, military, and political sources of power all work together.

[26] Large patent pools have been necessary to establish the technical foundations for interoperability in telecommunications and computing that underpin both the internet and smartphones. While it is very difficult to reliably estimate the number of patents embodied in smartphones, one widely reported number is on the order of 250,000, an estimate connected to the further estimate that somewhere around one-third of all currently active patents relate to smartphone technology in some way. For an accessible and thought-provoking discussion, see WIPO, *World Intellectual Property Report 2017: Intangible Capital in Global Value Chains* (Geneva: World Intellectual Property Organization, 2017), available at www.wipo.int/publications/en/details.jsp?id=4225 (accessed July 7, 2019). For further discussion of patent pooling and cross-licensing arrangements, viewed from the perspective of US antitrust policy-makers, see USDOJ & FTC, *Antitrust Guidelines for Licensing*, 30–32; see also US Department of Justice and the Federal Trade Commission, *Antitrust Enforcement and Intellectual Property Rights: Promoting Innovation and Competition*, April 2007 Report, available at www.justice.gov/atr/antitrust-enforcement-and-intellectual-property-rights-promoting-innovation-and-competition (accessed July 7, 2019), 1–13, 33–37, 57–85.

[27] Cf. Terrence C. Halliday and Bruce G. Carruthers, "The Recursivity of Law: Global Norm Making and National Law Making in the Globalization of Corporate Insolvency Regimes," *American Journal of Sociology* 112.4 (2007).

But analytically distinguishing the different sources of social power enables us to see distinctive patterns in the ways that they combine with one another, or, in Mann's words, *entwine* with one another. The patterns that emerge from distinctive *entwinings* Mann calls *forms* or *regimes*.[28]

Since this is a book about property, we should begin with the economic source of social power. In the modern world of global and industrial capitalism, economic power is in some ways the most fundamental source of social power. For Mann this source of social power arises because of the ways that people are linked together in their collective work to satisfy the material needs of human existence, and in their efforts to control nature. At a basic level human material needs involve things like food, shelter, and clothing. At a less basic level, we can think of things like money and credit.[29]

As we have seen in the case of Facebook, patents can play a significant role in the practical transition from great idea to successful business. The key to that transition is credit. While an inventor is moving from idea to functioning business – before she has revenues from sales that cover her costs – she will need loans. Unless she comes from a wealthy and generous family, or has wealthy and generous friends, she will need loans from strangers who are in the business of lending money. Typically, today, these strangers will work in banks or for venture capital firms, partnerships of people who lend money to start-ups and are willing to take higher-than-average risks with unestablished businesses. In return for taking these higher-than-average risks, venture capital firms will often ask for control over decision-making, that is, agenda-setting power, in the new business.[30]

We are used to thinking of lending primarily in economic terms, but there is also an important social side to lending. Every loan involves social relationships and ties (i.e., social bonds). Whether or not you get a loan may depend to a great extent on who you know. And, if you do receive a loan, you will be tied to your lender (and, through your lender, to the state) until you repay the loan. With credit card debt, the social tie is not so obvious, although we all realize at a certain level that we are obligated to repay a loan, and that this obligation is owed to a company. But with bank loans and start-up financing, where the obligations are large and tailored to the specifics of a start-up business, the social ties are quite obvious.[31]

Facebook's first major investment came in September 2004 from a man named Peter Thiel. Today, Thiel is a managing partner at a venture capital firm called

[28] Mann, *Sources, Vol. I*, 1–33, 518–24; Mann, *Sources, Vol.* 2, 1–3, 18–21; Mann, *Sources, Vol.* 3, 5–16; Mann, *Sources, Vol.* 4, 1–12, 400–32.

[29] Mann, *Sources, Vol. I*, 24–5; Mann, *Sources, Vol.* 2, 7–8, 23–34; Mann, Sources, Vol. 4, 401, 406–15.

[30] On the importance of loans – initially from family and friends, then from venture capital – for the early years of Facebook, see Kirkpatrick, *Facebook Effect*, 42–126.

[31] For further discussion of this sociological side to money and credit, see Bruce G. Carruthers and Laura Ariovich, *Money and Credit: A Sociological Approach* (Cambridge, UK: Polity Press, 2010); Viviana Zelizer, *Economic Lives: How Culture Shapes the Economy* (Princeton: Princeton University Press, 2011), 89–164.

Founders Fund. In 2004, when Thiel made his first loan to Facebook, he asked for a particular type of loan, one that would not be repaid with cash, but rather with an equity stake (i.e., property ownership) in the company, if the company was successful. (If Facebook had failed, it would have owed him repayment in cash, but as we all know, that eventuality never occurred.) With this loan, written out in the legal form of a contract, a social tie was created, one that has lasted until today, even though the loan has long since been repaid. As of August 2020, Peter Thiel remains a member of the board of directors for Facebook, and a major shareholder.[32]

Through the satisfaction of material and economic needs, then, social bonds are created, and these can become a significant source of social power because they join people together – get them working together – whether cooperatively or competitively. In a legal system that recognizes marriages, enforces contracts, and protects property, these bonds are often articulated using language of law. This is an important clue that formalities of law are working in the background, contributing through the distinctively meaningful, obliging force of law, to the formation of social bonds.

In Michael Mann's terminology, the social networks that are created on this legal basis are *classes*. Unlike Marxist classes, which are rooted strictly in conditions of production – the fact that some people own the means of production, like machines, while other people have no choice but to work on those machines and create value for the owners – Mann's classes are rooted in broader linkages of economic production with distribution, exchange, and consumption. Classes, in other words, are interconnected with regimes of social power, and they are therefore one analytical dimension of a broader and more complex pattern in the organization of social power. What is important is the fact that social power is expressed as economic power, the power to control resources and to affect others' material conditions of life. In the modern world, as in classical antiquity, law has been vitally important in defining and organizing economic powers, facilitating the agenda-setting powers of property and the existence of property-based classes.[33]

Venture capital firms, like the Founders Fund, create credit-based social bonds through the lending of property in the form of money. They are linked together through social ties with start-ups that receive their loans. The social networks and groups that are created in this way are social classes, linked together through their collective work to satisfy material, human needs. When we talk about Silicon Valley,

[32] Kirkpatrick, *Facebook Effect*, 88–9; Founders Fund website, https://foundersfund.com/team/peter-thiel/ (accessed August 21, 2020); Facebook board of directors, https://investor.fb.com/corporate-governance/default.aspx (accessed August 21, 2020).

[33] Mann, *Sources, Vol. 1*, 216–23, 520; Mann, *Sources, Vol. 2*, 23–34; Mann, *Sources, Vol. 4*, 26–66, 423–32. In Volume 3, Mann discusses "finance capital" as a "distinct capitalist class fraction." Mann, *Sources, Vol. 3*, 11, 64–5, 127–8, 208–40. In Volume 4, Mann builds on Greta Krippner's identification of "financialization," a social and economic phenomenon in which accumulation of capital and wealth occur "primarily through financial channels rather than through trade and commodity production." Greta Krippner, "The Financialization of the American Economy," *Socio-Economic Review* 3. 173–208 (2005): 174; Greta Krippner, *Capitalizing on Crisis. The Political Origins of the Rise of Finance* (Cambridge, MA: Harvard University Press, 2011); Mann, *Sources, Vol. 4*, 140–46.

then, we are often talking about an economic class, in Mann's sense, a network of people linked together through the financing and running of high-technology businesses.

Ownership of a strong patent on a new technology significantly increases the likelihood that a venture capital firm, like the Founders Fund, will lend money to a start-up like Facebook once was. But why? Here is where we see the power of culture (ideology).

In 2014, Peter Thiel published a book articulating his philosophy of the world, with the help of a Stanford law student named Blake Masters. In seeing the world through the eyes of Peter Thiel and Blake Masters, we gain insight into the social bonds that are rooted in shared ideas, ideals, interests, and hopes, which link people together at Facebook, and in the high-technology world of Silicon Valley.[34]

Thiel's book is called *Zero to One: Notes on Startups, or How to Build the Future*. It is a manifesto on the importance of new technologies for future prosperity, both in the narrow economic sense and in the broader sense of social well-being. New technologies, according to Thiel, are human "miracles," which take us in qualitatively new directions by enabling us "to do *more with less*, ratcheting up our fundamental capabilities to a higher level." Rather than adding more of what we already know and extending it to more people – which is what Thiel believes happens in globalization – new technology takes us somewhere we have not been before. It takes us, in his words, "from zero to one." The question that his book is written to address is: how can American companies perform human miracles, or at least recognize and support human miracle workers? Ironically, there is no formula or prescription, because, by definition, originality is unfamiliar. "The act of creation is singular, as is the moment of creation, and the result is something fresh and strange." There is no way to recognize something that we have never seen before, let alone to prescribe a formula for it. Nevertheless, it is in these mysterious and miraculous qualities of human creativity that our hopes for the future must rest.[35]

In Michael Mann's terminology, Thiel's book is a statement of ideology; in other words, it is a statement of cultural beliefs and values. It contains and communicates ideas at the level of a worldview – conceptions about what technology is, for example, and about how technology matters to the future of our societies. It also contains normative prescriptions and proscriptions – statements about what we should and should not do. We *should* invest in new technologies for the future, *not* place our hopes in globalization and old models for doing business. Novelty and evermore technological novelty are our best hope for the future, according to the worldview articulated by Peter Thiel.[36]

34 Peter Thiel with Blake Masters, *Zero to One: Notes on Startups, or How to Build the Future* (New York: Crown Business, 2014).

35 Thiel/Masters, *Zero to One*, 1–11.

36 Mann, *Sources, Vol. 1*, 22–4, 301–72, 379–90, 519–20; *Sources, Vol. 2*, xiv-xvi, 7, 39–42, 227–37, 571–5; *Sources, Vol. 3*, 6–9, 51–5, 227–36, 317–20, 334–6; *Sources, Vol. 4*, 1–8, 31–6, 67–85, 403–6, 428–9.

Thiel's book is based on a set of lectures that he gave at Stanford, and on the detailed notes that Blake Masters took in class, then circulated. Recognizing that there was a demand for the ideas presented in his lectures, Peter Thiel published them in a book. This enabled him to reach a wider audience, and to collect copyright royalties for sales of the book. (Just as a reminder, copyright protects tangible expressions of ideas, not ideas themselves. Peter Thiel cannot copyright the ideas articulated in a lecture, but he can (and did) copyright the book expressing those ideas.)[37]

Cultural forms of power come from social bonds based on shared ideas, beliefs, interests, morals, and values. In this form of social power, people are linked together primarily on the basis of things that involve the human mind, and the quest for meaning: ideas and ideals, intellectually cultivated habits, religious rituals, understandings, and worldviews. These can be matters of ultimate concern, and they are "values" because we care deeply about them.

Drawing on the Latin etymological roots of *culture* – that which is cultivated, cared for, and tended, as in *agriculture* or the shrine to a god – Hannah Arendt emphasized the spiritual connotations, the ways that our practices of joining together in caring for valued ideals and meaningful objects (e.g., books or paintings) indicate our deepest aspirations and commitments, as human beings. Cultural objects, the creative products of artists, musicians, and writers, for Arendt, are a testament to the animating "spirit" of an age, and to the history of humanity. They are beautiful or wise, and we love them for their beauty or wisdom. As objects existing in worldly forms, moreover, they give a tangible reality to our ethereal ideals, our transcendent hopes, and our complex worldviews.[38]

In the worldview expressed by Peter Thiel, which we can treat as a cultural manifesto for Silicon Valley venture capitalism, patents are important, valued protections against competition which help to enable a new technology to emerge. Competition is war, and it is wastefully costly to technology businesses. If you have to fight, do it decisively, but try to avoid it. Thiel advocates building monopoly businesses and using intellectual property to help in this. "Proprietary technology is the most substantive advantage a company can have because it makes your product difficult or impossible to replicate."[39]

The key to making technology proprietary is patent protection. Other forms of intellectual property can help – copyrights to prevent copying of source code, and trade secrecy to protect combinations of technological elements that are not themselves patent-eligible. Thiel also advocates strong protections of a brand, which

[37] Thiel/Masters, *Zero to One*, 3–4. The copyright notice at the front of the book names Peter Thiel alone.

[38] Hannah Arendt, "The Crisis in Culture: Its Social and Political Significance," in Hannah Arendt, *Between Past and Future: Eight Exercises in Political Thought*, edited by Jerome Kohn (New York. Penguin, 2006), 194–222.

[39] Thiel/Masters, *Zero to One*, 36–58.

come from trademark law, as we saw in the case of McDonald's Corporation. But the only way to guarantee that new technology will be given the protection afforded to property is to patent it. In Thiel's words, a patent is "a legally enforceable monopoly." If we are trying to build a monopoly business, as Thiel advocates, this is the place to focus our energies.[40]

If you are a venture capitalist like Peter Thiel, trying to decide where to invest your money for high-risk returns, you will look for start-ups with patents, or at least with the promise of obtaining patents. At the time Peter Thiel invested in Facebook, it did not have any patents, but, beginning in 2006, Facebook began filing a series of patent applications. As an agenda-setting shareholder in the company, Thiel perhaps exercised an influence in this decision to begin filing patent applications, which likely contributed, in turn, to the definition of a new class of patents at the USPTO, patents that claim property (and agenda-setting powers) in the "management of social interaction."

Why do patents have such powers? In order to answer this question, we need to see how economic and cultural powers are connected in modern patent law.

2.5 DRAWING BOUNDARIES WITH FORMALIZING WORDS FOR SOCIAL PURPOSES

Patents draw boundaries with formalizing words, and these words are loaded with cultural power. To see this more concretely, let's linger for a moment on the patent-claiming (prosecution) process, and on the drawing of boundaries with words that the process entails. There are two things to notice right away about the process: (1) its formalities involve a break with everyday social reality, and (2) the formal legal instrument that results from the process is legally connected to a set of justifications that legitimize the patent on the basis of its contribution to social goals. In the language of Max Weber, there is a *formal rationality* that stands behind the patent, as a legal instrument, which determines the strictly legal power (validity) that the patent has. There is also a *substantive rationality* that stands behind the patent, a set of social reasons that we can offer to explain, in terms of social policies, why the patent is legitimate: its effects are consistent with public goals that we uphold as morally responsible and even obligatory.[41]

[40] Thiel/Masters, *Zero to One*, 31–33, 47–57.

[41] The notion of formality as involving a break from everyday social reality borrows from Arthur Stinchcombe, *When Formality Works: Authority and Abstraction in Law and Organizations* (Chicago: University of Chicago Press, 2001), 9. Together with Stinchcombe, I am relying on Max Weber's famous distinction between formal and substantive rationality in law. Weber, *Economy & Society*, 654–8; Max Rheinstein (ed.), *Max Weber on Law in Economy and Society*, translated by Edward Shils and Max Rheinstein (New York: Simon & Schuster, 1967), 61–4. See also Chapter 1, section 1.5.

2.5.1 *Formalizing Words and Formal Rationality*

Remember that an inventor of new technology must pass five basic hurdles in order to receive a patent from the US government. Her patent application must describe a technology that is (1) new, (2) a nonobvious step beyond what was already known to people skilled in the particular area of technology, (3) useful, and (4) not within a category of things that cannot be patented, such as human beings, laws of nature, or abstract ideas. Each claim in the patent application must meet these hurdles. In addition, the patent specification, as a whole, must (5) adequately describe the technology so that a person with ordinary skill in the area could, on the basis of the verbal description, make the technology.[42]

Once the inventor files her patent application, a formal legal process begins by which US Patent Office examiners study the patent application, together with prior patents and scientific publications, to see whether the claims and specification meet the legal requirements. Looking at this process from the perspective of a patent applicant, it is called *prosecution*, because the applicant is pushing forward (prosecuting) her claims. In a typical process, the application will be initially rejected, and the applicant will have to revise her claims to get around the objections put forward by the patent examiner. A typical strategy by patent attorneys is therefore to draft broad claims, and then to narrow the claims in response to the examiner's objections.[43]

Why the initial effort to draft broad patent claims? Remember that the claims define the patented technology, so broader claims define a wider zone of exclusivity to keep competitors out, or to make them pay if they step over the line of a patented technology. A patent attorney's job is to draft broad claims which mark out a generous line around a new invention. The way to do this is to provide as little detail as possible in the claims, that is, to make them abstract.[44]

Here, in essence, is the trade-off in patent claim drafting. Claims that are stated more abstractly and with less detail claim much more, but in doing so they are more likely to extend into areas that are already covered by existing patents, or already known to people who are specialized in the particular area of technology. Broad claims are desirable because they create a wider zone of exclusivity, but they are harder to patent, because they are much less likely to meet the legal requirements for patent eligibility.[45]

When Mark Zuckerberg and his coinventors initially filed their News Feed patent application in August 2006, they included twenty-six claims. Their final patent, as issued in February 2010, included only twenty-five claims. In between, they received

[42] 35 U.S.C. §§ 101–103, 112; Lemley, Menell, and Merges, *Intellectual Property*, *Vol. 1*, 161–2, 168–316.

[43] 35 U.S.C. §§ 131–133; Rockman, *Intellectual Property Law*, 180–91 (despite being based on partially outdated patent law, this text is valuable in presenting the prosecution process from the perspective of a patent attorney, in dialog with his client).

[44] Rockman, *Intellectual Property Law*, 64, 161–3.

[45] Rockman, *Intellectual Property Law*, 64, 161–3.

two nonfinal rejections of their patent application. Each time they responded by amending the claims. This prosecution process took place through written filings by patent attorneys and responses by patent examiners. It left a paper trail, a *prosecution history*, which is a matter of public record. As you will see if you check out the record for yourself, the paper trail for Facebook's News Feed patent is long. The examiner's basic objection to the patent claims, as initially drafted, was that they were claiming technology that was already known, or was an obvious extension from what was already known. In order to respond to these objections, Facebook's patent attorneys were forced to draft narrower, more precise claims. Once the claims had been narrowed so that they no longer extended their verbal boundaries to technology that was previously known, or obvious, the patent could be issued.[46]

Patent claim drafting is a legal art. There are arcane rules about how claims are to be interpreted, which are partly articulated in court cases and partly developed through convention and custom among patent attorneys. Claims are drafted with an eye to the way that they will be interpreted by examiners and courts, as well as potential competitors, and with a recognition that the first response from the US Patent Office will probably be rejection. Skilled patent attorneys develop strategies for claim drafting, and pass these along to younger attorneys, who must not only develop these legal skills but also stay on top of a specialist field of technology, like computer programming or mechanical engineering.[47]

Whenever we look at an issued patent, we should keep in mind that there are years of debate and discussion, together with minute fine-tuning of the patent claims, standing behind it. The words really matter, and they are taken seriously by national governments, corporations, patent attorneys, inventors, and investors. The words matter because they claim technology as an intangible property, property that is carefully and formally defined in language. The patent claims stake out the boundaries of this property, a zone of exclusivity beyond which no one shall pass. And they do so as part of a legal process that breaks with everyday conventions of language, drawing on traditions of law that are passed along as teachings (doctrines, from the Latin *doctrina*, meaning *teaching*) from one generation of lawyers to the next.

2.5.2 *Legitimating Social Goals – Substantive Rationality*

The basic theory that substantively justifies patents today, as a matter of public policy, mainly comes from economics, but as we will see in this book, the underlying principles are much older than the modern discipline of economics. Lawyers and economists often explain the theory using the economic language of *public goods*.

46 The prosecution history is internet accessible through the USPTO's PAIR (Patent Application Information Retrieval) Portal, https://portal.uspto.gov/pair/PublicPair (accessed July 24, 2019). The only information that you need to access the history for Facebook's News Feed patent is the patent number, 7669123.

47 35 U.S.C. § 112; Rockman, *Intellectual Property Law*, 145–70.

To grasp the essence of the theory, we start from the premise that an invention, like a new vaccine or a social network like Facebook, is something that is socially valuable – we want to have inventions, and indeed we want to keep having more inventions, as many as possible, because these help solve social problems and grow our economy. Innovation, according to economists, is an engine that keeps our economies expanding as our population expands. But innovation is not easy – it takes time and costs money. Furthermore, ideas spread very easily, and can be available to many people all at once, unlike tangible things that can only be possessed by a few people at once. In the language of economic theory, a public good – like a public park, the chemical information for a new vaccine, or a social network – is "nonexclusive" and "nonrivalrous," meaning essentially that one person having more does not mean that another person has less; therefore, the regular assumptions about how people make choices under conditions of scarcity do not apply. This is the basic intuition for a public good – it is something that we think is good and valuable, yet it is something that is costly to make, and that, once made, can theoretically be freely available to everyone.[48]

And this explains the problem with public goods in a competitive, market-based society. As a society we want them. But if we rely on a competitive market to provide them, we will have too few of them. Why is this? Imagine there is no patent (or copyright) protection for Facebook's News Feed software. Another provider of social networking services, like Myspace, decides they want to cut Facebook down to size and steal away some of their customers. They have reason to believe that the News Feed is one of the things customers like about Facebook. So they design a News Feed exactly like Facebook's. Maybe they get their hands on the software code, or maybe their software designers do what is called *reverse engineering* – basically they work back logically from the way the software works to the way it is designed, and they design the same thing. Myspace could then compete directly with Facebook, and, especially if Myspace's service is cheaper or for some other reason more desirable, people might leave Facebook and go to Myspace.[49]

48 The contemporary economic theory of public goods is rooted in welfare economics, in which welfare has the sense of social well-being, or human flourishing. Welfare economics is concerned with the economic conditions for flourishing societies. The worry that economic growth will not keep up with population growth is as old as the discipline of economics itself. For a contemporary economic articulation of the centrality of innovation to economic growth, see Christine Greenhalgh and Mark Rogers, *Innovation, Intellectual Property, and Economic Growth* (Princeton: Princeton University Press, 2010).

49 Patent protection amounts to a legal prohibition on reverse engineering, which is part of what makes a patent so much stronger than copyright protection for software and computing-based innovations. I am ignoring, for the sake of simplicity, the existence of network effects, which entrench the socioeconomic dominance of internet-related technologies. In the case of Facebook, network effects may be seen in the fact that users value the sheer number of social connections they can make through the platform, beyond any question of the platform's technical features. This makes it much harder for Myspace to effectively compete, even if patent protections on software design features did not exist. However, patent protection is part of a corporate research and development strategy that enables

The experience of the twentieth century – particularly the competitive struggle between western capitalism and communism – taught many people to believe that national economies must be competitive and market based if they are to achieve maximum power. Desires for profit and success are like engines propelling market-based competition, and a capitalist economic system that harnesses these energies is the most powerful type of economic system we have ever seen. But economists also recognize that there are weaknesses in even the most powerful of competitive market systems. These weaknesses, or *market failures*, are ways in which the system is not perfectly self-regulating and can undermine itself. The failure of competitive markets to generate sufficient public goods is one type of market failure that is clearly recognized in economic theory.[50]

Patents, according to economic theory, exist as a solution to the public goods problem, the problem that we want two mutually incompatible things at once: (1) a competitive market system, and (2) strong incentives to create public goods, like new inventions in the form of antibiotics and social networks. Patents aim to help us have both, by creating a temporary form of governmental protection (or "franchise") for public goods, erecting property boundaries around the public good, for a limited time. Patents, in other words, transform something that would otherwise be freely available into something that is not freely available. They deploy the social power of nation-states to create zones of exclusivity around public goods. They do this for a limited time so that the inventor (or her company) can charge money for her public good and recoup her costs of invention.[51]

A theoretically perfect patent system would allow an inventor to recover just the amount that she spent in making her invention, together with just enough profit to give her an incentive to keep inventing. In the real-world patent system that we have, some patents are wildly powerful and profitable, and many are basically worthless. So companies in the business of inventing do the next best thing – they acquire as many patents as possible, consistent with legal and business strategies, building up large collections of patents that are sometimes called *patent portfolios*. They use a patent portfolio to build a defensive wall around a zone of technology that is important to their business, and sometimes they use the portfolio offensively to threaten competitors with lawsuits. Because litigation is

a company like Facebook to achieve dominance in the first instance, contributing a foundation to the network effects that then sustain the dominant position.

50 This paragraph summarizes what some people have called the "Washington Consensus," and what other people would call Neoliberalism. A standard account of Neoliberalism is found in David Harvey, *A Brief History of Neoliberalism* (Oxford: Oxford University Press, 2005). I am attempting to describe this intellectual position as a social fact – neither to endorse it nor to criticize it. As an intellectual position, which is hotly contested, but remains culturally widespread and influential in connecting people together in our contemporary world, this is a form of ideological power, from Michael Mann's theoretical perspective. His later volumes are explicitly critical of neoliberalism, for example, Mann, *Sources Vol. 4*, 400–32.

51 Greenhalgh and Rogers, *Innovation*, §§1.5–1.7, Chapter 2.

so expensive in the United States, a threat will often be enough to keep a potential competitor away.[52]

Facebook has a large and significant patent portfolio, although it trails far behind IBM, which annually tops the US list of highest patent acquisition. As of July 2019, approximately 3,000 US patents were listed by the US Patent and Trademark Office as being assigned to the Facebook Corporation. This probably represents only a portion of Facebook's overall patent portfolio, however, because the company owns other national patents – for example, Japanese, German, and French patents – and because it doubtless possesses rights to use (through licenses) many more patents, both US patents and international patents. Just by focusing on Facebook's US patents, though, we can see the significance of patent ownership to Facebook's overall business model.[53]

Patents, to reiterate, work as governmental limitations on market competition to incentivize invention and innovation. They provide a governmental solution to a systemic failure of competitive markets, without which, according to economic theory, we would not have enough innovation and economic growth. Ironically, despite extolling the virtues of market competition, the US government also works very hard to limit that competition through the issuance of patents. Indeed, as we will see in Chapter 9, the US government has done this work to limit market competition since its foundation.

2.5.3 *Formal Instruments of Legal Power*

A patent, then, is a formal legal document, issued by a national government, that describes the boundaries of an intangible property in new technology. Once the patent is issued, it serves as a legally validated promise by the government that anyone who steps across the verbally defined boundaries will be met with the power of the state. This promise is laid out in patent law, and it is this legal promise that helps to transform the document into an instrument of legal power. This legal power ultimately comes, I am arguing, from law's unique powers as a meaningful, obliging force.

One important support for these unique powers comes from the social rationale underlying the patent – the legitimating justification for the existence of patents that we have just discussed. But there is something important about the formalizing break from everyday social reality, which we have briefly explored through a focus on patent prosecution. In the theoretical language of Max Weber, logics of formal and substantive rationality stand in the background of patents as legal institutions, legitimating and empowering them as legal institutions. These logics are sometimes in tension with one another, but they nonetheless work together to provide a foundation for patents as instruments of legal power.

52 Rockman, *Intellectual Property Law*, 12–29.

53 A search of the USPTO website, conducted August 1, 2019, limited to issued patents assigned to Facebook, returned 3,394. This list includes design patents.

Even today, there are formal legal rituals that patent applicants must perform to initiate the prosecution process that will lead to a valid patent. One good example is the oath or declaration that an inventor must make, solemnly asserting that an invention is her own original creation. A version of this oath or declaration has been required of patent applicants ever since the US statutory framework of patent law was first revised in 1793, and it has survived, mostly intact, significant legislative changes enacted in 2011.[54]

Patent attorney Howard Rockman describes a typical scenario for administering the oath of invention as one in which a final meeting is held between the inventor and the patent attorney to review the patent application. Both parties read through the claims one last time, debating whether minute fine-tuning is appropriate or advisable. Once this final, careful review has been conducted, the "formal papers" are signed and the application is filed. These formal papers include an attestation that must be given by someone who is authorized under US law to administer oaths. This will be officially sealed, or otherwise attested through recognized procedures for the authentication of formal legal documents. Under the scenario that Rockman envisions, the patent attorney is also a notary public who attests the oath in that capacity.[55]

In theory, an oath is a solemn declaration, under penalty of perjury, to the truth of statements made in a document. According to the American Society of Notaries, the proper procedure for administering an oath involves a series of steps. First, the oath taker signs the document in front of the notary. Then there is a verbal ceremony. The notary should ask the applicant who has signed the document: "Do you swear under the penalties of perjury that the information contained in this document is the truth, so help you God?" This invocation of a "Supreme Being" is essential to the oath, but there is an alternative. "Persons who do not wish to invoke a Supreme Being in their pledge may make an affirmation ('I affirm that this is the truth.')." If the applicant responds "yes" to the oath or affirmation, the notary then completes the ritual by filling out the notarial certificate ("jurat"), signing and sealing it.[56]

54 Oath requirements in the 1793, 1836, 1870, 1952, and 2011 patent acts: 1 Stat. 318, 321 (1793); 5 Stat. 117, 119 (1836); 16 Stat. 198, 202 (1870); 66 Stat. 792, 799 (1952); 125 Stat. 284, 293–7 (2011). The US shift to a "first to file" system in 2011: The Leahy-Smith America Invents Act, Pub. L. 112–29, 125 Stat. 284 (2011). In shifting from a "first to invent" to a "first to file" system, the United States brought its patent law more closely in line with other globally powerful patent systems. This would have been a great opportunity to abandon the inventor's oath, which does seem like a relic of a more empirically formalistic age in US law. Nonetheless, although the requirement was softened to recognize the realities of large-scale corporate research and development, the basic requirement that an inventor must swear to the originality of her invention was retained, with alternative provisions for cases in which an inventor is dead or cannot be found, or in which the inventor is refusing to sign over her invention, under conditions in which she is obliged to do so. 35 U.S.C. § 115; 37 C.F.R. §§1.63, 1.64, 1.66, 1.68. For further discussion of the US legislative changes involving the shift to a "first to file" patent system, see House Report 112–98 (June 1, 2011), available at www.congress.gov/112/crpt/hrpt98/CRPT-112hrpt98.pdf (accessed August 18, 2019), 38–44.

55 Rockman, *Intellectual Property Law*, 153–4.

56 American Society of Notaries: Basic Notarial Duties: www.asnnotary.org/?form=basicduties (accessed August 18, 2019); *cf.* 37 C.F.R. 1.66.

In many cases, as we see in Facebook's News Feed patent, a group of joint inventors signs a statement, making no reference to God, but nonetheless solemnly declaring under penalty of perjury: "I believe I am an original, first, and joint inventor of the subject matter which is claimed and for which a patent is sought . . . ." The applicant also solemnly declares that she has reviewed the application, including the specification and claims. Importantly, she acknowledges an ongoing duty to disclose information that is relevant to the patentability of her invention, which might, for example, include patents or publications that she learns about after filing her patent application.[57]

While the administration of this oath or declaration by patent applicants may seem like an empty ritual, real consequences are attached. A patent application cannot proceed without the oath or declaration, and there is a possibility that a patent could be rendered null and void if dishonesty or fraud were somehow involved. Although much of the case law in this area goes back to the late nineteenth century, the principle still stands that the oath is "essential to the validity" of a patent. In the words of the US Supreme Court, penned in 1888 but quoted and cited repeatedly since:

> The patent law makes it essential to the validity of a patent that it shall be granted on the application, supported by the oath, of the original and first inventor, or of his executor or administrator, whether the patent is issued to him or to his assignee. A patent which is not supported by the oath of the inventor, but applied for by one who is not the inventor, is unauthorized by law and void, and, whether taken out in the name of the applicant or of any assignee of his, confers no rights as against the public.[58]

While theoretically the patent's validity depends on the truth of the inventor's oath, practically the most important implication of the oath is probably in the ongoing duty that is created between the patent applicant and the US Patent and Trademark Office. In acknowledging her duties to the USPTO, as part of her oath or declaration, an inventor acknowledges an ongoing relationship of obligation to a governmental organization, a relationship involving formalistic communications between attorneys but a real and ongoing relationship nonetheless.[59]

Focusing on medieval diplomas that issued property-related privileges from kings to their subjects, Geoffrey Koziol has emphasized the extent to which formalities are performative. By this he means that a solemn charter, written on parchment, witnessed by illustrious people, sacralized in a religious ritual, was enacting, constituting, and memorializing political and social relationships involving moral

57 37 C.F.R. § 1.56.

58 *Kennedy* v. *Hazelton*, 128 US 667, 672 (1888). Under the America Invents Act, patent applicants can be corporate entities rather than actual inventors, but the application must still be supported by the oath or declaration of the inventor(s), unless they are dead, otherwise unavailable, or refusing to comply with an obligation to assign an invention.

59 35 U.S.C. § 115; 37 C.F.R. § 1.56; *Wise* v. *Hubbard*, 769 F.2d 1, 3 (1st Cir. 1985).

obligation. In the ninth and tenth centuries, according to Koziol, formalistic definitions of property rights were relatively unimportant. But formalistic enactments of political relationships involving moral obligation were vitally important, and royal diplomas did precisely this.[60]

As we have just seen, formalistic enactments, performances, and memorials remain fundamental to modern instruments of legal power, like Facebook patents. Modern formalities are no less performative, although they are differently performative. And this performative dimension is not empty. Even if it is conducted pro forma, without invoking a Supreme Being, the inventor's declaration constitutes a solemn declaration, made in the presence of attorneys, creating an ongoing relationship of obligation to a governmental organization. The relationship is memorialized in the formal documents authenticating the obligation. And all are constituted "under penalty of perjury," the solemn threat of punishment for telling a legal lie, which sometimes turns out to be very real.

Empirical formalities in documentary practice are backed by semantic formalities in legal doctrine, together with substantive rationalities ranging from economic efficiency to righteousness and justice. All these come together in intellectual property law, as they do in all areas of law. *They are expressions of an order of obligation, which mobilizes social performances and relationships in formally configured ways.*

In short, instruments of legal power like modern patents and medieval diplomas mobilize, perform, and memorialize relations of social power. In helping to constitute, organize, and reinforce social relationships involving ongoing, mutual obligations, instruments of legal power help to actualize – as forms of social action and performance – coordinated social power, thereby facilitating the existence of property, as reflected in the exclusivity and the powers to "set the agenda" for a resource, as we have seen through careful study of a Facebook patent.

2.6 LEGAL INSTITUTIONS IN THE MODERN NATION-STATE SYSTEM

Modern instruments of legal power, like medieval ones, help to constitute social relationships of obligation. In this way they contribute to linkages between people, organized communities, and national governments, thereby becoming part of an infrastructure of state power. Legal institutions like intellectual property, in other words, are an important part of the infrastructure of the modern nation-state, part of the binding and bonding ties that connect governments, classes, corporations, citizens, and residents together within the nation-state, and that extend beyond the nation-state into global regimes of social power.

[60] Geoffrey Koziol, *The Politics of Memory and Identity in Carolingian Royal Diplomas: The West Frankish Kingdom (840–987)* (Turnhout, Belgium: Brepols Publishers, 2012).

For Mann, the modern nation-state is preeminently a form of political power – a network of social ties linking people together on the basis of *centralized, territorial regulation of social life*. Mann draws a careful, analytical distinction between political and military forms of social power, arguing that the latter come from social ties linking people together on the basis of joint participation in, or subjection to, *concentrated, lethal violence*. Because the social ties involved in national coordination and regulation do not always involve concentrated, lethal violence, Mann argues that we should keep military and political forms of social power separate in our analytical understanding, even though in practice they typically go together.[61]

Criminal law, of course, most directly foregrounds the violent, enforcement powers wielded by the nation-state. Max Weber famously argued that what makes the nation-state distinctive, as a modern type of political community, is the way in which it claims a monopoly on the legitimate exercise of violence. Only the state should have the right to use violence in punishing people, we think, although today this violent power is increasingly questioned. Gangs and mafias are illegitimate, we think, precisely because their violence infringes on the legitimate powers of the law-governed state.[62]

All of modern law, including intellectual property law, is ultimately backed by the violent, enforcement powers wielded by the state. Mann's important point, however, is that this violent, coercive power is only one, analytically distinguishable, aspect of the state's social power.

States are also seen in what we often call the "private sphere," as much as in the "public sphere." While this is to some extent true of all states, it is certainly true of the modern nation-state, which wields power through legal institutions extending deeply into everyday private life, like property. Since industrial capitalism depends on private property, legal institutions are an essential component (an "infrastructure") of the industrialized, capitalistic, nation-state. While legal ideology/culture, in Mann's view, is mostly conservative, and therefore mainly works to reinforce existing legal institutions, he recognizes that there are deeper and more open-ended layers of meaning in the legal traditions that have contributed – sometimes in revolutionary ways – to the foundations of the modern nation-state system.[63]

2.7 GOING BACK TO ROMAN LAW

Patents, then, are formal instruments of legal power that mobilize, enact, and memorialize – thereby constituting, configuring, and reinforcing – social relationships involving obligation and power, enabling zones of exclusivity around new technologies, together with agenda-setting powers that operate within the zones of exclusivity. Through a language-based system of signs, a patent

61 Mann, *Sources, Vol.* 2, 8–10, 44–88.

62 Weber, *Economy & Society*, 31–8, 901–26.

63 Mann, *Sources, Vol.* 2, 64–66, 145–6, 155–58, 175–97.

delineates boundaries around a new technology and serves as a formally validated promise by the government that anyone who steps across the formally defined boundaries will be met with the power of the nation-state. Because people mostly hold themselves outside of the boundaries, the state only occasionally needs to step in.

But where, after all, did these instruments of legal power come from? The answer, I believe, is that they developed out of legal instruments prevalent in the Roman empire. The important qualification is that Roman imperial grants were conceived very differently. Concepts of property did inform the way the grants were understood, but there was nothing like a legally granted property in new technology in ancient Rome.

A goal of this book is to explain how we got from the legal instruments of imperial Rome to modern patents and intellectual property. We must begin by taking ourselves back to the Roman empire, to see how instruments of legal power worked there.

For lawyers trained in European legal traditions, Rome holds a special place in the imagination. Rome is, in so many ways, a source of law for Europe. The great codifications of European law drafted during the late eighteenth and nineteenth centuries were profoundly inspired by Roman law, as was the twelfth-century renaissance of scholastic legal study across Europe. From the eighth century forward, Roman popes anointed European rulers, while extracting royal promises to protect God's law. For a millennium, stretching from the ninth to the nineteenth century, the Holy Roman Empire – a polity based in central Europe that laid important foundations for modern European nation-states, including Germany, Italy, Austria, Hungary, and Poland – was the heart of Europe.[64]

Rome, however, holds a very ambivalent place in the imagination of lawyers trained in Anglo-American legal traditions. American lawyers are trained in the common law tradition of England and (later) Great Britain, a tradition marked by periodic conflicts with Rome, culminating in the Reformation. For this common law tradition, Rome is the height of legal despotism. Emblematic of this despotism is the famous phrase of the great jurist Ulpian: "what pleases the prince has the force of law." Almost nothing could be more horrifying than this kind of arbitrary, autocratic legal power to an Anglo-American lawyer of the nineteenth century, whose imagination of law does so much still to shape our own. And yet, as we will see in this book,

64 Manlio Bellomo, *The Common Legal Past of Europe, 1000–1800*, translated by Lydia G. Cochrane (Washington, DC: Catholic University Press, 1995); Randall Lesaffer, *European Legal History: A Cultural and Political Perspective*, translated by Jan Arriens (Cambridge, UK: Cambridge University Press, 2009); Maurizio Lupoi, *The Origins of the European Legal Order*, translated by Adrian Belton (Cambridge, UK: Cambridge University Press, 2000); Peter Stein, *Roman Law in European History* (Cambridge, UK: Cambridge University Press, 1999); Franz Wieacker, *A History of Private Law in Europe*, translated by Tony Weir (Oxford: Clarendon Press, 1995); Peter H. Wilson, *Heart of Europe: A History of the Holy Roman Empire* (Cambridge, MA: Belknap Press, 2016).

Rome did a great deal to make England – especially the Church of England but also English law – what it is today. Hence the deep ambivalence.[65]

Anglo-American common law is typically defined as a legal tradition that emphasizes case law precedent, and that therefore heightens the power of judges who decide cases. Lawyers trained in this tradition learn to read cases and to extract the law by an inference from the "holding" of a particular case, in comparison with other cases. Knowing what the law is means knowing how the case law has developed, where it stands at present, and how it is likely to be interpreted by a judge in the future. Common law is contrasted with European civil law, which is based much more explicitly on Roman law, emphasizes statutes enacted by legislative bodies, and is codified. The contrast contains a great deal of truth, but it also exaggerates. American law obviously emphasizes statutory legislation, too, and, during the mid-twentieth century, American legislation was extensively codified, both federal and state law. Furthermore, case law is very influential in European legal practice, despite formal statements to the contrary in foundational codes, like the French Civil Code.[66]

Louisiana, where I received my legal training, is a mixed jurisdiction. French and Spanish law have been influential there, and first-year law students who plan to practice law in Louisiana still receive training in Roman law. Someone who will be interpreting Louisiana law for a living needs to understand both the contemporary case law and the evocations of Roman antiquity that, for a civilian legal thinker, infuse words like property and obligation with legal meaning. But the US Constitution establishes the supreme law in Louisiana, too. Louisiana lawyers must learn the common law tradition, because this is the legal tradition of the United States.[67]

This very brief introduction to the complicated place of Roman law in Anglo-American legal traditions has been necessary to set the stage for what follows. First, you need to know that you are reading a book written from a specific perspective – a perspective that sees deep influences from Rome, and that goes somewhat against the grain of Anglo-American legal scholarship. Second, you need to know why, for a book about a modern legal institution like intellectual property, it might be important to pay attention to what happened in Roman antiquity. Roman law was

65 What pleases the prince (Ulpian): Alan Watson (ed.), *The Digest of Justinian* (Philadelphia: University of Philadelphia Press, 1985), 1.4.1; *Justinian's Institutes*, translated by Peter Birks and Grant McLeod (Ithaca: Cornell University Press, 1987), 1.2.6. Latin text available online at The Roman Law Library, founded by Alexandr Koptev and Yves Lassard, https://droitromain.univ-grenoble-alpes.fr/ (accessed August 20, 2019). For a thoughtful and representative reflection on this quote from a preeminent English jurist, see F. W. Maitland, Introduction to *Bracton's Note Book*, Vol. 1 (London: C. J. Clay & Sons, 1887), 3–4.

66 Eva Steiner, *French Law: A Comparative Approach*, 2d ed. (Oxford: Oxford University Press, 2018), Chapter 4.

67 Warren M. Billings, "A Course of Legal Studies: Books That Shaped Louisiana Law," in *A Law Unto Itself? Essays in the New Louisiana Legal History*, edited by Warren M. Billings and Mark F. Fernandez (Baton Rouge: Louisiana State University Press, 2001), 25–39.

hugely influential for European law, and European legal institutions still bear strong Roman imprints. Intellectual property, too, might bear these imprints. But North Americans need reminding of this, because our legal system is based so largely on English law, which has spent a lot of time and energy denying the impact of Roman law.

Finally, you need to see from the outset how daunting is the task that stands in front of us. This book is the height of hubris: we will be surveying two millennia of history. Historians will be horrified.

This is one reason why Michael Mann is so helpful. We can build our hubris upon his. Mann's four-volume sociology of social power stretches from the beginning of time to today. And, moreover, Mann draws great inspiration from the classical sociological thinkers, who were themselves full of hubris. Max Weber surveyed the cultures of the world, seeking to explain what made the west so different. Christianity (especially of the western varieties) was a big part of his answer. Emile Durkheim surveyed the universal principles of social solidarity, identifying religion and law as essential elements of social groups. And Karl Marx narrated a story of universal history that begins with the original sin of property and ends in the heaven of communism. All three were profoundly inspired, in different ways, by Roman, Jewish, and Christian history.

Sociology, for better and worse, is a discipline that generalizes boldly from history and religion, especially the history and religion of ancient Rome.

And so, to Rome.

3

Instruments of Legal Power in the Roman Republic

In 189 BC, a man named Spurius Postumius Albinus sent a letter to Greece, conveying a decision of the Roman Senate. According to the Senate's decree, the polis of Delphi – site of an ancient, famous, and sacred temple to Apollo – was to be autonomous, free, and immune from taxation. The Delphians could live and govern themselves, "having dominion over the sacred territory and the sacred harbor, just as was their inherited right."[1]

We have the language of this letter/decree because the Delphians preserved it. They carved the words onto a big marble slab and displayed them publicly in their temple complex. Fragments of the marble remain today, pieced together by scholars, printed in modern editions, and translated from ancient Greek into modern English.[2]

At first glance, this ancient inscription seems to have nothing whatsoever to do with modern patents and intellectual property. However, if we focus a bit more closely on the form and content of the decree, some similarities do begin to appear. To preview the argument of this chapter, this letter constitutes a formal grant of civic exclusivity and property, one that works in some ways like intellectual property, and one that stands in a long line of development in legal practice that leads from ancient privileges to modern intellectual property.

[1] Spurius Postumius Albinus: T. Robert S. Broughton and Marcia L. Patterson, *Magistrates of the Roman Republic*, Volume I (New York: American Philological Association, 1951), 360. The letter/decree in English translation: Robert K. Sherk, editor and translator, *Rome and the Greek East to the Death of Augustus* (Cambridge, UK: Cambridge University Press, 1984), 14–15; Allan Chester Johnson, Paul Robinson Coleman-Norton, and Frank Card Bourne, *Ancient Roman Statutes* (Austin: University of Texas Press, 1961), 24–5; Naphtali Lewis and Meyer Reinhold (eds.), *Roman Civilization, Volume 1, The Republic and the Augustan Age*, 3d ed. (New York: Columbia University Press, 1990), 331. Commentary and partially reconstructed Greek text in Robert K. Sherk, *Roman Documents from the Greek East: Senatus Consulta and Epistulae to the Age of Augustus* (Baltimore: Johns Hopkins University Press, 1969), 21–5.

[2] The document was first edited by scholars in 1840. Sherk, *Roman Documents*, 21. For fascinating history of Delphi's archaeological uncovering, see Michael Scott, *Delphi: A History of the Center of the Ancient World* (Princeton: Princeton University Press, 2014), 253–85.

In this decree, Rome's authoritative body of governors, the Senate, granted the Delphians autonomy, freedom, and immunity from taxation. In other words, Rome granted Delphi powers of self-governance, both in a political and an economic sense. And Rome recognized the Delphians as having dominion (mastery or lordship) over their sacred territory and harbor. This sacred territory, indeed, was called an inherited right (patrimony) by the Romans. What did all this mean?[3]

It meant, in essence, that the Romans were asserting themselves as patrons of Greek freedom in Delphi. To be a patron, for the Romans, was to be a beneficent caregiver and legal superior, one to whom grateful service was owed by the client who had received a legal benefit, such as freedom from slavery. Patron–client relationships were an important form of governance in Roman society, and the relationship between a master and his freed slave was one that came to be explicitly delineated in law. If a freed person failed to live up to their obligations to a patron, they could be legally compelled. This background in Roman patronage, then, is important social context for making sense of the Roman Senate's decree for Delphi.[4]

But the Romans were not the first to proclaim themselves liberators of the Greeks. Hellenistic rulers, successors to Alexander the Great of Macedon (356–323 BC), had been doing this long before Rome came onto the scene. In order to fully make sense of this Roman decree for Greece, which is among our earliest direct witnesses to the development of Roman law, we need to situate ourselves in the period that modern historians have labeled a "Hellenistic Age." This is an era that runs (roughly) from Alexander the Great's lifetime to the death of Cleopatra (30 BC), last of the Ptolemaic rulers of Egypt.[5]

Alexander inaugurated the Hellenistic age through his military conquests, which ranged across lands that we today conceive as parts of Turkey, Syria and Armenia, Israel-Palestine and Egypt, Iraq, Iran, Afghanistan, and Pakistan. Through the establishment of administrative governance structures across these vast areas – which built

3 Johnson et al., *Ancient Roman Statutes*, 24–5; Sherk, *Roman Documents*, 21–5; Sherk, *Rome and the Greek East*, 14–15.

4 E. Badian, *Foreign Clientelae* (264–70 B.C.) (Oxford: Oxford University Press, 1958); Jane F. Gardner, *Being a Roman Citizen* (London: Routledge, 1993), 7–50; Richard P. Saller, *Personal Patronage under the Early Empire* (Cambridge, UK: Cambridge University Press, 1982). For later legal delineation, see Alan Watson (ed.), *The Digest of Justinian* (Philadelphia: University of Philadelphia Press, 1985), 37.14 –38.5. Latin text available online at *The Roman Law Library*, founded by Alexandr Koptev and Yves Lassard, https://droitromain.univ-grenoble-alpes.fr/ (accessed January 30, 2019).

5 Michel Austin, *The Hellenistic World from Alexander to the Roman Conquest: A Selection of Ancient Sources in Translation*, 2d ed. (Cambridge, UK: Cambridge University Press, 2006); Helmut Koester, *History, Culture, and Religion of the Hellenistic Age* (New York: Walter de Gruyter, 1995); F. W. Walbank, *The Hellenistic World* (London: Harper Collins, 1981). Notions of Hellenism and Hellenization are contested, but, despite controversy over how the processes occurred and who was responsible for them, there remains an underlying agreement that this was a period of dramatic political transformation, which involved references to Greek/Hellenic cultural models. Simon Hornblower, Antony Spawforth, and Esther Eidinow, *The Oxford Classical Dictionary*, 4th ed. (Oxford: Oxford University Press, 2012) [hereafter *OCD*], 656–7; Andrew Wallace-Hadrill, *Rome's Cultural Revolution* (Cambridge, UK: Cambridge University Press, 2008), 14–37.

in many ways on forms of governance inherited and developed from the Persian empire – Alexander and his successors linked societies and cultures of Asia with Greece and the eastern Mediterranean, in newly intensive ways. Alexander's successors established dynasties in Macedonia (the Antigonid dynasty), Syria and Mesopotamia (the Seleucid dynasty), and Egypt (the Ptolemaic dynasty), which lasted until Rome took them over. Cleopatra's suicide, in the wake of her defeat by Julius Caesar's heir, Octavian/Augustus, marks the end of this period, which is at the same time the beginning of a new period – that of the Roman empire, which lasted into the period of history that we call the middle ages.[6]

The Hellenistic age is essential to our understanding because it was the context in which Romans formed their legal ideas, governance structures, and practices for drafting legal instruments. Although Roman historians of the Hellenistic period believed that the foundations of Roman law stretched back to the eighth century BC, those beliefs rested on unreliable premises. When we go back very far beyond the Hellenistic age, Roman history starts to become myth. The myths are important and interesting for our understanding of Roman law, but they tell us about the legal culture of a much later age, not about anything we can reliably say about archaic Rome.[7]

Our opening, then, for understanding the development of Roman legal instruments, like the Senate's decree for Delphi, is in the Hellenistic age. That age, however, was profoundly impacted by events in the period that immediately preceded it, and especially by two things: (1) the violent encounter between Greece and Persia, and (2) the horrific wars between Greek city-states (poleis) – called collectively *The Peloponnesian War* – that occurred between 431 and 404 BC. According to

[6] Austin, *Hellenistic World*, Introduction; Koester, *Hellenistic Age*, 1–45; M. Rostovtzeff, *The Social & Economic History of the Hellenistic World*, Volume 1 (Oxford: Clarendon Press, 1941).

[7] Hellenistic Age as formative period for development of Roman law: Fritz Schulz, *History of Roman Legal Science* (Oxford: Clarendon Press, 1946), 5 ff.; *cf.* H. F. Jolowicz & Barry Nicholas, *Historical Introduction to the Study of Roman Law*, 3d ed. (Cambridge, UK: Cambridge University Press, 1972), 1–7. Critical approaches to early Roman history which have influenced my thinking: Tim Cornell, *The Beginnings of Rome* (Abingdon: Routledge, 1995); Harriet I. Flower, *Roman Republics* (Princeton: Princeton University Press, 2010); Gary Forsythe, *A Critical History of Early Rome* (Berkeley: University of California Press, 2005). Due to the impact of critical historiography, it has become much harder to say anything with confidence about the Twelve Tables, a codification of Roman law traditionally dated to the mid-fifth century BC, although scholars of Roman law have reestablished some of the traditional understandings. What is important for my chronology, however, is the fact that our versions of the Twelve Tables are scholarly reconstructions, based on the memories of authors writing in the Hellenistic period, like Cicero. The Hellenistic period is therefore a significant context for interpretation, even for older legal documents such as the Twelve Tables. In addition to the sources already cited, see Michael H. Crawford (ed.), *Roman Statutes* (London: Institute of Classical Studies, 1996), Vol. II; Bruce W. Frier, Libri Annales Pontificum Maximorum: *The Origins of the Annalistic Tradition*, 2d ed. (Ann Arbor: University of Michigan Press, 1999), 129–35; Alexandre Grandazzi, *The Foundation of Rome: Myth & History*, translated by Jane Marie Todd (Ithaca: Cornell University Press, 1997), 22; Alan Watson, *Rome of the XII Tables: Persons and Property* (Princeton: Princeton University Press, 1975). On the cultural importance of myths in Greco-Roman historiography, see also Jaclyn Neel, *Early Rome: Myth and Society* (Hoboken, NJ: Wiley Blackwell, 2017).

the documentary records that we have, the basic paradigm for grants like the one we see from Rome to Delphi – grants of autonomy, freedom, and tax immunity to a polis – developed in this period. Rome would later take over the basic form, emulating Hellenistic rulers who proclaimed themselves as liberators and patrons of the Greeks.[8]

Rome, too, became a patron of Greek art, science, and technology, and this profoundly changed Rome. An understanding of this process is vital for our understanding of modern intellectual property.[9]

3.1 A CONCEPTUAL MAP OF THE MEDITERRANEAN WORLD

Before we go any further into the cultural world of ancient patronage, I should briefly sketch a conceptual map of the ancient Mediterranean world. This is something we moderns tend not to have, and it is important for making sense of what follows. To do this, I will take you on a journey from Rome to Delphi and Athens, then to important Hellenistic cities (Pergamum, Antioch, Alexandria, and Carthage), and finally back to Rome. This mental journey circling the eastern Mediterranean will lay a foundation for the forthcoming narrative, one that can be readily supplemented with maps and atlases of the ancient world.[10]

Imagine yourself setting out from Rome to Delphi. Today, you might take a train across the Apennine mountains to Ancona, a port city on Italy's east coast. From Ancona, you can take a ferry across the Adriatic to Durrës, an Albanian city on the west Balkan coast. In Hellenistic Rome, Durrës was known as Epidamnus (later Dyrrachium), and it stood at the westernmost edge of what would become the *Via Egnatia*, the great Roman road leading east to Macedonia, Byzantium, and the Black Sea. (Romans typically sailed to Epidamnus/Dyrrachium from Brundisium (modern Brindisi), a coastal town on the heel of Italy's boot.)[11]

From Epidamnus/Dyrrachium, the easiest way to get to Delphi was by boat, since the Balkan Peninsula is very mountainous. Hugging the coastline, we would sail

[8] Martin Ostwald, *Autonomia: Its Genesis and Early History* (Chico, CA: Scholars Press, 1982).

[9] In the famous and poetic words of Horace (65–8 BC), "Conquered Greece took prisoner her rough conqueror and introduced the arts to rough Latium." *Epistles* 2.1.156 (translation by John Davie, 2011, Oxford edition).

[10] This mental journey is loosely inspired by a *periplus*, an account by ancient mariners, but it also builds on my own travel experiences. Authors from Mediterranean antiquity who drew inspiration from the *periploi* in constructing a literature of geography and travel include Josephus, Pliny the Elder, Pausanias, Polybius, and Strabo. See O. A. W. Dilke, *Greek & Roman Maps* (Baltimore: Johns Hopkins University Press, 1985), 130–44; James S. Romm, *The Edges of the Earth in Ancient Thought* (Princeton: Princeton University Press, 1992), 19–20, 121–22; Yuval Shahar, *Josephus Geographicus: The Classical Context of Geography in Josephus* (Tübingen: Mohr Siebeck, 2004), 3–4, 39–48. Today, such journeys can be plotted using ORBIS – The Stanford Geospatial Network Model of the Roman World, a joint project of Walter Scheidel and Elijah Meeks, available at http://orbis.stanford.edu/ (accessed February 15, 2019). Thank you to Lauren Curtis for making me aware of this site.

[11] OCD, 253, 481, 514, 1548.

south past the large island of Corcyra, site of an opening battle in the Peloponnesian War, and of a later Roman battle against pirates, which historians now see as the moment when Rome began conquering Greece. Further down the coastline, we would pass Actium, site of the great naval battle in which Octavian/Augustus defeated Antony and Cleopatra (31 BC), establishing himself as the sole ruler of the Roman world. Following the coastline as it turns east into the Corinthian gulf we would pass mountainous regions of Aetolia on our left, and Achaea on our right, before finally pulling into the tiny gulf of Cirrha (modern Itea) on our left. Facing northeast from this narrow gulf we would look up to a narrow plain, and then, clinging to the mountainside and hidden from view, to the dramatic Delphi temple complex.[12]

The great Athenian wise man Socrates (c. 470–399 BC), among many others, drew important lessons from the temple at Delphi. These lessons included two famous maxims inscribed on the marble face of Apollo's temple: "know thyself," and "nothing in excess," together with a lesser-known maxim, "an oath leads to perdition." According to the geographer Strabo (60s BC–AD 20s), Delphi was the mythical center of the inhabited world (what Greeks called the *oikumene*). In a tale rendered by Pindar (c. 518 –c. 440 BC), the great lyric poet, Zeus released two eagles (or maybe they were ravens), one from the east and one from the west. They met above Delphi, establishing this as the religious center (*omphalos*, belly-button) of the world. In Strabo's time, the temple complex was somewhat neglected, but Roman emperors beginning with Augustus lavished effort and resources to bring it back to its former glories. By the time of Pausanias, a travel writer of the mid second century AD, Delphi was a great, open-air museum, one that Pausanias led his Greece-loving (*philhellene*) Roman readers through in lush, narrative detail. We have much more to say about Delphi, but for now we continue our journey to Athens.[13]

Athens is roughly 75 miles southeast of Delphi. Returning to our boat, we might sail directly south to Corinth, which controlled the narrow isthmus leading from the Greek mainland to the Peloponnese, that large, southwestern extension of the Balkan Peninsula, shaped a bit like a human hand. For centuries, following their victory in the Peloponnesian War, the Spartans were the controlling power in the southern Peloponnese, but, by the Hellenistic era, Sparta was in decline. In 189 BC,

[12] OCD 10, 320; 373–4, 427–9; Simon Hornblower, *A Commentary on Thucydides*, Volume I: Books I-III (Oxford: Clarendon Press, 1991), 66–97; Robert B. Strassler (ed.), *The Landmark Thucydides: A Comprehensive Guide to the Peloponnesian War* (New York: Touchstone, 1996), 16–33; Scott, *Delphi*, 2–4.

[13] The inscriptions at Delphi: Scott, *Delphi*, 137. The importance of Delphi to Socrates: Plato, "Apology of Socrates," in *Plato: Five Dialogues*, translated by G. M. A. Grube, 2d ed., revised by John M. Cooper (Indianapolis: Hackett Publishing, 2002), 24 ff.; H. W . Parke and D. E. W. Wormell, *The Delphic Oracle*, Volume I: The History (Oxford: Basil Blackwell, 1956), 401–5. Delphi as the mythical and spiritual center of the world: Parke & Wormell, *Delphic Oracle* I, 1; Duane W. Roller, *The Geography of Strabo* (Cambridge, UK: Cambridge University Press, 2014), 9.3.6. Roman *philhellenes* touring Delphi: Scott, *Delphi*, 223–44; Pausanias : *Guide to Greece* 1: *Central Greece*, translated by Peter Levi (London: Penguin Books, 1971), 405–89.

when the Romans were extending their power into Greece, the dominant political force on the Peloponnese was the Achaean League, a northwesterly federation (*koinonia*) of poleis based in the relatively new polis of Megalopolis. To the east of Corinth, on the other side of the narrow isthmus connecting the Peloponnese with the mainland, is Athens, iconic Greek polis for ancient Romans and we moderns alike.[14]

Skipping, with regret, the wonders of Athens, we can walk (as Socrates did in Plato's *Republic*) down to Athens' connected port city, called the Piraeus, hopping onto another boat, this time bound for Asia Minor and the great city of Pergamum. Heading northeast across the Aegean Sea, we might stop briefly on the island of Lesbos, one of so many islands dotting the Aegean and home of the great poetess Sappho, before hopping across to the mainland of what is today Turkey, then heading up the Caecus River Valley to Pergamum. This glorious city was the metropolitan center of the kingdom of Pergamum, ruled by the Attalids, Hellenistic kings who became vital allies to Rome. This is one of so many cosmopolitan centers in western Asia, a region of cross-cultural encounter that was profoundly important for the development of Greek and Roman political life.[15]

From Pergamum, we can travel to many places in Asia by foot, as so many philosophers and religious teachers did in the Hellenistic age. Following in the intensively studied footsteps of the apostle Paul, we can travel east all the way to Antioch, an important center of early Christianity, passing through various regions of Asia Minor along the way, including Cilicia. Reaching Antioch, we experience a city that had been established on the Orantes River by one of the early Seleucid rulers: Seleucus I Nicator (358–281 BC), whose father and son were both named Antiochus. Antioch remained an important base for Seleucid rulers throughout the Hellenistic era, and the Romans made it the capital city of Syria, a vital center for their imperial rule in Asia. Looking east and slightly south from Antioch, we can gaze out toward Mesopotamia, the land between the Tigris and Euphrates Rivers, running southeast into the Persian Gulf. Here is the heartland of the Babylonian empire, and, more recently, part of the Persian empire.[16]

14 On Sparta's historical rise and fall, in the context of an overall introduction to the geography and history of Greece, see Sarah B. Pomeroy et al., *Ancient Greece: A Political, Social, and Cultural History*, 4th ed. (Oxford: Oxford University Press, 2018), 154–85, 489. The Achaean League and Megalopolis: OCD, 4–5, 924.

15 Walking like Socrates to the Piraeus: Plato, *Republic*, translated by G. M. A. Grube, rev'd by C. D. C. Reeve (Indianapolis: Hackett Publishing, 1992), 1–3 (327–29). Sappho & Pergamum: OCD, 1105–6, 1317.

16 The intensively studied footsteps of Paul: see Adrian Curtis, *The Oxford Bible Atlas*, 4th ed. (Oxford: Oxford University Press, 2007), "Paul's Journeys"; Jerome Murphy-O'Connor, *Paul: A Critical Life* (Oxford: Oxford University Press, 1996). Antioch: OCD, 103–4. The Seleucids, with particular focus on their activities in Asia Minor: John Ma, *Antiochus III and the Cities of Western Asia Minor* (Oxford: Oxford University Press, 2000). Roman Asia: David Magie, *Roman Rule in Asia Minor* (Princeton: Princeton University Press, 1950).

Turning to face directly south from Antioch, we are looking toward Jerusalem, center of so many hopes and conflicts across the centuries. But we are bound for Alexandria, in Egypt, so we hop back into a boat and sail there. In Alexandria, we stand at the northeastern tip of Africa, and, like Alexander and the Ptolemies who built this city, we can reflect on the astounding antiquity of this Nile-watered land. During the Hellenistic era, Alexandria became one of the greatest cosmopolitan centers, boasting one of the inhabited world's (*oikumene's*) finest libraries. The geographer Strabo, whom we have briefly met, did extensive research here, as did many other scholars through late antiquity. This was a vital center of trade and philosophy, and it would become one of the most influential and conflict-ridden centers of Christian theology under the later Roman emperors.[17]

Now, finally, we have a long journey west along the northern coast of Africa, bound for Carthage, passing the colonial polis of Cyrene on our way. Like Corinth, the proud, ancient city of Carthage was destroyed by the Romans in 146 BC. However, before its destruction, Carthage was among antiquity's great social, political, and economic centers, founded as a colony by trading peoples known to history as Phoenicians, based originally in Tyre and Sidon, coastal cities of what is today Lebanon. By the time of Augustine (AD 354–430), who spent significant periods of his life in Carthage, this was again a great city. Geographically, culturally, and economically, Rome and Carthage came to have very close ties. But the story about how that happened is, in many ways, the story about how Rome became an imperial power. We need to say more about this, but for now we will return to Rome, having circled around the eastern Mediterranean, and briefly introduced ourselves to the Hellenistic world.[18]

Before going further, though, a brief word on chronology, the *logos* of time (*chronos*). Up until now, I have been using the traditional Christian time markers of BC and AD. The time markers BCE and CE follow the same logic. Whether we mark the break by calling it the Year of the Lord (*anno domini*) or the Common Era, the break marks a time that came before, and a time that came after, the birth of Jesus of Nazareth, a man who lived and died in Judaea, under the imperial domination of Hellenistic Rome, and who was regarded by his early followers as the anointed son of God (*Christus*).[19]

Obviously, this way of marking time did not exist for Greeks and Romans who lived before Christianity came onto the scene. (In fact, this way of marking time only became conventional in western Europe between the eighth and eleventh centuries.) Greek historians developed a method of measuring time according to

17 Alexandria: OCD, 60, 830–31. Strabo in Alexandria: Roller, "Introduction," in *Geography of Strabo*, 8–10, 24–7.

18 Carthage and Cyrene: OCD, 283–5, 405–6. Augustine in Carthage: *Confessions*, translated by R. S. Pine-Coffin (London: Penguin Books, 1961); Peter Brown, *Augustine of Hippo: A Biography*, 2d ed. (Berkeley: University of California Press, 2000).

19 Leofranc Holford-Stevens, *The History of Time: A Very Short Introduction* (Oxford: Oxford University Press, 2005); Neel (ed.), *Early Rome*, 11–13.

Olympiads – periods between Olympic games. During the Roman Republic, new consuls were elected every year, and the passage of time was marked by the election of new consuls. Years were *consular* for Hellenistic Romans, and sometimes divided into periods of Olympiads, while for us they mark a historical descent to, and ascent from, a moment of birth. There is something very suggestive in this point, something that takes us down into the marrow of our cultural world.[20]

3.2 THE POLIS AND SOCIAL POWER

One thing that this brief journey around the Hellenistic, Mediterranean world has shown us is that this was a world of cities, poleis in Greek. To draw on Michael Mann's theoretical language, poleis were centers of intensive social power. They were places in which people lived in close proximity to one another, built families and lives together, and participated jointly in collective, religious rituals. The intimate interdependence of city life, combined with the ties of religion, military alliance, and trade that bound cities to one another, made social life highly energetic: tightly connected, generating high levels of personal commitment and engagement, and therefore highly mobilizing. Mann, drawing on Aristotle (384–322 BC), calls the ancient poleis "communities of place."[21]

Poleis were communities in which new levels of wealth were being generated and accumulated, and this made them vulnerable to plunder and violence. Poleis contributed to the development of newly monetarized economies, and new levels of economic and political fragility. For male citizens, these were communities in which a life of military action was required, and political performance became possible. This meant a life of great responsibility and danger, with the potential for glorious honor in living up to the responsibility, and in overcoming the danger. But this glorious and dangerous life was only for those men who, as citizens, fought side by side in war to defend the community through which they received a share in wealth. For these men, the polis enabled a new kind of economic power – the power, in Mann's words, of a person to control his own life chances, and those of others, through the control of economic resources. Struggles over such power made the

[20] On traditions of Greek and Roman historiography, including discussions of chronology, see Andreas Mehl, *Roman Historiography: An Introduction to Its Basic Aspects and Development*, translated by Hans-Friedrich Mueller (Chichester: Wiley-Blackwell, 2011); Thomas F. Scanlon, *Greek Historiography* (Chichester: Wiley-Blackwell, 2015). On the establishment of dating according to the Christian era (*anno domini*) in western Europe, see *Bede: The Reckoning of Time*, translated by Faith Wallis (Liverpool: Liverpool University Press, 1999); *Bede:* On the Nature of Things *and* On Times, translated by Calvin B. Kendall and Faith Wallis (Liverpool: Liverpool University Press, 2010); Georges Declercq, *Anno Domini: The Origins of the Christian Era* (Turnhout: Brepols, 2000); Alden A. Mosshammer, *The Easter Computus and the Origins of the Christian Era* (Oxford: Oxford University Press, 2008). For Bede's influence on Carolingian historiography and chronology, see Rosamund McKitterick, *The Frankish Kingdoms under the Carolingians*, 751–987 (London: Longman, 1983), 2–3.

[21] Mann, *Sources, Vol. 1*, 197.

Mediterranean poleis prone to destructive cycles of internal conflict, which the Greeks called *stasis*, and which modern theorists like Mann consider to be the first class-based conflicts – conflicts between networks of people whose social ties were rooted in economic resources, and whose relationships to economic resources determined life conditions involving wealth and luxury for some, and privation and domination for others.[22]

As socially bonded and bounded communities, the poleis created the essential social conditions for (somewhat) stable property relations to emerge. They were tightly organized social groups, which limited access to economic resources (especially land) to their own citizen-members, or to some extent to foreign traders (*metics*), who were permitted to live alongside them. The poleis also created inheritance patterns, which permitted property to be passed down from one generation to the next. Learning much from the older empires of Babylon, Persia, and Egypt, the Mediterranean poleis nonetheless created a new social world, one that was linked together through bonds of trade, military alliances, and internationally shared religious festivals, seen at sanctuaries like Delphi.[23]

The poleis were intensively powerful, in other words, because of the social methods by which they bonded people together and drew boundaries against those they defined as being outsiders and foreigners (*xenoi*). Not all poleis did this bonding and boundary-drawing in the same ways, even within Greece, let alone around the Mediterranean world. However, the Greeks came to see certain patterns as emerging across the vast array of poleis, a range of types that we could call *orders of obligation*, which contributed to different qualities of social existence within the polis, and different ways in which the polis could be said to be socially powerful. It was the reflection on these different types of polis, on the different types of social existence within the polis, and on the different ways that

22 Mann, *Sources, Vol. 1*, 190–230. Newly monetized economies: monetized in a new way, namely, with coins, which mark the involvement of the polis as an authority that oversees the use of money, bringing a level of stability, standardization, conventional valuation, and trust to monetary exchanges. John H. Kroll, "The Monetary Background of Early Coinage," in *The Oxford Handbook of Greek and Roman Coinage*, edited by William E. Metcalf (Oxford: Oxford University Press, 2012), 33–42. For a creative, thought-provoking, and deeply Marxist argument that the introduction of money into the Greek poleis was a condition enabling metaphysical philosophy to emerge, as unconscious projection, see Richard Seaford, *Money and the Early Greek Mind: Homer, Philosophy, Tragedy* (Cambridge, UK: Cambridge University Press, 2004). Seaford's analysis of "fiduciarity" brings analytical clarity to the role played by the polis and early Greek law, particularly their shared backgrounds in communal rituals of sacrifice, in conferring conventional value and trust on early Greek coins. Seaford, *Money*, 136–46.

23 M. I. Finley, *The Ancient Economy*, updated edition (Berkeley: University of California Press, 1999), 47–51, 95; A. R. W. Harrison, *The Law of Athens* (2 Volumes, London: Bristol Classical Press, 1998); Douglas M. MacDowell, *The Law in Classical Athens* (Ithaca: Cornell University Press, 1978); Weber, *Economy & Society*, 1212–46, 1260–62, 1285–91, 1311–17, 1359–63; Max Weber, *The Agrarian Sociology of Ancient Civilizations*, translated by R. I. Frank (London: Verso, 1988), 37–79, 147–219.

poleis were powerful, that gave rise to Greco-Roman history and moral philosophy, as we know them today.[24]

Religious centers like Delphi stood at the beginning of this reflective development. Dating back to the Archaic Age (c. 700–480 BC), Delphi had grown up with the myriad Greek poleis that dotted the eastern Mediterranean world, "like frogs around a swamp," in Plato's memorable words. Through religious centers like Delphi and Olympia, Greek poleis were linked together into a broader, social, and cultural world, one that came to extend well beyond Greece. In their religious centers, Greeks began to define themselves as Greeks (*Hellenes*), to think about who they were and how they differed from one another, and to draw distinctions with the non-Greeks they encountered, those they called barbarians because their unintelligible language sounded like *bar-bar-bar*.[25]

3.3 DELPHIC ARTS AND ORACLES – GREEK RELIGIOUS "TECHNOLOGY"

Two important things happened at Delphi. Periodically, the sanctuary polis hosted competitions, which involved music, poetry, and athletic games. It was for these periodic, competitive festivals held in honor of a god that the poets like Pindar composed their verses, celebrating an athletic victor, while also celebrating the Greek culture and society that had nourished the victor. However, the most important draw for Delphi, and the one that remained constant between the competitive cycles, was the oracle – the voice of divine wisdom and prophecy that ushered forth from women known as Pythias, and from the temple complex of priests (*prophetes*) who supported the Pythias' divining activity.[26]

No one knows exactly how the oracles worked, and speculations have been wide-ranging from antiquity to today. Scholars have argued that, in the classical period

[24] Aristotle, *Constitution of Athens & Related Texts*, translated by Kurt von Fritz and Ernst Kapp (New York: Hafner Press, 1974); Aristotle, *Nicomachean Ethics*, translated by Terence Irwin, 2d ed. (Indianapolis: Hackett Publishing Company, 1999), 1.2 and passim; Aristotle, *Politics*, translated by C. D. C. Reeve (Indianapolis: Hackett Publishing Company, 1998); Herodotus: *The History*, translated by David Grene (Chicago: University of Chicago Press, 1987), 1.5 and passim; *Thucydides*, 1.2–1.23 and passim; John David Lewis, *Solon the Thinker: Political Thought in Ancient Athens* (London: Bloomsbury, 2006); Glenn R. Morrow, *Plato's Cretan City: A Historical Interpretation of the* Laws (Princeton: Princeton University Press, 1993); *The Laws of Plato*, translated by Thomas L. Pangle (Chicago: University of Chicago Press, 1988); Scanlon, *Greek Historiography*, 7 ff.

[25] *Herodotus* 1.4, 2.158, 8.144; Plato, *Phaedo*, in *Complete Works*, edited by John M. Cooper with D. S. Hutchinson (Indianapolis: Hackett Publishing Company, 1997), 109; Walter Burkert, *Greek Religion*, translated by John Raffan (Maiden, MA: Blackwell Publishing & Harvard University Press, 1985), 8; Parke & Wormell, *Delphic Oracle*, I, 1; Pomeroy et al., *Ancient Greece*, 8, 97–8; Scott, *Delphi*, 31–70.

[26] Pindar and the Pythian Games: Pindar, *The Complete Odes*, translated by Anthony Verity (Oxford: Oxford University Press, 2007). The oracle: Parke & Wormell, *Delphic Oracle*, I, 1–45; Scott, *Delphi*, 9–30.

when the oracle was functioning regularly, understandings about how the oracle worked were perhaps so widely shared as to escape comment. The technique of the oracle was, according to this view, a matter of common sense, and, as a taken-for-granted thing, was not seen as requiring an explanatory account. However, at the time when Romans started systematically relying on the oracle, there was a new effort to make sense of the way that it worked, and to provide rationalizing explanations. This was not because Romans were inherently more rational than Greeks, but perhaps because Roman intellectuals were less comfortable with ecstatic, divine inspiration.[27]

Romans relied heavily on techniques of divination to discern the will of the gods, but their techniques were more algorithmic and "scientific," in the sense of an ancient body of teachable wisdom, like astronomy or mathematics. To divine the will of the gods, Romans relied especially on augury and haruspicy – systematic study of the heavens and of the internal organs of sacrificial animals. As Romans began supporting the Delphic oracle financially and relying upon it more extensively, they seem to have sought explanatory accounts of the oracle that would make it into a more comprehensible technology of divination. Or at least this is one way of accounting for the fact that our first "technical," materialistic explanations of the oracle come from the period of Roman imperial rule. In these accounts, the Pythia's cryptic words were attributed to physical causes, such as an intoxicating vapor.[28]

Physical and mechanistic accounts of the Pythia's inspiration have periodically reappeared, even to the present day, but they have not received very strong support from the extensive archaeological work at Delphi. No cleft in the rock from which intoxicating vapors might pour forth to inspire the Pythia has been found. Moreover, any notion that the oracle was simply a profitable hoax is belied by longstanding evidence of sincere belief from a large number of ancient sources, including Plutarch (AD 46–119), who was himself a priest at Delphi, but also including historians like Herodotus (c. 484–425 BC) and Thucydides (c. 460–400 BC), together with philosophers like Socrates, Plato, and Aristotle, none of whom was greatly given to credulity. It seems unlikely that a conspiratorial hoax could have lasted so long and been taken seriously by so many thoughtful people.[29]

27 Parke & Wormell, *Delphic Oracle*, I, 17–24; Scott, *Delphi*, 10, 17–23. Cicero's reflections on the differences between Greek and Roman divination: *On Divination*, Book 1, translated by D. Wardle (Oxford: Clarendon, 2006), 1.1–1.4 and passim.

28 Parke & Wormell, *Delphic Oracle*, I, 17–24; Scott, *Delphi*, 17–23. On Roman religion, including methods of divination and efforts to set boundaries on legitimate religious expression, see Mary Beard, John North, and Simon Price, *Religions of Rome, Vol. I: A History* (Cambridge, UK: Cambridge University Press, 1998), 18–30, 42–54, 62–3, 91–8, 211–36.

29 Parke & Wormell, *Delphic Oracle*, I, 17–24, 36–41; Scott, *Delphi*, 17–23. Plutarch as priest at Delphi: Frank Cole Babbitt, "Introduction" to Plutarch, *Moralia*, Volume I (Cambridge, MA: Harvard University Press, 1927), x. Plutarch's discussions of the oracle are scattered throughout his collected essays, traditionally titled *Moralia* in Latin. I rely on the 16-volume Loeb edition, which includes translations by Frank Cole Babbitt, Harold Cherniss, P. A. Clement, Phillip H. De Lacy, Benedict

What we are left with is the sociological truism that the Delphians acquired their social and cultural awareness in a world premised upon the shared understanding that there was an authentically divine manifestation in their temple complex. Young Delphian women would have been raised believing in the oracle, and some would perhaps have been chosen to serve in supporting capacities for the temple complex, which was a huge international draw and therefore something of an industry, requiring a supporting staff. Young women will have been trained here, and perhaps a few were selected for their evident capacity to serve as Pythias. The male priests (like Plutarch) who translated the Pythia's mysterious words into cryptic poetry are likely candidates for the selection committee. But the truth is that we will probably never know. The Delphic oracle partakes in the mysteries of antiquity and of "enchanted" phenomena across the whole sweep of human history.[30]

What is important for our purposes is to see that the oracle at Delphi was an internationally recognized method for ascertaining and interpreting the divine will. The earliest literary sources from Greek culture, dating from around the seventh century BC – Homer and the Homeric *Hymn to (Pythian) Apollo* – speak of Delphi as providing an interpretive portal between the realm of mortals and the realm of the gods. The oracle is closely connected with the beginnings of law and history, both in Greece and in Rome. Its first uses, however, may be seen in the Greek movements to establish colonies across the Mediterranean world, particularly in southern Italy and Sicily.[31]

Rome was profoundly influenced by these developments, although it is impossible to trace the processes of influence precisely. According to later Roman and Greek historians, Rome was founded during this early period of Greek colonization, around 750 BC. Although Rome was not a Greek colony, she was surrounded by them. To her north were the Etruscans (the Italian region of Tuscany is named after them), people who were in regular contact with Greek poleis. And to Rome's south were myriad Greek colonies, with some of which Romans would form early connections through trade and warfare.[32]

Einarson, Harold North Fowler, W. C. Helmbold, H. B. Hoffleit, Edwin L. Minar, Jr., Lionel Pearson, and F. H. Sandbach, together with an index by Edward N. O'Neil.

30 Parke & Wormell, *Delphic Oracle*, I, 34–41; Scott, *Delphi*, 23–29. On Greek religious phenomena involving ecstatic utterances, divination, and oracular prophecy, see Burkert, *Greek Religion*, 109–17.

31 *Homeric Hymns*, translated by Sarah Ruden (Indianapolis: Hackett Publishing Company, 2005), 25–37; Homer, *The Odyssey*, translated by Peter Green (Berkeley: University of California Press, 2018), 8.75–85; Parke & Wormell, *Delphic Oracle*, I, 49–79; Scott, *Delphi*, 31–70. For reflections on the propriety and utility of using the term "colonization" for these movements of people in antiquity, relative to modern colonization, see Henry Hurst and Sara Owen, *Ancient Colonizations: Analogy, Similarity and Difference* (London: Durkworth, 2005).

32 The official date recognized from the first century BC onward for Rome's founding was 753 BC. For discussion of this date and the corresponding timeline for Rome's development, see Forsythe, *Critical History*, 369–70. Etruscans, Romans, and their connections to the Eastern Mediterranean: Forsythe, *Critical History*, 9–10, 19–53; Martin Frederiksen, *Campania*, edited by Nicholas Purcell (Rome: British School at Rome, 1984). Greek colonies in Sicily and Southern Italy: T. J. Dunbabin, *The*

3.4 TRADITIONS OF LEGAL HISTORIOGRAPHY – THE BIRTH OF JURISPRUDENTIAL NARRATIVES

By 189 BC, when Spurius Postumius sent the Senatorial decree of freedom, autonomy, and tax immunity to Delphi, Rome had a long history of seeking prophetic wisdom from the Delphic oracle. According to Roman historical memory, consultation of the Pythia stretched back to the very beginnings of the Roman Republic, to the moment when a hero named Brutus freed the Romans from a tyrannical king, and thereby helped to usher in the period of rule by magistrates, transforming the city-state (*civitas*) into a free, public thing, or commonwealth (*res publica*). According to later historical reckoning, this happened in 509 BC.[33]

Although the actual events remain shrouded in legend, scholars accept elements of Roman historical traditions recognizing religious and legal influences from Delphi, and, more broadly, from Greece. These traditions record the establishment of a temple to Apollo at Rome, during the fifth century BC, reflecting Roman gratitude for Apollo's contributions to their young and growing city. The Roman historian Livy records several significant occasions upon which the Romans consulted the Pythia before the third century BC, each of which was an important turning point in his narrative.[34]

At Delphi, Roman and Greek history are intertwined and linked to a much wider, Mediterranean story. Indeed, the beginnings of Greek and Roman history-writing are intimately connected with Delphi. The earliest prose history-writers of Greece and Rome – Herodotus and Fabius Pictor – both visited Delphi, and Herodotus seems to have spent significant amounts of time there, studying records of the Pythia's prophecies. Beginning with Herodotus, and then extending forward to later Greek and Roman historians, we have access to a long tradition of history-writing, a tradition of humanistic reflection on what it is to live well (*eudaimonia*), and on the tragedies of human character and social convention that prevent us from living well. Law (*nomos* in Greek, *lex* and *ius* in Latin) is a central focus of inquiry for this tradition, as is the encounter with culturally distinctive peoples whose laws and conventions are recognized as being different in some ways, similar in others.

Western Greeks (Oxford: Oxford University Press, 1948); Forsythe, *Critical History*, 31–6. The theme of Greek influences on early Rome was fundamental to Dionysius of Halicarnassus' *Roman Antiquities*, written at the beginning of the first century AD. Emilio Gabba, *Dionysius and The History of Archaic Rome* (Berkeley: University of California Press, 1991), 16, 216.

33 Livy, *The History of Rome*, Books 1–5, translated by Valerie M. Warrior (Indianapolis: Hackett Publishing Company, 2006), I.56; R. M. Ogilvie, *A Commentary on Livy Books 1–5* (Oxford: Oxford University Press, 1965), 216–18. In addition to Valerie Warrior's translation, I rely on the Loeb Classical Library's 14-volume edition of Livy's *History of Rome*, including the translations of B. O. Foster (Books 1–10), Frank Gardner Moore (Books 23–30), J. C. Yardley (Books 31–40), Evan Sage, and Arthur C. Schlesinger (Books 40–45). I also rely on the Penguin Classics series of Livy translations – by Henry Bettenson, R. M. Ogilvie, A. H. McDonald, Betty Radice, and Aubrey de Sélincourt – including their valuable introductions.

34 Livy 1.56, 3.63, 4.25, 4.29, 5.13, 5.15–16, 5.21, 5.23, 5.25, 5.28; Ogilvie, *Commentary on Livy*, 574, 651–56; Parke & Wormell, *Delphic Oracle* I, 265–81.

History-writing, as it developed in Greece and Rome, was also inquiry into legal customs and manners of life among Mediterranean peoples, including their wondrous new discoveries and inventions, and their legal records.[35]

According to Herodotus, proclamations of freedom from military service and taxation were a legal device utilized by Persian rulers to show favor to groups of subjected peoples. With a tax and governance structure regularized under Darius I (c. 550–486 BC), the vast Persian empire was one that granted varying powers of self-governance, both legal and religious, to subjected peoples. However, tax exemptions and other freedoms could also be specially granted as ways to show unique favor and to garner loyalty. Regularized administrative mechanisms were developed for these and other types of royal communications. Essentially these were formal letters drafted by trained scribes and authenticated as communications from the king by elaborately carved seals pressed onto clay or wax. What was developing, in other words, was a regular method for issuing orders and favors by means of formal documents.[36]

An important turning point seems to have come with the Persian effort to subject Greece to imperial control, and with the formation of Greek defensive leagues, in response. This is the dramatic story that Herodotus builds up to in his *History*. From the Persian side, it looks like this could have been an effort to secure the Mediterranean end of trade routes extending from India and China to Thrace and Egypt – to bring order to the chaotic and often violent world of Greek and Phoenician poleis, which were economic exchange networks for the ancient world, as well as political communities. A significant provocation came from the Greek side with the destruction of Sardis (a polis on the Mediterranean coast of Asia Minor) by a league of Greek cities led by Athens. Part of the response to this provocation was the imposition, through "compact," of a requirement that the poleis of Asia Minor "should submit their quarrels with one another to law instead of plundering and harrying one another." Their territory was measured, and they were

[35] Fabius Pictor: Livy, 22.57, 23.11; Polybius, *The Histories*, translated by Robin Waterfield (Oxford: Oxford University Press, 2010), 1.14–15, 3.8–9; T. J. Cornell (ed.), *The Fragments of the Roman Historians*, Vol. 1, Introduction (Oxford: Oxford University Press, 2013), 160–78; *Fragments of the Roman Historians*, Vol. 2, Texts and Translations (Oxford: Oxford University Press, 2013), 32–105; E. H. Bispham and T. J. Cornell, "Commentary on Q. Fabius Pictor," in *Fragments of the Roman Historians*, Vol. 3, Commentary (Oxford: Oxford University Press, 2013), 13–49; Frier, *Libri Annales*, 201–84. Wondrous discoveries and inventions in Herodotus: 1.71, 2.4, 2.82, 2.92, 2.109, 2.160, 5.58.

[36] Herodotus on grants of freedom from taxation: 3.67, 3.97, 9.73. Taxation and administrative governance of the Persian Empire: *Herodotus* 3.89–96; Amélie Kuhrt, *The Persian Empire*, Vol. 2 (London: Routledge, 2007), Chapters 14–16. Formal, sealed documents: *Herodotus* 3.128; Kuhrt, *Persian Empire*, Vol. 2, Figure 16.7. The Biblical books of Ezra-Nehemiah are constructed around formal documentary exchanges with Persian imperial officials, including Cyrus, Darius, and Artaxerxes. The documents are edited and modified in order to incorporate them into the surrounding theological narrative, and their authenticity has been questioned, but many scholars accept them as authentic reflections of Persian imperial rule. Amélie Kuhrt, *The Persian Empire*, Vol. 1 (London: Routledge, 2007), 49, 84–5; H. G. M. Williamson, *Word Biblical Commentary: Ezra-Nehemiah* (Grand Rapids, MI: Zondervan, 2018) [1985].

subjected to a more regularized tax assessment. More worryingly for mainland Greece, however, the provocation of Sardis' destruction was festering into a plan of revenge and subjugation by the Persian king. The plan was hatched by Darius I but carried out on a massive scale by his son and successor, Xerxes I (519–465 BC).[37]

The language of freedom (*eleutheria*) acquires poignant meaning in Herodotus' account of the titanic struggle between Persia and Greece. Freedom is defined by its opposition to slavery, which in Herodotus is subjugation to the overwhelming and often arbitrary power of Persian rulers. The nomadic, tribal peoples of southern Russia (the Scythians) were able to remain free, according to Herodotus, because they were so mobile – they could lead the great Persian army on a wild-goose chase, slashing and burning as they went, and eventually exhausting the Persians into going back home to Susa (in today's Iran). For communities of place, like the poleis, this mobility was not possible. Their choice was between subjugation – which Herodotus portrays as an appealing option for those wishing to protect their city-based property and wealth – and violent struggle. In the end, the Greek poleis led by Athens and Sparta chose violent struggle, a cause that they defended as a struggle for freedom. For Rome, too, *libertas* was defined by its opposition to slavery, both legal and political.[38]

If freedom, for the Greeks, acquired its meaning in violent struggle against overwhelming imperial power, autonomy (*autonomia*) acquired its meaning in the relationship between poleis. More precisely, autonomy acquired its meaning when a treaty-based league of poleis – the Delian League – became so powerful and wealthy that its leader, Athens, came to seem like an overwhelming, imperial power. In the narration of this story, Thucydides takes over from Herodotus, as does a new kind of history-writing, one that focuses much less on the wondrousness of the wide Mediterranean world, and zeros in more analytically on political power dynamics. The great struggle for Thucydides was the Peloponnesian War (431–404 BC), the war in which the Hellenes nearly destroyed themselves.[39]

37 Herodotus 5.28–55, 5.97–126, 6.42, 6.94, 7.1–5. For Persian economic interests in Egypt and Thrace, see Hornblower, *Commentary on Thucydides*, Vol. 1, 177–78; Kuhrt, *The Persian Empire*, 181–5. Herodotus presents the Persian motivations much more in terms of conquest, but there is an economic dimension to this, as seen in the advice of Xerxes' cousin Gobryas that "Europe was a very fair land and bore every sort of cultivated tree, was high in its fertility, and it was the Great King, alone of mortals, who deserved to own it" 7.5 (Grene trans.).

38 Scythian freedom: *Herodotus* 4.1–4.143, especially 4.46, 4.126–8, 4.133, 4.136–42. Violent struggle for Greek freedom: *Herodotus* 6.94 ff. On the theme of freedom (*libertas*) in Livy's Roman history, see Ogilvie, *Commentary on Livy*, 30, 233–34. On the influence of Greek historiography on Latin historiography, particularly Livy, see S. P. Oakley, A *Commentary on Livy Books VI-X*, Volume 1 (Oxford: Oxford University Press, 1997), 72–5, 85, 114–22. On the importance of slavery in contributing to the formation of western conceptions of freedom, and on the development of freedom as a defining value in western culture, see Orlando Patterson, *Freedom in the Making of Western Culture* (New York: Basic Books, 1991).

39 OCD, 214–15, 1101; Ostwald, *Autonomia*, 1, 40–9; *Thucydides*, 1.1, 1.23.

According to Thucydides, the cause of the Peloponnesian War was Athens' rise to greatness and power within the Delian League, which made Athens a *hegemon* – a dominant polis. This unprecedented rise in Athenian political, economic, and military power frightened the Spartans. The spark that triggered war was a conflict between Athenian and Spartan allies in northern Greece and Illyria, concentrated at first around the island of Corcyra. The ultimate cause of war, however, was an imbalance of social power between Athens and Sparta, one that played out as a conflict between two types of civic culture and two orders of obligation.[40]

Delphi stood at the center of the Peloponnesian War, not least because the Delphian oracle and sanctuary were so religiously important to both Athens and Sparta. Spartans believed that their great lawgiver Lycurgus had been divinely inspired by Apollo at Delphi. Athenians traced their laws and political institutions to multiple lawgivers, but their iconic lawgiver Solon, too, had been inspired by Delphi. Furthermore, Athens had invested heavily in the sanctuary at Delphi, and had an important treasury there. This great importance of Delphi to both sides of the Peloponnesian War helps to explain why it was the focus of a treaty: one that brought a break in the hostilities, and one that helps shed light on Rome's privilege to Delphi from 189 BC.[41]

3.5 FREEDOM, AUTONOMY, AND IMMUNITY IN THE HELLENISTIC ERA

In the winter of 422–21, the tenth year of the Peloponnesian War, the exhausted combatants agreed to a truce, called often the Peace of Nicias after the general-statesman who helped bring it about. The terms of the peace treaty are transcribed by Thucydides. In this treaty, Athens, Sparta, and their allies agreed, among other things, to halt their devastating mutual destruction and to protect Greek religion for the benefit of all parties. Oracles and games could go ahead, with special provision for the oracle at Delphi.

> The temple and shrine of Apollo at Delphi and the Delphians shall be governed by their own laws (*autonomous*), taxed by their own state (*autoteleis*), and judged by their own judges (*autodikous*), the land and the people, according to the customs of their country.[42]

According to the scholar Martin Ostwald, the language of this treaty reflects the distinct political meaning that "autonomy" had recently acquired, a meaning that

[40] *Thucydides*, 1.23, 1.46–1.55, 1.67–88, 1.97–99.

[41] *Herodotus*, 1.29–33, 1.65–66; *Laws of Plato*, 624a, 630d, 632d, 738c, 858e; Lewis, *Solon the Thinker*, 13; Morrow, *Plato's Cretan City*, 18, 33–4, 68–70, 76–84, 402–411; "Lycurgus" and "Solon," in *Plutarch's Lives, the Dryden Translation*, edited by Arthur Hugh Clough, Vol. 1 (New York: The Modern Library, 2001), 52–80, 106–28; cf. Aristotle, *Politics*, 1273b.30–34. Athens' investments and treasury at Delphi: Scott, *Delphi*, 75–81, 100, 112–13, 128–32.

[42] *Thucydides*, 5.18; Simon Hornblower, *A Commentary on Thucydides*, Vol. II (Oxford: Oxford University Press, 1996), 469–89.

involved relations of mutual respect between allied poleis, where one polis was nonetheless superior in power. From this viewpoint, autonomy delineates a position of relative independence for a weaker polis, in relation to a stronger (imperial) power. The Greek phrase *kata ta patria*, translated into English as "according to the customs of their country," indicated normative principles that stood behind the agreement, providing the closest possible thing to a guarantee of validity, in an agreement between warring powers. These principles were traditional and religiously inflected, closely connected with customs allowing for the collection and burial of dead and dying soldiers after battle.[43]

This was merely a pause in the Peloponnesian War, which finally ended in 404 BC with the defeat of Athens and her allied poleis by Sparta and her allies. The mutual devastation that this war brought to Greece created an opening for Macedonia, in the north, which Philip II (382–336 BC) built into a powerful state, one that contained poleis but was not centered in a polis, in the way that the Greek polis leagues (*koinonia*) had been. When Alexander, Philip's son, defeated Persia's armies and conquered Persian territories, he initiated a long process of cultural and political interaction, one in which traditions of religious and military rulership from Asia both blended and clashed with Greek, Egyptian, and Phoenician traditions. It was during this Hellenistic era, as successors to Alexander the Great established their frameworks of imperial rule over Macedonia, the Near East, Greece, and Egypt, that the language of freedom, autonomy, and tax exemption began appearing in letter-based grants from rulers.[44]

An important and paradigmatic example comes from 311 BC, the year in which Alexander's warring successors (called *diadochi* by historians) agreed to a division of the massive territories that they had conquered with Alexander. The peace itself did not hold, and it seems not to have even included all the warring parties, but the notion of a territorial division did eventually take hold, as did the ideal of Greek freedom that was articulated as an overarching goal of the treaty. This ideal was articulated especially by Antigonus I ("the One-Eyed," *Monophthalmos*, 382–301 BC), whose letter to the town of Scepsis (in modern Turkey), announcing the terms of the treaty, was carved into marble and survived, buried in rubble, until the end of the nineteenth century.[45]

In his letter to Scepsis, Antigonus proclaimed his zeal for the freedom of the Greeks, described certain events leading up to the treaty, and articulated conditions

43 Ostwald, *Autonomia*, 1, 3–9, 40–41, 44–9; cf. Hornblower, *Commentary on Thucydides*, Vol. II, 472–3, 477.

44 OCD, 1128; Austin, *Hellenistic World*, Introduction; Ian Worthington, *Philip II of Macedonia* (New Haven: Yale University Press, 2008).

45 OCD, 102; Austin, *Hellenistic World*, No. 38; C. Bradford Welles, *Royal Correspondence in the Hellenistic Period: A Study in Greek Epigraphy* (New Haven: Yale University Press, 1934), xxxvii-l, 3–12. For other proclamations involving combinations of freedom, autonomy, and/or tax exemption, see Austin, *Hellenistic World*, Nos. 35, 48, 61, 117, 170, 230; Ma, *Antiochus III*, 150–74, with Epigraphical Dossier.

relevant to the making of the treaty. Among these conditions, according to Antigonus, were burdensome military services and expenses under which the people of Scepsis were being compelled. In order to give force to the liberating treaty, Antigonus stated that a clause had been included requiring the Greeks themselves to swear an oath, and thereby to "join together in protecting their mutual freedom and autonomy." Antigonus also noted that he was sending a copy of the oath that they should swear to the people of Scepsis, together with a man named Acius, who would discuss the terms and considerations with them. Antigonus promised that, as one of the "men in power," he would endeavor in the future to protect the interests of the people of Scepsis, and he asserted that the oath they should swear would help to guarantee protection of these interests in the future. Presumably these interests included the alleviation of the burdensome military obligations and expenses to which the people of Scepsis were being subjected.[46]

The people of Scepsis were so grateful to Antigonus that they established a religious site and festival to honor him, carving their resolution into the same marble slab that included Antigonus' letter. In this honorific decree, the people of Scepsis resolved:

> [S]ince Antigonus has been responsible for great benefits to the city and the other Greeks, to praise Antigonus and to rejoice with him in what has been accomplished ... that they shall live in peace henceforward enjoying freedom and autonomy; and so that Antigonus may receive honors worthy of his achievements and the people should be seen to be returning thanks for the benefits it has received, let it mark off a sacred enclosure (*temenos*) for him, build an altar and set up a cult statue as beautiful as possible, and let the sacrifice, the competition, the wearing of the wreath and the rest of the festival be celebrated every [year] in his honor as they were before.[47]

Gold crowns were to be provided for this festival, the citizens were to wear wreaths, and the polis treasurer was to allocate the appropriate funds so that this annual religious festival could go forward.

The people of Scepsis, in other words, were worshipping Antigonus in their gratitude for the freedom and autonomy that he claimed to be offering them. In reality, this good news of freedom and autonomy ended up being meaningless: Antigonus sometime later compelled the people of Scepsis to move to a new city that he founded and named after himself. However, the preservation of the letter and the corresponding expression of gratitude enable us to see a kind of paradigm for letter-based grants of freedom, autonomy, and tax immunity in development.[48]

This is a paradigm in which letter-based grants act as instruments of legal power – as written, declarative enactments by a ruler who is performing an idealizing zeal for

46 Austin, *Hellenistic World*, No. 38; Welles, *Royal Correspondence*, 3–12.
47 Austin, *Hellenistic World*, No. 39.
48 Welles, *Royal Correspondence*, 8–9.

freedom and autonomy, and who is seeking to generate a grateful response from a group of subordinate peoples. Later, Hellenistic rulers would emulate Antigonus, in his idealizing zeal for Greek freedom, and would also establish themselves as performative benefactors and patrons of Greek poleis. By around 200 BC, when Rome started to become actively involved in Greek affairs, paradigms for such patronage in Greek poleis were being translated to the Latin-speaking west. By 189 BC, when the Roman Senate sent its decree of liberation to Delphi, a standardizing Latin translation for the Greek *eleutheria* was *libertas*, which was also defined through its opposition to slavery and political domination.[49]

To be given an *immunity* was to be freed from civic obligations, which in Latin were often called *munera,* translated into Greek as *leitourgiai* (liturgies). In Rome's privilege to Delphi, the word that was used is *aneisphoria*, meaning something like an exemption from service obligations. *Munera* and *leitourgiai* were service obligations that were expensive and burdensome. To be given an *immunity*, then, was to be relieved in some way from an expensive and burdensome obligation. Often, the expensive and burdensome obligation involved conscription of soldiers and compulsion to pay taxes.[50]

The Roman Senatorial privilege for Delphi, then, defines a zone of civic exclusivity – a line beyond which neither Rome nor another state should pass in its relations with the Delphians. Conscription of Delphians as soldiers and compulsion to pay taxes would cross that line and would interfere with the sacred services that Delphi provided, both to Rome and to the wider Mediterranean world. Rome's privilege for Delphi enacted a liberation of the polis and created a bond of dependence that enabled Rome to exert influence over, and to benefit from, Delphian religious services. It also symbolized Rome's entry into a position of power in the eastern Mediterranean world.

3.6 ROME AND DELPHI: A UNIFYING WORLD

With the Delphians' ancient privilege, we are thrown into a world of Roman law and diplomacy, at precisely the moment when Roman military power was expanding beyond Italy. The trigger for Roman expansion was conflict with Carthage, which had established colonies and trading posts in Sicily and Sardinia. During the third century BC, as Rome was also establishing colonies and forming alliances with other city-states across Italy, conflict with Carthage began to seem inevitable. Over the course of the third and second centuries BC, Rome fought three terrible wars with Carthage, the last of which ended in the total destruction of the African city (146 BC).

[49] Austin, *Hellenistic World*, No. 35; Ma, *Antiochus III*, 81–2 and passim; Sherk, *Roman Documents*, 24.

[50] Sherk, *Rome and the Greek East*, 14; Sherk, *Roman Documents*, 22. Compare Johnson et al., *Ancient Roman Statutes*, 24–5, arguing that the immunity at issue in this decree was probably against military conscription, rather than taxes.

Historians call these the Punic Wars, drawing on the Latin word for Carthaginians (*Poeni*).[51]

The Punic Wars are a hinge of Roman history. In order to take the fight to Carthage, Rome had to venture onto the seas, and to build a navy. Carthage was located across that narrow stretch of the Mediterranean which separates Africa from Sicily. The sea that separated Rome and Carthage was, however, at the same time a great connector of the ancient world. This was the communications superhighway of antiquity, a transportation link that enabled exchanges of information, goods, and peoples from throughout the known world. This world included the powerful heirs to Alexander's empire: the Ptolemies of Egypt, the Seleucids of Syria, and the Antigonids of Macedonia. In venturing onto the seas, Rome was a young upstart, entering a venerable, profitable, and treacherous world. The Punic Wars, by drawing Rome onto the seas, made her part of a much larger, and much older, imperial story.[52]

By 189 BC, when Spurius Postumius sent his letter to Delphi, Rome had won her second great war with Carthage, which lasted from 218 to 201. Victory had partly come through alliances with Greek poleis. Macedonia had allied herself to Carthage, while Greek poleis hoping to free themselves from Macedonia had allied themselves with Rome. The southeastern corner of Europe, in other words, together with the western edges of Asia, had been drawn into Rome's titanic struggle with Carthage. Or, looking at this the other way around, Rome drew herself into older struggles for power in Greece and Asia in order to win her victory against Carthage.[53]

In the spring of 200 BC, a Roman assembly voted to authorize war with Macedonia. This Second Macedonian War would see extensive fighting across the Greek mainland. Although Roman soldiers had previously marched briefly along the western edge of the Balkan peninsula – in a fight with an aggressive Illyrian queen – they had not entered mainland Greece in such numbers. However, in the wake of the Second Punic War, energy and resources were available to do something about Greece, and especially about the perceived threat of Greek and Macedonian alliances with Carthage, or with the kingdoms of Egypt and Syria.[54]

51 OCD, 1239–41; Polybius, 1.3, 1.63–64, 3.1–5 and passim; F. W. Walbank, *A Historical Commentary on Polybius*, Vol. 1 (Oxford: Clarendon Press, 1970), 43–44; Walbank, *Hellenistic World*, Chapter 13. In addition to Robin Waterfield's translation, I rely on Ian Scott-Kilvert's translation (Penguin 1979) and on the Loeb Classical Library's 6-volume edition of Polybius' *Histories*, translated by W. R. Paton and revised by F. W. Walbank & Christian Habicht.

52 Taking the fight to Carthage and building a navy: Polybius, 1.20–29, 1.36–39, 2.1. The Mediterranean as information and transportation link: Finley, *Ancient Economy*, 30–32; cf. Michael McCormick, *Origins of the European Economy: Communications and Commerce*, AD 300–900 (Cambridge, UK: Cambridge University Press, 2001), 83–114. Ptolemies, Seleucids, and Antigonids: OCD, 102, 1234–36, 1341.

53 Polybius, 3.1–5, 4.28, 5.31, 5.100–105, 7.9, 15.20.

54 Livy 31.3–8; Polybius 18.12, 18.18–27; Philip Matyszak, *Roman Conquests: Macedonia and Greece* (Barnsley: Pen & Sword Books, 2009). Fight with the aggressive Illyrian queen, Teuta: Polybius, 2.2–12.

Rome was victorious in the Second Macedonian War, which was proclaimed as a war for the liberty of Greece. It did mean something like freedom for Delphi, which had come increasingly under the control of the Aetolian League, an alliance of northern Greek poleis. In 196 BC, Titus Flamininus celebrated his great victory over Macedonia in Delphi, dedicating a number of the instruments and spoils of war to Apollo. The grateful Delphians, in turn, sculpted a statue of the consul and placed it in the forecourt of the temple to Apollo. As the Romans increasingly became the protectors of Delphi, inscriptions were added to the base of this statute, including records of legal privileges granted from Rome to Delphi.[55]

While the Delphians were coming under the patronage of Rome, a boy named Polybius (c. 200–118 BC) was growing up in the Greek city of Megalopolis, near the center of the Peloponnese. Drawn into the story of Roman power because of Roman conquest in his native land, Polybius would go on to become one of Rome's greatest early historians. His personal experience and witness to the workings of Roman institutions, and to the text of Roman legal documents, make him an invaluable source of information and insight for us.

Writing toward the end of the second century BC, Polybius saw a world that had become unified. The ancient histories of Greece, Asia Minor, Persia, Syria-Palestine, Egypt, and North Africa had all become linked together with the histories of Italy, Sicily, Sardinia, and Spain. For the first time it had become both possible and necessary to tell a universal history, because all the world had become one through the power of Rome. Polybius considered this to be a radically new development of his own era, and one that begged for an explanation.[56]

We moderns have a tendency to think ourselves unique in the experience of globalization. However, Polybius reminds us that the experience of worldwide interconnection is not new. What is new is the way we imagine that worldwide interconnection – as links between territorially bounded, centrally administered, national states. Polybius, rather, imagined geographic clusters of peoples, poleis, and lands surrounding the Mediterranean. With the growth of Roman power, which began with the titanic struggle between Rome and Carthage, the fortunes of all peoples throughout the world had become linked, such that what happened in one Spanish town could affect a town in central Greece, Syria, or Egypt.[57]

According to Polybius, Rome's unique achievement of world domination was due to the methods by which Romans organized their social power. A method of organizing social power was what Polybius, following Aristotle, called a *politeia*, a Greek word that is often translated into English as *constitution*. (It is very close to what Michael Mann calls a *regime*.) For Polybius, influenced as he was by Greek philosophical traditions, as well as by his experiences of the Roman Republic, a *politeia* was an organized combination of military, political, and religious powers.

55 Livy, 31–33.35; Polybius 18.42, 18.44–51, 21.18; Scott, *Delphi*, 178–85.
56 Polybius 1.1–5, 3.1; Walbank, *Historical Commentary*, Vol. 1, 9, 43–6.
57 Polybius, 3.36–38.

The ways that powers were held in a *politeia* were highly regulated in the sense that strong normative principles governed the manner in which power was supposed to be acquired, exercised, and relinquished. In other words, there were rules that governed the exercise of power, which made its exercise rightful and just. The following of these rules was what made power organized and orderly rather than chaotic and arbitrary.[58]

Did people always follow the rules? Well, of course, they did not. But there were strong motivations for them to do so, or at least to successfully make it appear that they were doing so. For holders of constitutional powers, such as Roman magistrates, those powers were highly personal, in the sense that a man's manner of exercising power (his *virtus*, virtue) would define the way his personality and character were perceived, both by contemporaries and in historical memory. The virtuous exercise of constitutional powers, and the consequent earning of *gloria* for family (*familia*) and the Republic, was the goal of life for an elite Roman man. This was the ideal of human flourishing, a version of the well-lived life that philosophers like Plato and Aristotle had called *eudaimonia* (sometimes translated, confusingly, as *happiness*). This combination of highly personal and highly regulated performance of power is an important entry point into the Hellenistic, Mediterranean culture that was shared by Polybius, the Delphians, and the Romans.

The source of Rome's unique power, to reiterate Polybius' argument, was her constitution, particularly its combination of political, military, and religious powers. Aristocratic powers of the Senate balanced the more monarchical powers of senior magistrates (consuls and praetors), while popular assemblies and regular elections built in democratic elements. Militarily, Rome was strong in her reliance on citizen soldiers and formal allies, rather than mercenaries. And religiously, Rome was unique in harnessing a deep respect for the sacred through solemn rituals that were honored to a high degree even among elite, educated Romans.[59]

The Senate was the great council of the Roman polity, a body of elder statesmen – the word *senatus* is closely related in Latin to the word *senex*, which means *old*, so the Senate was, quite literally, a body of old men – who collectively met and engaged in debate about matters we would call *policy*. In language closer to that of the Romans themselves, the Senate made collective decisions and issued advisory opinions (*consulta*) on behalf of the Roman people (*populus*) and the Republic (*res publica*, literally *public thing*). The Senate was

58 Aristotle, *Politics*, Books III, VI and passim; Polybius, Book 6; Andrew Lintott, *The Constitution of the Roman Republic* (Oxford: Oxford University Press, 1999), Chapter 3; Andrew Lintott, *Imperium Romanum: Politics and Administration* (London: Routledge, 1993) [Kindle]. Mann on regimes of social power: Mann, *Sources, Vol. I*, 1–33, 518–24; Mann, *Sources, Vol.* 2, 1–3, 18–21; Mann, *Sources, Vol.* 3, 5–16; Mann, *Sources, Vol.* 4, 1–12, 400–32.

59 Polybius, Book VI; Lintott, *Constitution*, Chapters 3, 11–13; Walbank, *Historical Commentary*, Vol. 1, 659–62, 673–96, 741–2.

composed of elite Roman citizens (*cives*) who had served the Republic in public positions as magistrates and priests.[60]

Spurius Postumius, the sender of our Delphic privilege, was a *praetor*. A *praetor* was a high-level magistrate, one that played a central role in the development of Roman law. Praetors were annually elected by the Roman people in assemblies (the *populus*, organized so that they could act collectively). At this time in the Republic's history, the number of praetors elected each year was increased to six. Their service supplemented that of two senior magistrates, the *consuls*. Once the consuls and praetors had been elected, their spheres of responsibility and power (*provincia*) were then assigned in consultation with the Senate, often by drawing lots (a randomizing device, something like throwing dice). Since this was a time of frequent wars, the consuls and several of the praetors would typically be sent out as generals to lead armies and act as envoys. Two of the praetors, however, stayed in Rome to oversee judgments in private lawsuits: one to oversee disputes between Romans and foreigners (*peregrini*), and the other to oversee disputes arising between Roman citizens. These came to be known as the peregrine and urban praetors, respectively.[61]

The Senate and People of Rome (*senatus populusque romanus*, abbreviated *SPQR*) were the authority (*auctoritas*) behind the magistrates, but the magistrates held significant power (*potestas*), especially beyond Rome's sacred boundary, the *pomerium*. The Romans gave performative significance to a senior magistrate's powers with *lictors* and *fasces*. The *lictors* were men who marched in front of a senior magistrate carrying a bundle of sticks and axes (the *fasces*). These symbolized the *imperium*, the power of a Roman magistrate to give commands and to back them up with violence. Within the sacred boundary of the city, the *pomerium*, the axes were lowered as a symbolic display of the fact that a Roman commander's powers were limited when he dealt with Roman citizens.[62]

Extolling these unique aspects of the Roman constitution, Polybius noted something else – the fact that the constitution had not been instituted by a single man. Establishment (*institutio*) of a *politeia* by a divinely inspired lawgiver, like Lycurgus for Sparta, was a common founding myth for a Greek city-state. Rome, instead, had grown her constitution by accretion from many great lawgivers, as well as through *mores* and customs that developed on the basis of responses to crises and repeated practice. To Polybius, this rendered the growth and development of the Roman

60 Polybius, 6.13; Jolowicz & Nicholas, *Historical Introduction*, 30–45; Lintott, *Constitution*, Chapters 6, 10.

61 Livy 7.1, 31.4, 32.27; S. P. Oakley, *A Commentary on Livy*, Volume 2 (Oxford: Oxford University Press, 1998), 77; Polybius, 6.12; Jolowicz & Nicholas, *Historical Introduction*, 48–9, 97–101; Lintott, *Constitution*, Chapter 7.

62 Mary Beard, *SPQR: A History of Ancient Rome* (New York: W. W. Norton, 2015), Chapters 1–4. The pomerium: Beard, North, & Price, *Religions of Rome*, 177–81. Fasces: Livy 2.1; Ogilvie, *Commentary on Livy*, 235–6, 251, 463–4.

constitution as something natural and organic, something that emerged immanently through incremental, wise responses to the forces of historical and social change.[63]

Mos maiorum, the customary wisdom of the ancestors, was deeply respected in Rome, but there was also a pragmatic willingness to accept new practices as displacing those old and outdated. This pragmatic willingness to accept and adopt new practices may help us to understand the development of Roman legal documents, which seems to occur in conjunction with Rome's expansion into the eastern Mediterranean world. Some of our oldest Roman legal documents come from this time period. The legal letter from Spurius Postumius to Delphi is among these turning-point legal texts.[64]

3.7 THE DELPHIAN PRIVILEGE AS AN INSTRUMENT OF SOCIAL POWER

And so we return, at last, to the immediate context in which Spurius Postumius, praetor of the Romans, sent his letter to Greece, conveying a decision of the Roman Senate. This immediate context was one in which Rome, shortly after defeating Philip V in the Second Macedonian War, had turned her attention to Antiochus III (c. 242–187 BC) of Syria. An important trigger for Roman reentry into the eastern Mediterranean was the perfidy of her northern Greek allies, the Aetolian League of poleis that controlled Delphi. The Aetolians, disenchanted with Rome, had flirted with Syria, inviting Antiochus to invade Greece, adopting the tried-and-true ideal of a campaign for the liberation of Greece. Roman forces returned, one-upping them all in the liberation, once again, of Greece.[65]

The Delphians were doubtless pleased that a Roman general had freed them, but they wanted something more durable than the verbal declaration of a soldier in the field. They sent an embassy to Rome, where a meeting of the Senate was convened by Spurius Postumius. The Senate determined that the Delphians should have the freedom, autonomy, and immunity that the consul had declared. In effect, the Senate ratified and formalized the consul's decision. In keeping with administrative practices that seem to have been standardizing about this time, the Senate's decree was probably written by Spurius Postumius, in consultation with other Senators who

63 Polybius, 6.4–10; Walbank, *Commentary on Polybius*, Vol. 1, 635–63

64 Mos maiorum: Karl-J. Hölkeskamp, *Reconstructing the Roman Republic: An Ancient Political Culture and Modern Research*, translated by Henry Heitmann-Gordon (Princeton: Princeton University Press, 2010), Chapter 2. Pragmatic willingness to adopt new practices and methods: Polybius 1.20, 6.25; Walbank, *Commentary on Polybius*, Vol. 1, 75–6, 708. Development of Roman legal documents: Sherk, *Roman Documents*, 4–7, 24, 186–9.

65 Election of Spurius Postumius Albinus as praetor: Livy, 37.47, 37.50. Roman attention to Antiochus III: Livy, 33.13, 33.19–20, 33.27, 33.34, 33.38–41, 33.44–49, 34.43, 34.49, 34.57–60, 35.15–17, 35.23–25, 35.41; Polybius, 18.49–52; Aetolian disenchantment with Rome: Livy, 31.1, 33.13, 33.31, 33.35, 33.44, 33.49, 34.22–23, 35.12, 35.31–33; Polybius, 18.45, 20.9–11, 21.2, 21.4–5. Aetolian invitation to Antiochus: Livy, 35.33, 35.43–49. Roman forces returning to Greece: Livy, 36.5–35; Polybius, 20.8–10, 21.1–5; Scott, *Delphi*, 185–87.

had participated in and witnessed the debate, and then deposited in the Temple of Saturn. The decree that we have today comes from an official Greek translation of the original Latin text: one that Delphian ambassadors took back with them to Delphi, carved into marble, and publicly displayed.[66]

Decrees of the Senate were nothing new for the Romans, either in their domestic governance or in their foreign affairs. However, official letters like the one sent by Postumius do appear to be something new. Entering into the domain of Hellenistic powers, Roman magistrates seem to be emulating Hellenistic kings in developing and enacting forms of official correspondence. As we will see, this will become the foundation of imperial Roman law-giving, which will take the form of letters (*epistolae* and *rescripta*) from the Roman emperor.[67]

The Senate was the patriarchal council of the Republic, and counsel about divine honor and respect was a crucial function of the Senate. In recognizing and protecting a zone of political and economic exclusivity at Delphi, and in becoming a patron of Delphi, the Senate was doing what elite Roman men of virtue were supposed to do: honoring the religion of the ancestors, which included the worship of Apollo at Delphi. They were performing an act of traditional piety.

But the Senators were also performing the role of a Hellenistic ruler in proclaiming the "freedom of the Greeks," and this was new. The privilege for Delphi granted in 189 BC, then, which is among our earliest extant documents of Roman law, is a document in which the Romans were announcing themselves to the inhabited world (the *oikumene*) as the new, Hellenistic-style rulers on the block. Importantly, though, they were not doing so entirely on their own volition – they were responding to a request by Delphi, and this would become the pattern for Roman privileges, indeed a pattern for Roman imperial rule.[68]

In their privilege to Delphi, the Romans enacted and memorialized a beneficent grant of freedom, autonomy, and tax exemption. They did so in recognition of the sacred services that Delphi offered – the divine oracles from Apollo that the internationally important temple and polis provided. They asserted themselves as patrons to Apollo's prophetic messengers, thereby showing piety and beneficence, and earning for themselves the right to expect grateful services in return. They enacted an empowerment of Delphi, by subjecting the Delphians to their power, and in so doing further empowered themselves. This became a pattern for Roman expansion into the Greek east, an institutional structure that would knit Rome's complicated, multifaceted, cultural, economic, military, and political relations of power into something that approached a unitary, imperial state.

66 Sherk, *Roman Documents*, 4–19, 21–5, 221–28.

67 Lintott, *Imperium Romanum*, ll. 485; Sherk, *Roman Documents*, 4–7, 24.

68 Lintott, *Imperium Romanum*, ll. 223, 116–83, 621–81; Fergus Millar, *The Emperor in the Roman World*, 2d ed. (London: Duckworth, 1992); Sherk, *Roman Documents*, 184–97.

3.8 ZONES OF EXCLUSIVITY AND INSTRUMENTS OF LEGAL POWER: AN INITIAL COMPARISON

We have now looked at several legal documents, focusing especially on two: one from AD 2010, granting a zone of exclusivity to Facebook, and one from 189 BC, granting a zone of exclusivity to the sacred polis of Delphi. A world of difference seemingly separates these two legal documents. The question upon which the remainder of this book depends is the following: is there a connection between the two? Does it make sense to bring these two legal instruments alongside one another, to compare them, and even to draw a line of development that links them together across time?

I believe the answer to these questions is yes, and this book is my effort to justify that answer. I cannot give the full answer yet, but in order to persuade you to keep traveling along this path with me, I will offer an initial justification.

To begin with, we can focus on what these legal documents have in common. I have set the comparison up by noting the ways in which they each create a zone of exclusivity. Both legal documents draw boundaries with words. They say, in effect, to everyone who reads the document: "Here is a line. We shall not pass it. You shall not pass it. Everything inside the line belongs to Facebook/Delphi. They make the decisions about what happens there. So long as they do not violate binding principles of law and custom, they are free to decide about everything that happens within the line. And, by the way, if anyone should be so foolhardy as to step across that line, that one will be met with the full force of our high displeasure. Be thou warned!"

What makes these instruments of legal power is both: (1) the potent linkage of cultural, economic, military, and political power that stands behind that warning, and (2) the performative social action that dramatically enacts and memorializes this through formal, written documents. The political and social form seems to differ significantly: with the Facebook patent it is the nation-state, and with Delphi it is a Greco-Roman city-state complex, rapidly moving toward Mediterranean empire. But even between these different constitutional structures there is a common source of social power. That common source is both social-relational and cultural. It involves the formation of governing communities: bounded and bonded social relationship structures that explicitly define membership, and, in defining membership, define the social status of citizenship.

Two fundamental categories of social status end up being defined by such communities: insider and outsider. Insiders are those people who belong to the organization, who are protected by it, and who stand inside the boundary, while outsiders are those who do not belong, those who are not protected. Between the Facebook News Feed patent and the Roman privilege for Delphi, the source of social power enabling a zone of exclusivity to be created is ultimately a common, political form of social-relational power: a social group defining membership (insider status) based on citizenship.

We call this common form of governing community a *state*, and we have a tendency to think that states are universal. In all historical periods and across all types of cultural contexts, we think, people have organized themselves into groups. If we equate "state" with "stable group," then we can indeed argue that states are universal. But an important purpose of this book is to argue against this view, to argue instead that states are not universal, that they are a particular type of governing community that has been *universalized*. Once this type of social-relational organization was developed, it has been imitated and adapted across time, but it is a social and political project, not something that happens automatically. Rome, in fact, was a vital agent in a broader project and developmental process.

So, to summarize: a common pattern underlying Facebook's News Feed patent and Rome's Delphian privilege is one in which a particular form of governing community (a state) is creating a zone of exclusivity on behalf of a favored client, which is itself collectively organized. In the case of Facebook, the favored client is a business corporation. In the case of Delphi, the favored client is a city (polis). In fact, cities and business corporations have a great deal in common, legally speaking.

Two other important similarities underpin the Facebook News Feed patent and the Delphian privilege.

First, note how both grants are made for the purpose of securing social services. Patents, we have said, are granted in order to enable something that is considered a public good, one that, according to economic theory, would not otherwise be provided in sufficient quantities: technological innovation. Delphi's privilege was also being granted to enable a public good: civic and religious services, which were things that cities were good for, in the view of Roman and Greek thinkers. It is true that this is nowhere stated explicitly in the privilege itself, but then neither is the public good being served by Facebook's News Feed patent stated in the patent itself. Instead, this understanding that protection for a zone of exclusivity is being granted in return for the provision of a public good (social services) is part of a prevailing rationale that underpins the legitimacy of the institution, one that can be highlighted when the institution is viewed in its historical and social context.

Second, note how both grants are grants of property. Such grants are deeply ironic because they grant something that, according to the logic, the grantee already has: namely, property. This is explicit in the case of the Delphian privilege. The Senate granted the Delphians dominion over their sacred harbor and territory, "just as was their inherited right." We have to infer backward from the Greek text to the Latin original, which no longer exists, but this is made easier by the fact that standard translations existed for rendering Latin words into Greek, and by the fact that a stable, scribal practice already existed for drafting these legal documents. The Latin concepts being evoked with Greek words seem to be mastery/lordship (*dominium*) and patrimony (*patrimonium*), meaning inherited property. So the paradoxical sense is that Rome is granting something that Delphi already has, namely, her inherited property.[69]

There is a similarly paradoxical sense with modern patents for new technology. US patent law states that patents have the attributes of personal property during the period of time that they are valid. However, in order to have the attributes of property, patents must be granted after an examination/prosecution process that tests whether they meet the legal requirements. A patent application must first be filed, and the applicant must be the first to file the application, in order to receive the patent. Furthermore, once the time period of validity defined by law is over, the property disappears. This is property that the government grants, in order to serve purposes that are believed to be good for society, as a whole. In a way, this is a very public and communal type of property, even though, during the period that the property lasts, the owner has the powers of a private property owner.

The thing that is so different about a modern patent, of course, is the subject matter of the property – the fact that the property is for new technology. There is nothing quite like this in Roman antiquity, although in the following chapters we will see some privileges that come rather close. Romans did not celebrate novelty and originality the way that we do today. Although they could be quite pragmatic, and could recognize the value of new technology, they tended to celebrate the past, and to admire what was very old, rather than celebrating the future, and that which is radically new. Here is an important cultural difference between Roman privileges and modern patents.

Finally, notice the strikingly similar roles being played by the written documents themselves. The processes and contexts in which the documents were written are, of course, very different. But the documents are doing something very similar. They are performing and memorializing social relations of power. They are a kind of symbolic, social action, one that is oriented toward a prevailing order of obligation, and one that intentionally breaks with everyday patterns of speech and behavior in order to solemnize the relations of exclusivity that are being performatively enacted. In Geoffrey Koziol's sense, these are both instruments of legal power.[70]

There are, therefore, important differences between ancient privileges, like the privilege for Delphi, and modern patents. These differences have to do with changes at the level of culture, and with the scale and bureaucratic intensity at which social relationships are organized in the modern world of nation-states. What I have tried to do in this chapter, however, is to stress that there are, nonetheless, important similarities between ancient privileges, like the privilege for Delphi, and modern patents. Both types of legal document grant something that is considered in terms of property, in exchange for the provision of useful social services. This formal, structural pattern is something that we will see running across time, from antiquity

69 Sherk, *Roman Documents*, 7–19.

70 For Koziol's thesis about diplomas as instruments of power, see Chapters 2 and 6.

to today. The long-standing, historical experience with formal legal documents enabling this structural pattern of social power is an important factor to consider in seeing how modern intellectual property emerged.

3.9 CONCLUSION

In this chapter, we have studied a Roman privilege for the temple at Delphi, entering into the Mediterranean-centered world of ancient Rome, as a way to glimpse important, Hellenistic influences on the development of Roman legal instruments that I am arguing are comparable to, and foundational for, modern intellectual property. The document that we have mainly looked at is one in which freedom, autonomy, and tax immunity were granted to Delphi by the Roman Senate, a document through which, I have argued, the Romans declared themselves to the world as imperial rulers in the tradition of Hellenistic kings, as well as pious protectors of traditional religion. In making this legal declaration, Rome became a patron of Delphi, expecting grateful religious services in return.

Delphi was a sacred place, with sacred boundaries, which protected treasures and vast wealth. It was also an industrial center of divination, a place to which people traveled from all around the Mediterranean world, to seek divine counsel and advice. In patronizing the polis that housed this world-famous oracle, together with its wealth of sculptures, inscriptions, and other monuments, Rome was stepping onto the world stage as a patron of Hellenistic culture and religion. In the letter from Spurius Postumius to Delphi, Rome was emulating and adapting an already-ancient tradition of beneficence, granting privileges through formal letters, a tradition that the Romans would develop as they grew ever more imperial in their styles of governance.

What we see at Delphi in 189 BC is the beginning of a Roman tradition of letter-based privilege granting, one that stands at the heart of the much broader Roman legal tradition that grew up around it. In the next chapter, we will look at developments in this tradition, encountering some of the same cultural ideals pursued through modern intellectual property: protection of poets, artists, and learning.

4

Semantic Legal Ordering

Idealizing Roman Law

In 62 BC, Marcus Tullius Cicero (106–43 BC) stood up in court to defend his client, A. Licinius Archias, against the charge that, as a non-Roman citizen, he was wrongfully continuing to live in the city of Rome. The charge had been brought under a law enacted in 65 BC, providing that all non-Roman citizens residing in Rome should be expelled. Cicero, as a friend of Archias' patron (L. Licinius Lucullus), took on the case for the defense, and, in doing so, provides us with an insider's view of Roman patronage for the literary arts in the late Republic.[1]

Archias was a Greek-speaking poet from Syria. He was born in Antioch, and he had become famous throughout Greek-speaking areas of western Asia. According to Cicero, he had traveled to southern Italy and had been granted honorary citizenship by certain cities (poleis) there. These poleis were a vital, western outpost of Greater Greece (*Magna Graecia*), and they were following an established model for rewarding a service to the polis in granting honorary citizenship to Archias.[2]

In 102 BC, Archias found his way to Rome and was adopted into the household of Lucullus. The Luculli family became his patrons, and Archias probably became a tutor to Lucullus' teenage sons. At some point within the next several years, Archias traveled with Lucullus back to southern Italy, and Lucullus arranged for Archias to receive honorary citizenship from the city of Heraclea, which had a formal treaty of

[1] Cicero's speech *Pro Archia*: James E. G. Zetzel (ed. & trans.), *Ten Speeches* by Cicero (Indianapolis: Hackett Publishing, 2009), 168–86; Cicero, *Orations*, translated by N. H. Watts (Cambridge, MA: Harvard University Press (Loeb), 1923), 6–41; see also Dominic H. Berry, "Literature and Persuasion in Cicero's Pro Archia," in *Cicero the Advocate*, edited by Jonathan Powell and Jeremy Paterson (Oxford: Oxford University Press, 2004), 291–311; Gordon Williams, "Phases in Political Patronage of Literature in Rome," in *Literary and Artistic Patronage in Ancient Rome*, edited by Barbara K. Gold (Austin: University of Texas Press, 1982) [Kindle ed.], ll. 235–796. As a beneficiary of patronage from Lucullus, Archias was perhaps charged to curry favor with the powerful general Pompey, who was politically at odds with Lucullus. Zetzel, *Ten Speeches*, 168; compare Berry, "Literature and Persuasion," 294. Law of 65 BC: Cicero, *Pro Archia*, V.10; Berry, "Literature and Persuasion," 294.

[2] Cicero, *Pro Archia*, II.4–III.5, V.10; Richard Hunter and Ian Rutherford, "Introduction," in *Wandering Poets in Ancient Greek Culture: Travel, Locality and Pan-Hellenism*, (Cambridge, UK: Cambridge University Press, 2009), 1–22; Ian Rutherford, "Aristodama and the Aetolians: An Itinerant Poetess and Her Agenda," in Hunter & Rutherford, *Wandering Poets*, 237–48.

alliance with Rome. After the Social War (91–88 BC) – a war fought over extension of Roman citizenship to allied cities across Italy – a series of laws were enacted, enabling citizens of allied Italian cities to receive Roman citizenship. According to Cicero, Archias had complied with the requirements of the second of these laws – the *lex Plautia Papiria* – and formally became a Roman citizen. Unfortunately, however, the violence of the Social War meant that the official records of Heraclea were destroyed. Hence the problem about Archias' Roman citizenship.[3]

Cicero was the Roman version of a self-made man, a big fish from a small pond named Arpinum, someone who had financial resources but lacked elite status, and who nevertheless made his way to the pinnacle of Roman magistracy, to the Senate and then to the jointly held position of supreme power in Rome, the consulship. Cicero was a professional rhetorician and an amateur philosopher. (It should be remembered, however, that to call someone an amateur is to say that he was doing something he loved – *amatus* – something that he did not need to do to survive.)[4]

Cicero's arguments in the case of Archias are important to our investigation of an ancient lineage for intellectual property in several respects. First, they show us how citizenship could be used as a reward for one kind of social service that is involved in modern intellectual property, namely, creative written expression. They also suggest a plausible line of development in which this practice, developed in Greek poleis, found its way to Rome. Moreover, this case also shows us how patronage of artistic and literary expression worked in Roman society. In fact, this is a prime piece of evidence about Roman literary patronage. And, finally, in his arguments, Cicero provides us with a line of argument that remains relevant to modern intellectual property, namely, that creative scholarly work benefits the state and should therefore receive a benefit from the state. The benefit in both cases – ancient citizenship and modern legal status as author/creator and property owner – is at once economic, social, and political. And it is, quite intentionally, offered to encourage creative work that serves the state.[5]

The important contrast, however, between ancient Roman patronage and modern intellectual property is that the benefit was not described as property. And yet, Cicero's lifetime marks an important turning point toward increasing abstraction in conceptions of property that will become an important foundation for modern intellectual property.

In this chapter, we will see how Roman property law approaches modern notions of intellectual property – in recognizing the value derived from an artist's contribution to artistic work – but nonetheless does not quite reach modern notions of intellectual property. In Roman law, under the theory of accession (*accessio*), the

3 Cicero, *Pro Archia*, III.5–V.10; Berry, "Literature and Persuasion," 292–4.

4 Mary Beard, *SPQR: A History of Ancient Rome* (New York: W. W. Norton, 2015) [Kindle], ll. 207–28; J. G. F. Powell, "Introduction: Cicero's Philosophical Works and Their Background," in *Cicero the Philosopher*, edited by J.G.F. Powell (Oxford: Clarendon Press, 1995), 1–35. On the value of amateurism, see Edward W. Said, *Representations of the Intellectual: The 1993 Reith Lectures* (New York: Random House, 1994), 82.

5 Williams, "Phases in Political Patronage," ll. 235–54.

owner of a literary work remains the person who owns the materials, rather than the author. However, in the arguments of the jurists we also see that artistic works were coming to be recognized as valuable in virtue of their artistry, a point that was highlighted in polemics of Greco-Roman authors against literary "kidnapping," that is, plagiarism. We will see, in other words, how legal practices and ideals developed that look very much like modern intellectual property, while nonetheless lacking the kind of property-based rationale of cultural progress that is fundamental to modern intellectual property today.[6]

To see all this, however, we first enter the regime of social power that was involved in Rome's transition from Republic to Empire.

4.1 MILITARY AND ECONOMIC POWER IN LATE REPUBLICAN ROME

As we saw in the previous chapter, Polybius viewed Roman military organization as a vital source of Rome's power in unifying the world. In Polybius' time, the Roman army was a well-organized, but nonprofessional, citizen army – men left their farms to serve in the army and returned to their farms when their time of service was over. In Cicero's time, however, the composition and organization of the Roman army had changed. Soldiers were becoming full-time professionals, whose primary loyalty was to the great *imperium*-wielding general (typically a *consul*, but increasingly a governor whose service was extended into a multi-year position, a *proconsul*), who led them into the field of battle, and who rewarded them with land and booty for their loyal service.[7]

Leadership of the Roman state, in other words, was coming to mean charismatic leadership of professional men-at-arms, many of whom were not Roman citizens, but who hoped for citizenship as a reward for their military service. There is no better figure to reveal these patterns than Gaius Julius Caesar (100–44 BC), who is perhaps Rome's most famous citizen. But as innovative as he was, Caesar also followed

6 Plagiarism as literary kidnapping (*plagiarius*): Martial, *Epigrams*, 1.52, Loeb editions and translations by Walter C. A. Ker (London: William Heineman, 1919) and D. R. Shackleton Bailey (Cambridge, MA: Harvard University Press, 1993); also Victoria Rimell, *Martial's Rome: Empire and the Ideology of Epigram* (Cambridge, UK: Cambridge University Press, 2008), Chapter 1; J. Mira Seo, "Plagiarism and Poetic Identity in Martial," *The American Journal of Philology* 130(4) (2009): 567–93.

7 *Polybius: The Histories*, translated by Robin Waterfield (Oxford: Oxford University Press, 2010), 6.19–42; Frank W. Walbank, *A Historical Commentary on Polybius*, Vol. I (Oxford: Clarendon Press, 1970), 697–723. In addition to Robin Waterfield's translation, I rely on Ian Scott-Kilvert's translation (Penguin 1979) and on the Loeb Classical Library's six-volume edition of Polybius' *Histories*, translated by W. R. Paton and revised by F. W. Walbank and Christian Habicht. For the transition from a citizen army to "virtually professional soldiers" expecting rewards, see Brian Campbell, *The Roman Army, 31 BC–AD 337* (London: Routledge, 1994), 1–7. On proconsuls: Andrew Lintott, *The Constitution of the Roman Republic* (Oxford: Oxford University Press, 1999), Chapter 7(c). On governors: Andrew Lintott, *Imperium Romanum: Politics and Administration* (London: Routledge, 1993), Chapter 4.

patterns for charismatic generalship that had been established by earlier generations of Roman generals.[8]

These patterns developed partly because Roman military expansion had meant massive acquisition of wealth. In the last chapter we saw that expansion in its early phase, which was arguably defensive. However, as they marched across Spain, Greece, Macedonia, Asia Minor (Turkey), Syria, Palestine, North Africa, and Egypt, Roman armies and their *imperium*-wielding generals began to grow addicted to the wealth they acquired as booty. The Roman people came to share this addiction, as the triumphal ceremonies and gladiatorial games marking Roman victories in the east grew increasingly impressive. Economic interests began to attach themselves to military conquest and provincial administration, especially through the companies of tax collectors (*publicani*) who grew wealthy from tax-collection services they provided to the Roman state. A pattern developed that Max Weber called *political capitalism*, in which the provinces linked to Rome through military conquest became a source of profit for Roman senators and *equites* ("knights"), families that became something like a wealthy upper middle class, often through exploitation of Rome's dependent provinces.[9]

The late Republic was a time, in other words, when Rome's military power, organized as this was into legions of soldiers led by centurions, became inextricably linked to economic sources that fed and entertained the people of Rome, and that made Roman politicians rich. To capture the sociological implications of this development, Michael Mann has labeled Rome a "legionary economy." In this legionary economy, the wealth acquired as booty (especially in the eastern Mediterranean) was used to finance land acquisition in the west – north Africa, Italy, Spain, and Gaul – building up massive landholdings worked by plantation

[8] Caesar: Kurt A. Raaflaub and Robert B. Strassler (eds.), *The Landmark Julius Caesar* (New York: Pantheon Books, 2017); Julius Caesar, *The Gallic War*, translated by H. J. Edwards (Cambridge, MA: Harvard University Press, 1917); Julius Caesar, *Civil War*, translated by Cynthia Damon (Cambridge, MA: Harvard University Press, 2016); Plutarch, "Life of Caesar," in *Plutarch's Lives, the Dryden Translation*, edited by Arthur Hugh Clough, Vol. II (New York: The Modern Library, 2001), 199–244; *Plutarch's Lives*, Vol. VII, translated by Bernadotte Perrin (Cambridge, MA: Harvard University Press, 1919); Suetonius, *Lives of the Caesars*, I, Revised ed. (Cambridge, MA: Harvard University Press, 1998).

[9] Polybius on the profits from extending Roman dominion: 6.17. Classic republican critique of Roman addiction to wealth and luxury, fueled by conquest in the eastern Mediterranean: Sallust, *The War with Catiline*, translated by J. C. Rolfe, revised by John T. Ramsey (Cambridge, MA: Harvard University Press, 2013), 10–12. The *publicani*: Ernst Badian, *Publicans and Sinners: Private Enterprise in the Service of the Roman Republic* (Dunedin: University of Otago Press, 1972). Weber on political capitalism: Weber, *Economy & Society*, 164–66. Economic analysis of the Roman Republic: Tenney Frank, *An Economic Survey of Ancient Rome, Vol. I: Rome and Italy of the Republic* (Baltimore: Johns Hopkins University Press, 1933). For an older and valuable analysis drawing on Marxist terminology, see Michael Rostovtzeff, *The Social and Economic History of the Roman Empire*, 2nd ed. revised by P. M. Fraser (Oxford: Clarendon Press, 1957). Overview of the legal and economic developments, with transcription and discussion of legal texts revealing important aspects of efforts at reform: Andrew Lintott, *Judicial Reform and Land Reform in the Roman Republic* (Cambridge, UK: Cambridge University Press, 1992).

slavery, thereby generating further wealth for the landowners. Land across Italy that had previously belonged in a vaguely collective way to the Roman people – called *ager publicus* – was transformed into privately exploited land, and small farmers were driven out of business by large land owners. The small farmers had no choice but to either become soldiers, who might then hope for land in the provinces, or to become poor residents of Rome supported by a "basic income" of grain. These were people who lived on *panem et circenses* ("bread and circuses"), in Juvenal's famous line.[10]

An important turning point toward this legionary economy came when the last king of Pergamum, Attalus III (c. 170–133 BC), gifted his kingdom to Rome by will. Now Rome had property to protect in western Asia. And protecting this property meant confronting Hellenistic kings, particularly the king of Pontus, a region along the southern shore of the Black Sea. This king was Mithradates VI (120–63 BC), and he would become the figure who seemed most threatening to Rome during the early part of Cicero's lifetime. The great general who finally defeated him was Gnaeus Pompeius Magnus, known to us as Pompey (106–48 BC). In his rise to power, Julius Caesar at first allied himself to Pompey. And it was in defeating Pompey that Caesar established himself as the supreme ruler of Rome.[11]

Both Pompey and Caesar knew how to motivate soldiers to fierce loyalty on their behalf. The key to this was offering hope for advancement, as a result of their military service. This hope for advancement was both political and economic. It came in the form of rewards for service: rewards in war booty (often slaves, but sometimes also objects of movable wealth, which could range from gold or silver coins to great works of art), in land, and in citizenship.

4.2 GRANTS OF CITIZENSHIP AND PROPRIETARY PRIVILEGES IN A TRANSFORMING STATE

Rome had always been relatively generous in grants of citizenship to outsiders. However, the typical pattern was one in which rights were granted to an allied city, rather than to an individual. During the Social War, a law had been enacted at the behest of Caesar's older relative (Lucius Julius Caesar) to confer citizenship on allies who remained loyal to Rome. We do not have a copy of this law, but we can

10 Mann, *Sources*, *Vol. 1*, 250–300. Bread and circuses: Juvenal, Satire 10, in *Juvenal and Persius*, edited and translated by Susanna Morton Braund (Cambridge, MA: Harvard University Press, 2004), line 81.

11 Will of Attalus III and its effects: Badian, *Publicans*, 63; Allan Chester Johnson, Paul Robinson Coleman-Norton, and Frank Card Bourne, *Ancient Roman Statutes* (Austin: University of Texas Press, 1961), 37; David Magie, *Roman Rule in Asia Minor* (Princeton: Princeton University Press, 1950), 3, 31–33; Robert K. Sherk, *Roman Documents from the Greek East: Senatus Consulta and Epistulae to the Age of Augustus* (Baltimore: Johns Hopkins University Press, 1969), 59–62. Mithradates and Pompey: Magie, *Roman Rule*, 147–365. Caesar and Pompey: Suetonius, *Lives of the Caesars*, I.19–35; Cynthia Damon and Kurt A. Raaflaub, "Caesar's Life and Works," in *The Landmark Caesar*, xxvi–xxxvii; Magie, *Roman Rule*, 368–404.

infer that it authorized Roman magistrates – including generals in the field – to issue grants of citizenship to favored individuals. From 90 BC, we have an early example of this kind of administrative grant (*lex data*), a grant of citizenship made by Pompey's father to Spanish cavalrymen who had served him with distinction in southern Italy (Picenum). In addition to the grant of citizenship, these men were rewarded with objects of wealth that they could wear as marks of distinction, and with a double ration of grain.[12]

In the next year, 89 BC, Roman citizenship was extended to all freeborn Italians. In addition, the Plautio-Papirian law was enacted, granting citizenship to persons who already had citizenship in an allied city, who were resident in Italy, and who registered themselves with the praetor within sixty days. This was the law under which Cicero argued that the Syrian poet Archias held his Roman citizenship. As we have seen, Archias acquired citizenship in Heraclea as a reward for his poetry. This pattern of rewarding individual artists and writers with citizenship was therefore one that Romans drew in, as they incorporated citizens of allied cities under the Plautio-Papirian law.[13]

By 88 BC, Roman citizenship had been extended across the Italian peninsula. Transformed from a small city-state in west-central Italy, Rome was rapidly becoming something much closer to a territorial state. This territorially based extension of citizenship was unprecedented in the ancient world, and it brought Rome closer to the modern nation-state than anything yet seen. Focusing on the implications of such territorially based citizenship for social power, Michael Mann characterizes this as the "widest extent of collective commitment yet mobilized." Rome was moving into uncharted waters, harnessing new levels of social energy, and this meant new challenges of social organization. Rome's constitutional structure, however, remained that of a city-state, and this mismatch between constitutional structure and social reality was generating significant tensions.[14]

The personality who electrified and oversaw a constitutional transformation was Lucius Cornelius Sulla Felix, known to history simply as Sulla (138–78 BC). Like nearly all Republican politicians, Sulla earned his political distinction through military victories, ranging from north Africa to Gaul, Greece, and western Asia. By 88 BC, Sulla had earned enough political and military glory to be elected consul, but he soon became one of Rome's most notoriously brutal rulers, marching his soldiers into Rome to threaten his political enemies and issuing a decree of *proscription*. In this type of extreme decree, which would later be used to murder Cicero, men were named as enemies of the state, and sanction was given to anyone who would kill the enemy. Such proscriptions transformed political disagreements into deadly fights,

12 Johnson et al., *Roman Statutes*, No. 60.

13 Cicero, *Pro Archia*, IV.7; Johnson et al., *Roman Statutes*, Nos. 62, 71.

14 Mann, *Sources*, *Vol. 1*, 254. For valuable reflections on these constitutional tensions, as part of a broader reassessment of historical periodization in the republican period, see Harriet I. Flower, *Roman Republics* (Princeton: Princeton University Press, 2010).

instituting something like an atmosphere of gang warfare, which involved freedmen and dependents of powerful politicians, as well as the politicians themselves.[15]

In 81 BC, Sulla was elected *dictator*, an established position in the Roman constitutional structure that was used in times of crisis to generate stability under temporary, monarchical rulership. Sulla used his time as dictator to oversee the enactment of wide-ranging constitutional reforms. He increased the number of praetors and reorganized the Roman court system. He doubled the number of senators from 300 to 600, naming certain *equites* as his favorites and securing their election. Sulla also gave added strictness and definiteness to the *cursus honorum*, the series of offices through which an elite Roman man progressed in political office and position. From this time forward, election and service as a *quaestor* made a man senator for life. In order to weaken the often-demagogic plebeian tribunes, Sulla made senate approval necessary for enacting their proposed laws, and he made them ineligible for further positions as magistrates, which meant in practice that no one would want to run for this office. Beyond Rome, Sulla subjected holders of *imperium* to stricter senatorial controls, and he arranged for settlement of his veterans on confiscated lands, ranging from the rich lands of Campania in central Italy to Etruria in the north.[16]

Not all of these reforms would endure, but they did irreversibly change the Roman constitution, including its courts and legal system. Cicero made a name for himself, arguing in Sulla's newly constituted courts, and Cicero's earliest cases were overshadowed by the legacy of Sulla, particularly his proscriptions. The younger generation of charismatic generals, led by Pompey, were also in the background whenever Cicero stood up to argue a case in front of a Roman jury. For Cicero, there was always a delicate political balancing act underlying a set of arguments that superficially might seem to be simply about the dissolution of a partnership for profit (*societas*, the word from which we get our *society*), or the inheritance of property from a man killed under the proscriptions.[17]

One important effect of Sulla's reforms was to bring the Senate back into the controlling position in Roman political life, albeit in a much enlarged and altered form. Practices of granting citizenship privileges to reward behavior continued under the enhanced senatorial control. In 78 BC, for example, the Senate issued a decree granting privileges to three Greek ship captains who had loyally served Rome in wars against King Mithradates. Although citizenship was not formally granted to these captains, they were given nearly all the rights of citizenship, except the right to vote. These rights included tax exemption and immunities from public

15 Cicero, *Pro Sexto Roscio Amerino*, translated by John Henry Freese (Cambridge, MA: Harvard University Press, 1930), 112–263; Walter Kirkpatrick Lacey and B. W. J. G. Wilson, *Res Publica: Roman Politics and Society According to Cicero* (Oxford: Oxford University Press, 1970), 16–32; Arthur Keaveney, *Sulla: The Last Republican*, 2nd ed. (London: Routledge, 2005), 124–34.

16 Flower, *Republics*, ch. 7; Keaveney, *Sulla*, 134–55.

17 Cicero, *Pro Publio Quictio* and *Pro Rosio Amerino*, translated by John Henry Freese (Cambridge, MA: Harvard University Press, 1930), 10–263; Zetzel, *Ten Speeches*, Introduction.

services, rights that were coming to be seen as the distinguishing privileges of Roman citizens in a state that increasingly relied on the provinces for its taxes. The privileges were explicitly described as inheritable by the children and descendants of the Greek captains, and therefore they look a great deal like property, even though they are not named as property.[18]

4.3 CAESAR AND CICERO: DIVERGING TYPES OF SOCIAL POWER

Caesar and Cicero were almost exact contemporaries, but their paths to positions of social power were very different. Caesar earned his glory and popularity through military conquest, especially across parts of what are today France and Germany, extending briefly into Britain. Caesar became the great conqueror and discoverer of the west, for the Romans. And it was the loyalty of Caesar's soldiers, enriched with booty, that made him powerful. Cicero, on the other hand, earned his glory through words, words that were carefully chosen and delivered according to canonical principles of rhetoric, fashioned as elaborate arguments in court, in assemblies, and in the Senate.[19]

We should remember, though, that Caesar also studied rhetoric, and he also made arguments in courts and assemblies. In fact, Caesar's early political career was marked by efforts on behalf of provincial communities to secure convictions for extortion against provincial governors. Cicero likewise earned his first dramatic political points for prosecuting an extortionate governor of Sicily, a man named Verres. Caesar, furthermore, like Cicero, did sacred services for the Republic in earning his political glory. Sometime around 73 BC, Caesar was brought into a leading body of priests (the *pontifices*), and he would eventually become *pontifex maximus*, high priest of the Roman state religion. Cicero served as an augur, a professional diviner of the will of the gods, as seen in the heavens and in the entrails of sacrificial animals.[20]

Caesar's first elective position, in 72 BC, was as a military tribune, an officer who commanded a unit of a Roman legion. Making his way up through the army in the immediate aftermath of Sulla's anti-popular reforms, Caesar, despite his aristocratic birth, embraced a populist position in politics. He advocated restoration of citizenship to men who had lost it under Sulla, and a return to the old powers of the tribunes of the plebs. In 69 BC, Caesar was elected *quaestor*, and accordingly, under

[18] Johnson et al., *Roman Statutes*, No. 71. The constitutional effects of Sulla's reforms are helpfully summarized in Flower, *Republics*, chs. 7–9.

[19] Adrian Goldsworthy, *Caesar: Life of a Colossus* (New Haven: Yale University Press, 2006); Zetzel, *Ten Speeches*, Introduction.

[20] Damon and Raaflaub, "Caesar's Life," xxiv–xxv; Debra L. Nousek, "Caesar, Man of Letters," *Landmark Caesar*, Web Essay E, available at www.landmarkcaesar.com (accessed September 23, 2019); Cicero, *The Verrine Orations*, 2 Volumes, translated by L. H. G. Greenwood (Cambridge, MA: Harvard University Press, 1928, 1935); Cicero, *On Divination*, translated by William Armistead Falconer (Cambridge, MA: Harvard University Press, 1923).

Sulla's constitutional reforms, became a lifelong member of the Senate. In 59 BC, with help from Pompey's loyal soldiers, Caesar was elected consul.[21]

Cicero moved through the *cursus honorum* alongside Caesar but rose to the pinnacle first, becoming consul in 63 BC. Cicero's consulship was marked by the outing of a conspiracy centered around a man named Catiline, whom Cicero successfully presented as a mortal threat to the Republic. Unlike Caesar, Cicero embraced a conservative political position, and it was partly through his political pursuit of the Catiline conspiracy that he was able to demonstrate his loyalty to an aristocratic vision of the Republic. Caesar the aristocrat was a charismatic general and populist in his politics, while Cicero the self-made, "new" man embraced a more overtly intellectual and conservative style of politics. Caesar presented the way forward for Rome as one of reform, while Cicero proclaimed the ideals of the *mos maiorum*, the traditional way of the ancestors.[22]

But there is one very striking thing that these two men shared: a recognition that literary arts could serve useful purposes in support of political power. Both men deployed literary skills in service of their political careers – Cicero in publishing his speeches and philosophical treatises, and Caesar in publishing his ethnographic and autobiographical accounts of heroic warfare against ferocious and exotic western barbarians. Nonetheless, it was Cicero's advocacy on behalf of the poet Archias that provides us with the most explicit rationale about how literature can serve the state.

4.4 *PRO ARCHIA* – CICERO ON THE BENEFITS OF CREATIVE LITERATURE TO THE STATE

Cicero's speech on behalf of Archias was relatively short, and, formally speaking, the only question was whether or not Archias was entitled to remain in Rome as a citizen. As a good advocate, though, Cicero went well beyond the narrow, formal question in his speech. The documentary records supporting Archias' case for citizenship were not available, so this was not a slam-dunk case, and it was a panel of about seventy-five Roman jurors – men perhaps inclined to be skeptical about the value to their society of Greek-speaking poets from Asia – who would be casting the deciding vote. Cicero understood that he needed to make not only a formal case for citizenship, but also a substantive case – to persuade the jury that they should want to claim Archias as a citizen of Rome, and to grant him that status, even if he did not already possess it (which, of course, he did).[23]

[21] Damon and Raaflaub, "Caesar's Life," xxv–xxvii; Caesar as populist: Plutarch, *Life of Pompey*, XXV, in *Plutarch's Lives*, Vol. V, translated by Bernadotte Perrin (Cambridge, MA: Harvard University Press, 1917); Beard, *SPQR*, Chapter 7.

[22] Cicero, *In Catilinam* 1–4, translated by C. MacDonald (Cambridge, MA: Harvard University Press, 1976); Beard, *SPQR*, Chapters 1, 7.

[23] Cicero, *Pro Archia*, I–II; Berry, "Literature and Persuasion," 291–302; Zetzel (ed.), 168–74.

So Cicero sought to show the many ways in which Greek-speaking poets like Archias, and Archias himself, were useful to the Roman people. Cicero did this by first implying that Archias had been his own teacher. If Cicero had served the republic well – as, of course, he had only the previous year in outing Catiline's conspiracy – Archias was partly to be thanked for this. In making this argument, Cicero used language that would become technical in Roman property law, hinting slightly humorously that Archias would have the legal right (*ius*) to claim any profitable advantage (*fructus*) that Cicero might have earned as a successful rhetorician. The argument was a metaphorical joke, but it required a recognition that ingenuity/talent, skill, and intellectual understanding can be analogized to things that generate an advantageous return. This argument had a long and illustrious future.[24]

Cicero's main argument, though, was that Archias' poetry was serving, and would continue to serve, the Roman people, through the praise of great Roman generals like Pompey, in their military conquests and in their provincial governance. Archias had made his career by deploying his talent in praising the Roman people. He had chronicled the wars against Mithradates with the acquisition of valuable territory in Pontus. He had also glorified Lucullus, who had helped to lay the foundation for Roman rulership, greatness, and enrichment in Asia. Archias' praise of Lucullus had earned him the patronage of the Luculli family, but Archias had also praised the Roman people, as a group, and they too should be grateful.[25]

The fact that Archias wrote in Greek only enhanced the propaganda value of his work, because it meant a wide audience in the language most broadly shared throughout the eastern Mediterranean. The spread of this valuable propaganda was beneficial to the state, both for its provincial subjects and in spurring heroic action by its soldiers and generals.

> We should want our glory and reputation spread as far as our weapons have reached. Such rewards are important for the nations whose history is being recorded, but for the men who are fighting for their lives to gain glory, this is the greatest spur to enduring danger and toil.[26]

In addition to providing good propaganda for the Republic, poetry like that of Archias established models (*exempla*) of political virtue for young Romans to emulate. Moreover, the knowledge provided through literature provided essential resources that, when added to virtuous character, helped to make the greatness of Rome's heroes: Scipio Africanus and Cato the Censor, men of the "greatest generation," who had defeated Carthage and extended the Roman *imperium*, who were also known for their embrace of literary learning.[27]

24 Cicero, *Pro Archia*, I–V.12–14; Berry, "Literature and Persuasion," 298.
25 Cicero, *Pro Archia*, VIII–X; Berry, "Literature and Persuasion," 303–10.
26 Cicero, *Pro Archia*, X.23 (Zetzel trans.).
27 Cicero, *Pro Archia*, VI–VII; Berry, "Literature and Persuasion," 305–7.

Literary learning, in short, was useful and valuable to the state, both morally and intellectually. Like the myriad Greek cities that competed with one another to claim Homer as their own, Rome should claim Archias as their poet, as their property even, by recognizing his citizenship. To receive citizenship rights in the Roman Republic was to receive a great and valuable reward, and Archias had earned that reward. The Roman people should become his patrons, acknowledging the fact that he had earned the right to be legally protected by their laws, and thereby returning the benefits that he had given to them through his literary work. Metaphors of patronage, in other words, are working throughout this speech in addition to metaphors of monetary and propaganda value.[28]

Metaphors of property are also at work in this speech. We saw this at the beginning of the speech, with the metaphor of a "property right" to the advantages earned from literary knowledge and skill. And we see it again in the notion that the Roman people's claim of an individual as its citizen is something like a proprietary claim. In the wake of Sulla's proscriptions, which revoked protections of citizenship in order to enable state-sanctioned execution and plunder of wealth, it is no wonder that citizenship and property were semantically connected.[29]

In closing his speech, Cicero expressed his expectant hope that Archias would soon be publishing a poetic work praising Cicero's own labors on behalf of the Republic. In doing so, Cicero acknowledged that the longing for praise and glory was part of what had motivated him to work so hard on behalf of Rome. Greatness – whether this be the greatness of a general, an orator, or a poet – must be encouraged, and the way to encourage it is for the state to publicly reward it.

> Virtue wants no other reward for toil and danger than the reward of praise and glory; and once you remove that, members of the jury, what reason is there, since the course of life is short and narrow, to wear ourselves out in work like this? If the mind didn't anticipate the future and if the physical limits of our lives also marked the boundary of our consciousness, we certainly wouldn't batter ourselves on such great labors, or give ourselves pain from so much worry and wakefulness, or struggle so often for life itself. But every person of worth has within himself a virtue that night and day urges on the mind with the spurs of glory and warns us not to cast away the remembrance of our name at the end of life, but to make it last through all the generations to come.[30]

In rewarding poets of genius like Archias, the Romans would not only be showing piety to the gods who had granted them the gifts of poetic genius, but they would also be promising a like reward to other young men, like Cicero and Caesar, who would undertake great works on behalf of the state, if they saw a hope of glory and honor to be found in it.

[28] Cicero, *Pro Archia*, VIII–X; Berry, "Literature and Persuasion," 307–10.

[29] See also Quintilian, *The Orator's Education*, edited and translated by Donald A. Russell (Cambridge, MA: Harvard University Press, 2001), I.Pr.17–18.

[30] Cicero, *Pro Archia*, XI.28–9 (Zetzel trans.).

It seems that the jury members were persuaded – Archias was able to stay in Rome.[31]

4.5 REPUBLICAN CITIZENSHIP AND THE AUGUSTAN REVOLUTION

No magistrate or priest, least of all Augustus, pronounced a formal end to the Republic. But it is commonly agreed that Cicero witnessed its end, and this is how Cicero himself saw things. Cicero suffered a gruesome death on the orders of Mark Antony – his head and right hand were chopped off, and then nailed to the speakers' platform (*rostra*) in the Roman forum. In the years before his death, partly as a kind of self-comfort, Cicero wrote a series of treatises on philosophical and legal topics. Two of his earlier treatises, *The Republic* and *The Laws*, had been inspired by Plato's texts of the same name.[32]

In *The Republic*, Cicero offered the following definition of the Republic:

> A republic is the property (*res*) of a people . . . not any collection of human beings brought together in any sort of way, but an assemblage of people in large numbers associated in a shared understanding of rightness and a partnership for the common good (*iuris consensu et utilitatis communione societatus*).[33]

A republic, in our modern language, is a public good, a civil society, or "commonwealth," existing because of joint social power in an organized legal community. The legal community exists, according to Cicero, because there is consensus about what is right (*ius*), and because there is a partnership (*societas*) in the common good. In this definition of the Republic, moreover, we can see close semantic links between communal membership/belonging (citizenship) and property/possession.[34]

Romans developed their conceptions of citizenship in relation to people they did not consider to be citizens but with whom they often had intimate relations. These included slaves, as well as allies (*societates*). Relations with the allies had often been specified in treaties of alliance, or in the treaties by which fighting ceased with peoples defeated in war. Certain rights (*iura*) became identified as linking the Romans with allied peoples, in particular the right to enter into binding agreements that would be enforced according to Roman law (*ius commercium*), as well as the

31 Berry, "Literature and Persuasion," 295.

32 Cicero on the end of the Republic: *Letters to Atticus*, Volume II, edited and translated by D. R. Shackleton Bailey (Cambridge, MA: Harvard University Press, 1999), Letter 92 (IV.18). Cicero's death: Beard, *SPQR*, Chapter 9. Cicero's philosophical treatises: Charles Brittain, *Introduction to Cicero: On Academic Scepticism* (Indianapolis: Hackett Publishing Co., 2006); Cicero, *De Re Publica, De Legibus*, translated by C. W. Keyes (Cambridge, MA: Harvard University Press, 1928); James E. G. Zetzel, *Cicero on the Commonwealth and on the Laws*, 2nd ed. (Cambridge, UK: Cambridge University Press, 2017).

33 Cicero, *De Re Publica*, I.XXV.39 (following Keyes, with adaptation).

34 Zetzel, *Cicero on the Commonwealth*, xxxi, 32.

right to a legal marriage (*ius conubium*), which would mean citizenship and inheritance for children of the marriage.[35]

Furthermore, as Roman power was extending beyond the Italian peninsula, legal freedoms (*libertates*) were granted to the Greek, Asian, and north African cities that were being incorporated into Rome. These legal freedoms, as we saw in Chapter 3, were supposed to mean protection against onerous impositions by senior magistrates exercising *imperium*, such as burdensome taxes, military conscriptions, and the requirement to lodge and feed the Roman soldiers.

Citizenship and treaty-based rights, in other words, were like zones of protection. Within the zone of protection, magistrates wielding the power of *imperium* were supposed to hold themselves back. And, moreover, within the zone of protection, citizens were empowered to do certain kinds of things – to enter legal marriages, inherit property, and make binding agreements. Standing behind this zone of protection was the collective power of the Roman state (*res publica*), which grew alongside Roman military power. Paradoxically, then, citizenship was a zone of protection from Roman military power, a protection that was real and effective because of Roman military power.

Caesar's nephew and adopted heir, Octavian/Augustus, borrowed many strategies from his uncle in building an empire from the old and shattered *res publica*. In the wake of Caesar's murder on the Senate floor in 44 BC, Octavian had to fight his potential rivals for power – generals like Mark Antony who had once commanded soldiers alongside Caesar. In the year 31 BC, Octavian won his famous naval battle against Mark Antony and Cleopatra at Actium. Renamed Caesar Augustus, he quickly began taking steps to reorganize the Republic, steps that nominally preserved Republican institutions, while transforming them into supports for autocratic power.[36]

From the time of Caesar Augustus forward, the rulership of the emperor rested on a convergence of legal, military, and religious powers. At the core of these was the *imperium*, the power of a senior Roman magistrate to issue commands and to compel obedience to those commands through violence. Behind this stood the organized power of armies. There was also the sacrosanct power of the plebeian tribune, the quasi-religious figure who had become a popular agent of lawmaking

35 Jane F. Gardner, *Being a Roman Citizen* (London: Routledge, 1993); Herbert Felix Jolowicz and Barry Nicholas, *Historical Introduction to the Study of Roman Law*, 3rd ed. (Cambridge, UK: Cambridge University Press, 1972), 58–74; Adrian N. Sherwin-White, *The Roman Citizenship*, 2nd ed. (Oxford: Clarendon Press, 1973); *cf.* Orlando Patterson, *Freedom in the Making of Western Culture* (New York: Basic Books, 1991).

36 Adrian Goldsworthy, *Augustus: First Emperor of Rome* (New Haven: Yale University Press, 2014); Jolowicz and Nicholas, *Historical Introduction*, 321–52. Important narrative sources for the Augustan transformation: Appian, *The Civil Wars*, volumes 3–4 in the Loeb Classical Library edition by Horace White (Cambridge, MA: Harvard University Press, 1913); Cassius Dio, *Roman History* (Loeb Classical Library edition in nine volumes, edited by Earnest Cary); Suetonius, *Lives of the Caesars* (revised Loeb edition, edited by Jeffrey Henderson, 1998); Velleius Paterculus, *Compendium of Roman History*, edited by Frederick Shipley (Cambridge, MA: Harvard University Press, 1924).

during the later Republican period. This was reinforced by the *auspicia*, the authority to take auspices and divine the will of the gods. From these adapted, Republican foundations – the authority to command and compel obedience, together with religiously sanctioned powers of law-giving and law-finding – the emperor's constitutional position expanded.[37]

Augustus was deeply conservative in many of his reforms of family law and religion. Nonetheless, with the active cooperation of the Senate and the popular assemblies, he managed over time to concentrate the most important religious and legal powers in himself. By the time of his death, in addition to holding the powers of a plebeian tribune and a specially tailored *imperium* – valid both within and beyond the sacred boundary of Rome, the *pomerium* – he was the chief priest (*pontifex maximus*) and diviner (*augur*). After his death he was legally named a god and referred to as the deified (*divi*) Augustus.[38]

Because the army had become a significant source of instability in the late Republic – when soldiers followed charismatic and powerful generals like Julius Caesar into wars against other Romans – Augustus focused early energies on its reorganization. One of his most important steps was to complete the transformation of army service into a profession, increasing the number of noncitizen auxiliaries who were recruited for army service. Theoretically, the army remained a citizen militia, but in reality the men fighting and dying for Rome's protection were increasingly noncitizen provincials. Army camps at the edges of the empire became permanent towns which linked Roman citizens and barbarian outsiders, with dramatic implications for the future.[39]

Over time, the position of supremacy enjoyed by the emperor came to be called a "prerogative." One important way in which an emperor exercised his prerogative

37 *Res Gestae Divi Augusti*, edited and translated by Alison E. Cooley (Cambridge, UK: Cambridge University Press, 2009), chapters 1–7; Werner Eck, "The Emperor, the Law, and Imperial Administration," in *The Oxford Handbook of Roman Law and Society*, edited by Paul J. Du Plessis, Clifford Ando, and Kaius Tuori (Oxford: Oxford University Press, 2016), 98–110; Ronald Syme, *The Roman Revolution* (Oxford: Oxford University Press, 1939), 37, 337. For further discussions of the imperial constitution and religion, see J. H. W. G. Liebeschuetz, *Continuity and Change in Roman Religion* (Oxford: Clarendon Press, 1979), 1–54; Lintott, *Imperium Romanum*, ll. 501, 1102, 1228–48; Andrew Lintott, *Cicero as Evidence: A Historian's Companion* (Oxford: Oxford University Press, 2008); Millar, *Emperor*, 208–9, 509. Adrian Goldsworthy's narrative biography, cited in the previous note, is enormously helpful in chronologically tracing the development of Augustus' imperial powers, many of which were urged on him.

38 Mary Beard, John North, and Simon Price, *Religions of Rome, Vol. I: A History* (Cambridge, UK: Cambridge University Press, 1998), 182–92; Arnold Hugh Martin Jones, *Studies in Roman Government and Law* (New York: Barnes & Noble, 1968); Walter K. Lacey, *Augustus and the Principate: The Evolution of the System* (Leeds: Francis Cairns, 1996); Beth Levery, *Augustus and the Family at the Birth of the Roman Empire* (New York: Routledge, 2003); Liebeschuetz, *Continuity and Change*, 55–100.

39 Brian Campbell, *The Emperor & the Roman Army* (Oxford: Clarendon Press, 1984); Brian Campbell, *War and Society in Imperial Rome 31 BC–AD 284* (London: Routledge, 2002); Campbell, *The Roman Army*, 9–27; Adrian Goldsworthy, *The Roman Army at War, 100 B.C.–200 A.D.* (Oxford: Oxford University Press, 1998).

powers was in granting favors (*beneficia*, *privilegia*, *indulgentia*) to his soldiers and veterans. Soldiers joined the army in two ways: either by force or as volunteers. Conscription into the army by force would always be a necessary way to keep the number of soldiers up, but this could not be relied upon to produce loyal, effective soldiers. Young provincial men needed to believe that it was in their interest to join the army. One way to make them believe this was to promise them benefits (*beneficia*). At its core, the *imperium* was a military command, and socially it was only as powerful as the soldiers' obedience would make it.[40]

Perhaps the most highly prized *beneficium* received by veterans of the early imperial wars was land. However, the grant of land was administratively complex and expensive, and in any case the number of soldiers exceeded the plots of land available. But there were other privileges that emperors could grant to make army service appealing: tax exemptions and immunities from certain types of punishment for citizen legionaries, and citizenship for noncitizen auxiliaries. Beginning with Claudius (AD 41–54) – Augustus' third successor in the Julio-Claudian line of emperors – special diplomas (*diplomata*) granting legal privileges, including Roman citizenship and a legal right to legitimate marriage (*ius conubium*), were issued to reward veterans upon completion of their military service.[41]

A grant of Roman citizenship and the right to legitimate marriage would have been very valuable to soldiers. Citizenship and the right to legitimate marriage meant legal and economic rights for children and family: the capacity to begin building wealth that could be accumulated and inherited by future generations, and someday, perhaps, to become a family of honor and wealth in a local community.

40 During the Republican period, *praerogativa* had named a group of Roman citizens (a "century" or "tribe") who had the right to first register their votes in a legal assembly. From at least the fourth century, the word was used to indicate the Roman emperor's supremacy. Cicero, *On Divination*, 1.45.103; Anonymous, "Panegyric of Constantine," in *In Praise of the Later Roman Emperors: The Panegyrici Latini*, edited by Charles E. V. Nixon and Barbara Saylor Rodgers (Berkeley: University of California Press, 1994), 221, 573. On the relevance of *beneficia* in motivating soldiers, see Campbell, *War and Society*, chapters 2, 5.

41 For a general description of the *diplomata* for veterans and the privileges they granted, see Campbell, *The Roman Army*, 193–221. A prohibition against marriage before the end of military service had probably originated with Augustus, as part of an effort to promote military discipline and dedication after the civil wars of Republican collapse. Not surprisingly, however, soldiers nonetheless formed sexual unions with women during their time in service, and, when these resulted in children, the children would be born with the negative legal status of illegitimacy. Moreover, when the mothers of such children were not Roman citizens, which was likely to be the case with soldiers serving in the provinces, their children would not only not be citizens, but would also have a very hard time inheriting any property from their fathers. To disadvantage soldiers and their families in this way was recognized as a problem, and it was for this reason that emperors began issuing military diplomas that included the right to legitimate marriage. Brian Campbell, "The Marriage of Soldiers under the Empire," *The Journal of Roman Studies* 68 (1978): 153–66; Martin Goodman, *The Roman World 44 BC–AD 180*, 2nd ed. (London: Routledge, 2012), 56, 123–32. For a discussion of Claudius' role in consolidating and regularizing the imperial administrative framework, see Arnaldo Momigliano, *Claudius: The Emperor and His Achievement*, translated by W. D. Hogarth (Westport: Greenwood Press, 1981), 41–53.

This was a promise of socioeconomic mobility and status, a promise of full participation in the glory of Rome, including the zone of protection that it offered to its privileged citizens. Experience going back to the late Republic showed that such a promise was effective in producing soldiers who were willing to fight (and die) for Rome.[42]

Like patents, military diplomas were formal legal documents that promised a kind of intangible property: the inheritable right to be treated as a citizen of Rome, and to benefit from the legal protections of Roman law. This was a promise that bound foreign soldiers to the Roman *res publica* they protected. What was so obviously different about the military diploma was the way in which it tied the recipient personally to the emperor.

Today, a patent comes from an abstract entity, for example, the United States of America, which stands for the united power of approximately 300 million people. In imperial Rome, a military diploma came from the person of the emperor. It was to this person, first and foremost, that the soldier owed his loyalty and service, and to whom he swore his oath (*sacramentum*). It was from this person, likewise, that a barbarian provincial might receive his legal status, as citizen, upon completing his term of service.

4.6 LAW AND LETTERS IN IMPERIAL ROME

Caesar Augustus had continued Republican practices in working through the Roman voting assemblies, securing their cooperation in enacting laws and electing magistrates, using them to indirectly shape the Roman regime of social power. Under Augustus' stepson and adopted son Tiberius (AD 14–37), however, the electoral and legal functions of the assemblies were mostly taken over by the Senate. By the end of the first century, the assemblies were no longer called together in Rome. Performative debates and discussions did not take place, as in the time of Cicero, before a motley convention of the people but behind closed doors – either the doors of the Senate or those of an imperial palace.[43]

The form of empire was at first ambiguous, since the title (*princeps*) used by the early emperors was closely associated with their role as senatorial magistrates.

[42] Campbell, *The Roman Army*, 193–221; Campbell, "Marriage of Soldiers," 153–66; Margaret M. Roxan, *Roman Military Diplomas 1978–1984* (London: Institute of Archaeology, 1985).

[43] In addition to the primary sources already referenced, Tacitus now becomes an important narrative source, particularly the *Annals* and the *Histories*. I rely on the Loeb Classical Library editions, with translations by John Jackson and Clifford H. Moore. On Tacitus and the "Tacitean" historical tradition, see Ronald Syme's two-volume *Tacitus* (Oxford: Clarendon Press, 1958); Torrey James Luce and Anthony John Woodman, *Tacitus and the Tacitean Tradition* (Princeton: Princeton University Press, 2014). On the transfer of electoral and legislative powers to the Senate: *Annals* I:XV; Barbara Levick, *Tiberius The Politician*, 2nd ed. (London: Routledge, 1999). On the overall transition from a politics of public performance in motley conventions and assemblies to performances occurring behind closed doors, see and compare Cassius Dio, *Roman History*, 53.19; Syme, *Roman Revolution*, 406–11.

Nevertheless, the combination of *imperium*, priesthoods, and tribunician powers made the emperors a primary source of public law, popular appeal, and privilege-granting, backed by the cooperation of the Senate, as well as magnates in the provinces and cities of the empire. In practice, however, the emperor's legal authority was often exercised through written documents coming out of his palace (or his army camp): letters (*epistula*), responses to written requests called *rescripts*, *edicts* addressed to an entire group of people, and *mandates* to officials, often provincial governors, to carry out specific actions.[44]

In the empire, in other words, letters became an essential legal vehicle, one that served both to articulate law and to grant privileges. Such letters could speak very generally, or they could speak quite specifically, to one single petitioner, who might range in status from the lowliest freedman to the most illustrious of senators. The emperor's range of lawmaking and law-finding powers was thus breathtakingly wide, but it is important to remember that it depended, fundamentally, on the cooperation of wealthy families, on the army, on a growing class of civilian functionaries (who were often freedmen or *equites*), and on local political communities – colonies (*colonia*), cities (*municipia*), and towns – throughout the empire.[45]

Letter-based privileges provided a legal foundation, in other words, for constituting a new, imperial society, one that built on Republican traditions while nonetheless forming something new. We have seen already how this process worked in forming an army that depended upon and served the emperor. Equally important, however, was the transformation of Rome's senatorial aristocracy into an order (*ordo*) that would serve the emperor with the inherited wealth and honor of its families,

44 Eck, "The Emperor," 98–110; Tor Hauken, *Petition and Response: An Epigraphic Study of Petitions to Roman Emperors 181–249* (Bergen: The Norwegian Institute at Athens, 1998), 296–317; William Warwick Buckland, *A Text-Book of Roman Law: From Augustus to Justinian*, 3rd ed. Revised by Peter Stein (Cambridge, UK: Cambridge University Press, 1963), 1–39; Simon Corcoran, "The Codex of Justinian: The Life of a Text through 1500 Years," in *The Codex of Justinian: A New Annotated Translation*, edited by Bruce W. Frier (Cambridge, UK: Cambridge University Press, 2016), cvi–cx; Simon Corcoran, *The Empire of the Tetrachs: Imperial Pronouncements and Government AD 284–324*, Revised paperback ed. (Oxford: Clarendon Press, 2000); Michael H. Crawford (ed.), *Roman Statutes* (London: Institute of Classical Studies, 1996); Tony Honoré, *Emperors and Lawyers*, 2nd ed. (Oxford: Clarendon Press, 1994), 1–32; Dario Mantovani, "More than Codes: Roman Ways of Organizing and Giving Access to Legal Information," in *Oxford Handbook of Roman Law and Society*, 23–41; Millar, *Emperor*, 203–72, 368; Richard J. A. Talbert, *The Senate of Imperial Rome* (Princeton: Princeton University Press, 1984), 431–59.

45 Mantovani, "More than Codes," 33–4; Millar, *Emperor*, 275–549. An additional category of letter-based law-giving, the *decretum*, was an imperial verdict given at the end of a public hearing. Hauken, *Petition and Response*, 298–9. On the role of slaves and freedmen in imperial administration, see Syme, *Roman Revolution*, 408–10. For focus on the later Roman empire, see Arnold Hugh Martin Jones, *The Later Roman Empire 284–602* (Baltimore: Johns Hopkins University Press, 1964), 321–65. For patterns of continuity and change in late antique and early medieval Italy, see Truesdell Sparhawk Brown, *Gentlemen and Officers: Imperial Administration and Aristocratic Power in Byzantine Italy A.D. 554–800* (Hertford: British School at Rome, 1984).

together with the reinforcement of a wealthy, upper-middle rank of families ("equestrians"), who would serve as economic and governmental agents for the empire.[46]

Acting with the powers of the ancient censors, before whom Romans had been periodically required to render an accounting of their property and their morality, Augustus consolidated this constitutional process by reducing the number of senators. He also developed new channels for entry into the Senate, channels that depended on a grant of favor from the emperor. By controlling entry into the Senate, Augustus and his successors controlled the composition of this legal body of privileged families, who, despite their dependence, remained vital to the functioning of imperial society into the sixth century AD.[47]

4.7 PRIVILEGED ORDERS, LOCAL COMMUNITIES, AND EARLY PRECURSORS FOR INTELLECTUAL PROPERTY

Entry into the "senatorial order" (*ordine senatorio*) became a favor (*beneficium, indulgentium*) that was within the emperor's prerogative to grant. In a society that marked social rankings through articles of dress, this elevation of legal and social status was symbolized through the grant of a broad purple stripe (*latus clavus*), to be worn with the *toga virilis*, the garment of an elite Roman man. Although election to a magistracy would still have been required in most cases, a grant of the *latus clavus* marked a man as someone whose aspirations to the Senate had been blessed by the emperor. Successful entry into the senatorial order meant entry into a system of honors (*honores*) and loyal service (*officia*) that constituted Rome's civilian and military administration.[48]

This ideal of honor and loyal service was also available to equestrian families that were not able to reach the senatorial *ordo* but who nonetheless put forward fathers and sons for service in imperial and/or municipal offices, beginning often with military service in the provinces and rising to the honor of service in Rome or in

46 Millar, *Emperor*, 275–361. Rome's class and status hierarchies had been fundamentally transformed by a combination of legal and social factors, which are traditionally viewed as beginning with reforms initiated around 133 BC by the Gracchi brothers. The Social Wars leading to expansion of Roman citizenship across Italy can be seen as an outcome of increasing political violence and unwillingness to conform to Republican norms for political disagreement, extending from 133–88 BC. The Senate of Cicero's day had, according to this view, already become a very different type of body, compared to the Senate that Polybius would have known. For more detailed discussions, see Badian, *Publicans*, 82–118; Flower, *Republics*, chs. 4–6; Jones, *Studies*, 3–26.

47 Millar, *Emperor*, 293–361; Talbert, *Senate*, 15–16; Richard J. A. Talbert, "Augustus and the Senate," *Greece and Rome* 31(1) (1984): 55–63. On early foundations for the Senatorial *ordo*, as a status-grouping distinct from the Senatorial body of political functionaries, see Cassius Dio, *Roman History*, 52.42; Suetonius, *The Deified Augustus*, 35; Goldsworthy, *Augustus*, 219–20. For later development of the Senatorial status group, seen from the perspective of fourth-century Christianization in the western empire, see Michele Renee Salzman, *The Making of a Christian Aristocracy: Social and Religious Change in the Western Roman Empire* (Cambridge, MA: Harvard University Press, 2002).

48 Jones, *Studies*, 30–2, 180 n.15; Millar, *Emperor*, 275–361; Richard P. Saller, *Personal Patronage under the Early Empire* (Cambridge, UK: Cambridge University Press), 50–78; Talbert, *Senate*, 9–16.

local civic councils (*curia*), which were modeled on the Roman Senate. Here again, grants of favor from the emperor provided the foundation for a social system of rank, privilege, and obligation, one that constituted imperial society both within and beyond Rome, from Britain to north Africa and western Asia.[49]

In the early second century AD, for example, the emperor Trajan (98–117), through a grant of special legal privilege (*beneficio indulgentiae*), recognized a "free and confederated" (*libera et foederata*) city called Amisus, located in what is today western Turkey, on the southern shore of the Black Sea. In common with other cities of the province (Bithynia-Pontus) to which Amisus belonged, citizens over age 22 were eligible to serve as minor magistrates in their city and could stand for election to their civic council (*curia*). In addition, however, citizens were recognized as members of a self-governing city. This meant that their town council held specific privileges, including the right to create local organizations (*collegia*) that might perform a range of economic and social functions in the town.[50]

The earliest developments in imperial prerogative, privilege-granting, and diplomatic practices are difficult to trace due to limited sources. There are good reasons to believe, though, that legal practice and scholarship had been developing into a specialized, intellectual discipline, a development that is especially clear under Trajan's successor Hadrian (117–38), and that continued through the period of the "Antonine" and "Severan" imperial dynasties (AD 138–235). Legal texts and scholarship from this period have left traces in European legal traditions, and, in hindsight, are viewed as the pinnacle of "classical" Roman law. This was also the period in which Roman citizenship was finally extended to all freeborn men within the empire (AD 212).[51]

During this period of classical Roman jurisprudence, categories of legal privilege were defined more formally. One of these involved rights to hold markets and fairs, sometimes including tax exemptions for these markets and fairs. Another developing category of legal privilege involved rights to participate in religious associations and guilds (*collegia*). According to the jurist Gaius, writing sometime in the later second

49 Millar, *Emperor*, 300–61. For a window into the social and legal world of Senatorial and equestrian elites, including their relations with provincial and municipal elites, the letter collection of the Younger Pliny is an outstanding source: Pliny, *Letters*, Loeb Classical Library edition in two volumes, translated by Betty Radice (Cambridge, MA: Harvard University Press, 1969); Adrian Nicholas Sherwin-White, *The Letters of Pliny: A Historical and Social Commentary* (Oxford: Clarendon Press, 1966).

50 Pliny, *Letters*, 10.79–80, 10.92–3, 10.114–15; Sherwin-White, *Commentary*, 669–75, 686–9. Julian Bennett, *Trajan Optimus Princeps: A Life and Times* (London: Routledge, 1997).

51 Honoré, *Emperors and Lawyers*, 1–32; Tony Honoré, *Ulpian: Pioneer of Human Rights*, 2nd ed. (Oxford: Oxford University Press, 2002); Jolowicz and Nicholas, *Historical Introduction*, 321–468; Jones, *Later Roman Empire*, 3–36; Mantovani, "More than Codes," 35–6. For explanation of Hadrian's importance for later developments in Roman law, see Jill Harries, *Law and Empire in Late Antiquity* (Cambridge, UK: Cambridge University Press, 1999) [Kindle ed.], ll. 228–97; Fritz Pringsheim, "The Legal Policy and Reforms of Hadrian," *Journal of Roman Studies* 24 (1934): 141–53.

century, the general rule was that corporate associations like *collegia* could only be constituted through special permission, which would typically be granted through imperial privilege. There was an exception to the general rule, however, for lower-ranking citizens (and slaves), if they only met once a month and paid a small fee. Exceptions were also recognized for certain religious groups, and for traders or craftsmen who served the community, such as bakers and ship owners. These could form guilds, and some of these guilds were able to grant their members a further valued privilege: freedom from civic obligations.[52]

Ominously, service in the local senate or town council was increasingly perceived as a burden to escape rather than a benefit to prize. Local civic obligations of town councilors, *munera* in the Latin-speaking west and *leiturgeia* in the Greek-speaking east, included a range of services required to keep local communities functioning. Rather than being funded from collective tax revenues, as is typically the case for local governments today, these expenses were paid from the inherited wealth (*patrimonium*) of local town councilors.[53]

At the best of times, *munera* and liturgies had been expensive, but they had been compensated by the glory and honor of patronage, which also meant a capacity to generate further wealth. To be a patron was to be a father, so to speak, of one's local community, and to earn glory by glorifying the community. However, when tax burdens increased within the empire, and when money became inflated or scarce, the families of town councilors were burdened by the requirement to fund both the taxes for imperial armies and their local communities. Exceptions from *munera* ("immunities") were actively sought and could be granted as privileges to men who caught the eye and favor of the emperor.[54]

As part of a broader, cultural reaction against the excesses and moral degeneration epitomized by the *imperium* of Nero (AD 54–68), the Flavian dynasty of Vespasian (AD 69–79) and his two sons – Titus (AD 79–81) and Domitian (AD 81–96) – inaugurated a series of legal reforms. According to Suetonius, Vespasian showed a special concern for legal records and privileges granted to individuals, initiating a search for

52 Relatively early evidence for market privileges in the empire is found in an inscription based on an imperial rescript issued in 238 to the village of Scaptopara, located in what is today Bulgaria, then the Roman province of Thrace. Hauken, *Petition and Response*, 74–139, especially 115–17. See also Pliny, Letters, V.4, 8; Bruce W. Frier (ed.), *The Codex of Justinian* (Cambridge, UK: Cambridge University Press, 2016, hereafter abbreviated CJ), 4.60.1; Alan Watson (ed.), *The Digest of Justinian* (Philadelphia: University of Philadelphia Press, 1985), 50.11; L. De Light and P. W. De Neeve, "Ancient Periodic Markets: Festivals and Fairs," *Athenaeum* 66 (1988): 391–416. Latin text for classical Roman law texts available online at *The Roman Law Library*, founded by Alexandr Koptev and Yves Lassard, https://droitromain.univ-grenoble-alpes.fr/ (accessed Jan. 30, 2019). On the *collegia*: *Digest* 3.4.1; cf. 47.22; J. A. Crook, *Law and Life of Rome* (Ithaca: Cornell University Press, 1967), 264–68; Fergus Millar, "Empire and City, Augustus to Julian: Obligations, Excuses, and Status," *The Journal of Roman Studies* 73 (1983): 76–96.

53 *Digest* 50; Jones, *Later Roman Empire*, 11–14, 724–66; J. H. W. G. Liebeschuetz, *The Decline and Fall of the Roman City* (Oxford: Oxford University Press, 2001), 2–3.

54 *Digest* 50; Jones, *Later Roman Empire*, 724–66.

copies and restoring the bronze tablets upon which such privileges were recorded, as part of a broader restoration of Roman civic architecture. Beyond material infrastructure and legal records, Vespasian showed a marked concern for legal process, initiating a reform of the Roman courts, connected with a censorial reform of the senatorial and equestrian orders that staffed the courts and served on Roman juries. Most notably for our purposes, however, Vespasian also established a system of salaried chairs for Latin and Greek rhetoricians, rewarding outstanding artists and an inventive engineer with prizes for their creative efforts.[55]

Rescripts from Vespasian and Domitian offer further evidence for imperial efforts to encourage literary, rhetorical, technical, and artistic work through grants of privilege. A jurist named Arcadius Charisius later recalled that both Vespasian and Hadrian had issued rescripts "to the effect that teachers who are released from civil *munera* and grammarians and orators and doctors and philosophers had been granted immunity from billeting [of soldiers] by the emperors." As a later recollection, this conflates privileges granted by Vespasian and Hadrian, but it nonetheless attests to a striking shift toward prioritizing the encouragement of literary and technical work, through grants of imperial privilege.[56]

Pliny's letter collection provides striking evidence for the way in which such privileges might be claimed by a provincial intellectual. According to a letter exchange between Pliny and Trajan, a philosopher named Flavius Archippus had tried to wriggle out of onerous jury services, claiming immunity on the basis of his status as a philosopher. Due to questions about Archippus' legal standing, Pliny forwarded imperial letters from Domitian and Nerva (AD 96–98), the former attesting to privileges for Archippus personally, and the latter attesting to a policy of affirming Domitian's privileges. Taken together, these ambiguously supported Archippus' claim for privileged exemption from jury service, which Trajan upheld, subject to the possibility that further evidence might come to light.[57]

What we see here is the beginning of a movement toward the privileging of intellectual activities, whether these be the teaching of grammarians, the knowledgeable work of doctors, or the literary work of rhetoricians. Privileges providing exemptions from burdensome obligations (*munera*) are being granted in order to encourage learned, literary, and technical activities. The vision of Cicero, so admired by the younger Pliny, is being realized in the imperial priorities of the Flavians and their successors.

55 Suetonius, *The Deified Vespasian*, 8–19; Andrew Wallace-Hadrill, *Suetonius*, 2d ed. (London: Bristol Classical Press, 1995).

56 M. McCrum and A. G. Woodhead, *Select Documents of the Flavian Emperors*, AD 68–96 (Cambridge, UK: Cambridge University Press, 1961), 135-6; *Digest* 50.4.18.30; Sherwin-White, *Commentary*, 287.

57 Pliny, *Letters*, 10.58–60; Sherwin-White, *Commentary*, 639–46. It is noteworthy, however, that Domitian had expelled philosophers from Rome and Italy toward the end of his *imperium*. Suetonius, *Domitian*, 10.

The development of law, as an intellectual discipline, is part of this broader movement for prioritizing learned, literary, and rhetorical activities.

4.8 *IUS RESPONDENDI* – THE RIGHT OF RESPONDING

According to the later recollection of a jurist named Pomponius – writing in the early second century AD – the principate of Caesar Augustus had marked an important turning point in the scholarly writings of jurists, and in the advisory role played by jurists. Before the time of Augustus, the activities of jurists were unregulated, and therefore their authority as jurists was entirely of their own making. People might consult them as to the meaning and application of the law, and they might give opinions in response, but their standing as jurists came from their own learning and social position, not from the emperor's oversight and approval.[58]

During the reign of Augustus, however, things had changed. According to Pomponius:

> It was the deified Augustus who, in order to enhance the authority of the law, first established that opinions might be given under his authority. And from that time this began to be sought as a favor (*beneficium*). As a consequence of this, our most excellent emperor Hadrian issued a rescript on an occasion when some men of praetorian rank were petitioning him for permission to grant opinions; he said that this was by custom not merely begged for but earned and that he [the emperor] would accordingly be delighted if whoever had faith in himself would prepare himself for giving opinions to the people at large.[59]

Augustus, in other words, transformed the giving of juristic opinions about the meaning of the law into an officially granted privilege, or *beneficium*. The legal power "to say what the law means" became a privilege controlled by the emperors, one that was evidently desirable. From what Pomponius says, it sounds like at some point an official seal was issued by the emperors to the privileged jurists, who held the right of responding (*ius respondendi*). They presumably used this seal to authenticate their juristic opinions as being officially sanctioned and therefore authoritative. These juristic opinions became a source of law, alongside statutes, plebiscites, and resolutions of the Senate. Hadrian's innovation, as Pomponius described it, was to require some specialized education and preparation, as a prerequisite for holding this considerable legal authority.[60]

As Gaius describes them, the juristic opinions were responses of practical wisdom (*responsa prudentium*). They were "the opinions and advice of those entrusted with the task of building up the law (*iura condere*)." Where they all agreed, their opinion was equivalent to a statute enacted by the Roman people, a *lex*. Where the jurists

58 *Digest* 1.2.2.48–53.
59 *Digest* 1.2.2.49.
60 *Digest* 1.2.2.49.

disagreed with one another, magistrates and judges had a choice about which jurist to follow, according to another decision by the emperor Hadrian.[61]

As we can see from this discussion about the legal privileges and powers of jurists, the principate of Augustus was also a turning point in the development of jurisprudence. The decisions and communications of one man, holding supreme power in the state, had become a source of law. As the jurist Ulpian would later say, "A decision given by the emperor has the force of a statute. . . . Therefore, whatever the emperor has determined by a letter over his signature or has decreed on judicial investigation or has pronounced in an interlocutory matter or has prescribed by an edict is undoubtedly a law (*lex*)." Because the emperor was a source of law, his letters became a vehicle for communicating law, which was a matter of his own personal determination.[62]

There was, then, a close parallel between the *responsa prudentium* of the jurists and the legal determinations of the emperors. Both were answers given in response to questions that were asked about the law. Whatever the emperor decided in response to a question that was put to him by a petitioner was law, and, by virtue of their privilege from the emperor, whatever the jurists said in response to a question put to them was valid as to the meaning of the law.

In the case of privileges from the emperor, moreover, questions arose about how they should be interpreted. According to a decision from the emperor Nerva (AD 96–8), letter-based enactments of previous emperors were to be treated as binding precedents by subsequent emperors. According to the jurist Ulpian, however, in cases where a decision of the emperor was only applicable to an individual – either in granting him a special privilege or indulgence, or imposing a special penalty – no precedent was established by the emperor's decision. Such enactments were purely *ad hominem* and should not be considered laws. At the same time, though, according to the jurist Javolenus, privileges (*beneficia*) from the emperor should be interpreted as broadly as possible, since they proceed from the emperor's "divine generosity."[63]

4.9 RATIONALIZING ROMAN LAW

These differences of opinion show us that the world of Roman law was becoming complex. Part of the complexity, it should be emphasized, comes from the fact that the jurists' writings are preserved only in fragments. As we will see in the next chapter, projects of legal codification undertaken in the period of the late Roman empire involved fragmentary preservation of the jurists' writings, with recontextualization of the fragments in ways that made sense for Roman societies in late

61 *The Institutes of Gaius*, translated by W. M. Gordon and O. F. Robinson, Latin text of Seckel and Kuebler (Ithaca: Cornell University Press, 1988), 1.1.7.

62 *Digest* 1.4.1.

63 Pliny, *Letters*, 10.58; *Digest* 1.4.

antiquity. It is therefore quite difficult to use the jurists' writings, in the form that we have them now, to reconstruct the world of the classical Roman law.

There is one exception, however. In 1816, the German historian Barthold Niebuhr discovered a manuscript among the records of the cathedral chapter at Verona, in Italy. The parchment leather manuscript contained writings of the patristic scholar Jerome (AD 347–420). Niebuhr could tell, however, that the manuscript was a palimpsest, meaning that the text copied from Jerome had been written over an even older text. By carefully studying the imprint left behind by the older letters, a famous German scholar of Roman law and legal history – Friedrich Carl von Savigny (1779–1861) – was able to decipher the older text. The palimpsest turned out to be a nearly complete copy of a legal textbook from sometime in the second century AD, called the *Institutes*, written by the jurist Gaius. Supplemented with more recent fragments of the text discovered in the first half of the twentieth century, we now have a nearly complete edition of this text.[64]

Because it is an introductory textbook, the *Institutes* of Gaius provides us with something like a conceptual map of Roman law. Drawing on Gaius, then, we can enter the world of Roman law, and especially of Roman property law. This was a wide-ranging, complex, and surprisingly modern world, one that brings us close to conceptions like modern intellectual property law, but not all the way there.

Gaius' opening to his four-volume treatise is very revealing: "All peoples who are governed by laws (*leges*) and customs (*mores*) use law (*ius*) which is partly theirs alone and partly shared (*commune*) by all mankind." Gaius goes on to define the law that is specific to a given people (*populus*) as "state law" (*ius civile*): law that is specific (*proprium*) to a particular state (*civitas*). On the other hand, Gaius says, the law that is shared by all human beings is law that is constituted by natural reason (*ratio naturalis*), and it is applied the same way everywhere. Because it is common to all nations (*gentes*), it is also called the law of nations (*ius gentium*).[65]

For Gaius, writing during the period of a flourishing Roman empire, law had become universal. There were different laws for different states, but there was also a common law rooted in shared human nature – a law that was valid between people of different nations. An example of a nationally specific body of law might be the body of law that applied to the Jewish nation, which Rome had dispersed under the emperor Vespasian but which was nonetheless permitted to retain certain rights of national self-governance. Between Romans and Jews, peoples whose national laws differed but who were both part of the Roman empire, the law that applied was the law of all peoples, the *ius gentium*, a law in which principles were universal because they were based in a universal, natural reason.

64 Jolowicz and Nicholas, *Historical Introduction*, 389; A. Arthur Schiller, *Roman Law; Mechanisms of Development* (The Hague: Mouton Publishers, 1970), 43.

65 Gaius, *Institutes*, 1.1.

This notion of a universal, natural law will become a vital foundation of modern intellectual property law. Here is a foundation for semantic formality in Roman law, for semantic legal ordering.

4.10 SEMANTIC FORMALITY IN LAW: TYPES OF LAW AND CATEGORIES OF THINGS

Gaius began his treatise by describing the sources of law. Identifying and distinguishing sources of law helps us to see where the law comes from, and especially where the law derives its authority and validity. This information becomes especially important when a law is questioned in the course of its application to a dispute, or when we need to decide how to read laws together that might conflict. Distinguishing sources of law is essential, in other words, when it comes time to formally interpret laws, to decide what they mean, and to determine whether (or to what extent) they are binding.

After telling us about where law comes from, and how its authority is derived, Gaius tells us that there are three basic types or categories of law. "All our law is about persons, things, or actions."[66]

With respect to persons, the main distinctions are between free persons and slaves, and between citizens and foreigners. Of equal importance for us is Gaius' second category: the law of things (*res*). Here there are two fundamental categories: things that can constitute private wealth passed down through inheritance (*patrimonium*) and those that cannot. In talking about the law of things, in other words, we are talking about the law of property. Suddenly we can see in a deeper way what Cicero was talking about when he said the Roman Republic (*res publica*) was a kind of public property, a common wealth.[67]

The part of Roman property law that was most significant to the emergence of intellectual property was the part dealing with acquisition of property, particularly the acquisition of property that did not yet belong to anyone, which the jurists called a *res nullius* – a thing belonging to no one. Some things belonging to no one were public things, belonging to the whole body of the people. These could never be transformed into private property, and would always remain *res nullius*. However, some things could be transformed into private property if they were acquired in a legally recognized way.[68]

One legally recognized way of acquiring property that had previously belonged to no one was by occupancy – *occupatio* – literally being the first to seize upon something, and to keep it under control. The example that Gaius and many afterward often used was the example of a wild animal. Previously the animal belonged to no one – it was a *res nullius* – but the first person to capture the animal

66 Gaius, *Institutes*, 1.2.8.
67 Gaius, *Institutes*, 2.1.
68 *Ibid.*, 2.9, 2.11.

and keep it under his control became the legitimate owner of the animal, by right of occupancy. According to the law of nature, the same general rule applied to property seized from enemies in war, including other human beings. They became property by right of occupancy.[69]

Closely connected with occupancy was accession – *accessio* – the acquisition of property by adding to property that already belongs to someone. According to the law of nature, buildings placed upon landed property, and plants added to landed property, become the property of the person who owns the land. From these principles of accession, Gaius noted, a debate had arisen among jurists about two analogous cases: the case where an artist paints something on material owned by another person, and the case where someone writes a text on material owned by another person. Who owns the painting or the text? At the time Gaius was writing, the debate seems to have been unresolved: one school of jurists argued that the person who owned the materials should own anything artistic or literary that was made from those materials, while another school of jurists argued that the maker should own the literary or artistic work.[70]

According to the emperor Justinian's later adaptation of the *Institutes*, the overall debate had been resolved by adopting a "middle view": if the thing could be returned to its constitutive materials, then the owner was the owner of the materials, but otherwise the owner was the maker. If the maker had used another's materials without permission, of course, he would have to compensate the owner of the materials, but he owned the product of his making. Furthermore, where the materials themselves were partly owned by the maker, and partly owned by another, then it was clear that the owner should be the maker. "He contributes not only his own work but also even part of the material."[71]

In the case of writers, however, it remained true that their writings "acceded" to the material they were written upon, meaning that even a great poem or history written on parchment belonging to another would be owned by the owner of the parchment. The owner of the parchment would, nonetheless, be obligated to compensate the writer for his expenses. On the other hand, in the case of a painting, the opposite rule held: a great artist would own the painting, rather than the owner of the board upon which it was painted. "It would be ridiculous for a picture by Appelles or Parrhasius to accede to a board worth almost nothing." The artist would, however, have to compensate the owner of the board for its cost.[72]

In these legal discussions about how property ownership is legally acquired by artists and writers, we see classical Roman law approaching, but not quite reaching, our modern theory of intellectual property. There does seem to be a recognition that

69 *Ibid.*, 2.66–7, 2.69.

70 *Ibid.*, 2.73–6, 2.77–9. The noun *accessio* seems to be later than Gaius (he uses a verb, *cedere*).

71 *Justinian's Institutes*, translated by Peter Birks and Grant McLeod with Latin text of Paul Krueger (Ithaca: Cornell University Press, 1987), II.1.25.

72 *Ibid.*, II.1.33–34.

artistic work, especially, can have economic value that far exceeds the value of the materials from which it is composed. This constitutes a recognition that artistic work has value, simply in virtue of its artistry, and that because of this economic value it would be unfair for ownership to vest in the person who owns the materials, under principles of accession. However, literary works are treated differently, and the overall principles are presented as a kind of compromise – or "middle view" – about how to adjudicate between two different people who each seem to have a case for owning the thing that has been made.

The modern theory of intellectual property, articulated by William Blackstone, will go a step further, conflating occupation and accession, arguing that the creator of a literary or artistic work has a property-based right to that which she has created, because she has brought something into existence that did not exist before, through her labor. As in the case of occupancy, she has acquired a *res nullius*. Here is the formalistic part of the argument. But it is the value of that which she has created, and the labor she has expended in creating it, that justifies or legitimates her ownership. Underlying this justification is the labor theory of value, articulated by John Locke, who drew on Roman law reasoning, as we will see.[73]

But this is to look far into the future. In the case of Roman law, as we see it articulated in the *Institutes* of Gaius and Justinian, there is only a rather ambivalent compromise, with occupancy and accession remaining separate bases for legal acquisition of property.

Nonetheless, what we do clearly see in Gaius is an early foundation for semantic formality in law, and for its combination with substantive rationality. Abstract legal categories and definitions of legal principles are combined with arguments about fairness and justice, together with pragmatic compromises that are presented as bringing us to a fair result, even if they do not offer strict consistency. Why should an artist be treated differently from a writer? We are not told, and doubtless it reflected cultural judgments about the relative values of their creative work.

4.11 CONCLUSION

In this chapter, we have moved from the late Republic of Cicero to the classical period of Roman jurisprudence, highlighting the important theme of membership and belonging that is reflected in Roman writings of the time. Questions of citizenship were controversial and divisive in the early Roman empire, as they are in our time. The implications of a loss of citizenship – seen in the proscriptions of the late Republic – show how vital the civic protection of the state can be, simply for personal security, but also for stability in property ownership.

[73] See Chapters 7–9.

To be a citizen (*cives*) is to be a protected member of a governing community (*civitas*), and to share in the possibilities for security of material sustenance afforded by the governing community. This is part of the sense conveyed by that very classical, Roman word – *republic* – meaning public thing, public property, or common wealth. Governing communities enable us to exist as legal persons, and as property-owning agents. In the jurists of imperial Rome, we see the implications of this, explored in ways that, with the benefit of hindsight, provide a foundation for the much later development of the modern nation-state system, linked together through intellectual property law.

By the time we reach the end of the second century AD, Roman law is flourishing as a field of scholarly and practical endeavor. The development in Roman law paralleled the development of the empire itself, from the important foundations laid by Julius Caesar and his nephew Caesar Augustus, to the periodic reforms by emperors who followed in their footsteps. From one imperial dynasty to another – Julio-Claudian to Severan – emperors and their growing cadre of personally dependent officers managed to oversee reforms that kept the basic imperial framework of legal administration functioning.

The Roman *imperium* became a stable social regime, a Roman Peace (*Pax Romana*), held together by armies overseen by praetorian prefects and by families overseen by senatorial councils, radiating outward from the central *curia* in Rome to provincial *curiae* across the empire. Grants of privilege and patronage relationships, idealized systems of beneficence and grateful service, held the system together, with the emperors at the top, theoretically accessible to all. Law, articulated rhetorically and performatively through imperial letters, became a professionalized, intellectual discipline that helped to solidify the social framework.

To be a citizen of this social world might mean many things, but one thing it clearly meant was participation in a legal community, a community that promised order and peace, with the possibility of status and wealth. Social mobility was possible to a notable degree. A barbarian outsider could acquire citizenship through service in the army, could have children who would be citizens and who might be able to acquire an advanced education in the liberal arts, becoming teachers of grammar or rhetoric, and perhaps catching the eye of powerful elites, including the emperor himself. Sponsored by those powerful elites, a rhetorician might find his way to one of the top positions in the imperial administration, perhaps even advising the emperor himself or writing his legal correspondence. A slave, too, might hope for a similar trajectory, beginning with the privilege of freedom itself.

Instruments of legal power, like privileges from the emperor, came to serve purposes that we can recognize as being very close to modern intellectual property. Such privileges functioned as an infrastructure of state power, in Michael Mann's sense, helping to bind the Roman empire together. In the letters of the younger Pliny, we can see how imperial privileges constituted a bridge between public service in positions of imperial or local responsibility – such as service in the

Senate or in a provincial governorship – and the private realm of the domestic household. When the imperial privileges extended to immunities for intellectual services – such as privileges for teachers of grammar – we can see how close the imperial legal practices involving instruments of legal power came to modern intellectual property.

But imperial legal privileges for intellectual services are not quite the same as modern intellectual property, as we can clearly see in the debates faintly preserved from classical jurisprudence. As had already been recognized by Cicero, intellectual and artistic labors have economic and political value. In the jurisprudential theory of *accessio*, granting ownership (*dominium*) to the painter of a painting, rendered upon materials belonging to another, we have come almost to the threshold of modern intellectual property, but not quite there. Fundamentally, and for the foreseeable future, intellectuals will depend upon discretionary patronage from imperial and royal elites, whose position is secured by military power.

During the first two centuries of its existence, the Roman social order came to extend over large parts of Europe, north Africa, and western Asia, establishing a set of shared cultural and social presuppositions for thinking and talking about law. While the Romans did not use our contemporary language of territorial states, governed by the rule of law, their imperial language could be quite similar. From the time of Cicero to the time of Ulpian – the age in which citizenship was extended to all freeborn men within the empire, and the age in which Roman jurists came to see themselves as priests of a new sacred calling – articulate, elite Romans established a literary tradition conveying powerful ideals of Roman law. According to these cultural ideals, Roman law is a sphere of meaningful order, of justice and rightness, debated and developed through speaking and writing and shared, to some extent, by all human beings.

The Roman law of the classical period left a significant imprint for the future, particularly in the realm of formal rationalities in law. Indeed, we can now start to distinguish two separate types of formal rationality in law: empirical formality, depending on the presence of empirically ascertainable marks of validity (like the seal of authentication on an indulgence from an emperor), and semantic formality, depending on meaning and logical coherence in legal concepts and principles. Basic categories of law and logical methods for drawing meaning from those categories were recognized that have endured into the present day. Property and legal belonging (citizenship) became semantically linked through categories of legal personhood and methods for acquiring property. And creative products of the human intellect – artistic and literary works, in particular – were ambiguously recognized as objects with value that are subject to legal analysis using the language of property acquisition by legal persons: *occupatio* and *accessio*.

In chapter 1, I defined the thesis of semantic legal ordering as a thesis about how enduring legal meanings, received through legal traditions, exercise causal power in forming and solidifying our patterns of social activity and social relationships. In classical Roman jurisprudence, we have a foundation for legal meanings that have endured. In the personalities of Cicero, Caesar, Pliny, and Gaius, moreover, we have started to see how these legal meanings can have causal power: through the power of human words and ideas, in rhetorical speech and writing, which bind people together and contribute to their sense of shared obligation to cultural ideals.

Beginning with Cicero's speech on behalf of Archias, and extending into the *Institutes* of Gaius, we have seen early forms of semantic formality in law. We have also seen early forms of substantive rationality in law, which come close to our modern ideas about intellectual property. In Cicero, this involved a line of argument about how creative, artistic work is good for the state. While Cicero's argument is in many ways quite different from our modern theories of artistic works as public goods, there is a recognizable thread that can take us from Cicero's arguments to our modern theories that justify intellectual property. In the *Institutes* of Gaius, moreover, we see early foundations for a labor theory of value, which has been so important to substantive ethical theories about justice and fairness, in property ownership, including intellectual property ownership.

By the classical period of Roman law, then, we have in place all three layers of legal tradition that comprise the modern institution of intellectual property: empirical formality in legal documents, semantic formality in legal culture, and substantive rationality in political ideals. Now we will see how these layers were culturally transformed in an earthquake of religious inspiration.

5

Cultural Transformations

Christianizing Legal Power

On February 28, 380, the emperors Gratian (367–83), Valentinian II (375–92), and Theodosius I (379–95) jointly issued an imperial edict to the people of Constantinople, the city that we know today as Istanbul. The edict opened with the words "All peoples" – *Cunctos populos* in Latin – and this is its name today. In this edict, the three emperors declared their desire, will, and order that all peoples in the empire should be Catholic Christians, and should follow the law (*lex*) of the Christian religion (*religio*). All those who did not embrace this law were insane; they should "suffer the infamy of heretical doctrine." As heretics, they would be stricken by vengeance, both divine and imperial, "in accordance with the judgment of heaven."[1]

With this edict, Christianity – as doctrinally defined in the councils beginning with Nicaea (325) – became the established religion of the Roman imperial state, the source of imperial law, enforceable both through ecclesiastical tribunals overseen by bishops and by the imperial structures of civil and criminal law. While this imperial decision applied by its terms only to Constantinople, its broad statement and its inclusion in later codifications meant that it came to be seen, over time, as a statement for the whole empire. At least that is how it is read now, when we look back to the transformative period in which Christianity received the mixed blessings of imperial power.[2]

[1] *The Codex of Justinian: A New Annotated Translation, with Parallel Latin and Greek Text*, based on a translation by Justice Fred H. Blume, edited by Bruce W. Frier (Cambridge, UK: Cambridge University Press, 2016) (hereafter *CJ*), 1.1.1; *The Theodosian Code and Novels and the Sirmondian Constitutions*, translation with commentary by Clyde Pharr (Princeton: Princeton University Press, 1952) (hereafter *CT*), 16.1.2; P. R. Coleman-Norton, *Roman State & Christian Church: A Collection of Legal Documents to A.D. 535* (London: Society for Promoting Christian Knowledge, 1966), No. 167 (pp. 353–6). For helpful overviews, see J. H. W. G. Liebeschuetz, *Introduction to Ambrose of Milan: Political Letters and Speeches* (Liverpool: Liverpool University Press, 2010); John Matthews, *Western Aristocracies and Imperial Court, AD 364–425* (Oxford: Oxford University Press, 1975); Stephen Williams and Gerard Friell, *Theodosius: The Empire at Bay* (London: B. T. Batsford, 1994). For online access to Roman law resources, including Latin texts, see The Roman Law Library, https://droitromain.univ-grenoble-alpes.fr/ (accessed September 23, 2019).

[2] Coleman-Norton, *Roman State*, 353–4; W. H. C. Frend, *The Rise of Christianity* (Philadelphia: Fortress Press, 1984), 636–7. The Council of Nicaea: Norman P. Tanner, S. J. (ed.), *Decrees of the*

The establishment of Christianity as the law and religion of the empire was by no means a foregone conclusion, even 20 years earlier, when the emperor Julian (361–3) was seeking to reestablish traditional Roman religion. However, with Julian's death and the ascendancy of emperors who were committed to Nicene Christianity, initial steps toward Christianization taken earlier by Constantine (307–37) became the foundation for more radical developments, following the grooves laid down by recent projects in administrative reorganization that aimed to extend state power much more deeply into the daily lives of imperial citizens.[3]

Taken together, imperial reorganizations with Christianization effected a transformation in the governing communities of the Roman empire. Christianity became a legal religion that bound communities and societies together across the empire, and it would remain so, even as the empire was dissolving in the west. In the process, Christianity was also transformed, absorbing many of the social patterns and ideals of empire, including those of imperial Roman law. Roman law would live on after the Roman empire, in the west, and would become a traditional source of legal life for the church. In the realm of property law, this meant that Roman structures of property transfer survived as traditional legal practices within the church, becoming a customary source of law for the kings and queens of the west. As part of this process, Roman instruments of legal power became instruments for the performance and memorialization of Christian piety.[4]

At the same time, logics of salvation – logics about what it means to live well, to flourish as a human being, together with logics about where we should place our trust and hope in our efforts to live well – were built into the meaning of legal instruments themselves, as well as the law that supported them. These logics ultimately came from the Jewish scriptures, which Christians interpreted as covenantal promises extending to them from the God of Abraham. The salvation logics were mediated, however, by jurisprudential narratives in Christian scriptures, an ongoing tradition of Biblically inspired history-writing that began with stories about Jesus of Nazareth and the people of Israel, and expanded into stories about God's relationship with the entire inhabited world (*oikumene*). Originally written in Greek, situated in Hellenistic-Roman communities around the Mediterranean, and later translated into Latin, these jurisprudential narratives constituted a fundamental source of Christian attitudes toward law. In the western empire,

Ecumenical Councils, Volume I (London and Washington, DC: Sheed & Ward and Georgetown University Press, 1990), 1–23.

3 Emperor Julian and the effort to revive traditional Greco-Roman religion: Coleman-Norton, *Roman State*, Nos. 111–123; Frend, *Rise of Christianity*, 594–609; Wilmer C. Wright, Introduction to Volume III of the Loeb Classical Library's 3-Volume Edition of Julian's Works (Cambridge, MA: Harvard University Press, 1923), vii-lxix.

4 Mann, *Sources, Vol. 1*, 301–40; Peter Brown, *The Rise of Western Christendom: Triumph and Diversity, A.D. 200–1000*, 10th Anniversary Edition (Chichester: Wiley-Blackwell, 2013), 12–17; Chris Wickham, *The Inheritance of Rome: A History of Europe from 400–1000* (New York: Penguin Group, 2009).

they would contribute to a new order of obligation, oriented by faith in Biblical law and Christian traditions of authority.[5]

Over the next five chapters, I will trace a cultural process of development in law, one that is entwined with developments in the administrative structures for governing communities and the performance of obligation through instruments of legal power. In this process, formal and substantive rationalities of law will be transformed through a cultural synthesis of Roman and Biblical law. This developmental process will lead us through the legal establishment of royal prerogative powers that, with the rise of early modern nationalism, will be revolutionarily interpreted as the foundation of modern intellectual property. Ultimately, however, I will be arguing that the long and complex synthesis of Biblical and Roman law has given rise to a deeply ambivalent legal culture, our legal culture, one that valorizes human creativity while critically depersonalizing human authority. This is the cultural synthesis that stands behind our modern institution of intellectual property.

5.1 IMPERIUM CHRISTIANORUM

Christians perhaps initially appeared to Romans as a kind of illicit association (*collegium*) or religious club (*hetaeria*), one that might combine the threat of political insurrection with "superstition" (*superstitio*) and irreverence to traditional Roman religion. During the first two centuries of imperial rule, Christians were primarily dealt with by provincial administrators, and there was probably significant variation from one province to another in the way they were treated. Aside from a brief episode of violent scapegoating under Nero (54–68), the first imperial legal notice of Christians came in letter-based rulings from the emperors Trajan (98–117) and Hadrian (117–38). These established a legal precedent that Christians should be killed for avowing their novel religion, but also demonstrated a concern with procedural justice: anonymous allegations, for example, should not be relied upon in outing people as Christians, and subjecting them to capital punishment.[6]

5 Max Weber on salvation logics, with their implications for the experience of social obligation and for the administrative structures of governing communities: "Introduction to the Economic Ethics of the World Religions," in Sam Whimster (ed. & trans.), *The Essential Weber: A Reader* (Abingdon: Routledge, 2004), 62–70, 75, 77–9; Max Weber, "The Social Psychology of the World Religions," in H. H. Gerth and C. Wright Mills, *From Max Weber: Essays in Sociology* (New York: Oxford University Press, 1946), 294–99; Max Weber, "Intermediate Reflection on the Economic Ethics of the World Religions," in Whimster, *Essential Weber*, 215–44; Weber, *Economy & Society*, 437–8.

6 Robert L. Wilken, *The Christians as the Romans Saw Them* (New Haven: Yale University Press, 1984). Ruling by Trajan: Pliny, *Letters*, Loeb Classical Library edition in 2 volumes, translated by Betty Radice (Cambridge, MA: Harvard University Press, 1969), 10.96–7; A. N. Sherwin-White, *The Letters of Pliny: A Historical and Social Commentary* (Oxford: Clarendon Press, 1966), 691–712, 772–87. Eusebius on rulings by Hadrian and Antoninus Pius: Eusebius, *Ecclesiastical History*, Vol. I, translated by Kirsopp Lake (Cambridge, MA: Harvard University Press, 1926), 4.8–13; Eusebius, *The Church History*, translated by Paul L. Maier (Grand Rapids, MI: Kregel Publications, 2007), 124–8. For Latin translation of Eusebius by Rufinus, which some scholars have believed may have incorporated original Latin decrees, see *Eusebius Werke*, edited by Eduard Schwartz and Theodor Mommsen (Leipzig:

Things changed, however, over the course of the third century, culminating in the establishment of a new imperial framework by Diocletian (284–305). Following several decades of imperial conflict – including a brief but violent episode under the emperor Decius (249–51) – Diocletian enacted significant administrative reforms, establishing a four-person imperial rulership structure (the "Tetrachy"), and reorganizing provincial administration into dioceses. With Diocletian's reforms, the imperial command (*imperium*) extended further into everyday life. Craftsmen were to be legally tied to their guilds, peasant farmers (*coloni*) were to be legally tied to the land that they farmed, and town councilors (*decuriones*) were to be personally liable for local tax collection.[7]

In this environment of militarization and administrative reorganization, religion, always a marker of political loyalty in Roman civic culture, seems to have become a matter of heightened, imperial concern. The emperor, after all, was Rome's chief priest (*pontifex maximus*). The perception of threat to traditional piety, together with the belief that such a threat needed to be countered through imperial lawmaking, became intense.[8]

This is the environment in which Constantine rose to power. As the son of a caesar, he was groomed for war and imperial service. Around 305, when his father Constantius became a senior coemperor (Augustus), Constantine joined him in Britain to help in battles against the Scottish Picts. Upon his father's death the next year at York, Constantine was acclaimed by the army as Augustus. Between 306 and 312, Constantine consolidated his position through marriage and battle, culminating in victory at the Milvian Bridge in Rome. This final battle occurred with a Christian symbol on the soldiers' shields, and from that moment forward Constantine's approach to law and letters reflected growing Christian commitments.[9]

J. C. Hinrichs, 1903), 319–31. For the current scholarly consensus on the legal basis for persecuting Christians, see T. D. Barnes, "Legislation against the Christians," *The Journal of Roman Studies* 58 (1968), 32–50; G. E. M. de Ste. Croix, "Why Were the Early Christians Persecuted?," *Past & Present* 26 (1963), 6–38; *cf.* Coleman-Norton, *Roman State*, Nos. 1–3.

7 Eusebius, *Ecclesiastical History*, Books 5–8 (Vol. II translated for the Loeb edition by J. E. L. Oulton, Cambridge, MA: Harvard University Press, 1932). Administrative reorganization of the empire: Simon Corcoran, *The Empire of the Tetrarchs: Imperial Pronouncements and Government AD 284–324*, 2d ed. (Oxford: Oxford University Press, 2000); Jill Harries, *Imperial Rome AD 284 to 363: The New Empire* (Edinburgh: Edinburgh University Press, 2012); A. H. M. Jones, *The Later Roman Empire, 284–602* (Baltimore: Johns Hopkins University Press), 25–70; Ramsey MacMullen, *Roman Government's Response to Crisis A.D. 235–337* (New Haven: Yale University Press, 1976), 153–81. Examples of imperial pronouncements extending into everyday life: CT 14.7.1 (guild members), 5.17 (fugitive *coloni*), 14.3.1 (bread makers); C. Dickerman Williams, "Introduction," in CT, xx. Striking illustration of the increasing impact of state organization on everyday life: Geoffrey Rickman, *The Corn Supply of Ancient Rome* (Oxford: Clarendon Press, 1980).

8 Mary Beard, John North, and Simon Price, *Religions of Rome, Vol. I: A History* (Cambridge, UK: Cambridge University Press, 1998), 91–5, 211–44.

9 Noel Lenski, "The Reign of Constantine," in *The Cambridge Companion to the Age of Constantine* edited by Noel Lenski (New York: Cambridge University Press, 2006) [Kindle ed.], ll. 1583–2462; A. H. M. Jones, *Constantine and the Conversion of Europe* (London: English University Press, 1948).

Legal source materials become fuller from the time of Constantine's *imperium*, so that it is easier to discern attitudes and goals pursued through the grant of legal privileges. The Theodosian *Codex*, which was compiled and issued between 429 and 438 under Theodosius II (402–50), included imperial letters and orders going back to Constantine. One century later, the emperor Justinian's (527–65) *Codex* included edicts, mandates, and rescripts going back to the second century, while nonetheless emphasizing the period of the Tetrarchy and the *imperia* that followed.[10]

Christianity did not become the established religion of the empire until the 380s, but, beginning immediately after Constantine's victory at the Milvian Bridge in Rome, Christianity was increasingly privileged. Already in 313, in the "Edict" of Milan, the Christian church was recognized as a collective social body (*corpus*) that could own property in its own name. Property that had been seized from churches during the time of persecution was to be returned to them. Individual churches, many of them overseen by bishops, were recognized as corporate entities, and some were even subsidized with imperial funds.[11]

In 321, Constantine issued an edict permitting donations by will to Christian churches. His own donations, especially to the churches in Rome and Constantinople, were extremely generous. Over time, the corporate property of the church, much of it acquired through gifts of the faithful, came to be viewed as a patrimony – an inheritance of wealth – administered by bishops and their deacons in a manner analogous to the corporate *fiscus* of the empire. This patrimonial treasury included donations for hospices, monasteries, orphanages, poorhouses, and other similar institutions.[12]

The first steps toward establishment of a Christian legal system were also taken under Constantine, beginning in 313. The trigger for this came from a conflict that erupted in the wake of harsh persecution in the north African church, centered at

10 Simon Corcoran, "The Codex of Justinian: The Life of a Text through 1500 Years," in CJ, cvi-cx; Corcoran, *Empire of the Tetrarchs*, 3–5; Jill Harries, "Introduction: The Background to the Code," in *The Theodosian Code: Studies in the Imperial Law of Late Antiquity*, edited by Jill Harries and Ian Wood, 2d ed. (Bristol Classical Press, 2010), 1–16; "Chronological List of the Constitutions in Justinian's Codex," in CJ, 3088–3176.

11 Coleman-Norton, *Roman State*, Nos. 4 ff., especially Nos. 12, 15; Jill Harries, "The Many Voices of Roman Law," in Philip L. Reynolds (ed.), *Great Christian Jurists and Legal Collections in the First Millennium* (New York: Cambridge University Press, 2019), 63–4; Susan Wood, *The Proprietary Church in the Medieval West* (Oxford: Oxford University Press, 2006), 9–11. Although it is typically called an edict, the famous Edict of Milan was closer to a mandate, since it was addressed to a provincial governor. Coleman-Norton, *Roman State*, No. 30. The edict establishing Christianity as the imperial religion was *Cunctos populos*, discussed earlier.

12 CJ 1.2.1; Coleman-Norton, *Roman State*, No. 36. The *Liber Pontificalis* ("Book of the Popes") records generous donations from Constantine to the Roman church. Raymond Davis, *The Book of Pontiffs* (Liber Pontificalis): *The Ancient Biographies of the First Ninety Roman Bishops to AD 715*, translated by Raymond Davis, 2d ed. (Liverpool: Liverpool University Press, 2000), 14–27. Hospices and other similar institutions: CJ 1.2.17–19. Discussion of the legal principles: W. W. Buckland, *A Text-Book of Roman Law from Augustus to Justinian*, third edition revised by Peter Stein (Cambridge, UK: Cambridge University Press, 1963), 177–79.

Carthage. Known as the Donatist Schism, this dispute centered on questions of ecclesiastical purity and authority. The question was whether a bishop who had succumbed to fear during persecution, such that he handed over Christian scriptures or sacred objects to inquisitors, was so defiled by this betrayal that his sacred acts (e.g., ordination or baptism) became ineffectual. The rigorists and purists, aligning themselves with a bishop named Donatus, said yes. But the orthodox Catholic position, defended by the bishop of Carthage and (later) by Augustine, bishop of Hippo, was more understanding of human frailty. A bishop who had succumbed to persecution should lose his office, yes, but his acts of ordination and baptism were still valid, as sacred acts. These depended on his office, not his personal purity of character.[13]

This conflict was shaking the north African church at the very moment that Constantine won his great victory at the Milvian Bridge. The Donatists were losing the fight for legitimacy and purity, so they sought justice from the new western emperor, a step that was in keeping with understandings of an emperor's responsibilities to his subjects. Constantine's first step was to refer the case to the bishop of Rome, Miltiades (311–14), requesting that a panel of bishops be convened to decide the case in accordance with the church's "most revered law," and transmitting records from north Africa. The bishop of Rome, however, had his own ideas about who should decide the case, and assembled a different panel, one dominated by Italian bishops. The Donatists lost the case.[14]

Constantine's first effort to respect Christian customary law and jurisdiction had not worked out according to plan, but he seems to have been convinced that recognition of a separate sphere of Christian jurisdiction was the right way forward for empire and church. In 318, he issued an edict authorizing transfer of cases being heard in civilian courts to episcopal courts, so that cases might be heard according to "Christian law." In 333, just four years before his death, Constantine confirmed the development of a separate system of Christian jurisdiction, overseen by bishops, ordering that verdicts of Christian courts should be enforced through secular courts. The result was a judicial system overseen by bishops, which, within its sphere, was to be unappealable, and which evidently

[13] H. A. Drake, "The Impact of Constantine on Christianity," in Lenski (ed.), *Age of Constantine*, ll. 2888–3408; Frend, *Rise of Christianity*, 488–92; W. H. C. Frend, *The Donatist Church: A Movement of Protest in Roman North Africa* (Oxford: Oxford University Press, 2000). Scholars often note the sociological significance of this dispute. Among other things, it involved questions of social identity and boundary-drawing for the early Christian church. Peter Brown, *Augustine of Hippo: A Biography*, 2d ed. (Berkeley: University of California Press, 2000); J. Patout Burns Jr. and Robin M. Jensen, *Christianity in Roman Africa: The Development of Its Practices and Beliefs* (Grand Rapids, MI: Wm. B. Eerdmans, 2014), 47–51, 195–8, 224–30; Mann, *Sources, Vol. 1*, 331–5.

[14] Coleman-Norton, *Roman State*, Nos.17–22; Eusebius, *Ecclesiastical History*, 10.5. On conceptions of an emperor's responsibilities, as reflected in responses to petitions and specifically in the Donatist controversy, see Fergus Millar, *The Emperor in the Roman World*, 2d ed. (London: Duckworth, 1992), 584–90 and passim.

was actively used by litigants, as Augustine, bishop of Hippo in the late fourth century, would bitterly complain.[15]

Under Constantine, then, bishops were acting as judges and mediators. At the same time, however, they were also diocesan administrators. They were furthermore acquiring valuable economic privileges. In the same year as his victory at the Milvian Bridge, Constantine issued the first of many letters granting exemption from local civic obligations (*munera*) to clerics, so that they might devote themselves more wholeheartedly to their Christian duties. They were given free access to the empire's public conveyance system, so that they might attend synods and councils. In 320, clergy and clergy-in-training, together with their agents, were exempted from commercial taxes, with the understanding that the profits of their commercial endeavors would be used to benefit the poor.[16]

Constantine, in short, was undertaking a Christian reorganization of the empire, building on the organizational patterns and "ancient custom" (*antiqua conseutudo*) of his imperial predecessors.[17]

5.2 PARALLELS TO INTELLECTUAL PROPERTY IN LATE ROMAN LEGAL PRIVILEGES

In some ways the purposes pursued through legal letters by Constantine and his successors bear a striking resemblance to modern intellectual property, but in other ways they are diametrically opposed. One resemblance is in the recognition of a valuable public good that will be gained through the exercise of intellectual and technical skills, together with an effort to harness such skills for the economic benefit of the imperial "community" (*res publica*). Constantine, for example, issued privileges freeing artisans – including architects, painters, glassworkers, and potters – from all compulsory public services, so that they might spend their leisure in further learning and training others. In the case of architects, especially, privileges issued by

15 Coleman-Norton, *Roman State*, No. 28 (CT 1.27.1) and No. 65 (CT, Sirmondian Constitution No. 1). The authenticity of these constitutions is doubted, and related/later provisions add complexity. CT 1.27.2; CT, Novels of Valentinian 35. For Augustine's complaints about his judicial obligations, see Brown, *Augustine*, 190–2, 222. For a thorough discussion of the evidence, drawing nuanced conclusions, see Caroline Humfress, *Orthodoxy and the Courts in Late Antiquity* (Oxford: Oxford University Press, 2007), Chapter 6; *cf.* H. A. Drake, *Constantine and the Bishops: The Politics of Intolerance* (Baltimore: Johns Hopkins University Press, 2000, 315–36; Harries, *Imperial Rome*, 161–2.

16 Dioceses as an administrative unit carried over from the pre-Christian empire: Andrew Lintott, *Imperium Romanum: Politics and Administration* (London: Routledge, 1993), Chapter 4. Exemptions and immunities: Coleman-Norton, *Roman State*, Nos. 16, 29–30, 32, 60 (CT 16.2.1–2, 16.2.7, 16.2.10). Free access to public conveyance system: Coleman-Norton, *Roman State*, Nos. 18–19. Tax exemption for benefit of poor: Coleman-Norton, *Roman State*, No. 32 (CT 16.2.7).

17 For language of ancient custom and tradition as support for the privileges/prerogatives (*privilegia*), honors (*honores*), and dignities (*dignitates*) of bishops, see the canons issued at the Council of Nicaea (325), particularly canons 6–8. Tanner, *Ecumenical Councils*, 6–16.

Constantine and his successors indicate that the overarching goal was to increase the number of trained architects available for work across the empire.[18]

Professors of studies deemed necessary or liberal were also granted broad privileges to further their intellectual and technical capacity for the training of others. Such arts included medicine, grammar, literature, rhetoric, and painting. Physicians and professors of literature (together with their families) were granted extensive privileges, including freedom from compulsory services, and tax exemptions. Many of these privileges were also extended to grammarians, orators, and teachers of philosophy.[19]

Painters, in particular, were granted freedom from business taxes on the sales of their paintings, on condition that they use their studios and workshops exclusively for the production of art. As we saw in the previous chapter, debates between two early "schools" of Roman law register a recognition that the artistry of a painting is a primary source of the value that a painted work possesses.[20]

Nevertheless, while intellectual and technical skills were clearly recognized as valuable to the political community, fostered through economically valuable grants of privilege to the bearers of such skills, originality and innovation were *not* encouraged. Furthermore, the general approach to economic and industrial policy relied on a degree of punitive compulsion that is difficult for us to fathom.

Textile and arms production, for example, were organized into guilds of conscript laborers, who were physically branded with an official state mark (*stigmata nota publica*), in order that they might be recognized and apprehended should they try to escape. Many of these workers were slaves. With the transformation of guilds under the Tetrarchy, moreover, even once-privileged trades became like slavery. Bread makers, for example, became tied to city guilds and burdensome public services, particularly in Rome and Constantinople. Shipmasters and miners, likewise, were tied to the profession of their fathers, although they continued to enjoy periodic grants of privilege, as well.[21]

One striking case connected with shipping enables us to see how the Roman empire of late antiquity approached the issue of "trade secrets." In 419, a mandate from the emperors Honorius (394–423) and Theodosius II was issued to the praetorian prefect of the east, sanctioning the release of a group of unnamed persons who had "transmitted to barbarians the previously unknown practical knowledge of shipbuilding." A bishop named Asclepiades had intervened on their behalf, so they were to be released, but, for the future, capital punishment was prescribed for anyone who should transmit such arts to non-Romans.[22]

18 CT 13.4.1–3; CJ 10.66. For the copyright-like character of a rescript appended to the CT, see John Matthews, "The Making of the Text," in Harries & Wood, *Theodosian Code*, 19–20.

19 CT 13.3; CJ 10.47, 10.53.

20 CT 13.4.4; *Justinian's Institutes*, translated by Peter Birks and Grant McLeod with Latin text of Paul Krueger (Ithaca: Cornell University Press, 1987) (hereafter *IJ*) II.1.25–7.

21 CT 10.20–10.22, 13.5; CJ 11.10; Jones, *Later Roman Empire*, 795–872.

22 CT 9.40.24; cf. CJ 9.47.25.

What we see in the late Roman empire, then, is a pattern of legal, social, and economic organization that bears certain resemblances to later forms of intellectual property, while nonetheless reflecting conceptions and practices that were strikingly different. Privileges were granted to encourage intellectual arts and technical skills, and there did seem to be a sense that this would work in some way to the benefit of the imperial polity. But the overall approach to economic organization was heavily dependent on slavery and compulsion. Professors of rhetoric were highly privileged, but many industrial artisans were enslaved, or they were inter-generationally tied to guilds to a degree that approaches slavery, to our modern eyes.

5.3 THE GOOD BARBARIAN KING

Over the course of the fifth century, imperial government in western Europe and north Africa was assumed by militant, "barbarian" groups of people believed to have come from the north and the east. In Italy and north Africa, the militant groups were known as "Goths" and "Vandals." In 402, Goths were threatening northern Italian cities, and, in 410, the Gothic leader Alaric famously sacked the city of Rome. This traumatic event, blamed by some on the empire's embrace of Christianity, led a north African bishop, Augustine, to begin composing his famous treatise on Christian social and political philosophy, *The City of God*.[23]

In late Roman Britain and Gaul, towns were transforming from centers of imperial militarization, with traumatic memories of Roman glory, into forts of promised spiritual comfort, occasional exchange, and small-scale consumption, surrounded by agricultural estates and forests. Waves of migration by peoples known as Angles, Saxons, and Jutes unsettled southeast Britain. In northwest Gaul, a warrior king named Clovis converted to catholic Christianity, inaugurating a long and dramatic history for an alliance of peoples who called themselves Franks. This name apparently came to mean, to them, that they were free. Beginning with Clovis, the Franks would claim to be free, orthodox (catholic) Christians.[24]

[23] Brown, *Augustine*, 285–339, 428–30; Peter Heather, *Empires and Barbarians: The Fall of Rome and the Birth of Europe* (Oxford: Oxford University Press, 2009); Jones, *Later Roman Empire*, 170–265; Peter Sarris, "Introduction" to *The Novels of Justinian: A Complete Annotated English Translation*, edited by David J. D. Miller and Peter Sarris (Cambridge, UK: Cambridge University Press, 2018), 1–51; Herwig Wolfram, *The Roman Empire and Its Germanic Peoples*, translated by Thomas Dunlap (Berkeley: University of California Press, 1997). For an overview and introduction to the revisionist history about who the "Germanic barbarians" were, see Thomas F. X. Noble, "Introduction: Romans, Barbarians, and the Transformation of the Roman Empire," in Thomas F. X. Noble (ed.), *From Roman Provinces to Medieval Kingdoms* (Oxford: Routledge, 2006).

[24] Transformation of towns and the broader Mediterranean economy: J. H. W. G. Liebeschuetz, *The Decline and Fall of the Roman City* (Oxford: Oxford University Press, 2001); Michael McCormick, *Origins of the European Economy: Communications and Commerce, AD 300–900* (Cambridge, UK: Cambridge University Press, 2001). Roman and post-Roman Britain: Anthony R. Birley, *The Roman Government of Britain* (Oxford: Oxford University Press, 2005); K. R. Dark, *Civitas to Kingdom: British Political Continuity 300–800* (London: Leicester University Press, 1994); Robin Fleming, *Britain after Rome* (London: Penguin Books, 2010); David Mattingly, *An Imperial Possession: Britain in the Roman*

Sometime near the end of this transformative century, a man named Cassiodorus, whose family background may have been Syrian, was elevated to the status of patrician and recommended to the Roman senate by the Gothic king Theoderic (493–526). Theoderic and his army had probably been sent to Italy by the emperor Zeno (474–91) with the promise that, if they would defeat Odoacer (476–493, deposer of the last western emperor), they could live as free peoples in Italy, under the leadership of their own king. With a pinch of deadly deception, Theoderic did defeat Odoacer, and he would go on to rule as an imperially recognized king (*rex*). Cassiodorus, who had served as a financial officer under Odoacer, also served Theoderic, first as governor (*rector*) in Sicily and later as praetorian prefect in Ravenna, a position combining something like prime minister with chief legal officer. It was this distinguished service for Theoderic that earned Cassiodorus the reward of patrician status, and commendation to the Roman Senate.[25]

Cassiodorus' son, whose name (Cassiodorus Senator) reflected his father's distinction, began serving Theoderic from a relatively young age. Like his father, Cassiodorus Senator would ascend through the ranks of office to the peak of praetorian prefect. By the time he reached this high point, however, Theoderic had died, and his regent daughter, Amalasuntha, would soon be killed, giving the new eastern emperor, Justinian, a good justification to invade Italy, seeking to fulfill his dream of a reestablished Roman empire stretching from the borderlands of Persia to Britain. As wars raged around him, Cassiodorus retired to a monastery (*Vivarium*) on his family's property in southern Italy (Squillace). Before this retirement, however, he collected, edited, and published a series of letters, which he called the *Variae*. These collected letters seem to have been published, at least in part, as a tribute to the legal ideals of King Theoderic and his Gothic

Empire, 54 BC–AD 409 (London: Penguin Books, 2007); J. N. L. Myres, *The English Settlements* (Oxford: Clarendon Press, 1986); Peter Salway, *Roman Britain* (Oxford: Oxford University Press, 1984). Roman and post-Roman Gaul: J. F. Drinkwater, *Roman Gaul: The Three Gauls, 58 BC–260 AD* (Abingdon: Routledge, 1983); Patrick J. Geary, *Before France & Germany: The Creation & Transformation of the Merovingian World* (Oxford: Oxford University Press, 1988); Edward James, *The Origins of France: From Clovis to the Capetians, 500–1000* (Basingstoke: Macmillan Press, 1982); Alexander Callander Murray, *From Roman to Merovingian Gaul: A Reader* (Toronto: University of Toronto Press, 2008). The Franks: Edward James, *The Franks* (Oxford: Basil Blackwell, 1988); Herwig Wolfram, *The Roman Empire and Its Germanic Peoples* (Berkeley: University of California Press, 1997), 41–2.

25 S. J. B. Barnish, Introduction to *Cassiodorus*: Variae (Liverpool: Liverpool University Press, 1992), ix–liii; Sean D. W. Lafferty, *Law and Society in the Age of Theoderic the Great* (Cambridge, UK: Cambridge University Press, 2013); John Moorhead, *Theoderic in Italy* (Oxford: Clarendon Press, 1992); Wolfram, *Roman Empire*, 183 ff.; James J. O'Donnell, *Cassiodorus* (Berkeley: University of California Press, 1979); Herwig Wolfram, *History of the Goths*, translated by Thomas J. Dunlap (Berkeley: University of California Press, 1988). Office of the praetorian prefect: *Cassiodorus: The* Variae: *The Complete Translation*, by M. Shane Bjornlie (Berkeley: University of California Press, 2019), Letters I.4, VI.3, Books XI-XII; Thomas Hodgkin, *The Letters of Cassiodorus* (London: Henry Frowde, 1886), 93–114; Jones, *Later Roman Empire*, 448–62.

successors, together with the administrators who had served them faithfully, including the Cassiodori.[26]

Under King Theoderic and his Gothic successors, as evidenced by the *Variae* of Cassiodorus, diplomatic traditions from the Roman empire were adapted to new social conditions. One of these adaptations involved encouraging the expenditure of wealth and labor in rebuilding Italy. We see this, for example, in orders sent to Rome to embellish the Eternal City, and to reinforce the city's walls. We see it also in orders to build forts along the northwestern passages leading into southern France (Gaul). In their collective efforts to build defensive structures, Gothic rulers promised, Romans and Goths alike would receive a reward, both individual and communal. Such rewards included honors and income connected to public office. They might also include a right to property that had been improved.[27]

In several of Theoderic's letters, as presented by Cassiodorus, we see an explicit connection between the king's beneficent grant and industrious activity by the grant's recipient. For example, sometime around 510, Theoderic sent a letter to an administrative officer named John, seeking to ensure that swamp-draining efforts in an area along the road between Rome and Ravenna should move forward. At some point previously, Theoderic had apparently granted the land in this area to two "distinguished gentlemen," Spes and Domitius, permitting them to profit from the land on condition that they first cleared the swamps. However, the king had learned from Spes that Domitius was failing to pay his fair share of the expenses. The king ordered his agent John to investigate, and, if necessary, to require Domitius to hand over his share in the property to Spes, so that the work could move forward. In this way, Spes would receive, as deserved, the "fruits of his labor" (*fructu laboris*), and the proper reward for his hard work (*industria*).[28]

Similar language about ensuring the receipt of deserved fruits from labor can be seen in a grant from King Theoderic to a skilled marble worker in Ravenna. Pronouncing himself to be delighted by the marble worker's artistry (*artis*), the king granted him an exclusive privilege to practice that art in making and selling

[26] M. Shane Bjornlie, *Politics and Tradition Between Rome, Ravenna and Constantinople: A Study of Cassiodorus and the "Variae", 527–554* (Cambridge, UK: Cambridge University Press, 2013); O'Donnell, *Cassiodorus*, 15–103, 177–222; Walter Pohl, "Justinian and the Barbarian Kingdoms," in Michael Maas (ed.), *The Cambridge Companion to the Age of Justinian* (New York: Cambridge University Press, 2005). The Latin text of Cassiodorus' *Variae*, edited by Theodor Mommsen, is digitally accessible through the *Monumenta Germaniae Historica* (MGH) website: www.dmgh.de/ (accessed January 8, 2020): MGH, *Scriptores, Auctores antiquissimi (Auct. ant.) XII, Cassiodori Senatus Variae* (Berlin, 1894).

[27] *Variae*, Letters I.17, I.21, I.25, I.28, IV.30, IV.51. Inheritable property: Letter III.29, Formula VII.44. Emphasis on discovery and grant for public utility: for example, Letters III.31, III.52. See also Lafferty, *Law and Society*, 233–38.

[28] *Variae*, Letter II.21, with commentaries by Barnish and Bjornlie, Latin from Mommsen's edition (1894, 58). This language about a grant from the king rewarding the hard work of the recipient, thereby ensuring that the recipient received the fruits of his labor, will have a very important impact in the development of intellectual property law. This language, or very similar language, was used in several other letters from Cassiodorus' *Variae*: I.3, II.32–33; III.19, V.35, XI.30.

coffins to the people of Ravenna. Recognizing that this monopoly would give a power to charge high prices, the king urged him to exercise moderation in his pricing, so that he would not add to the grief of his customers.[29]

As we see an emphasis on *industria* in Cassiodorus' collection of royal letters, we also see an emphasis on learning, discovery, creation, and even invention. Letters and privileges from the king were sent, according to Cassiodorus, to encourage both. Most famously, perhaps, we see this in the letters from Theoderic to the ill-fated Roman senator and author Boethius (c. 480–524).

Sometime around 506, Theoderic wrote to Boethius, asking him to exercise his ingenuity in overseeing the making of two extraordinary timekeeping devices: a water clock and a sundial. These were to be given as a gift to Gundobad, king of the Burgundians, whose son had married Theoderic's daughter. Around the same time, Theoderic requested Boethius' help in locating a skilled lyre player to send as a gift to Clovis, king of the Franks. Several years afterward, Theoderic seems to have sought Boethius' learned help in addressing problems with inflated coinage.[30]

As drafted and published by Cassiodorus, the letters sent to Boethius constitute lengthy panegyrics to liberal and mechanical arts, invention, and discovery. Years later, the values enshrined in these letters, including the value of arts discovered and mechanical inventions, would also be reflected in Cassiodorus' program for monastic and scholarly education, *The Institutions of Divine and Secular Learning*, drafted after the imperial armies of Justinian had ended Gothic rule in Italy.[31]

The high value placed on learning, discovery, and mechanical arts by Cassiodorus is presented as having been held by Theoderic and his short-lived successors. Letters and privileges evidently aimed at rewarding or encouraging such arts are plentiful in the *Variae*. Especially numerous are letters aimed at encouraging metallurgy and mining (iron, gold, and other buried treasures, presumably coins and precious metals). Mathematical arts, geometry, and land surveying were also emphasized, together with music. Literary study, grammar, and rhetorical arts were also praised and encouraged.[32]

Efforts to encourage trade and commerce through legal letters are likewise evident under the Gothic rulers of Italy, as seen through Cassiodorus. In 527, for example, Theoderic's grandson Athalaric (526–534) issued a letter to his governor in southern Italy, seeking to ensure that adequate protection, both for physical security and for guaranteeing payment, was provided for an annual fair near the site of an ancient city in Lucania. By cooperating with local landowners and

29 *Variae*, Letter III.19 (Hodgkin 1886, 207; Mommsen 1894, 89); *cf.* Letters III.53, IX.5, X.28.

30 *Variae*, Letters I.10, I.45–6, II.40–1.

31 Cassiodorus, *Institutions of Divine and Secular Learning*, translated by James W. Halporn (Liverpool: Liverpool University Press, 2004), I.XXX, II.V.

32 Metallurgy & Mining: *Variae*, Letters III.25–6, III.31, IV.34, IX.3. Math, Geometry, Surveying, Music: Letters I.10, I.45–6, II.40–1, III.52–3. Literary Study, Grammar, and Rhetoric: Letters II.16, VIII.12, IX.21, IX.24–25. See also the formulae for appointment of architects and armourers, Formulae VII.5 & VII.18, and the panegyric on papyrus, Letter XI.38.

leaseholders, and through a show of physical force against any violators of the peace, the great commerce of the fair would be protected. In this way, profit (*proficuus*) would be assured to the local community, and the merchants' wealth would be protected.[33]

There is scholarly debate about the reliability of Cassiodorus' *Variae* as a historical source of knowledge about Theoderic and the Italian Goths. This need not concern us. Whether or not Cassiodorus' letters precisely reflect the values of the kings and regent queen he served, they nevertheless speak for the legal ideals of a high-level Italian officer and an influential personality in the development of western monasticism. Cassiodorus would be copied and studied in new monasteries springing up from Italy to Ireland. The emphasis that his letters placed on the role of a good "barbarian" king in fostering and encouraging learning, creativity, and discovery, as well as investment in industrial activity, would survive to influence future generations.[34]

5.4 THE FOUNDATIONAL POPE – GREGORY THE GREAT

Over the course of the sixth century, as we have seen, the old Roman empire was painfully transforming. Efforts on the part of Roman emperors – especially Justinian – to bring the empire back to its former glory had devastated lands and peoples in regions we view as the Spanish and Italian peninsulas, southern France, north Africa, and the middle east, preparing the way for acceptance of new rulers, new religions, and new patterns of trade. In the city of Rome, and in other towns throughout what are today Italy, Switzerland, France, and Spain, links to imperial Rome (centered increasingly in Constantinople) were nonetheless maintained through bishops and their families, many of whom were closely connected to senators and high-ranking imperial officers. It was through one aristocratic Roman bishop, Gregory ("the Great," c. 540–604), that Roman legal letters were transmitted west, reaching all the way to Britain.[35]

33 *Variae*, Letter VIII.33 (Mommsen 1894, 261–2); *cf.* I.10. A policy of favoring creditors and encouraging commerce is also evidenced by the Edict of Theoderic. Lafferty, *Law and Society*, 85–8.

34 George A. Kennedy, *Classical Rhetoric & Its Christian and Secular Tradition*, 2d ed. (Chapel Hill: University of North Carolina Press, 1999), 199–200; O'Donnell, *Cassiodorus*, 185, 239–51.

35 CJ 1.27 (Justinian's orders for governing north Africa); Miller & Sarris (eds.), *Novels of Justinian* (NJ), Appendix 7 (provisions for governing Italy); T. S. Brown, *Gentlemen and Officers: Imperial Administration and Aristocratic Power in Byzantine Italy A.D. 554–800* (British School at Rome, 1984); Yitzhak Hen, "The Church in Sixth-Century Gaul," in Alexander Callander Murray (ed.), *The Brill Companion to Gregory of Tours* (Leiden: Brill, 2016); Frank Stenton, *Anglo-Saxon England*, 3d ed. (Oxford: Oxford University Press, 1971), 103 ff. It is difficult to overstate Gregory's cultural, social, and legal influence in European history. For a recent assessment, see Conrad Leyser, "The Memory of Gregory the Great and the Making of Latin Europe, 600–1000," in Kate Cooper and Conrad Leyser (eds.), *Making Early Medieval Societies: Conflict and Belonging in the Latin West, 300–1200* (Cambridge, UK: Cambridge University Press, 2016), 181–201.

As pope, Gregory was responsible for a monastic mission sent to Britain through *Francia* (the land of the Franks) at the end of the sixth century, and for initiating the spread of Roman Christianity that followed in the wake of this mission. He was later remembered as a hero of English history, not only by a monk named Bede ("The Venerable Bede," 672–735) who recorded so much of England's early history, but also by Alfred the Great (849–899), founding hero of the Wessex dynasty, which unified and ruled England – with a few significant interruptions – from the tenth century to the coming of the Normans in the eleventh century.[36]

Gregory was born into a Roman senatorial family and served as a high-ranking legal officer in Rome and Constantinople before becoming pope in 590. He was also a monk, the first monk to become bishop of Rome. He was a foundational and epoch-making pope, and more of his letters have been preserved than any other pope before the eleventh century. In his letters, as we will see, Gregory behaved very much like an emperor, granting privileges and "indulgences," and urging the retention of legal records (*breve*). In so doing, he established precedents that would become legally important throughout medieval Europe.[37]

During Gregory's time, a new "barbarian" threat was looming – the Lombards. The Roman emperor, Maurice (582–602), was involved in Italian affairs, especially through his primary agents (the exarchs), located in Ravenna and Carthage, and his praetor of Sicily. However, the emperor's attention was focused eastward, toward a resurgent Persia. Through Gregory's letters, we see a situation in which the residents of Italian cities were left to their own devices, negotiating with Lombard

36 Gregory as Bede's "hero": Michelle P. Brown, "Bede's Life in Context," in Scott DeGregorio (ed.), *The Cambridge Companion to Bede* (Cambridge, UK: Cambridge University Press, 2010), 18. Alfred as translator of Gregory's *Book of Pastoral Rule*: Janet M. Bately,"Alfred as Author and Translator," in Nicole Guenther Discenza and Paul E. Szarmach (eds.), *Brill Companion to Alfred the Great* (Leiden: Brill, 2015), 113–42. For a modern English translation of Alfred's Old English translation, see Henry Sweet, esq., *King Alfred's West Saxon Version of Gregory's Pastoral Care* (London: The Early English Text Society, 1871). For an introduction to the latest scholarship on Alfred the Great and his West Saxon (Wessex) dynasty, see Nicole Guenther Discenza and Paul E. Szarmach (eds.), *A Companion to Alfred the Great* (Leiden & Boston: Brill, 2014). Simon Keynes provides an overview of the political context and accomplishments during Alfred's reign, based especially on recent archaeological evidence from coins, and on diplomatic evidence. Keynes, "Alfred the Great," in Discenza and Szarmach (eds.), *Companion to Alfred*, 13–46.

37 R. A. Markus, *Gregory the Great and His world* (Cambridge, UK: Cambridge University Press, 1997), 8–14; John R. C. Martyn, "Introduction," *The Letters of Gregory the Great*, translated by John R. C. Martyn (Ontario: Pontifical Institute of Medieval Studies, 2004), 1–2. Latin text of Gregory's letters, edited by Paul Ewald and Ludo Moritz Hartmann (Berlin, 1887–1889), is digitally accessible through the MGH website: *MGH, Epistolae, Epistolae (in Quart) (Epp.)*, available at www.dmgh.de (accessed January 14, 2020).Gregory's autobiographical letter, written to Leander, Bishop of Seville: Letter 5.53a (July 595). Letters referring to records, indulgence, and emphasizing the firmness of writing: 3.41, 5.59, 8.37, 9.67, 9.83, 9.113. Legal precedents: John Albert Eidenshink, *The Election of Bishops in the Letters of Gregory the Great* (Washington, DC: The Catholic University of America Press, 1945), 22 ff.; Martyn, "Introduction," 14, 81.

military leaders and kings, ransoming captives taken in Lombard raids, and paying soldiers for defense of threatened cities.[38]

As bishop of Rome, Gregory was responsible for overseeing the church's vast patrimony of agricultural estates, located especially in Sicily, but extending across Italy into Illyria (southeast Europe), north Africa, and what is today southern France. He was also responsible for ensuring that churches had adequate pastoral care, and for maintaining order in monasteries. In addition, he sought to address schismatic and heretical doctrines being taught by certain bishops, who often disagreed about the precisely correct language for describing God.[39]

In short, Gregory was responsible for doctrine and discipline in the region that would become western Christendom. In carrying out these responsibilities, he brought considerable legal and diplomatic training, which he had gleaned from his upbringing, his legal service in Roman secular affairs, and his years as a papal ambassador in Constantinople (579–86). In his letters, Gregory followed imperial protocols, and, because of the precedents that his letters established, he brought imperial legal protocols into the office of the papacy.[40]

5.5 BUILDING A NEW SOCIAL MODEL OF ORDERS AND OFFICES

We can see Gregory's legal transformations of the papal office, for example, in the precise way his terms of address are calibrated to the social rank of his addressees. As we have seen, Roman society was highly sensitive to order and rank. Such sensitivities had been handed down through legal traditions, especially within the senate and in families of high-ranking Romans. Such traditions were also reflected in imperial codifications of Roman law, and in the episcopal hierarchy of the church itself.[41]

External symbols of rank and authority were marked not only by titles of address, but also by items of dress and personal adornment. Imperial letters going back to

38 Lombard threat: Martyn, "Introduction," 30–2; Letters 1.30, 5.39–40. Maurice in Italy and the emperor's western agents: Martyn, "Introduction," 20–30, 32–42; Letters 1.31, 1.32, 1.46–7, 1.59, 7.19; NJ 37, 75, 104, Appendix 9. Maurice and Persia: Michael Whitby, *The Emperor Maurice and His Historian: Theophylact Simocatta on Persian and Balkan Warfare* (Oxford: Clarendon Press, 1988). Left to their own devices: Martyn, "Introduction," 20–22, 30–2; Letters 2.4, 2.27–8, 2.38, 2.47, 3.16, 4.17, 5.34, 5.36, 5.39, 6.32–3, 7.23, 9.9, 9.11, 9.44, 9.66, 9.68, 9.85, 9.196.

39 Patrimony: Martyn, "Introduction," 26–8, 32–42, 91–2; Edward Spearing, *The Patrimony of the Roman Church in the Time of Gregory the Great* (Cambridge, UK: Cambridge University Press, 1918); Letters 1.42, 1.44, 1.53, 2.50, 5.31–3. Pastoral care: Letters 1.46, 1.48, 1.54–6, 2.31, 3.3, 4.40, 6.43–4, 7.32, 9.108, 9.205, 11.6. Doctrinal responsibilities: Letter 1.24, 1.41, 1.72–5, 4.2–4, 4.33, 5.52, 5.59, 6.2, 6.14, 6.65, 7.4; compare *CT* 16.10.13 (395).

40 Gregory's role in contributing to western Christendom: Brown, *Rise of Western Christendom*, 198–216. Legal and diplomatic training, years in Constantinople: Letter 5.53a. Imperial protocols: Martyn, "Introduction," 3–4, 14; Letters 4.2, 5.53a. Through the imagery employed in his letters, Gregory also contributed to a distinctively imperial and judicial imagination of the Christian God. Letters 1.2, 1.17, 1.24, 1.26, 1.38a, 1.42, 1.75, 3.44, 5.46, 6.48, 7.26, 8.34, 9.157, 9.225, 9.232, 10.20, 11.18, 37, Appendix 9.

41 Martyn, "Introduction," 103–5; Letter 9.157; CJ Book 12.

Constantine had established legal standards about the wearing of rings, specific colors, and garments edged with gold. Honors connected with such external symbols were sometimes even granted through imperial diplomas, such as the "diploma of ex consul," for which someone known personally to Gregory was willing to pay 30 pounds of gold. In 598, Gregory himself addressed a papal letter to the bishop of Syracuse, directing him to prevent deacons in that church from wearing kid leather boots, a privilege that had only been allowed by Gregory's predecessors to the deacons of Messina, in Sicily.[42]

This context can help us to understand the significance of the *pallium*, which was one of the most important privileges granted by Gregory to his highest-ranking ecclesiastical officers, the metropolitan bishops of the west. The *pallium*, as it is worn today, is a white wool cloth, something like a scarf, adorned with crosses. It is a liturgical item of dress ("vestment"), to be worn only on certain occasions and for certain sacred rituals, which symbolizes the jurisdictional authority of senior bishops, like the pope himself. It is reminiscent of the *cingulum*, which was a belt or sash symbolizing service in the emperor's *militia*.[43]

According to Roman ecclesiastical traditions, which are recorded in the *Book of the Popes* (*Liber Pontificalis*), the papal granting of the *pallium* extends back to the fourth century, to the time of pope Marcus (336). However, the oldest document providing evidence of contemporary practices and beliefs surrounding the *pallium* comes from the sixth century (569), when the vestment was used to designate the bishop of Arles as an official agent, or *Vicar*, of the pope in Gaul. By the time Gregory was first ordained as deacon in 578, the grant of the *pallium* was coming to symbolize the pope's conferral of episcopal authority and jurisdiction on his metropolitan bishops and vicars. Gregory's own letters would, in turn, provide the basis for later formulas governing the grant of the *pallium*, which are preserved in the earliest papal formulary book, the *Liber Diurnus*.[44]

42 Martyn, "Introduction," 19; Letters 9.6, 9.17, 11.27. Diploma of ex consul: Letter 2.49. Kid-leather boots: Letter 8.27.

43 Most important privilege granted by Gregory: Martyn, "Introduction," 9. *Pallium* as worn today: John Albert Eidenschink, *The Election of Bishops in the Letters of Gregory the Great* (Washington, DC: Catholic University of America Press, 1945), 101. Different theories/speculations about the origin of the *pallium* are discussed by Eidenschink at 101–4. In early Roman imperial times, an item of dress called a *pallium* (often translated as "cloak") was associated with Greek philosophers, and with learned persons who provided a public benefit from their learning (teachers of letters, grammarians, rhetors, doctors, poets, musicians, astronomers, and diviners); in the second century, it also came to be associated with the dress of Christians. Cassiodorus, *Variae*, 1.45.3, 9.25.5; Tertullian, *De Pallio*, translated with commentary by Vincent Hunink (J. C. Gieben: Amsterdam, 2005); John Moorhead, "Boethius' Life and the World of Late Antique Philosophy," in John Marenbon (ed.), *The Cambridge Companion to Boethius* (Cambridge, UK: Cambridge University Press, 2009). *Cingulum*: Gregory Letter 10.16; *cf.* CJ 1.1.4 (452), 2.3.29 (531); Cassiodorus, *Variae*, 3.23; Coleman-Norton, *Roman State*, 807.

44 Davis (ed. & trans.), *Book of Pontiffs*, 63, 110. In 514, Pope Symmachus (498–514) granted the *pallium* to the Bishop of Arles, using this grant as a way to establish that Bishop (Caesarius) as patriarch over all

From the moment of Gregory's election as pope, judicial and episcopal authority were a central focus of his attention and his letters. As may be seen from the encyclical letter that he sent after his election as pope, for Gregory the priestly vestments signified the highest priestly powers of divining God's will, both in judging cases and in serving as a pastoral *rector* in the Petrine office of supreme authority (*summa auctoritas*). In granting the *pallium*, Gregory saw himself as conferring a great honor and a privilege, one that belonged to the papal office, and that could be revoked as punishment for wrongful behavior by a senior bishop. The grant served as a recognition of the jurisdictional position that a metropolitan or vicar occupied in the church, of the authority connected with that position, and of the supremacy of the papal office in granting it. Invoking the customary practices of his predecessors, and developing his own formulas, Gregory was defining the organizational structure of senior episcopal offices, especially in relation to jurisdiction.[45]

In addition to imperial legal protocols, with their recognition of an elaborate system of social ranking, Gregory was incorporating Roman jurisdictional concepts into the papal office. Gregory was closely linked to the imperial family of Justinian and was only a generation removed from Justinian's massive overhauling of Roman law, the *Corpus Juris Civilis*. One scholar, Giuseppe Damizia, has studied the extent

other bishops in France and Spain. In 530, Pope Felix IV (526–30) tried to use the grant of the pallium as a way to designate his successor, but this was deemed to be illegal by the Roman clergy and Senators who controlled papal elections at this time. J. N. D. Kelly and M. J. Walsh, *Oxford Dictionary of the Popes*, 2d ed. (Oxford: Oxford University Press, 2010), 47–9, 52–4. Symbolism for Gregory and *Liber Diurnus*: Martyn, "Introduction," 74–81; Eidenschink, *Election of Bishops*, 105–48; Reginald L. Poole, *Lectures on the History of the Papal Chancery* (Cambridge, UK: Cambridge University Press, 1915).

45 Focus on judicial and episcopal authority: Letters 1.1, 1.2, 1.36, 1.38a, 1.60–2, 2.5, 2.37, 2.42, 6.11, 11.24. Postelection encyclical letter and symbolism of vestments: Letter 1.24. Gregory seems to have seen a symbolic connection between the *pallium* and the vestments prescribed for the Mosaic priesthood in the Bible. For similar attitudes in early medieval Francia, see Michael Edward Moore, *A Sacred Kingdom: Bishops and the Rise of Frankish Kingship*, 300–850 (Washington, DC: Catholic University Press, 2011), 172–80. Through Gregory's letters, early principles of canon law were being developed about which church officials were to wear the *pallium*, and about the occasions upon which it should be worn. Eidenschink, *Election of Bishops*, 101–48; Martyn, "Introduction," 78. Other letters dealing with the *pallium* – 1.27 (Anastasius, ex-patriarch of Antioch); 1.45 n., 5.58, 60 (Bishop of Arles, pallium addressed in footnote by Martyn); 2.17–9, 44, 8.36, 9.177, 9.231, 234 (Bishop of Salona, threatened revocation, penance, and reconciliation); Appendix 7, 3.54, 54a, 5.11, 15, 5.61, 6.31, 9.168 (Bishop of Ravenna, customs of rightful wearing); 4.1 (Bishop of Milan, honor and divine nature); 5.10, 16 (Prima Justiniana & Illyria, confirmation of consecration); 5.57a (Gregory's Papal Decree, prohibiting simony in the granting of the pallium); 5.62–3 (Bishop of Corinth & Achaea); 6.7 (Bishop of Nicopolis & Epirus, confirmation of privileges); 6.8 (Bishop of Messina, order of ancient custom); 6.18 (Bishop of Syracuse, order of ancient custom, confirmation of privileges); 8.4, 9.214, 9.220, 9.223 (Bishop of Autun, as special favor to Queen of the Franks, with specific instructions); 8.37, 11.39 (Bishops of England & Gaul, general instructions to Augustine about the structure of English and French churches); 9.221 (Bishop of Vienne, search for records of grant); 9.228, (Bishop of Spain, Seville);13.38 (Bishop of Palermo, honor and privilege). Importance of Gregory's encyclical letter in establishing western adherence to the first four ecumenical councils: Tanner, *Ecumenical Councils*, 23.

to which Justinian's legal *Corpus* is reflected in Gregory's letters, identifying twelve extensive quotations, and over a hundred references. Especially in his letters dealing with donations to the church, but also in other contexts, Gregory shows both an extensive knowledge of Roman law and a great respect for it.[46]

Gregory brought a Roman legal conception of office into his language about the papacy and papal administration. In one of his most famous treatises, the *Moralia in Job*, Gregory had argued that respect is for an office, not for the person who holds the office. According to his conception of senior episcopal offices, especially the papacy, these offices entailed obligations, powers, and responsibilities that were acquired through succession, irrespective of personality. The bishop's charismatic powers, in other words – his powers of God's divine favor, or grace (*gratia*), referred to as the "power of the keys" and the Petrine succession – were conferred through official ordination, not earned through personal qualities, and Gregory often expressed great diffidence about his own personal qualifications for the papal office. Authority was separate from the person and could be granted by Gregory to his episcopal agents, in the form of licenses and privileges sent by means of formal letters, in a manner analogous to the granting of the *pallium*.[47]

Gregory's senior administrators of the patrimonial estates were known as *rectors*, a term borrowed from Roman imperial administration. Most often, however, Gregory worked through *defensores*, an office that was probably modeled after the *defensor plebis*, an office of Roman urban administration. Gregory was, in fact, quite familiar with the structure of Roman civic administration, having served as the senior legal officer (*praetor urbanus*) and administrator (*prefect*) of the city of Rome before becoming pope. As the senior administrator of the western church, in dialog with emperors and empresses, kings and queens, he worked through legal clerks (*notarii*), secretaries (*cancellarii*), record-keepers (*chartularii*), and other administrative officers.[48]

46 Connections to Justinian: Letter 5.57a. *Corpus Juris Civilis* in Gregory's letters: Martyn, "Introduction," 20, 34; Corcoran, "Codex of Justinian," cxx; Letters 1.9, 2.6, 2.11, 2.45, 3.3, 3.49, 4.6, 4.43, 6.1, 6.12, 6.30, 6.35, 7.20, 7.36, 8.3, 8.5, 8.12, 9.23, 9.35, 9.40–42, 9.48 ("rule of law"; also 9.183); 9.52–3 (respect for privileges and customary law), 9.58–9, 9.72, 9.90, 9.181, 9.195–6, 9.198, 9.229c, 13.16, 13.49.

47 Roman concept of office into the papacy: Martyn, "Introduction," 45; Letters 5.57a, 8.7, 11.4, 13.32, 39–40. The *Moralia*: Gregory the Great, *Moral Reflections on the Book of Job*, Vol. 5, translated by Brian Kerns (Collegeville, MN: Cistercian Publications, 2019), 160 (25.16.37). Power of the keys, Petrine succession: 4.41, 5.37, 6.5, 7.37, 9.26, 11.27. Authority separate from person, granted through licenses and privileges: Letter 1.24, 5.39, 3.20, 4.16, 6.9, 6.11, 6.65, 9.29, 9.79, 9.81–2, 9.98, 9.167, 13.3, 13.14, 19, 14.3, 9. The concept of charisma is Weberian. It may seem strange to couple charisma with law, but Weber did recognize that charisma can be institutionalized. Weber, *Economy & Society*, 241–54, 954, 1121–48.

48 When Gregory refers to the office of the bishop, including the papal office, he sometimes uses the word "rector." Letters 1.24, 7.38; *cf.* Moore, *Sacred Kingdom*, 187. Defensors: 8.16; 5.26 (office of defensor as privilege), 9.28–30, 9.75, 9.98. Familiarity with Roman civic administration: Martyn, "Introduction," 3, 92–3; Letters 1.25, 1.26, 3.3, 4.2. Work through administrative officers: Martyn, "Introduction," 93–4; Letters 1.42, 1.67–8, 1.70, 1.82, 2.1, 3.5, 3.40, 5.34, 6.12, 6.24, 7.11, 9.111.

5.6 UNITY IN DIVERSITY AND SEPARATION OF AUTHORITIES

Like the Christian emperors of the east, Gregory considered the kings and queens of western Europe as holding a basic responsibility for the unity and peace of their subject peoples. The ultimate source of that unity rested in the church (*ecclesia*), but temporal rulers provided necessary supports to the church, particularly through the exercise of military power. Standing at the head of armies, temporal rulers exercised the imperial power of command (*imperium*). That *imperium*, as Gregory wrote to the king of the Franks, was needed to stamp out heresy and support the unifying authority (*auctoritas*) of the church. When kings deployed their power (*potestas*) to support the church's *auctoritas*, the divine plan orchestrating harmony from a diversity of orders and ranks was carried out.[49]

Gregory, like the emperor Constantine whom he held up as an exemplar for western kings, was deeply committed to Christian unity. This is especially evident in his letters to fellow patriarchs of the church, and to the emperor Maurice. It is also evident in his letters to schismatic bishops – like the bishop of Aquileia in northeast Italy – and to subordinate members of the clergy who joined them. As in Augustine, the binding force of union in the church is love – love is a unifying social force that can make two minds and souls into one, and that can constitute an entire society as a solidary unit, a "harmonious concord" of unity from diversity.[50]

Nevertheless, committed as he was to Christian unity, Gregory also upheld a separation between spheres of authority within Christendom. There was a line at which the emperor's authority stopped, and the pope's began. The emperor was God's designated agent, a primary source of unity and peace in the world. Through him all nations were to be pacified. But the pope was supreme when it came to matters of doctrine and discipline within the church. Gregory's assertion of this supremacy was subtle and deferential, but it was ultimately grounded on a belief that, as a matter of law, the papacy possessed a sphere of authority over the church that should remain free from imperial interference.[51]

49 Letters 5.59–60. Duties of princes: Martyn, "Introduction," 72–3; Letters 1.41, 5.37, 5.39, 5.60, 6.5–6, 6.64, 8.4, 9.68, 9.213ff, 11.35ff, 11.51; 13.7; Gregory the Great, *Moral Reflections on the Book of Job*, Vol. 2, translated by Brian Kerns (Collegeville, MN: Cistercian Publications, 2015), 265–66 (9.16.25–6).

50 Letters to fellow patriarchs emphasizing unity: 1.24, 6.61, 7.4, 24, 31. Letters to Bishop of Carthage, who was technically subject to Papal oversight but whom Gregory treated with some degree of independence: 2.40, 6.63. Letters to Emperor Maurice emphasizing unity: 3.61, 64, 5.37, 41, 44, 6.16, 64, 7.6, 30; see also Martyn, "Introduction," 18. Letters to schismatic bishops and their followers emphasizing unity: Letters 1.16, 2.43, 3.10, 5.56, 6.65, 12.13. Binding force of love: Letters 3.48, 3.65, 5.59, 6.61, 63, 8.2, 9.223. On Augustine and the binding force of love, see Philip Cary, "United Inwardly by Love: Augustine's Social Ontology," in *Augustine and Politics*, edited by J. Doody, K. L. Hughes, and K. Paffenroth (Lanham, MD: Lexington Books, 2006), 15–36.

51 Emperor as God's agent in pacification: Letter 5.30, 7.5. Papal supremacy: Letters 4.20, 5.36–39, 6.25, 9.27, *cf.* 8.10. This supremacy was affirmed by the Emperor Phocas, in a letter to Gregory's successor, Boniface III. Martyn, "Introduction," 89. W. H. C. Frend regards the view of separating spheres of authority between church and state as developing in the fourth century, and to a degree that was distinctive in the west. Frend, *Rise of Christianity*, 522–650.

Two bodies of law were cited in support of this papal supremacy – imperial and canonical. In Gregory's time the canon law was in its earliest moments of development, but Gregory does cite it, and his letters are a valuable source for investigating the early foundations of this law, which would later be further elaborated through papal letters (decretals) and church councils. As the metropolitan bishop of Peter's church, Gregory was the ultimate overseer and defender of the canon law, at least in the west.[52]

According to Gregory, canon law and imperial law were complementary bodies of law, both of which might need to be applied by a bishop in resolving a dispute or controversy. One specific area in which imperial enforcement and canonical discipline might need to cooperate was that of penance. Gregory refers in several of his letters to cases in which officers and servants of the church, as well as laity, have been sent to monasteries to "do penance." In a letter referring to the case of a lapsed monk, Gregory elaborates on the meaning of penance: "in accordance with apostolic sentence," the penitent's spirit would be "saved through carnal affliction," so that "with a continuous flow of tears he can wash away the earthly disease of sins, which he is said to have contracted through wicked deeds." While in many cases the external enforcement of penance could be carried out by church officials exclusively under canon law, at times imperial assistance and imperial law were also needed.[53]

One type of penance to which Gregory refers, again in the case of a lapsed monk, involved a return to slavery. In other cases, as for the "country folk" (*paganos*) of Corsica who reverted to non-Christian religious rituals, the penance was more limited. In many (if not most) cases there are hints that penance involved some type of bodily suffering, externally imposed, which contributed to the penitent's sorrow over his guilt. Although he did not prescribe pilgrimage in any of his letters, Gregory did recognize it as a "good deed," and as obligatory if avowed.[54]

The beneficial outcomes from penance involved purification (purgation) of the individual person and reconciliation to the community from which his sin had separated him. As in the case of the bishop of Salona, for example, the swearing of an oath before the relics of a saint might also be required to complete the required purgation and reconciliation. Through such means, the "correction" of the developing canon law would contribute to discipline and a "righteous way of life" in the church, in monasteries, and throughout society.[55]

[52] Letters 3.52, 4.7, 5.39, 5.57a, 11.29.

[53] Cooperation of Christian and imperial Roman law: Letters 2.25, 3.6, 8, 6.24–6, 7.35, 8.3, 8.12, 9.52, 9.69–70, 9.111, 205, 10.11, 11.3014.7–8. Certain cases, of course, would exclusively implicate Biblical principles and canon law. Letters 2.26, 3.9, 3.38, 7.39, 9.157, 203, 219, 10.2, 13. Doing penance: Letter 3.49 (former Bishop), 9.25 (priests and deacons), 13.46, 13.48 (laity?). Letter of apostolic sentence: Letter 4.24; see also Letter 7.31, Appendix 9. Imperial assistance: Letter 3.49, 13.49.

[54] Return to slavery: Letter 5.28. *Paganos*: Letter 8.1. Bodily suffering to enhance sorrow: Letters 8.36, 11.18, 11.27, 12.3. Pilgrimage: Letters 2.24, 4.44.

[55] Correction and return to righteous way of life: Letter 13.47. Bishop of Salona and swearing of oath to complete purgation: Letter 8.1, 9.177–9, 9.231. The swearing of an oath before the body of a saint might also be required in order to prove one's innocence, or to establish the truth of an asserted fact or

5.7 A RECIPE FOR THE FUTURE: POPES AND KINGS, INDULGENCES AND BULLS

Gregory believed that the world was going to end very soon. This gave him a powerful sense of mission and drove him to send the good news of Christianity to the barbarians of the west. Gregory focused especially on the Franks of northwest Gaul and the Anglo-Saxons of southeast England, working through patrician agents of his patrimonial estates, through bishops, and through teams of monks sent to establish churches and monasteries.[56]

In the farthest reaches of the barbarian west, Gregory used the grant of the *pallium*, together with other privileges, to cement alliances with powerful kings and queens, and to strengthen the church's organizational position within their kingdoms. In a letter to Childebert, the king of the Franks, Gregory invoked his grant of the *pallium* to the bishop of Arles, as a way of ingratiating himself with the king. By Gregory's time, a grant of the *pallium* to the bishop of Arles was becoming a matter of customary canon law, but it had also been requested by the king, and Gregory was careful to note that he was responding favorably to the king's request. This, after all, was Childebert II (575–96), grandson of Clovis, that dynastic king of the Franks whose conversion to orthodox Christianity may have raised the papacy's hopes for a western protector. The papal response had been a stamp of legitimacy on the Frankish lineage of Merovingian kings, and Gregory was continuing in this tradition through the granting of papal favor. Likewise with Reccared, king of the Visigoths in what is today Spain, Gregory invoked his grant of the *pallium* to the bishop of Seville, as an honor and privilege rewarding the king's conversion of his "nation" to orthodoxy.[57]

Gregory's most striking instance of this "papal beneficial diplomacy" involved a grant of the *pallium* to the bishop of Autun, at the request of queen Brunhilde, who was formally acting as regent for Childebert's nephews and successors. Under principles of canon law that were developing, the bishop of Autun would not normally be entitled to the *pallium*. However, rather than standing on the principle

custom. Letter 2.29, 11.16. In order to allay all doubt, a panel of mature and respected men might be called to swear an oath before the body of a saint about an asserted fact or custom. Letter 6.31. Alternatively, the oath might be sworn on the "holy gospels," and the "judgment by a selected jury" thereby obtained. Letter 9.170, 9.210. Oaths were often used to secure promises, both for officers of the church and for formerly schismatic members of the church who promised to remain within the unity of the church community. Letter 12.7, 13.35.

56 Apocalyptic mission: Letter 3.61, 4.23, 7.26, 8.2, 9.157, 9.232, 10.20. Patrician agent: Letter 5.31. Episcopal and monastic agents: Letter 5.58, 6.51–60, 8.4, 8.29, 8.37, 13.5. For further discussion of Gregory's apocalyptic worldview and his western missions, see Martyn, "Introduction," 17–18, 47–61; Gregory the Great, *Moral Reflections on the Book of Job*, Vol. 1 (Collegeville, MN: Cistercian Publications, 2014), 48(Letter to Leander of Seville).

57 Letter 5.60 (Childebert II, King of the Franks); (Reccared, King of the Visigoths, in reference to the Bishop of Spain/Seville); Letters of alliance with western kingdoms: 6.5–6, 6.51–60, 8.4, 9.68, 9.212ff, 11.35ff, 13.5 (confirmation of privilege). For discussion of Gregory's use of the pallium and other gifts in papal diplomacy, see Martyn, "Introduction," 9–10, 51–61, 74–81.

of office hierarchy in this case, Gregory granted the queen her request, seeking thereby to establish an alliance of concern for protecting the Frankish church, and for maintaining high standards within the church.[58]

The papally recognized right of wearing the *pallium* was evidently viewed as a great honor and privilege, not only to the bishop who wore it, but also to his church, to his territorial region of episcopal oversight, and to the secular powers with whom he served. Once granted, honors and privileges like the wearing of the *pallium*, as well as the sacred relics sent by the pope, often came to be viewed as possessions of the bishopric.[59]

Honors and privileges, however, were not always acknowledged, and, if questions were raised, it was important to offer documentary proof of the grant. In several of his letters, Gregory refers to an assertion of privileges by a church, and to a search through documentary archives to verify the existence of such privileges. Sometimes this indicates a search through papal archives, and sometimes Gregory urges a bishop to search through his own church's archives for records of privileges.[60]

In the case of the Frankish church, for example, the grant of the *pallium* to the bishop of Autun seems to have triggered a conflict with the bishop of Vienne, who also asserted a right to wear the sacred vestment. Gregory responded to this assertion by stating that he had conducted a search through the Roman church's records, seeking evidence that in former times the *pallium* had been granted to the bishop of Vienne. He had found nothing, but he urged the bishop to "apply vigilant care in searching through the manuscripts of your church, and if any documents can be found there that could inform us, make sure you send them over here." Acknowledging the grant of "new honors," Gregory assured the bishop of his willingness to restore "old ones."[61]

In Gregory's time, the documents used to grant papal privileges were coming to be known as papal bulls (*bullae*). Gregory recognized this development explicitly in 595, in a decree issued from Saint Peter's Basilica in Rome. In this decree, Gregory ruled that, "following the ancient rule of the fathers," no fee should be accepted for ordination into clerical orders, "nor for the allotting of a *pallium*, nor for the delivery of letters, nor for what a new falsity has found ambitiously, called a papal 'bull.'"[62]

58 Letters 8.4, 9.214 (Brunhilde, Queen of the Franks, in reference to the Bishop of Autun); Martyn, "Introduction," 56.

59 Gifts of relics and proprietary attitudes: Letters 1.25, 1.29, 1.30, 1.52, 3.33. 3.47, 4.27, 4.30, 6.58, 7.23, 7.25, 8.33, 9.45, 9.49, 11.37, 43, 57, 12.2, 13, 13.43.

60 Church privileges reviewed/granted: Letters 11.40, 8.24 (Zara), 9.207 (Gallipoli), 9.220–1, 14.13, 14.

61 Letter 9.221.

62 Letter 5.57a(5). The *bulla* was a seal, corresponding to the Greek *boullon*, which might be gold or lead. For discussion of sealed documents in tenth-century Byzantium, see Rosemary Morris, "Dispute Settlement in the Byzantine Provinces in the Tenth century," in Wendy Davies and Paul Fouracre, *The Settlement of Disputes in Early Medieval England* (Cambridge, UK: Cambridge University Press, 1986), 125–47. For an early use of lead seals worn around a Roman soldier's neck and bearing his name, see Brian Campbell, *The Roman Army*, 31 BC–AD 337 (London: Routledge, 1994), 12.

Although he was very willing to grant privileges, including the new fangled papal bulls, Gregory was staunchly opposed to the purchase and sale of such privileges. This commerce in the church's spiritual gifts, positions, and privileges was known as "Simony" from a person named Simon Magus in the *Acts of the Apostles*. Simony had been officially defined as a heresy in the fifth-century Council of Chalcedon. Gregory considered it to be an egregious sin and labored to eliminate it.[63]

As we can see from Gregory's early decretal, the granting of papal privileges was beginning to extend well beyond the granting of the *pallium*. With Gregory there was an emphasis on privileges to monasteries and nunneries, which is not surprising from a pope who was himself a monk, and who had grown up as a young contemporary of the monastic *Rule of Benedict*. Important privileges granted to monasteries and nunneries through Gregory's letters include (1) privileges of self-governance, (2) recognition of corporate existence, together with corporate property, (3) receipt of church revenues, and (4) protection and care, where needed, from nearby bishops. Gregory also granted privileges recognizing the corporate existence of hostelries, with other pious monastic establishments, founded by Frankish kings and queens.[64]

Gregory especially appreciated the role that monks could play in missionary efforts directed to the west. He sent a group of monks from his own monastery in Rome to plant the church in England and gave the leader of this group, Augustine, detailed instructions about how to organize the new English church. He viewed monks as soldiers (*militia*) of Christ and sought to ensure their relative independence from secular clerics, to preserve their capacity to undertake their distinctive tasks. In the estimation of the Venerable Bede, writing in the eighth century from a monastery in northern England, Gregory was the founder of the English nation, because he had enabled its transformation into a church of Christ.[65]

In 601, approximately six years after he had begun laying the groundwork for his English mission, Gregory sent letters to Ethelbert and Bertha, the English king and queen who had welcomed Augustine to Kent and supported his mission from Canterbury. Bertha, a Frankish princess whose marriage cemented an alliance

63 Martyn, "Introduction," 84; Letters 5.16, 5.58, 5.60, 5.62, 5.65, 6.3, 6.7, 6.26, 8.4, 9.214, 9.216, 9.219, 11.28, 38ff, 12.8–9. For the decrees of the Council of Chalcedon, see Tanner, *Ecumenical Councils*, 77–103, and see further in the chapter.

64 Monastic privileges: Martyn, "Introduction," 81–3; Letters 1.23, 3.17, 5.47, 6.1, 6.41, 7.12, 7.32, 8.5, 8.17, 8.30, 8.32, 9.58–9, 9.72, 9.88, 9.97, 9.172, 9.181, 9.233, 10.18, 14.17; Appendix 2; cf. 1.8, 2.40 (Gregory's philosophy of privilege-granting); 6.46; 6.65 (grant of license to return to monastery after period of heresy); 7.36 (direction to Bishop to adjudicate boundary between to monastic establishments); 8.12; 9.18; 9.163, 9.165; 9.166; 10.9; 11.13; 11.15 (grant to an abbot of the right of making a will). Corporate existence of Frankish hostelries and monasteries: Letters 9.217, 13.513.9–11.

65 Instructions to Augustine: Martyn, "Introduction," 61–66; Letter 6.10, 6.51–60. Treatment of monks: Martyn, "Introduction," 81–3; Letters 1.40, 1.67, 4.11, 6.28, 7.40, 9.142. Bede's view of Gregory: Bede, *Ecclesiastical History of the English People*, edited by Bertram Colgrave and R. A. B. Mynors (Oxford: Oxford University Press, 1969), Preface, 1.23–32, 2.1, 5.24; J. M. Wallace-Hadrill, *Bede's Ecclesiastical History of the English People: A Historical Commentary* (Oxford: Clarendon Press, 1988), 49; Martyn, "Introduction," 61–72.

between Anglo-Saxon and Frankish kings, had been raised a Christian, but Ethelbert had only recently converted to Christianity. Gregory wrote to congratulate Ethelbert on his baptism and to offer guidance about his duties as a Christian king. Extolling the example of Constantine, Gregory urged Ethelbert to deploy his regal powers in converting and training the English people in Christian faith and morality. If he acted in accordance with this elevated duty of Christian princes, then the grace (*gratia*) that God had given him would also be conferred as heavenly benefits (*beneficia*) upon the English nation (*gens Anglorum*) that was subject to him.[66]

Gregory periodically referred to his letters as "encouraging" a particular attitude or behavior. In so doing, the letters might also encourage someone in the possession of *beneficia*, thereby protecting property. In one especially poignant case, Gregory's letter was to serve as a "Charter of Manumission" for two slaves of the church who were being freed in order that they might serve the church as free Roman citizens: one as a nun, and the other as a notary. In all of these cases, there is a recognition that papal letters and decretals carry with them a capacity to grant, by means of letter, a particular legal position, and at the same time to impact the behavior, attitudes, and social relations of the recipient.[67]

In addition to their recognition of slavery, as a social institution, Gregory's letters lend the seal of papal legitimacy to two other institutions of great significance for the medieval economy: guilds and serfdom. More broadly, they support an idealizing model for society: the model of the "Three Estates." Perhaps referencing Plato's *Republic*, and certainly influenced by the Pauline model of diversity in spiritual gifts, Gregory affirmed a unitary model of society, in which hearts are joined by love. This was a unity in diversity, however, one in which individuals were called to serve in different ways. Here is a Greco-Roman and Christian ideal of *Concordia*, adopted and adapted by a bishop and lawgiver.[68]

Already in Gregory we see an early version of the theory that some are called to pray, some are called to fight, and some are called to work. In the ninth century, an Anglo-Saxon translator of Boethius articulated the model in a manner that centered it around service to the king. For this Anglo-Saxon, perhaps even King Alfred himself, "a king's raw material and instruments of rule are a well-peopled land, and he must have men of prayer, men of war, and men of work."[69]

66 Martyn, "Introduction," 58–61; Letters 11.35–7; MGH, *Epp.* 2, 305–10.

67 Letter 9.50 (encouraging cooperation), 9.55 (zeal in justice), 9.93 (generosity in spending). Encouragement in possession of *beneficia*: Letter 9.62. Charter of Manumission: Letter 6.12; *cf.* Letter 9.99.

68 Guilds and serfdom: Letters 9.114, 9.129. References to Platonic image of society: Letter 3.65, with Martyn commentary. *Cf.* Henry Sweet, Esq., *King Alfred's West-Saxon Version of Gregory's Pastoral Care* (London: N. Truebner & Co., 1871), 232. Roman religious ideal of *Concordia* and its transformation: J. H. W. G. Liebeschuetz, *Continuity and Change in Roman Religion* (Oxford: Clarendon Press, 1979), 51–2, 177. The Pauline model of diversity in spiritual gifts: 1 Corinthians 12:4–11.

69 *The Old English Boethius*, edited and translated by Susan Irvine and Malcolm R. Godden (Cambridge, MA: Harvard University Press, 2012), 98–99(Prose 9).

5.8 THE BIRTH OF ENGLISH LAW AND LETTERS

The ecclesiastical precedents and foundations that Gregory helped to lay in England were important for the church of England, and for the development of English law. It is here that we find the roots for a complex lineage of legal documents leading from Anglo-Saxon to Anglo-Norman charters and writs, later developing into letters patent. Concepts of the royal prerogative itself can be traced back to this papal root, and through that root to their imperial Roman soil.[70]

Gregory prepared the way for his English mission by ordering a priestly agent in France (Candidus) to use monetary proceeds from the church's patrimony to purchase English boys in the slave markets. These English boys would be trained as monks and then sent with Augustine to help establish the English mission from Canterbury. French coins were relatively worthless in Rome, but English slaves provided a currency that Gregory could use.[71]

At the beginning of the seventh century, when Gregory's mission to England departed from Rome, slaves were among the most important items of global commerce. Captured and enslaved persons constituted one of the few saleable objects that the west could offer in exchange for goods from the more economically developed east. Slaves were exchanged for relics from eastern churches, Byzantine coins, and Indian spices. As economic historians have reminded us, this was an era when the volume of trade between east and west had reached a low ebb, but patterns were developing that would be significant for the centuries of growth to come, patterns in which international merchants played an important role.[72]

In the west, slaves worked on large manors, which had grown out of the agricultural estates of late antiquity. In the regions surrounding London, for example, agricultural estates had emerged in the early second century, extending south into the territories of Kent and Surrey, and linking southeastern England to London through social and economic ties that persisted through the Anglo-Saxon movements and Viking raids. A limited number of tablets recording and cementing these ties have endured, revealing the work of lawyers and notaries from the classical period of Roman law.[73]

London itself had been born circa AD 50, as an appendage of Roman military transport lines, leading across the river Thames from ports in the southeast to front lines in the north and west of England. Roman London grew in prosperity through mercantile trade in the multifarious products and supports of military conquest:

70 Letters 3.54, 9.223, 10.1. For further discussion of diplomatic lineages stretching back to Gregory, see Chapter 7.

71 Letters 5.31, 6.10, 6.51.

72 McCormick, *Origins of the European Economy*, 27–30, 237–70, 571–798.

73 David Bird, *Roman Surrey* (Tempus Publishing 2004); Dominic Perring, *Roman London* (London: Routledge, 1991), 40, 48–55, Michael Rhodes, "Inscriptions on Leather Waste from Roman London," *Brittania* 18 (1987): 173–81; Roger Tomlin, "A Five-Acre Wood in Roman Kent," in J. Bird et al. (eds.), *Interpreting Roman London: Essays in Memory of Hugh Chapman* (Oxford: Oxford University Press, 1996), 209–15.

slaves, soldiers, craftsmen, engineers, lawyers, sex workers, tax collectors, civilian administrators, millers, bakers, animals, grain, wine, oil, fruits, salt, vegetables, pottery, textiles, metals, glass, and precious stones. By the early second century, London was becoming a center of industrial production in salt, iron, and leather.[74]

With increasing commercial and industrial wealth came the capacity to invest in landed property. As Christianity and monasticism spread across the empire from east to west, gifts of property to establish and support local churches and monastic houses increased. From the fourth century onward, ecclesiastical foundations were recognized under imperial Roman law as corporate entities, with the capacity to own and dispose of property. When London and southeastern England reappear to history under Anglo-Saxon rulers, it is primarily through legal records of gifts to monasteries and churches.[75]

5.9 THE LAW IN BOOKS: COUNCILS, *LEGES*, AND *HISTORIA*

The legal ideals expressed in Cassiodorus' and Gregory's writings are very much those of Roman late antiquity. The king or pope acts wisely and beneficently through his decrees, like a Roman emperor, as he seeks, among other things, to encourage valued behaviors: industry, artistry, learning, and religiosity. The king or pope does not act alone, however. Rather, he seeks to elicit cooperation from administrative officers, senators, citizens of ancient cities, and local magnates. He elicits this cooperation through his performative beneficence in the granting of privileges and property, and through edicts addressed to specified recipients, declaring his will.

These decrees are always personal, even when they speak broadly to large groups of people. They are an expression of the lordly will and *persona*, even as they are also an expression of the law. They elicit cooperation through personal beneficence, obedience, and loyalty. They do not attempt to speak in the abstract and impersonal voice of rightness (*ius*) itself.

But there was a place where rulers might participate in a more universal form of law-giving: a church council. The Christian scriptures contained a record of such councils in *The Acts of the Apostles*, which later writers of Christian history like Eusebius (263–339), Jerome (349–420), Gregory of Tours (538–594), Isidore of Seville (560–636), and Bede interpreted as the foundation for a sustained tradition. Bede, for example, included an account in his *Ecclesiastical History* from a council held in 664 (the synod of Whitby), which made a final determination about when Easter should be celebrated in Northumbria. Although the king (Oswiu, 654–670) presided and rendered his decision after hearing arguments from both sides, his

74 Gustav Milne, *The Port of Roman London* (London: Routledge, 2000); Perring, *Roman London*, especially chapters 1–2.

75 N. P. Brooks and S. E. Kelly, *Charters of Christ Church Canterbury* (Oxford: Oxford University Press, 2013), 1–3 and passim; Stenton, *Anglo-Saxon England*, 140–41 and passim.

decision about which side was right (the "truer tradition") was determined by conformity with the true practices (*mores*) of the "universal church" (*universalis ecclesiae*). Following the king's declaration, according to Bede, "all present, both high and low," indicated their willingness to abandon their imperfect custom (*institutio*) and to adhere to the better one.[76]

Church councils were truly universal, however, only when they were ecumenical, that is, when they included an assembly of bishops representing the whole Christian world. Most church councils were regional or local, addressing issues of concern to a local community. However, beginning with Constantine, Roman emperors, acting in consultation with the pope and other leading bishops, had periodically attempted to bring the entire church leadership together to address issues of concern to the worldwide community. The first such issues had been primarily doctrinal and had focused on the definition of correct belief. At the same time, however, beginning already with the council of Nicaea (325), disciplinary canons had been issued in the great church councils. Although these canons primarily concerned issues of church governance, their implications were always broader in an age that drew no firm distinctions among church, state, and society.[77]

Church councils in the west-Gothic kingdom (later to become Spain) joined bishops and kings together in their efforts to establish stable institutions for their people. An influential figure here was Isidore, bishop of Seville. Younger brother to Gregory's close friend Leander, Isidore served as a leading bishop during the early seventh century, overseeing several important church councils. These culminated in the Fourth Council of Toledo (633), which helped to establish a liturgical ritual for anointing a new king, while also declaring that kings should be elected by "the whole people along with the priests ... in common council." Emphasis on the "whole people" of the kingdom, as a unitary people, was reinforced by reference elsewhere in the canons to an associated people (*gens*) and homeland (*patria*). Some scholars have seen evidence here for the emergence of a new political and quasi-national identity in the west-Gothic kingdom.[78]

76 Bede, *Ecclesiastical History*, III.25; Wallace-Hadrill, *Bede's Ecclesiastical History*, 124–29.

77 The Council of Chalcedon (451), fourth of the councils adjudged ecumenical, is the first of the ecumenical councils from which a full record of proceedings has been preserved. For a recent English translation, see Richard Price and Michael Gaddis (trans.), *The Acts of the Council of Chalcedon*, 3 Volumes (Liverpool: Liverpool University Press, 2005). For discussion of the "new conciliar fundamentalism" that emerged in conjunction with public dissemination of these records, see Richard Price, "The Council of Chalcedon (451): A Narrative," in Richard Price and Mary Whitby (eds.), *Chalcedon in Context: Church Councils 400–700* (Liverpool: Liverpool University Press, 2009), 70–91. The disciplinary canons issued as part of the conciliar proceedings are also published in Tanner, *Ecumenical Councils*, 77–103. It is important to reiterate the imperial view that councils presided over by the emperor carried the status of imperial law. CT 16.1.2; NJ 131; Sarris, "Introduction" to *Novels of Justinian*, 9–10.

78 Roger Collins, *Visigothic Spain*, 409–711 (Malden, MA: Blackwell Publishing, 2004), Chapters 1 and 9; *cf.* Moore, *Sacred Kingdom*, 159.

Church councils were important sources of legal authority for the kingdoms and peoples of western Europe as they were developing their distinctive, post-Roman, governing communities. In parts of the territories we know today as Spain and France, councils were held regularly from the sixth century onward. According to the canons of Nicaea (325) and Chalcedon (451), such councils were to be held twice each year, but this was relaxed at the seventh ecumenical council of Nicaea ("Nicaea II"), held between 786 and 787. Going forward, the canonical rule was that provincial synods should be held annually. Any ruler discovered to be preventing observance of this rule was to be excommunicated.[79]

Nicaea II was called to address a violent controversy over the use of artistic images in Christian worship. In the eastern church, religious art had become a source of intense conflict. The conflict was so intense, in fact, that the council convened to address the controversy was threatened with violence. This seventh ecumenical council was the last to be recognized by the churches of east and west alike. For us, the council is especially significant because it addressed the production of art. Speaking for the universal Christian church, the council defined the church's position in favor of religious art and images, prohibiting as heretical any art-destroying (iconoclastic) doctrine.[80]

Speaking generally to the Christian faithful, church councils articulated legal principles that were meant to govern belief and practice throughout Christian society. This is perhaps the closest that we come to statutory law in the early Middle Ages. Conciliar "legislation" coexisted with legal letters and decrees from kings, emperors, and popes, granting privileges and property. Early forms of Christian history-writing, moreover, preserved both types of law, often verbatim, as evidentiary support for their narratives about the formation of Christian peoples (*gentes, nationes*). *Jurisprudential narratives*, in other words, were an important way in which the "law in books" was transmitted to future generations, together with stories and myths about the peoples who had lived in accordance with (or violated) the laws.[81]

79 Tanner, *Ecumenical Councils*, 8, 96, 143–45 (Nicaea I canon 5; Chalcedon canon 19; Nicaea II canon 6). This canon cites an earlier council, the "Quinisext" council of 692, held in Constantinople. For more on the Quinisext council, see Judith Herrin, "The Quinisext Council (692) as a Continuation of Chalcedon," in Price & Whitby, *Chalcedon in Context*, 148–68.

80 Richard Price (trans.), *The Acts of the Second Council of Nicaea (787)* (Liverpool: Liverpool University Press, 2018); Tanner, *Ecumenical Councils*, 133–56.

81 Eusebius laid an important foundation for these jurisprudential narratives in describing Christians as a new people in world history (a new nation (or race): Greek *ethnos*, *gens* in Rufinus' Latin translation). Eusebius, *Ecclesiastical History*, 1.4. The theme of "new nations" was carried forward by the great "narrators of Barbarian history," who were churchmen familiar with Eusebius' work. Walter Goffart, *The Narrators of Barbarian History (A.D. 550–800): Jordanes, Gregory of Tours, Bede, and Paul the Deacon* (Notre Dame: University of Notre Dame Press, 2005). Bede's *Ecclesiastical History* illustrates this interweaving of legal documents and jurisprudential narratives, as part of a broader story about the formation of a nation.

A connection between mythical history and law is particularly evident in the "Germanic law codes," which were preserved from the sixth to ninth centuries, and which have constituted an important source of information about peoples encountered at the northwestern edges of the Roman empire. Questions have been raised about whether these laws applied very extensively in practice, or whether they rather served as symbolic declarations, operating more in the realm of aspiration than reality. For our purposes it is not necessary to take a strong position on this question, and we can assume for the sake of argument that these laws were primarily aspirational. The legal ideals and rules that they recorded are nonetheless interesting and significant, leaving an imprint in European historical developments.[82]

We do not see anything like intellectual property in these early forms of law (*leges*). What we do see, however, are broad-based rules for the protection of church property, for hierarchical principles of social peacemaking, and for recognition of legal relationships of various kinds. We see, in other words, a conception that law is an ordering and obliging force in society, and that the king in council with his wise men has a responsibility for ensuring that the society under his protection has good laws. Concepts of divinity, sacrality, and mythical history underpin this notion of law as an ordering and obliging social force.[83]

An especially potent combination of sacred history and law is evident in the prologue to the Bavarian Laws (*Leges Baiwariorum*, c. 745), which were described in the opening title as a decree (*decretum*) of the king and his princes, together with "all the Christian people who live under [or within, *infra*] the Merovingian kingdom." In the *Bavarian leges*, Moses is described as the first and greatest lawgiver, preeminent in a long series of legislators for specific peoples (*gentes*). New laws began with the emperor Constantine, but these were disordered (*inordinatae*) until they were arranged in books (*codices*), culminating in the Theodosian Code (438). After this, each people (*gens*) developed their own law from their long-standing customs (*consuetudines*).[84]

82 Patrick Wormald, *Legal Culture in the Early Medieval West: Law as Text, Image, and Experience* (London: The Hambledon Press, 1999); Moore, *Sacred Kingdom*, 262. The level of Christian influence seems to develop over time, with the earliest of the Frankish law codes showing relatively little influence from Christianity. J. M. Wallace-Hadrill, *The Frankish Church* (Oxford: Clarendon Press, 1983), 27. Drawing on the scholarship of Patrick Wormald, however, it is important to add that the very motivation to render laws in writing testifies to influences from Roman and Biblical legal culture. Wormald, *Legal Culture*, xii, 1–43.

83 In using the phrase "mythic history," I mean to indicate a narrative describing a "higher time" of origins. On the notion of higher times, see Charles Taylor, *A Secular Age* (Cambridge, MA: Harvard University Press, 2007), 54–61. In the Biblical tradition, the archetype for such narratives is found in the Genesis accounts of creation, which Biblical scholars have described as a hybrid between myth and epic history. Frank Moore Cross, *Canaanite Myth and Hebrew Epic: Essays in the History of the Religion of Israel* (Cambridge, MA: Harvard University Press, 1973).

84 Theodore John Rivers (trans.), *Laws of the Alamans and Bavarians* (Philadelphia: University of Pennsylvania Press, 1977), 109–18. Latin text, edited by George Henry Pertz & John Merkel, is digitally accessible through the *Monumenta Germaniae Historica* (MGH) website: www.dmgh.de/

Lex after all is a written constitution (*constitutio scripta*). *Mores* are old and tested customs, unwritten, but manifested in traditional social practices. *Mores* are nonetheless a type of law which derives from common and long-standing usage. Written law (*lex*) should be universal. It should be established with reason (*ratio*), contribute to orderly social action (*disciplina*), and produce well-being (*saluti*). In accordance with these principles, the kings of the Franks, Alamans, and Bavarians, counseled by their wisest men, gave good and ordered law to each people (*gens*) under their rule. Pagan customs were changed in accordance with Christian law, and the best ancient laws were written down. What followed was the law of a particular people, the Bavarians.[85]

Here we see evidence that the Bible was conceived as a source of law, since Moses was described in the Bavarian *leges* as the preeminent lawgiver. The defining conceptions of law articulated in the Bavarian *leges* echo Isidore of Seville's *Etymologies*, an encyclopedia of words and concepts from antiquity. Relying on Isidore, the Frankish and Bavarian lawgivers were placing themselves within a "tradition of legislation beginning with Moses, and running through Egyptian, Greek and Roman law, culminating in the Theodosian Code."[86]

Isidore's *Etymologies* had offered mythical and historical (etiological) explanations for the meaning of Latin, Greek, and Hebrew words while also constituting a compendium of ancient learning ranging from agriculture to mining, law to philosophy. One area of learning with which Isidore was particularly concerned was technology and the arts. Like the Elder Pliny, whom he imitated and referenced, Isidore was concerned with the origins of arts, skills, and bodies of learning. But, as a Christian bishop schooled in Biblical traditions, Isidore blended a Greco-Roman fascination with the origins of technology and civilization with an emphasis on *genesis*, on creation of the radically new. Isidore's inventors were divine and human agent-creators rather than discoverers of timeless arts.

Stories of invention are everywhere in the *Etymologies*. Where the traditional Greco-Roman account of origins relied on a divine inventor (e.g., Saturn), Isidore might accept this, but he downgraded the Greco-Roman deities to human beings. Saturn may have invented the stamping and marking of gold coins, for example, but Saturn was simply a man turned into a god by his people after his death, because they so valued his contributions to their society. Vulcan came to be worshiped as a god because he invented the art of forging metals, Asclepius because he invented the art of medicine. Inventors were human creators, for Isidore, and he celebrated their authorship and originality, even as he denied their divinity. He also recognized the

(accessed January 31, 2020): MGH, *Leges (in Folio) (LL)* 3: *Leges Alamannorum. Leges Baiuwariorum. Leges Burgundionum. Lex Frisionum* (Hannover, 1863), 257–69.

85 Rivers, *Law of the Bavarians*, 109–10; MGH, *Leges* 3, 257–60; Moore, *Sacred Kingdom*, 234–9.

86 Ian Wood, *The Merovingian Kingdoms, 450–751* (Abingdon: Routledge, 2014) [Kindle], location 3689; *cf.* Moore, Sacred Kingdom, 239. *The Etymologies of Isidore of Seville*, translated by Stephen A. Barney, W. J. Lewis, J. A. Beach, Oliver Berghof (Cambridge, UK: Cambridge University Press, 2006), V.i.

value to human communities, particularly to cities, that came from new arts, technologies, and writings.[87]

The legacies of west-Gothic law and church councils, together with the writings of Isidore, would endure in Frankish culture through the revolutionary upheaval that ushered in the Carolingian kings, a new Frankish dynasty called by historians after their early founder Charles Martel, grandfather of Charles "the Great" (Charlemagne).

But that is the story for the next chapter.

5.10 CONCLUSION: WESTERN LEGALITY AND RATIONALITIES

In this chapter, we have traced the Christianization of the western Roman empire, focusing on key episodes from the fourth to the eighth century. Emphasizing the impacts of this Christianization on instruments of legal power, we have also witnessed a transformation in jurisprudential narratives and early legal codes. A revolution in the sources of social power took place in these centuries, and its causes were both spiritual (cultural) and material. The church became a privileged beneficiary, from emperors and kings, and from pious persons, rich and poor alike. The massive accumulation of wealth, especially of landed property, that this involved transformed bishops and monasteries into great landlords and judges.

Christianity became an order of obligation, and performances of social obligation drew upon a synthesis of Roman and Biblical legal traditions. When a Frankish king like Clovis granted judicial immunities to churches, monasteries, or powerful laymen, he was performing and memorializing what he perceived to be an obligation for a Christian king: to protect the property of the church, to preserve law and order, and to ensure a continuous stream of prayers on behalf of his family and the kingdom. When bishops and monasteries preserved the legal documents granting these immunities, surrounding them with mythical and historical accounts in chronicles and cartularies, they were contributing to jurisprudential narratives which would become parts of the legal tradition transmitted to future generations of western kings.

A western tradition of legality was coming into being.

This western tradition of legality, we might say, is an order of obligation, one in which legitimating rationales for obligations and privileges are offered through jurisprudential narratives that draw on Biblical and Roman legal traditions. The granting of privileges through instruments of legal power continues a line of practice

[87] *Etymologies of Isidore* VIII.xi; vi.viii; xvi.xviii; cf xvi.xvi.6; Wallace-Hadrill, *Frankish Church*, 19. Isidore may be building on a literature on "first discoveries" (labeled heurematography by contemporary scholars), which seems to go back to the Peripatetic school of Aristotle, and which was influential among early Muslim scholars. William F. McCants, *Founding Gods, Inventing Nations: Conquest and Culture Myths from Antiquity to Islam* (Princeton: Princeton University Press, 2012), 6 n.18, 63–4.

stretching back to the republican period of Rome's expansion, one involving both social performances and written memorials. The performances draw on a combination of Christian ideals for relations of authority, and Roman lordly powers. The Christian ideals for relations of authority contribute to a separation of *officium* from *persona*, duty/obligation from personality. And privileged lordly powers center around jurisdiction and courts.[88]

We are witnessing the rise of a distinctive order of obligation, one involving faith in legality. This is an order of obligation that combines a deep confidence in the ordering powers of law with tendencies toward acquisitiveness in matters of property and wealth. The emphasis on God's creation within Christianity is being combined with Hellenistic Roman traditions celebrating wondrous discoveries, and this will enable new substantive rationalities that valorize invention and creativity for the benefit of the state. Any such possibility is held in check for the moment by the strong subordination of all goal-oriented behavior to Biblically inspired purposes involving heavenly salvation and ultimate well-being, but this subordination is fragile, subject to displacement by the pragmatics of power politics.[89]

In the next chapter, we will witness such displacement in Venice, in an early precursor to modern intellectual property.

[88] For further discussion, with focus on transformations in the tax structure of Roman late antiquity, see Walter Goffart, "Old and New in Roman Taxation," *Past & Present* 96 (1982): 3–21; Alexander Callander Murray, "Merovingian Immunity Revisited," *History Compass* 8.8 (2010): 913–28; Alexander Callander Murray, "Immunity, Nobility, and the Edict of Paris," *Speculum* 69.1 (1994): 18–39.

[89] For evenhanded assessment of arguments that a new Christian cultural context contributed to medieval emphases on technological innovation in Western society, see George Ovitt, Jr., *The Restoration of Perfection: Labor and Technology in Medieval Culture* (New Brunswick: Rutgers University Press, 1986); *cf.* George Ovitt, Jr., "The Cultural Context of Western Technology: Early Christian Attitudes Toward Manual Labor," in Allen J. Frantzen and Douglas Moffat (eds), *The Work of Work: Servitude, Slavery, and Labor in Medieval England* (Glasgow: Cruithne Press, 1994), 71–94. For the development of Christian theological views on creation ex nihilo, see Wilken, *Christians as the Romans Saw Them*, 83–93; *Theophilus of Antioch* Ad Autolycum, text and translation by Robert M. Grant (Oxford: Oxford University Press, 1970), I.4, II.4, II.10. For an extended argument that the rise of market-oriented societies in the west was due to a displacement of normative (legal, political, and religious) controls on acquisitive, goal-oriented activity, see Karl Polanyi, *The Great Transformation: The Political and Economic Origins of Our Time* (Boston: Beacon Press, 2001).

6

Privileges and Immunities in a Sacramentalizing Order

On September 18, 1469, five lord councilors of Venice issued a privilege to Master John of Speyer, granting him the exclusive right, good throughout the city of Venice and its dominions, to practice the novel art of printing. Five years later, in 1474, Venice's chief councilors voted to issue a broader decree, one that many have considered the world's first patent law. In this decree, Venice promised that any author and inventor of "new and ingenious contrivances," not seen before in the Venetian dominions, would be granted the exclusive freedom (*libertà*), for a period of up to ten years, to make his ingenious device. In this way, the lord councilors reasoned, inventors of new and ingenious artifices (*artificii*) would be encouraged and their great city would be enriched.[1]

[1] Johannes of Speyer's Printing Monopoly, Venice (1469), translated by Joanna Kostylo, at Primary Sources on Copyright (1450–1900), edited by Lionel Bently and M. Kretschmer, www.copyrighthistory.org (hereafter *Primary Sources*); Venetian Statute on Industrial Brevets, Venice (1474), translated by Joanna Kostylo, *Primary Sources*.

Now-classic statements about Venice's claims to enacting the world's first patent law were published in the *Journal of the Patent and Trademark Office Society* (JPTOS) during the mid-twentieth century, and were foreshadowed in the work of P. J. (Pat) Federico, a long-time editor and historian for the JPTOS, USPTO examiner, and architect of the US Patent Act of 1952, which remains the statutory foundation of US patent law today. P. J. Federico, "Origin and Early History of Patents," *Journal of the Patent Office Society* 11 (1929): 292–305; P. J. Federico, "Commentary on the New Patent Act [of 1952]," *Journal of the Patent and Trademark Office Society* 75 (1993): 161–231; Maximilian Frumkin, "The Origin of Patents," *Journal of the Patent Office Society* 27 (1945): 143–9; Giulio Mandich, "Venetian Patents (1450–1550)," translated by F. D. Prager, *Journal of the Patent Office Society* 30 (1948): 166–224; Giulio Mandich, "Venetian Origins of Inventors' Rights," translated by F. D. Prager, *Journal of the Patent Office Society* 42 (1960): 378–82; F. D. Prager, "A History of Intellectual Property from 1545 to 1787," *Journal of the Patent Office Society* 26 (1944): 711–60; F. D. Prager, "The Early Growth and Influence of Intellectual Property," *Journal of the Patent Office Society* 34 (1952): 106–40. For earlier arguments and parallels in British historiography, see E. W. Hulme, "The History of the Patent System under the Prerogative and at Common Law," *Law Quarterly Review* 12 (1896): 141–54; E. W. Hulme, "History of the Patent System under the Prerogative and at Common Law. A Sequel." *Law Quarterly Review* 16 (1900): 44–56; Maximilian Frumkin, "Early History of Patents for Invention," *Transactions* 26 (1947): 47–56. For important refinements, see Christopher May, "The Venetian Moment," *Prometheus* 20:2 (2002): 159–79; Ted Sichelman and Sean O'Connor, "Patents as Promoters of Competition: The Guild Origins of Patent Law in the Venetian Republic," *San Diego Law Review* 49 (2012): 1267–82.

In these two Venetian decrees, we can see elements of modern intellectual property law. However, we are seeing only a tentative development – one that displayed significant continuities with older forms of privilege-granting, and one that should be carefully differentiated from modern intellectual property. Like the emperors, popes, and kings we have already studied, the Venetian lord councilors were granting privileges, not property – the decree provided that the city retained complete discretion to appropriate the invention, at any time, without compensation – and they were granting these privileges for the "utility and benefit" of their civic community (*stado*).[2]

Nevertheless, there are important new elements here. Something like modern statutory law, albeit at the level of a city and not a nation-state, is being used to prospectively promise a reward for invention, in general terms. The promise of a privileged position is offered to Venetian citizens and residents according to conditions that are laid out explicitly. There is a shift here, in other words, toward uniformity, publicity, and generality, rather than private discretion and particularized judgment. There is also a shift in orientation toward the future, with a corresponding sense of value in novelty, rather than a traditional orientation toward the past, with a corresponding emphasis on stability.[3]

Invention and authorship are presented as coming from the "most clever minds" of ingenious men. A form of civic, statutory law is to be deployed in encouraging such men to exercise their ingenuity. The mechanism of such encouragement will be the city's promise of cooperative protection against imitation by others in making an invention, for up to ten years, in this way ensuring that ingenious inventors are not deprived of their honor (*l'honor*). By granting honor and reward to inventors, "men of such kind" will "exert their minds, invent and make things" that will be "of no small utility and benefit to our state."[4]

The emphasis placed on *honor* in the Venetian statute is an important clue that we are not quite in the same social world as our own. Language of honor takes us into a field of semantics associated with the aristocratic lordship of the high Middle Ages. So, in the Venetian statute of 1474, we see a kind of hybrid regulation, one that holds potential for development into the world of modern intellectual property law, but one that is also rooted in the social world of late European feudalism and urban aristocracy. In this chapter, we will seek to understand how these elements of urban

[2] "But our Government (*Signoria*) will be free, at its complete discretion, to take and use for its needs any of the said contrivances and instruments, with this condition, however, that no one other than the authors shall operate them." Kostylo (trans.), Venetian Statute of 1474, *Primary Sources*. Joanna Kostylo strongly emphasizes continuities with older privilege-granting practices in her detailed commentary, while also noting new directions in the generality and prospective character of the legislation, as well as the emphasis on individual inventors. Joanna Kostylo, "Commentary on the Venetian Statute of 1474," *Primary Sources* (2008), §5.

[3] Joanna Kostylo, "Commentary on the Venetian Statute of 1474," *Primary Sources* (2008), §5; May, "Venetian Moment," 162.

[4] Kostylo trans. (Et se'l fosse prouisto … e tuor l'honor suo, simel homeni exercitariano l'ingegno, trouoriano, et fariano de la chosse, che sariano de non picola utilità et beneficio ad stado nostro.)

aristocratic lordship and European feudalism came together, in such a way that they held the potential for development into modern intellectual property law. In order to do this, though, we must grapple, albeit minimally, with the concept of *feudalism* itself, a concept that is highly contested among medieval scholars.[5]

Consistent with the work of Max Weber and Michael Mann, we can follow recent historians of the European Middle Ages, who have argued that a "feudal transformation" took place, with local variations, between roughly 800 and 1200 across western Europe. This transformative development, which we can only describe with the benefit of hindsight, injected new cultural meanings and methods of political coordination into social relationships, enabling possibilities for new levels of social power. We can think of these new cultural meanings and methods of political coordination, in combination, as a *sacramentalizing order of obligation*, the development of which we will trace in this chapter. The developmental process begins with an ambitious project of religious and legal reform, one that placed high value on learning and education, albeit with primary emphasis on sacramental theology. The energizers of this cultural and political project are known to history as the Carolingians, a dynastic lineage named after their progenitor, Charles Martel, "The Hammer" of European history.[6]

In one chapter we cannot hope to do justice to the Carolingians and their legacy, but there are at least two related ways in which they matter for the story of intellectual property that we are tracing in this book. First, the Carolingians carried forward traditions from imperial and papal Rome, transforming those traditions in the forging of a new type of governing community. And second, with the Carolingians, a new emphasis on learning led to new types of communities aiming at the support of learning. While many aspects of Carolingian governance had

[5] Language of *honor*: Heinrich Fichtenau, *Living in the Tenth Century: Mentalities and Social Orders*, translated by Patrick J. Geary (Chicago: University of Chicago Press, 1991), 7, 141–4. Scholarly contestation over the concept of *feudalism*: Elizabeth A. R. Brown, "The Tyranny of a Construct: Feudalism and Historians of Medieval Europe," *The American Historical Review* 79.4 (1974): 1063–88; Susan Reynolds, *The Middle Ages without Feudalism: Essays in Criticism and Comparison on the Medieval West* (London: Routledge, 2012); Susan Reynolds, *Fiefs and Vassals: The Medieval Evidence Reinterpreted* (Oxford: Clarendon Press, 1994).

[6] New understandings of the feudal transformation: Jean-Pierre Poly and Eric Bournazel, *The Feudal Transformation 900–1200*, translated by Caroline Higgitt (New York: Holmes & Meier, 1991); Charles West, *Reframing the Feudal Revolution: Political and Social Transformation between the Marne and Moselle, c. 800–c. 1100* (Cambridge, UK: Cambridge University Press, 2013). Ideologies and political coordination in the Carolingian project of reform: Mayke de Jong, *The Pentitential State: Authority and Atonement in the Age of Louis the Pious, 814–840* (Cambridge, UK: Cambridge University Press, 2009); Geoffrey Koziol, *The Politics of Memory and Identity in Carolingian Royal Diplomas* (Turnhout, Belgium: Brepols Publishers, 2012); Rosamond McKitterick, *The Carolingians and the Written Word* (Cambridge, UK: Cambridge University Press, 1989); Rosamond McKitterick, *The Frankish Church and the Carolingian Reforms, 789–895* (London: Royal Historical Society, 1977); Janet L. Nelson, *Politics and Ritual in Early Medieval Europe* (London: Hambledon Press, 1986). My concept of a "sacramentalizing order" builds especially on Mayke de Jong's portrayal of the Carolingian "Penitential State," in combination with Max Weber's conception of law as a cultural *Ordnung* (order).

collapsed by the end of the ninth century, the new communities of learning would endure and develop into the universities of the high Middle Ages, which are a very mixed blessing for us today.

To understand how something like modern intellectual property was created, we need to understand how Europeans came to see originality and creativity as activities to be encouraged through economic privileges. While the Carolingians did not emphasize novelty, they did treat learning as something to be encouraged. Moreover, this encouragement was given a new level of cultural and organizational force. What is interesting, however, is that the Carolingian encouragement of learning was part of a grand vision for the Christianization of society. Learning and education were to serve the cause of Christian sacraments and salvation. Legal patterns (forms) for the religiously inspired encouragement of learning in governing communities would endure, carried by a new brand of legal professionals, to become a foundation for modern intellectual property law.

In Venetian privileges of the fifteenth century, we will see one early outgrowth of these developments, which some scholars have identified as a foundation for modern intellectual property.

6.1 CULTIVATING A SACRAMENTAL ORDER OF OBLIGATION

In 753–4, when a Frankish boy known to history as Charlemagne – "Charles the Great" – was about six years old, Pope Stephen II (752–7) made the first-ever journey by a pope across the Alps to the land of the Franks, seeking support from Charlemagne's father, Pippin (III), in an ongoing struggle against the Lombards. After concluding a treaty of friendship, the pope traveled with the Frankish king, his wife Bertrada, and their sons to the abbey of St. Denis near Paris; there he consecrated them by pouring sacred oil (*chrism*) on their heads. Biblical in inspiration, the rituals carried out by pope and king together on this sacred occasion were modeled on Roman-Byzantine forms of ordination. Just shy of fifty years later, on Christmas day in the year 800, Charlemagne would again be consecrated by a pope, but this time it would be as emperor (*imperator*), and the sacramental ritual would take place in Rome.[7]

During Charlemagne's lifetime, a momentous realignment was taking place in the realms of military and political power. The popes were allying themselves with the Franks, as their military protectors, deliberately replacing the emperors in Constantinople. As we can see from the anointing of the young Charlemagne, this

[7] Raymond Davis (ed. & trans.), *The Lives of the Eighth-Century Popes (Liber Pontificalis)*, 2nd ed. (Liverpool: Liverpool University Press, 2007), 50–67; Johannes Fried, *Charlemagne*, translated by Peter Lewis (Cambridge, MA: Harvard University Press, 2016), 41–50; Rosamund McKitterick, *Charlemagne: The Formation of a European Identity* (Cambridge, UK: Cambridge University Press, 2008), 1, 70–5; Thomas F. X. Noble, *The Republic of St. Peter: The Birth of the Papal State, 680–825* (Philadelphia: University of Pennsylvania Press, 1984), 87–8; J. M. Wallace-Hadrill, *The Frankish Church* (Oxford: Clarendon Press, 1983), 166–70.

realignment involved an important cultural dimension: the granting of a sacramental character to the Frankish kings. Donations of property and authority solidified a sacramental alliance between imperial kings and popes, laying the foundation for a relationship between the papacy and the rulers of Europe that would hold, even in periods of intense struggle, until the sixteenth century, when a new European order was forged.[8]

Charlemagne initiated a program of religious reform during the last quarter of the eighth century, not long after victory in northern Italy brought Lombardy into his kingdom (774). In that same year, Pope Hadrian I (772–95) gave a compilation of canon law to Charlemagne, encouraging him as an anointed Christian king to undertake reforms for his kingdom. In 789, during a break in his endless wars of conquest, Charlemagne oversaw the issuance of a *capitulary* that is known to historians as the *General Admonition*. Central to its canonical vision for church reform was an educational campaign to raise the standards of learning throughout the kingdom, particularly the learning of clerics. Through clerics, learning was to extend also to the laity. New forms of law-giving – especially royal legislation organized into chapters (*capitula*) – were part of this reforming vision.[9]

6.2 LEGAL LETTERS AND RELIGIOUS REFORM

Law was an important instrument for the Carolingian kings, and for those who cooperated with them in their ambitious project to build a more Christian community. One early supporter was a missionary from the British Isles, Winfrid, later named Boniface. In Boniface's letters we see striking evidence of continuity in practices and performances connected with letters as instruments of legal power.

[8] Eleanor Shipley Duckett, *Alcuin, Friend of Charlemagne: His World and His Work* (New York: The MacMillan Company, 1951), 39–79; Clemens Gantner and Stefan Schima, "The Papacy," in Philip L. Reynolds (ed.), *Great Christian Jurists and Legal Collections in the First Millennium* (Cambridge, UK: Cambridge University Press, 2019), 145–54; Noble, *Republic of St. Peter*, xxi and passim.

[9] The Latin text of the *General Admonition* is digitally accessible through the *Monumenta Germaniae Historica* (MGH) website: www.dmgh.de/ (accessed September 12, 2019). I refer to MGH volumes by website headings and shortened titles, together with the editor. For the General Admonition, edited by Alfred Boretius (Hannover, 1883): MGH, *Leges, Capitularia Regum Francorum (Capit.) I*, 52–62. An English translation is available in P. D. King, *Charlemagne: Translated Sources* (Lancaster: University of Lancaster, 1987), 209–20. Charlemagne's victory in northern Italy: Davis, *Eighth-Century Popes*, 132–9. The compilation of canon law (*Dionysio-Hadriana*): Lotte Kéry, *Canonical Collections of the Early Middle Ages: A Bibliographical Guide to the Manuscripts and Literature* (Washington, DC: The Catholic University of America Press, 2013); Rosamund McKitterick, "Knowledge of Canon Law in the Frankish Kingdoms before 789: The Manuscript Evidence," *The Journal of Theological Studies*, 36 (1): 97–117 (1985), 98; Michael Edward Moore, *A Sacred Kingdom: Bishops and the Rise of Frankish Kingship, 300–850* (Washington, DC: Catholic University Press, 2011), 265; Robert Somerville and Bruce C. Brasington, *Prefaces to Canon Law Books in Latin Christianity* (New Haven: Yale University Press, 1998), 59–62. Connections between canon law, church reform, and the Carolingian "renaissance" in learning: Giles Brown, "Introduction: The Carolingian Renaissance," in Rosamund McKitterick (ed.), *Carolingian Culture: Emulation and Innovation* (Cambridge, UK: Cambridge University Press, 1994), 1–51; McKitterick, *Frankish Church*, and passim.

At the same time, however, we see how these are being adapted in accordance with the new, sacramental culture.[10]

One of Boniface's letters, for example, describes a ritual connected with an oath of loyalty to Pope Gregory II (715–31). Boniface's oath had been written out on parchment and placed on the altar at St. Peter's cathedral in Rome, above the relics of St. Peter himself. After administering the oath, Pope Gregory drafted letters of commendation for Boniface to carry with him, investing him with the authority of a bishop, and threatening excommunication against anyone who did not lend him their support. Charlemagne's grandfather, Charles Martel, added his support, issuing a letter to his agents (*missi*) throughout the kingdom, instructing them to protect Boniface and ensure that he received justice. In 732, Pope Gregory III (731–41) raised Boniface to the status of archbishop and granted him the *pallium*.[11]

By 742, Boniface's letter collection indicates that the Carolingians were undertaking ambitious reforms of ecclesiastical law and organization in the Frankish realms. Church councils were held in 742 and 743, announcing general principles for church governance, given with the advice of priests and nobles, including a rule that synods should thereafter be held annually, "so that in our presence the canonical decrees and the laws of the Church may be reestablished and the Christian religion purified."[12]

Under the Carolingian kings, church councils were an important occasion for public assemblies and legal hearings, for the issuance of charters and privileges, and for the issuance of capitularies. Writing to Boniface in 745, Pope Zacharias (741–52) had urged that church councils continue, considering them to be vital for "the unity of the Church of God," and for the spreading of Christian discipline, "even in the extreme West." For the pope this "extreme West" likely extended to the British Isles, whose bishops, abbesses, and kings remained in active correspondence with Boniface, their fellow Briton.[13]

Hints at reform in practices connected with property donation are apparent in Boniface's letters. The endowment of monasteries was a way that wealthy families could ensure spiritual and material support for themselves, and this was a system that could be abused. Bede was scathing about comparable practices in northern

10 *The Letters of Saint Boniface*, translated by Ephraim Emerton (New York: Columbia University Press, 2000), Latin edition by Michael Tangl (Berlin, 1916) available at MGH, *Epistolae (in Qaurt)* (*Epp.* 3), *Epistolae Merowingici et Karolini aevi (I)*, 215–433. Context for Boniface's letters: Thomas F. X. Noble, "Introduction," in *Letters of Boniface*, 7–35. I cite Emerton's translation as *Letters of Boniface*, using Emerton's numeration in Arab numerals.

11 *Letters of Boniface* 4, 8–14, 17, 20. Boniface drew instruction from Gregory the Great's letters, including his instructions to Augustine of Canterbury. *Letters of Boniface* 24, 59.

12 *Letters of Boniface* 43–4; *also* Moore, *Sacred Kingdom*, 221–3.

13 *Letters of Boniface* 48–9, 51–2, 62, 65, 76–7. "From its inception, the Carolingian dynasty was conceived in terms drawn from the social thought of episcopal councils." Moore, *Sacred Kingdom*, 244. On the new forms of state and social power achieved by the Carolingians and expressed through their performative acts of law-giving, see Moore, *Sacred Kingdom*, 243–85; *also* McKitterick, *Frankish Church*, 16–25.

England, viewing some of the resulting monastic establishments as morally compromised retirement homes for the wealthy. One solution to this problem, as we can see from the letter of Pope Zacharias, was to ensure oversight from the local bishop. However, if the bishop himself was compromised by family ties of loyalty, episcopal oversight was an ineffective solution.[14]

A more radical solution was to place a monastery directly under the oversight and jurisdiction of the papacy, and to protect the monastery from local interference by granting it an immunity. In the previous chapter, we saw Gregory I do this on an ad hoc basis for certain monasteries, and his grants were afterward treated as precedents. By the Carolingian period, paradigms were developing for joint papal and royal protection of monasteries through grants of immunity. In 751, the same year that he approved the Carolingian replacement of the Merovingian dynasty, Pope Zacharias approved Boniface's request to establish a new monastery in the middle Rhine region, to be known as Fulda, and issued a charter of privilege granting exemption from episcopal oversight to the new monastery.[15]

Carolingian kings, like their Merovingian predecessors, actively cooperated with the papacy in seeking to immunize monasteries from various types of interference by local lords, which could weaken a monastery by undermining the authority of its abbot or by depleting the revenues that it could otherwise collect from economic activities on its lands. Documentary forms for royal grants of immunity are included in the *Formulary of Marculf*, a collection that may have been originally compiled by a monk of St. Denis near 700; it was continually copied, edited, and circulated into the tenth century. Charters of immunity from kings were also preserved as originals by monasteries, or recopied within jurisprudential narratives, in cartularies.[16]

In granting immunities, popes and kings alike endeavored to ensure material and social support for a recipient who was to be favored because of a social good being provided by the recipient. In the case of monasteries, the social good being provided was heroic spirituality and prayer, which was believed to merit favor from God,

[14] Reform of property: *Letters of Boniface* 44, 48, 67; Wallace-Hadrill, *Frankish Church*, 61–2; Noble, "Introduction," in *Letters of Boniface* 22–23. Bede on comparable critiques in northern England: Letter to Egbert, translated by D. H. Farmer, in Bede, *Ecclesiastical History of the English People*, translated by Leo Sherley-Price, revised by R. E. Latham (London: Penguin Books, 1990), 335–51.

[15] *Letters of Boniface* 70–1, 73; Susan Wood, *The Proprietary Church in the Medieval West* (Oxford: Oxford University Press, 2006), 101.

[16] *The Formularies of Angers and Marculf: Two Merovingian Legal Handbooks*, translated by Alice Rio (Liverpool: Liverpool University Press, 2008), 104–244. For helpful discussion of the different types of immunity, including episcopal immunities for monasteries, see Alexander Callander Murray, "Merovingian Immunity Revisited," *History Compass* 8.8 (2010): 913–28; *also* Alexander Callander Murray, "Immunity, Nobility, and the Edict of Paris," *Speculum* 69.1 (1994): 18–39; Wallace-Hadrill, *Frankish Church*, 60, 62 69–74, 101. For a cartulary preserving documents from the early eighth to the early twelfth centuries, see *The Cartulary of Flavigny, 717–1113*, edited by Constance Brittain Bouchard (Cambridge, MA: The Medieval Academy of America, 1991). For discussion of the role of immunities, both royal and episcopal, in strengthening the monastery of Corbie, see David Ganz, *Corbie in the Carolingian Renaissance* (Sigmaringen: Jan Thorbeke Verlag, 1990), 14–35.

spilling over for the good of the entire community, and most especially for the founder and his family.[17]

Important economic benefits flowed to the recipients of immunities. The grants created an exceptional legal status, ensuring a revenue stream, either directly or indirectly. A common pattern was that the immunity permitted the grantee to collect revenues or fees that would otherwise be collected by a local overlord, or by the king himself. According to a typical example, the grantee might be permitted to collect court payments, which would otherwise be collected by a local count or bishop. In addition to economic effects, moreover, immunities might result in direct access to justice from the king or the pope, rather than from a local lord.[18]

Most of the actual grants like these, which have been preserved, were given to monasteries or churches. This does not mean that grants were not made to laypeople, however. In fact, the generic forms preserved in formularies like the *Formulary of Marculf* indicate that grants of various kinds were probably made in significant numbers to laypeople. However, only monasteries and churches had the kind of institutional longevity that enabled records to be preserved into our own time. With medieval history, as indeed with all history, we only see part of the story.[19]

However, for our purposes, the part of the story that we can most readily recover is important and relevant. This is because ecclesiastical immunities supported social communities that were preeminent, in their own time, for intellectual production. It was in the great monasteries, like Fulda and St. Denis, as in cathedral churches like Rheims, that manuscripts were copied and that elite thinkers of the day were educated. It was monasteries and cathedral churches that were given the economic resources enabling them to house kings and entourages on itineraries, as well as the growing numbers of men and women on pilgrimage. Monasteries and cathedral churches were the privileged intellectual and economic centers of their time, and it is important to see that this was actively fostered by popes and kings, through legal grants of privilege and immunity, together with grants of landed property. These grants by popes and kings were greatly aided by a continuous stream of donations

17 Wallace-Hadrill, *Frankish Church*, 58–61, 126–30.

18 Wallace-Hadrill, *Frankish Church*, 128–30, 138. I am following the interpretation of Alexander Callander Murray in "Merovingian Immunity Revisited," 915–18.

19 For further discussion of the evidence from formulae, see Alice Rio, *Legal Practice and the Written Word in the Early Middle Ages: Frankish Formulae, c. 500–1000* (Cambridge, UK: Cambridge University Press, 2009). For early Frankish charters, some of which were still written on papyrus, see Albert Bruckner and Robert Marichal (eds.), *Chartae Latinae Antiquiores: Facsimile-Edition of the Latin Charters Prior to the Ninth Century*, Parts XIII–XVI: France (Dietikon-Zürich: URS Graf Verlag, 1981–2, 1986); also MGH, *Diplomata [Urkunden], Merowinger (DD Mer.)*, 2 volumes edited by Theo Kölzer (Hannover, 2001); MGH, *DD Mer. 1872*, edited by George Heinrich Pertz (Hannover, 1872). Review essays: David Ganz and Walter Goffart, "Charters Earlier than 800 from French Collections," *Speculum* 65.4 (1990): 906–32; Alexander Callander Murray, "The New MGH Edition of the Charters of the Merovingian Kings," *The Journal of Medieval Latin* 15 (2005): 246–78.

from clerics and Christian laity, ranging from wealthy dukes and counts to humbler women and men.[20]

Carolingian grants of privilege, immunity, and property offer an important comparison point to modern intellectual property. From the perspective of legal form, they constituted an ongoing pattern of legal practice, with roots stretching back to imperial Rome. And, in their economic substance, they were very similar to modern intellectual property: they created a kind of exclusive, protected position in the provision of valued services in order to ensure a revenue stream and to thereby provide material support for an intellectual activity that was seen as a social good. In the case of the monasteries and cathedral churches, the social goods being provided were primarily spiritual, whereas, in the case of contemporary intellectual property, the social goods are primarily technological, artistic, and commercial. The social substance differs, but the legal and economic form is very similar.

6.3 BISHOPS, PROPERTY, AND HONOR

Bishops had played a formative role in constituting the authority structure for western kingdoms since the days of the Roman empire. However, during the reign of Charlemagne, bishops became vital agents in a specific project of religious and legal reform, a project that emphasized learning and education, as well as behavior, and that focused both directly and indirectly on the laity. Ideals and social realities of property were developed in important ways through this process of reform, impacting prevailing understandings of law and social order, and providing a foundation for legal and communal conceptions of the civic community, based on idealized models of the church.[21]

A specific, communal vision for church reform radiated outward from the *civitas* of Metz, a cathedral town located within the ancient ecclesiastical province of *Belgica Prima*, under the metropolitan bishop of Trier. Focusing especially on the cathedral churches of bishops, the reforms also extended more broadly to people served by the cathedral churches, primarily the clergy, but also to widows, orphans, and other similarly vulnerable persons who depended on the church. Echoing later in conciliar legislation for the whole kingdom, this reforming vision became a kind of communal blueprint, one that included specifications for property and inheritance.[22]

[20] Overview in Rosamond McKitterick, *The Frankish Kingdoms under the Carolingians, 751–987* (London: Longman, 1983), 200–27; also see Ganz, *Corbie*, 14–35, 121–3. On monasteries as spiritual and material supports for itinerant Carolingian rulership, see Mayke de Jong, "The Sacred Palace, Public Penance, and the Carolingian Polity," in Reynolds, *Great Christian Jurists*, 155–81.

[21] Moore, *Sacred Kingdom*, 328–67; Nelson, *Politics & Ritual*, 133–71, esp. 146–7, 170.

[22] For the Merovingian and Carolingian ecclesiastical structure, which followed the outlines of late Roman diocesan organization, see McKitterick, *Frankish Kingdoms*, 372–3; Alexander Callander Murray, *From Roman to Merovingian Gaul: A Reader* (Toronto: University of Toronto Press, 2008), 665–9. For an archaeological and historical survey, providing context for ecclesiastical

This reforming vision was premised on an understanding of episcopal structure and authority adapted from late antiquity. Popes like Gregory the Great had strongly influenced this understanding, but so had other important bishops, such as Isidore of Seville, Ambrose of Milan (c. 340–397), Caesarius of Arles (c. 470–542), and Augustine of Hippo. Isidore's influence was especially strong. In addition to his *Etymologies*, Isidore had written a handbook for bishops, *On Ecclesiastical Offices* (*De Ecclesiasticis Officiis*). This handbook offered an explanatory account – one that is characteristically etymological – for duties and rituals undertaken by bishops in the west-Gothic church. This text was later picked up and used by eighth-century Frankish clerics, as they searched for clarity about their obligations.[23]

What was drawn upon by the Frankish reformers, and articulated by Isidore, was nothing less than a theory of society, one in which bishops occupy the center of authority, and one in which society and church are equated. This is a society that is idealized as being held together by bonds of peace and love (*pax et concordia*), a society that is overseen by bishops, and a society that comes alive in liturgical performance. This is also a society in which community is constituted through humility and obedience to an overarching system of rules (*regulae*), articulating principles, and exemplary ideals that are meant to guide social action and govern virtuous practices in everyday life. Such an overarching system of principles and rules can be conceived as a moral order (*Ordnung*), an order of obligation.[24]

The duties (*officia*) and authority (*auctoritas*) of bishops are fundamental in this order of obligation. Bishops, according to Isidore of Seville, are high priests who

governance in Metz, see Guy Halsall, *The Merovingian Region of Metz: Settlement and Social Organization* (Cambridge, UK: Cambridge University Press, 1995). Despite the fact that Metz was not the site of an archbishopric, Chrodegang had been granted the *pallium* by Pope Stephen II around 751, together with the privilege of relics from Rome. This made him something like an archbishop in his personal capacity, and meant that he was a key intermediary between the papacy and the king, something like a papal legate. Metz was given a heightened prominence in the Carolingian court by Angilram, chief advisor (archchaplain) to Charlemagne, who was also bishop of Metz and archbishop in his personal capacity. Around 784, Angilram commissioned a Lombard intellectual in Charlemagne's court, Paul the Deacon, to write a historical account of Metz's bishops. In carrying out this commission, Paul constructed a genealogy for Charlemagne that made him the great-great-great grandson of Metz's twenty-ninth bishop, Arnulf. This genealogical account stands behind references to Charlemagne's family as Arnulfings. Damien Kempf (trans.), Paul the Deacon, *Liber de episcopis Mettensibus* (Paris: Peeters, 2013), 1–39, 73–5.

23 Isidore of Seville, *De Ecclesiasticis Officiis*, translated by Thomas L. Knoebel (New York: Newman Press, 2008) ("DEO"); Christopher M. Lawson (ed.), *St. Isidore, Bishop of Seville's* De Ecclesiasticis Officiis, Corpus Christianorum, Series Latina 113 (Brepols: Turnholt, 1989). For further discussion of the imprint of this text on Frankish political culture, see Moore, *Sacred Kingdom*, 147–60, 243–85.

24 Jerome Bertram, *The Chrodegang Rules: The Rules for the Common Life of the Secular Clergy from the Eighth and Ninth Centuries, Critical Texts with Translations and Commentary* (Abingdon: Routledge, 2017), 85–94, 175–83; M. A. Claussen, *The Reform of the Frankish Church: Chrodegang of Metz and the* Regula canonicorum *in the Eighth Century* (Cambridge, UK: Cambridge University Press, 2004), 1–18, 46–57, 206; Moore, *Sacred Kingdom*, 147–60, 243–85; Wallace-Hadrill, *Frankish Church*, 170–231.

follow the typological pattern of the ancient Israelite priesthood, and who share with St. Peter and his successors both disciplinary and doctrinal authority. They receive this office through merit, which is manifested in a life that honors God. In order to carry out their episcopal duties, bishops were to be "learned in teaching and speaking." They were also to be practiced in the arts of justice, so that they could rightly judge a case "by merit and not by favor," and be vigorous advocates in "begging pardon before God for the crimes of [their] subjects."[25]

Transported into Frankish monasteries by the beginning of the eighth century, Isidore of Seville's programmatic statement for episcopal office strongly influenced reforming efforts. Following the pattern set forth by Isidore, the emphasis was on performative liturgical practices, including baptism, which marked an identity-forming ritual, the entrance into Christian society, sealed with chrism on the forehead. Emphasis was also placed on the marking out and blessing of sacred spaces (sanctuaries), where special protections were promised to those who fled the rigors of law and justice. Such sacred spaces could sometimes extend outward to include the entire territory served by the bishop's cathedral church, the *civitas* with its surrounding countryside.[26]

These episcopal foundations for new patterns of civic life are evident in a communal rule authored by Chrodegang of Metz. Written probably around 755, this was a *regula* intended to govern the communal life of secular canons, men who were serving the church of Metz, working in the world (*saeculum*), while living in accordance with the church's canonical legislation. Closely tracking the *regula* of St. Benedict, which was becoming the gold standard for monastic life, Chrodegang's *regula* is especially interesting in the way it governs property ownership.[27]

Chrodegang's *regula* was intentionally drafted to constitute a new kind of community, one in which the order and honor governing social life proceeded strictly according to merit and seniority, rather than inherited social status. Those who entered this community voluntarily, many of whom may have come from elite families, were required to leave their social status at the door: to submit themselves to a new kind of social system, one in which obedience and humility were the orienting virtues. Unlike monks, however, the canons were not required to renounce their property. Instead, they were given legal options that would enable them to benefit from the use and revenues of property (*usufruct*) during their lifetimes, while at the same time leaving the ownership to the church (rather than their families) after they died.[28]

25 Isidore, *DEO*, II.V; *cf.* Paul the Deacon, *Liber*, 69. For discussion of Isidore of Seville as a theologian of legal obligation, whose vision for ecclesiastical society was actualized by the Carolingians, see Luca Loschiavo, "Isidore of Seville," in Reynolds, *Great Christian Jurists*, 381–96.

26 Moore, *Sacred Kingdom*, 161–202, 226–7, 279–85.

27 Bertram, *Chrodegang Rules*, 1–8, 12–26; Claussen, *Reform*, 58–165.

28 Bertram, *Chrodegang Rules*, 12–26, §§2, 31; Claussen, *Reform*, 66–113, 195–6, 206–47, and passim.

Chrodegang's *regula* has been identified as an early foundation of the western *prebend* system, which became a widespread institution for materially supporting clerics (later university professors) from church revenues. In Chrodegang's *regula*, early hints at the later system can be seen in the allocation of tax revenues to the cathedral clergy, and in the reference to benefices from the bishop, as one way in which the clergy were to be supported in their secular ministry. In the concluding section of the *regula*, we see that the material supports allocated to this clerical community were meant to extend outward to "almsfolk," a category of persons who were in some way dependent upon the cathedral church, for material support, for spiritual services, and for education. Overseeing this community of clergy and dependent layfolk was the bishop, assisted by his archdeacon and *primicerius*, "teachers according to the law of God."[29]

Chrodegang's vision was shared by his younger contemporary, Theodulf of Orleans, whose episcopal statute for a canonical community on the upper Loire River was perhaps even more influential. Writing probably around the year 800, Theodulf envisioned an episcopal community that bound together clerics, monks, and laity in a legally binding unity of love and peace. Theodulf wrote his episcopal statute to provide instructions for all the priests of his diocese who worked with the laity, baptizing them into the church community, teaching them what it meant to be a member of the community, and carrying out the liturgical rituals that performatively brought the community to life. Copied widely throughout the Frankish kingdoms, this communal vision became influential as an organizational ideal across the empire.[30]

Theodulf's communal vision emphasized the spiritual importance of arts and literature. His viewpoint on the arts comes through especially clearly in the responses, drafted on behalf of Charlemagne, to a Latin translation of the records from the Council of Nicaea (II, 787), the council that had ruled against iconoclasm. In this Carolingian response to a Byzantine council, Theodulf acknowledged valuable ways in which the arts and literature might contribute to Christian communities. On the other hand, however, he expressed vivid repugnance – with Charlemagne's vigorous approval – at any veneration or worship of such images. In the passionate and sometimes violent debates over images and "manufactured things," as Ann Freeman and Thomas Noble have shown, important and revealing divergences were opening between the orders of obligation in Byzantium, Italy, and the emerging empire of northwestern Europe.[31]

29 Bertram, *Chrodegang Rules*, 83 nn. 124, 126, §§ 25, 29, 34. On the influence of Chrodegang's rule in England, see Robert E. Rodes, Jr., *Ecclesiastical Administration in Medieval England: The Anglo-Saxons to the Reformation* (Notre Dame: University of Notre Dame Press, 1977), 24.

30 Carine van Rhijn, *Shepherds of the Lord: Priests and Episcopal Statutes in the Carolingian Period* (Turnhout: Brepols, 2007), 104–5 and passim; also see Susan A. Keefe, *Water and the Word: Baptism and the Education of the Clergy in the Carolingian Empire* (Notre Dame: University of Notre Dame Press, 2002).

31 Ann Freeman, *Theodulf of Orléans: Charlemagne's Spokesman against the Second Council of Nicaea* (Aldershot, Hampshire: Ashgate Publishing, 2003); Thomas F. X. Noble, *Images, Iconoclasm, and the*

The debate over images was connected by Carolingian elites to a new "proto-imperial" vision of the Christian community. Until recently, it has often been argued that this was an ethnic and nationalist vision in which the Franks were understood as the heirs of Israel in God's vocational plan for the world. However, some scholars have argued that the Carolingian vision was more imperial and universal. This was a vision in which the Carolingian Franks were defenders of Christian orthodoxy, opposing themselves to a perceived Byzantine heresy.[32]

To venerate and adore images is to wrongly elevate the products of human skill into salvific objects, endowing them with spiritual powers that they do not have. The Carolingians, as spokesmen for universal Christian orthodoxy, presented their vision for Christian imperial community as the orthodox one, demeaning Byzantium with an anti-Jewish rhetoric of carnal materiality, irrationality, and ignorance. This was a new, western vision of Christian empire, one in which artistry and craftsmanship would be embraced for their usefulness in changing the world, but not because they were worthy of veneration as sacred and active revelations from God.[33]

Words, however, were a different story.

6.4 INSTRUMENTS OF LEGAL POWER IN CAROLINGIAN EUROPE

In contrast to images, the Carolingians upheld the power of words to reveal spiritual realities, and to reform them. This is a striking aspect of the debate over images, one that is evident in Charlemagne's responses to Theodulf's writings, and in the reign of Louis the Pious (813–840), Charlemagne's son. Words, unlike images, *do* have sacramental power. This is a conviction that the Carolingians entrenched, and left as a legacy for European Christendom.

For the Carolingian intellectuals whose writings have survived, words of law are connected to powerful spiritual realities. Words can do things not because they are magical but because they connect us – in a way that is ontological or metaphysical – to spiritual, divine realities that transcend material life. Material objects, such as art and technology, on the other hand, can only and at best serve as signs and symbols of transcendent realities. They have no power in themselves, and certainly no power to save. They can remind and they can direct attention, but they cannot do anything. They are utterly different from words that can do things. When pronounced by

Carolingians (Philadelphia: University of Pennsylvania Press, 2009); also see Moore, *Sacred Kingdom*, 268–71, 275. Ann Freeman's new edition of the *Libri Carolini* (edited with assistance from Paul Meyvaert) is digitally accessible through the MGH website, MGH, *Leges, Concilia (Conc.) 2, Supp. 1, Opus Caroli regis contra synodum (Libri Carolini)* (Hannover, 1998).

32 Conor O'Brien, "Empire, Ethnic Election and Exegesis in the *Opus Caroli* (*Libri Carolini*)," *Studies in Church History* 54 (2018): 96–108.

33 This might, therefore, be a key moment in the "disenchantment" of the west. Charles Taylor sees sources for this disenchantment in the "rage for order" that he traces back to Hildebrand (Gregory VII, 1073–85). Arguably, we should go back further to the "mania for order" and "quest for order" that reached their apex in the age of Louis the Pious (813–840). Noble, *Images*, 351, 357; Charles Taylor, *A Secular Age* (Cambridge, MA: Harvard University Press, 2007), 63, 76, 85, 143–5, 242–4, 265.

a priest who has been properly educated and elected into the divine purpose and plan, words are transcendently powerful.[34]

Words pronounced in the sacrament of baptism effectuate the joinder of a person into the church, conceived as the sacred community of God. And words written in a charter can be sacramentalized through rituals that connect them to transcendent sources of power, such as the relics of saints. To us, this might seem like magic, but the Carolingian intellectuals would have drawn a sharp distinction between magic and sacrament. They were as adamantly opposed to the former as they were vigorously committed to the latter.

Inscribed onto parchment, marked with crosses and sacramentalized through performative rituals, charters donating property and privilege did things with words. The words recognized transfers of property through gift and marked out boundaries for exclusivity. The exclusivity was often judicial. Monasteries were granted judicial powers, which were an important source of revenue and protection for the monastery. The revenue came from the charging of fees for judicial services, and the protection came from the sacramentally declared exclusivity: other local rulers who also wished to charge fees for their judicial services must stay *out*.

Geoffrey Koziol has made a powerful case for treating medieval diplomas as performative acts. As performative acts, charters and diplomas are a kind of social action, one that takes place through writing and witnessing. Because diplomas and charters were often produced in connection with important political occasions, they offer a record of social behaviors invested with legal and political meanings, formulaic interpretations of the events they record, and rhetorical set-pieces in a larger symphony of social activities connected with major social and political events. And, moreover, because they were used as a memorial and legal record, these texts continued to carry their performative activity into future generations, long after the people who initially drafted and enacted them had exited the worldly stage. As Koziol emphasizes, these performative legal acts helped to constitute the meaning of sacramental rulership and community in the heartland of western Europe.[35]

We can see an early version of this performative legality, in connection with artistic skill, in royal charters granted to Einhard, who served as a senior adviser to Charlemagne and wrote the king's first biography. Einhard had earned for himself a reputation as a master craftsman, although scholars today think that this was probably for his skill in *overseeing* the work of craftsmen, rather than in carrying out the work of craftsmanship himself. Art and technical skill almost always remained anonymous in the early Middle Ages, and it was the patron or high-ranking overseer who received credit for the artistry or craftsmanship. In Einhard's

34 Laura Carlson, "Adoption, Adaptation, & Authority: The Use of Isidore in the Opus Caroli," in Andrew Fear and Jamie Wood, *Isidore of Seville and His Reception in the Early Middle Ages* (Amsterdam: Amsterdam University Press, 2016), 209–30.

35 Geoffrey Koziol, *The Politics of Memory and Identity in Carolingian Royal Diplomas: The West Frankish Kingdom (840–987)* (Turnhout, Belgium: Brepols Publishers, 2012).

case, the reputation was earned especially for architectural and artistic work contributing to Charlemagne's new palace at Aachen. Alcuin of York and Theodulf of Orléans also considered Einhard a master craftsman, nicknaming him Bezalel, Moses' divinely recognized craftsman.[36]

In January of 815, Louis the Pious granted to Einhard and his wife Emma a place (*locus*) in the German part of his kingdom. The landed properties were near the Main River, not far from today's Frankfurt. The charter described their *locus*, together with appurtenances, including churches, natural resources, and dependent persons (serfs or slaves). These properties were granted to Einhard and Emma with full ownership rights, including the right to transfer the property to their heirs, in order to honor Einhard as he deserved, "for with every effort and at every moment he has striven faithfully to submit to our service and our demands."[37]

In June 815, Louis the Pious granted an immunity to the monastery of Blandin, located near Ghent, in today's Belgium. Einhard had been named as an abbot of this monastery, and he would later be remembered in the records of the monastery as a heroic restorer. Einhard donated properties to the monastery and ensured that there were sufficient revenues to support the monks. According to tenth-century records, Einhard "devised a wise plan about all the things that seemed to belong by law to the monastery he ruled," and Louis responded to this plan by granting an immunity to the monastery, marking the charter with his signet ring. According to the text of the charter, it was granted to confirm a previous immunity granted by Charlemagne. No one holding judicial powers was to "infringe upon the churches, places, fields or other possessions of the monastery," or to enter the property to hear cases, impose fines, or collect taxes. In 819, a similar set of privileges was issued to the nearby monastery of St. Bavo, from the palace at Aachen.[38]

Among the charters of Louis the Pious, we see grants of privileges, properties, and immunities, given to honor and reward those who served the king well, in capacities that included artistry and technical skill, as well as spiritual services. In Einhard's privileges, we also see how immunities of various kinds, for example, against judicial incursion, could work to support the economic, social, and political independence of a religious organization, enabling it to flourish and provide for the spiritual good of king and kingdom. Rapacious attention to St. Bavo's Abbey by Viking raiders later in the ninth century supports an inference that the immunities did effectively contribute to an economically flourishing community.[39]

36 Paul Edward Dutton (ed.), *Charlemagne's Courtier: The Complete Einhard* (Peterborough, Ontario: Broadview Press, 1998). Bezalel: Exodus 31:1–5.

37 Dutton, *Complete Einhard*, 3.7.

38 Dutton, *Complete Einhard*, 3.8, 3.9.

39 Janet L. Nelson (trans.), *The Annals of St. Bertin* (Manchester: Manchester University Press, 1991), 73 (851). Latin text for the Annals of St. Bertin is digitally accessible through the MGH website, MGH, *Scriptores, Scriptores rerum Germanicarum in usum scholarum seperatim editi* (SS rer. Germ.) 5, edited by G. Waitz (Hannover, 1883). On semantic linkages between honor, office, benefice, and property being made in this period, see Nelson (trans.), *Annals of St. Bertin*, 18, 45 (839).

6.5 LEGAL BONDS AND THE SACRAMENTAL STATE

A view of law as an ordering and morally binding social force – one that is ontologically powerful and socially performative – underpins the Carolingian sacramental state, an understanding that received further specification from Hincmar of Rheims (c. 805–882). Heir to the religiously legalizing rhetoric of the earlier Carolingians, Hincmar furthered that legalization, deploying legal texts as authorities in his writings and issuing legal treatises on the important political and religious issues of his day. Among these were questions about authority structures within the church, as well as the degree to which kings were bound by their marriage obligations. In his writings about law, Hincmar articulated a vision of an order of obligation, a social force both fundamental and overarching – one that is wielded preeminently by bishops and that binds all lawgivers. Backing up this vision was an ultimate penalty, one that Hincmar did not hesitate to use: excommunication.[40]

In 860, Hincmar wrote a series of responses to legal and religious questions concerning the divorce of Lothar II (855–869) from his wife Theutberga. The case involved political and religious conflict on the grandest of scales, involving all the regional kingdoms into which the Carolingian empire was dividing: (1) the western kingdom ruled by Charles the Bald (840–877), son of Louis the Pious, which would eventually become France; (2) Lothar's "middle kingdom" (Lotharingia), which extended from Frisia in the north (what is today the Netherlands) to the mountains of northern Italy (in what is today Switzerland); (3) the north Italian kingdom ruled by Emperor Louis II (855–875); and (4) the eastern kingdom ruled by Louis "the German" (840–876), Louis the Pious' other living son, including large parts of what is today Germany.[41]

Lothar had repudiated his wife Theutberga, whose family controlled strategically important lands just north of the Italian Alps. Evidently preferring a woman named Waldrada to Theutberga, Lothar tried to rid himself of Theutberga. The fact that he was ultimately unsuccessful, and that law was cited as a reason, demonstrates the moral and social power that law was beginning to have in northern Europe. Even a king was bound by law, as Hincmar so forcefully argued. And, furthermore, even a pope could act illegally.[42]

Hincmar was asked to respond to a series of questions, which identified legal and religious issues raised by the divorce. As in his other treatises, Hincmar did so by

[40] Rachel Stone and Charles West (eds.), *Hincmar of Rheims: Life and Work* (Manchester: Manchester University Press, 2015); Charles West, "Hincmar of Reims," in Reynolds, *Great Christian Jurists*, 429–43. Hincmar's sentences of excommunication: Rachel Stone and Charles West, "Introduction" to *The Divorce of King Lothar and Queen Theutberga: Hincmar of Rheims's* De Divortio (Manchester: Manchester University Press, 2016), 33; Elisabeth Vodola, *Excommunication in the Middle Ages* (Berkeley: University of California Press, 1986), 1–20.

[41] McKitterick, *Frankish Kingdoms*, 169–96; Stone & West, "Introduction" to *Divorce of King Lothar*, 1–6.

[42] Stone & West, "Introduction" to *Divorce of King Lothar*, 1–10; also see Nelson (trans.), *Annals of St. Bertin*, 121, 123–6 (864–5).

citing a range of legal authorities, including papal decretals, church canons, collections of Roman law, royal charters, capitularies, and broader principles of "natural law." His arguments about the moral and legal force that these sources should have are themselves important, as is the evidence that his arguments provide about the sources of law available in ninth-century northern Europe. For our purposes, however, Hincmar's arguments are especially important for the light that they shed on a sacramental understanding of legal obligations and on legal principles connected with property ownership. Directly at issue in the case were marriage bonds, but a broader range of legal bonds were implicated, including those created through mutual oaths (*coniurationes*) by clerics and laity alike, as well as the bonds of loyalty and obedience that tied subjects to their immediate lords, and to their king, defining powers and obligations with respect to landed properties and positions in the church.[43]

The social theory of law as a morally binding force, one that could tie different persons together such that they became a solidary social unity, was strongly influenced by Augustine of Hippo. Hincmar cited Augustine extensively in his treatise on Lothar's divorce. Augustine's treatise on *Christian Teaching* (*De Doctrina Christiana*) had identified learning and understanding as essential to proper Christian living, for clerics and laity alike, and had furthermore articulated a theory of social reality according to which such learning contributed to the formation of social bonds. This theory depended on a conception of love and will, as orienting and directing forces in the lives of individual human persons, and as connecting forces that unify them with the persons or things that they love. Teaching, a social process by which human beings learn from other human beings, is a necessary condition for love (*caritas*), "which ties people together in the bonds of unity, to make souls overflow and as it were intermingle with one another."[44]

A human community has existence as a social collectivity (*civitas*), as something more than the sum of its individual parts, according to Augustine, in virtue of

[43] Stone & West, *Divorce of King Lothar*, 10–81, 119, and passim; Wood, *Proprietary Church*, 804–12. On Hincmar's presentation of natural law as a "norm" linking judicial, religious, and moral concepts of normativity, see Sylvie Joye, "Family Order and Kingship According to Hincmar," in Stone & West (eds.), *Hincmar of Rheims*, 190–209, esp. 192–3. An early form of lay *conjuratio* is briefly mentioned in the *Annals of St. Bertin*, as a response to Viking raids. Nelson (trans.), *Annals of St. Bertin*, 89 (859): "The Danes ravaged the places beyond the Scheldt. Some of the common people living between the Seine and the Loire formed a sworn association (*conjuratio*) amongst themselves and fought bravely against the Danes on the Seine. But because their association had been made without due consideration (*incaute*), they were easily slain by our most powerful people."

[44] Augustine, *On Christian Teaching*, translated by R. P. H. Green (Oxford: Oxford University Press, 1997), Preface § 6; Phillip Cary, "United Inwardly by Love: Augustine's Social Ontology," in John Doody, Kevin L. Hughes, and Kim Paffenroth, *Augustine and Politics* (Lanham, Maryland: Lexington Books, 2005), 3–34. On the Carolingian reception of Augustine, focused on implications for conceptual models of the Carolingian state, see Sophia Moesch, *Augustine and the Art of Ruling in the Carolingian Period: Political Discourse in Alcuin of York and Hincmar of Rheims* (London: Routledge, 2020).

a shared understanding and reasoning about the things or beings that are loved. Unless this rational agreement exists about what or whom is loved, there is in fact no community. Therefore, according to Augustine, shared understanding about the good that is loved is vital to the very existence of a human community. Societies, *civitates*, are made into solidary social communities in virtue of an inward binding force of love, which ties together many different people into one community, governed under authority that is ultimately divine, if it is legitimate.[45]

Sacred words and actions (*sacramenta*) can serve as outward signs of this inward love, and as reminders of it, when short human memories are tempted to forget. No matter how scripted they may be, such statements of will, when carried out with proper intentionality, change the cognitive directionality of the persons who make them, stamping a mark (*character*) on the person, making them different, and drawing them like a magnet into the thing or person to which they have declared their love. Oaths and formal promises are a matter of deep seriousness in such a theory. Added to the Carolingian view that words can be ontologically powerful, in ways that other outward symbols cannot, this theory makes legal promises and bonds into a potent social force.

In seeking to repudiate his wife Theutberga, Lothar seemed to be setting himself against the ideals underpinning a sense of shared community in the Christian west, which was absorbing Augustinian social theory into its marrow. Formalized, sacred promises were assuming great importance in binding together kings, dukes, and counts, archbishops and their suffragen bishops, and in binding bishops to their king. Christian society was held together by these sacred bonds of love and will, symbolized by legal *formulae*, and, if such bonds were subject to easy repudiation based on selfish desire, the very constitution of society could be threatened. This can help us to understand why Lothar's divorce was such a big deal.

In the end, Lothar failed to obtain his divorce, but only after continued efforts culminating in a trip to Rome. It is possible that he managed to secure the pope's consent to annulment of his marriage during this trip, but he died during the treacherous return journey, leaving his middle kingdom to be carved up by his uncles. In 870, the treaty of Meerson drew a line down the middle of Lotharingia, dividing the Carolingian realm of western Europe in half, marking something close to what would become the conflict-ridden boundary between France and Germany.[46]

45 Augustine, *The City of God against the Pagans*, edited and translated by R. W. Dyson (Cambridge, UK: Cambridge University Press, 1998), for example, II.21, XIV.28, XIX; *cf.* IV, XIV.22; Cary, "United Inwardly," 3–34; Moesch, *Art of Ruling*, 20–66. For evidence that this conception carried forward to the end of the tenth century, with legal elaboration drawing upon the writings of Hincmar and the Novels of Justinian, see *The Letters of Gerbert with His Papal Privileges as Sylvester II*, translated by Harriet Pratt Lattin (New York: Columbia University Press, 1961), Letter 201, 236–62.

46 Nelson (trans.), *Annals of St. Bertin*, 167–72 (870), 213–15 (878).

6.6 NEW LEGAL COMMUNITIES AND RADICAL SOCIAL CHANGE

In the ninth and tenth centuries, pilgrimage helped to mobilize wealth, centered in monasteries and the church, and in the secular lords that drew on their revenues. Europeans were traveling in search of saints and their relics, and this generated competition between the holders of relics. Visitors meant fees, and fees meant necessary material supports for a monastery or church in carrying out its spiritual mission. These developments can be seen in dramatic form at Cluny.[47]

The abbey of Cluny was established in 910 by a solemnly attested charter of donation. The donor – William I ("the Pious"), duke of Aquitaine and count of Burgundy – executed his legal gift in the city of Bourges in a public assembly of important personages, 42 of whom signed the charter as witnesses. The first signatory was Ingelberga, William's wife. Befitting his importance as primate of the city, the archbishop, Madalbertus, signed next. The other signatories were priests and nobles, including a count, William, who was uncle to the donor. At the end of the document, Oddo, priest and vice chancellor, signed as writer and subscriber of the charter.[48]

The monastery was established on the site of a villa near Mâcon, along a branch of the Saône River, to the west of Geneva and the Alps, in the region of Burgundy. Unlike the plantation-style villas of the late Roman period, this was probably a small village, with a population of peasants working the land, whose legal status stood somewhere between slavery and freedom. During the tenth century, military power and cultural authority had been devolving onto local dukes, counts, and bishops. In this development, associated with the rise of a new European nobility, the un-freedom of serfs was clarified and hardened, even while outright slavery declined. William's charter of donation explicitly granted the lordly ownership of the "serfs of both sexes" (*mancipii utriusque sexus*) – together with the other appurtenances of the villa, including court and demesne manor, a small church (*capella*) dedicated to Mary and St. Peter, vines, mills, incomes, and revenues – to the apostles Peter and Paul.[49]

[47] Lester K. Little, *Religious Poverty and the Profit Economy in Medieval Europe* (Ithaca: Cornell University Press, 1978), 8–18. On Cluny: Barbara H. Rosenwein, *Rhinoceros Bound: Cluny in the Tenth Century* (Philadelphia: University of Pennsylvania Press, 1982); idem, *To Be the Neighbor of Saint Peter: The Social Meaning of Cluny's Property, 909–1049* (Ithaca: Cornell University Press, 1989).

[48] Auguste Bernard and Alexandre Bruel (eds.), *Recueil des chartes de l'abbaye de Cluny* (Paris, 1876–1903), available at Cartae Cluniacenses electronicae: Database of the Charters of the abbey of Cluny (802–1300), www.uni-muenster.de/Fruehmittelalter/Projekte/Cluny/CCE/ (accessed February 24, 2020), No. 112, pp. 124–8; English translation available in Ernest F. Henderson, *Historical Documents of the Middle Ages* (London: George Bell and Sons, 1903), 329–33. For further discussion of the liberty/immunity, see H. E. J. Cowdrey, *The Cluniacs and the Gregorian Reform* (Oxford: Clarendon Press, 1970); Barbara H. Rosenwein, *Negotiating Space: Power, Restraint, and Privileges of Immunity in Early Medieval Europe* (Ithaca: Cornell University Press, 1999), 156–83.

[49] The language of donation invokes full ownership rights, in very lordly terms: *res juris mei ... de propria trado dominatione* ("I hand over from my own rule/ownership ... the possessions/property over which I rule"). I have slightly adapted this translation from Henderson's. Bernard & Bruel,

Over the next century, under the leadership of strong reforming abbots, paralleled by the rise of radically reformist popes, Cluny would be built up into an idealized system of monastic freedom from all interference, secular or episcopal, under the direct headship and jurisdiction of the pope. Duke William's charter of foundation had been generous in its grant of freedom from interference, by laity or clergy, and later privileges from the papacy added a strong and actively enforced exemption from episcopal interference. Partly because it was elevated into an ideal, this was a model of communal freedom that was, for its time, radical; it was a model of freedom from all local authority, which would be significant for European cities, and for European society more generally.[50]

Cluny would grow into a gigantic system of monasteries, churches, manors, and hostels. It received extensive privileges from French kings, as well as popes, and its papal exemptions were also encouraged by the German emperors. As Cluny's fame grew, so did its donations, which might range from churches and manors given by wealthy and powerful patrons to small plots of land, saving time-limited rights to uses and fruits to sustain a poorer donor during his lifetime. As conflicts with the local bishop (of Mâcon) waxed and waned, the abbey also began receiving visitations from papal legates. One legate who came to visit was Hildebrand, who would become Pope Gregory VII (1073–85). Under Gregory VII and his fellow reformers, Cluny was elevated into an idealized system of religious governance.[51]

In the hands of Gregory and his fellow reformers, however, the cause of church reform also became, paradoxically, a seed of secularization. In their efforts to clarify the supremacy of papal authority, the reformers undermined the authority of bishops and incited rebellion from secular rulers, including the new German king, Henry IV (1053–1105). The reforming popes were convinced that secular interferences with the church, especially secular ownership interests, were a corrupting force, and they were prepared to go to ultimate lengths in their effort to eliminate this corruption. But, in their uncompromising vigor, the reformers unleashed social forces that would ultimately not remain within the control of either popes or kings, let alone bishops.[52]

For our immediate purposes, three outcomes of the eleventh-century church reform movement, centered as these were in the papacy and in the Cluniac conglomerate, were of greatest significance. First, in Germany, the Holy Roman

CCE, 125; Henderson, *Historical Documents*, 330. On the rise of the new nobility in these regions, see Constance Brittain Bouchard, *Sword, Miter, and Cloister: Nobility and the Church in Burgundy*, 980–1198 (Ithaca: Cornell University Press, 1987). For an important chronicle of the period, see *History and Politics in Late Carolingian and Ottonian Europe: The* Chronicle *of Regino of Prüm and Adalbert of Magdeburg*, translated by Simon MacLean (Manchester: Manchester University Press, 2009).

50 Cowdrey, *Cluniacs*, 3–43.

51 Cowdrey, *Cluniacs*, 47, 51, 148–50; H. E. J. Cowdrey, *Pope Gregory VII, 1073–1085* (Oxford: Clarendon Press, 1998), 29–30, 253–64; Rosenwein, *Neighbor of Saint Peter*, and passim.

52 Cowdrey, *Gregory VII*, 119–21, 253–64, and passim; Kathleen G. Cushing, *Papacy and Law in the Gregorian Revolution: The Canonistic Work of Anselm of Lucca* (Oxford: Clarendon Press, 1998); 11–39; Taylor, *Secular Age*, 63, 76, 85, 143–5, 242–4, 265.

Emperor began granting privileges of immunity directly to cities. Up until this time, privileges had been granted to bishops, and had indirectly benefited their cities. But from this time forward, privileges would increasingly be granted to cities directly, and would thereby contribute to other social forces potentially undermining to the authority of bishops.[53]

At the same time, the papacy encouraged forms of popular protest against "simoniac" bishops, who were perceived as corrupted by having received their position through donation to a secular lord. The political pressures even extended to kings, who were not taking adequate care of churches, monasteries, pilgrims, and merchants in their kingdoms. As seen in the Milan-based *Pataria* movement, the laity of cathedral churches were encouraged to boycott their bishop, inviting a broader questioning of authority on the part of the laity. This is seen by many historians as the beginning of a new series of religious movements, deemed heretical by the church hierarchy, social movements involving independent interpretation of the Bible by the laity, together with popular return to ancient metaphysical questions.[54]

A wave of communal movements began spreading across western Europe during the latter half of the eleventh century, gathering strength into the twelfth. In northern Italy, this took the form of rural and urban "communes," which were paralleled under different names in Spain, France, and Germany. In northwestern Europe, in the regions of Flanders and Frisia (modern-day Belgium and the Netherlands), there were also communal movements, taking a slightly different form. There the developing cities were younger, centered less often around a bishopric, more typically around a count's castle. Their earliest period of economic growth often built on their role as grain markets. By the twelfth century, however, these cities, too, became caught up in communal social movements.[55]

At the same time, a related social movement was also developing: the Crusades. In order to encourage participation in a crusade, popes developed the legal traditions of privileges in new directions, creating a new instrument of legal power that we can see, in hindsight, as especially significant for later events of European history: the indulgence.

53 This is an inference based on a survey of royal diplomas and charters (*Urkunden*) in the MGH.

54 *The Register of Pope Gregory VII*, 1073–1085, translated by H. E. J. Cowdrey (Oxford: Oxford University Press, 2002), for example, Nos. 2.5, 2.30, 2.55a, 3.6* (a text of Gregory's sentence upon Henry IV that circulated with 3.6), 4.1, 4.12, 5.15, 6.1, 6.5 6.10, 7.2, 7.14a, 8.9; Edward Colman, "Representative Assemblies in Communal Italy," in P. S. Barnwell and Marco Mostert, *Political Assemblies in the Earlier Middle Ages* (Turnhout, Belgium: Brepols, 2003), 193–210; A. Demyttenaere, "Galbert of Bruges on Political Meeting Culture: Palavers and Fights in Flanders during the Years 1127 and 1128," in Barnwell & Mostert, *Political Assemblies*, 151–92; Malcolm Lambert, *Medieval Heresy: Popular Movements from the Gregorian Reform to the Reformation*, 3rd ed. (Oxford: Blackwell Publishing, 2002).

55 David Nicholas, *The Growth of the Medieval City: From Late Antiquity to the Early Fourteen Century* (London: Longman, 1997); Chris Wickham, *Sleepwalking into a New World: The Emergence of Italian City Communes in the Twelfth Century* (Princeton: Princeton University Press, 2015).

In its fully developed form, the indulgence offered blanket immunity from the need to perform penance for forgiveness from sin, in effect a guarantee of salvation for those who would undertake holy war on behalf of the church. The indulgence was complemented, in turn, by a range of more direct economic privileges: protection of property during absence, freedom from the obligation to make debt service payments during the period of Crusade (effectively, a degree of debt forgiveness), and generally the opportunity to benefit from a protected legal status, the status of a pilgrim. In the crusading movements, in other words, legal privileges became an instrument of military mobilization for the Christian laity.[56]

For roughly the first 1,000 years of European history, the people (*populo*), namely, the nonclerical laity, had been considered by literate elites primarily as objects of righteous power and religious community. Now, however, the people were being encouraged to consider themselves as self-conscious and legally privileged agents. Models of monastic community, especially the Rule of St. Benedict, were taken as models for lay communities as well, ranging from communities of righteous warriors, protectors of pilgrims and strangers – such as the Templars and Hospitalers – to the laboring craftspeople in cities, who organized themselves into guilds. Underpinning all these developments was the notion that legal bonds can work as a unifying force, joining a symbolic outer form to an inward intentional directedness, linking people together in new types of community, and endowing them with a legally privileged status. In the cities developing across western Europe, this legally privileged status drew on a word loaded with meaning from the history of republican Rome: *civis*, citizen.

6.7 CLERICS TO LAWYERS

It was during this period of intensive community building among the laity that a revival of Roman law learning began in northern Italy. The earliest shadows of evidence associate a learned practitioner of Roman law ("Pepo") with Countess Matilda of Tuscany (1046–1115), and credit Pepo with a decisive court victory, turning on Roman law, in a case heard before Henry IV. Clearer evidence relating to the legal career and teaching of Irnerius (c. 1055–1125), the legendary founder of Roman law studies at Bologna, also associates him with Countess Matilda, as well as Henry V (1099–1125), in whose court he served as a judge (*iudex*). By the second half of the twelfth century, there is decisive historical evidence for the fact that learned scholars in Bologna were teaching Roman law to students from all over Europe, including a man who would become archbishop of Canterbury, Thomas Becket

56 James A. Brundage, *Medieval Canon Law and the Crusader* (Madison; University of Wisconsin Press, 1969); Nelson (trans.), *Annals of St. Bertin*, 73 (864) (letters of indulgence from Pope Nicholas).

(c. 1118–1170); these "doctors" of Roman law were brought in as advisors to a new German emperor, Frederick I ("Barbarossa") (1152–90).[57]

According to the medievalist Brian Tierney, Roman jurisprudence came to medieval intellectuals "with the force of a revelation." What was particularly powerful was the idea that a "body of laws" (*corpus*) could be formed as a coherent intellectual system. This "revelatory" conception, tied to renewed study of Justinian's sixth-century codification of Roman law, electrified Europe. By the thirteenth century, universities with curricula modeled on Bologna's were popping up all over Europe, as far away as England. Organized into guild-like brotherhoods called "nations" and colleges, granted the legal privileges of clerics, Europe's new jurists poured over Justinian's sixth-century texts, producing "glosses" that reflected interpretive application of Roman law principles to medieval social conditions.[58]

One of the most important careers for a jurist trained in Roman law was to be found in Europe's growing cities. Returning from their studies of Roman law at Bologna, well-born young men became "professional administrators" (*podestà*) of cities, often traveling from city to city with a coterie of judges, notaries, and secretaries. The jurists also became professional advisors to secular rulers, including the emperor. At the same time, their fellow students were returning to the service of the church. Indeed, many graduates obtained a degree that signified their capacity to apply Roman law in both spiritual and the secular jurisdictions: *doctor utriusque juris* ("doctor of both laws").[59]

The fact that the Roman law tradition formed a basis for both religious and secular law in Europe is enormously important. The belief that "the Church lives by the Roman law" lent sacred legitimacy to this cultural tradition and to the legal institutions that could be founded upon it. Ironically, it was for this very reason that the Roman law tradition could eventually be drawn upon to distinguish religious and secular powers. Although there was a tremendous amount of conflict involved in this separation, the parties could draw upon a shared cultural tradition in their disputes and in the resolutions of their disputes. These disputes and resolutions could then be given the status of legal "precedents," which were viewed in retrospect as forming part of Europe's constitutional history.[60]

57 James A. Brundage, *The Medieval Origins of the Legal Profession: Canonists, Civilians, and Courts* (Chicago: University of Chicago Press, 2008), 78–89; *cf.* Harold J. Berman, *Law and Revolution: The Formation of the Western Legal Tradition* (Harvard: Harvard University Press, 1983), 85–164.

58 Brian Tierney, *The Crisis of Church and State 1050–1300* (Toronto: University of Toronto Press, 1988), 97; also see Brian Tierney, *Religion, Law, and the Growth of Constitutional Thought, 1150–1650* (Cambridge, UK: Cambridge University Press, 1982), 13–19; Jacques Verger, "Patterns," in Walter Rüegg & H. de Ridder-Symoens (eds.), *A History of the University in Europe*, Vol. I (Cambridge, UK: Cambridge University Press, 2003), 35–68.

59 Peter Moraw, "Careers of Graduates," in Rüegg & Ridder-Symoens, *History of the University*, 244–79.

60 Berman, *Law & Revolution*, 520–58 and passim; Brundage, *Medieval Origins*, 488–92 and passim; Kenneth Pennington, *The Prince and the Law: Sovereignty and Rights in the Western Legal Tradition, 1200–1600* (Berkeley: University of California Press, 1993); Tierney, *Growth of Constitutional*

Many law students were clerics, financing their legal education by an ecclesiastical benefice. Even nonclerical students enjoyed a privileged quasi-clerical status by virtue of the *Authentica Habita* issued by Frederick Barbarossa in 1155. This imperial privilege ("constitution") extended to professors and students of civil law the *privilegium fori*: the privilege of being tried in a bishop's court, rather than a local court. It also gave them protected status, so that they could freely move among, and live securely in, seats of learning throughout the empire, with freedom from vicarious liability for the debts of their fellow nationals. Frederick ordered that this constitution be placed in Justinian's Code, to be studied alongside the earlier imperial constitutions in that Code. This privilege was followed by a number of important papal and imperial constitutions issued to regulate the study of canon and civil law in universities across Europe.[61]

Enjoying a privileged, quasi-clerical status and living on the revenues of their benefices, the students called themselves "clerks," adopting the clerical tonsure and *cappa clausa*: the cape and hood of the secular clergy. They lived in the air of relative "academic freedom," safe in the knowledge that their freedoms from taxation, military service, and arbitrary legal process were protected by a right of final appeal to the pope, who might very well be a fellow alum. Within their corporate nations and colleges, they lived according to statutes, governed and judged by a rector whom they had elected.[62]

Although there were some differences in the curricula of canon law and civil law students, all European law students received a basic grounding in a combination of Roman and canon law (*ius commune*). On the civil law side, the focus was on Justinian's codification (the *corpus iuris civilis*). These texts were supplemented by medieval constitutions and codes, referred to as the "Feudal Books" (*Libri feudorum*) or "Feudal Customs" (*Consuetudines feudorum*). On the canon law side, the focus was on papal and episcopal "decretals": Gratian's twelfth-century collection, known as the *Decretum*, supplemented by additional papal decretals, collected ultimately in a Paris edition of 1500 (the *corpus iuris canonici*).[63]

Over the period stretching from the twelfth to the sixteenth century, three basic "schools" of commentary on these texts emerged to shape the ways the texts were

Thought, 8–28; Walter Ullmann, *Law and Politics in the Middle Ages* (Ithaca: Cornell University Press, 1975).

61 Aleksander Gieysztor, "Management and Resources," *in* Rüegg & Ridder-Symoens, *History of the University*, 108–43; Paolo Nardi, "Relations with Authority," in Rüegg & Ridder-Symoens, *History of the University*, 77–107.

62 Gieysztor, "Management," 108–42; Pearl Kibre, *The Nations in the Medieval Universities* (Cambridge, MA: Mediaeval Academy of America, 1948); idem, *Scholarly Privileges in the Middle Ages: The Rights, Privileges, and Immunities, of Scholars and Universities at Bologna, Padua, Paris, and Oxford* (Cambridge, MA: Mediaeval Academy of America, 1962); H. Koeppler, "Frederick Barbarossa and the Schools of Bologna," *The English Historical Review* 54 (1939): 577–607; Rainer Christoph Schwinges, "Admission," in Rüegg & Ridder-Symoens, History of the University, 171–94.

63 Antonio García Y García, "The Faculties of Law," in Rüegg & Ridder-Symoens, *History of the University*, 388–408, esp. 393–4.

interpreted by jurists. The earliest school was that of the Glossators, based in Bologna and Orléans, who "regarded Justinian's texts as sacred and ascribed to them almost biblical authority." They assumed that the texts reflected general principles that were just, applicable to their societies, and logically coherent with one another; their interpretive practices aimed at drawing these general principles and logical relations out of the texts. They focused on word-by-word interpretation, writing "glosses" in the margins and between lines of text to expound the meaning of important words (e.g., *proprietas*). Over time, these glosses were extended into exegetical treatises aimed at elucidating basic interpretive principles and intentions standing behind a legal text. In the thirteenth century, one collection of these extended glosses became particularly authoritative: the *Glossa ordinaria* of Accursius. The practical significance of the Accursian Gloss is reflected in the maxim: "What the Gloss does not recognize, the Court does not recognize."[64]

After the Glossators, a related school of interpretation developed which drew on Aristotelian logic in interpreting the Roman law texts. This school is known as the *mos Italicus*. The scholars identified with this school tended to produce a different type of interpretive text: treatises or monographs elucidating a more general, overarching meaning from the legal texts. What the *mos Italicus* shared with the Glossators, however, was a noncritical, nonhistorical reading of Roman law. They seemed to assume that the Roman law applied timelessly to their contemporary social worlds, and they drew on the interpretive techniques they had learned to fill gaps, "stretching the sense of the old legal texts to fit medieval conditions."[65]

With the spread of humanist learning, however, a new school of interpretation associated with French law schools (the *mos Gallicus*) began to develop, which applied more critical readings to the Roman law texts, identifying "interpolations" and distinguishing the genuine sources of authentic Roman law from distasteful "medieval" ideas. These scholars did not assume that the Roman law applied directly to their contemporary social conditions, studying the texts instead from historical and philological perspectives. At the same time, however, humanistic legal education built on Platonist idealism, aiming to lead the student to general principles of law by enabling him to recognize his "inborn ideas of law." Since the process by which the student came to recognize these inborn ideas involved critical engagement with the texts of Roman law, students naturally came to associate universal ideals of law with elevated concepts and principles of Roman law.[66]

If the university represented an institutional location within which students were inducted into the cultural tradition of Roman law and trained to orient themselves to that tradition in resolving contemporary social problems, the administrative

64 García Y García, "Faculties of Law," 390–92; also see Peter Stein, *Roman Law in European History* (Cambridge, UK: Cambridge University Press, 1999), 46, 49; Franz Wieacker, *A History of Private Law in Europe*, translated by Tony Weir (Oxford: Clarendon Press, 1995), 38–46.

65 García Y García, "Faculties of Law," 391–2.

66 García Y García, "Faculties of Law," 392; Wieacker, *History of Private Law*, 63–4, 173.

chancery represented the institutional location where legal practices relevant to the emergence of intellectual property took shape and developed. As preeminent legal advisors to emperors, popes, kings, and princes, the chancellors of Europe contributed to the formalization of an institution that was founded on the imperial traditions of Rome.[67]

Chancellors developed a basic pattern, which the Carolingians had carried from their Merovingian predecessors, and ultimately from late antique Rome. This basic pattern involved the grant of a privilege by a ruler to create an exceptional legal status that was politically and economically valuable. As we have seen, the content of this grant could vary widely. It could be a recognition of corporate status, an exemption from incursions by wielders of authority, a freedom from taxes or tolls. The basic pattern was one by which a privileged recipient received political powers to collect economic revenues, in order to pursue objectives that were valued by the leaders of the governing community.

In Venice, this pattern developed into a statutory protection for new inventions.

6.8 PRIVILEGED REPUBLICANISM

Venice's story is somewhat unique, playing out on the borderlands of Christendom. This borderland existence enabled Venetian leaders, mobilized initially under dukes (*doges*), to operate as *de facto* sovereigns, negotiating treaties with Frankish and Byzantine emperors alike, and compartmentalizing religious obligation in ways that favored economic and political expansionism.

The institutional structures for Christianity were very peculiar in the region of the Veneto. The center of Venetian religious life, from the earliest period of her history, was a church established by the doge, which housed the relics of St. Mark, patron saint of the city. These relics had been stolen from Alexandria in one of the more infamous cases of reliquary theft (*furta sacra*). At the same time, due to doctrinal and political conflicts stretching back to the time of Gregory the Great, the region had two metropolitan bishops: one of Aquileia and one of Grado.[68]

The patriarchs of Aquileia had been especially favored by the Carolingian emperors, although the patriarch of Grado seems also to have received valuable economic privileges from Charlemagne. The patriarch of Grado was claimed by the Venetians as their archbishop, but his cathedral church was located on an island far

[67] In overseeing and interpreting a wide range of laws for different groups, the chancellors bore a particular responsibility for maintaining Christendom's complex society of orders, kingdoms, and principalities. On the extent to which their training in Roman law informed their understanding of this office, from the fourteenth into the sixteenth centuries, see John M. Headley, *The Emperor and His Chancellor: A Study of the Imperial Chancellery under Gattinara* (Cambridge, UK: Cambridge University Press, 1983), 8–12.

[68] Patrick J. Geary, *Furta Sacra: Thefts of Relics in the Central Middle Ages*, 2nd ed. (Princeton: Princeton University Press, 1990), 87–93. Gregory VII treated the patriarch of Grado as the patriarch of Venice in his letters. *Register of Pope Gregory VII*, Nos. 2.39, 4.26–27; *compare* 9.8.

removed from the center of Venetian political life. During the eleventh and twelfth centuries, conflicts between the patriarchs of Grado and Aquileia neutralized their authority. As Venice became increasingly wealthy and powerful in her own right, moreover, the conflict over episcopal primacy became irrelevant to power politics. In 1451, the patriarchal see of Grado was eliminated entirely. Already by the early thirteenth century, Venice was effectively independent of episcopal control, except where this was exercised through the papacy directly.[69]

Venice had been claimed as part of the Republic of St. Peter, the papal dominions established under Charlemagne, but in fact had operated relatively independently from the popes. Venice's closest political and religious loyalties were often to the Byzantine emperors, and, beginning in the late tenth century, these were linked to generous privileges granted in the form of a Golden Bull (*chrysobulla*).

In a *chrysobull* from the eastern empire, granted in 992, Venetian merchants had received a privileged status in harbor taxes and litigation. In return, the lagoon city was obligated to provide ships for Byzantine military services in Italy. Based on an inference from the value of taxes on goods being shipped from Venice to Constantinople, relative to those being shipped back to Venice – 2 solidi upon entering and 15 at departure – it can be seen that, in this early period, Venice was primarily exporting basic commodities and trading these for higher-valued goods. Venetian exports to Byzantium likely included salted fish, timber, slaves, and wool, while her imports likely included silks, spices, drugs, sugar, and weapons.[70]

Over the next century, however, Venice grew increasingly wealthy and powerful. In 1082 or 1092 – the date and context are debated – Venice received another set of trading privileges from Byzantium. These were much more extensive, laying a foundation for the unique trading status that Venice would enjoy in Constantinople for another century. Among many other privileges, Venice was granted the rights to a trading quarter in the imperial city, together with exclusive locations for shops and wharves. Tax exemptions and litigation-related privileges were also specified along with exalted titles for the Venetian doge and the patriarch of Grado.[71]

69 MGH, *Diplomata, Die Urkunden der Karolinger (Pippin, Karlmann und Karl der Große (DD Karol. I)*, Nos. 200–201, pp. 269–70 (immunity from Charlemagne to patriarch of Grado, referencing relics of St. Mark, August 803, plus toll freedom for four ships). For narrative discussion of the Veneto's peculiar episcopal politics, see Thomas E. A. Dale, *Relics, Prayer, and Politics in Medieval Venetia* (Princeton: Princeton University Press, 1997), 7–11, 48–56; Frederic C. Lane, *Venice: A Maritime Republic* (Baltimore: Johns Hopkins University Press, 1973), 88.

70 Daphne Penna, *The Byzantine Imperial Acts to Venice, Pisa and Genoa, 10th–12th Centuries: A Comparative Legal Study* (Groningen: Eleven International Publishing, 2012); also see Horatio Brown, "The Venetians and the Venetian Quarter in Constantinople to the Close of the Twelfth Century," *The Journal of Hellenic Studies* 40(1) (1920): 68–88; Michael McCormick, *Origins of the European Economy: Communications and Commerce, AD 300–900* (Cambridge, UK: Cambridge University Press, 2001), 731, 768, and passim.

71 Penna, *Byzantine Imperial Acts*, 26–34; *cf.* Peter Frankopan, "Byzantine Trade Privileges to Venice in the Eleventh Century: The Chrysobull of 1092," *Journal of Medieval History* 30 (2004): 135–60 (arguing for a corrected date).

Between the tenth and thirteenth centuries, Venice acted as a uniquely privileged agent of commerce between east and west, bringing crafts, techniques, and sciences that were much more highly developed in the eastern Mediterranean. This is readily apparent in the case of the silk industry, for example, which did not exist in the west before the ninth century, but which would grow into one of Italy's primary manufacturing exports by the thirteenth century. Venice's service to east–west communication is also evident in the case of paper production, which would provide a necessary foundation for printing technology in the fifteenth century.[72]

In short, Venice managed to generate grants of privilege from both western and eastern secular rulers, as from popes. These privileges often enabled Venice to act as a monopolistic supplier of goods and services, including goods that were increasingly in high demand within Europe, such as spices and silks. More nefarious transports on Venetian ships included slaves and crusading warriors.[73]

Infamously, Venice managed to coopt the social energies of sacred warfare in the Fourth Crusade (1198–1204), channeling them into the sacking of Constantinople (1204). In this shocking act of violence against an ancient Christian city, Venice signaled increasingly imperial intentions, which would also be directed against mainland Italy, in the coming centuries. The Venetians and the crusaders established a new Latin state, the Empire of Romania, defining commercial privileges for Venetian traders to match those of the Byzantine *chrysobull*. Venice's commercial empire in the eastern Mediterranean had been secured, at least for a time. Vengeance would eventually come, however, in the form of losses to the Ottoman Turks, who seized the opportunities that a ravaged Byzantine empire had given.[74]

By the fifteenth century, then, Venice had centuries of experience with the use of instruments of legal power to mobilize wealth-generating activity and political power. What had changed dramatically, however, was the geopolitical context. With the rise of Ottoman power in the east, and the absorption of Constantinople into a Muslim society, Venice turned westward. The recent invention of the printing press had shown how revolutionary new technologies could be, and, as Venetian merchants shifted their investments, they likely saw possibilities in encouraging the search for other, as-yet-unknown techniques.[75]

[72] Luca Molà, *The Silk Industry of Renaissance Venice* (Baltimore: Johns Hopkins University Press, 2000). On the Byzantine development of a domestic silk industry as a state monopoly, see Constantin Zuckerman, "Silk 'Made in Byzantium': A Study of Economic Policies of Emperor Justinian," *Traveaux et mémoires, Volume XVII: Constructing the Seventh Century* (2013): 323–50; *cf.* Robert Sabatino Lopez, "Silk Industry in the Byzantine Empire," *Speculum* 20.1 (1945): 1–42.

[73] Two other north Italian cities successfully sought Byzantine chrysobulls with trade privileges: Pisa and Genoa. These two cities became chief rivals of Venice.

[74] D. S. Chambers, *The Imperial Age of Venice, 1380–1580* (London: Thames and Hudson, 1970); Lane, *Venice*, 42–3, 234–6; Peter Lock, *The Routledge Companion to the Crusades* (Abingdon: Routledge, 2006); Thomas F. Madden, *Enrico Dandalo and the Rise of Venice* (Baltimore: Johns Hopkins University Press, 2003), 117–299.

[75] Lane, *Venice*, 144–7, 203–73, 309–21.

In 1469, the Venetian Council had granted a five-year monopoly on printing to Johannes Speyer, an immigrant from Mainz, where the printing press had recently been invented. As Joanna Kostylo has emphasized in her commentary on this privilege, the Venetian councilors probably regarded this as a simple variant of monopolistic privileges granted to immigrants bringing skills deemed beneficial to the republic. It would have been difficult to imagine the extent to which this particular new technology would transform the social world. Speyer died shortly after his privilege was granted, and his monopolistic privilege was not granted to anyone else, enabling printing to quickly become a flourishing industry in Venice.[76]

Indeed, Venice was an early leader in the printing industry, far outstripping other Italian city-states in the number of presses. Before the mid-sixteenth century, moreover, there was little in the way of censorship, and regulation was primarily maintained to ensure quality, rather than to control content. This made Venice an early and important exporter of printed editions that would have been censored elsewhere, such as the "Ultraquist Bible," printed in Czech for export to Bohemian Hussites, moderate followers of Jan Hus (1372–1415), an advocate for church reform who had been burned for heresy at the Council of Constance (1414–1418).[77]

Other early "protestant" books were published in Venice, together with books that proved vital to the Renaissance and Reformation more broadly: books by humanist authors, Hebrew and Greek Bibles, ever-widening ranges of classical literature. Literary treasures from Greek-speaking Christianity and philosophy were transmitted into western literary culture through the pathbreaking labors of Aldus Manutius (1449/52–1515), among others, while erudite social critiques from university-trained scholars raised profound questions about the validity of traditional doctrines and rituals.[78]

As printing presses proliferated, it became increasingly important to ensure quality in printed editions. At least for highly respected authors whose fame was spreading across Europe, such as Erasmus of Rotterdam (1466–1536), an important aspect of quality control required that a printed edition actually reflected the author's work. A way to achieve this was to grant exclusive printing privileges, ensuring that only one printer held the public responsibility for printing a particular work. For a printer-publisher, this made the time and expense invested in a high-quality edition much less risky. Here is the logic behind the printing privileges that developed, in Venice and elsewhere, forming a precursor to modern copyrights.[79]

76 Johannes of Speyer's Printing Monopoly, Venice (1469), translated by Joanna Kostylo, *Primary Sources*; Joanna Kostylo, Commentary on Johannes of Speyer's Printing Monopoly, Venice (1469), *Primary Sources*.

77 Kostylo, Commentary on Johannes of Speyer's Printing Monopoly; Alessandro Marzo Magno, *Bound in Venice: The Serene Republic and the Dawn of the Book*, translated by Gregory Conti (Rome: Edizione e/o, 2013).

78 Chambers, *Imperial Age*, 147–56; Martin Davies, *Aldus Manutius: Printer and Publisher of Renaissance Venice* (Tempe, Arizona: Arizona Center for Medieval and Renaissance Studies, 1999).

79 Kostylo, Commentary on Johannes of Speyer's Printing Monopoly, *Primary Sources*.

Until recently, scholars of copyright history have emphasized the significant differences between printing privileges and modern copyrights. Printing privileges primarily protected publishers, not authors, and they did not use the language of property in describing the temporary rights that were granted. They certainly did not recognize authors' rights, as property rights, in their creative written work. However, in a careful study of sixteenth-century papal printing privileges (in the Vatican Secret Archives), Jane Ginsburg has shown that the merits of creative authorship were increasingly stressed to justify a grant of privilege. While the privileges were not property, and while authors' creativity was typically of secondary importance in justifying the grant, the papacy did nonetheless give its imprimatur to the argument that literary creativity merited legal protection.[80]

As printing spread across Italy and Europe, authorship rights were increasingly claimed in forms that look very similar to modern copyright. In Chapter 10, we will meet one such argument from sixteenth-century Paris, which drew an explicit analogy between the sovereign lordship of divine and human creators as a justification for recognizing authorial rights. But that came in a social context in which conflicts within western Christendom over the political implications of religious divisions had become violent, a context in which popular religious revolt was contributing to national consciousness and republican revolution. That was a context inflamed by the Printing Revolution, a revolution that came early to Venice, and that has played its due part in revolutions ever since.

6.9 CONCLUSION

By the twelfth century, instruments of legal power involving privileges and immunities were being used to mobilize members of the laity, creating economic incentives to go on crusade, together with spiritual incentives to boycott local clergy in favor of ambitious, reforming popes. Instruments of legal power developed by European clerics were turned back against them as part of conflictual processes in which the rulership structures of cities, universities, and nations were constituted and increasingly "laicized."

The development of law, as a medieval profession, illustrates a broader process in which the organizational structure of the clergy became gradually secularized. However, for many centuries, lawyers and clerics would train together and would claim clerical status together, remaining only partially distinct. Law and theology grew up together, influencing one another, even as conflicts between popes and kings, clergy and laity, encouraged the increasing separation of secular and religious spheres. Sacramental semantics lending an elevated legal meaning to words and

[80] Jane C. Ginsburg, "Proto-Property in Literary and Artistic Works: Sixteenth-Century Papal Printing Privileges," in Isabella Alexander and H. Tomas Gomez-Arostegui (eds.), *The History of Copyright Law: A Handbook of Contemporary Research* (Cheltenham: Edward Elgar, 2015). Thank you to Dr. Péter Mezei for this reference!

organized rulership for governing communities under constitutive rules (*regulae*) would remain powerful as aspirational ideals within the world of law, even as processes of secularization weakened the authoritative connections to clerical hierarchies.

In the case of Venice's civic statute promising a privilege to any inventor of a new device, we can see elements of European law that are both old and new. The city-based system of civic law was old, and by the late fifteenth century it was already secularizing. The system of privileges was also old, and we have seen how, across the sweep of European history, privileges were used for many different types of purposes: to establish judicial powers of bishops, or create exceptions to those powers, to encourage the establishment of religious foundations, to encourage people to go on crusade, or to build up cities and imperial states in opposition to reforming popes. Europe has a long experience in the use of instruments of legal power to incentivize valued behaviors.

What was new about Venice's privilege granting, however, was the use to encourage *inventive* activities together with the use of statutory law to accomplish this goal. Venice was making a generalized promise rather than simply exercising the discretion to grant a privilege. And this generalized promise was made in the effort to encourage novel technologies, which would bring both prosperity and honor to the lagoon city.

We have come a long way from the seventh and last ecumenical council, and particularly from the Carolingian response, which declared in no uncertain terms that material objects cannot save. We are at a turning point in European history, a tipping forward into a future in which material objects – and especially inventions – will come to be seen as salvific, as "human miracles," in the words of Peter Thiel.

Among the first of these human miracles was the printing press, an invention that quickly spread from the Rhineland to Venice, enabling the lagoon city to act as an early leader in humanist and reformation printing. Without this invention, it is hard to see how an obscure monk named Martin Luther (1483–1546) could have contributed to a revolutionary conflagration that, over time, contributed to a radical transformation in orders of obligation and structures of social power across Europe.

But we are peering into the future. For now, we need to look northwest to England, where intellectual property will emerge when Protestant interpretations of English legal traditions facilitate a kind of nationalization in the royal prerogative, a leveling transformation of feudal properties belonging traditionally to the king. We need to return to the feudal transformation and to follow a nationalization in the royal prerogative power made possible by that transformation.

This is the story to which we now turn.

7

Administrative Kingship and Covenantal Bonds

Early Roots of Intellectual Property in England

In 1542, King Henry VIII of England (1509–47) granted to a man named Anthony Marler, "citizen and haberdasher of our city of London," the exclusive right to print English Bibles for four years. Henry gave this legal privilege through *letters patent*, notifying the kingdom's printers, officers, ministers, and subjects that no other person – subject or stranger, "within these our dominions" – was to print an English Bible. If anyone should presume to do so in contravention of the king's privilege and command, they would be met with "punishment and high displeasure." This exclusive privilege to print Europe's most intensively studied book was granted – "for certain causes convenient to our grace especial" – to Henry's "well beloved subject" *or* his assignees, meaning that, for as long as it endured, the privilege could be transferred and sold like an object of property.[1]

In this printing patent, the infamous Tudor king was using his letters patent to accomplish something new, namely, the royal control of printers and religious publications. However, the legal form through which he accomplished this goal was nothing new. In England, continuity in the use of formalized letters to grant exclusive privileges, often called *liberties* or *franchises* (i.e., freedoms), stretches backward from Henry VIII all the way to his Angevin predecessor and namesake, Henry III (1216–72), and even beyond into the Anglo-Norman and Anglo-Saxon periods of English history.[2]

[1] Paul L. Hughes and James F. Larkin (eds.), *Tudor Royal Proclamations, Volume I, The Early Tudors (1485–1553)* (New Haven: Yale University Press, 1964), no. 210, p. 309. On the Bible as Europe's most intensively studied (and therefore highly demanded) book, see Beryl Smalley, *The Study of the Bible in the Middle Ages*, 2nd ed. (New York: The Philosophical Library, 1952), xi; *cf.* Nicholas Vincent, *A Brief History of Britain: The Birth of the Nation* (London: Robinson, 2011), 197. On the early printing of English Bibles, see H. S. Bennett, *English Books & Readers, 1475–1557* (Cambridge, UK: Cambridge University Press, 1952), 75–6; A. W. Pollard, *Records of the English Bible* (Oxford: Oxford University Press, 1911).

[2] The Angevin dynasty, beginning with Henry II (1154–89), takes its name from the Counts of Anjou, a region in what is today western France. Henry II's father was Geoffrey, Count of Anjou, who had married Matilda, daughter of Henry I (1100–1135), herself a claimant to the throne of England under her father's publicly declared will. Henry I was the son of William I (lived c. 1028–1087), the conqueror from Normandy, who reigned as king of England from 1066 to 1087. While historians draw a distinction between the Angevin dynasty, beginning with Henry II, and the earlier Anglo-

Nonetheless, despite striking continuities in the legal form of privilege granting that connect the England of Henry I (1100–35) to Henry VIII, dramatic transformations had occurred in regimes of social power. Michael Mann narrates these transformations as phases in the emergence of industrial capitalism, linked to nation-state formation. During the early, "intensive" phase – stretching between the ninth and mid-twelfth centuries – Roman law was studied in new ways, with strong cultural support from Christianity and Biblical scholarship. During the second, "extensive" phase, relations of obligation were transformed in ways that spread broadly across Christendom, laying the foundations for the modern nation-state system and legal conceptions of property that are still with us.[3]

In England, new forms of legal property were recognized within corporate boroughs like London and town-based guilds across the island. Zones of exclusivity were constituted in patterns that supported development of new technologies, including the windmill, which appeared in England sometime around 1185. Some scholars have connected these developments with an industrial revolution of the Middle Ages. While this may go too far, we will see organizational innovations in royal administration, facilitated by developments in English law, lending new life to economic privileges and franchises, supporting new technologies, and establishing a foundation for modern intellectual property.[4]

To see the long thread of historical connections, though, we need to wrap our minds around the unfamiliar world of Anglo-Norman privileges. These were granted through charters and writs, which were the legal and diplomatic foundations for later letters patent and corporate charters. In ways that are challenging to pinpoint precisely, the development of these new legal forms was catalyzed by the Norman Conquest, part of a new paradigm for royal administration, and a basis for the

Norman dynasty beginning with William I, there was a continuous, family line leading from William I to Henry III. The partial exception was Stephen (1135–54), who was Henry I's nephew, son of Henry I's sister Adela and the Count of Blois-Champagne, who seized the throne before Matilda could effectively claim it. For a simplified family tree, and for valuable historical context, see Robert Bartlett, *England under the Norman and Angevin Kings 1075–1225* (Oxford: Clarendon Press, 2000), 5 and passim.

3 Mann, *Sources, Vol. 1*, 373–449, especially 375–6, 419, 423, 430–6, 441, 445–6.

4 E. M. Carus-Wilson, "An Industrial Revolution of the Thirteenth Century," *The Economic History Review* 11(1): 39–60 (1941). Helpful reviews of the scholarly debates over the thesis of an "industrial revolution of the Middle Ages" are available in John Langdon, *Mills in the Medieval Economy, 1300–1540* (Oxford: Oxford University Press) and Adam Lucas, *Ecclesiastical Lordship, Seigneurial Power and the Commercialization of Milling in Medieval England* (London: Routledge, 2016). On boroughs as medieval corporations, see Adolphus Ballard, *British Borough Charters, 1042–1216* (Cambridge, UK: Cambridge University Press, 1913); Adolphus Ballard & James Tait, *British Borough Charters, 1216–1307* (Cambridge, UK: Cambridge University Press, 1923). English guilds, towns, and boroughs, broadly surveyed: Susan Reynolds, *An Introduction to the History of English Medieval Towns* (Oxford: Clarendon Press, 1977).

precisely defined royal, prerogative powers that constitute the foundation for modern intellectual property.[5]

7.1 BRIDGING THE NORMAN CONQUEST: CHARTERS AND WRITS IN ANGLO-NORMAN LEGAL GOVERNANCE

The Norman Conquest of 1066 was one of the great watersheds in English legal history. William the Conqueror (1066–87) left his powerful duchy in northern France, and – with the help of Norman, Flemish, and Breton warriors – won an English kingdom. The conquest had dramatic impacts on English law, but the impacts were more gradual than we might initially imagine. Continuities are important, too, and these matter for our understanding about how intellectual property developed. In fact, many of the chartering practices and theoretical approaches to law that we saw developing in Carolingian Europe were developing in England, too, and these continued to play a role in shaping English society, both before and after the Norman Conquest.[6]

There is no question, however, that the conquest was traumatic and transformative. William engaged in major "harrying" campaigns – briefly around London in the southeast, and much more extensively in northern England – to put down revolts, and these were devastating in the areas they occurred. There were also significant threats of invasion from the relatives of former king Cnut (1016–35) in Scandinavia. Four times William assembled armies to respond to the threats. The repeated efforts to assemble military resources may have stimulated a greater awareness of the wealth that his new kingdom offered, as well as a sense that some resources remained unmeasured and untapped. Perhaps it was ultimately a sense of military and political insecurity that provided an impetus for William's massive project in inquiry-based surveillance, a measure of his new kingdom's power structures and material resources, resulting in the records we know as *Domesday*.[7]

[5] C. Warren Hollister and John W. Baldwin, "The Rise of Administrative Kingship: Henry I and Philip Augustus," *The American Historical Review* 83(4) (1978): 867–905. On the shift from medieval, household-based administrative kingship to national bureaucracy, initiated in the wake of the Reformation under Henry VIII and Thomas Cromwell, see Geoffrey R. Elton, *The Tudor Revolution in Government: Administrative Changes in the Reign of Henry VIII* (Cambridge, UK: Cambridge University Press, 1953).

[6] For a classic description of the Norman Conquest on English legal history, see Sir Frederick Pollock and Frederic William Maitland, *The History of English Law before the Time of Edward I*, 2nd ed. (Cambridge, UK: Cambridge University Press, 1952), 79–110; also see David Bates, *William the Conqueror* (Stroud, Gloucestorshire: The History Press, 201); Judith A. Green, *The Aristocracy of Norman England* (Cambridge, UK: Cambridge University Press, 1997); Ann Williams, *The English and the Norman Conquest* (Woodbridge: Boydell Press, 1995). For discussion of Breton and Flemish elements in William's entourage, see Bates, *William the Conqueror*, ll. 190; Elizabeth M. Hallam & Judith Everard, *Capetian France 987–1328*, 2nd ed. (Abingdon: Routledge, 2013).

[7] *Domesday Book: A Complete Translation*, Alecto Historical Editions, edited by Ann Williams & G. H. Martin (London: Penguin Press, 2003); Elizabeth M. Hallam, *Domesday Book through Nine Centuries* (Public Record Office, 1986), 17; Sally Harvey, *Domesday: Book of Judgment* (Oxford:

The Domesday inquiry was carried out with rapidity and efficiency in 1086–7, and records even beyond the Domesday "books" resulted. The record-generating activities involving Domesday were only the most visible manifestation of a broader process of inquiry that the Normans were carrying out in their new land, drawing to varying degrees on models of legal inquiry (*inquisitio*, inquest) that were developing in Anglo-Norman and canon law. The Normans were seeking to understand their newly colonized country, to learn about its legal traditions, and to gain a measure of its property holdings. Such a project was a powerful stimulus to the gathering and production of legal records. It also stimulated the writing of legal treatises. However, we will begin with the legal records, because these are the direct ancestors of letters patent, and because they are an important part of the material from which the new treatises were prepared.[8]

Here we come to a vital foundation of English common law: the writ. The English word *writ* comes from the Old English *gewrit*, which simply meant a writing or document. The English writ is the ancestor of *letters patent*, like we saw Henry VIII granting in 1542, and it is accordingly the distant ancestor of a modern patent, like the kind that Facebook owns today. Viewed in its historical context by scholars as a formal legal text, however, the writ is a type of diploma, together with charters and other types of letter-based legal documents.[9]

Writs were short, formulaic texts written on parchment, which issued orders to subordinate officers or granted property-related privileges. They were sealed for purposes of authentication and their use was already a developed legal tradition in

Oxford University Press, 2014); Bruce R. O'Brien, *God's Peace and King's Peace: The Laws of Edward the Confessor* (Philadelphia: University of Pennsylvania Press, 1999), 8; David Roffe, *Decoding Domesday* (Woodbridge: Boydell Press, 2007); Sir Frank Stenton, *Anglo-Saxon England*, 3rd ed. (Oxford: Oxford University Press, 1971), 581–618.

8 Domesday inquiry and resulting records: H. C. Darby, *Domesday England* (Cambridge, UK: Cambridge University Press, 1977), 3–9 and passim; David C. Douglas and George W. Greenaway (eds.), *English Historical Documents 1042–1189*, 2nd ed. (London and New York: Eyre Methuen and Oxford University Press, 1981) [hereafter EHD II], 855–73, 911–59; V. H. Galbraith, *Domesday Book: Its Place in Administrative History* (Oxford: Clarendon Press, 1974), 18–99; Harvey, *Domesday*, 96–100. Broader process of legal inquiry (*inquisitio*) and colonization: Galbraith, *Domesday Book*, 18, 33–46; J. C. Holt, "The Origins of the Constitutional Tradition in England," in *Magna Carta and Medieval Government* (London: The Hambledon Press, 1985), 8–9; O'Brien, *God's Peace*, 26. Stimulus for the writing of legal treatises: Patrick Wormald, *The Making of English Law: King Alfred to the Twelfth Century* (Oxford: Blackwell Publishers, 2001), 465–83.

9 For introduction to the world of Anglo-Saxon writs, see Frances E. Harmer, *Anglo-Saxon Writs* (Manchester: Manchester University Press, 1952). For the connection to letters patent, see Harmer, *Writs*, 1–118. While Harmer's text remains foundational, important additional discussions may be found in Pierre Chaplais, "The Anglo-Saxon Chancery: From the Diploma to the Writ," in *Prisca Munimenta: Studies in Archival and Administrative History Presented to Dr. A.E.J. Hollaender*, edited by Felicity Ranger (London: University of London Press, 1973), 43–62; M. T. Clanchy, *From Memory to Written Record: England 1066–1307*, 3rd ed. (Chichester: Wiley-Blackwell, 2013); R. C. Van Caenegem, *Royal Writs in England from the Conquest to Glanvill* (London: Bernard Quaritch, 1959), 107–34; Dorothy Whitelock, "Introduction to Part II, Charters and Laws," in Dorothy Whitelock (ed.), *English Historical Documents, Volume I, c. 500–1042*, 2nd ed. (London and New York: Eyre Methuen and Oxford University Press, 1979) [hereafter EHD I], 357–90.

England at the time of the Norman Conquest. Going back to the time of Alfred the Great, there is evidence that writs accompanied by a seal (*insegel*) may have been used in England as a documentary conveyance of the king's command. From the time of Aethelred II ("the Unready," 978–1016) – Alfred's fourth-generation descendant – a tradition of Anglo-Saxon royal writs is weakly attested in surviving copies of documents. This tradition is more firmly attested from the reign of Aethelred's Danish successor, Cnut, and from the subsequent reign of Edward the Confessor (1042–66), in whom the House of Wessex came back briefly to the English throne. The tradition continued with William the Conqueror and his Anglo-Norman successors, from whom we have rapidly increasing numbers of original writs.[10]

Today, scholars often distinguish writs from writ-charters, separating those that issue commands from the king to his subordinates (the former) from those that grant property and privileges (the latter). During the Anglo-Norman period inaugurated by the Norman Conquest, the writ-charters gradually replaced an older diplomatic form that stretches back much further in English history, perhaps all the way to Gregory the Great or perhaps to a bishop named Theodore, who came from Constantinople by way of Rome to help stabilize the English church in the seventh century. Because the form of the older charters differs significantly from the later writs and writ-charters that would give birth to letters patent, diplomatic historians are careful to distinguish them.[11]

However, while there are important differences in diplomatic form between the oldest Anglo-Saxon charters and the later Anglo-Saxon writs, there are continuities in function and content. The older charters had also been used to convey property and privileges, which came under the Normans to be called franchises and liberties.

[10] Harmer, *Writs*, xiii, 10–19, 235–43, 372–96 (including transcriptions of two writs (copies, likely forgeries) from Aethelred II, one for St. Paul's Cathedral in London and the other for Winchester Cathedral); *cf.* Chaplais, *Anglo-Saxon Chancery*, 50–62 (Chaplais is skeptical about the existence of sealed writs prior to the reign of Edward the Confessor). See also *Frank Barlow, The English Church 1000–1066: A Constitutional History* (Hamden, Connecticut: Archon Books, 1963), 126–9; John Hudson, *The Oxford History of the Laws of England, Volume II* (Oxford: Oxford University Press, 2012) [Kindle ed.], ll. 639–1064; Simon Keynes, "Royal Government and the Written Word in Late Anglo-Saxon England," in Rosamond McKitterick (ed.), *The Uses of Literacy in Early Medieval Europe* (Cambridge, UK: Cambridge University Press, 1990), 248 (Keynes sees "no reason to dissent from Harmer's belief that the surviving writs are but the rump of a long tradition of administrative letters stretching back at least as far as the reign of King Alfred the Great"); Simon Keynes, *The Diplomas of King Aethelred "The Unready" 978–1016* (Cambridge, UK: Cambridge University Press, 1980), 140–5; van Caenegem, *Royal Writs*, 113–20; Wormald, *Making of English Law*, 398–402, 435. On the life and reign of Edward the Confessor, see Frank Barlow, *Edward the Confessor*, 2nd ed. (New Haven: Yale University Press, 1997).

[11] On the distinction between writs and writ-charters, see Mark Haggor, "The Earliest Norman Writs Revisited," *Historical Research* 82.216 (2009): 181–205; W. H. Stevenson, "Yorkshire Surveys and Other Eleventh-Century Documents in the York Gospels," *The English Historical Review* 27.105 (1912): 1–25; van Caenegem, *Royal Writs*, 4, 107–34. Development of charters and writs: Chaplais, *Anglo-Saxon Chancery*, 50–62; Harmer, *Writs*, 34–8; Keynes, *Diplomas of King Aethelred*, 140–5; van Caenegem, *Royal Writs*, 113–26; Patrick Wormald, *Bede and the Conversion of England: The Charter Evidence* (Jarrow Lecture, 1984); Wormald, *Making of English Law*, 398–402, 435.

Such franchises and liberties could have very similar effects – or at least they seem to intend similar effects – whether they were granted in the seventh century or in the twelfth.

For example, ten charters granting freedom from payment of shipping tolls survive from the eighth century. Grants of freedom from tolls remained important under the early Norman kings, offering a legal means for the king to provide economic support to favored monks, bishops, or merchants, without paying any money out of pocket. The eighth-century grants from Kings Aethelbald and Offa of Mercia, as from King Eadberht of Kent, offer a fleeting glimpse into trading patterns during the "Dark Age" of Europe. Hinting at a world that is mostly unrecoverable today, these grants pertained to markets, ports, and trading areas (*wics*) in London, and along the southeast coast of Kent.[12]

For our purposes, it is important to emphasize that there are Roman law roots for both the older charters and the newer writs. While there are debates about the precise lines of descent, scholars generally agree that both developed from late Roman diplomatic models, as mediated by the church and perhaps by Carolingian practices. Based on formulaic appearance, the oldest Anglo-Saxon charter form seems to have been modeled on late Roman forms of property transfer, especially deeds of gift, while the later writs look more like adaptations from Roman imperial mandates.[13]

William and his two sons, William Rufus (1087–1100) and Henry I, mainly relied on writs and writ-charters to issue orders and grant privileges, but they occasionally reverted back to the older charter forms. Today we are fortunate to have many of their charters and writs available to read and study. The reason we have them, of course, is that the cathedral churches, monasteries, and laypeople who received them were careful to keep them. The charters and writs constituted

[12] N. P. Brooks & S. E. Kelly, *Charters of Christ Church Canterbury, Part I* (Oxford: Oxford University Press, 2013), 360–2, no. 15; Susan Kelly, "Trading Privileges from Eighth Century England," *Early Medieval Europe* 1.1 (1992): 3–28; Neil Middleton, "Early Medieval Port Customs, Tolls and Controls on Foreign Trade," *Early Medieval Europe* 13.4 (2005): 313–58. For a growing electronic collection of Anglo-Saxon charters and translations, see *The Electronic Sawyer: Online Catalogue of Anglo-Saxon Charters*, available at www.esawyer.org.uk/about/index.html (accessed September 28, 2017). For additional translations of preconquest charters, see EHD I; A. J. Robertson (ed.), *Anglo-Saxon Charters*, Digitally Printed Edition (Cambridge, UK: Cambridge University Press, 2009).

[13] Wormald, *Bede*, 9–19. "[P]rivate acta in the sub-Roman west had a common origin, and long retained many similarities in the various charter traditions that gradually evolved. What may positively be said about the Anglo-Saxon charter is that it too belongs to this extended family in its own independent right, and shares a variety of family traits with several other members. We can be confident about its distant ancestor, the founder of the line, which was Roman, but we need to be more cautious about the genealogical details which link the two .... England in the seventh century established its own idiosyncratic relationship with the Roman world." *Ibid.* 19; Wormald, *Making of English Law*, 398–402, 435; *cf.* van Caenegem, *Royal Writs*, 107–35; Ben Snook, "Who Introduced Charters into England? The Case for Theodore and Hadrian," in Bruce O'Brien and Barbara Bombi (eds.), Textus Roffensis: *Law, Language, and Libraries in Early Medieval England* (Turnhout: Brepols, 2015), 257–89.

precious evidence of privileges and immunities, which protected rights to revenues and wealth. And, to repeat, they are the distant, diplomatic ancestors of our modern patents.[14]

7.2 NEW LEGAL CULTURES AND THE ROYAL PREROGATIVE

Influences from Italy and northern France were significant under the new Norman rulers, and, through the clerics they brought over to serve in England, those influences were felt in both royal and ecclesiastical administration. Lanfranc's time of service as archbishop of Canterbury (1070–89) is widely seen as a turning point. Lanfranc *could* have brought with him from Pavia, by way of Normandy, connections to the legal learning of northern Italy. In Bologna, as we saw in the previous chapter, a small collection of legal scholars would soon coalesce into one of Europe's first universities. During the twelfth and thirteenth centuries, legal learning from Bologna would spill across western Europe, reaching all the way to England. Pavia was also a center of legal learning, with traditions of law and notarial practice stretching back to the Lombard kings whom Gregory the Great had known.[15]

Much more certainly, however, Lanfranc brought with him connections to new learning in canon law, most directly from northern France and less directly from imperial Germany. Lanfranc introduced into England a collection of canon law texts that scholars today call the Pseudo-Isidorian Decretals. This was a collection that included some genuine papal letters going back well before the time of Gregory the Great, interspersed with forgeries laying emphasis on the powers of bishops, especially the bishop of Rome. Scholars today identify the collection as originating

[14] David Bates (ed.), *Regesta Regum Anglo-Normannorum: The Acts of William I (1066–1087)* (Oxford: Clarendon Press, 1998), A systematic project by David Carpenter and Richard Sharpe is currently ongoing to collect, edit, transcribe, and translate the charters and writs of William II and Henry I. The edited and translated documents are readily available through the Anglo-Norman Royal Charters website, https://actswilliam2henry1.wordpress.com (accessed March 6, 2020).

[15] On Lanfranc's background in Pavia, see H. E. J. Cowdrey, *Lanfranc: Scholar, Monk, and Archbishop* (Oxford: Oxford University Press, 2003), 1–8, 13; Margaret Gibson, *Lanfranc of Bec* (Oxford: Clarendon Press, 1978), 1–15. On the new scholastic humanism, with its social ideals of philosophically and Biblically informed engagement in legal administration and governance, see C. Stephen Jaeger, *The Envy of Angels: Cathedral Schools and Social Ideals in Medieval Europe, 950–1200* (Philadelphia: University of Pennsylvania Press, 1994), 27–52, 83–7, 292–329; R. W. Southern, *Scholastic Humanism and the Unification of Europe, Volume I: Foundations* (Oxford: Blackwell, 1995); Ronald G. Witt, *The Two Latin Cultures and the Foundations of Renaissance Humanism in Medieval Italy* (New York: Cambridge University Press, 2012); Wormald, *Making of English Law*, 469–76. On the linkages between England and continental Europe – extending through pilgrimage to Byzantium and Jerusalem – during the period leading up to the Norman invasion, viewed from the perspective of economic, ecclesiastical, and constitutional developments, see Barlow, *English Church 1000–1066*, 10–23, 62–95. On continuities in legal development under the English clergy, especially the bishops, see ibid. 30–40, 62–158

in northern France, probably in the mid-ninth century. A version of the collection was available at Bec, and Lanfranc brought it with him from Bec to England.[16]

Controversies among secular and regular clergy over jurisdiction and hierarchical authority had given new life to the Pseudo-Isidorian Decretals, and to the development of legal arguments based on papal letters and church councils. A center of the new canon law learning that developed from these controversies was Chartres, where Ivo of Chartres had been invested as bishop in 1090. Ivo became famous as the compiler of canon law collections known as the *Decretum* – based on a previous collection by Burchard of Worms with the same name – and the *Panormia*. By the time that Anselm (1033–1109) – a charismatic theologian and successor to Lanfranc as abbot of Bec – was invested as archbishop of Canterbury in 1093, the trickle of canon law learning spreading from northern France to England was becoming a flood. Records of library holdings at Rochester Cathedral from the early twelfth century, for example, testify to close connections between canon law developments in England and northern France.[17]

These legal developments became practically significant in England with efforts by Lanfranc and Anselm to clarify Canterbury's jurisdictional boundaries, particularly the primacy of Canterbury over York. Based on his review of the records and canonical authorities, Lanfranc was convinced that England's ecclesiastical structure was monarchical, with Canterbury as overseer to London and York, together with all other bishoprics throughout the British Isles. Drawing on legal principles articulated in papal letters and imperial capitularies – some of them coming from the Pseudo-Isidorian Decretals – Lanfranc obtained a temporary victory, extending ambiguously into the period of Anselm's governance as archbishop. Although the claims to primacy over the bishops of York and Ireland did not last, claims over the bishops of Wales and London became permanent, symbolized formally in written professions of obedience. Beginning in 1126, moreover, popes named the archbishops of Canterbury as papal legates for England and Scotland, making them papal agents exercising many of the pope's legal powers and giving them an effective primacy of jurisdiction.[18]

16 Z. N. Brooke, *The English Church and the Papacy: From the Conquest to the Reign of John*, 2nd ed. (Cambridge, UK: Cambridge University Press, 1989), 57–83; Cowdrey, *Lanfranc*, 138–43; Clara Harder, "Pseudo-Isidorus Mercator," in Philip L. Reynolds (ed.), *Great Christian Jurists and Legal Collections in the First Millennium* (Cambridge, UK: Cambridge University Press, 2019), 397–411; R. H. Helmholz, *The Canon Law and Ecclesiastical Jurisdiction from 597 to the 1640s: The Oxford History of the Laws of England, Vol. I* (Oxford: Oxford University Press, 2004), 70–4; Wormald, *Making of English Law*, 469–76.

17 Christof Rolker, *Canon Law and the Letters of Ivo of Chartres* (Cambridge, UK: Cambridge University Press, 2009); Mary P. Richards, *Texts and Their Traditions in the Medieval Library of Rochester Cathedral Priory* (Philadelphia: The American Philosophical Society, 1988). Rolker's study of reliance on canon law collections in Ivo's letters raises significant doubts about whether the *Panormia* has been rightly attributed to Ivo. Anselm of Canterbury: R. W. Southern, *Saint Anselm: A Portrait in a Landscape* (Cambridge, UK: Cambridge University Press, 1990).

18 *The Letters of Lanfranc Archbishop of Canterbury*, translated by Helen Clover and Margaret Gibson (Oxford: Oxford University Press, 1979), Nos. 3–13, 47, 49–50, 59; James A. Brundage, *Medieval Canon Law* (London: Routledge, 2013), 25–43; Cowdrey, *Lanfranc*, 87–103, 144–8; Michael Richter (ed.),

We can see here one dimension of the new legal culture that was developing through jurisdictional disputes of the early twelfth century. The issues concerned both canon and secular law, and they were ultimately about the sources of authority and obligation, both secular and religious. The effort to distinguish canon law from the secular law of the kingdom was, indeed, an important part of the disputed terrain. The disputes rapidly broadened to include kings and emperors, as secular rulers, and the pope, as the head of the church. In England, these disputes prompted the Anglo-Norman and Angevin kings to explicitly, and self-consciously, assert their royal prerogative as a response to assertions of primacy by bishops and the pope.[19]

In tracing the early disputes in England, we are fortunate to have what are, in effect, legal briefs from each side. On the Canterbury side, we have a history by an English monk named Eadmer (c. 1060–1126), who was devoted to archbishop Anselm. On the York side, we have a history written by a Norman canon, a kind of ecclesiastical officer (*precentor*) of the cathedral church, named Hugh (c. 1080–1139). This has survived in a single manuscript, which is basically a cartulary – a narrated collection of legal records and privileges – for York Cathedral. Hugh's *Historia* constitutes a narrative core for that cartulary. Both legal arguments begin with the Norman Conquest, although Eadmer, as the older of the two, does more to place the conquest in its context.[20]

Eadmer looked back to the days of King Edgar of Wessex (959–975) as a golden age, a time when the whole realm of England was "governed diligently … with righteous laws" (*totum regnum sanctis legibus strenuo gubernantuo*). Edgar had ruled cooperatively with archbishop Dunstan of Canterbury, who "ordered the whole of Britain by the administration of the law Christian" (*Christianae legis moderamino totam Brittaniam disponebat*). This time of peace and happiness was broken by the

Canterbury Professions (Torquay: Devonshire Press, 1973), lvii–xcvi, 26–108; Southern, *Saint Anselm*, 330–64.

19 Scholars often refer to these disputes under the heading of "the investiture dispute." Investiture was the sacramental ritual according to which authority was conferred on bishops and, by analogy, on secular rulers. Like a profession of obedience, the symbolism of investiture indicated lines of authority and fidelity/loyalty, therefore of social power. In England, the investiture dispute was resolved by distinguishing feudal homage, as a secular expression of loyalty to the king, from investiture, as a religious ritual. Kings were permitted to demand the former from their clergy, although they were prohibited from involvement in the latter. This distinction of a secular source of social power (homage) from religious ritual (investiture) clarified the sacred purity of clerical authority, enabling an important step toward our modern division of religion from political power. *Cf.* Harold J. Berman, *Law and Revolution: The Formation of the Western Legal Tradition* (Cambridge, MA: Harvard University Press, 1983), 86–119, 434–38; Uta-Renata Blumenthal, *The Investiture Controversy: Church and Monarchy from the Ninth to the Twelfth Century* (Philadelphia: University of Pennsylvania Press, 1988), 142–59.

20 *Eadmer's History of Recent Events in England*, translated by Geoffrey Bosanquet (London: Cresset Press, 1964); *Eadmeri Historia Novorum in Anglia et Opuscula Duo*, edited by Martin Rule (London: Longman & Co, 1884); M. Brett, C. N. L. Brooke, and M. Winterbottom, *Introduction to* Hugh the Chanter, *The History of the Church of York 1066–1127*, translated by Charles Johnson (Oxford: Clarendon Press, 1990), xiii–xlv, lv–lxi; also see *The Life of St. Anselm, Archbishop of Canterbury by Eadmer*, translated by R. W. Southern (Oxford: Oxford University Press, 1962), 1.

unrighteous rule of Aethelred, "the Unready." Renewed violence from Viking warriors, whom Aethelred bribed through "crushing exactions" placed upon the English people, was the divine punishment. England passed into a period of devastation and chaos, culminating in William's conquest.[21]

William imposed "usages and laws" from Normandy. These involved a new level of royal centralization: subjection of all magnates – ecclesiastical and secular alike – to the ruler. According to Eadmer, William ensured his supremacy by four specific measures. First, he prohibited anyone from recognizing a new pope, unless they had received instructions and permission to do so. Second, he forbade anyone to receive a letter from the pope, unless it was first delivered to (and approved by) him. Third, he prohibited the archbishops from issuing any ordinances or prohibitions without his approval. And fourth, he set limits on the capacity of bishops to punish or excommunicate his barons or ministers (officers). William, in short, was insisting on a primacy of legal governance. Eadmer saw this as a dangerous novelty for England.[22]

William refused to perform a ritual of fidelity (fealty) to Pope Gregory VII (1073–85). In this refusal, he was negating the pope's claim of feudal primacy and insisting on the retention of his supremacy. At the same time, however, he demonstrated his loyalty to the pope by promising that payments of "Peter's Pence," a tax collected in England for payment to Rome, would be renewed. William also demonstrated his loyalty and willingness to work cooperatively with the papacy in his holding of church councils.[23]

William Rufus, the Conqueror's son, claimed his royal powers in a much less compromising spirit, aggressively pursuing a fiscal strategy that would later be interpreted as a foundational element of the royal prerogative. The new king, according to Eadmer, appropriated the revenues of bishoprics and monasteries, purposely delaying the appointment of new bishops and abbots, so that he could collect the revenue streams from lands and privileges belonging them in the period of vacancy. During the twelfth century, the king's power to collect these revenues was defended as a core element of the king's regalian right, sometimes referred to in the plural as the *regalia* and sometimes referred to in the language of prerogative (*praerogativa*).[24]

William Rufus' perceived abuses of his prerogative, however, would also contribute to a new legal practice: the issuance of a charter of liberties for the entire kingdom.

21 *Eadmer's History* (Bosanquet trans.), 3–9; Rule (ed.), *Eadmeri, Historia Novorum*, 3–9.

22 *Eadmer's History* (Bosanquet trans.), 9–10; Rule (ed.), *Eadmeri, Historia Novorum*, 10; *cf.* Hugh the Chanter, *History of York*, 183.

23 *Letters of Lanfranc*, Nos. 38–9; also see EHD II, 692–4; *Eadmer's History* (Bosanquet trans.), 10–26; Rule (ed.), *Eadmeri, Historia Novorum*, 10–25.

24 *Eadmer's History* (Bosanquet trans.), 26–8; *Dialogus de Scaccario (The Dialogue of the Exchequer)*, 2nd ed., translated by Emilie Amt and S. D. Church (Oxford: Clarendon Press, 2007), 127, 141–7; Margaret Howell, *Regalian Right in Medieval England* (London: The Athlone Press, 1962).

7.3 MOSAIC TRADITIONS IN ENGLISH LEGAL HISTORY – THE POWER OF A COVENANTAL IDEAL

William the Conqueror and William Rufus had asserted their prerogative powers against bishops and the growing power of the pope. At the same time, they recognized an idealized conception of English law as it had existed before the Norman Conquest. We can see this conception in the Domesday Book, which repeatedly marks a "before and after" with the acronym TRE – Latin for "in the time of King Edward" (*Tempore Regis Edwardi*).[25]

William the Conqueror, in his charters, reinforced this idealized conception of "Edwardian law." For example, in a writ-charter for Abingdon Abbey, issued probably within a few years of the conquest, William granted the right to restore "all the customs of their lands," those applying either "in borough or out of borough," as these had existed "by gift of King Edward." The abbot would have to prove by "writ or charter" that the customs by gift of Edward had existed but so long as he could do so, those privileges would be reinstated.[26]

The promise to reinstate the law as it had existed in the time of Edward the Confessor was also given in William the Conqueror's "charter of liberties" for London, issued shortly after the conquest (sometime between 1066 and 1075). In this charter, issued to the bishop of London, the portreeve, and to "all the burgesses of London," William declared that Londoners were to be "worthy" (i.e., deserving) of "all the laws you were worthy of in the time of King Edward." William granted the right for sons to inherit property from their fathers and promised legal protection to the burgesses of the city. In referring to the Londoners as burgesses, William implicitly recognized London as having the status of a *burgh*, tethering that conception to the laws of King Edward's time.[27]

An idealizing conception of England's "good old laws" had already been powerfully articulated by Wulfstan (d. 1023), whose service in the English church extended across the reigns of Aethelred II and Cnut. For Wulfstan, as for Eadmer, the ideal went back, in turn, to the time of Edgar, that righteous king who had ruled under the teaching and guidance of reforming churchmen. Wulfstan exercised an extraordinary level of cultural power in England, as has been recently emphasized by historians of English law. He was the drafter of laws issued under the names of Aethelred and Cnut, as well as homilies and treatises that circulated under his own name. Collected after the conquest by anonymous Anglo-Norman scholars into manuscripts, Wulfstan's idealizing vision of English royal law, stretching back to king Edgar and before him to king Alfred, survived in

25 Williams & Martin (eds.), *Domesday Book*, 1435.

26 *Historia Ecclesie Abbendonensis: The History of the Church of Abingdon*, Vol. II, edited and translated by John Hudson (Oxford: Clarendon Press, 2002), 2–3.

27 Bates (ed.), *Regesta . . . Acts of William I (1066–1087)*, No. 180, p. 593; EHD II, 1012; Wormald, *Making of English Law*, 398–9

English legal history, packaged together under the sanctifying halo of Edward the Confessor.[28]

Wulfstan's legal vision for England had been both Mosaic and apocalyptic. His service as bishop began at the opening of a new millennium, when threats of annihilation from Viking Danes seemed very real. Millenarian themes were powerful in ecclesiastical and monastic scholarship of this period, and they were heightened in England with the periodic, terrifying violence. Millenarian themes were acute in Wulfstan's writings, and they seem to have contributed to his powerful sense that English society must be reformed, according to God's Biblical legal pattern. If English society could be reformed in this way, the English would become God's holy nation, as Israel had been. Like the Israelite kings, England's kings had an especially important role to play in this legal reformation, as both givers and implementers of laws governing church and worldly society alike.[29]

All of this could have disappeared with the conquest, but instead it was preserved and reinterpreted, in an intensified formulation of legal obligations for those subjected to the power of kings, lords, and bishops. The formulation was accomplished through a manuscript tradition of Anglo-Saxon legal "codes." This interpretive process of "inventing tradition" coalesced through the work of anonymous writers under Henry I and his successors. They contributed to an ideal of English legislation, modeled on divinely given, Biblical law, with an interpretive context in emerging studies of Roman and canon law.[30]

A significant, performative moment in this new development of Anglo-Norman royal law occurred in 1100, with Henry I's coronation charter. While it had long been traditional for a new English king to swear a solemn oath at the time of his

28 Andrew Rabin, *The Political Writings of Archbishop Wulfstan of York* (Manchester: Manchester University Press, 2015); Wormald, *Making of English Law*, 27, 185–203, 218–19, 222, 264, 328–65, 389–97, 449–65.

29 Wulfstan, "God's Threat to a Sinning Israel," translated in Rabin, *Political Writings*, 173–6; idem, "The Institutes of Polity," translated in Rabin, *Political Writings*, 101–24; idem, "The Laws of Edward and Guthrum," translated in Rabin, *Political Writings*, 35–60; Wormald, *Making of English Law*, 27, 111–483 (esp. 162–263 (on the manuscripts) and 264–415 (on the "codes," as reconstructed from the manuscripts), 449–65 (on Wulfstan and God's law)).

30 L. J. Downer (ed. & trans.), *Leges Henrici Primi* (Oxford: Oxford University Press, 1972); O'Brien, *God's Peace*, 26–61; O'Brien (ed. & trans.), "The Laws of Edward the Confessor," in *God's Peace*, 158–203; Richard Sharpe (trans.), "The Prefaces of '*Quadripartitus*,'" in George Garnett and John Hudson (eds.), *Law and Government in Medieval England and Normandy: Essays in Honour of Sir James Holt* (Cambridge, UK: Cambridge University Press, 1994), 148–72; Patrick Wormald, "*Quadripartitus*," in Garnett & Hudson (eds.), *Law and Government*, 111–47; Wormald, *Making of English Law*, *passim*, esp. 19, 27, 111–43, 162–483, esp. 197 ("Holy Writ and royal precept had the same objective: the holiness of God's people. The English kingdom's basic law book opened with extensive excerpts from the law God gave Moses. Its kings' laws were part of the ongoing story of Divine legislation. To enshrine royal law beside God's was not blasphemy. It was a statement, at once blunt and profound, of their common purpose."), 308 ("The pulsing heart of all this was an ideology finding new legislative expression in what the king said about his rights and God's."), 398–429, 444–76, 481–3. Critical edition of the codes: Felix Libermann (ed.), *Die Gesetze der Angelsachsen*, Vol. I (Halle: Max Niemeyer, 1903).

coronation, Henry seems to have been the first to issue a coronation *charter*, one that his grandson Henry II (1154–89) would affirm at his own coronation. As Henry II would look back to the good old days of his grandfather – before the civil wars between Matilda and Stephen (1135–54) had so disrupted life in the Anglo-Norman realms – Henry I looked back with his father William to the good old days of Edward the Confessor.[31]

In Henry I's charter of liberties, the "laws of Edward" became a kind of bedrock for the "good old laws" of England even though the actual content of these laws was very undefined. Henry promised a "firm peace," and to restore "the law of King Edward," subject to such rightful amendments "as my father made with the counsel of his barons." Laws made with wise council, rooted in the time of Edward, were the foundation for promissory legal obligations spreading continuity, stability, and justice from the king to his churchmen and lay vassals.[32]

Beyond his general promise of legal stability and justice, Henry promised to curtail practices that leading men regarded as abuses of the king's prerogative powers. He vowed to respect and protect the liberty of the church: he would not exploit episcopal vacancies, in the ways his brother William had, by selling or leasing the church's properties during a period of vacancy. Analogous promises were made to the barons and earls, indicating royal practices that would also be identified as part of the prerogative: compelling payment (*auxilium*) from an heir to one of the kingdom's great landed estates, as a condition for his inheritance, and collecting fees in exchange for royal permission to the marriage of an heiress daughter.[33]

Copies of the charter were sent to the shires, addressed to leading clergy and laymen, forming a foundational element in legal records that have survived until today in county archives. In 1101, threatened by his elder brother Robert, Henry confirmed the provisions of the charter while also demanding an oath of allegiance from the great men of his kingdom.[34]

With Henry I's charter of liberties, we see an adaptation of the Anglo-Norman writ-charter that will be of enormous significance as a precedent (*exemplum*) for the future. At the time it was issued, it was probably seen as a modest adaptation of the traditional, performative practice, in which the king took an oath at the opening of his reign. The adaptation was to put the oath in writing and to issue the writing in the form of a solemn charter, the same legal form that was used to convey property and privileges. The use of this legal form would have added to the solemnity of the king's promises, emphasizing the ways in which his reign would be different from that of

31 Richard Sharpe, "Charter of Liberties and Royal Proclamations," Charters of William II and Henry I Project, October 2013, available at https://actswilliam2henry1.files.wordpress.com/2013/10/h1-a-liberties-2013-1.pdf (accessed April 5, 2020), 1–70; Wormald, *Making of English Law*, 134, 228 ("The reign of Henry I was the most important period in the history of Old English law from 1066 itself to the reign of Elizabeth.), 252, 400–1.

32 Sharpe, "Charter of Liberties," §§ 12–13; Wormald, *Making of English Law*, 134, 228, 252, 400–1.

33 Sharpe, "Charter of Liberties," §§ 1–3; EHD II, 432–5; Howell, *Regalian Right*.

34 Sharpe, "Charter of Liberties," 2–76.

his brother. This idealizing vision of a king cooperating with his bishops to implement Godly rule throughout society reaches back to Wulfstan and Alfred.[35]

The reign of Henry I nonetheless marks a dramatic turning point in the history of English law and governance, a development that is partly reflected in the early legal treatises written by unknown Anglo-Norman clerics. Henry promised to restore the good old laws of righteous kingship and social obligation, which bound the kingdom together and made it strong enough to withstand all trials of invasion and conquest. At the core of this bonded kingdom was the royal prerogative itself, a foundation of landed property, titles, and the source of justice. Surrounding this core of the royal prerogative, moreover, was an intensifying and broadening array of social ties created through vows and oaths, bonds of obligation created intentionally through performative promises, which would be used to build an increasing panoply of social structures and economic institutions in the following centuries.[36]

7.4 CONSOLIDATING PATTERNS IN ANGLO-NORMAN AND ANGEVIN LAW: PREROGATIVES AND PROPERTY

Among many things that the Normans brought with them from northern France was a growing recognition that grants of legal privilege could stimulate economic exchange and the accumulation of taxable wealth. Under the fragmented political conditions of northern France, regional princes were learning that they could supplement their political powers by fostering centers of trade and industry: hosting and protecting fairs and ports and aiding in the development of mercantile towns. Counts of Flanders, Boulogne, and Blois-Champagne all supplemented their political positions this way, and the king of France followed suit in his efforts to grow his kingdom beyond the region around Paris. In Normandy, too, duke William fostered

[35] Wormald, *Making of English Law*, 134, 228, 252, 400–1.

[36] In addition to the sources cited in note 30, see Nichlas Karn, "*Textus Roffensis* and Its Uses," in O'Brien & Bombi (eds.), Textus Roffensis, 49–67; Richards, *Texts and Their Traditions*, 43–60; Mary P. Richards, "The *Textus Roffensis*: Keystone of the Medieval Library at Rochester," in O'Brien & Bombi (eds.), Textus Roffensis, 19–48; Peter Cramer, "Ernulf of Rochester and Early Anglo-Norman Canon Law," *Journal of Ecclesiastical History* 40(4): 483–510 (1989). Evidence for theologically grounded conceptions of a strong royal prerogative can be seen from a text probably composed in Normandy around 1100, which made its way to northern England: the *Norman Anonymous*. This collection of texts bears witness to a strong reaction against papal claims of supremacy on the part of a northern French cleric, who assembled arguments and authorities in favor of (1) the equality of all bishops, including the pope, and (2) the royal authority of the king, as personifying the authority of Christ. The author was particularly opposed to monastic privileges exempting monasteries from the oversight of their bishop, placing them under the direct oversight and jurisdiction of the pope. The claims to primacy and jurisdiction being made by the activist, reforming popes was sinful and Satanic, and rightly resisted. Royal law, rather than papal law, was to be followed, since the former in preference to the latter enabled true Christian freedom. George Williams, *The Norman Anonymous of 1100 A.D.: Toward the Identification and Evaluation of the So-Called Anonymous of York* (Eugene: Wipf & Stock 2008 [1951]); *cf.* Karl Pellens, *Die Texte des Normannischen Anonymus* (Wiesbaden: Franz Steiner Verlag, 1966).

the generation of taxable wealth through the granting of fair and market privileges, and he carried an early awareness of these practices with him when he colonized England.[37]

By the end of Henry I's reign, transformations in the cross-channel economy are evident in the legal records. Transactions and penalties were increasingly specified in precise, monetary terms. The coining of money was controlled through a system of exclusive privileges (together with harsh punishments for infringement). And new types of economic privileges were being recognized. Near the end of William Rufus' reign, London's "Cnightengild" had been confirmed, with its land and customs, on the same terms as it had existed during the time of Edward the Confessor and William the Conqueror. Then, toward the end of Henry I's reign, a craft guild was recognized in Rouen. The privilege, probably issued around 1131, is striking in creating a zone of exclusivity for Rouen's cordwainers and shoemakers.[38]

According to a town official of Rouen, who in 1267 certified that he himself had seen (*vidimus*) the document, Henry I had issued a charter addressed to the "justices of Normandy," and to the sheriff, barons, and burgesses of Rouen. In the charter,

37 Hallam and Everard, *Capetian France*, 37–66, esp. 49–52; Charles Gross, *The Gild Merchant: A Contribution to British Municipal History*, 2 Vols. (Oxford: Clarendon Press, 1890), 2–5. Scholarship on the origins of commercial revival in northern France, Flanders, and England involves fierce debate over the precise role of northern continental influence, and this is intertwined with debate about whether the sources of change came from royal privileges or from local initiatives. I don't intend to revisit these debates here, but only to emphasize signs of novelty in royal privileges, which doubtless responded in many (if not most) cases to local movements. For an overview, see Reynolds, *English Medieval Towns*, 16–108; James Tait, *The Medieval English Borough: Studies on Its Origins and Constitutional History* (Manchester: Manchester University Press, 1999 [1936]), 130–220.

38 H. W. C. Davis (ed.), *Regesta Regum Anglo-Normannorum, 1066–1154*, Vol. I (William the Conqueror & William Rufus) (Oxford: Clarendon Press, 1913), no. 444. This was confirmed by Henry 1 c. 1100–1103. Charles Johnson and H. A. Cronne (eds.), *Regesta Regum Anglo-Normannorum, 1066–1154*, Vol. II (Henry I) (Oxford: Clarendon Press, 1956), no. 663. Control of "moneyers" through exclusive privileges: ibid., nos. 501, 760, 1430, 1472. Development toward specification of monetary penalties: ibid., nos. 568–9 (specification of monetary privileges for infringement of privileges for church and canons of Colchester, 1100–1102); 585 (specification of monetary privilege for violation of trading privileges to Thorney church and monks, 1100–1102); 814–15 (specification of monetary penalty for failure to repair the abbot of Abingdon's broken sluice, 1107); 938 (specification of monetary penalty for violating tax exemptions of Abingdon, which apply to "all the property" (*res propriae*) of the abbot and monks, 1110); 1167 (specification of monetary penalty in privilege for monks of St. Mary, Thorney); 1674 (specification of monetary penalty for violating a Dover trading privilege); 1725 (specification of monetary penalty for infringement of trading privilege, notified to justiciars, reeves, and officials throughout England and Wales, 1131). Other evidence of monetization: ibid., nos. 1580–81 (grants of "money of Rouen" to nuns of Fontevrault, 1129), 1669 (reference to "coinage-tax" of Romney), 1698 (grant of "money of Rouen" to Augustinian canons, 1131); 1799 (command to all sheriffs and servants in England to seek out fugitives from Abingdon Abbey and to seize their "money and chattels" (*pecunia et catallo*)). The cordwainers and shoemakers of Rouen: ibid., no. 1695 (noting *vidimus* inspection in 1267); J. Horace Round (ed.), *Calendar of Documents Preserved in France 918–1206* (London: Her Majesty's Stationery Office, 1899), no. 107 (Seine Inférieure, Part 1). The *cnihtengild* was rooted in private jurisdictional privileges, and represents a brief continuation from the Anglo-Saxon period, the proprietary inheritance of which eventually passed to a priory of Augustinian Canons (Holy Trinity, Aldgate). EHD II, 1015–1021.

Henry granted to two men, together with their companions (*sociis*), that they might have a guild "for their mystery" (*de ministerio suo*), as well and honorably and fully as ever they had it. No person was to exercise this mystery within the *banlieu* of Rouen, except with their permission.[39]

In other words, only members of the royally protected guild would be permitted to exercise the craft of shoemaking, within the recognized borders of the town of Rouen. Here is a zone of exclusivity for an industrially defined social group, which is being recognized and defined through legal letters from the Anglo-Norman king, defining boundaries around a set of economic skills, and in effect making those skills the legally protected possessions of a guild. The privileges were confirmed by Stephen and Henry II.[40]

During the reign of Henry II, privileges of this kind became more plentiful. The Angevin king's economic privileges often looked back to the reign of his grandfather, as in the privilege recognizing a merchant guild for the men of Chichester, in Sussex. But there is a dynamic and novel dimension in the consolidating patterns of Henry II's legal grants, in which exclusive privileges to practice a trade are recognized within specified boundaries, often the boundaries of a borough. And the preeminent English borough, of course, was London.[41]

Sometime between 1154 and 1162, Henry II issued a charter to "the weavers of London," notifying his bishops, justiciars, sheriffs, and barons, together with "all his servants and liegemen of London" that he had granted the weavers their craft guild in London, "with all the liberties and customs" that they had in the time of his grandfather. No one was to carry on the occupation of weaver without the permission of the guild and unless they belonged to the guild. The privilege extended throughout London, to Southwark, south of the Thames. As we can see from this document, such valuable privileges were not free. The weavers of London were to pay the king 2 marks of gold each year at Christmas.[42]

By the reign of Henry II, the quantity of charters and writs available for historical study becomes overwhelming. A definitive edition has been in progress since the

[39] Round (ed.), *Calendar*, no. 107. English merchant guilds recognized by Henry I: Johnson & Cronne (eds.), *Regesta* 2, nos. 1137 (gild-merchant of Beverley); 1275 (gild-merchant at Wilton); Gross, *Gild Merchant*, Vol. I, 5–20, 114, 196.

[40] H. A. Cronne and R. H. C. Davis (eds.), *Regesta Regum Anglo-Normannorum*, 1066–1154, Vol. III (Matilda, Stephen, and early Henry II) (Oxford: Clarendon Press, 1968), nos. 727–8 (confirmations by Stephen (1137) and "Duke Henry" (1150–51)).

[41] Chichester privileges: Nicholas Karn and Richard Sharpe, "Men of Chichester," Charters of William II and Henry I Project (2014); *Calendar of the Patent Rolls Preserved in the Public Record Office, Edward III*, Vol. XVI (1374–77) (London: Her Majesty's Stationery Office, 1916), 289 (inspeximus and confirmation June 26, 1376). London as preeminent English borough: 25 Edward I, Magna Carta § 9, 1 Stat. 115 (1297) (§13 of 1215 Magna Carta); Ballard, *British Borough Charters*, 4–5, 10, 12–15. The acknowledgment of London's liberties and privileges, together with those of the Cinque Ports, is one of three provisions in Magna Carta that remain valid and binding under UK law. See Nicholas Vincent, *Magna Carta: Origins and Legacy* (Oxford: Bodleian Library, 2015), 15–16.

[42] EHD II, 1014–15, within broader survey of town-related documents, especially mercantile privileges, 1011–44.

1970s, and the documents number over 3,000. Given the quantity of records and the absence of a complete edition, it is not possible to draw final conclusions. However, based on comparison between the privileges granted by Henry II and those of his Anglo-Norman predecessors, it seems probable that the foundational pattern for royal protection of economic exclusivity in practices of a trade, like that which we see in the cloth guilds, was established during the reign of Henry II, building on looser foundations laid by Henry I. The combination of political and military stability, together with strong economic privileges, supported England's early cloth industry, enabling privileged, commercial cells to begin emerging well beyond London, from Beverley and York in the north, to Bristol in the west and Chichester in the south.[43]

The impacts of Anglo-Norman and Angevin economic "policies" were starting to become evident toward the end of Henry II's reign, when William fitz Stephen published his *Life of Thomas Becket*, opening with a prologue to celebrate "the most noble city of London."

> Among the noble and celebrated cities of the world that of London, the capital of the kingdom of the English, is one which extends its glory farther than all the others and sends its wealth and merchandise more widely into distant lands.[44]

William wrote of London because it was the birthplace of Thomas Becket (1118–70), who had been killed by men acting for Henry II.[45]

Thomas Becket's life and violent death highlighted important transformations in law, economy, and society that were coalescing during the reign of Henry II and his

[43] J. C. Holt, "The Writs of Henry II," in John Hudson (ed.), *The History of English Law: Centenary Essays on "Pollock and Maitland," Proceedings of the British Academy* 89 (Oxford: Oxford University Press, 1996), 47–64; Nicholas Vincent, J. C. Holt, and J. Everard, *The Acta of Henry II* (Oxford: Oxford University Press, forthcoming). For a cautious assessment of Henry's approach to feudal privileges and franchises, see W. L. Warren, *Henry II* (Berkeley: University of California Press, 1973), 376. I am not drawing a sharp distinction between merchant guilds and craft guilds, a distinction that did not sharpen until a later period. Gross, *Gild Merchant*, Vol. I, 106–16. For discussion of Henry II's stimulus to the cloth industry through writ-charters, see Austin Lane Poole, *From Domesday Book to Magna Carta, 1087–1216*, 2nd ed. (Oxford: Clarendon Press, 1955), 85–8; also *Calendar of the Patent Rolls Preserved in the Public Record Office, Edward III, Vol. 7 (1345–48)* (London: Her Majesty's Stationery Office, 1908), 199–200 (inspeximus and confirmation to the weavers of York October 24, 1346); *Royal Charters and Liberties Granted to the Burgesses of Nottingham* (London and Nottingham: Borough of Nottingham, 1890), 2–5. For an analogous pattern in the early history of Amsterdam, with stimulus in a grant of toll freedom from the Count of Holland, see Carl Bangs, *Arminius: A Study in the Dutch Reformation*, 2nd ed. (Grand Rapids: Zondervan, 1985), 83–4.

[44] EHD II, 1024–30. For a helpful introduction to the *vitae* of Thomas Becket, see Michael Staunton, *The Lives of Thomas Becket* (Manchester: Manchester University Press, 2001). A critical edition of the Latin sources, both lives and letters, was produced in seven volumes for the Rolls Series by James Craigie Robertson, a canon of Canterbury Cathedral. William fitz Stephen's life is in volume 3: James Craigie Robertson, *Materials for the History of Thomas Becket*, Vol. III (London: Longman, 1877), 1–154. This life is also available in English translation: Leo T. Gourde, *An Annotated Translation of the Life of St. Thomas Becket by William Fitzstephen* (Master's Thesis, Loyola University Chicago, 1943).

[45] Frank Barlow, *Thomas Becket* (Berkeley: University of California Press, 1986), 251–75; Anne Duggan, *Thomas Becket* (London: Hodder Education, 2004), 224–36.

sons, Richard I (1189–99) and John (1199–1216). Becket's titanic clash with Henry challenged the prerogative power of English kings, and, in the settlement with the church leadership that came afterward, an unprecedented level of industrial activity poured into the building of churches and monasteries, with quarrying and mining activities generating enough pollution to leave traces still visible today in Swiss ice cores.[46]

In so many ways, Thomas Becket personified the crystallizing tensions between royal and ecclesiastical law. He served as the "chief lawyer of the church," as well as chancellor, chief lawyer, and head diplomatist of the king. He had received the elite legal education of his time, in the newly developing university at Bologna, and had honed his practical legal skills as archdeacon of Canterbury, before catching the king's attention and being named as chancellor of England. As Henry's chancellor, furthermore, he had labored vigorously for the cause of royal law and privileges rooted in the royal prerogative. But, upon receiving the pallium as archbishop of Canterbury, Becket became the church's advocate in England, a position that set him on a collision course with England's vigorous young king.[47]

Henry had made the establishment of royal legal power in England a high priority, and he is credited by historians as largely succeeding in his efforts. It is from his reign that England's royal courts and its common law tradition begin to take shape. In his reign, royal writs began to be routinized in ways that facilitated use of the king's courts, rather than ordeals and military combat, for settling disputes. But the king also wanted to establish a coherent and consistent system of criminal law, which would apply to all his English subjects regardless of their legal status. This brought him into conflict with the church, which claimed jurisdiction over ordained clerics.[48]

46 Nick Barratt, "Finance and the Economy in the Reign of Henry II," in Christopher Harper-Bill and Nicholas Vincent (eds.), *Henry II: New Interpretations* (Woodbridge: Boydell Press, 2007), 242–56; Elizabeth M. Hallam, "Henry II as a Founder of Monasteries," *Journal of Ecclesiastical History* 28(2) (1977): 113–32; Christopher P. Loveluck et al., "Alpine Ice and the Annual Political Economy of the Angevin Empire, from the Death of Thomas Becket to Magna Carta, c. AD 1170–1216," *Antiquity* 2020: 1–18 (2020), including supplementary materials published online (78 pages); Poole, *Domesday Book to Magna Carta*, 80–1; also see Martin Allen, "Henry II and the English Coinage," in Harper-Bill & Vincent, *Henry II*, 257–77.

47 Eleanor Searle (ed. & trans.), *The Chronicle of Battle Abbey* (Oxford: Clarendon Press, 1980); also see Eleanor Searle, *Lordship and Community: Battle Abbey and Its Banlieu, 1066–1538* (Toronto: Pontifical Institute of Medieval Studies, 1974). Nicholas Vincent has raised important questions about the Battle Abbey chronicle's historical reliability. However, the chronicle's portrait of Henry as aggressively protecting his prerogative power in performative moments of juridical discussion has been deemed consistent with the *persona* of the king, from the chronicler's own day until today. There seems, therefore, no reason to doubt the general conclusion, even if the chronicle is factually unreliable. Nicholas Vincent, "King Henry II and the Monks of Battle: The Battle Chronicle Unmasked," in Richard Gameson and Henrietta Leyser (eds.), *Belief and Culture in the Middle Ages: Studies Presented to Henry Mayr-Harting* (Oxford: Oxford University Press, 2001), 264–86.

48 Paul Brand, "Henry II and the Creation of English Common Law," in Harper-Bill & Vincent, *Henry II*, 215–41; G. D. G. Hall (ed.), *The Treatise on the Laws and Customs of the Realm of England Commonly Called Glanvill* (Oxford: Clarendon Press, 1965); Pollock & Maitland, *History of English*

Charters, writs, and questions of patrimony had contributed to the material basis for this conflict, because they had enabled wealthy laypersons, especially kings, to establish churches and monasteries over which they claimed lordship rights, including property-related rights (*Eigenkirchen*). The effort to combat proprietary attitudes toward churches, and more broadly to protect the church from corrupting involvement on the part of wealthy laypeople, was central to the successive efforts at ecclesiastical reform leading to an increasingly aggressive papacy and a zealous archbishop of Canterbury.[49]

This reformist ecclesiastical zeal was part of the reason why Henry was so determined to solidify the position and power of his own courts. The Constitutions of Clarendon had included several provisions that evidently sought to limit appeals to Rome, including the requirement that appeals from an archbishop's court should go the king himself, and should not proceed further without his consent. However, in his negotiations at Avranches, in the wake of Becket's murder, Henry was forced to make concessions.[50]

Acknowledging his responsibility for Becket's murder, Henry agreed to do penance, and to retreat from some of the victories he had achieved with respect to royal jurisdiction in the Constitutions of Clarendon. One of the main things that he lost was royal jurisdiction over "criminous clerks." In criminal cases, clerics would be tried by church courts. However, in civil law cases, including those relating to property law, Henry's victory remained. Disputes over property, including the property of churches and monasteries, would be tried increasingly in the king's courts. In general, jurisdiction would be determined according to the subject matter in dispute, rather than the personal status of litigants. And, with the development of the writ of prohibition (a writ issued to the church's courts, prohibiting them from hearing a case and ordering that it be transferred to the king's courts), church courts would be increasingly placed on the defensive, even in areas formally conceded to their jurisdiction.[51]

It was during the reign of Henry II that a new technology appeared in England: the windmill. Wealthy monasteries were among the primary investors in this new technology. Their wealth had been acquired through centuries of privileges and accumulated donations. Newly privileged monastic orders like the Templars would use windmills as part of their widening industrial horizons. Organizational sophistication was growing, in monastic orders, in the church, and in the household of the king. And, as the geographic reach of increasingly formalized organizations

Law, 136–69; Nicholas Vincent, "Introduction: Henry II and the Historians," in Harper-Bill & Vincent, *Henry II*, 1–23.

49 Helmholz, *Canon Law and Ecclesiastical Jurisdiction*, 100–4; Susan Wood, *The Proprietary Church in the Medieval West* (Oxford: Oxford University Press, 2006), 851–933.

50 Helmholz, *Canon Law and Ecclesiastical Jurisdiction*, 110–18, 139.

51 Helmholz, *Canon Law and Ecclesiastical Jurisdiction*, 106–46, 301–9.

extended ever more widely, the political challenges of holding an organization together – whether cultural, economic, or military – correspondingly increased.[52]

7.5 IMPERIAL AMBITIONS AND THE BIRTH OF THE ADMINISTRATIVE STATE

The administrative core of the English state emerged out of the household of the Plantagenet kings. The process was long, complex, and contested. We can only describe it meaningfully with the benefit of hindsight. But, with the benefit of hindsight, a portrait emerges in which administrative branches gradually acquired a degree of independence, becoming functionally defined and differentiated. In the time of Henry I, there was simply the court of the king (*curia regis*). By the death of Henry II in 1189, however, we can see the hazy outlines of a secretarial chancery, exchequer (treasury), and courts, surrounding an inner core of the household, which later also developed into departments.[53]

The reigns of Richard and John marked a turning point in which ministers began to establish offices underneath the king, as well as procedures, defining a continuously functioning administration, through documented acts. Under Henry III, these fitful developments consolidated. The combination of Henry's lengthy minority – in which ministers exercised power – with a lengthy reign, in which tentative steps could be defined and recognized as institutional patterns – was vital. Dramatic memories of crusading kingship were also significant.[54]

A defining ambition of the Plantagenet kings was to maintain a cross-channel empire, and this meant that they were partly absentees in England. They depended on ministers, who gradually acquired titles and offices, in carrying out their activities of rulership. The coordination of local governance in bishoprics, counties, and hundreds, with tightening central administration, enabled a capacity to extract resources through taxation that was unparalleled in Europe. The agency of resource extraction was the exchequer, and the agencies of coordination were the chancery and courts. Our focus is on the chancery,

[52] John Langdon, "The Birth and Demise of a Medieval Windmill," *History of Technology* 14 (1992): 54–76; Lucas, *Ecclesiastical Lordship*, passim; Lynn White, Jr., *Medieval Technology and Social Change* (Oxford: Oxford University Press, 1962), 87. For discussion of Henry's economic privileges to new monastic orders, with attention to their implications for tax revenues, see *Dialogus de Scaccario (The Dialogue of the Exchequer)*, edited and translated by Emilie Amt and S. D. Church (Oxford: Clarendon Press, 2007), 78–9.

[53] T. F. Tout, *Chapters in the Administrative History of Mediaeval England*, Vol. I (Manchester: University Press, 1920), 12–22, 100–19, 127–39 ; *cf.* Amt & Church, Introduction to *Dialogus de Scaccario*, xxv–xxvii.

[54] Pierre Chaplais, *English Royal Documents, King John-Henry VI, 1199–1461* (Oxford: Clarendon Press, 1971); V. H. Galbraith, *An Introduction to the Use of the Public Records* (Oxford: Oxford University Press, 1934), 15–52; Tout, *Administrative History*, Vol. I, 176 ff.; W. L. Warren, *The Governance of Norman and Angevin England, 1086–1272* (London: Edward Arnold, 1987), 105–229.

because it was from here that letters patent and charters, authenticated with the great seal, were issued.[55]

During the reign of Henry II, an inspection process (*inspeximus*) had begun by which the holder of a franchise could have it examined and reissued under the authority of a new ruler. Under Richard I, this became a compulsory way of raising money. By the reign of Henry III, and especially under Edward I (1272–1307), investigations were carried out in conjunction with regional court processes to examine "by what warrant" (*quo warranto*) privileged subjects held their privileges from the king. In cases where charters had faded or patents were questionable, new ones might be purchased at the right price, if the king was inclined to be graceful. All of this meant an increasing emphasis on careful documentation and rigorous investigation of privileges granted through charters and letters patent.[56]

If the money raised to finance Richard's crusade had been burdensome, the ransom required to rescue him from the clutches of the German emperor was even more so. Military glory was purchased at a high price, extracted from the agricultural produce of peasants, from merchants trading across the channel, from commercial towns, and from Jews who lent money at great risk to their Christian neighbors. The barons and knights who went on crusade with Richard also needed to raise money, and this they might do by borrowing from Jews, or later (after Jews had been expelled from England) from Italians and southern Frenchmen. When push came to shove and the king needed money, he could call on moneylenders, who then needed to call on their debtors to raise the necessary sums. Social conflicts, some litigated through the kings' newly emerging courts and some litigated through the church's courts, were a frequent result.[57]

55 Bartlett, *England under Norman and Angevin Kings*, 11–28; Michael Prestwich, *Plantagenet England, 1225–1360* (Oxford: Oxford University Press, 2005), 55–77; Francis West, *The Justiciarship in England, 1066–1232* (Cambridge, UK: Cambridge University Press, 1966). Royal documents from the chancery: Thomas Duffus Hardy, *A Description of the Close Rolls in the Tower of London* (London: George Eyre and Andrew Spottiswoode, 1833); Thomas Duffus Hardy, *A Description of the Patent Rolls in the Tower of London* (London: by King's Command, 1835); Thomas Duffus Hardy (ed.), *Rotuli Chartarum in Turri Londinensi* (London: by King's Command, 1837); also see G. R. Elton, *England: 1200–1640: The Sources of History* (Ithaca: Cornell University Press, 1969), 33–89.

56 Helen M. Cam, *The Hundred and the Hundred Rolls: An Outline of Local Government in Medieval England* (London: Methuen & Co., 1930), 29 ff.; idem, "The Quo Warranto Proceedings under Edward I," in Helen M. Cam, *Liberties & Communities in Medieval England* (Cambridge, UK: Cambridge University Press, 1944), 173–82; Prestwich, *Plantagenet England*, 125–9; Donald W. Sutherland, *Quo Warranto Proceedings in the Reign of Edward I, 1278–1294* (Oxford: Clarendon Press, 1963); Nicholas Vincent, "The Charters of King Henry II: The Introduction of the Royal *Inspeximus* Revisited," in Michael Gervers (ed.), *Dating Undated Medieval Charters* (Woodbridge: Boydell Press, 2000), 97–120.

57 The "king's ransom" required to redeem Richard: John Gillingham, *Richard I* (New Haven: Yale University Press, 1999), 222–53; Sydney Knox Mitchell, *Taxation in Medieval England*, edited by Sidney Painter (New Haven: Yale University Press, 1951), 1–62, 285–320; Poole, *Domesday Book to Magna Carta*, 365–6. Jews in England from 1066–1290: Robin R. Mundill, *The King's Jews: Money, Massacre and Exodus in Medieval England* (London: Bloomsbury, 2009); Cecil Roth, *A History of the Jews in England*, 3nd ed. (Oxford: Clarendon Press, 1978); Pollock & Maitland, *History of English*

And so we can see an administrative state developing in the form of household servants and officers, personally answerable to the king, a state with the power to extract unprecedented levels of wealth from the kingdom, financing wars that brought moments of glory to the king and nobility, at the cost of great suffering to many of the king's people, with the corresponding enrichment of a few.

7.6 NATURAL LAW AND PREROGATIVE RIGHT

Around the middle of the thirteenth century, an enormous treatise on English common law began circulating. The treatise has traditionally been attributed to one of Henry III's justiciars, Henry de Bracton, and it is often called *Bracton*. The full title, as published today in scholarly, critical editions, is *On the Laws and Customs of England*. The treatise marks a fruitful period in the development of English common law, one in which there was a high level of openness to Roman and canon law. Very soon, English common law, like the English legal profession, started to become more closed to outside influences.[58]

Two aspects of *Bracton* are especially relevant to our inquiry: (1) its theory of law, especially of natural law, and (2) its theory of franchises. *Bracton* is also important, however, in illustrating the close connections with theology, Roman law, and canon law, in the early history of English common law.[59]

Bracton opens with a traditional reflection on the king's need for two types of support in ruling well: arms and laws. Through these mutually dependent supports, times of war and peace are rightly ordered. If arms should fail, the realm would be vulnerable to depredation by hostile enemies. If laws should fail, justice would be eliminated, and there would no longer be any people to render just judgments.[60]

Justice and judgment, for *Bracton*, were dependent upon laws, which, uniquely in England, were unwritten, deriving from usage and custom. At the national level, these unwritten laws nonetheless deserved the title of *leges*, since "whatever has been rightly decided approved with the counsel and consent of the magnates and the general agreement of the *res publica*, the authority of the king or prince having first

Law, 468–75. Cases of debt litigated in royal and church courts: Helmholz, *Canon Law & Ecclesiastical Jurisdiction*, 355–86. Most debts to Jews would probably have been litigated in the specialized court attached to the Exchequer of the Jews: Mundill, *King's Jews*, Chapter 2 and passim; Pollock & Maitland, *History of English Law*, 468–75.

58 Samuel E. Thorne (ed.), *Bracton on the Laws and Customs of England*, 4 volumes, with revisions to an earlier edition by George E. Woodbine (Cambridge, MA: Harvard University Press, 1968).

59 Survey of the debates regarding Bracton's familiarity with Roman and canon law: Thorne (ed.), *Bracton*, Vol. I, xxvi–xl. Close connections with theology, Roman law, and canon law: Francis de Zulueta, *The Teaching of Roman Law in England around 1200* (London: Selden Society, 1990); Jason Taliadoros, *Law and Theology in Twelfth-Century England: The Works of Master Vacarius* (c. 1115/20–c. 1200) (Turnhout: Brepols, 2006). Intellectual and social context: Southern, *Scholastic Humanism: Foundations*, 1–13, 102 ff.; R. W. Southern, *Scholastic Humanism and the Unification of Europe, Vol. II: The Heroic Age* (Oxford: Blackwell, 2001), 151–218.

60 Thorne (ed. & trans.), *Bracton*, Vol. II, 19.

been added thereto, has the force of law (*lex*)." At the local level, customs of various counties, cities, boroughs, and villages constituted a supplementary source of law, one that must be learned by any justice seeking to offer just judgments.[61]

Bracton described his enormous work as a *summa*, one that was being offered to support wisdom in judgments by judges. The methodology it described was essentially inductive:

> I, Henry de Bracton, to instruct the lesser judges, if no one else, have turned my mind to the ancient judgments of just men, examining diligently, not without working long into the night watches, their decisions, *consilia* and *responsa*, and have collected whatever I found therein worthy of note into a *summa*, putting it into the form of titles and paragraphs . . . by the aid of writing to be preserved to posterity forever.[62]

The extent to which *Bracton* relied upon inductive study of actual cases decided in English courts in preparing his great text was brought out by F. W. Maitland (1850–1906), who published a three-volume study of *Bracton's Notebook*, a collection of reports on cases decided by justices. As an inductive study of English legal cases, *Bracton* was a very English law book.[63]

But, ironically, this was also a Romanesque law book. The basic framework and intellectual spirit of rationalization reflected in the text came from a recognized model: Azo of Bologna. "The Englishman's work both in its general structure and in many details has been influenced by Roman jurisprudence."[64]

Maitland identified three specific ways in which *Bracton* borrowed from Roman law. First, *Bracton* borrowed at the level of general principles "some of the highest premises of all civilized law expressed in neat and accurate phrases."[65] Second, *Bracton* borrowed some particular rules "as solutions for concrete cases." But third, and most important, *Bracton* borrowed a basic approach to thinking about law, which was new and culturally powerful. This most important debt of Bracton to Azo involved "spirit rather than substance, not these or those rules, but a method of reasoning about law, of perceiving the interdependence of rules, of making them take their places as members of a body."[66]

For Maitland, it was the precocity of English legal borrowing from Rome that ultimately protected against a more full-scale reception of Roman law, which scholars have identified especially in German law, and in parts of French law. There is much that has been debated about Bracton's law book, including its

[61] Ibid.
[62] Ibid.
[63] F. W. Maitland, *Bracton's Note Book: A Collection of Cases Decided in the King's Courts during the Reign of Henry the Third, Annotated by a Lawyer of that Time, Seemingly by Henry of Bratton*, 3 Vols (London: C. J. Clay & Sons, 1887).
[64] Maitland, *Bracton's Note Book*, Vol. I, 9.
[65] Ibid.
[66] Ibid., 10.

authorship. But there is no debate about the fact that, at least in its organizing principles, it is a very Roman law book. And yet, somehow, this does not stop it from being a very English law book. This paradox is, itself, suggestive.[67]

Bracton's basic theory of law, set forth in his introduction, is Roman. His definition of justice is quoted verbatim from Justinian's *Institutes*: "Justice (*justitia*) is the constant and unfailing will to give to each his right (*jus*)." Justice means getting what we deserve, and what we deserve is our right. Justice comes from God, and law (*lex*) – while it may be manifested in general commands, judicious decisions, or the consensus of the community, seen sometimes in local customs – is fundamentally a "just sanction, ordering virtue and prohibiting its opposite." The defining standard for this justice, law, and right is ultimately, therefore, "the disposition of God which in all things rightfully orders and justly disposes." Law is the "art of what is fair and just, of which we are deservedly called the priests, for we worship justice and administer sacred rights." In practice, however, this righteous law may be manifested in many ways: in natural law, in the law that is common to all nations (*jus gentium*), in the civil law of states, in the law that results from a particular judgment, in the "feudal" ties of personal connection and affinity, and in the ownership (*proprietas*) or possession (*possessio*) of a thing.[68]

Ownership and lordship (*dominium*) are protected by the law of nations (*jus gentium*), in addition to civil law and natural law, for they are ultimately rooted in the rightful disposition of God, which governs all peoples alike.

Individual ownership was not effected de novo by the *jus gentium* but existed of old, for in the Old Testament things were already mine and thine, theft was prohibited, and it was decreed that a man should not retain his servant's wages. By the *jus gentium* boundaries were set to holdings, buildings erected next to one another, from which cities, boroughs, and vills were formed. And generally, the *jus gentium* is the source of all contracts and of many other things.[69]

Bracton's theory about how ownership is acquired in things is very Roman. We see here a developed discussion of the natural law methods by which ownership is acquired, one that closely tracks the discussion in Gaius' *Institutes* that we saw in Chapter 4, which was later echoed in Justinian's *Institutes*. In this discussion, natural law and the law of nations (*jus gentium*) are essentially treated as equivalent, as the "older law," providing the underpinning for civil law, "which came into existence later, after states came to be founded, magistrates created and laws reduced to writing." According to the older, natural law of all nations, ownership (*dominium*) may be acquired, first, by taking possession of something that belongs to no one (a *res*

67 Ibid.

68 Thorne (ed. & trans.), *Bracton*, Vol. II, 22–5; *Justinian's Institutes*, translated by Peter Birks and Grant McLeod with Latin text of Paul Krueger (Ithaca: Cornell University Press, 1987) (hereafter *IJ*), 1.1.

69 Thorne (ed. & trans.), *Bracton*, Vol. II, 28.

nullius). However, Bracton immediately qualifies by noting that this rule is now nullified by civil law, which makes any *res nullius* the property of the king.[70]

The principle of accession still governs acquisition of ownership, however, even though the king's prerogative has displaced the principle of acquisition by occupation. By operation of the accession principle, both natural and human forces may add to the existing property of an owner. In the case of human acts, which join things together by soldering and welding, the combined material becomes the property of the person who owned the components with the greatest value, although he will nonetheless owe compensation to the person whose materials were added to his.[71]

This "right of accession by the labor of human beings" also applies to buildings where someone builds on his own land using materials belonging to someone else. Bracton then discusses the cases of writings and paintings following the Roman jurists nearly verbatim:

> This kind of accession produced by the intervention of human action may be seen in connection with letters. For writing, though in letters of gold, becomes part of parchments and charters exactly as things built upon land or crops sown become part of the soil. But a contrary rule will apply to paintings. It would be ridiculous if by accession a valuable painting became part of a worthless panel. Thus the panel cedes to the painting [as explained more fully in the *Institutes*].[72]

Bracton and his copier-editors are here evidently following the *Institutes* of Justinian. But Bracton emphasized an application of great interest, given what we know about economic developments in England around this time. He echoes Justinian in stating that the same principle applies to textiles:

> The same sort of accession may be seen in connection with textiles, for if one has woven the purple thread of another into his vestment, though the purple is more valuable it nevertheless becomes part of the vestment by [right] of accession.[73]

Here the labor in combination with the raw materials outweighs the value of the purple thread.

In addition to these examples involving acquisition of ownership by the method of accession, Bracton noted the methods of specification – "as where one makes a new object out of another's material; he will be the owner of the new object he made" – and by finding or discovery, *inventio* in Latin. "Dominion is also acquired by finding (*inventio*), as where treasure is found." All this is Roman law, some directly taken from the *Institutes* and some mediated by the scholars of Bologna but transposed into a thirteenth-century English context; there is a foreshadowing of developments to come. Here we are not yet in the world of industrially produced new inventions,

70 Ibid., 42.
71 Ibid., 43–7.
72 Ibid., 46.
73 Ibid; *IJ*, 2.1.25–26.

for invention is an accidental stumbling upon treasure that is buried, but we are inching closer.[74]

Even when Bracton moves beyond the methods of acquiring ownership by natural law and the *ius gentium*, to methods of acquisition by civil law, he remains in very traditional (Roman) territory. For the main method of acquisition remains acquisition by gift, rather than sale. But the content of the discussion becomes more concrete, and Bracton begins to draw on English cases in illustrating his principles. He offers extensive discussions of charters – differentiating types of charters, their role in providing evidence of property transfers, and the ways in which their words should be interpreted.

> A gift in writing is made in these words, "Know all men, present and future, that I, such a one, have given, granted, and by this my present charter confirmed to such a one, for his homage and service, so much land with the appurtenances in such a vill etc.[75]

Bracton goes on to specify what each of these phrases means. The "I have granted" indicates the will of the donor, by which the property is transferred. The homage and service are the *causa*, the reason in consideration of which the gift was given. We are approaching the mysterious "consideration" and "cause" that first-year law students struggle mightily to understand, whether their courses be in Anglo-American contract law or civilian obligations.

But what if the grantor is the king? What may he rightfully grant as a gift by way of his own charters? Here we come to legal boundaries that are evidently being placed on the king's prerogative powers, in this case, his power to grant franchises (or liberties).

> Now we must turn to liberties [and see] who can grant liberties, and to whom, and how they are transferred, how possessed or quasi-possessed, and how they are retained by use. Who then? It is clear that the lord king [has all] dignities, rights or jurisdictions in his hand.

A later annotator, probably, added the following elaboration:

> [It is the lord king] himself who has ordinary jurisdiction and power over all who are in his realm. For he has in his hand all the rights belonging to the crown and the secular power and the material sword pertaining to the governance of the realm. And also justice and judgment [and everything] connected with jurisdiction, that, as minister and vicar of God, he may render to each his due. Also everything connected with the peace, that the people entrusted to his care may live in quiet and repose.

This basic responsibility of the king for justice, jurisdiction, and protecting the peace implied a limitation in the kinds of things that he could grant as gifts by means of letters patent or charters.

[74] Thorne (ed. & trans.), *Bracton*, Vol. II, 47.
[75] Ibid., 47–112. The words of the charter and their explanation: ibid., 111–12.

> Those concerned with jurisdiction and the peace ... cannot be transferred to persons or tenements, neither the right nor the exercise of the right, nor be possessed by a private person .... *Those called privileges, however, though they belong to the crown, may nevertheless be separated from it and transferred to private persons, but only by special grace of the king himself.*

Examples of transferable liberties, inhering in the Crown, included grants "to a *universitas*, as to citizens or burgesses or others, that they may have a market and fair in the vill, city or borough, and may take customs and tolls and be quit of rendering toll or any other customary due throughout the whole of [the king's] realm." The normal method of transferring such liberties, from the era of Bracton to the era of William Blackstone (1723–80), was by charters or letters patent.[76]

Writing in his much later era, aiming to revive the university-based study of English common law after centuries in which it had been the exclusive preserve of practically oriented jurists trained in the Inns of Court, Blackstone wrote admiringly of Bracton, specifying his work as authoritative on matters of common law. Authors like "Glanvil and Bracton, Britton and Fleta, Littleton and Fitzherbert" were given "great veneration and respect" by "students of the common law" partly because their treatises served as "evidence that cases have formerly happened in which such and such points were determined, which are now become settled and first principles."[77]

With Blackstone, we have flashed dramatically forward, but it is important to see that there is a long thread of jurisprudence connecting the thirteenth to the eighteenth century. The line was interrupted, and Blackstone was doing new things with his old authorities. But he, like Edward Coke (1552–1634), John Selden (1584–1654), and William Lambarde (1536–1601) before him, was drawing self-consciously on a legal tradition – one that stretched back well beyond the twelfth century and one that he saw as echoing meaningfully in his own age.

With Blackstone, we arrive at a fully articulated, natural law theory of intellectual property, and we need to juxtapose it with Bracton in order to hear the echoes. Blackstone wrote of ways to acquire ownership by natural law in his second volume of *Commentaries on the Laws of England*. For Blackstone, "the doctrine of property arising from accession is also grounded on the right of occupancy." Accession and occupancy have been combined. Blackstone neatly and concisely summarized the Roman law doctrine from the *Institutes*, before adding that "these doctrines are implicitly copied and adopted by our Bracton, in the reign of king Henry III," noting further that the doctrines had been many times confirmed in the courts ever since. Immediately after this affirmation of Bracton, Blackstone went on to discuss "another species of property, which, being grounded on labor and invention, is more properly reducible to the head of occupancy than any other." This is the right

76 Ibid., 166–70 (emphasis added).

77 William Blackstone, *Commentaries on the Laws of England: A Facsimile of the First Edition of 1765–1769*, Vol. I (Chicago: University of Chicago Press, 1979), 72; *cf.* idem, Vol. IV, 418.

of literary property, what we today call copyright, "the right, which an author may be supposed to have in his own original literary compositions."[78]

We have arrived at an explicit argument for intellectual property which has been used in courts from the time of Blackstone to today. And that line of argument draws directly on Roman law, as mediated by the Roman law-based scholarship of the twelfth and thirteenth centuries.

7.7 THE TUDOR REVOLUTION AND CLAIMS TO LITERARY PROPERTY

The establishment of the new Tudor dynasty under Henry Tudor, earl of Richmond (reigning as Henry VII of England from 1485–1509), coincided with the importation of movable-type printing into England by William Caxton. Caxton trained in Cologne and Bruges, under the patronage of Margaret, duchess of Burgundy, establishing his first press in England at Westminster in 1476–7. Early regulation of printing began in the 1520s, under Henry VIII, with protections for English printers against foreigners, and with efforts to prevent contagion from Lutheran heresies. An early, performative moment in these efforts came in 1521, when Cardinal Wolsey (1515–30), acting under orders from a papal bull, staged a public burning of Martin Luther's writings.[79]

By 1524, moreover, an informal regime for censorship had been established through the cooperation of London-based booksellers and church authorities (Cardinal Wolsey, the archbishop of Canterbury, and the bishop of London). Between 1529 and 1538, this was formalized through proclamations instituting a national system of licensing by the Privy Council. Pursuant to these regulations, licensed books were printed with an indication of royal permission: *cum privilegio regali ad imprimendum solum*. This licensing regime was supplemented with printing patents: letters patent granting exclusive permission to print books in high demand, such as English Bibles, liturgical service books, and law books.[80]

The English Reformation, in fact, was a catalyst for formalizing, nationalizing control of printed publications. An initiator of the transformation was Thomas Cromwell, Henry's chief minister from about 1530 to 1540. Stretching between the reigns of Edward VI (1547–53) and Elizabeth I (1558–1603), and into the reign of James I (1603–25), the transformation was implemented under William Cecil (Lord Burghley, 1572–98) and his son, Robert Cecil (Earl of Salisbury, 1608–12). Especially under the Cecils, prerogative-based patents and charters were used to create or oversee national monopolies in trade and industry. Domestically, these monopolies

78 Idem, Vol. II, 404–5.

79 Bennett, *English Books and Readers*, 9–33.

80 Ibid., 30–9; Hughes & Larkin (eds.), *Tudor Royal Proclamations*, Vol. I, nos. 122, 129, 161, 186, 192, 272, 371. Under Edward VI, a licensing regime overseen by the Privy Council was affirmed. John Roche Dascent (ed.), *Acts of the Privy Council of England*, Vol. II (London: Her Majesty's Stationery Office, 1890), available at British History Online, www.british-history.ac.uk/acts-privy-council/vol2/pp301-325 (last accessed May 6, 2020), 311–12 (August 13, 1549).

were used to break down and unify the local regulatory frameworks of cities and guilds, to create proto-administrative agencies, and to reward favorites. Globally, these monopolies were used to contest the commercial ambitions of continental monarchs, and to appropriate industries, laying the foundations for imperial trading companies and markets.[81]

It is in this context that the Stationers Company emerged into the light of historical record. The company received its corporate charter in 1557, during the brief reign of Mary Tudor (1553–8). Sir William Petre was then acting as privy councilor and principal secretary, having been reappointed by Mary following her accession to the throne in 1554. Petre, William Cecil, and Sir Thomas Smith had served together as secretaries and privy councilors under Edward VI, overseeing the council's licensing regime for book publication since 1549. In 1559, the Stationers' corporate charter was confirmed by Elizabeth, with Cecil at the helm as principal secretary. Beneath the dramatic changes in the monarchy during this period, in other words, we see a line of policy in prerogative-based corporate chartering practice, and William Cecil (soon to become Lord Burghley) was a central bearer of that continuity.[82]

Pursuant to its corporate charter, the Stationers Company was erected as a corporate community with "perpetual succession," meaning that company would henceforth own property in a corporate capacity for as long as it endured. The company was also endowed with the capacity to sue and be sued under its own name in any court, and to make "ordinances, provisions, and statutes" for "the good

[81] On Cromwell as initiator of a bureaucratizing transformation in English administration, see Elton, *Tudor Revolution*, 66–71, 124–7, 316–69, 415–27, and passim; *cf.* Robert Bucholz & Newton Key, *Early Modern England 1485–1714: A Narrative History*, 2nd ed. (2009), 82–91, 156; Diarmaid MacCulloch, *Thomas Cromwell: A Revolutionary Life* (New York: Viking, 2018); Alan G. R. Smith, *The Emergence of a Nation State: The Commonwealth of England, 1529–1660*, 2nd ed. (London: Longman, 1997), 87–97. The Cecils: Peter Blayney, "William Cecil and the Stationers," in Robin Myers & Michael Harris (eds.), *The Stationers' Company and the Book Trade* (Winchester: St. Paul's Bibliographies, 1997), 11–34; Conyers Read, *Mr. Secretary Cecil and Queen Elizabeth* (New York: Alfred A. Knopf, 1955); Conyers Read, *Lord Burghley and Queen Elizabeth* (New York: Alfred A. Knopf, 1960); Alan G. R. Smith, *William Cecil: The Power behind Elizabeth* (1982); Alan G. R. Smith, "The Secretariats of the Cecils, circa 1580–1612," *English Historical Review* 83: 481–504 (1968). Use of monopolies for national regulatory purposes: Blayney, "William Cecil," 16–30; Chris Dent, "Patent Policy in Early Modern England: Jobs, Trade, and Regulation," *Legal History* 10: 71–95 (2006); Harold G. Fox, *Monopolies and Patents: A Study in the History and Future of the Patent Monopoly* (Toronto: University of Toronto Press, 1947), 24–42; Thomas B. Nachbar, "Monopoly, Mercantilism, and the Politics of Regulation," *Virginia Law Review* 91(6): 1313–79 (2005), 1318–27; Smith, *Emergence of Nation State*, 239–41; Stephen D. White, *Sir Edward Coke and 'the Grievances of the Commonwealth,' 1621–1628* (Chapel Hill: University of North Carolina Press, 1979), 4–7, 284–90. Imperial trading companies: P. E. H. Hair and Robin Law, "The English in Western Africa to 1700," in Nicholas Canny (ed.), *The Origins of Empire: British Overseas Enterprise to the Close of the Seventeenth Century* (Oxford: Oxford University Press, 1998), 241–63; P. J. Marshall, "The English in Asia to 1700," in Canny (ed.), *Origins of Empire*, 264–85.

[82] Edward Arber (ed.), *A Transcript of the Registers of the Stationers Company of London, 1554–1640*, Vol. I (London: Private Printing, 1875), xxix; Blayney, "William Cecil," 13; Read, *Mr. Secretary Cecil*, 42–3, 45, 55, 57, 103, 117ff.

and sound rule and government" of the incorporated community. Most significantly, the articles of incorporation provided further that:

> [n]o person within this our realm of England or the dominions of the same shall practise or exercise by himself or by his ministers, his servants or any other person the art or mistery of printing any book or any thing for sale or traffic within this our realm of England or the dominions of the same, unless the same person at the time of his foresaid printing is or shall be one of the community of the foresaid mistery or art of Stationary of the foresaid City, or has therefore license of us, or the heirs or successors of us the foresaid Queen by the letters patent of us or the heirs or successors of us the foresaid Queen.

By its act of incorporation, then, the Stationers Company was established as a community exclusively privileged to practice the "art or mystery" of printing throughout England and England's "dominions." At the same time, the company was given broad search and seizure powers to enforce this exclusive privilege. In other words, the charter gave the company "nation-wide powers, almost as if it were an executive arm of the Government."[83]

By the reign of Charles I (1600–49), on the eve of the English civil war, the Stationers Company had become an administrative agent for the monarchy, in its attempts to regulate and censor printing. The powerful position that this created for the Stationers Company would have a profound effect on the company and would encourage its members to begin viewing their rights to copy as a kind of property that they were entitled to hold in perpetuity, to transmit to their heirs, and to use for the benefit of Stationers Company widows and orphans.[84]

What is important to emphasize, however, is the way in which the monarchy's regulation and censorship of printing was premised on the royal prerogative tradition. That tradition, in other words, provided the legitimating foundation for a new set of rulership-related activities: overseeing the materials that are printed and distributed within the kingdom. The context for this new set of rulership-related

83 Arber, *Transcript, Vol. I*, xxx–xxxi; Cyprian Blagden, *The Stationers Company* (London: George Allen & Unwin, 1960), 31; see also W. S. Holdsworth, *A History of English Law*, Vol. VI (London: Methuen & Co., 1924), 360–70. For discussion of patents for the printing of common law books, which created a monopoly position that was separate from that of the Stationers Company, see Sir John Baker, *The Oxford History of the Laws of England, Vol. VI, 1483–1558* (Oxford: Oxford University Press, 2003), Ch. 27. Beginning in 1557, the Stationers Company recorded the internal allocations of "Copyes as be licyensed to be printed by the master and wardyns of the mystery of stacioners." Next to an individual's name and the "copy" allocated to the individual (e.g., "To William pekerynge a ballet called *a Ryse and wake*") the records present a monetary figure, which indicates the fee paid by that individual to the company for the license of the copy (e.g., 4 pence). These records were placed alongside annual records of expenses, which were regularly incurred for the annual dinner connected with livery pageantry, and periodically incurred to provision the monarchy (e.g., with grain or ships). Regular accounts were also kept of fines imposed on members, which prominently included fines for printing without license. Arber, *Transcript, Vol. I*, 74 & passim.

84 Lyman Ray Patterson, *Copyright in Historical Perspective* (Nashville: Vanderbilt University Press, 1968), 114–42; see also Holdsworth, *History of English Law*, 360–70.

activities was, of course, the growth of printing technology, which had radically intensified the political, religious, and legal conflicts of the Reformation.[85]

Henry VIII's "Reformation from Above" had been based to a large degree upon the prerogative tradition and had, in turn, added greatly to that tradition. Two centuries later, the English jurist Matthew Bacon described the "Supremacy of the Crown of England, in Matters Ecclesiastical" as a "most unquestionable Right" forming part of the royal prerogative. The development of this supremacy, under the Tudors, played a vital role in defining the sphere of English royal jurisdiction and executive authority, and therefore in defining the English state. According to Bacon:

> All Jurisdiction exercised in these Kingdoms that are in Obedience to our King, is derived from the Crown; and the Laws, whether of a Temporal, Ecclesiastical, or Military Nature, are called his Laws; and it is his Prerogative to take Care of the due Execution of them. Hence all Judges must derive their Authority from the Crown, by some Commission warranted by Law; and must exercise it in a lawful Manner, *and without any the least Deviation from the known and stated Forms.*

The jurisdictional and executive authority of the monarchy – its authority to engage, in other words, in what Gianfranco Poggi has called the "business of rule" – was asserted and legitimated through the prerogative tradition. And that tradition was greatly expanded in the crisis of the Reformation.[86]

The ecclesiastical rulership of the king – his prerogative supremacy over the English church – was powerfully asserted through the writ of *praemunire*, a writ originally developed in the fourteenth century to protect the royal jurisdiction against papal assertions, and used with dramatic effect to threaten Cardinal Wolsey with death. In 1530, following Wolsey's downfall, the writ was used to initiate legal proceedings against a handful of prelates and clergy, and, in 1531, the writ was widened to threaten all of the English clergy. A series of parliamentary statutes, issued at the behest of the king and drafted largely by Thomas Cromwell, then proceeded to affirm and elaborate the prerogative supremacy of the king. Pursuant to that supremacy, England's clergy were divorced from Rome and "subjected to the royal will." From this time forward, the English clergy would hold their offices, like other officers of the crown, pursuant to the royal prerogative, and would be answerable in the royal courts.[87]

85 Bennett, *English Books and Readers*, 26–39; *cf.* Eamon Duffy, *The Stripping of the Altars: Traditional Religion in England 1400–1580* (2d ed. 2005), 77–87.

86 Matthew Bacon, *New Abridgment of the Law*, Vol. IV (London: Catherine Lintot, Royal Printer, 1759), 171–2; Gianfranco Poggi, *The Development of the Modern State* (1978); see also W. S. Holdsworth, "The Prerogative in the Sixteenth Century," *Columbia Law Review* 21: 554–71 (1921); F. W. Maitland, *The Constitutional History of England* (Cambridge, UK: Cambridge University Press, 1908), 418–21.

87 "Subjected to the Royal Will": G. R. Elton, *The Tudor Constitution: Documents and Commentary* (Cambridge, UK: Cambridge University Press, 1960), 329–69. Fourteenth-Century Statutes of Praemunire: A Statute against Annullers of Judgments of the King's Court, 27 Edw. III, St. 1, c.1

Thus an elevation of the prerogative tradition was key to the definition and legitimation of the Crown's rulership over the printing and sale of books, and to the Crown's assertion of state control over the English church. But there was also another, more proprietary, side to the prerogative tradition. Indeed, the prerogative was frequently described in proprietary language: it belonged to the royal person bearing the Crown, and it passed as part of the royal inheritance to the next rightful bearer of the Crown. Elements of the prerogative could be sold or leased by the Crown through charters and letters patent. The content of these grants could include a wide range of things, including judicial and administrative offices, rights to hold a market, privileges to practice a trade, and rights for the "sole liberty of printing." Here, on this proprietary side of the prerogative tradition, was the prerogative copyright, a copyright that received extensive attention from common law courts during the Restoration era (1662–88).[88]

Indeed, early common law cases raising the question of literary property all involved conflicts deriving from prerogative grants. The first case – *The Stationers* v. *The Patentees about the Printing of Roll's Abridgment*, or "Atkins' Case" (1666) – involved a patent to print "all law books that concern the Common Law." The patent had been granted to someone who did not belong to the Stationers Company. It was transmitted through inheritance and marriage and enforced against the Company, which had printed a common law treatise by an eminent judge – Henry Rolle's *Abridgment des Plusieurs Cases* – in violation of the patent. Judgment had been given in chancery on behalf of the patentees (Colonel Atkins, through his heiress wife, "and his assigns"), and an injunction was issued to prevent the Stationers from selling the *Abridgment*. The Stationers appealed to Parliament, and judgment in favor of the patentee was ultimately given based on the royal prerogative underlying the patent grant.[89]

The subsequent case of *Roper* v. *Streater* (House of Lords 1672) was viewed, at least in retrospect, as definitively resolving the question: the exclusive printing and publishing of law books were within the royal prerogative and could therefore be granted by means of letters patent and enforced, even against the Stationers Company. Although multiple arguments originally supported this printing prerogative in law books, the later consolidation of these arguments, by the Court of King's Bench, relied fundamentally on the prerogative supremacy: "matters of law and religion ought and always was [sic] under the immediate care and government of the King."[90]

(1353) and 16 Richard II c. 5 (1392–93). Use of *praemunire* to destroy Wolsey: J. A. Guy, "Henry VIII and the Praemunire Manoeuvres of 1530–1531," English Historical Review 97: 481–503 (1982).

88 Bacon, *New Abridgment*, 149–66, 174, 203–10.

89 The Stationers against the Patentees about the Printing of Roll's Abridgment, Carter 89, 124 Eng. Rep. 842 (1666) (hereafter *Atkins' Case*); *Millar*, 98 Eng. Rep. at 208 (Willes); Bacon, *New Abridgment*, 208.

90 *The Company of Stationers* v. *Parker*, Skinner 233, 90 Eng. Rep. 107–8 (King's Bench 1685); *The Company of Stationers* v. *Seymour*, 1 Modern 256, 86 Eng. Rep. 865–6 (Court of Common Pleas 1677); Bacon, *New Abridgment*, 208–9; *Atkins' Case*, 842–4. *The Company of Stationers* v. *Parker*,

In the *Company of Stationers* v. *Seymour*, the prerogative copyright was held to extend to almanacs partly due to their religious content and partly because, as compilations, they had no identifiable author. By implicit analogy, just as tangible things belonging to no one belonged to the monarch, according to the prerogative tradition, so the copies of a text without an author belonged to the monarch. Thus the copyrights to almanacs, Psalters, Bibles, Year-Books, and Books of Common Prayer were all within the royal prerogative, and, along with law books, subject to grant by letters patent. In fact, with the exception of the patent pertaining to common law, all these patents came to be held and enforced by the Stationers Company.[91]

7.8 CONCLUSION

What is so striking to us today about the prerogative tradition is the fusion of property with rulership conceptions. This fusion of proprietary and rulership conceptions is, in fact, characteristic of the prerogative tradition. Reaching back to the thirteenth century, in *Bracton*, we have seen that ownership (*dominium*) over certain things belonging to no one – which according to the law of nations (*jus gentium*) or natural law would belong to the first person to take possession of ("occupy") them – belonged to the king under English common law.

All property was held from the king; he was the lord of lords. In its real property law, England, in the words of F. W. Maitland, was "the most perfectly feudalized" of European states.[92]

And so the much-contested concept of feudalism is important for our purposes as we are seeking to understand the legal and formalistic roots of modern intellectual property law. Those roots are found in the prerogative tradition, which was developed in the fusion of Anglo-Norman canon law, Roman law, and customary law, the foundations of English common law. The cultural process in which Roman law and legal power were Christianized and transformed into the basis for a new, sacramentalizing order of obligation is the background that helps us to understand and explain the emergence of a prerogative tradition. We have traced the roots of that tradition in the preceding chapters.

The prerogative tradition, with its synthesis of administrative kingship, grants of privilege through letters patent, and covenantal social bonds linking people together through vows of faith, will, in turn, become foundational for modern intellectual property as an infrastructure of state power in a developing nation-state system. In our brief flash forward to the time of William Blackstone, writing

Skinner 233, 90 Eng. Rep. 107 (King's Bench 1685); see also *The Company of Stationers* v. *Seymour*, 1 Modern 256, 86 Eng. Rep. 865–6 (Court of Common Pleas 1677).

91 1 Modern 256, 86 Eng. Rep. 865 (Court of Common Pleas 1677); see also Bacon, *New Abridgment*, 208–9; *The Company of Stationers* v. *Lee*, 2 Shower 259, 89 Eng. Rep. 927 (King's Bench 1681).

92 Maitland, *Constitutional History of England*, 156; Pollock & Maitland, *History of English Law*, 235.

in the eighteenth century, we have seen how a logic of Roman law was transformed into a logic of valuable mental labor, which underpins modern, "substantive" justifications of intellectual property law. The logic relies on Christianized Roman law, which was universalized into a basis for natural law and the "law of nations" (*ius gentium*).

But the actual implementation of this logic required a further transformation in political power: national legislation enacted by representatives of national social groups, imposing legal obligations on all members of the nation. In England, this came about through the rise of Parliament, and it is to this development that we now turn.

8

Intellectual Property in a Nationalizing Order

On May 29, 1624, an English parliament under a Scottish king – James I (1603–25), ruling Scotland as James VI (1567–1625) – issued a law against monopolies, the foundation of modern patent law for the United Kingdom and its colonial heirs. The law prohibited monopolies while carving out an exception for "new inventions." Monopolies issued by the king to protect new inventions would continue to be a legitimate exercise of the king's prerogative power, as would monopolies issued to create corporations, but other types of royal monopolies would henceforth be illegal.[1]

Less than a century later, in 1710, a parliament of James' great-granddaughter, queen Anne (1702–14), issued a law "for the encouragement of learning." This was Britain's first copyright law. Litigation over the meaning of this law, which was finally resolved by the House of Lords, established the foundation for modern, Anglo-American copyright law.[2]

By 1710, the newly defined United Kingdom of Great Britain had undergone a series of legal, political, and social revolutions. Efforts to cement a legal union between England and Scotland constituted an important dimension, as did the Protestant Reformation, beginning in Henry VIII's "Reformation from Above" and culminating in the "Glorious Revolution" of 1688–89, which paved the way for queen Anne's reign. On the European continent, devastating wars over political and religious power were finally ended by treaty in 1648, in a negotiated division of territorial power. Western Christianity was being "confessionalized": compartmentalized within nation-states, according to the decisions of kings or aristocratic rulers, integrating religious confessions into political projects of disciplinary, popular control. Around the world, a struggle for political

[1] 21 James I, Ch. 3; 4 Stat. 1212. For discussion of the debate in Parliament, see Chris R. Kyle, "'But a New Button to an Old Coat': The Enactment of Statute of Monopolies, 21 James I cap. 3," *The Journal of Legal History* 19(3): 203–23 (1998).

[2] 8 Anne, Ch. 1; 9 Stat. 256. Litigation over the meaning: *Millar* v. *Taylor*, 4 Burrow 2303, 98 Eng. Rep. 201 (1769). Final resolution by the House of Lords: *Donaldson* v. *Becket*, 4 Burrow 2408, 98 Eng. Rep. 257; 2 Brown 129, 1 Eng. Rep. 837; William Cobbett's *Parliamentary History of England*, Vol. XVII (London: T. C. Hansard, 1813), 953–1003.

and economic control was intensifying through extended trading networks, as part of the effort to establish national colonies. These are the seventeenth-century foundations of the modern nation-state system, and of modern intellectual property law.[3]

A decisive shift toward treating patents and copyrights as legal property, as objects that can be owned, was made by the British parliament, as part of this constitutional transformation. But the movement toward embracing intellectual property was fitful and ambivalent. It was not until questions were raised about whether this new type of property was truly property, as defined under English common law, that the full implications of nationalization became explicit.

8.1 CULTIVATING A NATIONAL ORDER OF OBLIGATION

The birth of Parliament and of English statutory law came during the reigns of Henry III (1216–72) and his son, Edward I (1272–1307). Edward, indeed, has been called the "English Justinian" because of the way in which he consolidated English statutory law. But the creation of Parliament and of English statutory law was not solely attributable to English kings. It was also attributable to aristocratic laity and churchmen who, in revolt, pressured their kings to concede a "higher law" that bound them all. In the course of these revolts, and of defining this "higher law," institutional patterns for the calling of Parliaments, and for representation of the political nation in those Parliaments, were created. In practice, Parliaments still had to concede much to their kings, and strong kings from Edward I to Henry VIII could direct their Parliaments through performative leadership and subtle manipulation. But paradigms were established that, under changing social conditions, enabled

[3] Efforts to cement a legal union and impacts of the Glorious Revolution: Geoffrey Holmes, *The Making of a Great Power: Late Stuart and Early Georgian Britain, 1660–1722* (London and New York: Longman, 1993), 307–21 and passim. Henry VIII's Reformation from above: G. W. Bernard, *The King's Reformation: Henry VIII and the Remaking of the English Church* (New Haven: Yale University Press, 2005); G. R. Elton, *Reform and Reformation: England 1509–1558* (Cambridge, MA: Harvard University Press, 1977); W. G. Hoskins, *The Age of Plunder: King Henry's England, 1500–1547* (London and New York: Longman, 1976). Devastating continental wars of religion and the 1648 settlement: Frederic J. Baumgartner, *France in the Sixteenth Century* (New York: St. Martin's Press, 1995); James B. Collins, *The State in Early Modern France* (Cambridge, UK: Cambridge University Press, 2009); Geoffrey Parker et al., *The Thirty Years' War* (London: Routledge, 1997); Joachim Whaley, *Germany and the Holy Roman Empire: Volume I: Maximilian I to the Peace of Westphalia* (Oxford: Oxford University Press, 2012); Peter H. Wilson, *Heart of Europe: A History of the Holy Roman Empire* (Cambridge, MA: Belknap Press, 2016). Confessionalization, national compartmentalization, and the "disciplinary revolution": Philip Gorski, *The Disciplinary Revolution* (Chicago: University of Chicago Press, 2003). Globalizing struggle for economic and political power: Nicholas Canny (ed.), *The Origins of Empire* (Oxford: Oxford University Press, 1998); J. A. Fernández-Santamaria, *The State, War and Peace: Spanish Political Thought in the Renaissance* (Cambridge, UK: Cambridge University Press, 1977); Jonathan Israel, *The Dutch Republic: Its Rise, Greatness, and Fall, 1477–1806* (Oxford: Clarendon Press, 1995), 307–27; George Masselman, *The Cradle of Colonialism* (New Haven: Yale University Press, 1963).

Parliaments to exercise increasing levels of independence from their kings and (eventually) queens.[4]

The iconic baronial revolt went against King John (1199–1216), and its resolution came in the *Magna Carta* (the "Great Charter") of 1215. John, like his older brother Richard (1189–99), had subjected the barons and their tenants to burdensome taxes and arbitrary exercises of royal power. But, unlike Richard, John was also seen as an unsuccessful (weak and vacillating) king – he lost much of the land in France that had sustained the cross-channel empire of his father, Henry II. At a low point in his struggle against his barons, John agreed to terms for governing the kingdom that were recorded in 63 clauses of the Great Charter. Some of these would be of enduring significance. But, beyond *Magna Carta*'s specific terms, there was also the covenantal sense that the king was bound by a higher, even divinely given, law in the way that he governed his kingdom. This was an ideal, one that was often compromised in the realities of power politics, but it was an ideal that would endure.[5]

One clause in *Magna Carta* is especially significant for the definition of England, as a political community. This was clause 61, which laid out an enforcement mechanism for the Great Charter's terms. According to this clause, the barons were to select a committee of 25 who would oversee compliance with the terms of the Charter. If compliance was not maintained, they were to notify the king or his justiciar. If the violation was not rectified, the barons, in concert with "the commune of all the land" (*cum communa tocius terre*), were empowered to "distrain" the king by seizing his castles, lands, and possessions, that is, his property. Distraint was a traditional method of legal enforcement, but what was so striking here was its linkage with the idea that there was a "community" of England, which should join with the 25 barons in compelling the king, through distraint of his property, to adhere to his legal obligations.[6]

John died in 1216, still fighting his barons, his obligations under *Magna Carta* nullified by his feudal overlord, the pope. He left behind a nine-year-old son, Henry

[4] Birth of Parliament and English statutory law: J. R. Maddicott, *The Origins of the English Parliament, 924–1327* (Oxford: Oxford University Press, 2004), especially 106–276. Edward I as the English Justinian: William Blackstone, *Commentaries on the Laws of England: A Facsimile of the First Edition of 1765–1769*, Vol. IV (Chicago: University of Chicago Press, 1979), 418 (Book IV, c. 33); Caroline Burt, *Edward I and the Governance of England, 1272–1307* (Cambridge, UK: Cambridge University Press, 2013); Patrick Wormald, *The Making of English Law: King Alfred to the Twelfth Century* (Oxford: Blackwell Publishers, 2001), 5. Baronial revolutions: Adrian Jobson, *The First English Revolution: Simon de Montfort, Henry III and the Barons' War* (London: Bloomsbury, 2012); J. R. Maddicott, *Simon de Montfort* (Cambridge, UK: Cambridge University Press, 1994); R. E. Treharne & I. J. Sanders (eds.), *Documents of the Baronial Movement of Reform and Rebellion, 1258–1267* (Oxford: Oxford University Press, 1973).

[5] J. C. Holt, *Magna Carta*, 3rd ed. (Cambridge, UK: Cambridge University Press, 2015); Maddicott, *Origins*, 106–56; NicholasVincent, *Magna Carta: Origins and Legacy* (Oxford: Bodleian Library, 2015).

[6] Holt, *Magna Carta*, App. 6 (Magna Carta 1215), § 61, 394–97; Maddicott, *Origins*, 139–47; Vincent, *Magna Carta*, 70–1.

III, who would rule England for most of the thirteenth century. During Henry's minority, several important ministers functioned as the real governing powers in the kingdom, including Stephen Langton, as archbishop of Canterbury, and Hubert de Burgh, as justiciar, together with papal agents (legates) named Guala (or Wala) and Pandulf. During Henry's minority, *Magna Carta* was reissued twice, and, in 1225, upon Henry's assumption of full royal powers, the Charter was reissued in a modified, abbreviated form. Certain of the king's prerogative powers were limited through definition, and privileges – such as those of London – were affirmed. Taxes ("scutages") to fund the fighting of wars were to be limited by the customs set in the time of Henry II.[7]

With the loss of French lands, the English kings became committed to fighting costly wars in France, seeking to win back property that they claimed as their own. With *Magna Carta*, however, two basic principles had also been asserted: (1) that taxation was to be limited by "necessity," and (2) that taxes should be imposed with "the common council of our realm." More broadly, there was the transcendent appeal to divine law, an overarching law of God, to be recognized by the English kings as safeguarding the "liberties" of the church, together with certain specific rights and principles of justice for English subjects. What these liberties, rights, and principles meant, of course, and whether they would hold, remained open to wide-ranging questions.[8]

A second baronial revolt, led in important respects by the charismatic Simon de Montfort (c. 1208–65), contributed to answering the questions. The revolt began in the swearing of an oath and the formation of a confederacy. It ended in the violent death of Simon de Montfort. King Henry and his son, the lord Edward, successfully reasserted their rulership through military power. But even though the revolt both depended upon and ended in assertions of military power, it was also cultural and political in character. It was the cultural and political legacies that were of lasting importance for English law.[9]

Politically, the revolt consolidated the growth of Parliament, as a periodic assembly through which the king sought council from his leading subjects, together with consent to taxation. As an assembly, Parliament could act as a court of judgment, as well as a deliberative body. In France, the *Parlements* developed primarily into courts, whereas in England, political deliberation and lawmaking became central.

7 David Carpenter, *Henry III: The Rise to Power and Personal Rule, 1207–1258* (New Haven: Yale University Press, 2020); Holt, *Magna Carta*, App. 12 (Magna Carta 1225), 420–8; Maddicott, *Origins*, 147–53; Sir Maurice Powicke, *The Thirteenth Century, 1216–1307*, 2nd ed. (Oxford: Oxford University Press, 1991), 23–4, 28–30; Vincent, *Magna Carta*, 71–82, 274–80.

8 David L. D'Avray, "'Magna Carta': Its Background in Stephen Langton's Academic Biblical Exegesis and Its Episcopal Reception," *Studi Medievali* 1 (1997): 423–38; R. H. Helmholz, "The Church and Magna Carta," *William and Mary Bill of Rights Journal* 25(2) (2016): 425–36; Vincent, *Magna Carta*, 32, 65–82; *also* Michael Prestwich, *Plantagenet England, 1225–1360* (Oxford: Oxford University Press, 2005), 28–44, 278–80.

9 Maddicott, *Simon de Montfort*, 4–5, 77–105, 124–91, 342–5; Maddicott, *Origins*, 157–276; Treharne & Sanders (eds.), *Documents of the Baronial Movement*, 4–5, 77–113.

However, in the mid-thirteenth century, as these institutions were developing on both sides of the Channel, the two trajectories were not clearly differentiated. What mattered most in the baronial revolt of 1258–67 was the fact that leading men from throughout the kingdom were assembling together in order to argue with the king and with each other about the appropriate practices for governing the community of the realm. As in the French Revolution of 1789, the assembly itself presented possibilities in the form of social performances involving idealistic words and (ultimately) legal documents that have endured.[10]

The beginning of the revolt came in April 1258 at a London assembly, held at Westminster. The king needed more money than he could possibly raise from his own landed wealth, or from issuing privileges. In this instance, his needs were especially high because of his crusading commitments, which had been renegotiated into an obligation to extend English lordship into Sicily, a step that the pope, as feudal overlord to both England and Sicily, was vigorously promoting. For Englishmen of the rising "gentry" class, as well as some vocal barons, monastic chroniclers, and churchmen, the king's continual wars in France were starting to seem like expensive folly. An extension of English commitments into southern Italy went well beyond reasonability, let alone necessity.[11]

The answer to the king's request for money, and not for the first time, was no. However, in this instance, the barons who met with the king did not say no with finality. Instead, they held out the possibility of funds in exchange for a project in "rectification" of the "state of the realm." Through writs issued by letters patent in May 1258, the king proclaimed to all (*omnibus*), on behalf of himself and his barons, that the great and leading men of the kingdom would assemble in Oxford to further debate the grant of an aid. The king also promised, in turn, that, taking the advice of his leading men, he would ordain (*ordinatio*) for the reform of the "state of the realm" ordinances that would be faithfully observed both by himself and his son, the lord Edward.[12]

The assembly at Oxford occurred in conjunction with a mustering for battle in Wales, and the combination of military and political assembly meant heightened attention and attendance. In the background was a tentative agreement with Louis IX of France (1226–70) for a settlement of perennial warfare between kindred kingdoms, a draft treaty that would be ratified in 1259. Territorial boundaries for

[10] Maddicott, *Simon de Montfort*, 151–72; Maddicott, *Origins*, 233–76, 376–452, and passim; Ulrike Muessig, "Superior Courts in Early Modern France, England, and the Holy Roman Empire," in *Judges and Judging in the History of the Common Law and Civil Law*, edited by Paul Brand and Joshua Getzler (Cambridge, UK: Cambridge University Press, 2012), 210–11; Prestwich, *Plantagenet England*, 98–120, 131–3, 185–7, 278–89.

[11] Jobson, *First English Revolution*, Chs 1–2; Maddicott, *Simon de Montfort*, 151–72; Maddicott, *Origins*, 233–76; G. E. Mingay, *The Gentry: The Rise and Fall of a Ruling Class* (London: Longman, 1976); Treharne & Sanders (eds.), *Documents of the Baronial Movement*, 72–5.

[12] Jobson, *First English Revolution*, Ch 2; Maddicott, *Simon de Montfort*, 151–6; Maddicott, *Origins*, 171–8, 233–6; R. F. Treharne, *The Baronial Plan of Reform, 1258–1263* (Manchester: Manchester University Press, 1971), 64–9; Treharne & Sanders (eds.), *Documents of the Baronial Movement*, 72–7.

France and England were being defined which were approaching the boundaries we recognize today for these two nations. The English kings would relinquish their Norman and Angevin claims in northwestern France. They would hang onto Gascony, in southwestern France, but hold it as a fief from the French king, thus recognizing him as lord of the territory, while retaining the power to practically rule the territory and enjoy its bounty, especially its wines.[13]

In June 1258, at Oxford, a wide cross section of Anglo-French society met together. There was a committee selected to propose legal reforms, including a few leading churchmen and more powerful laymen. In addition, there was an array of barons (churchmen and laity) summoned to the Oxford Parliament. And, finally, there may have been as many as 137 tenants-in-chief of the king, together with their knightly entourages, met in answer to the king's summons for war in Wales. This wide cross section of society, which came together almost by accident, brought a greater range of perspectives to bear on the legal documents drafted and discussed at Oxford. Viewing these with the benefit of hindsight, we can see the legal culture for a national state beginning to emerge.[14]

Establishing the framework for discussion at Oxford was a *Petition of the Barons*. The petition elaborated a range of injustices that affected classes well beyond the titled nobility and high-ranking churchmen. Speaking first for their own class, the baronial lords sought to limit the feudal powers of chief lords, pointedly the king, which became especially onerous in moments of transition between property holding, for example, as a son (or daughter) was stepping up to assume an inheritance. The barons sought to regularize this moment of transition, defining the proprietary right of a feudal overlord as a limited (*simplex*) possession and setting explicit boundaries on the powers he could exercise in situations of inheritance. Going beyond the regulation of feudal powers, however, they sought to limit the king's prerogative powers more generally, for the benefit of "true-born Englishmen" (*de natione regni Anglie*), for the sake of justice to merchants and townspeople, and for people summoned to court proceedings who could not afford specialized legal advice.[15]

13 Pierre Chaplais, "The Making of the Treaty of Paris (1259) and the Royal Style," *English Historical Review* 67(253) (1952): 235–53; Jobson, *First English Revolution*, Ch 2; Maddicott, *Simon de Montfort*, 151–91; Maddicott, *Origins*, 233–45. On the broader, geopolitical and international context, see Powicke, *The Thirteenth Century*, 80–128; Björn Weiler, "Introduction" *to England and Europe in the Reign of Henry III (1216–1272)* (Abingdon: Routledge, 2016), 1–11. On the significance of the southwestern French wine trade, see Mingay, *Gentry*, 33; Powicke, *Thirteenth Century*, 108–28, 669 n.3; Prestwich, *Plantagenet England*, 292–4, 492–3.

14 Jobson, *First English Revolution*, Ch 2; Maddicott, *Simon de Montfort*, 151–65; Maddicott, *Origins*, 236–45; Treharne, *Baronial Plan*, 67–76; Treharne & Sanders (eds.), *Documents of the Baronial Movement*, 77–97.

15 Treharne & Sanders (eds.), *Documents of the Baronial Movement*, 77–91. The expulsion of high-ranking "foreigners" with close connections to king Henry and the lord Edward occurred shortly afterward. Treharne, *Baronial Plan*, 76–81; Treharne & Sanders (eds.), *Documents of the Baronial Movement*, 90–7.

A memorandum perhaps edited in the wake of the Oxford Parliament, the *Provisions of Oxford*, treated the implications for rightful governance of a national community even more sweepingly. These *Provisions* contemplated dramatic reforms that would be administered under the oversight of an elective council, with authority exercised by oath-bound officers implementing justice in the interests of the "community" (*ex parte communitatis*). The *Provisions* were described in this memorandum as having been accepted by Henry III and Edward I "for the correction and reform both of their own affairs and of the state of the [English, *Anglie*] realm."[16]

After naming twelve chosen representatives (*electi*) for each side, the *Provisions* transcribed five oaths sworn on the Bible. First was an oath of the whole "community of England [*Engletere*] at Oxford." This was performatively sworn and proclaimed as a mutual binding of all together, solemnly promising in good faith to help each other against all men, to do justice and to respect property both in land and in moveable wealth. The second oath was for the twenty-four representatives at the Oxford Parliament, promising in honor of God, in fealty to the king, and for the benefit (*profit*) of the realm, to negotiate in good faith for reform and amendment in the state of the realm (*estat del reaume*). These two communal oaths were followed by separate oaths for three major officers: the chief justiciar, the chancellor, and the keepers of the king's castles. The chief justiciar was to uphold right (*de dreiture tenir*) to all people (*a tute genz*), for the benefit of king and realm, in accordance with provisions established by the twenty-four, by the council, and by the great men of the land. The chancellor was to limit his writs to standardized "routine writs" (*bref de curs*), except under orders from the king in council, and he was to limit the application of his seal in accordance with ordinances made by the council. The overseers of castles were to conduct their responsibilities in accordance with written commissions, limited to fixed terms.[17]

Parliaments were to be held three times each year, and local justice was to be overseen in the county courts by "prudent and law-worthy knights," residents of the county in question. The state of the church was to be amended, and sheriffs were to be paid a salary by the king, so that they would not be tempted to extract revenues in onerous and corrupting ways. The charter of liberties (*Magna Carta*) was to be firmly observed, the mints of London were to be reformed, and the state of all cities of the king, impoverished by his exactions, was also to be reformed. Grants of privilege and property from the king were henceforward to be made under the oversight of an elective council.[18]

There is a breathtaking comprehensiveness in reformist idealism here, paralleled in the nationalizing conception of the English realm as a legal community, and in the conciliar limitation of the king's prerogative powers. There is also a recognizable

16 Treharne, *Baronial Plan*, 82–101; Treharne & Sanders (eds.), *Documents of the Baronial Movement*, 96–113.

17 Treharne & Sanders (eds.), *Documents of the Baronial Movement*, 100–3, 106–9.

18 Treharne & Sanders (eds.), *Documents of the Baronial Movement*, 98–99, 106–11.

formalism, both in the procedures to be followed in nominating political representatives and in the use of written laws to define and limit ministerial discretion. The range of purposes to be served by royal writs and letters patent, for example, was to be explicitly limited to those forms already established, except where the king decided otherwise with the advice of his councilors. Right/justice (*jus*) was to be upheld for all people of the realm by judicial officers extending from the chief justice of the king to county courts overseen by local, knightly magistrates.[19]

The *Provisions of Oxford* were communicated throughout England through writs and letters patent from the king, to be read and recorded in county courts. While the *Provisions* were only briefly and marginally "in force," they nonetheless contributed to an intensely held ideal of legal obligation and rightful governance in national community, guaranteeing right to each member of the community and protecting the community against "foreigners." The class-based concerns of the barons – especially against arbitrary and heavy taxation – had clearly contributed to this legal ideal, but the ideals extended beyond property-based groupings. In March 1259, the barons swore to adhere to the same standards, upholding right and justice, in governing their own franchises, liberties, and manors, and in their relations with their neighbors.[20]

The *Provisions of Oxford* had an enduring effect on English legal culture not so much through their specific terms as through the way that they entrenched *Magna Carta* as a foundation for good governance, and because of their legacy for later legislation. In 1264, Henry's efforts to reassert his prerogative powers were mediated by Louis IX of France. The memoranda put forward by the English king and the reformers looked back to the *Provisions of Oxford*, as to *Magna Carta*, for standards defining the legitimacy of prerogative powers. The Great Charter (together with the closely related charter of the forest law) became a kind of bedrock for legal legitimacy, even in Louis' settlement decision, which purported to annul the *Provisions of Oxford*, while preserving the validity of "charters, liberties, statutes, and laudable customs" in effect before the *Provisions*.[21]

As the culminating struggle over feudal and prerogative powers gathered in intensity between king Henry, the lord Edward, and the reforming barons, Parliaments were held and planned, and paradigms were established for

[19] Jobson, *First English Revolution*, Ch 2; Treharne & Sanders (eds.), *Documents of the Baronial Movement*, 96–111. With respect to judicial process, however, it is important to note that a relatively informal querela procedure enabled poorer people in the shires to bring complaints in the special eyre courts assembled under the justiciar, Hugh Bigod. A. H. Hershey, "Justice and Bureaucracy: The English Royal Writ and '1258'," *English Historical Review* 113(4): 829–51 (1998); Jobson, *First English Revolution*, Ch 2.

[20] Jobson, *First English Revolution*, Ch 2 and passim; Treharne & Sanders (eds.), *Documents of the Baronial Movement*, 116–19, 130–57. It should be noted, however, that the idealism did not extend to adequate protections for Jews. Cecil Roth, *A History of the Jews in England*, 3nd ed. (Oxford: Clarendon Press, 1978), 59–64.

[21] Maddicott, *Simon de Montfort*, 256–70; Treharne & Sanders (eds.), *Documents of the Baronial Movement*, 252–91.

summoning knights of the shire, together with borough representatives, for Parliamentary counsel. In 1266, a final settlement was reached, with formal terms anchored in *Magna Carta*, as well as in canon law and the common law of the realm. In 1267, the Statute of Marlborough gave legal definition to certain of the reforming ideals, with enduring echoes in the final years of Henry's reign.[22]

After Henry's death in 1272, Edward's first Parliament (April 1275) ratified a set of statutory provisions inspired by the *Provisions of Oxford*, signifying the new king's intention to selectively embrace the reforming vision, working through Parliament and statutory law in governing a nationalizing community of clerics and laity, both through centralizing administration and through local governance by an increasingly self-conscious gentry: the "knights of the shire," together with the esquires and local landowners who might be called upon to act as keepers and justices of the peace.[23]

The baronial reform movement of 1258–67 helped to consolidate an idealistic legal transformation, establishing a trajectory in which *Magna Carta*, county courts, and Parliamentary legislation became the institutional foundations for a national legal community. A governing community was being defined through the assertion of a common law that gave legal definition to (often onerous) obligations between fellow members of that community. And an English king, an "English Justinian," was recognizing that his prerogative powers could be stably supported, even while they were definitionally limited, in the organized administration of justice and in the strategic deployment of legislation and legal privileges.[24]

8.2 CHRONICLERS AND NATIONAL LEGAL CONSCIOUSNESS

We can see the impacts of this nationalizing legal revolution in the thought-world of the great monastic chroniclers at St. Albans, a Benedictine abbey located about 20 miles from London, on the old Roman road (Watling Road) heading northwest, out of the city. From the beginning of the thirteenth to the fifteenth century, St. Albans maintained a sequence of nearly continuous chronicles, revealing close connections with major actors and events of the time, from the issuance of *Magna Carta* and the baronial revolt led by Simon de Montfort to the later peasant revolts and religious radicalism of "Lollardy." The chronicles bridge the Black Death of the mid-fourteenth century, coming to renewed life under the authorship of Thomas Walsingham, and then finally ending with the funeral of Henry V (1386–1422).

22 Maddicott, *Simon de Montfort*, 263–371; Treharne & Sanders (eds.), *Documents of the Baronial Movement*, 290–337.

23 Maddicott, *Origins*, 277–98.

24 Jobson, *First English Revolution*, passim; Anthony Musson, *Medieval Law in Context: The Growth of Legal Consciousness from Magna Carta to the Peasants' Revolt* (Manchester: Manchester University Press, 2001); T. F. T. Plucknett, *Legislation of Edward I* (Oxford: Clarendon Press, 1949); Prestwich, *Plantagenet England*, 93–8, 554–75.

The chronicles of St. Albans thus lead us very nearly into the Tudor period of English history.[25]

During the mid-thirteenth century, the St. Albans chronicler was Matthew Paris. Following in the footsteps of his predecessor Roger of Wendover, Paris took in the wide sweep of secular history, from political and legal events in England, Wales, Ireland, and Scotland to letters and reports from France, Germany, Rome, and the Holy Lands. His hostility to Islam was nearly matched by his hostility to Franciscans and Dominicans, and he offered institutional histories of all three. His attitude to the papacy is especially revealing, since it shows the degree to which Rome could be seen, even by devoutly religious figures, as a rapacious and oppressive source of foreign influence.[26]

The conflict with the papacy over nomination ("provision") of clerics for benefices in the English church, as Matthew Paris portrays it, is exemplary of the way in which English national consciousness could be highlighted in legal struggles with Rome. Wheeling from a dramatic and closely documented narrative about the pope's excommunication of the German emperor, Paris highlighted the extraordinary devotion of the English church, especially in the face of "the daily oppressions of the Romans." He told a brief story about a knight from northern England, Robert de Twenge, who became so desperate that he made the long journey to Rome, "refusing with all his efforts to bend his neck to the yoke of these Romans." This heroic English knight was seeking to vindicate his right of patronage in "a certain church which belonged to him, on which the Romans had, through the archbishop of York, laid the hands of cupidity."[27]

Robert was only the tip of the iceberg. Matthew Paris went on to describe a general indignation, shared by "earls, barons, and other nobles of England," deprived of their property rights in the patronage of English churches by "foreigners," unjustly enriched by English benefices. These angry earls and barons, deprived of their patronage rights, sent a letter with Robert de Twenge to present on their behalf to the pope. Matthew Paris transcribed copies of the nobles' letter, and of the pope's responses.[28]

25 Chronicles of St. Albans: J. A. Giles (trans.), *Roger of Wendover's* Flowers of History, 2 Volumes (London: Henry G. Bohn, 1849); J. A. Giles (trans.), *Matthew Paris's English History*, 3 Volumes (London: George Bell & Sons, 1889 (Vol. I), Henry G. Bohn, 1853–4 (Vols. II–III)); Henry Richards Luard (ed.), *Chronica Majora*, 7 Volumes (London: Longman et al., 1872–83); Henry Thomas Riley (ed.), *Chronica Monasterii S. Albani, Thomae Walsingham*, 2 Volumes (London: Longman et al., 1863–4); John Taylor, Wendy R. Childs, and Leslie Watkiss (eds. & trans.), *The St. Albans Chronicle: The* Chronica maiora *of Thomas Walsingham*, 2 Volumes, 1376–1422 (Oxford: Clarendon Press, 2003 & 2011).

26 Giles, *Matthew Paris's English History*, Vol. I, 5–6, 14–28, 37–8, 50–1; see also R. W. Southern, *Western Views of Islam in the Middle Ages* (Cambridge, MA: Harvard University Press, 1962); Richard Vaughan, *Matthew Paris* (Cambridge, UK: Cambridge University Press, 1958).

27 Giles, *Matthew Paris's English History*, Vol. I, 54–5, 96–8. For the persistence of these nationalizing tensions into the time of the Reformation, see A. G. Dickens, *The English Reformation*, 2nd ed. (University Park, Pennsylvania: The Pennsylvania State Press, 1989), 108–12.

28 Giles, *Matthew Paris's English History*, Vol. I, 230–4.

According to Paris's transcript, the barons cried out against the infringement of their liberty, "which has been gained by the blood of our ancestors," and they begged the pope to "allow to each of us his right." The barons then proceeded to elaborate the legal foundations for these rights, citing papal bulls and feudal law. They concluded with a veiled threat, premised on the fact that Robert de Twenge was "necessary to the management of the king's business": if their petition did not receive the desired response, affirming their liberties and rights, they would be "obliged" to seek the assistance of the king, "who is bound to protect and cherish the rights and liberties of laymen."[29]

The pope conceded, reiterating the principle asserted by the English nobles: that it would be strictly unlawful, henceforward, for a bishop or archbishop to grant benefices in churches, for which laymen held the legal right of patronage (advowson), without the consent of the patron. The pope pleaded mistake in the nomination. But Matthew Paris nonetheless concluded:

> By these, and such like examples, it can be clearly weighed in the balance of reason, how disrespected was the severity [rigor] of law (*jus*) at that time slumbering, and the reverence of the Church and the piety of religion: for the possessions of ecclesiastics and peaceful, religious men, were given only as plunder and booty; and the world threatened now to fall into its old state of chaos.[30]

St. Albans often hosted royal retinues traveling into and out of London, and the monks were well-informed about developments in secular law. Parliamentary assemblies were noted and discussed by the chroniclers, as were reports concerning the activity of royal justices, both those of the itinerant courts (*eyre*) and from the "bench" (*banco*) in Westminster. In 1240, Paris reported a response of the bench (*rescriptum de banco*), concerning a case of women's inheritances in Ireland. Since there was some question about the applicable customary law in Ireland, in the specific case where multiple sisters inherited property held from the king, the king's bench instructed that English customary law should be applied. Shortly afterward, Paris noted that the itinerant justices were sent out on eyre throughout England, extorting massive sums for the king, "under the pretext of administering justice."[31]

Given his evident interests in law, it will come as no surprise that Paris reported very fully on a case involving privileges granted to St. Albans. The privileges concerned rights of "warren": exclusive hunting rights. Such privileges are numerous in the patent rolls of Henry III, and the litigation at St. Albans provides a valuable insight into the way these were interpreted at the time. Moreover, because Paris copied the legal documents, the case also provides insight into legal processes of the time.[32]

29 Ibid., 231–2.

30 Ibid., 232–4; Luard, *Chronica Majora*, Vol. III, 614.

31 Giles, *Matthew Paris's English History*, Vol. I, 263–4, 280; Luard, *Chronica Majora*, Vol. IV, 12–13, 34–5; Vaughan, *Matthew Paris*, 11–18.

32 Giles, *Matthew Paris's English History*, Vol. I, 291–5; Luard, *Chronica Majora*, Vol. IV, 50–4.

The case was initiated by a complaint of the abbot to the king, who issued a writ of summons to the knights alleged to be infringing the abbey's privilege in hunting rabbits. The case was heard before a jury assembled at Cambridge. A charter from Henry II was introduced into evidence, and the jury found for the abbey. Upon the assessment of money damages for infringement of the abbey's rights, a warrant was issued to the county sheriff to ensure that the damages were actually paid.[33]

As we can see quite vividly, English law was rapidly developing during the lifetime of Matthew Paris. The reigns of Henry III and Edward I, encompassing the century from 1216–1307, were foundational, not only for the forms of law that would become English common law, but also for the English legal profession. Canon law was developing and professionalizing alongside common law, and a focus on the full range of law applied in a privileged monastery helps us to see the complex and overlapping character of common law and canon law during this period. The centralization of royal control over a developing, national system of courts was a significant factor in the professionalization and differentiation of both types of law.[34]

At first, the king's courts had primarily been experienced by ordinary people as itinerant courts, ranging around the country on eyre, overseen by agents of the king, and judged according to conventional standards by local men. But the standardizing processes involving writs and detailed records that are evident in Matthew Paris' chronicle were contributing an increasingly technical character to royal justice, affecting a wider range of the population. Rules, standards, and principles were recognized, entailing an increasing expertise for royal justices, on the one hand, and an increasing need for experienced advice, on the other hand. The possibility of avoiding trial by battle was one appeal of these courts, but this was only the most vivid illustration of an increasingly formal rationality in law and procedure that drew increasing numbers of litigants into the royal courts.[35]

8.3 INDUSTRIALIZATION AND THE BLACK DEATH

Into the middle of this increasingly legalistic world of wealth and privilege came a devastating agent of transformation, the impacts of which were felt from China to

33 Giles, *Matthew Paris's English History*, Vol. I, 291–5; Luard, *Chronica Majora*, Vol. IV, 50–4.

34 Development of the English legal profession: Paul Brand, *The Origins of the English Legal Profession* (Oxford: Blackwell, 1992), 27–9, 50–160; Musson, *Medieval Law*, 36–75. One very important development, in which canon law and common law were inextricably linked, was the ending of ordeals by fire and water. The Fourth Lateran Council of 1215 had prohibited clergy from participating in these ordeals. In 1219, Henry III issued orders to his justices on eyre, acknowledging papal prohibition of ordeals, and providing for alternatives in criminal cases. H. C. Maxwell Lyte (ed.), *Patent Rolls of the Reign of Henry III*, Vol. I (London: Her Majesty's Stationery Office, 1901), 186; Norman P. Tanner (ed.), *Decrees of the Ecumenical Councils*, Vol. I (London: Sheed & Ward, 1990), 244 (§18); Robert Bartlett, *Trial by Fire and Water: The Medieval Judicial Ordeal* (Oxford: Clarendon Press, 1986), 100 and passim.

35 Brand, *Origins*, 8–9, 14–32; Sir Frederick Pollock and Frederic William Maitland, *The History of English Law before the Time of Edward I*, 2nd ed. (Cambridge, UK: Cambridge University Press, 1952), 109, 154–6, 169–70, 190, 198–207; see also Musson, *Medieval Law*, passim.

London: the Black Death. The social historian David Herlihy has called this fourteenth-century global pandemic – probably the bubonic plague carried by rats – "the great watershed" of medieval history, a turning point that tips us over into the modern world. Recognizing a fundamental shift in economic power dynamics, Michael Mann agrees with this view, although for him it is important to qualify that this was a change radiating outward from only one of the four sources of social power.[36]

According to the rough estimates of medieval population that are available for England, the Black Death – which returned in waves after its initial devastation in 1348–9 – perhaps halved the population of England. It is difficult to overstate the impacts of sudden death in these numbers, involving this scale of gruesome suffering. All institutions were affected, none more than the church. Because of their religious and social responsibilities, priests and friars died in large numbers. The cultural ideal of estate society, which had placed clerics at the top of an organic vision for social cooperation – among those who pray, those who fight, and those who work – had already been losing its tarnish, but now it seemed to collapse altogether, as is evident in the sharply satirical *Canterbury Tales* of Geoffrey Chaucer.[37]

In terms of strictly economic dynamics, the most fundamental change was in the relationship between the human population and the land supplying material resources for sustenance. Before the Black Death, population had been increasing to new heights, and this meant that people were competing with one another, at new levels of intensity, for access to the land. In economic terms, prices for land were being driven up, and prices for labor (wages) were being driven down. Workers were getting the short end of the stick, and landlords were doing well.[38]

But the Black Death radically changed things, making land suddenly plentiful (relative to human population), and workers in short supply. The economic situation of landlords – the men who owned the crucial economic resource of the Middle Ages – altered almost overnight. The workers who were left alive were in a much stronger position to seek higher wages, or greater levels of access to the land.[39]

This had important implications for political power and legal culture, because the English system of local governance by county and hundred had meant that landlords were the holders of enormous political authority in their local communities. Everyday power dynamics were still very local. Nevertheless, networks of diplomacy

36 David Herlihy, *The Black Death and the Transformation of the West* (Cambridge, MA: Harvard University Press, 1997); Mann, *Sources* Vol. I, 408–13; see also John A. F. Thomson, *The Transformation of Medieval England, 1370–1529* (London: Longman, 1983).

37 Thomson, *Transformation*, 9–16; Jill Mann, *Chaucer and Medieval Estates Satire* (Cambridge, UK: Cambridge University Press, 1973).

38 J. L. Bolton, *The Medieval English Economy, 1150–1500* (London: The Garden City Press, 1985), 45–206.

39 Bolton, *Medieval English Economy*, 207–45.

and exchange between merchants were developing into trading patterns that would carry over into the globalized, modern world. In Michael Mann's terms, the tracks were being laid for the modern nation-state system and modern capitalism.[40]

Viewed in the macroscopic lens of a broad narrative like ours, the century that stretches from Chaucer to the Tudors – roughly the fifteenth century – looks very chaotic. This was the period of the "Wars of the Roses," a period in which struggles over political and economic power repeatedly destabilized the English kingdom. But, as scholars like John Watts have argued, this was also a creative period, a period in which new forms for binding together political communities were developing. In the yet-conjoined realms of English canon and common law, this was a stabilizing period, one in which procedural legal forms involving writs and trials settled into patterns that echo to today.[41]

Writing under King Edward IV (1461–83), the jurist John Fortescue praised the laws of England and formulated principles for the governance of England, seeking in the new paradigm of "Renaissance" scholarship to offer advice about how to design a powerful kingdom. An important priority, Fortescue wrote, was to protect the prosperity and wealth of the kingdom, and to ensure that common people had an opportunity to share in this prosperity. This was ultimately the greatest security to the kingdom, ensuring widespread investment in the wealth and well-being of the kingdom.[42]

Promising common people an opportunity to rise from poverty to wealth would mean that impoverished people ("our poor archers") would support the kingdom militarily, with loyalty to the great king who had enriched them.

> Likewise, it is the king's honour, and also his duty, to make his realm rich .... God defend our king, and give him grace to augment his realm in riches, wealth, and prosperity, to his perpetual laudation and worship .... The greatest safety, truly, and also the most honour that may come to the king is that his realm should be rich in every estate. For nothing shall make his people arise, except lack of goods or lack of justice. But yet certainly when they lack goods they will arise, saying that they lack justice. Nevertheless if they are not poor, they will never arise, unless their prince so leaves justice, that he gives himself all to tyranny.

Wealth, in other words, is a close proxy for justice. When they are enjoying prosperity, people will forgive a prince all but the grossest of tyrannies.[43]

Fortescue, like Machiavelli, was a realistic advisor to his prince. And this realism carried over to advice about the granting of privileges through patents. Fortescue advised that grants should formally state that they were granted "by the advice" of the king's council. This would have two benefits. First, applicants for favors would give

40 Mann, *Sources* Vol. I, 408–13.

41 Gerald Harriss, *Shaping the Nation: England 1360–1461* (Oxford: Oxford University Press, 2005); John Watts, *The Making of Polities, 1300–1500* (Cambridge, UK: Cambridge University Press, 2009).

42 Sir John Fortescue, *On the Laws and Governance of England*, edited by Shelley Lockwood (Cambridge, UK: Cambridge University Press, 1997)

43 Fortescue, *Governance of England*, Ch. 12 (Shelley, ed., 108–10).

greater thought to their request. This would enhance the quality and "merits" of the requests. And, second, resentment at the denial of a request would not be focused upon the prince personally, but rather on the council, as a whole.[44]

Fortescue was writing in an age when letters patent were often issued for purposes – for example, grants of office in church and state – that look very different from modern patents. But since the reign of Edward III (1327–77) – in the context of the "Hundred Years War" between France and England – patents had also been granted to enable transfers into the kingdom of industrial know-how, for example, of cloth-making techniques. This was done by offering privileges to foreigners who would come to work in the kingdom, training the English to share in their skills and "working knowledge."[45]

In the struggles between France and England for national power, economic wealth for the nation was increasingly recognized as a priority for effective rulership. Strategies for the granting of privileges through patents were an important part of this effective rulership. A substantive rationality was developing to support a strategy of national, economic investment, with a conscious sense that the benefits needed to flow broadly throughout the nation. The national development of industrial know-how was something to encourage, and Parliament became the central institution through which strata of society familiar with this industrial know-how could communicate with their king, and consent to his taxation of their growing wealth.[46]

8.4 INVENTING THE ANTI-MONOPOLY TRADITION

As a means of overseeing economic development and creating bonds of patronage, the patent framework had the obvious advantage of requiring no payment on the part

44 Fortescue, *Governance of England*, Ch. 20 (Shelley, ed., 122–3).

45 Harold C. Fox, *Monopolies and Patents: A Study in the History and Future of the Patent Monopoly* (Toronto: University of Toronto Press, 1947), 43–56; William Hyde Price, *The English Patents of Monopoly* (Boston: Houghton, Mifflin and Company, 1906), 5–6. Patent-granting practices under Edward IV: *Calendar of the Patent Rolls Preserved in the Public Record Office, Edward IV (1461–67)* (London: Her Majesty's Stationery Office, 1897). Clothmaking patent for Flemings: *Calendar of the Patent Rolls Preserved in the Public Record Office, Edward III, Vol. II (1330–4)* (London: Her Majesty's Stationery Office, 1893), 161 (July 23, 1331, Lincoln: "Protection, during pleasure, for John Kempe of Flanders, weaver of woolen cloths, his men, servants and apprentices, to exercise and teach his trade in this country; with promise of the same for any other merchants of that mistery who choose to come here"), reinforced as part of a broader statutory framework for encouraging cloth exports, 11 Edw. III, 1 Stat. 280–1 (1337). Edward III's industrial policies, as part of his strategy for financing wars with France: Harriss, *Shaping the Nation*, 256–79; T. H. Lloyd, *The English Wool Trade in the Middle Ages* (Cambridge, UK: Cambridge University Press, 1977), 144 ff.; *cf.* Bolton, *Medieval English Economy*, 287–344. On "working knowledge," see Catherine L. Fisk, "Working Knowledge: Trade Secrets, Restrictive Covenants in Employment, and the Rise of Corporate Intellectual Property, 1800–1920," *Hastings Law Journal* 52: 441–535 (2001).

46 Harriss, *Shaping the Nation*, 256–309; G. L. Harriss, *King, Parliament, and Public Finance in Medieval England to 1369* (Oxford: Clarendon Press, 1975); W. M. Ormrod, *The Reign of Edward III: Crown and Political Society in England 1327–1377* (New Haven: Yale University Press, 1990), 196 and passim.

of the crown: patent holders were compensated, instead, through their ability to control an industry and charge high prices; their self-enforcement privileges made prerogative-based privileges an effective substitute for an extensive, government-run, administrative apparatus. Some patents even provided a revenue stream to the crown.[47]

During the Elizabethan and early Stuart period, however, patent practices were increasingly perceived as abusive. Moreover, the self-enforcement methods of patent holders were viewed as destructive and punitive. The English anti-monopoly tradition emerged as a reaction to these perceived abuses.

A jurist whose name is closely connected to the early English anti-monopoly tradition is Edward Coke. From 1589 to 1628, Coke was ubiquitous throughout the Elizabethan and Jacobean legal system, Parliament, and administration. In 1592, Coke became solicitor general and began serving in an advisory capacity for the privy council. That same year, he gave a reading at his alma mater, the Inner Temple, on the Statute of Uses (1536), which had strengthened the royal prerogative in settling a problem of feudal law. From the 1580s onward, Coke was closely tied, both personally and professionally, to the Cecils. His close connection with Lord Burghley meant that Coke was frequently asked to undertake special investigations, on behalf of the privy council, into the economic affairs of the kingdom. In this capacity, Coke gained extensive knowledge of national finances, and of the workings of English industry, a knowledge that he would draw upon in Parliamentary debates of the 1620s.[48]

As Elizabeth's attorney general, Coke argued the "Case of Monopolies" – *Darcy v. Allen* (1603) – on behalf of the queen's patentee and groom of the privy chamber, Edward Darcy. Although Coke argued in support of Darcy's patent, his report of the case, appearing alongside another anti-monopoly case (concerning the Tailors of Ipswich guild) in the eleventh volume of his reports (1615), provided a conceptual framework for *opposing* monopoly patents. Coke drew on this framework a few years later (1621–24) in drafting and supporting the Statute of Monopolies (1624) in Parliament.[49]

47 Chris Dent, "Patent Policy in Early Modern England: Jobs, Trade and Regulation," *Legal History* 10: 71–95 (2006); Fox, *Monopolies*, 43–85; Price, *English Patents*, 6–7; Alan G. R. Smith, *The Emergence of a Nation State: The Commonwealth of England, 1529–1660*, 2nd ed. (London: Longman, 1997), 121–6, 240–1, 260–1, 282–3.

48 Stephen D. White, *Sir Edward Coke and "The Grievances of the Commonwealth," 1621–1628* (Chapel Hill: University of North Carolina Press, 1979), 4–11, 86–141, 284–90; see also David Chan Smith, *Sir Edward Coke and the Reformation of the Laws: Religion, Politics and Jurisprudence, 1578–1616* (Cambridge, UK: Cambridge University Press, 2014), passim. On the Statute of Uses (3 Stat. 539 (1536)), see Margaret McGlynn, *The Royal Prerogative and the Learning of the Inns of Court* (Cambridge, UK: Cambridge University Press, 2003).

49 The Case of Monopolies, 11 Coke's. Reports 84b, *English Reports* 77: 1260–6 (Edinburgh: William Green & Sons, 1907); Jacob I. Corré, "The Argument, Decision, and Reports of Darcy v. Allen," *Emory Law Journal* 45: 1261–1327 (1996).

The *Darcy* case had involved a patent on playing cards. It included three specific types of privilege, allocating each of them to the patentee Edward Darcy (along with his agents and assigns): (1) the exclusive right to domestically manufacture cards and sell them, (2) the exclusive right to import cards and sell them, and (3) the right to enter and search buildings where it was suspected that cards imported in violation of the patent were being held, and to seize and carry away any cards found (i.e., a right to self-enforcement). The defendant in the *Darcy* case, Thomas Allen, was a London "haberdasher" who admitted to manufacturing a small number of cards in violation of the patent. In his defence, he alleged that as a freeman of the "society of Haberdashers," he was a citizen of the City of London and entitled to its ancient liberties, which included the manufacture and sale of playing cards.[50]

The court ruled against Edward Darcy but gave no reasons for its holding. In a thorough study of the ruling, Jacob Corré has shown that the actual reasons for the court's holding may have been procedural: the court may have considered Darcy's reliance on the "action on the case" an impermissible extension of this form of action, especially given the specification of remedies provided in the patent itself. Be that as it may, due to the influence of Coke, the case has come to stand as a precedent establishing the invalidity of monopoly patents.[51]

Coke reported the case in 1615, in a form that makes it appear as if the judges gave an extended set of reasons for their holding, reasons that articulated distinctions between valid and invalid patents. According to Coke's report, the grant of an exclusive right to practice a particular trade, by excluding all others from practicing the trade, violated the ancient rights of Englishmen to practice their respective trades and thereby to contribute to the English commonwealth. Moreover, Coke argued, all such monopolies on the practice of a particular trade have three inevitable effects on the product of the trade: the price of the product is increased, the quality of the product is reduced, and the tradesmen who previously practiced the particular trade are impoverished, along with their families.[52]

If, as Corré argues, the court's actual holding was premised on a procedural basis, the ruling may have avoided confrontation with the royal prerogative: the court may never have reached the question about the patent's validity. However, as Coke reported the *Darcy* case, it presumes the power of a common law court to declare limits on the royal prerogative, limits premised on inherent, trade-related rights of Englishmen, and on the legal sovereignty of Parliament (vis-à-vis the monarchy) in addressing trade-related issues. According to Coke, only Parliament has the legal power to restrain an Englishman from practicing his trade by granting a trade-related monopoly. The granting of trade-related monopolies, Coke later argued in Parliament, was an exercise of the royal prerogative that implicated what is "mine

[50] *Case of Monopolies*, 77 Eng. Rep., 1260–1.
[51] Corré, "Argument," 1265, 1267–72, 1285–92, 1325–7.
[52] *Case of Monopolies*, 77 Eng. Rep., 1260–5.

and thine" (*meum et tuum*); this meant that, unlike other exercises of the prerogative, it could be legally challenged in courts and in Parliament.[53]

The crown and council saw things differently. In 1601, when vociferous challenges to trade-related "monopolies" had been raised in the House of Commons, Elizabeth had promised her subjects their "ordinary remedy" under "her highness' laws of this realm." This promise was made in a proclamation preceding Elizabeth's "Golden Speech," a speech that cooled the commons' debates by dramatically highlighting the queen's love and concern for her subjects.[54]

However, Elizabeth's *Proclamation Reforming Patent Abuses* had carefully preserved the prerogative power to invalidate patents based on two reasons: the applicants had made "false and untrue suggestions" about their effects, and the execution of the patents had been "extremely abused." The notion that her courts had the power to declare legal limits on her prerogative, and thereby to invalidate her patents, was forcefully resisted by Elizabeth and her advisors. Just the previous month, her privy council had issued a letter to the Court of Common Pleas, ordering the court to stay a hearing on Darcy's playing card patent, and making them to "understand her Majesty's pleasure ... that her Prerogative Royall may not be called in question."[55]

Elizabeth's *Proclamation Reforming Patent Abuses* deflected the issue of monopolies to the reign of her successor, James VI of Scotland, who would become James I of England. During the course of his journey from Scotland to London, after the queen's death, James received many expressions of grievance which pertained to monopolies. Immediately upon his arrival in London, in May 1603, James issued a *Proclamation inhibiting the use and execution of any Charter or Grant made by the late Queen Elizabeth, of any kind of Monopolies, &c.* This proclamation provided for review of all Elizabeth's patents by the king and his privy council.[56]

[53] *Case of Monopolies*, 77 Eng. Rep., 1264; Corré, "Argument," 1265, 1285–92, 1321–7; White, *Sir Edward Coke*, 119–20, 122–5, 139–40.

[54] Paul L. Hughes and James F. Larkin (eds.), "Proclamation Reforming Patent Abuses," *Tudor Royal Proclamations, Volume III, The Later Tudors* (1588–1603) (New Haven: Yale University Press, 1969), 235–8; see also J. E. Neale, *Elizabeth I and her Parliaments, 1584–1601* (New York: St. Martin's Press, 1958), 376–93.

[55] Hughes & Larkin (eds.), *Tudor Royal Proclamations*, 236. "[S]o her Majesty doth notify and signify by these presents that if any of her subjects shall seditiously or contemptuously presume to call in question the power or validity of her prerogative royal annexed to her imperial crown in such causes; all such persons so offending shall receive severe punishment according to their demerits." Ibid., 237. In the previous Parliament, Elizabeth's language had been more conciliatory, but less had been conceded: "Her Majesty ... hoped that her dutiful and loving subjects would not take away her prerogative – which is the chiefest flower in her garland and the principal and head pearl in her crown and diadem – but that they will rather leave that to her disposition .... [T]hey shall all be examined to abide the trial and true touchstone of the law." Neale, *Elizabeth I and her Parliaments*, 355. Privy Council letter: John Roche Dascent (ed.), *Acts of the Privy Council of England*, Vol. 32 (London: Her Majesty's Stationery Office, 1907), available at British History Online, www.british-history.ac.uk/acts-privy-council/vol32/pp226-250 (last accessed June 23, 2020), 237 (October 7, 1601).

[56] James F. Larkin and Paul L. Hughes (eds.), *Stuart Royal Proclamations of James I* (Oxford: Oxford University Press, 1973), 1–6, 11–14; see also Kyle, "But a New Button," 205; Dascent (ed.), *Acts of the*

James also acted quickly to ensure administrative continuity from Elizabeth's reign, a goal that he furthered through the elevation of Robert Cecil to the peerage, as the Earl of Salisbury. Cecil/Salisbury would serve as James' principal secretary, overseeing his administration, leading his privy council, and serving him in the House of Lords, until his death in 1612.[57]

Exactly one month after James' proclamation regarding monopolies was issued, the king-in-council proceeded to review their first patent: a patent issued by Elizabeth to Thomas Brigham and Humphrey Wemes "for the pre-emption of tin." Shortly thereafter, James issued a *Proclamation concerning the Patents for Tin*, which declared as follows:

> We, after long debate thereof before our self and our Privy Council, where objections of either side were made, and where the inconveniences were laid open, have resolved not only to consider how the generality of our subjects might be relieved in suspension of this grant, but how the same might be done without any injustice to any particular person, who is interested therein by virtue of Letters Patents under the Great Seal of England, whereof we never intend to seek any course of revocation, but by an ordinary course of justice, in which all our people are equally interested. In which respect having commanded the Lords and others of our Privy Council to call before them the patentees, and then to offer them all such trial for the maintenance of that patent, as the justice of this our realm affordeth, the said patentees have rather yielded in their own duty and discretion, to surrender the patent, than to go about to maintain it.

Offered the option of a trial, in other words, the patentees chose to surrender the patent.[58]

The story of the tin patent did not end with its surrender, however. The following year it was reissued, by order of the privy council, to the same patentees. In November 1606, the Lord Treasurer Dorset noted certain "points to be considered, in the question of the King's right to the preemption and exportation of tin," which had been challenged by Richard Glover and the London Pewterers' Company. On November 14, 1606, the Star Chamber issued a decree upholding the patent, against Glover and the Pewterers, "for endeavoring to frustrate a patent

Privy Council, Vol. 32, 497 (May 4, 1603) (naming a special commission "to take knowledge and consider of all monopolies and grants that are offensive to the subjects of this land, and to informe his Majestie of the same, that such order may be taken for the calling in of those that are greivous and burdensome to the subject as his Majestie in his princely wisedom shall thinke fitt and convenient").

57 Larkin & Hughes (eds.), *Stuart Royal Proclamations*, "A Proclamation signifying his Majesty's pleasure, that all men being in Office of Government at the death of the late Queen Elizabeth, should so continue till his Majesty's further direction," 4–6 (April 1, 1603); Smith, *Emergence of a Nation State*, 226–8; Alan G. R. Smith, "Secretariats of the Cecils, circa 1580–1612," *The English Historical Review* 83(328): 481–504 (1968).

58 Mary Anne Everett Green (ed.), *Calendar of State Papers Domestic: James I, 1603–1610* (London: Her Majesty's Stationery Office, 1857), *available at* www.british-history.ac.uk/cal-state-papers/domestic/jas1/1603-10/pp13-26 (last accessed June 24, 2020), 13 (June 7, 1603); Larkin & Hughes (eds.), *Stuart Royal Proclamations*, 29 (June 16, 1603).

granted to Thomas Brigham and Humphrey Wemes for preemption of tin in Cornwall and Devon." Pursuant to this decree, Glover and the Pewterers were ordered to be imprisoned, fined, and to publicly confess their guilt to the privy council.[59]

The problem of monopoly patents and licenses, it turned out, was inseparable from the crown's broader, fiscal problems. Despite an apparently genuine intention to address the grievances that these patents brought to his subjects, James desperately needed the revenue that they might provide. In many cases, moreover, it seems that the monopolies served regulatory purposes.[60]

In 1621, in a proclamation to repeal patents relating to inns, alehouses, and the manufacture of gold and silver thread, James declared that his intentions with his patents "were no other but the increase of profitable Arts and Inventions, the repressing of vice and disorder, and reformation of sundry enormities and abuses." Shortly thereafter James issued a much broader proclamation, including the promise that all subjects grieved or injured by a lengthy list of patents "may take their remedy . . . by the Common Laws of the realm, or other ordinary course of justice."[61]

The grievances of James' subjects, provoked partly by his patents and more generally by the conditions of economic stress connected with the European wars over religiously inflected politics, had been widely discussed in the first session of the 1621 Parliament, which met from January to June. By March, Sir Edward Coke had drafted a bill to address the issue. The bill referenced James' "Book of Bounty" (1610), which was essentially a proclamation declaring monopolies to be "things contrary to our lawes." Drawing on this legal support, Coke's bill proceeded to "declare and enact" that all grants of monopoly were "utterly void" and should be tried "by the laws of this realm in the King's courts of record"; the bill also prescribed treble damages and double costs against anyone who would attempt to exercise the monopolies prohibited by the act. Strikingly, the bill provided for a further penalty against anyone attempting to exercise the prohibited monopolies: *praemunire*. This

59 Larkin & Hughes (eds.), *Stuart Royal Proclamations*, 29, 352–4; Green (ed.), Calendar of State Papers Domestic: James I, 1603–1610, *available at* www.british-history.ac.uk/cal-state-papers/domestic/jas1/1603-10/pp328336 (last accessed June 24, 2020), 334–5 (November 1606).

60 David L. Smith, *The Stuart Parliaments* (London: Arnold Publishers, 1999), 47–56, 101–13; Larkin & Hughes (eds.), *Stuart Royal Proclamations*, 29 n.2 (tin); 163–6, 188–92, 224–7, 237–41, 250–3, 473–5 (starch); 182–4 (transportation of leather); 224–7, 319–22, 380–4 (alum); 233–6 (pepper); 293–5 (French wines); 300–2, 312–14, 327–9, 371–3 (cloth); 287–90, 308–10 (farthing tokens); 342–3, 464–6 (glass); 365–9 (wool); 384–89, 441–6 (gold and silver thread); 393–5 (peddling); 401–1 (manufacture of pins); 409–13 (ale-houses); 446–9, 457–60, 478–84 (tobacco); 470–2 (glossing of "new drapery" cloths); 490–3 (apothecaries). Regulatory purposes: Larkin & Hughes (eds.), *Stuart Royal Proclamations*, 446–9, 457–60, 478–84 (tobacco); 490–3 (apothecaries); see also Dent, "Patent Policy," 89–93.

61 Larkin & Hughes (eds.), *Stuart Royal Proclamations*, 503–5 (March 30, 1621); ibid., 511–19 (July 10, 1621) (A proclamation declaring His Majesty's grace to his subjects, touching matters complained of, as public grievances).

was, in effect, a form of legal outlawry, a threat of legalized murder and wholesale expropriation, analogous to the proscriptions that killed Cicero.[62]

This bill was debated in the Parliaments of 1621 and 1624, and in the course of the debates, particularly in conference with the House of Lords, a number of provisos were added in an attempt to delineate the difference between an illegal "monopoly" and a legal, trade-related patent or charter. The final result was the Statute of Monopolies.[63]

The goal of the Statute of Monopolies was to articulate the legal boundaries of the prerogative power to issue trade-related patents and charters, boundaries which Coke considered to be determined (and determinable) by common law and Parliament. During the debate, some had suggested defining the word "monopoly," since "the etymology of the word may be larger than the true definition or civil description of the thing." However, Coke successfully resisted such efforts, while at the same time compromising on the insertion of specific provisos.[64]

First among the provisos was the exception for new inventions: "any Patent and Grant of Privilege … of the sole working or making of any manner of new Manufacture within this Realm, to the first and true Inventor or Inventors of such Manufactures." The terms of such patents and grants of privilege were explicitly limited: twenty-one years (or under) for patents already granted, and fourteen years (or under) for future patents. These exceptions provided a clear statement of the belief, held certainly by Coke and apparently held by many of his contemporaries in Parliament and in the courts, that the common law sanctioned such patents as legitimate exercises of prerogative power.[65]

According to this belief, Parliament was only declaring in the Statute of Monopolies what had always been true under common law, while perhaps adding some clarity in delineating specific patent terms. Nevertheless, it remains true that this is the first statutory statement of the principle that patents for new inventions are legally permitted, and distinct from illegal "monopolies." It is thus the first canonical text in the British legal tradition pertaining to patents of new invention, and to the

62 Chris Dent, " 'Generally Inconvenient': The 1624 *Statute of Monopolies* as Political Compromise," *Melbourne University Law Review* 33: 415–53 (2009), 438; Elizabeth Read Foster, "The Procedure of the House of Commons against Patents and Monopolies, 1621–1624," in *Conflict in Stuart England: Essays in Honour of Wallace Notestein*, edited by William Appleton Aiken and Basil Duke Henning (New York: New York University Press, 1960), 59–85; Mark Kishlansky, *A Monarchy Transformed: Britain 1603–1714* (London: Penguin Books, 1996), 88–111; Kyle, "But a new button," 205–7; Smith, *Stuart Parliaments*, 109–10; White, *Sir Edward Coke*, 86–141, esp. 128–9. The Book of Bounty: Fox, *Monopolies*, 330–5 (Appendix VII); Robert Steele (ed.), *A Bibliography of Royal Proclamations of the Tudor and Stuart Sovereigns*, Vol. I (Oxford: Clarendon Press, 1910), 130.

63 An Act Concerning Monopolies and Dispensations with Penall Lawes and the Forfeyture Thereof, 21 Jac. I c. 3, 4 Stat. 1212 (1624); White, *Sir Edward Coke*, 128–35; Kyle, "But a new button," 207–16.

64 White, *Sir Edward Coke*, 115–35, esp. 133; see also Sir Edward Coke, *The Institutes of the Laws of England*, Vol. III (London: Clarke and Sons, 1817), 181–5; Foster, "Procedure of the House," 76–7; *cf.* Kyle, "But a new button," 204, 211, 216–17.

65 4 Stat., 1213, §§ v–vi; Coke, *Institutes* III, 183–4; Fox, *Monopolies*, 125, Kyle, "But a new button," 206–16; White, *Sir Edward Coke*, 129–35.

later institutions of modern patents and intellectual property. Occupying this prime position in the British patent tradition, the Statute of Monopolies is also a canonical text in the patent traditions of Britain's colonies.[66]

8.5 PARLIAMENTARY SUPREMACY

The story of the English anti-monopoly tradition is also a story about the assertion of Parliament's share in supremacy and sovereignty. It is, accordingly, part of the story of Britain's constitutional development. Intellectual property law and modern constitutionalism emerged together in British legal history.[67]

The anti-monopoly tradition, as we have seen, emerged from the common lawyers and from Parliament, but it was narrowly targeted to the declaration of limits on the exercise of royal prerogative. However, during the long series of political events now identified with the English Reformation, an important development took place in the legal traditions pertaining to patents and copyrights: these came to be rooted statutes that positively asserted proprietary status. The foundational stage of this line of development leads through the Glorious Revolution (1688–89) to the Statute of Anne (1710).[68]

During the "Long Parliament" – which began in 1640 and formally continued through the "Interregnum" to 1660 – Parliament took over the prerogative tradition pertaining to printing, continuing the basic framework for censorship and regulation that had strengthened the Stationers Company's exclusive rights in printing and publishing. However, Parliament made two important changes to the regulatory framework: (1) they substituted themselves, as overseers of the regulatory regime, for the privy council and prerogative courts (the "High Commissioners in Causes Ecclesiastical" and the Star Chamber), and (2) they introduced the justices of the peace, as well as other secular officials, into the framework for enforcement, as a support to the Stationers Company's own deputies, who continued to serve as the primary enforcers.[69]

66 Dent, "Generally Inconvenient," 415–17 (discussing the significance of the Statute of Monopolies for Australian patent law); Foster, "Procedure of the House," 76–7; Kyle, "A New Button," 203.

67 Charles Howard McIlwain, *Constitutionalism: Ancient and Modern*, 2nd ed. (Ithaca: Cornell University Press, 1958), 127–8 (the Statute of Monopolies is "the first statutory invasion of the royal prerogative"); Foster, "Procedure of the House," 76–7; F. W. Maitland, *The Constitutional History of England* (Cambridge, UK: Cambridge University Press, 1908), 260–1; Smith, *Emergence of a Nation State*, 402 (the Statute of Monopolies is "the first important statutory limitation on the royal prerogative during the seventeenth century").

68 An Act for the Encouragement of Learning by Vesting the Copies of Printed Books in the Authors or Purchasers of such Copies during the Times therein mentioned, 8 Anne, c. 21, 9 Stat. 256 (1710).

69 C. H. Firth and R. S. Rait (eds.) *Acts and Ordinances of the Interregnum, 1642–1660* (London: His Majesty's Stationery Office, 1911), "An Ordinance for the Regulation of Printing," 184–7 (June 14, 1643) (*The 1643 Ordinance*); ibid., "An Act against Unlicensed and Scandalous Books and Pamphlets, and for Better Regulating of Printing," 245–54 (September 1649) (*The 1649 Ordinance*). Scholars often refer to individual "Parliaments" between 1640 and 1660 using separate names (e.g., "Barebone's Parliament"). Smith, *Emergence of a Nation State*, at 233–4, 305–8. However, in lumping these

Most significantly, Parliament began referring to the Stationers Company members as "*Owners* of the Copies" of books registered in their names in the registry books of the company. Since the preceding regulatory framework under a 1637 Star Chamber decree did not use the language of "ownership" when referring to the members of the Stationers Company registered as rightful printers of the copy, we can pinpoint the shift in legal language – from the language of registered licensing to the language of "ownership" – to this precise moment in time: 1637–43. At the same time, we see in 1637 and 1649 the first regulatory discussions of the "mark" of the Stationers Company, in prohibitions against "counterfeiting" the "name, title, marke or vinnet" of the company.[70]

So Parliament was in some ways continuing the framework in place since the Tudors, while it was in other ways introducing changes. For our purposes, the most important continuity relates to the Stationers Company: excepting the universities of Oxford and Cambridge, the king's printer(s), and any independent holders of printing patents, the Stationers Company remained the sole authorized printer in England, and the primary enforcer of this privileged status. Most significantly, the Stationers Company's registry books remained the sole record of licenses to print: they indicated which individuals were the holders of copyrights. From a semantic perspective, the most dramatic change introduced by Parliament was the legal description of these copyright holders as "owners."[71]

According to Stephen D. White, a decisive shift in Parliament's conception of its constitutional role and relationship to the monarchy occurred in the 1620s. In the Parliaments of 1625 and 1628, leaders in the House of Commons (prominent among them Edward Coke) began to lose confidence in the monarchy; they increasingly believed that more explicit recognition of Parliament's privileged role in protecting the rights of citizens and the common good would be required if such rights and the common good were to be preserved at all. The rights of property were particularly emphasized: Parliament began to conceive of itself as the primary guardian of citizens' rights, especially their property rights and personal liberties.[72]

Parliamentary speeches, bills, and negotiations with the king began to focus also on the establishment of Parliament's constitutional privileges and roles. Crucially, these privileges and roles were not presented as new; they were rather presented as

Parliaments together under one name, I am following the Long Parliament's own statutory prescription, and the example of Thomas Hobbes. Act against dissolving the Long Parliament without its own assent, 17 Charles I, c. 7 (1641); Thomas Hobbes, *Behemoth, or The Long Parliament* (1889); see also Maitland, *Constitutional History*, 293.

70 Firth & Rait (eds.), *The 1649 Ordinance*, 250; ibid., *The 1643 Ordinance*, 185; Lyman Ray Patterson, *Copyright in Historical Perspective* (Nashville: Vanderbilt University Press, 1968), 126–34.

71 Firth & Rait (eds.), *The 1643 Ordinance*, 184–7; ibid., *The 1649 Ordinance*, 245–54.

72 White, *Sir Edward Coke*, 187–274; see also Smith, *Stuart Parliaments*, 111–20, 229 (quoting a 1628 resolution of the House of Commons: "the ancient and undoubted right of every free man is that he hath a full and absolute property in his goods and estate, and that no tax, tallage, loan, benevolence, or other like charge ought to be commanded or levied by the King, or any of his minister [sic], without common assent by act of Parliament.").

having been established and continued through ancient precedents, traceable ultimately to the Great Charter (*Magna Carta*) of 1215. However, even when both sides conceded these precedents, the question of their legal interpretation remained. For Parliament, especially the Commons, it became increasingly important to establish that these privileges could not be retracted, that they existed as a matter of ancient "rights," vested in Parliament, independent from and of equal weight with the royal prerogative.[73]

The men who acted in Parliament at this time were predominantly members of the "landed gentry": owners of real property throughout the "shires" and "boroughs" of England, and extending into Ireland, Scotland, and Wales. Their rise to power since Henry VIII's supremacy had constituted one of the "seismic" social shifts of the preceding century: one made possible by the massive redistributions of land connected with Henry's expropriation of church property. Their political and ecclesiastical authority had been decisively elevated through their legislative support of the Reformation, and their economic position depended on the continuing stability of that Reformation. Parliament was, in other words, heavily invested in the Tudor Reformation, even if it was beginning to undermine the prerogative supremacy that had lent the support of legal power to that Reformation.[74]

As Parliament met, warfare between Catholic and Protestant rulers was devastating Continental Europe, and it was perceived as an imminent threat at home. To make matters worse, Archbishop William Laud (1573–1645) – a man whose religious views were seen as "Arminian" and therefore as doctrinally threatening – was undertaking a comprehensive reform of the church's episcopal organization, seeking to strengthen the administrative authority of bishops. Laud was among the most influential members of the privy council and a primary advisor to King Charles I (1625–49). These were the circumstances under which Scotland revolted against its Scottish king, and Parliament began its slide into military dictatorship.[75]

With this as background, we can better understand the changes introduced by the Long Parliament into the framework for regulation of printing and publishing. Parliament was substituting itself for the monarchy, and for the ecclesiastical powers under the royal supremacy. At the same time, Parliament was rhetorically elevating the legal position of copyright holders. In its position as guardian of the rights of citizens, particularly their property rights, Parliament was elevating the Stationers' copyrights from (1) temporary privileges vested by operation of the royal prerogative to (2) property recognized as such by Parliamentary act.

73 White, *Sir Edward Coke*, 187–274.

74 Smith, *Stuart Parliaments*, 19–31.

75 Caroline Hibbard, *Charles I and the Popish Plot* (Chapel Hill: University of North Carolina Press, 1983); Conrad Russell, *The Causes of the English Civil War* (Oxford: Clarendon Press, 1990); Smith, *Emergence of a Nation State*, 284–86, 296–302; Smith, *Stuart Parliaments*, 111–20.

This rhetorical elevation of copyrights to the status of property continued after the Restoration under Charles II (1660–85). In 1662, Charles II, with the advice and consent of Parliament, imposed restrictions on printing through the Licensing Act of 1662: an "Act for preventing the frequent Abuses in printing seditious and unlicensed Bookes and Pamphlets and for Regulating of Printing and Printing Presses." This licensing act returned in many ways to the framework established by the 1637 Star Chamber decree. Ecclesiastical officers once again took their place as the primary licensors of printing and as overseers of the Stationers Company. *Nevertheless, the proprietary language of copyright introduced during the Long Parliament remained:* the act prohibited the printing or importing of any copy, with respect to which another had a right by virtue of a patent or an entry in the Stationers Company registry books, without the consent of the "Owner or Owners Proprietor or Proprietors of such Copy." Here we see the entry in the Stationers Company registry books placed on parity with a printing patent, and the rights established by either method being referred to in the language of ownership.[76]

With the Statute of Anne (1710), the transition to a statute-based, proprietary concept of copyright was nearly complete: the act explicitly declared its intention to "secure" to the "Proprietor" the "Property in every such Book" addressed by the act. The "Proprietor" whose security was provided for under the act might be an author, or he might be the purchaser of the copyright from the author. The act declared that copyrights are "vested" first in the authors of books, and only secondarily in purchasers (i.e., printers and booksellers). Here, as scholars have noted, is the beginning of *authorial* copyright.[77]

Nevertheless, an important question might still be posed, and was posed by the Stationers Company: might not the Statute of Anne merely "secure" copyrights that already existed by virtue of another source of law, operating alongside statutory law, such as the common law or natural law? Or did the Statute of Anne provide the statutory basis for the right itself? If this latter view were the correct one, copyright was strictly a creature of statute: pursuant to the statute, some kind of proprietary right was born with the act of authorship, but it died at the end of twenty-eight years, the birth and death occurring by operation of the statute.[78]

In the next chapter, we will see this question answered, on the eve of the American Revolution.

[76] 14 Char. II, c. 33, 5 Stat. 428 (1662), §§2, 5. The act also continued the prohibition against counterfeiting the "mark" of a licensed printer, along with the use of the justices of the peace as a supplement to the enforcement powers of the Stationers Company. Ibid., §§ 6, 13.

[77] Act for the Encouragement of Learning by Vesting the Copies of Printed Books in the Authors or Purchasors of such Copies during the Times therein mentioned. 8 Anne, c. 21, 9 Stat. 256 (1710), §§ 1, 2; see also Ronan Deazley, *On the Origin of the Right to Copy: Charting the Movement of Copyright Law in Eighteenth-Century Britain* (1695–1775) (Oxford: Hart Publishing, 2004), 31–50; Patterson, *Copyright*, 143 ff.; Mark Rose, *Authors and Owners: The Invention of Copyright* (Cambridge, MA: Harvard University Press, 1993), 31–66.

[78] 8 Anne, c. 21 §§1, 11.

8.6 CONCLUSION

In this chapter, we have followed a long train of historical development, one leading from the issuance of *Magna Carta* under King John, through the institutional beginnings of the English Parliament in the Barons' Revolt, past the dramatic events of the English civil wars, to the legal establishment of ownership rights in literary works, under a revolutionary Reformation Parliament. In the process, to draw on Michael Mann's language, we have been tracing a development toward the modern, nation-state system, entwined with modern, industrial capitalism.[79]

With the rise of Parliament, combined with the Tudor Revolution in the English administrative state, law is becoming statutory and national: a uniform voice, speaking for the King-in-Parliament to the nation. A powerful illustration of the impacts this could have in transforming cultural ideals into social reality is visible in the Acts of Uniformity, enacted under the Parliaments of Edward VI (1547–53), Henry VIII's son. By operation of statutory law, a *Book of Common Prayer* was imposed on the English nation, a prescribed liturgy for religious services ranging from baptism at birth to prayers offered at death. Revising traditional Roman Catholic liturgies in accordance with the commitments of Thomas Cranmer and his fellow evangelicals, *The Book of Common Prayer* prescribed a language of solemn ritual and recitation that helped to bind the English people together, in their marriages and in their communions, becoming over time a cultural foundation for social and political life in the Anglo-American world.[80]

This cultural and liturgical framework was imposed by statutory law, in accordance with the king's prerogative power, combined with the new powers of England's widening political classes. As a compromise between Roman Catholicism and Protestantism, *The Book of Common Prayer* was highly controversial. Only with the passage of time has its language come to be beloved and familiar for a surprisingly wide cross section of the world's population touched by the legacies of Anglicanism.[81]

The English Reformation effected a national, legal separation of England from Rome. Monasteries were dissolved and a Court of Augmentations was created to redistribute their wealth. Statutes regularized the operation of English property law. While this law would retain some of its feudal aspects, it was nonetheless significantly reformed, in ways that enabled property transfers to become more uniform, alongside liturgical religious practice.[82]

79 Mann, *Sources* Vol. I, 397–517.

80 For example, 2 & 3 Edw. VI c. 1, 4 Stat. 37; Brian Cummings (ed.), *The Book of Common Prayer: The Texts of 1549, 1559, and 1662* (Oxford: Oxford University Press, 2011); Alan Jacobs, *The Book of Common Prayer: A Biography* (Princeton: Princeton University Press, 2013).

81 Jacobs, *Book of Common Prayer*, 45 ff.

82 Court of Augmentations: 27 Hen. VIII c. 27, 3 Stat. 569 (1535–6). Dissolution of the Monasteries: 27 Hen. VIII c. 28, 3 Stat. 569 (1535–6); An Act for Dissolution of Monasteries, 31 Hen. VIII c. 13, 3 Stat. 733 (1539). Regularizing property law: Act Governing Joint Tenancy, 31 Hen. VIII c. 1, 3 Stat. 718

It is this uniformity of property law that Michael Mann highlights as a decisive contribution to the emergence of modern, rational capitalism. In order for capitalism to work in the way that it does today, all (or at least most) forms of wealth must be exchangeable with one another, for the right price in money. Property, in Mann's terms, must be commodified. Before the English Reformation, real property law was primarily feudal and covenantal, limiting transferability. With the formal break from Rome, however, and with the assertion of the king's prerogative supremacy, statutory laws imposed increasing uniformity from above, with the increasingly vocal consent of a new political class that benefitted from a dramatic redistribution in the church's wealth. Parliament became a great protector and investor for the English common-wealth – a governing community overseeing increasingly mobile forms of property – binding together a political class of legally privileged persons who were committed, spiritually and materially, to the Reformation.[83]

The Statute of Monopolies, which became the foundation of Anglo-American patent law, was one outgrowth of these developments, as was the Parliamentary recognition that copyright holders were "owners" of their copy-rights. This language of ownership is part of the movement toward uniformity, a departure from the more feudal language of *tenure* and *seisin*, a departure that entails an embrace of abstract conceptions of property derived from Roman law. With this embrace of Roman law-based conceptions of property, there is a close semantic linkage with lordship and dominion. Nonetheless, with the rise of statutory laws governing property in increasingly uniform and standardizing ways, across a widening political "nation," lordship and dominion are being nationalized. In the process, lordship and dominion are also becoming more impersonal and abstract.

The most radical moment in England's break from traditional law came in the execution of its king, Charles I (1649). Ironically, part of the justification for this radical, anti-traditional act was a line of legal tradition, interpreted as establishing a fundamental law, stretching back to *Magna Carta* of 1215. When a king became a tyrant, threatening the Protestant commitments of the newly established church, he could rightfully be executed, in accordance with the covenantal, higher law that bound the English nation together.[84]

For Edward Coke, writing the second part of his *Institutes of the Lawes of England* only a few years before these dramatic events, *Magna Carta* was the touchstone and bedrock of English law, a higher authority than judgments from the king's courts, which themselves were the language of law, *Juris Dicta*. Together with the Charter of the Forest, *Magna Carta* had been upheld by Parliamentary legislation under Edward I, which in Coke's interpretation had made these charters into a supreme

(1539); Act Changing the Custom of Gavelkind, 31 Hen. VIII c. 3, 3 Stat. 719 (1539); An Act How Land May be Willed by Testament, 32 Hen. VIII c. 1 (1540) (and many more)

83 Mann, *Sources Vol. I*, 397–9.

84 T. B. Howell, *A Complete Collection of State Trials*, Vol. IV (London: Longman et al., 1816), 990 ff.

legal standard. Any legal judgment or Parliamentary statute at odds with the great charters "shall be undone, and holden for nought."[85]

With the passage of time, however, the language of *Magna Carta* had become increasingly removed from everyday life, and professional lawyers and judges had become its expert interpreters. Under such circumstances, Coke argued, "the resolutions of Judges in Courts of Justice" served for English law as the "glosses and Commentaries" of learned scholarship served for continental "Civill Law." Providing certainty of legal interpretation, such case law records were like "a trustworthy safe-harbor for the learned" (*Statio bene fida peritis*). Despite the security of legal certainty that such case law records might offer, however, Coke was direct about the supremacy of Parliamentary legislation. "The highest and most binding Laws are the Statutes which are established by Parliament."[86]

Coke's own writings served, over time, to help consolidate this statutory supremacy within the common law tradition. But Henry VIII's Reformation from above had been crucially important. In elevating the king's prerogative through a statutorily defined supremacy, King Henry, Thomas Cromwell (1485–1540), and the English Parliament had transformed the King-in-Parliament into an *imperium*, the Supreme Head of an Imperial Realm.

> "[B]y diverse and sundry old, authentic histories and chronicles it is manifestly declared and expressed that *this Realm of England is an Empire*, and so hath been accepted in the world, governed by one Supreme head having the dignity and royal estate of the imperial crown of the same, unto whom a body politic compact of all sorts and degrees of people, divided in terms and by names of Spirituality and Temporalty, have been bound and ordered to bear next to God a natural and humble obedience."[87]

In the context of the times, this *imperium* defined a legal and religious power that was independent from the pope. But in the course of history, it also helped to establish a new kind of legal formalism: one that Max Weber theorized in his sociological treatments of law and rulership (*Herrschaft*) as positive legality.[88]

Positive legality involves semantic and empirical formalities in law that are shorn of sacramentality. During the Middle Ages, sacramentality linked outward signs with inward transformations, empirical formality with semantic formality. Outward signs, performed by qualified persons, could both indicate and effectuate an inward transformation, a transformation of intentionality and character, of heart, mind, and soul. The real agent in this transformation was God, but priests provided a necessary mediation, enabling cooperation between God and human beings. Semantic

85 Steve Sheppard (ed.), *The Selected Writings of Sir Edward Coke*, Vol. II (Indianapolis: Liberty Fund, 2003), 746–54.

86 Ibid., 751–2.

87 Act Against Appeals, 24 Henry VIII c. 12 (1533). I have modernized the language, and added the emphasis.

88 Weber, *Economy and Society*, 36–8.

formality (formality of meaning), both in the realm of law and in the realm of religion, was mediated by priests, learned persons who had received special training enabling a higher and deeper understanding of God's laws.

But the Protestant Reformation broke with its priests, as it broke with its monks. There was now to be no human mediator between humans and their God, and the causal relation between sign and inward, intentional reality was reversed. Outward signs became performative displays of inward, spiritual realities. This is part of the story for our remaining chapters, as we turn to the impacts of Protestantism in the New World, and on the European Continent.

The Anglo-American tradition of intellectual property law is complicated. It reaches deeply into the past of royal prerogatives and privileges, a tradition that is indebted to the imperial culture of Roman law and the Christianized culture of feudal law, while stretching forward into a legal culture of positive, secular legality, a culture in which hopes for a future of national prosperity are sought in national legal protections for creative genius and inventive industry. A vital strand in these cultural traditions was the transcendently idealistic commitment to a higher, covenantal law that bound the soon-to-be British nation together, limiting the powers of government, and enabling the recognition of certain "inborn, natural rights," tracing their lineage to the Great Charter of English liberties.

With the rise of Parliament, combined with the royal supremacy effectuated by the Henrician Reformation, we have the foundation for a statutory power that could recognize new types of legal property, and render them part of English common law. And we have a nationalizing sense that the securing of wealth is a foundational goal, one that will ensure peace and stability for the good of a national community.

In the next chapter, we will see how these developments spread to the American colonies of the New World. And we will see how the Christianizing of legal power, which was a legacy of the feudal transformation, carried over into a new culture of Christian liberalism, which is still with us today. The arguments for intellectual property, as a "right" under principles of natural law, are a legacy of these developments, to which we now turn.

9

Cultural Transformations

Naturalizing Intellectual Property

The Congress shall have the Power ... To promote the Progress of Science and useful Arts, by securing for limited Times to Authors and Inventors the exclusive Right to their respective Writings and Discoveries.

– *US Constitution, Article I, Section 8, Clause 8* (1787)

On November 9, 1787, a young attorney named James Kent wrote a letter to Nathaniel Lawrence, delegate to the New York convention debating ratification of a proposed US Constitution. Kent later became the first professor of law at Columbia University, attaining prominence as a New York jurist and early theorist of US law. At this time, however, he wrote as a young, practicing attorney. He disagreed with Lawrence about the constitution's potential to foster "aristocracy" in the United States. Seeking to persuade his friend that the constitution would not foster aristocracy, Kent closed his letter by inquiring about Lawrence's professional success, and by mentioning that he had just finished reading Adam Smith's new book *The Wealth of Nations* (1776). Kent wrote of Smith: he "has taught me to look with an unfavorable eye on monopolies – But a monopoly of the mental kind I take to be laudable & an exception to the Rule."[1]

Between 1787 and 1788, Americans engaged in a vigorous debate about the proper form of governance for a new political community. They could have remained a confederation, as they had been since the revolutionary break with Great Britain in 1776. That they should remain more loosely confederated, with fewer powers granted to a central (national) government, was a principled conviction of many "Anti-Federalist" resisters to ratification. Public endorsement of the 1787 constitution was by no means assured. The constitution's advocates nearly abandoned hope

[1] John P. Kaminski, et al. (eds.), *Documentary History of the Ratification of the Constitution*, Vol. XIX (Madison: Wisconsin Historical Society Press, 2003), 245–7. The reference here is oblique and jesting, but the joke seems to refer to something like intellectual property. *Cf.* Dotan Oliar, "Making Sense of the Intellectual Property Clause: Promotion of Progress as a Limitation on Congress's Intellectual Property Power," *Georgetown Law Journal* 94 (2006): 1771–1847, 1803 n. 164.

at various points over the summer of 1787, and during the contentious ratification process.[2]

Nevertheless, the constitution was ratified in 1788, and, ever since, has defined a "supreme law" for the United States of America. This supreme law explicitly enables a legal framework for the granting of patents and copyrights by a national legislature, and Congress acted promptly (in 1790) to give legislative specification to this framework. Trademarks came later in the nineteenth century, justified ultimately under the commerce clause, rather than the "intellectual property clause." Nonetheless, since 1790, intellectual property has been part of a national legal framework for the United States of America.[3]

In this chapter, I argue that the formation of intellectual property in the United States was enabled by a cultural transformation, *natural legality*, a transformation that parallels, in significant respects, the Christianization of imperial Rome. In this cultural transformation, traditions of Roman law were rediscovered as a naturalistic foundation for sociability and national economic life. The commodification of human creativity and inventive discovery, through "mental monopolies" (as Kent described them), made sense, within the culture of natural legality, as a justified response to natural, but extraordinary, powers of human creativity, and became part of a broader strategy for national empowerment. Adam Smith's "invisible hand," ordering society and economy in accordance with natural human propensities, can be seen as an archetypal expression of this naturalizing transformation, one that helped to launch the modern discipline of economics, and that is strangely influential in contemporary sociological theory.[4]

Adam Smith (1723–90), we should recall, was a scholar of moral philosophy and jurisprudence. And he offered his theory of natural sociability as a theory of moral and legal obligation. Smith drew on natural law theories developed in the Protestant Reformation, which took exceptionally influential forms in the liberal theories of John Locke (1632–1704). Smith also developed his arguments in dialog with his friend David Hume (1711–76), a proponent of "natural religion." In all three of these

[2] For a narrative of the ratification process, one that identifies this as the beginning of American national politics, see Pauline Maier, *Ratification: The People Debate the Constitution, 1787–1788* (New York: Simon and Schuster, 2010). I also rely throughout this chapter on the multi-volume *Documentary History of the Ratification of the Constitution*, abbreviated hereafter as *Documentary History*, edited by Merrill Jensen, John Kaminski, and others, published by the State Historical Society of Wisconsin.

[3] US Constitution Art. VI: Congressional Research Service, *Constitution of the United States: Analysis and Interpretation* (hereafter *CRS, Constitution Annotated*), https://constitution.congress.gov/browse/article-6/ (accessed May 31, 2020). Constitutional enablement of national intellectual property law: US Constitution Art. I §8 Clause 8. Federal legislation creating first US national frameworks for patent and copyright law: An Act to Promote the Progress of Useful Arts, 1 Stat. 109 (April 10, 1790); An act for the encouragement of learning, 1 Stat. 124 (May 31, 1790).

[4] Adam Smith, *The Wealth of Nations* (New York: The Modern Library, 2000), 485. For Smith's influence on sociological theory, by way of pragmatist philosophy, see Lewis A. Coser, *Masters of Sociological Thought: Ideas in Historical and Social Context*, 2nd ed. (Long Grove, IL: Waveland Press, 2003), 350–1.

writers, frameworks of natural law, with roots ultimately in Roman law and Hellenistic culture, became a universal foundation for principles of law and justice, which could be treated as primary foundations for human sociability. Natural legality could replace Biblical and ecclesiastical legality, providing a foundation for moral and legal obligation posited in human nature, rather than divine teaching. And "spiritual" powers, seen in human creativity and invention, could become natural objects for appropriation.[5]

In this chapter, we focus on the ways that this naturalizing and commodifying cultural transformation enabled the recognition of intellectual property as a new type of legal property. We first trace the emergence of the new, natural legality, focusing on contributions from Roman law and liberal Christianity. The combination of Roman law with interpretations of Christian obligation that emphasized natural sociability and legality gave new form to a natural rights tradition, one that became politically powerful in Anglo-American revolutionary contexts. Early forms of intellectual property, particularly copyrights, became part of this broader tradition. In the writings of William Blackstone (1723–80) and Samuel Stanhope Smith (1751–1819) – an influential US moral philosopher and president of the college that became Princeton University – John Locke's synthesis of Roman law and liberal Christianity became an explicit, natural law foundation for intellectual property-related rights.[6]

We will center our attention on the famous cases of *Millar* v. *Taylor* and *Donaldson* v. *Becket*, decided in England just before the US war for independence. These cases, in combination, solidified the legal foundation for copyrights under British law, a foundation that extended by analogy also to patents. The reasoning of these two cases, especially the argument by Lord Mansfield in *Millar* v. *Taylor*, reveals the revolutionary significance of natural legality, with its optimistic faith in natural human powers of reason and will to order societies beneficently, a cultural orientation that hovers ambivalently between an ethics of moral absolutes in matters

[5] John Locke, *An Essay Concerning Human Understanding*, edited by Peter H. Nidditch (Oxford: Clarendon Press, 1975), 348–62; Adam Smith, *Lectures on Jurisprudence*, edited by R. L. Meek, D. D. Raphael, and P. G. Stein (Indianapolis: Liberty Fund, 1978); Adam Smith, *The Theory of Moral Sentiments*, edited by D. D. Raphael and A. L. Macfie (Indianapolis: Liberty Fund, 1976); also Knud Haakonssen, *The Science of a Legislator: The Natural Jurisprudence of David Hume and Adam Smith* (Cambridge, UK: Cambridge University Press, 1981); idem, *Natural Law and Moral Philosophy: From Grotius to the Scottish Enlightenment* (Cambridge, UK: Cambridge University Press, 1996); Albion Small, *Adam Smith and Modern Sociology* (Chicago: University of Chicago Press, 1907); Luigi Turco, "Moral Sense and the Foundations of Morals," in Alexander Broadie (ed.), *The Cambridge Companion to The Scottish Enlightenment* (Cambridge, UK: Cambridge University Press, 2003), 136–56.

[6] Samuel Stanhope Smith, *The Lectures, Corrected and Improved, which Have Been Delivered for a Series of Years, in the College of New Jersey, on the Subjects of Moral and Political Philosophy*, Vol. II (Trenton: Daniel Fenton, 1812), 189–200; Noah Webster, "Origin of the Copyright Laws in the United States," in *A Collection of Papers on Political, Literary, and Moral Subjects by Noah Webster* (New York: Webster & Clark, 1843), 173–74.

of right and an ethics of consequentialism, between semantic formality and substantive rationality.[7]

Finally, in the drafting and ratifying of the US Constitution, we will identify the sources of social power that have given organizational form to these cultural developments. We will see that men with legal training – jurists – played significant roles both in drafting and in defending the US Constitution, including its "intellectual property clause." James Madison (1751–1836), architect of both the intellectual property clause and the first US patent office, was a graduate of the college that Samuel Stanhope Smith helped to establish. Like Madison, the drafters and early defenders of the US Constitution largely shared the new cultural orientation, the optimistic belief that natural human capacities, harnessed through reason and well-designed legal incentives, can provide the social basis for a powerful and beneficent national state.[8]

In the American Revolution, liberalism and natural legality became vital elements in a constitutional framework and a national economy. In our well-designed constitutional framework, Americans have believed, tendencies toward unequal social ordering ("aristocracy") can be corrected by a paradigm for political and social governance that is wisely adapted to naturalistic structures of human freedom and equality. Rights to intellectual property, deservedly allocated to creators and inventors, are an intrinsic part of this constitutional framework, vital incentives in the paradigm for a powerful, yet good, national state.

9.1 THE NEW NATURALISM

The culture of natural rights draws strength from legal and religious traditions, in combination. It is an order of obligation, one that has been revolutionary in the modern west, and that today spreads its revolutionary fingers around the world. Paradoxically, it is an order of obligation that purports to free all social obligations from traditionalism and oppression, and, at the extreme, to eliminate the oppressiveness of obligation altogether. To understand this paradoxical order of obligation in its early form, as seen in Britain, we begin with the writings of John Locke and his friend John Tillotson (1630–94), archbishop of Canterbury from 1691 to 1694.[9]

John Locke's well-known arguments for property in a "state of nature" are found in the second of his *Two Treatises on Government*, first published anonymously in 1689. In his *Second Treatise*, Locke articulated his famous theory of a "social compact," by

7 *Millar* v. *Taylor*, 2 Brown 129, 1 Eng. Rep. 837; 4 Burrow 2408, 98 Eng. Rep. 201 (King's Bench 1769); *Donaldson* v. *Becket*, 98 Eng. Rep. 257; 1 Eng. Rep. 837; William Cobbett's *Parliamentary History of England*, Vol. XVII (London: T. C. Hansard, 1813), 953–1003.

8 Ralph Ketcham, *James Madison* (Charlottesville: University Press of Virginia, 1990), 25–50; Mark A. Noll, *Princeton and the Republic, 1768–1822* (Vancouver: Regent College Publishing, 1989), 32, 62, 69–72.

9 Isabel Rivers, "John Tillotson," in *The Oxford Dictionary of National Biography*, Online Edition (Oxford: Oxford University Press, 2004).

which people give up some of the freedom they possess in a state of nature, in order to form a community, which he alternatively called a *commonwealth*, or a *civil/political society*. The reason people consent to sacrifice some of their freedom, in civil society, is to achieve a greater level of security and personal agency, capacities that Locke associated with property. However, the very existence of property was something that Locke needed to explain, given his starting premise that God gave the earth to human beings in common.[10]

Locke's argument for the existence of property, under a natural law that governs the state of nature, is essentially the argument we have already encountered in Roman law, the argument from occupation, with emphasis on the role that labor plays in establishing a right to property. That in which we invest our labor and industry, so long as it does not already belong to someone else, becomes ours in virtue of the fact that we own ourselves. We have the capacity to extend that ownership by devoting an aspect of ourselves – our labor – in possessing and improving something. In a state of nature, this capacity is naturally limited, so that logically there is no worry about one person (or one group of people) acquiring too much. In a state of civil society, however, the social conventions enabling the existence of money also enable the economic and political aggrandizement of some at the expense of others. Positive laws created through legislation, so long as they are enacted with political consent, legitimately set limits to such aggrandizement, setting boundaries on the power of property through political power. But the laws of nature continue to operate in the background, setting limits on the legitimacy of political power, and undergirding a right to use lethal violence in self-defense, both in protection of personal freedom and property.[11]

This argument is almost numbingly familiar, but it can be read anew when we remind ourselves that Locke founded it upon an explicitly *theological* tradition of natural law. This is evident from Locke's reliance on the "judicious" Richard Hooker (1554–1600), whom he cites at crucial junctures in his argument, and from his Biblical citations. When we read Locke from this angle, we realize that he was universalizing, as "natural," a tradition shaped by Roman and Biblical law, a tradition that had previously been referenced as explicitly Christian and ecclesiastical. Scarred by the traumatic experiences of religiously justified civil war, Locke and his generation were seeking sources of social stability, peace, and tolerance in naturalistic interpretations of Christian legal traditions, which they offered as principles for moral obligation in social harmony, according to universal reason.[12]

Richard Hooker's *Laws of Ecclesiastical Polity* (published partly posthumously in separate books between 1593 and 1662) had offered a theology of law for the church of England, first under the Elizabethan settlement and then at crucial moments of

[10] John Locke, *Two Treatises of Government*, edited by Peter Laslett (Cambridge, UK: Cambridge University Press, 1988),269–78, 285–302.

[11] Ibid., 269–349 (Second Treatise, Chs. 2–8).

[12] Ibid., 270, 277–8 (§§ 5, 15).

re-settlement, in 1648 and 1662. It was essentially Hooker's framework of natural law that offered a legitimizing background for John Locke's liberal principles of national government in inter-national society, as seen in the *Second Treatise of Government*. In Hooker's debates with Puritan theologians, Locke found a framework for normative egalitarianism, from which he could launch his liberal political theory.[13]

Scholars have noted that Locke's published works do not actually articulate a theory of natural law, although they do depend on natural law-based arguments. Many years before his *Two Treatises on Government* were published, Locke had written a series of essays on natural law, but these were not published until the mid-twentieth century, when they were rediscovered among his papers. These early essays were written in the early 1660s, in the context of the Stuart Restoration, the period in which Charles II (1660–85, son of the beheaded Charles I) returned to England to reestablish monarchical rule, and to return the nation to the time of its discipline under the church of England. These early essays have been shown to be significant, not only for the *Two Treatises on Government*, but also for Locke's *Essay on Understanding* (1689), his philosophical dissertation about how knowledge is naturalistically generated within the human mind.[14]

In his early essays on natural law, Locke confronted fundamental questions that he later avoided in his *Second Treatise of Government*, questions about *how* law obligates us. Indeed, he offered a theory of obligation, one that addressed the binding force of divine laws, as well as human laws, and that rooted all human obligation ultimately in God. Divine laws, according to Locke, are the ultimate basis of moral obligation, and they are known in one of two ways: either through revelation in Biblical law (divine positive law), which we may come to know through trust in tradition and social teaching, or through natural sensory powers combined with human reason (divine natural law). All laws are founded ultimately on these divine laws, which alone are intrinsically binding, and which stand behind all human, "civil" laws. Divine law therefore binds us in multiple ways: (1) through a ruler's power and authority, which is founded upon divine law by right of divine gift, (2) through our human societies protecting natural law-based rights to property, which are also founded upon divine law, and (3) through our conscience and reason, which are the only sources of moral obligation not ultimately founded upon fear.[15]

Beyond the important influence of Hooker, evident in Locke's early essays as well as his later, published work, Locke's conception of legal and moral obligation was informed by the teachings of Robert Sanderson, bishop of Lincoln from 1660–63 and previously a professor of theology at Oxford. Sanderson had delivered a series of

[13] Richard Hooker, *Of the Laws of Ecclesiastical Polity: A Critical Edition with Modern Spelling*, edited by Arthur Stephen McGrade (Oxford: Oxford University Press, 2013), I:xv–cv, 42–102 and passim.

[14] Peter Laslett, "Introduction," in Locke, *Two Treatises*, 79–92; John Locke, *Essays on the Law of Nature and Associated Writings*, 2nd ed., edited by W. von Leyden (Oxford: Oxford University Press, 1988), 1–7, 10–11, 60–82.

[15] Locke, *Law of Nature*, 181–89 and passim.

lectures on oaths and promises that relied on concepts of legal obligation derived from Justinian's *Corpus Iuris Civilis*, extending them into principles of natural law. Locke's early essays also show influences from Christian-Platonist theories of natural law, which had been developed in Protestant directions by the Cambridge scholar Nathaniel Culverwell (1619–51), author of a posthumously published treatise on the "Light of Nature" (1652), which argued for a divinely illuminated, intellectual source of legal and moral obligations in human mental powers. Locke was also influenced by Samuel von Pufendorf (1632–94), a jurist who had recently (1660) been appointed to a newly inaugurated chair of natural law at the University of Heidelberg.[16]

Through scholars like Sanderson and Hooker, Culverwell and Pufendorf, Locke was exposed to principles of Roman law, which he generalized into natural law-based foundations for civil society and government. While Locke was by no means the first to do this, he was doing it in a way that broke with traditional Christian doctrines, both in the realm of politics and in the realm of epistemology, the theory of human knowledge. In his early essays, Locke sought to balance emphasis on sovereign divine will (voluntarism), as the source of natural law, with rationalism, a balance that close and sympathetic readers have concluded is ultimately incoherent. He would later move in a more overtly liberal and voluntarist direction, especially under the influence of early Whig politicians like the first Earl of Shaftesbury, but his convictions about the existence of a theologically grounded source of law and obligation would remain, providing a basis for his later arguments on behalf of natural law-based "property rights."[17]

Locke's developing commitment to liberalism was closely related to a position that was called (at first derogatively) Latitudinarian. "Latitude-men" became influential within the church of England during the later seventeenth century, rising finally to the highest positions in the church's leadership. They embraced a kind of establishment ("Erastian") Protestantism that emphasized morality and natural philosophy. Their God was a rational designer whose laws and works could be seen to the eye of the mind in contemplating an orderly universe. Early forms of natural scientific reasoning were closely associated with this intellectual movement,

[16] Von Leyden, "Introduction," in Locke, *Law of Nature*, 30–43; also Sarah Hutton, "Nathaniel Culverwell," *The Oxford Dictionary of National Biography*, Online Edition (Oxford: Oxford University Press, 2008); idem, "The Cambridge Platonists," *Stanford Encyclopedia of Philosophy*, available at https://plato.stanford.edu/entries/cambridge-platonists (accessed July 9, 2020). Influence of Pufendorf: Knud Haakonssen, *Natural Law and Moral Philosophy: From Grotius to the Scottish Enlightenment* (Cambridge, UK: Cambridge University Press, 1996), 38 ff.

[17] Von Leyden, "Introduction," 43–82; *cf.* Laslett, "Introduction," 79–92. The logical challenge involved in balancing voluntarism with rationalism, as Locke was trying to do, is succinctly described in Eric Nelson, *The Theology of Liberalism: Political Philosophy and the Justice of God* (Cambridge, MA: Harvard University Press, 2019), 1–4.

as seen in the works of Robert Boyle (1627–91) and Isaac Newton (1643–1727), and in Locke himself.[18]

This cultural orientation is also often exemplified in the sermons of John Tillotson. Before becoming archbishop of Canterbury, in 1691, Tillotson had served for nearly thirty years as chaplain of Lincoln's Inn, one of the Inns of Court in which English common lawyers were trained. In the momentous winter of 1688–89, Tillotson had dedicated to the gentlemen of this honorable society a sermon of thanksgiving, preached on January 31, celebrating England's deliverance by the victorious, Protestant royal couple William of Orange (William III, 1689–1702) and Mary Stuart (1689–94). Tillotson's sermon on this glorious occasion – he was among those who expressed joy at "the merciful design of this wonderful revolution" – was a reflection on the sinful past of the nation, a reflection guided by Biblical history, which was taken as a repository of lessons for the English people. England should humbly accept God's chastisement for her sins, and should establish herself anew in righteousness, as Israel had done upon returning from Babylon.[19]

Themes of national destiny, for good and for ill, were strong in the sermons of John Tillotson. These were rooted both in the Bible and in natural reason, supported by wide reading, especially in philosophy, but also in Roman and canon law. One of Tillotson's earliest published sermons had argued for the "wisdom of being religious," asserting that true happiness, in the philosophical sense, is to be found in the Christian religion, together with the rules for just and righteous living. Arguing sharply against the "atheism" of thinkers like Thomas Hobbes (1588–1679), Tillotson nonetheless agreed that logical arguments about ultimate obligation and duty could be derived from the natural desires for self-preservation and happiness that are part of the human condition. Tillotson taught that fear is the "strongest bond of law" and that the ultimate grounding for our social obligations rests in the law of God, as found in the Bible. Like Locke, however, Tillotson affirmed the reasonableness of Christianity, arguing from citations to scripture and philosophical writings, drawing inferences from what he took to be the natural social condition, and always returning to the implications for duty and obligation. Duty and obligation were both personal and national. We can easily see how the two would be conflated in preaching to elite lawyers.[20]

John Tillotson taught that there are positive consequences for national society in lives structured by religious obligation. A sermon on the "advantages of religion to society," preached on Proverbs 14:32, argued that God's judgments on human

18 Isabel Rivers, *Reason, Grace, and Sentiment: A Study of the Language of Religion and Ethics in England, 1660–1780*, Vol. I: Whichcote to Wesley (Cambridge, UK: Cambridge University Press, 1991), 25–88. On the significance of these intellectual lineages for later secularization, see Charles Taylor, *A Secular Age* (Cambridge, MA: Harvard University Press, 2007), 221–95.

19 Thomas Birch (ed.), *The Works of Dr. John Tillotson*, Vol. III (London: Richard Priestley, 1820), 2–28.

20 Birch (ed.), *Works of Dr. John Tillotson*, Vol. I (London: Richard Priestley, 1820), 317–89.

societies are seen in this life. Unlike individual human beings, who will be judged beyond the grave, nations are judged in this world. God's judgment may therefore be inferred from the evidence of worldly success or failure, in the course of events that we see, drawing on our natural endowments of reason. National prosperity is a sign of God's favor, and national suffering a sign of God's anger. The terrible violence that Britons had inflicted upon each other during the times of civil war was ultimately a chastening from God, one that should be humbly accepted under the newly secure, Protestant ordering of William and Mary.[21]

On December 11, 1694, John Locke wrote a letter to his Dutch friend Philipp van Limborch (1633–1712), lamenting the death of John Tillotson, mourning the loss of a "great and candid inquirer after truth," whom he had consulted freely upon "theological uncertainties." Tillotson's death was a great loss to the "English nation" (*respublica Anglicana*), and to the whole reformed church. And the loss was also personal: "I have assuredly lost, to my very great hurt and grief, a friend of many years, steadfast, candid, and sincere."[22]

In the friendships and lives of these liberalizing "latitude men," we can see reflections of a culturally formative movement, one in which the English legal and religious establishment embraced a form of liberal, Protestant Christianity, closely allied with Roman law and Greek philosophy, rooting national identity and moral obligation in the order of nature itself, which reflected God's design. Religious faith and social obligation were anchored in natural legality, which was also divine positive legality. This is the religion that was preached to common lawyers-in-training, in the Inns of Court. And it was the same religion that later offered comfort, guidance, and "authority" to Abigail (1744–1818) and John Adams (1735–1826), as they corresponded through the world-transformative events of the American Revolution.[23]

The importance of studying Roman law, in order to understand natural, foundational principles of obligation, was emphasized throughout the eighteenth-century world of British legal culture, as can be seen in Lord Mansfield's advice to law students, published near the end of the century. William Murray, first Earl of Mansfield (1705–93), recommended to young English lawyers in training that they begin their legal studies with basic principles of ethics, learning from Aristotle, Xenophon, and Cicero, and from William Wollaston's *Religion of Nature Delineated* (1722), a text that is widely seen as a foundational statement of English deism. Following this, Mansfield next recommended study in the law of nations (*ius*

21 Ibid., 409–23.

22 E. S. de Beer (ed. & trans.), *The Correspondence of John Locke*, Vol. V (Oxford: Clarendon Press, 1980), 237–8.

23 Letter of Abigail Adams to John Adams dated May 18, 1777, in *The Familiar Letters of John Adams and His Wife Abigail Adams during the Revolution*, edited by Charles Francis Adams (New York: Hurd and Houghton, 1876), 274–6. In another letter to John, dated October 20, 1777, Abigail refers to Tillotson as "our favorite." Ibid., 318.

gentium), focusing on the writings of Hugo Grotius (1583–1645), Samuel Pufendorf, and Jean-Jacques Burlamaqui (1694–1748), a Genevan jurist.[24]

After grappling with the foundational principles of ethics and jurisprudence, Mansfield recommended that students move to a historical study of "systems of positive law that have prevailed in their turn," concentrating on Roman and feudal law. For Roman law studies, Mansfield recommended that students start with an Italian jurist, Giovanni Gravina (1664–1718), who wrote on the development of Roman law. He then recommended that students read Justinian's *Institutes*, with commentary by the Dutch jurist Arnold Vinnius (1588–1657). Students should dip gradually in the *Digest* ("pandects"), and should avoid long commentaries on Roman law, which "will only confound you, and make your head spin around." The feudal law, according to Mansfield, "is so interwoven with almost every constitution in Europe that, without some knowledge of it, it is impossible to understand modern history." After these foundations had been laid, Mansfield finally recommended study of "municipal law," the laws that are specific to a modern nation.[25]

What is noteworthy in the shift from Locke and Tillotson to Mansfield is that Roman law has been historicized. Roman law, like feudal law, has become a historical basis for the constitutional development of legal systems, whereas for Locke the philosopher, Roman law had provided a set of categories and principles that defined a natural law for civil society, a law that empowers the magistrates of civil societies and that establishes a foundation for natural rights. The moral, and especially the religious, aspects of law are more muted in Mansfield as compared to Locke.

But Roman law, interestingly, comes into Mansfield's educational framework at two levels. As we will see further in the remaining chapters of this book, Roman law forms the foundation for the modern law of nations, as formulated by Hugo Grotius and Samuel Pufendorf, among others. For Mansfield, then, Roman law was both a foundational system of historically formative positive law and a conceptual framework for legality in inter-national relations. Roman law was, to summarize, a foundation for jurisprudence, ethics, and historical legal development.

William Blackstone, Mansfield's slightly younger contemporary, stands somewhere between Locke and Mansfield in his approach to Roman law. Blackstone had studied Roman law at Oxford, and he used the categories of Roman law to organize the subject matter for his great treatise on English common law, *The Commentaries on the Laws of England*. We have already encountered Blackstone as an early proponent of "literary property," drawing on Locke's adaptation of Roman law principles to articulate a basis for property in original literary creations.

24 *A Treatise on the Study of the Law: Containing Directions to Students, Written by Those Celebrated Lawyers, Orators, and Statesmen, the Lords Mansfield, Ashburton, and Thurlow, in a Series of Letters.* (London: Harrison, Cluse, and Co., 1797), 49; Norman S. Poser, *Lord Mansfield: Justice in the Age of Reason* (Montreal: McGill-Queen's University Press, 2013), 39–41.

25 [Mansfield], *Study of the Law*, 49–53; Poser, *Lord Mansfield*, 41.

We now encounter Blackstone again, as we turn to the great case that recognized intellectual property in English common law: *Millar* v. *Taylor* (King's Bench, 1769), a case in which Blackstone acted as an advocate, and Mansfield as senior judge.[26]

9.2 SCOTTISH VERSUS ENGLISH BOOKSELLERS

In 1769, England's highest common law court – the Court of King's Bench – came to a final decision in a lengthy dispute between two men: Andrew Millar, a member of the London-based Stationers Company, and Robert Taylor, a bookseller from Berwick – a fortress town in the contested borderland between England and Scotland – who made a regular practice of purchasing books in Scotland for resale in England. The dispute concerned poems written by James Thomson, which were being sold by both parties under title of *The Seasons by James Thomson*. The justices were called upon to decide whether Andrew Millar was indeed a "proprietor" of this poetic work, a determination that would render Robert Taylor's publication and sale of the work to be unlawful. The legal question to be decided by the Court of King's Bench concerned the nature of "literary property": was it really a form of property recognized and protected by common law, as was being claimed by the Stationers Company?[27]

The jury was persuaded that Mr. Millar had complied with customary practice by purchasing (for "valuable and full consideration") the "copyright" to James Thomson's poetic work, and had complied with Stationers Company bylaws by entering his copyright into the company's account books. For these reasons, the jury concluded that Mr. Millar had been wronged by Robert Taylor's unlicensed publication of that work. However, the jury professed ignorance as to whether this could be recognized and remedied by English common law.[28]

Andrew Millar died on the morning of June 8, 1768, one day after the second set of oral arguments in his case. The *Donaldson* case concerned a portion of his estate: copyrights to a number of literary works by James Thomson, including the *Seasons* poems, which had been transferred to Mr. Millar's heirs pursuant to his will. As reported in the *Donaldson* case, these copyrights had been acquired by Mr. Millar over a number of years, beginning in 1729 with a purchase of the tragedy *Saphonisba* and the poem *Spring*. In 1738, Mr. Millar purchased the rights to additional poems

26 William Blackstone, *Commentaries on the Laws of England: A Facsimile of the First Edition of 1765–1769*, Vol. II (Chicago: University of Chicago Press, 1979), 404–7.

27 *Millar* v. *Taylor*, 4 Burrow 2303, 98 Eng. Rep. 201 (King's Bench, 1769), 201–5. As noted by the court reporter Burrow, the case in controversy was one of "first impression" for the English common law. Andrew Millar was among the most prominent publishers of his day, known for his generosity to the authors (including David Hume) whose works he published. He had become "free" of the Stationers Company in 1738. Hugh Amory, "Millar, Andrew (1705–1768), *Bookseller*," in Oxford Dictionary of National Biography (Online Edition 2008). Robert Taylor: Richard B. Sher, *The Enlightenment and the Book: Scottish Authors and Their Publishers in Eighteenth-Century Britain, Ireland, and America* (2006), 470.

28 *Millar*, 98 Eng. Rep., 203–5.

by James Thomson – including *Summer*, *Autumn*, and *Winter* – from a Mr. Millan, who had in turn purchased them in 1729 from Mr. Thomson. The rights to all these works were sold in 1769, at an auction held in St. Paul's churchyard, to fellow members of the Stationers Company, including one Thomas Becket.[29]

Meanwhile, since 1768, Alexander Donaldson and an unnamed partner based in Edinburgh had been printing and selling a volume titled *The Seasons, by James Thomson*. Having paid a large sum of money for their copyrights, Becket and his Stationers Company associates sought an injunction to prevent Donaldson and his partner from further printing. Becket and his associates instituted an action in the Chancery court in 1771, obtaining a perpetual injunction in 1772. A special master was appointed to assess how much Donaldson and his partner had profited by their sales, and to determine the damages payable to Becket and his associates, but before this decision could be made, the case was appealed to the House of Lords.[30]

The judges involved in the *Millar* and *Donaldson* cases had been called upon to decide, once and for all, whether a new, "intellectual" type of property really fit within the English common law system, one that was, since 1707, somehow part of a treaty-based legal union between England and Scotland. The Chancery courts seemed to be behaving, at least at times, as though this new form of property did fit within the common law system. However, the Chancellors had until recently been relatively free to make their decision based on their perception of "equity" in a particular case, and they could not render an authoritative decision as to the common law. It was the justices of the King's Bench and the Lords who would have to engage in the difficult project of determining whether England's common law really sanctioned this new, "intellectual" form of property.[31]

Perhaps the most influential argument *against* the idea that the common law recognized copyrights as property was given in the House of Lords by Lord Camden. When it came to principles of "sound policy," Camden argued from the general premise that "science and learning are in their nature *publici juris*, and they ought to be as free and general as air or water." Glory, not profit, is the reward of science. Given this basic principle, the Stationers' efforts to claim literary works as property was nothing other than an abhorrent attempt to continue a monopoly. The

[29] *Millar*, 98 Eng. Rep., 201–2; see also *Donaldson* v. *Becket*, II Brown 129, 130; 1 Eng. Rep. 837, 838 (1774).

[30] *Millar*, 98 Eng. Rep., 201–2; *Donaldson*, 1 Eng. Rep., 838–9.

[31] The use of the adjective "intellectual" to characterize this admittedly new type of legal property occurred with some frequency in the *Millar* case. See, for example, *Millar*, 98 Eng. Rep., 251 (Mansfield). On the Chancery court decisions, and on the broader legal background to these cases, see Ronan Deazley, *On the Origin of the Right to Copy: Charting the Movement of Copyright Law in Eighteenth-Century Britain (1695–1775)* (Oxford: Hart Publishing, 2004), 51–85, 111–47; Lyman Ray Patterson, *Copyright in Historical Perspective* (Nashville: Vanderbilt University Press, 1968), 158–63; Mark Rose, *Authors and Owners: The Invention of Copyright* (Cambridge, MA: Harvard University Press, 1993), 49–66. On the freedom of Chancellors to decide in accordance with their own perception of equity, see Theodore Plucknett, *A Concise History of the Common Law* (London: Butterworth & Co., 1956), 673–707.

consequence of continuing this monopoly, which would follow if the Lords decided for the Stationers, would be "exorbitant price . . . for every valuable author will be as much monopolized by them as Shakespeare is at present."[32]

Lord Effingham, likewise, saw dangerous policy effects flowing from a decision for the Stationers, but for him the danger was to the freedom of the press and to the political health of the commonwealth:

> Lord Effingham rose last, and begged to urge the liberty of the press, as the strongest argument against this property; adding, that a despotic minister, hearing of a pamphlet which might strike at his measures, may buy the copy, and by printing 20 copies, secure it his own, and by that means the public would be deprived of the most interesting information.[33]

Economically, the common law copyright would sanction a monopoly; politically, it would stifle the press and thereby suppress politically relevant information. For both consequentialist reasons, the property should not exist.

Justice Yates, the second most senior judge of the King's Bench, agreed that copyright was not property under common law, and he also gave arguments based on politically significant consequences. However, his most powerful arguments approached the question from a formalist direction. Justice Yates began his opinion by defining the basis for property under English common law: "however peculiar the laws of this and every other country may be, with respect to territorial property, I will take upon me to say, that the law of England, with respect to all personal property, had its grand foundation in natural law."[34]

Justice Yates, in other words, agreed with the Stationers Company's lawyers that the general question about the proprietary status of copyrights could only be answered by looking to "the general principles of property." And these general principles were rooted in natural law. These general principles also, however, included the requirement that the object being claimed as property must have identifiable boundaries, and an "intellectual" property, like copyright, could not meet this requirement.

> All property has its proper limit, extent, and bounds. Invention or labour (be they ever so great) cannot change the nature of things; or establish a right, where no private right can possibly exist. The inventor of the air-pump had certainly a property in the machine which he formed; but did he thereby gain a property in the air, which is common to all? or did he gain the sole property in the abstract principles upon which he constructed his machine? and yet these may be called the inventor's ideas, and as much his sole property as the ideas of an author. To extend

32 Cobbett's *Parliamentary History*, Vol. XVII, 958 (note), 992–1001. Prerogative precedents were, for Lord Camden, "the very last places in which I should have dreamt of finding the least trace of the Common Law of this kingdom." Ibid., 992.

33 Ibid., 1003.

34 *Millar*, 98 Eng. Rep., 229–30, 249–50.

> this argument, beyond the manuscript, to the very ideas themselves, seems to me very difficult, or rather quite wild. Indeed the invention and labour, which are ranked among the modes of acquiring specific property in the subject itself, are that kind of invention and labour, which are known by the name of occupancy. In that sense, invention is defining or discovering a vacant property: and labour is the taking possession of that property, and bestowing cultivation upon it. *Property is founded upon occupancy*. But how is possession to be taken, or any act of occupancy to be asserted, on mere intellectual ideas? .... The occupancy of a thought would be a new kind of occupancy indeed. By what outward mark must the property denote appropriation? and if these are void of that which the act of occupancy requires, it is a proof to me they cannot be the object of property.[35]

Indeed, Justice Yates interpreted the natural law tradition as limiting the objects of property to *tangible* ("corporeal") objects. He recognized, of course, that intangible rights (e.g., easements) might exist in relation to tangible objects. However, with respect to the object itself, "it is a well-known and established maxim (which I apprehend holds as true now, as it did 2000 years ago,) 'that nothing can be an object of property, which has not a corporeal substance.'"[36]

Ultimately, it was his insistence on the tangible character of legal property that determined Justice Yates' conclusion. The other three justices of the King's Bench did not agree, and they were therefore able to conclude that intellectual property was, in principle, no different from any other type of property recognized by English common law.

Justice Aston focused on the common law concept of trespass, as it related to Andrew Millar's claim to literary property. Admitting that the object of property being claimed was a new "species," Justice Aston went back to the earliest foundations of the common law tradition to argue that the tradition had always been willing to draw new objects of property into its ancient grasp:

> In respect to the several species of property; though the rules touching them must ever have been the same, yet the objects of it were not all at once known to the Common Law, or to the world: and many have been disputed, as not being objects of property at Common Law, which yet are now established to be such; as, gunpowder, &c, &c, &c.[37]

Drawing on legal treatises and cases from the time of Henry VIII and Elizabeth I – cases that addressed questions, for example, about whether an action would lie to recover stolen dogs – Justice Aston argued that the common law tradition permitted

35 Ibid., 229–30 (emphasis added).

36 Ibid., 232–3; also 245: "But goods must be capable of possession; and must, of course, have some visible substance: for nothing but what has visible substance is capable of actual possession. The author's unpublished manuscript will indeed very properly fall under this class of property; because that is corporeal. But after publication of it, the mere intellectual ideas are totally incorporeal; and therefore incapable of any distinct separate possession."

37 Ibid., 223.

use of the action of trespass, even where the property at issue was new. From the common law authorities he assembled, Justice Aston concluded that an action for trespass was appropriate, since all that was requisite was that there be some "distinguishable property" with a "determinate owner." This standard was clearly met in the present case, "for, I confess, I do not know, nor can I comprehend any property more emphatically a man's own, nay, more incapable of being mistaken, than his literary works."[38]

But this was a radical argument, one that was not explicitly endorsed by Justice Willes or Lord Mansfield. The most conservative argument in favor of the case for intellectual property was the argument based on legal precedent. And here is where the prerogative tradition comes back to demonstrate its relevance to modern intellectual property.

The case for copyrights, as common law property, was, *as a matter of case law precedent*, strongest based on the prerogative tradition, whereby royal privileges, freedoms, and powers were granted from monarch to subject through instruments of legal power. As we have seen, this strength was rooted in the prerogative tradition's long-standing premise that the granted privileges, freedoms, and powers are the property of their monarchical grantors. When the king by means of letters patent or charters granted to his favored subjects "privileges and immunities" to incorporate cities, or "liberties" in forming corporate guilds for the exclusive exercise of a particular trade, he was granting something that originally belonged to him. This beneficent king or queen was bestowing upon the favored subject some element of his patrimony, her property.[39]

In the *Millar* case, the prerogative tradition was discussed by all the judges, albeit with ambivalence. One senses that they would have preferred not to draw on the tradition at all, since the prerogative was highly distasteful to Whiggish Britons only a few generations removed from the Stuarts, the civil wars, and the Glorious Revolution. Justice Willes, for example, looked back critically on the age of the Stuarts as "times when the Prerogative ran high."[40]

However, the earliest legal authorities relevant to the issue of literary property were unquestionably part of this prerogative tradition. These legal authorities were (1) decrees of a "Prerogative Court," the Star Chamber, and (2) the Restoration case law pertaining to prerogative-based copyrights. Moreover, by introducing its royal charter of incorporation as evidence, together with the by-laws and usages constructed pursuant to that charter, the Stationers Company had invoked the prerogative tradition that brought it into being. There was, therefore, no way to avoid addressing it.[41]

38 Ibid., 223–4.

39 *Millar*, 98 Eng. Rep., 208–9; Blackstone, *Commentaries*, Vol. II, 409–11.

40 *Millar*, 98 Eng. Rep., 209.

41 *Millar*, 98 Eng. Rep., 203–4, 206–9. On the characterization of the Star Chamber as a Prerogative Court, see Plucknett, *Concise History*, 176–97.

The same Justice Willes who looked critically on the times when prerogative "ran high" took responsibility for assembling the legal authorities relevant to the question of literary property, and addressing them in his written opinion. Beginning with the earliest council orders and Star Chamber decrees, as "Acts of State," Justice Willes construed the authorities together as establishing the existence of a common law copyright, which existed prior to the statutory framework created by the Statute of Anne (1710), and which remained supplementary to that statutory framework. For Justice Willes, England's common law was not reducible to "positive law," whether that was derived from Parliamentary statute or cases. England's common law, rather, underlay various English "usages" and practices, including those of the crown, its courts, and the Stationers Company. It was, in other words, a kind of immanent, legal tradition.[42]

And, prior to 1640, that immanent legal tradition very clearly recognized a prerogative authority vis-à-vis printed texts. This had been reflected in an order of Elizabeth's council (1566) and two Star Chamber decrees (1586 and 1637). These conciliar orders and decrees, Willes reasoned, built upon the earlier foundation laid by Henry VIII, delineating a framework for the censorship and regulation of printing, while they sanctioned the Stationers Company's exclusive rights in printing and publishing.[43]

William Blackstone's *Commentaries*, which probably indicate his arguments in the *Millar* case, hint at the way that the prerogative tradition could be interpreted as a legal foundation for literary property. While preferring to base his arguments in favor of intellectual property on natural law and chancery precedents, Blackstone nevertheless considered the case for literary property to be significantly bolstered by "those adjudged cases at Common Law, wherein the crown hath been considered as invested with certain Prerogative copyrights." The argument proceeded by way of analogy: "if the crown is capable of an exclusive right in any one book, the subject seems also capable of having the same right in another." For Blackstone, then, copyrights constituted a legally legitimate form of property within the common law system, a system that was at once a constitutional system of public law, and a system of private law.[44]

Lord Mansfield, Chief Justice of the King's Bench, regarded the argument from the prerogative tradition as "equally conclusive" with the argument from natural law. Like Blackstone, Lord Mansfield read the prerogative tradition as one that established limitations on the powers of the monarchy. However, his reading emphasized the historical effects of the Glorious Revolution more than Blackstone's.[45]

42 *Millar*, 98 Eng. Rep., 205–18, esp. 206, 209–10. Statute of Anne: 9 Stat. 256 (1710).
43 *Millar*, 98 Eng. Rep., 206–7.
44 Blackstone, *Commentaries*, Vol. II, 407.
45 *Millar*, 98 Eng. Rep., 253–4.

Examining the precedents carefully, Lord Mansfield drew a line between the cases decided before the Revolution and those decided after. Conceding that the Restoration cases had been decided on the basis of the prerogative tradition, Lord Mansfield distinguished royal property from the royal prerogative, arguing that the former basis for the decisions continued to survive a post-Revolution case that he regarded as decisively rejecting the prerogative as a basis for the "Crown copyright," even while it was never actually decided.[46]

Lord Mansfield, in other words, excised the proprietary conception of the prerogative tradition away from the rulership conception, equated the prerogative tradition to the rulership conception alone, and argued from the implicit premise that this had been destroyed by the Revolution as a legitimate foundation for the crown copyright. The common law precedents establishing the crown copyright over law books, statute books, English Bibles, year books, and prayer books remained valid, according to this interpretation, because they did not *solely* depend on royal prerogative (as equated with the rulership conception alone) but also depended on the "power" that "rests in property." The proprietary basis underlying these valid precedents, according to Lord Mansfield, derived from the king's payment, which operated as a transfer of property. This property was paid for by the king and transferred to him, and he could therefore grant it by means of letters patent to any of his subjects.[47]

Having interpreted these precedents as providing a proprietary basis for the crown copyright, Lord Mansfield then made the argument by analogy: "Whatever the Common Law says of property in the King's case, from analogy to the case of authors, must hold conclusively, in my apprehension, with regard to authors." Thus, reinterpreting a portion of the prerogative tradition as an egalitarian, proprietary tradition, Lord Mansfield argued that it survived the dramatic events of the seventeenth century: the civil wars, Restoration, and Revolution. Surviving to support the crown copyright, this reinterpreted tradition must also support an author's copyright, since the king could have no greater proprietary right than his subjects. "Crown-copies are, as in the case of an author, civil property." This argument, alongside arguments from natural law, was "conclusive," in Lord Mansfield's opinion, in determining that literary property existed as a matter of common law.[48]

Justice Yates adamantly disagreed with the notion that an analogy could be drawn between the crown and the subject, thereby enabling a conclusion about an author's copyright under common law. For Justice Yates, the prerogative copyright was an entirely different type of property, one rooted in the supremacy. No analogy could be drawn between the king and the subject here. "The King's right to all these is, as head of the Church, and of the political constitution." For Justice Yates, then, the

[46] Ibid., 254. The post-Revolution case: *Stationers Company* v. *Partridge*, 88 Eng. Rep. 647 (1709).

[47] *Millar*, 98 Eng. Rep., 256.

[48] Ibid., 254–6.

prerogative tradition survived the Revolutions of the seventeenth century, and it continued to ground the crown copyright in ways that could not ground a common law copyright for the king's subjects.[49]

The final ruling as to the question of "literary property" was given by the Court of Parliament (i.e., the House of Lords, acting in its judicial capacity) in the *Donaldson* case. A narrow majority of the Lords concluded that the effect of the Statute of Anne had been to substitute its statutory framework for the common law basis of literary property that existed prior to 1710. However, the Lords left no official record of the legal reasons for their decision, and the *Millar* case was not "overruled," in the narrow sense of that term. Thus, while it was clear from *Donaldson* that an author's literary property in *published* works would endure only for the period prescribed by statute, there was still room to argue that some form of copyright existed, at least with respect to an unpublished manuscript, irrespective of the Statute of Anne and its temporal limitations. Around the edges of the statutory right, in other words, and perhaps beneath it, lurked the possibility for a natural law argument about the ultimate foundation for intellectual property rights.[50]

In the disagreement between Justice Yates and Lord Mansfield, we can see that the question of intellectual property's legitimating foundations under the English common law system turned, to a significant degree, on interpretation of the prerogative tradition, as impacted by the new, natural legality. Influenced by the new legal and political culture, particularly as it had been legislatively embraced in the Glorious Revolution, Lord Mansfield was willing to reinterpret the prerogative tradition, while Justice Yates was not. Thus, for Lord Mansfield, the natural law argument could coexist with the prerogative tradition, which had survived the Revolution as an egalitarian, proprietary tradition. For Justice Yates, the prerogative tradition implicitly excluded any natural law argument for proprietary copyrights.[51]

9.3 NATIONAL ORGANIZING IN THE NEW WORLD

Two short years after the *Donaldson* decision, the culture of natural legality lent explosive meaning to an American Revolution. Thomas Jefferson's *Declaration of Independence* (in)famously drew on a natural law framework to articulate an ideal of republican freedom from colonial tyranny. During the existential struggle to make their revolution real, colonial Americans embraced the new culture of natural legality, as a foundation for their new governing community.[52]

[49] Ibid., 243–5.

[50] For a more recent discussion, see *Felter* v. *Columbia Pictures Television*, 523 US 340 (1998).

[51] Note, however, that Justice Yates had used a more traditional conception of natural law to argue that property can only inhere in tangible objects.

[52] Merrill Jensen (ed.), *Documentary History*, Vol. I, 72–6; US National Archives and Records Administration, *Founding Documents: Declaration of Independence*, available at www.archives.gov/founding-docs/declaration (accessed July 10, 2020).

In the 1783 Treaty of Paris, the success of their revolution was formally affirmed: thirteen colonial corporations, provinces, and proprietary holdings were to be transformed into independent, sovereign states. But the precise form these states would take, in relation to each other, remained an open question. Efforts at definition had begun, however, even before independence was declared, in the 1774 congress of colonial delegates held in Philadelphia (the "First Continental Congress"). From this time forward, according to the American jurist Joseph Story (1779–1845), the United States began to act as a "national organization."[53]

One of the most consequential results of this First Continental Congress was the formation of an "Association" to boycott British goods. Economic historians view this association as the first stage in the emergence of America's national economy. Pursuant to the "Articles of Association" voted on by the colonial delegates, an association was created to pursue and enforce a "non-importation, non-consumption, and non-exportation agreement" against Great Britain and Ireland. To compensate for the absence of British imports of finished goods, the contracting colonies agreed to "encourage frugality, economy, and industry, and promote agriculture, arts, and the manufactures of this country, especially that of wool."[54]

If the United States were to become a "national organization," however, something beyond the legal framework of "association" would be required. To call their union an "association" was to conceive of the states as members of a partnership, joined together for particular purposes, perhaps even holding some property and obligations in common, but not as unified into a single entity with the legal capacity to act and dispose of property under its own name. Lest it be doubted that the drafters of the Articles of Association had in mind such a technical, legal view, it should be emphasized that the committee of five tasked with drafting the Articles included two distinguished American jurists: Thomas Johnson of Maryland (1732–1819) and Thomas Cushing of Massachusetts (1725–88).[55]

During the revolutionary period from 1776 to 1783, the operating framework for the association was "confederacy": a political alliance of sovereign states, prominent models of which were to be found in ancient Greece and Rome, as well as in continental Europe. However, to certain members of the assembled Continental Congress, including James Madison, it quickly seemed apparent that an

[53] Joseph Story, *Commentaries on the Constitution of the United States*, reprinted with an introduction by Ronald D. Rotunda and John E. Nowak (Durham: Carolina Academic Press, 1987), 85. At the time of the Revolution, there were seven royal provinces (New Hampshire, New York, New Jersey, Virginia, North Carolina, South Carolina, and Georgia), three proprietary holdings (Maryland, Pennsylvania, and Delaware), and three colonial corporations (Massachusetts, Rhode Island, and Connecticut). Story, *Commentaries*, 67–83.

[54] *Journals of the Continental Congress*, edited by Worthington Chauncey Ford, Vol. II (Washington: Government Printing Office, 1904), 62–81; John McCusker & Russell R. Menard, *The Economy of British America, 1607–1789* (Chapel Hill: University of North Carolina Press, 1991), 358–77; Curtis P. Nettels, *The Emergence of a National Economy, 1775–1815* (Armonk, New York: M. E. Sharpe, Inc. 1962), 1–22.

[55] *Journals of the Continental Congress*, Vol. I, 53.

organizational structure of confederal alliance was insufficient, given the very real exigencies of a fledgling nation poised between European great powers.[56]

Commerce and industry suffered under the confederated organizational structure. Shortly after military peace had been agreed, moreover, imports from Britain flooded into American ports, leading to cash shortages and economic depression. Some interpreted this flood of British imports as an intentional strategy to destroy American industries and "manufactures," which had sprung up during the Revolutionary War.[57]

Responding partly to the sustained advocacy of James Madison, Virginia issued a call for a "convention" of state delegates to discuss whether the states' commercial relations should be placed on the foundation of a "uniform system." The recommendation of the delegates to this convention, held at Annapolis in 1786, was a constitutional convention to be held at Philadelphia in May 1787. Once prickly New York had grudgingly agreed to go along, the Continental Congress issued a recommendation for a convention "for the purpose of revising the articles of confederation."[58]

Delegates from a small number of states began their discussions in Philadelphia on May 14, 1787, and all twelve signatory states had representatives at the convention by June. Over the course of the summer, fifty-five men participated in drafting, oratory, and argument. The result of their labors was a written text, signed by thirty-nine delegates on September 17. The text of the constitution provided a semantic formulation for a new form of union ("a more perfect Union"), one that allocated

56 Story, *Commentaries*, 96–162; James Madison, *The Writings of James Madison in Nine Volumes*, edited by Gaillard Hunt (New York: Online Library of Liberty, 1900). See especially in Volumes 1 and 2: (1) Letter to Thomas Jefferson, dated April 16, 1781 (lamenting the absence of a Congressional power to punish states that violate the embargo against Britain); (2) Letter to Edmund Randolph dated May 29, 1782 (describing the threat to commerce from an absence of a unitary treaty power); (3) Notes of Speech delivered to the Continental Congress on January 28, 1783, concerning the impossibility of timely payment of national debts with "13 separate and independent governments"; (4) Letter of August 7, 1785, to James Monroe (concerning the impossibility of uniform regulation of trade by the confederated states); (5) Letter of August 20, 1785, to Thomas Jefferson concerning the need for a uniform regulatory basis of trade in order to retaliate against Great Britain); (6) Notes for Speech in the Virginia House of Delegates, November 1785; (7) Letter to Thomas Jefferson of March 18, 1786 (regarding the efforts by the confederated states to retaliate against Great Britain). Madison's writings are a prime example of the salience of Greek and Roman organizational models to leaders of Revolutionary America. Additional examples may be found in the writings of John Adams. For contemporary scholarly discussion of this point, see Bernard Bailyn, *The Ideological Origins of the American Revolution* (Cambridge, MA: Harvard University Press, 1992), 23–6; Gordon Wood, *The Creation of the American Republic 1776–1787* (Chapel Hill: University of North Carolina Press, 1998), 48–53.

57 Story, *Commentaries*, 99–101. Post-war depression and imports from Great Britain flooding American ports: William R. Bagnall, *The Textile Industries of the United States* (Cambridge, MA: Riverside Press, 1893), 81; Victor Selden Clark, *History of Manufactures in the United States 1607–1860* (Washington: Carnegie Institution of Washington, 1916), 227–9; Nettels, *Emergence*, 45–88.

58 Story, *Commentaries*, 105–7; *cf.* Jensen (ed.), *Documentary History*, Vol. I, 176–95.

substantial powers to a federal government, while broadening its electoral base to a "national" citizenry.[59]

Among the powers allocated to the lawmaking body of the federal government (the "Congress") was the power to "secure for limited times to authors and inventors the exclusive rights to their respective writings and discoveries," that is, to create a legislative framework for the granting of copyrights and patents.

9.4 CONSTITUTIONALIZING INTELLECTUAL PROPERTY

Given their shared sense of confederate crisis, the delegates to the constitutional convention mostly agreed that some transfers of state power and authority to a centralized, federal government were necessary. Nevertheless, their beliefs varied, widely concerning the extent to which power and authority should be relinquished by the states. Even more fundamentally, perhaps, their basic conceptions about the meaning of words being used to evoke institutionalized locations of power and authority – national, federal, republican, supreme – differed significantly. The "force and extent" of such words was an important focus of thought, writing, and discussion among the delegates, as can be seen from the notes and letters written by debaters and observers.[60]

Drawing on Greek and Roman legal traditions, as well as their own colonial and state legal traditions; drawing on their experience with British government and their understanding of English legal traditions; referencing Montesquieu's *Spirit of the Laws*, the "Law of Nations," and European legal history; drawing on all these traditions, the assembled delegates wrote, debated, and discussed their way toward a shared language for conceiving and disagreeing over their new nation-state. Here is an archetypal example of semantic legal ordering, one with very real effects in the material organization of economic, military, and political power.[61]

What these discussions fully meant, however, was yet to be worked out in writing. On July 26, the convention adjourned to enable this task to be performed by a Committee of Detail. Together, these five men produced the first draft of the US Constitution, a draft that would give direction to the remaining constitutional debates. One effect of the committee's draft was to shift the debate from *representation* in Congress to the *powers* of Congress.[62]

The draft constitution significantly limited Congress' powers by explicitly enumerating them. Such explicit enumeration, together with the carefully limited expansion of the "necessary and proper clause," would implicate, for a well-trained lawyer, a traditional principle of statutory interpretation: "express inclusion

59 Max Farrand (ed.), *The Records of the Federal Convention of 1787*, Vol. I (New Haven: Yale University Press, 1911), 1–92; idem, Vol. III, Appendix B; Jensen (ed.), *Documentary History*, Vol. I, 230, 304–17.

60 Farrand, *Federal Convention*, Vol. I, 20 n.12, 24, 29–44, 185, 263–5, 281–353.

61 Ibid., for example, Vol. I, 71, 282–333, 391, 485, 580, and passim.

62 Farrand, *Federal Convention*, Vol. I, xxii; idem, Vol. II, 85–7, 95–8, 106, 116–75.

of one thing excludes all others" (*expressio unius est exclusio alterius*). And the Committee of Detail was full of well-trained lawyers.[63]

By replacing a broad and general enablement of Congressional powers with enumerated powers, while also providing for the supremacy of federal law, the Committee of Detail created a set of circumstances in which the range of possibilities for intellectual property in the United States had become narrower: either Congress would now be given the explicit authority to grant federal copyrights and patents or copyrights and patents would be the creatures of state law, if they could be granted at all.[64]

On August 18, two delegates stepped forward to propose amendments to Congress' powers enabling federal patents and copyrights: James Madison of Virginia and Charles Pinckney of South Carolina. The official journal of the Convention, kept by the secretary William Jackson, simply records a list of "additional powers proposed to be vested in the Legislature of the United States" and their referral to the Committee of Detail. These included the following proposed powers:

- To grant charters of incorporation in cases where the public good may require them, and the authority of a single state may be incompetent
- To secure to literary authors their copy rights for a limited time
- To establish a university
- To encourage, by proper premiums and provisions, the advancement of useful knowledge and discoveries
- To establish seminaries for the promotion of literature and the arts and sciences
- To grant charters of incorporation
- To grant patents for useful inventions
- To secure to authors exclusive rights for a certain time
- To establish public institutions, rewards, and immunities for the promotion of agriculture, commerce, trades, and manufactures[65]

Madison's journal helps to explain the obvious overlaps: the first group of four powers (among others) was proposed by Madison, while the second group of five (among others) was proposed by Pinckney. According to Madison's records, these proposals were moved unanimously and referred to the Committee of Detail without debate.[66]

Meanwhile, John Rutledge of South Carolina (1739–1800) had voiced concern over "the length of the Session, the probable impatience of the public and the

[63] Expressio unius: A *Law Dictionary* by Henry Campbell Black, 2nd ed. (West Publishing, 1910), 468. The Committee: John Rutledge of South Carolina, Edmund Randolph of Virginia, Nathaniel Gorham of Massachusetts, Oliver Ellsworth of Connecticut, and James Wilson of Pennsylvania. Farrand, *Federal Convention*, Vol. II, 128–75; David O. Stewart, *The Summer of 1787* (New York: Simon & Schuster, 2007), 163–89.

[64] Farrand, *Federal Convention*, Vol. II, 176–89.

[65] Ibid., 321–2.

[66] Ibid., 324–33.

extreme anxiety of many members of the Convention to bring the business to an end." Although the delegates continued to work systematically through the Committee of Detail's draft, the debates took on a sharper edge.[67]

On August 21 and 22, they focused on the power to tax imported slaves. The debates were framed in terms of a divide between North and South, with the Southern states (South Carolina in particular) threatening to walk away if their interests were not recognized and protected. The compromise coming out of these debates favored the mercantile North by permitting protectionist "navigation acts" to be enacted by simple majority vote, while sanctioning the Fugitive Slave Clause and the South's continued importation of African slaves through 1808.[68]

Consideration of the additional matters assigned to the Committee of Detail had been postponed while these negotiations continued. However, on August 31, faced with additional threats to abandon the convention, the delegates approved a motion to create a committee that would deal with all the parts of the constitution that had been postponed. This "Committee on Postponed Parts," chaired by David Brearley of New Jersey, included delegates from each of the remaining ten participating states.[69]

The Committee on Postponed Parts worked quickly, issuing partial reports between September 1 and 5, proposing language for remaining sections of the constitution. A substantial focus was the Presidency. However, they also addressed the proposals for Congressional powers, which had been offered by Madison and Pinckney. In place of those wide-ranging proposals was a single provision defining Congressional powers to grant copyrights and patents:

> To promote the progress of science and useful arts by securing for limited times to Authors and Inventors the exclusive right to their respective writings and discoveries.

This proposed language was adopted without debate, remaining untouched by the Committee of Revision (often referred to as the "Committee on Style"), which produced a final, polished draft of the constitution. The final, "enrolled" constitution, which included the authorization for patents and copyrights in the language adopted by the Committee on Postponed Parts, was signed by thirty-nine delegates

67 Ibid., 328.

68 Ibid., 352–79, 396–421; Stewart, *Summer of 1787*, 191–204. On September 10, John Rutledge secured a provision protecting these provisions against amendment through 1808. Farrand, *Federal Convention*, Vol. II, 555, 559.

69 Farrand, *Federal Convention*, Vol. II, 368, 376, 473, 481. Committee on Postponed Parts: Nicholas Gilman of New Hampshire, Rufus King of Massachusetts, Roger Sherman of Connecticut, Gouverneur Morris of Pennsylvania, John Dickenson of Delaware, Daniel Carroll of Maryland, James Madison of Virginia, Hugh Williamson of North Carolina, Pierce Butler of South Carolina, and Abraham Baldwin of Georgia. No records are available to indicate how the Committee on Postponed Parts worked. As chairman and reporter of the committee's work, David Brearley probably took final drafting responsibility. Donald Scarinci, *David Brearley and the Making of the United States Constitution* (Trenton: New Jersey Heritage Press, 2005), 197.

on September 17, 1787, then transmitted to the Continental Congress, meeting in the same building.[70]

The signing of the constitution, however, marked only the beginning of a wider, national debate. The constitution was not yet legally effective.

According to its own terms, the constitution would only become effective once nine states had ratified it. The constitution's drafters had recommended a process of ratification that, by design, would involve the establishment of ad hoc ratification conventions for each state. It was believed by some that a ratification process left to the established state legislatures would probably be a failure: sufficient numbers of legislators could never be persuaded to undermine their own positions and responsibilities. And the delegates agreed that a constitution drafted in secret could not be implemented without some process of deliberative endorsement by the public.[71]

During the ratification process, jurists and lawyers who had participated in drafting the constitution stepped forward to present their interpretations of the text. Interestingly, the allocation of a power to the federal Congress to grant patents and copyrights generated relatively little debate, even during the contentious ratifications of Pennsylvania, Massachusetts, Virginia, and New York. Nevertheless, the discussions that are recorded shed light on then-developing concepts and principles related to intellectual property – and of the nation-state within which that property was to be enclosed – which would help to shape the broader culture and social powers of the new American nation.

9.5 INTERPRETING THE NEW CONSTITUTION

The first state to schedule a ratification convention was Pennsylvania. As a primary drafter of the constitution and a prominent Pennsylvania jurist, James Wilson (1742–98) undertook a central role as advocate for ratification. On October 6, at a meeting held by the city of Philadelphia to elect delegates to the Pennsylvania ratifying convention, Wilson gave a lengthy commentary on the constitution, a summary of which was published three days later in the *Pennsylvania Herald*. By December 29, this commentary had been republished in thirty-four newspapers from Vermont to Georgia. Wilson's commentary thus became the first nationally communicated, authoritative interpretation of the constitution, and, as such, a prime focus for later interpretations, defenses, and critiques.[72]

[70] Farrand, *Federal Convention*, Vol. II, 483–516, 505, 509–10, 595, 641–67. The Committee on Revision was selected on September 8 and comprised of William Samuel Johnson (Connecticut), Alexander Hamilton (New York), Gouverneur Morris (Pennsylvania), James Madison (Virginia), and Rufus King (Massachusetts). Ibid., 547, 553–4 565–603.

[71] Article VII; Farrand, *Federal Convention*, Vol. II, 478–9.

[72] Merrill Jensen, John P. Kaminski, and Gaspare J. Saladino (eds.), *Documentary History*, Vol. II, 20, 128, 167–72; John P. Kaminski and Gaspare J. Saladino (eds.), *Documentary History*, Vol. XIII, 337–43. Alexander Dallas, the editor of the *Pennsylvania Herald*, declared Wilson's Commentary to be "the first authoritative explanation of the principles of the NEW FEDERAL CONSTITUTION." Ibid.,

Although he never mentioned them, Wilson was responding to sixteen Pennsylvania assemblymen who had published their objections to the constitution – and to the strong-arm tactics used in scheduling Pennsylvania's ratification convention – in a widely reprinted pamphlet. Among other things, the dissenting assemblymen worried that the new "legislature consisting of three branches" threatened to annihilate their state, or to reduce it to a "mere corporation." They also argued that a "declaration of rights," particularly to protect the "liberty of the press," was necessary.[73]

Wilson responded by relying on a variation of *expressio unius* principle: Congress' powers were explicitly enumerated in a positive, written grant, and, therefore, "every thing which is not given is reserved." There was no reason to fear for the liberty of the press, according to Wilson, because no power to regulate the press had been given to Congress in the constitution.[74]

This argument was countered, however, by a pseudonymous New York "Republican," who read a reprint of Wilson's commentary in the *New York Daily Advertiser*. "A Republican" took issue with Wilson's argument, inquiring rhetorically:

> Does this constitution possess, as you assert, no influence whatsoever on the press? Is there not a provision in it "to secure for a limited time to authors and inventors the exclusive right to their respective writings and discoveries"? I do not mean to call in question the propriety of this provision, but I would ask, whether under it the press may not be considered subject to the influence and controul of this government? – Will it be denied that this power includes in it (in some measure) that of regulating literary productions?[75]

This response to Wilson was reprinted (among other places) in Philadelphia's *Independent Gazetteer* on October 30. Robert Whitehill, a drafter of Pennsylvania's 1776 constitution and one of the dissenting Pennsylvania assemblymen, drew on the Republican's argument in bolstering his case that a constitution without a bill of rights posed a threat to fundamental liberties, including liberty of the press.[76]

Apparently, the "Anti-Federalist" opponents of the US Constitution did not question the legal foundations of copyright protection, but they were concerned

337; also Bailyn, *Ideological Origins*, 328; Kermit L. Hall and Mark David Hall (eds.), *Collected Works of James Wilson*, Vol. I (Carmel, Indiana: Liberty Fund, 2007), 171.

73 Merrill Jensen, John P. Kaminski, and Gaspare J. Saladino (eds.), *Documentary History*, Vol. II, 112–17, 128.

74 Ibid., 167–8; Kaminski & Saladino (eds.), *Documentary History*, Vol. XIII, 339.

75 Kaminski et al. (eds.), *Documentary History*, Vol. XIX, 130–3.

76 Ibid., 130; Jensen, Kaminski & Saladino (eds.), *Documentary History*, Vol. II, 454, 468. Despite being defeated in the Pennsylvania Convention, Whitehill and twenty other men sharing his concerns published a lengthy "Dissent of the Minority of the Pennsylvania Convention" on December 18, 1787; this "Dissent" was republished and circulated widely throughout the States, and it helped generate significant momentum behind the movement to amend the Constitution with a bill of rights. John P. Kaminski, Gaspare J. Saladino, and Richard Leffler (eds.), *Documentary History*, Vol. XV, 7–36.

about its implications for a free press. They were also concerned about "monopolies," as would become clear in the Massachusetts ratifying convention. Before turning to the Massachusetts convention, however, one other argument in James Wilson's Commentary deserves emphasis.

Wilson had also responded to the concern that the constitution's provisions for a strengthened federal union would reduce the states to "mere corporations." His response reflects the significance of corporate legal traditions for the organizational structure of a newly forming United States of America:

> Those who have employed the term corporation upon this occasion, are not perhaps aware of its extent. In common parlance, indeed, it is generally applied to petty associations for the ease and conveniency of a few individuals; but in its enlarged sense, it will comprehend the government of Pennsylvania, the existing union of the states, and even this projected system is nothing more than a formal act of incorporation.[77]

Wilson, in other words, agreed with Charles Pinckney that the United States was, from a legal perspective, a corporate entity.[78]

Historians of the revolutionary period have drawn attention to the power of republican traditions in shaping American understandings about the new national society they were building. These same historians have also noted, however, that the "republican" concept was not a formal, organizational concept: it did not primarily evoke a particular form of society and government but rather the qualities (or "spirit") of the people making up the society and government.[79]

Granted, as Americans knew from reading Montesquieu and Polybius, a republican conception did imply some dispersion of political power and authority throughout a social collectivity. However, the significant point was more normative than organizationally descriptive: the people holding power and authority should be virtuous and reasonable. Their primary orientation should be to the public good (the common wealth, or *res publica*), rather than to private gain or selfish interest. Otherwise, the republic would collapse into a monarchical tyranny, as Rome had. To be a "republican" in this sense was to embrace a heroic virtue-ethic, to be supremely "value rational" in partaking of the commonwealth's resources and responsibilities. American "republicanism" was, therefore, a very particular type of

77 Jensen, Kaminski & Saladino (eds.), *Documentary History*, Vol. II, 170; Kaminski & Saladino (eds.), *Documentary History*, Vol. XIII, 342.

78 Pinckney had proposed an amendment to the draft constitution specifying that "[t]he United States shall be for ever considered as one Body-corporate and politic in law, and entitled to all the rights, privileges, and immunities which to Bodies Corporate do, or ought to appertain." Farrand, *Federal Convention*, Vol. II, 335, 340–2.

79 Bailyn, *Ideological Origins*, vi, 281–379; Wood, *Creation of the American Republic*, 46–90; *cf.* Mark A. Noll, *America's God: From Jonathan Edwards to Abraham Lincoln* (Oxford: Oxford University Press, 2002), 3–92, 447–51.

normative idealism, one infused with an understanding of Greco-Roman and Biblical history.

But within this framework of virtuous idealism, there was a wide range of possibilities for the formal structure of society and government. For two primary contributors to the text of the constitution – Charles Pinckney and James Wilson – the concepts and principles giving meaningful form to the federal government's formal structure were drawn from corporate legal traditions, traceable ultimately to Roman legal traditions, but interpreted in relation to more recent British traditions connected with colonial corporations and state charters. From this perspective, the Americans would, through their new constitution, move from a structure of partnership to a corporate structure, from an unincorporated "association" of states to an incorporated "Union" of states, which could hold property and incur obligations under its own name. Among the first obligations that this Union would incur under its own name were the states' crippling debts.[80]

But for jurists trained in English common law, corporate legal traditions were closely related to anti-monopoly traditions. The English Statute of Monopolies (1624) had prohibited monopolies while creating exceptions for corporate charters and patents for "new manufactures." Several of Sir Edward Coke's famous reports delineating the prohibition of monopolies under English common law had involved corporate charters. Indeed, the English charters incorporating guilds (like the Stationers Company) and colonial companies often granted monopolies explicitly – monopolies of trade, and, in the case of the colonies, monopolies of landed territory. Although the English anti-monopoly tradition carried with it a great deal of hostility to monopolies, it also enabled certain types of monopoly to be viewed as positive exceptions. Corporations (of certain types) and patents were, for jurists trained in this tradition, two such exceptions.[81]

But we can also see why some revolutionary Americans, whose "rights" and "liberties" had become so salient in their struggle with Britain, might have been worried. The Massachusetts delegates, who ultimately voted 187 to 168 to ratify the constitution, expressed pointed concern about its potential to sanction monopolies. Their concerns did not focus on the Congressional power to create patents and copyrights, but rather on Congress' potential to create corporations, either pursuant to its power to regulate commerce or its power to make all laws "necessary and proper for carrying into Execution" the other powers given in the constitution. Elbridge Gerry (1744–1814, of "gerrymandering" fame) had raised this concern at the end of the constitutional convention, and the concern echoed in Massachusetts newspapers during the period leading up to that state's ratifying convention. This concern was addressed by proposing an amendment to the constitution that would

80 Jason Kaufman, "Corporate Law and the Sovereignty of States," *American Sociological Review* 73(3): 402–25 (2008); Wood, *Creation of the American Republic*, 53–65.

81 For fuller discussion see Chapter 8.

prohibit Congress from erecting a "company of merchants with exclusive advantages of commerce."[82]

Concerns about mercantile monopolies were also raised in the Virginia and New York ratification conventions, as were concerns about liberty of the press. However, in neither convention were these concerns provoked by the constitutional clause authorizing the federal Congress to issue copyrights and patents. Indeed, in conventions marked by contentious debate over Congressional powers, the absence of debate in Virginia and New York over the intellectual property clause is striking.[83]

The letter from James Kent to Nathaniel Lawrence, with which this chapter opened, might help to shed light on the apparent acceptance of a Congressional power to issue copyrights and patents, even among opponents to the constitution who were concerned about its potential to sanction mercantile monopolies. Kent had written that Adam Smith "has taught me to look with an unfavorable eye on monopolies – But a monopoly of the mental kind I take to be laudable & an exception to the Rule."[84]

While there was a jesting element in this closing to a letter that had mainly focused on other issues, it also seems probable that the "mental monopolies" to which Kent was referring to were patents and/or copyrights, and that is how he has been interpreted by others. Such monopolies, according to Kent, are not only an exception to the general "Rule" against monopolies, but are also positively praiseworthy (laudable).[85]

James Madison echoed and elaborated this view as "Publius" in Federalist 43, which was first published in the *New York Independent Journal* on January 23, 1788. Addressing Congress' "miscellaneous" constitutional powers, Madison wrote of the power to grant copyrights and patents:

> The utility of this power will scarcely be questioned. The copyright of authors has been solemnly adjudged, in Great Britain, to be a right of common law. The right to useful inventions seems with equal reason to belong to the inventors. The public good fully coincides in both cases with the claims of individuals. The States cannot separately make effectual provision for either of the cases, and most of them have anticipated the decision of this point, by laws passed at the instance of Congress.[86]

82 John P. Kaminski et al. (eds.), *Documentary History*, Vol. IV, 14, 288–90, 426–8; John P. Kaminski et al. (eds.), *Documentary History*, Vol. V, 576–80, 653–4, 720–6, 770–2, 797–8; John P. Kaminski et al. (eds.), *Documentary History*, Vol. VI, 1382, 1414, 1470, 1478. Most of the newspaper articles were published in the *Massachusetts Gazette* under the pseudonym "Agrippa." Some have argued that "Agrippa" was, in fact, Elbridge Gerry (see Kaminski et al. (eds.), *Documentary History*, Vol. IV, 303–6).

83 John P. Kaminski, Gaspare J. Saladino, and Richard Leffler (eds.), *Documentary History*, Vol. IX, 672–3; John P. Kaminski et al. (eds.), *Documentary History*, Vol. X, 1191, 1316–17, 1325–6; John P. Kaminski et al. (eds.), *Documentary History*, Vol. XXII, 2069, 2110–12.

84 Kaminski et al. (eds.), *Documentary History*, Vol. XIX, 247.

85 Oliar, "Making Sense of the Intellectual Property Clause," 1803 n. 164.

86 John P. Kaminski, Gaspare J. Saladino, and Richard Leffler (eds.), *Documentary History*, Vol. XV, 439.

In arguing that "the public good fully coincides" with private benefit in the case of patents and copyrights, Madison was articulating the principle that underwrote their exceptional status. Consistent with the anti-monopoly tradition of English law, patents and copyrights were viewed as exceptions to the general prohibition, as beneficial monopolies granted for a limited time to "encourage" invention and cultural production, which would ultimately be for the public good.

In arguing that the individual States "cannot separately make effectual provision for" patents and copyrights, Madison was echoing an argument that Thomas McKean, Chief Justice of Pennsylvania, had made during the Pennsylvania ratification process. According to McKean, the effective granting of patents and copyrights could only be accomplished by the federal Congress:

> For, sir, the laws of the respective states could only operate within their respective boundaries, and therefore, a work which had cost the author his whole life to complete, when published in one state, however it might there be secured, could easily be carried into another state in which a republication would be accompanied with neither penalty nor punishment – a circumstance manifestly injurious to the author in particular, and to the cause of science in general.

Roger Sherman had formulated a similar argument during Connecticut's ratification debates, in an article published in the *Connecticut Courant* on January 7, 1788.[87]

In asserting that copyright had been "solemnly adjudged ... to be a right of common law," Madison was no doubt referring to the *Millar* case discussed earlier. His familiarity with the *Millar* decision, and with recent state-level patent and copyright laws, dated from his time in the Continental Congress and the Virginia House of Burgesses. Conversations with Noah Webster, author of a new dictionary of American English, and awareness of the struggle to secure steamboat patents within several states would likely have made the public and private benefits, as well as the "utility," of Congressionally granted patents and copyrights very salient to Madison.[88]

Although Madison had ultimately decided against a professional legal career, he had nonetheless engaged in sustained study of the law as a young man, and he had

87 Jensen, Kaminski & Saladino (eds.), *Documentary History*, Vol. II, 415; Merrill Jensen, John P. Kaminski, and Gaspare J. Saladino, *Documentary History*, Vol. III, 524–7. "These powers appear to be necessary for the common benefit of the states and could not be effectually provided for by the particular states." Ibid., 525.

88 Madison had served on the committee of the Continental Congress that recommended to the states that they provide copyright protection for "literary property." *Journals of the American Congress*, Vol. 4, 1823, at 219; Bugbee 1967, at 113, 189. He had also served on committees in the Virginia House of Delegates that, between 1785 and 1786, considered (and rejected) a patent application for a steamboat engine by John Fitch, and that drafted and presented Virginia's copyright law (see Bugbee 1967, at 96–7, 121). Just prior to the Constitutional Convention, Madison had noted the need for national uniformity in matters of commerce, including in relation to "literary property" (see Madison 1900 (Vol. II), Observations by J.M., #5, dated April 1787).

spent years as a legislator in dialog with statesmen like Thomas Jefferson and Edmund Randolph. He had, moreover, studied with Samuel Stanhope Smith at the College of New Jersey (Princeton), which formed the center of a powerful interweaving of Reformed (Calvinist) Christian and Scottish ethical traditions. In this interweaving, an ideal of natural legality had been articulated and supported. Building on the strength of this ideal, Madison and his fellow Americans reinterpreted legal traditions inherited from Britain and Rome, producing the foundation for US intellectual property law.[89]

9.6 NATURAL LAW AND THE EARLY ADMINISTRATION OF US INTELLECTUAL PROPERTY LAW

In the wake of their successful revolt against Britain, Americans found new ways of reconciling their deep religious convictions, rooted in Reformed traditions of Christianity, with republican conceptions of their polity, and a frenetic quest for freedom and prosperity. For us today, it is almost impossible to understand why they seemed to see so little moral conflict in a vigorous pursuit of property and power, on the one hand, and a prayerful worship of their redeeming God, on the other. Seeing the social implications of natural legality as a cultural paradigm of values and ideals might help us to make sense of this.

We can see this culture of natural legality, in microcosm, at Princeton University (then the College of New Jersey), and in a form with direct implications for recognition of intellectual property rights. We see it in the writings of Samuel Stanhope Smith, president of Princeton from 1795 to 1812, a former classmate of James Madison. And we see it, more broadly, in the republican ideology that flowed through centers of higher learning in the fledgling United States.[90]

A new worldview was created, one that is still with us today. This is the worldview for a nation that has been intentionally designed to work together in power for wealth generation. Its architects were men like James Madison and Thomas Jefferson, men who confidently believed that established Christianity should be disempowered, for the good of the nation. With the disestablishment of Christianity, in the "separation of church and state," went the empowerment of national commerce and industry, as well as early forms of federal administration to nurture their development. Among the earliest federal administrative agencies created to pursue these national goals were a post office and a patent office, sharing the same building in the new national capitol.[91]

89 Noll, *America's God*, 128, 203–4, and passim.

90 Samuel Stanhope Smith, *The Lectures, Corrected and Improved, which Have Been Delivered for a Series of Years, in the College of New Jersey, on the Subjects of Moral and Political Philosophy*, Vol. II (Trenton: Daniel Fenton, 1812), 189–200; Noah Webster, "Origin of the Copyright Laws in the United States," in *A Collection of Papers on Political, Literary, and Moral Subjects by Noah Webster* (New York: Webster & Clark, 1843), 173–4; Noll, *Princeton*, passim.

91 For further discussion, see Laura R. Ford, "Intellectual Property and Industrialization: Legalizing Hope in Economic Growth," *Theory & Society* 46: 57–93 (2017).

As president of the United States (1809–17), James Madison supported his neighbor Dr. William Thornton (1759–1828) in overseeing the new patent office. Dr. Thornton did so with vigor, establishing foundational practices for the office and issuing guidelines in what was becoming a national press. These guidelines were issued to help Americans in their applications for patents and copyrights, to protect their works of "genius." One of the practices that Dr. Thornton helped to establish, in conformity with early patent laws, was the oath of novelty.[92]

Dr. Thornton "superintended" the Patent Office for twenty-six years, from 1802 until his death in 1828. Interpreting Congress' patent and copyright acts, while drawing on his own experiences as an artist and inventor, Dr. Thornton contributed to early administrative frameworks that were maintained by the Patent Office, the Library of Congress, and the Copyright Office. Together with the federal courts, these were the institutional foundations of US patent and copyright law, and among the earliest foundations of America's administrative state.[93]

The arguments that had supported these early institutional foundations were ultimately arguments from natural law, which had been developed from older traditions of Roman and Biblical law, combined with English common law and British legal experience. John Locke's adaptations of arguments from natural law in support of liberal political theory spoke persuasively to men who were self-consciously creating a new legal order. On the basis of such arguments, men like Samuel Stanhope Smith and James Madison considered it both just and nationally advantageous to grant patents and copyrights, for limited times, to inventors and authors. And they embedded the Congressional power to legislatively enable such grants into the constitutional design for a powerful nation-state, one that endures, in tarnish and struggle, to this day.

9.7 CONCLUSION

As Chief Justice of the English Court of King's Bench, Lord Mansfield concluded that intellectual property (of the copyright variety) really is property, according to the principles of English common law. He came to this conclusion for two reasons: (1) it was the conclusion that he believed was logically coherent and just, and (2) it accorded with common law principles of property, *as these had developed in the Glorious Revolution*. In this second argument – "equally conclusive" with the first, he believed – Lord Mansfield implicitly recognized that the seventeenth-century's Parliamentary Revolution had impacted the property principles of English common law. Prerogative copyright – which, in his view, was property – survived the Revolution but only in a nationalized form. From this point forward, the king's property was "civil" property and could only be rooted in principles that were also

92 Ibid., 86.; also Kenneth W. Dobyns, *The Patent Office Pony* (Fredericksburg: Sergeant Kirkland's Museum and Historical Society, 1994).

93 Dobyns, *Patent Office Pony*, 79.

applicable to the king's subjects. Any special proprietary privilege belonging to the king, such as prerogative property in a thing belonging to no one (*res nullius*), had been eliminated by the Revolution, in Lord Mansfield's view.[94]

Lord Mansfield, in this reading of him, acknowledged that the events leading up to and growing out of the Glorious Revolution – events stretching from the Parliaments of Coke, through the civil wars, and ending with the Hanoverian succession – constituted a cultural, social, political, and legal revolution, one that did not leave principles of property untouched.

By concluding that copyrights are a form of "intellectual" property, limited in time and created by statute in a manner analogous to patents, the *Millar* and *Donaldson* decisions laid a foundation in the British legal tradition for fusing them together under a common category of "intellectual" property. Ultimately, these cases addressed a categorical question: did the English common law category of property include intellectual property within its conceptual boundaries? The answer was a complicated yes.[95]

Standing together, the *Donaldson* and *Millar* cases left an ambiguous legacy. At a minimum, however, two things were clear. First, the "intellectual" objects at issue were, in some new sense (however limited), property. Second, this property was basically created pursuant to statute, and it would come to an end pursuant to statute. This would mean that it could be used to support legislatively approved goals that might include economic protectionism for national industries and creative developments in literature.

On the other side of the Atlantic Ocean, meanwhile, a new national state was being created out of formerly British colonies. The new US Constitution gave the national Congress the power to "secure" to authors and inventors the "exclusive right to their respective writings and discoveries." As in Britain, copyrights and patents would be time-limited grants from the national state. From the beginning, however, they would be treated as grants "by right," rather than discretionary grants "by grace."

No one doubts the importance of natural law for the US Revolution. What is sometimes forgotten, however, is the extent to which the cultural ideals of natural law borrow from Roman law, and from a Christianity sustained over centuries through traditional syntheses of Biblical and Roman law. The natural rights ideals drawn from this legal tradition were vital in the Glorious Revolution of 1688–89, and in Britain's ambiguous embrace of intellectual property law. They were naturalized and radicalized in the revolutionary new world of Britain's American colonies.

94 *Millar*, 98 Eng. Rep. at 250–7.

95 The fusing of patent and copyright together under the heading of intellectual property would be completed as a result of future interpretive activity. At this point, the outcomes were, strictly speaking, more limited. They were: (1) copyrights are a form of literary property created by statute, limited in time, and vested in authors, and (2) patents are analogous to copyrights because they also are created by statute, limited in time, and vested in another type of intellectual laborer: inventors.

But there was also a movement of radicalism which spread across the European Continent. Here responses to liberalism and natural legality took dramatically idealistic and "romantic" turns, which nonetheless help us to see the extent to which intellectual property is fundamental to, and dependent upon, legal uniformity in the social bonds that ultimately empower the modern nation-state.

And so we turn our attention to Revolutionary France.

10

Semantic Legal Ordering

Idealizing Intellectual Property

In 1774 – the same year *Donaldson* v. *Beckett* was decided in the British House of Lords – a young French king, Louis XVI (1754–92), opened his reign with an ambivalent movement in the direction of liberal reform, nominating Anne-Robert-Jacques Turgot (1727–81) – a leading advocate for new economic approaches to policy-making – to direct the finances of his administration. Within the space of two short years, Turgot undertook a series of radical reforms, including the abolition of guilds throughout France. Although the unpopularity of Turgot's reforms quickly led to his replacement, and to the temporary reinstatement of the guilds, the reforms would ultimately become permanent in the French Revolution.[1]

Intellectual property emerged in France as part of the Revolution. Indeed, France in 1791 and 1793 went further than either Britain or the United States in declaring inventions and products of authorship to be part of the "natural rights" of their authors. To this day, French intellectual property law is traced back to these revolutionary declarations. However, the formal legal basis for French intellectual property rests in ever-changing legislation – the Intellectual Property Code – and in the interpretations of French courts, administrative bodies, and legal academics. In the French legal system, these interpretations are known as "jurisprudence" and "doctrine."[2]

[1] Louis XVI and the nomination of Turgot: John Hardman, *The Life of Louis XVI* (New Haven: Yale University Press, 2016), Chapters 1–2. Turgot as a leading advocate for the new "physiocratic" theories of the economy: William H. Sewell, Jr., *Work and Revolution in France: The Language of Labor from the Old Regime to 1848* (Cambridge, UK: Cambridge University Press, 1980), 72. Turgot's reforms: Douglas Dakin, *Turgot and the Ancien Régime in France* (London: Methuen & Co., 1939), 149–251; Robert Perry Shepherd, *Turgot and the Six Edicts* (New York: Columbia University Ph.D. Thesis, 1903).

[2] Revolutionary developments of French intellectual property law: French Literary and Artistic Property Act of 1793, available in translation by Andrew Counter at Primary Sources on Copyright (1450–1900), edited by Lionel Bently and M. Kretschmer, www.copyrighthistory.org (hereafter *Primary Sources*); Carla Hesse, *Publishing and Cultural Politics in Revolutionary Paris, 1789–1810* (Berkeley: University of California Press, 1991), 83–124 and passim. French Intellectual Property Code, consolidated version as of May 22, 2020, available from the World Intellectual Property Organization's WIPO-Lex database: https://wipolex.wipo.int/en/legislation/profile/FR (accessed July 13, 2020). WIPO is discussed further

In contrast to the United States, France's constitutional framework has undergone a series of fundamental transformations, some of them quite radical, since the time intellectual property was first recognized. A significant source of overall legal stability in France has therefore been the Civil Code, which was instituted in 1804 under Napoleon. Although that code did not mention intellectual property specifically, it did provide foundational and nationally uniform legal principles for the recognition and protection of property, which have endured until today.[3]

Under the approach to legality established by the French Civil Code, cases are not formally a binding source of law, although they are persuasive. Nevertheless, since legislation relating to important areas of intellectual property law was not enacted until long after the Revolution, French courts took actual responsibility for the development of important intellectual property doctrines during the nineteenth century. This contribution of French jurisprudence has had an enduring impact, well beyond France's national boundaries, in the development of "moral rights," which take intellectual property in an idealizing direction by positing a transcendent dimension to human creativity and authorship, implicating an inalienable proprietary bond between authors and their creative works. In German-speaking lands, the implications of this idealizing development may be seen in Romantic theories of authorship, which are closely connected to communitarian and nationalizing legal theories that have played an important role in German legal history, for better and for worse.[4]

In jurisprudence and legal doctrine, as in so many areas, the French Revolution was earth-shaking. In this jurisprudential earthquake, intellectual property was recognized, both as national property and as a natural right, while legal concepts of sovereignty were reinterpreted, in doctrinal activities involving semantic legal ordering. Under the pressure of events, and in the opening of radical new possibilities, old legal concepts, received through legal traditions, exercised a formative influence, while yet being given new interpretive meanings, with social implications extending well beyond France.

in Chapter 12. Jurisprudence and doctrine in the French legal system: John Bell, Sophie Boyron, and Simon Whittaker, *Principles of French Law*, 2nd ed. (Oxford: Oxford University Press, 2008), 24–34; Eva Steiner, *French Law: A Comparative Approach*, 2nd ed. (Oxford: Oxford University Press, 2018), chs. 1, 4, 9, and passim.

3 French Constitution of 1958, as amended in 2008, available from the WIPO-Lex database: https://wipolex.wipo.int/en/legislation/details/5560 (accessed July 13, 2020). French Civil Code, available from the WIPO-Lex database: https://wipolex.wipo.int/en/legislation/details/19413 (accessed July 13, 2020). French Civil Code, as enacted in 1804 under Napoleon, translated anonymously by a barrister of the Inner Temple: www.napoleon-series.org/research/government/c_code.html (accessed July 13, 2020). Property principles in the Civil Code: Steiner, *French Law*, ch. 15.

4 Christopher Aide, "A More Comprehensive Soul: Romantic Conceptions of Authorship and the Copyright Doctrine of Moral Right," *University of Toronto Faculty of Law Review* 48(2) (1990): 211–28; Russell J. DaSilva, "*Droit Moral* and the Amoral Copyright: A Comparison of Artists' Rights in France and the United States," *Bulletin of the Copyright Society of the U.S.A.* 28(1) (1980): 1–58; Irma Sirvinskaite, "Toward Copyright 'Europeanification': European Union Moral Rights," *Journal of International Media and Entertainment Law* 3(2) (2011): 263–88.

Frameworks of property and national sovereignty were reformed, in the French Revolution, in meaningful connection with radicalizing and idealizing conceptions of the rights and obligations inherent in human creativity. As many have noted, some in amusement and some in disgust, there are overtly religious dimensions in the "spiritualizing" of intellectual property (*geistiges Eigentum*, spiritual property), which was recognized by jurists and political actors, as an outgrowth of the Revolution.[5]

There were earlier roots for this, however, as we will see in a sixteenth-century case, argued in the *Parlement* of Paris in 1586, when deepening fragmentations over politicized religion were becoming increasingly violent in France. In this case, which involved a new edition of writings by the Stoic philosopher Seneca (c. 4 BC–AD 65), the jurist Simon Marion drew an explicit analogy between divine and human creation, arguing that, just as God exercises sovereign lordship over his creation, a human author or inventor should have the sovereign right (*droit*) to decide what happens with his creation. Authors accordingly have the sovereign power to make their creations freely available, and Marion sought to nullify a royal privilege that had been granted to protect a new edition of Seneca's works. Here, *in nuce*, is an argument for authorial rights as moral rights, with legal powers closely analogous to sovereign powers, totally independent of economic considerations. And here we can see an explicitly religious argument for the sovereign lordship of spiritually gifted authors and inventors, as creators. Linkages to new concepts of state sovereignty, articulated only a few years before by the jurist Jean Bodin (1529/30–1596), have been noted by recent commentators, as we will see.[6]

In this chapter, I endeavor to weave together a complex series of European legal developments connected with the emergence of intellectual property. I begin by tracing the emergence of intellectual property in France, focusing on the context for this development in the revolutionary processes through which a new French nation was formed, and on the ambivalent implications of national codification for intellectual property in France. I then go back to the Reformation, pointing out the significance of Calvinist and Lutheran legal doctrines for jurisprudential traditions carrying new conceptions of sovereignty and natural rights. Shifting to the legacies of these traditions for legal and administrative theories that developed in German-speaking lands, we will briefly glimpse early foundations for a jurisprudential narrative that becomes vital to the substantive rationale of intellectual property in our own time: progressivism.

5 Russell DaSilva quotes the Belgian legal scholar Pierre Recht in translation: "When *droit moral* fanatics discuss moral rights, they take the attitude of a religious zealot talking of sacred things, or a Girondin reading the Declaration of the Rights of Man." DaSilva, "*Droit Moral*," 7 (*translating* Pierre Recht, *Le Droit d'Auteur: Une Nouvelle Forme de Propriété* [Gembloux: J. Duculot, 1969], 281).

6 Simon Marion's plea on privileges (1586), translated by Andrew Counter, *Primary Sources*; Frédéric Rideau, "Commentary on Simon Marion's Plea on Privileges" (2008), *Primary Sources*.

Intellectual property is good because it helps us to economically and culturally progress. In nineteenth-century Germany, the jurisprudential narrative underpinning this argument came out of Kantian philosophy, and the focus was on moral progress. In Chapter 12, we will see that the concept of progress, especially in the United States, has become much more narrowly economic. But that is the story for our final chapter. What I hope to show in this chapter is the way that sixteenth-century developments in religious and legal consciousness, triggered in the complex dialectic between Protestant Reformation(s) and Catholic Counter-Reformation(s), contributed to a line of legal tradition extending into the early nineteenth century, with significant implications for the development of intellectual property and national sovereignty in western Europe.

The upshot of these complex developments, as seen with particular clarity in the development of moral rights doctrines, is a paradoxical linkage between bureaucratic impersonalism in the formal application of legal doctrines (the "rule of law") and an idealizing personalism in the agentive capacities of individual human beings (the idolizing of "genius"). This paradoxical combination can ultimately be traced to influences from Reformation-era legal doctrines, which generated new conceptions of legal and moral obligation. Under the secularizing influences of liberalism and Romanticism, this paradoxical combination enabled an idealization of human creative agency, on the one hand, in combination with increasingly impersonal concepts of state sovereignty, on the other.

In the radicalizing crucible of the French Revolution, intellectual property crystallized into an infrastructure of state power bridging public and private dimensions of social, political, and economic life. Reformation-era developments in legal doctrines linking Roman and Biblical law were interpreted anew, supporting a combination of "absolute" national sovereignty and Romantic individualism. Intellectual property was idealized, and state power was distinguished from the moral community of civil society. Positive and natural legality were synthesized and revolutionized, joined in supporting a jurisprudential narrative of progress, with troubling implications that haunt us today.

10.1 LA PROPRIÉTÉ LITTÉRAIRE, ARTISTIQUE, ET INDUSTRIELLE

Anne-Robert-Jacques Turgot, a friend of *philosophes* and *économistes*, took on an impossible task in attempting to address the economic crisis of France's Bourbon monarchy, which had held dynastic power since the sixteenth century. Nonetheless, as a minister of the king, Turgot sought to introduce the legal and economic reforms which he believed were desperately needed for the benefit of French society. He focused at first on the legal framework governing purchases and sales of "grain" (an expansive concept that included wheat, rye, flour, peas, beans, lentils, and rice). Having served for over twelve years as chief royal administrator (*Intendant*) in the rural province of Limousin, Turgot had been sensitized to the need for agrarian reforms throughout provincial France, especially in the food supply for Paris. Painfully aware of the monarchy's dire financial situation, Turgot also undertook financial reforms. However, it was his attempt at industrial reform that generated the greatest opposition to his ministry. This opposition was expressed through the *Parlements*, the preeminent judicial institutions of prerevolutionary France.[7]

Turgot's industrial philosophy was cogently expressed in his preamble to the 1776 decree abolishing guilds and their privileges, issued under the name of the king. This preamble declared the purpose of the decree to be the assurance of full and complete "rights" to the king's subjects, especially the rights to labor and "industry" among those who have none but these to sell. The preamble inveighed against the "monopolies" and "domination" of the guild-masters, recounting the history of growth in strength and exclusiveness of French guilds. It declared "the right of labor the property of all men," and it identified a chief evil of guild monopolies to be this: they "retard the progress of the arts by the difficulties which inventors find multiplied by the guilds."[8]

Turgot's commitment to liberalism in natural rights and innovation was shared by a younger man, who would extol Turgot's mentorship and friendship as "the sweetest perhaps I ever felt": Nicolas de Caritat, marquis de Condorcet (1743–94). In his *Life of Turgot* (1786), Condorcet presented the thoughts and activities of his late mentor, expressing his views on Turgot's policies in their prerevolutionary social context. Condorcet's perspectives on prerevolutionary French legal administration reveal patterns that would be significant to revolutionary lawmaking, contributing to the legal paradigms for French patent and copyright law. Indeed, Condorcet probably contributed to the drafting of an unenacted forerunner to the 1793 decree declaring writings to be the "property" (*propriété*) of their authors. Furthermore, as a member of the Royal Academy of Sciences, Condorcet would have observed firsthand the examination processes for "new and useful" inventions submitted to the king for royal privileges.[9]

[7] Dakin, *Turgot*, 92–103; Sewell, Jr., *Work and Revolution*, 72–7; Joseph Hugh Shennan, *The Parlement of Paris*, 2nd ed. (Thrupp: Sutton Publishing, 1998), 320–5; Shepherd, *Six Edicts*, 75, 162–75. Broader perspective on the *parlements*: Bailey S. Stone, *French Parlements and the Crisis of the Old Regime* (Chapel Hill: University of North Carolina Press, 1986); idem, *The Parlement of Paris, 1774–1789* (Chapel Hill: University of North Carolina Press, 1981).

[8] Sewell, *Work and Revolution*, 72–3; Shepherd, *Six Edicts*, 182–92.

[9] *Vie de Monsieur Turgot*, English translation published anonymously as *The Life of M. Turgot* (London: J. Johnson, 1787), 3; Jane C. Ginsburg, "A Tale of Two Copyrights: Literary Property in Revolutionary France and America," *Tulane Law Review* 64 (1990): 991–1023, 1009–14; Hesse, *Cultural Politics*, 102–121; David Williams, *Condorcet and Modernity* (Cambridge, UK: Cambridge University Press, 2004), 17–22. Condorcet and the Royal Academy: Frank D. Prager, "An Award and a Law Obtained by Caron de Beaumarchais," *Journal of the Patent Office Society* 44 (1962): 147–74, 148–9; Williams, *Condorcet*, 11–12, 14–16; also Maurice Crosland, *Science under Control: The French Academy of Sciences 1795–1914* (Cambridge, UK: Cambridge University Press, 1992), 14–18; Roger Hahn, *The Anatomy of a Scientific Institution: The Paris Academy of Sciences, 1666–1803* (Berkeley: University of California Press, 1971).

Condorcet did not initially embrace a concept of *propriété intellectuelle*. He wrote with approval of his mentor that he (Turgot) "never . . . bestowed a patent" during the period of his ministry, choosing instead to reward inventors with gifts, pensions, or a guaranteed purchase of their "machines" in substantial quantities. Condorcet also expressed regret that Turgot had been compelled to carve out an exception for booksellers and printers in his decree abolishing the guilds. The advantages of "rendering free the trade of the printer and bookseller" to authors and to the French nation would, in his judgment, have been substantial.[10]

In his *Fragments sur la liberté de la presse* (1776), Condorcet had argued that "[literary property] is not a property derived from the natural order and defended by social force, it is a property founded in society itself. It is not a true right, it is a privilege." In his *Life of Turgot*, moreover, Condorcet stated flatly that "a privilege can never be property." Nevertheless, as Carla Hesse has argued, Condorcet was apparently persuaded by 1790 to join with the abbé Emmanuel Sieyès (1748–1836) in declaring that "the progress of enlightenment, and consequently the public good, [unite] with notions of distributive justice to necessitate that the property of a work should be guaranteed to the author by law."[11]

Just what were the circumstances that led Condorcet to shift his position? Carla Hesse has argued that Condorcet may have been influenced by the social and economic conditions resulting from the collapse of the Old Regime's framework of governance for printing, a development that crystallized around a revolutionary decree of August 4, 1789, implicating the abolition of guild-based privileges throughout France. Bringing Turgot's brief measures to fruition, and indeed going further than he had dared, this decree threatened all the privileges that had been so jealously guarded by France's powerful guilds, including privileges relating to the printing of written works (i.e., the sphere of later literary property) and to the making, use, and sale of inventions (i.e., the later sphere of patent protections). A subsequent decree of March 17, 1791, made the threat a reality.[12]

The economic and social instability following in the wake of these decrees appears to have been a factor in Condorcet's ambivalent embrace of literary property. However, unlike Denis Diderot (1713–84) – who had transcendently idealized the individual's property "right" flowing from authorship, even to the extent of making it superior to the right flowing from physical labor – Condorcet insisted

[10] *Life of M. Turgot*, 144–5, 117–23 (note).

[11] Ibid., 140; Hesse, *Cultural Politics*, 103, 105–6 (quoting B.J.B. Buchez et Prosper-Charles Roux, *Histoire parlementaire de la Révolution française*, Tome 4 (Paris: Paulin, 1834), 283). On the abbé Sieyès: Michael Sonenscher, "'Introduction' to Sieyès," in *Political Writings*, edited by Michael Sonenscher (Indianapolis: Hackett Publishing Co., 2003), xxii–xxiii, xxxiv–xxxv; William H. Sewell, Jr., *A Rhetoric of Bourgeois Revolution: The Abbé Sieyes and What Is the Third Estate?* (Durham: Duke University Press, 1994), 8–21 and passim.

[12] Hesse, *Cultural Politics*, 20–56, 63–82, 85–100, 106; also Ginsburg, "Tale of Two Copyrights," 1009–14.

on the superior right of the French nation. He seems to have been finally persuaded that it was for the good of the French nation to permit a limited property right to authors, in order to incentivize creativity and innovation. However, this was no absolute property right: it was derived from the nation, subject to the will of the nation, and it would return to the nation upon the expiration of its term. This was, after all, the same Condorcet who had approved of his mentor Turgot's statement that "the whole nation is the true proprietor of . . . wealth."[13]

It was quite naturally in revolutionary France that the rhetoric of "intellectual property" was most dramatically articulated and elevated into a transcendent ideal. In January 1791, the National Assembly's "will and order" was ratified by the ill-fated king, making it the case that:

> [A]ny new idea, the manifestation or development of which may become useful to society (*la société*), belongs basically to the one who has conceived it, and . . . it would be a violation of the rights of man (*droits de l'homme*) in their essence, not to regard an industrial discovery (*une découverte industrielle*) as the property (*propriété*) of its author (*auteur*).[14]

Peter Kurz, in his *World-History of Invention-Protection*, has identified this as the first complete codification of "intellectual property" (*geistiges Eigentum*) vis-à-vis industrial inventions. The law was drafted by the marquis Stanislas de Boufflers (1738–1815), a representative of the nobility from the province of Nancy (Lorraine). It was adopted by the National Assembly on December 31, 1790, after only a brief discussion.[15]

To persuade his fellow assemblymen to vote for his proposed law, de Boufflers presented a memorandum "On the property of authors of new discoveries and inventions in every type of industry." In this memorandum, de Boufflers drew on the natural law tradition to argue that "discovery" is the original source of ownership. At the same time, however, he drew on Rousseau's "social contract" theory (itself rooted in a particular interpretation of the natural law tradition) to argue that exclusive rights, limited in time, are granted to the inventor through a kind of "reasonable agreement" (*pacte raisonnable*) with the sovereign state. By analogizing the discoverer/inventor of industrial techniques to the "author" of a book, de Boufflers drew strength from the support for authors' rights among adherents to the natural law tradition in the National Assembly. At the same time, he avoided all

[13] Diderot's Letter on the Book Trade, Paris (1763), *Primary Sources*; *Life of M. Turgot*, 35, 381–97; Hesse, *Cultural Politics*, 100–5; Frédéric Rideau, "Commentary on Diderot's Letter on the Book Trade, Paris (1763)," *Primary Sources*.

[14] *Lois et Actes du gouvernement*, Tome II, l'Imprimerie Impériale (1806), reprinted in Peter Kurz, *Weltgeschichte des Erfindungsschutzes: Erfinder und Patente im Spiegel der Zeiten* (Köln: Carl Heymanns Verlag, 2000), 242–8, English translation in Frank D. Prager, "A History of Intellectual Property from 1545 to 1787," *Journal of the Patent Office Society* 26 (1944): 711–60, 756–7.

[15] Kurz, *Weltgeschichte*, 236–51, esp. 238; *cf.* Prager, "Caron de Beaumarchais," 171–2.

references to "monopolies" and "privileges," which were now held in deep opprobrium by so many members of the Assembly.[16]

Indeed, it is clear from the law itself, and from de Boufflers' memorandum, that where the inventor's "natural right" comes into conflict with the "rights" of the French nation, the latter is in the superior legal position: "it is in no way the goal of society to enrich the inventor, but rather to enrich itself through the invention." The clearest indication of this is, perhaps, the limitation in time: at the expiration of a patent (*les patentes*) – which would occur within five, ten, or fifteen years – the discovery or invention would become the property of "the society," that is, of all French citizens (*tout citoyens*) (§§ 8, 15). Furthermore, the first importers into France of new inventions or discoveries were to be treated as if they were the actual inventors or discoverers (§3); the French national interest in obtaining the industrial techniques clearly trumped any "original rights" of the actual (foreign) inventor(s).[17]

Returning to the Condorcet–Sieyès proposal for the treatment of literary and artistic works, we see the same basic paradigm prevailing there. This proposal had been placed before the National Assembly by Sieyès on January 20, 1790. The proposal (in Article XIV) recognized a proprietary right in authors of literary works, but it restricted the term of this right to the author's life plus ten years, a period that was calculated to ensure sufficient time to complete and sell an edition. The recognition of this authorial right was justified on the basis of the "public good" (*l'utilité publique*). Moreover, importers of works from abroad were explicitly permitted to engage in the "counterfeiting" of foreign works (Article XV). Five years after the death of a playwright, his works were to be deemed a "common good" (*bien commun*) of all theaters (Article XVIII). While this proposal was never enacted, it formed a basis for the 1791 law enacted to govern the "property" of playwrights, and the 1793 law enacted by the National Convention, which applied to writings, musical compositions, paintings, and engravings.[18]

France's 1793 law relating to literary and artistic property is generally regarded as the foundation of contemporary French copyright law. In order to secure its enactment, Joseph Lakanal proclaimed to the Convention:

> Of all properties, the most incontestable, the one whose increase is in no way injurious to Republican equality and which gives no offence to liberty, is undeniably the work of genius; it is if anything surprising that it should have proved necessary to recognize this property and secure its free exercise by a positive law, and that a great Revolution like ours should have been required to return us, in this as in so many matters, to the simplest elements of common justice .... It is after

16 Kurz, *Weltgeschichte*, 238–41.

17 Ibid; Prager, "History of Intellectual Property," 756–7.

18 "Sieyès' Report, Paris (1790)," translated by Freya Baetens, *Primary Sources*; Hesse, *Cultural Politics*, 97, 105–14.

careful consideration that this Committee advises you to create dedicated legislative provisions which will form, in a sense, the declaration of the rights of genius.[19]

Lakanal's sweeping rhetoric of the "work" and "rights of genius" has supported an interpretation of France's 1793 law as a proclamation of absolute authorial right (*droit d'auteur*), rooted in a creative "workmanship" model of natural law, analogous to, but more radical than, the Lockean theory that we have already encountered in England and the United States.[20]

And yet, despite its dramatic rhetoric, the French law (like the Condorcet–Sieyès proposal) limited the proprietary right to the lifetime of the author plus ten years (Arts. 1 & 2). Moreover, in order to obtain enforceable proprietary rights, authors were required to deposit copies of their works with the National Library or the "Cabinet des Estampes"; absent compliance with this requirement, authors lacked standing to enforce their rights (Art. 6). By imposing a "condition precedent" to obtaining an effective proprietary right, and by limiting the term of that right, even this most revolutionary of law reveals the national origin of the rights being granted.[21]

Limited proprietary rights were granted by the nation, subject to conditions imposed by the nation, and all for the benefit and enrichment of the nation. Ultimately, then, the French nation was lord and owner of the revolutionary *Propriété Littéraire, Artistique, et Industrielle*.

In the *Declaration of the Rights of Man and Citizen*, issued on the eve of the Revolution in August 1789, the Assembly had forthrightly declared the nation to be the source of all sovereignty: "no body (*corps*) nor individual may exercise any authority which does not proceed directly from the nation" (Art. 3). Despite declaring property to be an "inviolable and sacred right," the Declaration had also acknowledged that "public necessity" might override this right, so long as the process was legal and the owner was "justly indemnified" (Art. 17).[22]

"Sovereignty" and "property" are not so easily distinguished: even in our time, the concept of "dominion" (*dominium*) evokes both ownership and sovereignty. In the process of French nationalization, sovereignty, property, and lordship were located fundamentally in the nation. The fact that the "rights of genius" are, at root, derived from the nation is revealed by the fact that the nation can decide, albeit not arbitrarily, to remove those rights. The national state, in American English terms, is the bearer of "eminent domain." This is simply more obvious in the case of

19 "French Literary and Artistic Property Act, Paris (1793)," including an extract from Joseph Lakanal's Report, translated by Andrew Counter, *Primary Sources*.

20 Ginsburg, "Tale of Two Copyrights," 991–2; Hesse, *Cultural Politics*, 104. On the Lockean theory of knowledge as a "creationist" or "workmanship" model, see Ian Shapiro, *The Moral Foundations of Politics* (New Haven: Yale University Press, 2003), 9–12.

21 French Literary and Artistic Property Act, Paris (1793), translated by Andrew Counter, *Primary Sources*.

22 French Constitutional Council, Founding Documents, Declaration of Human and Civil Rights of August 26, 1789, www.conseil-constitutionnel.fr/en/declaration-of-human-and-civic-rights-of-26-august-1789 (accessed August 18, 2020).

intellectual property, which is limited in time, and subject to conditions precedent imposed by the national state.

10.2 SEMANTIC LEGAL ORDERING IN THE EARLY REVOLUTIONARY PERIOD

With the exception of the 1793 law relating to literary and artistic property, all the laws we have looked at so far were enacted before the Revolution, or in its earliest, least radical period: the period between August 1789 and September 1791, when the *Assemblée Nationale Constituante* was governing in conjunction with the king. Furthermore, as Carla Hesse has argued, the basic framework for the 1793 law relating to literary and artistic property had been worked out in this early period through the draft of Condorcet and Sieyès. Thus, in seeking to understand the role of legal thought and action vis-à-vis the emergence of intellectual property in France, we can concentrate our attention on the roles and positions of jurists and legal advocates in the period just preceding the Revolution, and into the first two years of the Revolution (from 1774 to 1791).[23]

Recent historical scholarship on the French Revolution has pointed to a significant shift in juristic orientation and practice that occurred in the years leading up to this period. Reacting to the chancellor René Nicolas de Maupeou's (1714–92) efforts to tame the *Parlements*' resistance to attempted reforms – culminating in temporary banishment of the *Parlements* and their replacement with a "council of state" – prominent jurists intensified their publication of legal memoranda (*mémoires judiciaires*) connected with cases they were arguing in the *Parlements*, linking their legal arguments to interests of the broader French "public," and positioning themselves as advocates for that broader "public" and "nation." According to David Bell, these jurists used the *mémoires judiciaires* "to present their clients as universal paradigms whose experiences had relevance to society as a whole." The *mémoire judiciaire* was "implicitly democratic and universalistic" because it "addressed itself to a socially indistinct 'public', and, by the very fact of publicizing the details of trials, implied that 'public opinion' should have a supervisory role over justice, traditionally the prerogative of the king alone."[24]

23 Hesse, *Cultural Politics*, 119–21. Least radical period: Timothy Tackett, *Becoming a Revolutionary, 1789–90* (Princeton: Princeton University Press, 1996); Peter A. J. Van den Berg, *The Politics of European Codification: A History of the Unification of Law in France, Prussia, the Austrian Monarchy and the Netherlands* (Groningen: Europa Law Publishing, 2007), 183–95. Narrative chronology of the Revolution: William Doyle, *The Oxford History of the French Revolution*, 3rd ed. (Oxford: Oxford University Press, 2018).

24 David A. Bell, "Lawyers into Demagogues: Chancellor Maupeou and the Transformation of Legal Practice in France 1771–1789," *Past and Present* 130 (1991): 107–141, 110, 117; also idem, *Lawyers and Citizens: The Making of a Political Elite in Old Regime France* (Oxford: Oxford University Press, 1994); Lucien Karpik, "Lawyers and Politics in France, 1814–1950: The State, the Market, and the Public," *Law & Social Inquiry* 13(4) (1988): 707–36; Sarah Maza, *Private Lives and Public Affairs: The*

Through their quasi-corporate Order, Parisian jurists had obtained an exemption from censorship rules, which were established from the time of the Reformation. Because of their exemption from these rules, jurists were in the unique position of being able to publish their memoranda without preliminary review by a censor. After Maupeou's attempted reforms, moreover, the traditional discipline of the Order began to break down, such that more radical jurists began to question the importance of "erudition, deference and respect for the law codes," advocating instead that the juristic role be opened to all men who displayed "genius" and the capacity to persuade. In the wake of Maupeou's reforms, according to Bell, "the men who had led the Order, represented its institutional continuity, and enforced its unwritten code, remained absent from the courts." This break in institutional continuity at the highest level of the judiciary contributed to a significant change in the style of legal practice, which was remarked upon by jurists and ministers of the time. In place of sustained study of French and Roman legal traditions, premised on the belief that authority resided in these traditions, French jurists began to turn toward the "public" and the "national will" as the source of legal authority, and to view themselves as advocates for this "public" and "nation."[25]

The constitutional conflict between monarchy and ministry, on the one hand, and the *Parlements*, on the other, has long been discussed as a contributing factor in the French Revolution. Contemporary historians trace an important strand of this discussion back to Alexis de Tocqueville (1805–59), who pointed to the influence of the *Parlements* on the "ways of the nation" at the dawn of the Revolution, and to their prerevolutionary role as protectors of "liberty" vis-à-vis the ministry. David Bell adds to this discussion by pointing to the role that this constitutional conflict played in transforming French legal culture and practice: rather than primarily acting as advocates for particular clients, jurists came to envision themselves as advocates on behalf of the "society" or "nation," as a whole.[26]

More recently, Amalia Kessler has pointed to a parallel development in French commercial law: responding to conflicts adjudicated in Parisian merchant courts, judges in these courts came to articulate a vision of "commerce" as a sphere of social activity functioning within "society" as a whole, rather than as the preserve of particular, "corporate" bodies. Putting these studies together with Timothy Tackett's detailed study of the National Assembly between 1789 and 1790, we can conceptualize a revolutionary process of semantic legal ordering, a reframing of the

Causes Célèbres of Prerevolutionary France (Berkeley: University of California Press, 1993); Tackett, *Becoming a Revolutionary*, 58–60.

[25] Bell, "Lawyers into Demagogues," 123, 134; Bell, *Lawyers and Citizens*, 138–63; Tackett, *Becoming a Revolutionary*, 80.

[26] Alexis de Tocqueville, *The Ancien Régime and the French Revolution*, translated by Gerald Bevan (London: Penguin Books, 2008), 68–9, 120; Bell, "Lawyers into Demagogues," 123, 134, and passim; Bell, *Lawyers & Citizens*, 138–63 and passim.

basis for social obligation, one that broke with certain legal traditions in order to radically reform others.[27]

Witnessing the dismantling and collapse of legal traditions and institutions that had sustained the social world that they knew, and witnessing at the same time the expanding possibilities for communication with a broader, more abstract, national public, French jurists drew on customary traditions of law, on doctrinal traditions and jurisprudence, and on the natural law tradition, to articulate the semantic foundations for a new, national order. According to these semantic foundations, as we find them in the documentary artifacts, the fundamental social relationships were to be national, with property rights allocated to individual members of the nation-state. No corporate bodies or privileges would stand between the individual, the family, and the nation. While property would be sacralized with the language of natural, "workmanship-based" rights, the national origin of property rights was revealed in the nation's rights of eminent domain, in the term limits placed upon certain of such rights, and in the conditions precedent enabling such rights. Proprietary legal capacities would be the result of laws and policies determined by the national will, justified in their benefit to the nation.

As Timothy Tackett's study of the Constituent National Assembly shows, the men who gathered for the meeting of the "Estates General" in the spring of 1789, and who had transformed themselves into a National Assembly by the summer of that year, were predominantly jurists. Although there were few men with legal training among the "Second Estate" (the nobility), the "First Estate" (the bishops and clergy) contained a sizable number with training in canon law, and approximately two-thirds of the "Third Estate" were jurists. Among those who spoke with the greatest frequency in the Constituent National Assembly, the vast majority were jurists.[28]

Like their American counterparts, these men were engaging in performative social acts involving meaningful language, seeking through their words and rhetoric to give conceptual form to a reformed constitution. However, as traditional sources of authority collapsed around them, the deputies were forced to also take on administrative and legislative responsibilities. With the abolition of the guilds and the elimination of privileges, the institutional structures regulating industrial, literary, and artistic production had broken down. Thus, the deputies must have perceived themselves to be responsible for providing an alternative. Consistent with their proclamation of national sovereignty, and perhaps with an eye to developments in Britain and the fledgling United States, the delegates elected to constitute a "national" framework for intellectual property. This "national" model enabled them to idealize the rights granted to individual authors and inventors as the

[27] Amalia D. Kessler, *A Revolution in Commerce: The Parisian Merchant Court and the Rise of Commercial Society in Eighteenth-Century France* (New Haven: Yale University Press, 2007); Tackett, *Becoming a Revolutionary*, passim.

[28] Tackett, *Becoming a Revolutionary*, Appendix III.

"natural" reward of "genius," while at the same time fundamentally rooting those rights in the national state.[29]

10.3 CODIFYING FRENCH PROPERTY

Aside from the *Declaration of the Rights of Man and Citizen*, which is incorporated by reference into the 1958 French Constitution, the basis for French property law today is the *Code Civil*, which was issued in 1804 under Napoleon. The French Civil Code, in other words, established the national foundations for French property law that have endured. It also established a model for modern civil codes that has since been emulated or referenced in many other nations around the world. At the time of its drafting, however, the code was primarily intended to provide a uniform set of laws governing the social relations between Frenchmen.[30]

Previously, French civil law had been divided between regions (primarily in the north) that relied fundamentally on customary law (*coutume*) and regions (primarily in the south) that relied on a "written law" (*droit écrit*) derived from Roman law; on top of these were layered a variety of royal ordinances and Parliamentary determinations. Seeking to provide a uniform, written source of civil law to "govern the relationships ... that bind every individual to one or more individuals," Napoleon and a small coterie of legal draftsmen represented their twin goals as the stabilization and unification of the French nation.[31]

Aside from Napoleon and his jurists, no other person was more responsible for the enactment of this code than the abbé Emmanuel Sieyès, whom we have already encountered as a key figure in the establishment of revolutionary literary property. As an abbé, Sieyès was a member of the clergy, that is, the first estate. However, on the eve of the Estates General, he had written a powerful pamphlet articulating a vision for a unitary nation based in the "national will" and the third estate. He had also written pamphlets advocating the establishment of a uniform code of law.[32]

In 1799, Sieyès was appointed to membership in the *Directoire*, the executive body governing postrevolutionary France. Together with one of his allies in the *Directoire*, Sieyès recruited the help of Napoleon – at the high point of his popularity, in the

29 Tackett, *Becoming a Revolutionary*, 211–39; *cf.* Hesse, *Cultural Politics*, 97–124.

30 Jean-Louis Halperin, *The French Civil Code*, translated by Tony Weir (New York: UCL Press, 2006), 1–15, 88–95, and passim; Peter Stein, *Roman Law in European History* (Cambridge, UK: Cambridge University Press, 1999), 114–15; Steiner, *French Law*, ch. 15; Van den Berg, *European Codification*, 4–6, 24–6, 125–211, 263–73; see also Rafael La Porta, Florencio Lopez-de-Silanes, and Andrei Shleifer, "The Economic Consequences of Legal Origins," *Journal of Economic Literature* 46(2) (2008): 285–332.

31 Preliminary Address on the First Draft of the Civil Code, available in English translation at www.justice.gc.ca/eng/rp-pr/csj-sjc/ilp-pji/code/index.html (accessed July 14, 2020); Halperin, *French Civil Code*, 9–15.

32 Emmanuel Joseph Sieyès, "What Is the Third Estate?" in *Political Writings*, edited by Michael Sonenscher (Indianapolis: Hackett Publishing Co., 2003), 92–162; Van den Berg, *European Codification*, 167–71, 185–9.

wake of military victories against France's European enemies – in staging a *coup d'etat*. For the sake of establishing a nationally uniform legal framework for France, Sieyès helped bring a dictator to power.[33]

The French Civil Code represents the supremacy of national legislation over judicial authority, an expression of lawmaking power vested in the common "will" of the people. Article 5 of the code, indeed, expressly prohibits judges from pronouncing their decisions as "general or regulative dispositions," and from a formal perspective, the case law of French courts is a merely persuasive source of law.[34]

As a fundamental restatement of French private law, self-consciously elaborating the foundations for that law, and as the product of a legislative process, the code did not provide citations to its legal sources. Moreover, once the code was finally promulgated in 1804, all previous laws pertaining to its subject matter were formally revoked. Nevertheless, the drafters of the code explicitly acknowledged their reliance on prior legal sources in drafting the code. Indeed, Jean-Étienne-Marie Portalis (1746–1807), writing on behalf of all four draftsmen, stated that the code would not have been possible had its draftsmen not drawn from "the experience of the past and from that tradition of good sense, rules and maxims which has come down to us and informs the spirit of centuries."[35]

In 1973, Tulane Law Professor Rodolfo Batiza undertook a systematic study of the contents of the French Civil Code. This study examined the language of the code title by title, comparing the language of the 1804 promulgated text to the 1801 draft, and to texts by two prominent French jurists: Robert Joseph Pothier (1699–1772) and Jean Domat (1625–96). On the basis of this systematic study, Batiza confirmed that the contents of the code had been substantially influenced by French customary law (primarily the *Coutume de Paris*) and Roman law (particularly in relation to the regimes of property ownership, obligation, and contracts), with additional influences from royal ordinances, revolutionary legislation, canon law, and parliamentary determinations. Batiza also showed, however, that these sources (other than the revolutionary sources) were primarily indirect, that is, that they were mediated through the writing of the two French jurists Pothier and Domat. From this study, Batiza drew the conclusion that "most provisions of the French Civil Code trace their source to doctrinal texts rather than to customary, historical, and enacted laws, as respectively represented by French customs, Roman law, and royal ordinances."[36]

The concepts of property articulated in the French Civil Code are deeply rooted in the Roman law tradition. Since 1804, that code has provided the foundation for

33 Sewell, Jr., *Bourgeois Revolution*, 19–20, 195–7; Van den Berg, *European Codification*, 204–5.

34 Bell, Boyron, and Whittaker, *Principles*, 14, 24–32.

35 Halperin, *French Civil Code*, 11, 15; Portalis, *Preliminary Address*, 3.

36 Rodolfo Batiza, "Domat, Pothier, and the Code Napoleon: Some Observations Concerning the Actual Sources of the French Civil Code" (Typewritten Manuscript in Cornell Library, 1973), 4 and passim.

French property law, and for property law in the nation-states that have drawn on French law, either as colonies or as emulators. Ironically, however, despite the Revolution's enthusiastic embrace of *propriété intellectuelle*, that property is neither recognized nor mentioned in the Civil Code of 1804. In fact, the code's traditional treatment of *accessio*, together with its reformation of *occupatio*, point to a retreat from the revolutionary embrace of intellectual property.[37]

The code's embracing of traditional (Roman) principles of accession emphasizes a presumption of ownership in favor of the original owner of materials (rather than the creative artist), subject to exception only where a creation can be shown to be very valuable. The pressure against intellectual property-related conceptions is heightened further by the code's treatment of *occupatio*, which formed such an important foundation for William Blackstone's defense of intellectual property. In place of the principle that the first occupant is the owner of a thing that previously belonged to no one (*a res nullius*), the Napoleanic Code declared that "property having no owner belongs to the nation."[38]

In 1810, principles related to intellectual property were recognized to some extent in a new Penal Code. Section 425 of this code declared that "Every edition of writings, of musical compositions, of drawings, paintings, or any other production, wholly or in part, printed or engraved, *in contempt of the laws and regulations relative to the property of authors*, is a counterfeiting; and every counterfeiting is a delict." This provision, in other words, recognized literary and artistic property and defined the theft of such property as a form of wrongdoing ("counterfeiting"). By acknowledging "laws and regulations relative to the property of authors," the code gave statutory recognition to the revolutionary principles articulated in 1793, relative to copyrights. However, it left an open-ended ambiguity about which "law and regulations" were relevant, and about what, precisely, they protected.[39]

And what about patents? In 1810, the US attorney Thomas Fessenden asserted that, in France, "no patent is now granted without a special decree from Napoleon." Fessenden also described "tedious and complex formalities to be fulfilled in obtaining a patent" in France. Thus, while French law still presumably recognized a natural right of inventors to their property in patents, the reality in administration appeared quite different. As emperor, Napoleon had elevated himself into the personification of France's national will. And, in keeping with the Roman imperial traditions that he emulated, he arrogated to himself the discretion to award patents, as a matter of imperial favor, rather than as a matter of proprietary right.[40]

37 Bell, Boyron, and Whittaker, *Principles*, 269–77.
38 Book II, Title II, §§ 570–1, 713; *cf.* CJ 2.2.25.
39 The Penal Code of France, translated into English with a preliminary dissertation (London: Butterworth, 1819), available at www.napoleon-series.org/research/government/france/penalcode/c_penalcode.html (accessed August 18, 2020), §§ 425–9 (emphasis added).
40 Thomas G. Fessenden, *An Essay on the Law of Patents* (Boston: D. Mallory, & Co., 1810), 212.

The declaration that "property having no owner belongs to the nation" (rather than the individual discoverer, or the king by royal prerogative) neatly captures the nationalizing force of France's Civil Code. In the code, we can see a process of semantic legal ordering at work: Roman and French doctrinal traditions, in synthesis with jurisprudential traditions, revolutionary laws, and performative acts, are being interpreted together in nationalistic directions. Under the influence especially of Roman concepts of lordship (*dominium* and *imperium*), in a national revolutionary context, the nation is conceived in formal legal doctrine as the primary governing community and the primary owner of property, with semantic implications for nationalistic social closure. A national order of obligation, contributing to a national uniformity in the legal treatment and protection of property – that is, to the national commodification of property – was an evidently intended result.

We can see a dramatic illustration of this commodification in the nationalization of church property, effected by the National Assembly in late fall 1789. The motion came from Charles-Maurice de Talleyrand-Périgord, bishop of Autun (1789–1802). A recipient of legal training from the church, Talleyrand nonetheless argued that church property was actually the property of the nation, the body of the catholic faithful, which had assigned the property to the church and clergy as compensation for their spiritual labors, while retaining the ownership and the corresponding right to recover the property, if it was needed. Under the present circumstances, faced with crippling debts, the French nation needed its property back and could legally recover a portion of that property, leaving the remainder to the clergy.[41]

The proposal was developed by Mirabeau, who argued that all church property should be nationalized, subject only to an obligation to compensate the church and clergy for the loss of their property. The proposal was voted into law on November 3, 1789, and the church's property – including roughly 7 percent of France's landed territory – became security for a new paper currency, the *assignats*, which would finance France's upcoming war efforts.[42]

Note that Talleyrand's argument depends on equating the nation with the church, the social body of the Christian faithful. That argument is suggestive of ways that Christian conceptions of society continued to underpin later conceptions of the nation, even as the nation was being secularized. In the Napoleanic Code, the social body of the French nation had received a uniform law to govern their "private" social relations with one another: their marriages and family life, their contracts and business associations, and their transfers of property. That nationally uniform law remains valid today despite being thickly overlaid with treaty-based, legislative, jurisprudential, doctrinal, and administrative adaptations.

41 Charlotte Lady Blennerhasset, *Talleyrand*, translated by Frederick Clarke (London: John Murray, 1894), 106–34, esp. 116–17; Duff Cooper, *Talleyrand: A Biography* (New York: Fromm International Publishing, 1986), 33–8; Doyle, *French Revolution*, 131–4; Louis S. Greenbaum, "Talleyrand and Vergennes: The Debut of a Diplomat," *The Catholic Historical Review* 56(3) (1970): 543–50.

42 Doyle, *French Revolution*, 131–4.

Those adaptations depend, fundamentally, on principles underpinning the code, principles rooted in European legal history, and especially in doctrinal developments of state sovereignty and natural rights that had developed out of the legal and religious ferment of the Protestant Reformation.

10.4 LORDSHIP AND CONSCIENCE: POSITIVE LEGALITY AND NATURAL RIGHTS IN THE FRENCH REFORMATION

The radicalism and anti-clericalism, and even some of the national consciousness, which were dramatically enacted in the French Revolution, had much older roots, stretching back into the later Middle Ages. Philip the Fair (1285–1314) and his lawyers had already ignited proto-"Gallican" resistance to papal supremacy, culminating in horrific destruction of the Templar Order (1307–14), with which Pope Clement V (1305–14) collaborated under some duress.[43]

In Gallicanism, an early form of national consciousness was emerging in resistance to papal controls exercised over the church in France. However, a broader catalyst for violent social energies came in the politicization of Reformation doctrines pouring into France from Lutheran Germany and Calvinist Geneva, galvanized by conservative Catholic reaction. A formal response to these challenges came in the Council of Trent (1545–63), which was captive, throughout its prolonged and intermittent discussions, to power struggles between French kings and German emperors. A crescendo of violence came in the Wars of Religion (1559–98) and the Thirty Years' War (1618–48), terrible European precedents for the totalitarian violence of twentieth-century world wars.[44]

Despite its violence and disorder, or perhaps rather because of them, the Reformation was a period of intensely creative development in European jurisprudence, including for natural law-based adaptations of Roman law traditions, as for legal doctrines about state power. Two developments are particularly important as early foundations for the emergence of intellectual property, and for the legal

[43] Malcolm Barber, *The Trial of the Templars*, 2nd ed. (Cambridge, UK: Cambridge University Press, 2006); Franklin J. Pegues, *The Lawyers of the Last Capetians* (Princeton: Princeton University Press, 1962), 27, 38–9, 47–56, 226–9, and passim; Joseph R. Strayer, *The Reign of Philip the Fair* (Princeton: Princeton University Press, 1980), 299–300; Julien Théry, "A Heresy of State: Philip the Fair, the Trial of the 'Perfidious Templars', and the Pontificalization of the French Monarchy," *Journal of Medieval Religious Cultures* 39(2) (2013): 117–48.

[44] Norman P. Tanner, S. J. (ed.), *Decrees of the Ecumenical Councils*, Volume II (London and Washington, DC: Sheed & Ward and Georgetown University Press, 1990), 657–799; Thomas I. Crimando, "Two French Views of the Council of Trent," *The Sixteenth-Century Journal* 19(2) (1988): 169–86; Wim Decock, "Charles Dumoulin (1500–1566)," in *Great Christian Jurists in French History*, edited by Olivier Descamps and Rafael Domingo (Cambridge, UK: Cambridge University Press, 2019), 97–116; Donald R. Kelley, "'Fides Historiae': Charles Dumoulin and the Gallican View of History," *Traditio* 22 (1966): 347–402; Van den Berg, *European Codification*, 126–7. Wars of religion and Thirty Years' War as terrible precedents: Hannah Arendt, *Imperialism* (San Diego: Harcourt Brace, 1968), 147; Robert Jean Knecht, *The French Wars of Religion, 1559–1598*, 3rd ed. (London: Routledge, 2010); Geoffrey Parker (ed.), *The Thirty Years' War*, 2nd ed. (London: Routledge, 1997).

establishment of a nation-state system. These are (1) the articulation of a new conception of state sovereignty, seen in the doctrinal work of Jean Bodin (1529/30–1596), and (2) an early but dramatic defense of authorial rights, premised on a logic closely analogous to Bodin's logic of sovereignty. Indeed, the early argument for authorial rights was an argument for a special kind of sovereignty, a sovereign lordship of human creators over that which they have created, by explicit analogy to the sovereign lordship of a creator God.[45]

Bodin's legal conception of state sovereignty was articulated in his famous treatise *Six Books of the Republic (Commonwealth)*, published first in French (1576) and later in a Latin translation (1586). What is especially significant about Bodin's conception, for our purposes, is the way it links an impersonal theory of state power ("sovereignty"), on the one hand, with a command theory of positive legislation, on the other. A Roman law-based theory of *imperium*, combined with Christian understandings of divine lordship, ultimately underpins Bodin's vision of sovereign public law and government, which are conceived in a kind of principle–agent relationship, where government magistrates are the agents holding the powers exercised in their offices as a kind of temporary guardianship or loan. If magisterial office holders are like temporary guardians of property, however, it is the sovereign state itself that is the lordly owner of public authorities and powers.[46]

At the core of the sovereign state's "absolute" power is a unique kind of ownership right, focused particularly in the legislative power, the exclusive power to impose law that is binding on everyone, by command, and, by implication, to be absolved from (independent of) subjection to any other sovereign's positive law. Legislation issues as the command of the sovereign, and subjects are bound to obey, in virtue of the general relationship of obligation that constitutes their social bond, as subjects, to the sovereign. This obligation does not depend on consent, and the sovereign legislator is not obligated by his own legislation, although he *is* bound by higher obligations from divine law, natural law, and the contractual law of nations. This command theory of legislation, in other words, is a theory in which the basis for an

45 Harold J. Berman, *Law and Revolution II: The Impact of the Protestant Reformations on the Western Legal Tradition* (Cambridge, MA: Harvard University Press, 2003), 1–28 and passim; Christian Hattenhauer, "Hugues Doneau (1527–1591)," in Descamps and Domingo (eds.), *Great Christian Jurists*, 173–90; Mathias Schmoeckel, "François Hotman (1524–1590)," in Descamps and Domingo (eds.), *Great Christian Jurists*, 149–72; John Witte, Jr., *Law and Protestantism: The Legal Teachings of the Lutheran Reformation* (Cambridge, UK: Cambridge University Press, 2002); John Witte, Jr., "John Calvin (1509–1564)," in Descamps and Domingo (eds.), *Great Christian Jurists*, 117–32.

46 Julian H. Franklin (ed.), *Bodin on Sovereignty* (Cambridge, UK: Cambridge University Press, 1992), I.8; Myron Piper Gilmore, *Argument from Roman Law in Political Thought, 1200–1600* (Cambridge, MA: Harvard University Press, 1941), 93–132; Daniel Lee, "Jean Bodin (1529/1530–1596)," in Descamps and Domingo (eds.), *Great Christian Jurists*, 191–209; M. J. Tooley, *Bodin on Sovereignty: Six Books of the Commonwealth* (Oxford: Basil Blackwell, 1955), 25. For discussions of early modern "absolutism," compare James B. Collins, *The State in Early Modern France*, 2nd ed. (Cambridge, UK: Cambridge University Press, 2009) with Julian H. Franklin, *Jean Bodin and the Rise of Absolutist Theory* (Cambridge, UK: Cambridge University Press, 1973).

obligation to obey positive law comes from a hierarchical relationship of social power, as reflected, for example, in the relationship of a king to his subject peoples. From Bodin's perspective, it would be incoherent and problematic to bind a sovereign by his own prior legislation, since that would not leave the sovereign sufficiently free to issue new legislation, under appropriate circumstances.[47]

The "absolute" conception of sovereignty in legislative power that Bodin articulated here was, according to a recent interpreter, intended to remedy "the inevitable imperfection, and even injustice, bound to emerge in any legal system, a problem especially devastating in democracies." The remedy is to allow legal changes, where social circumstances change or inequities are recognized.

> Amending and even "overriding" [*deroger*] ordinary legislation – what Bodin, citing the lawyer-pope Innocent IV, regarded as the very essence of a sovereign's absolute power – embodied the moral purposes of sovereignty, which was to serve as an agent of justice by *continuously engineering a system of legislation* thought to be in harmony with the higher law of equity.[48]

Bodin, like other Christian jurists of his time, considered the ultimate lordship and sovereignty to rest in God, and he regarded divine and natural law as important limits on the worldly sovereignty of kings. Nonetheless, in articulating a command theory of legislative power, as part of a general theory of state sovereignty rooted in Roman law-based concepts of *imperium*, Bodin helped to lay the foundations for modern, positive legality: a faith in state-issued laws to "continuously engineer" solutions to social problems.[49]

In the same year that Bodin's treatise on sovereignty was published in its Latin translation (1586), an argument was made before the Paris *Parlement* by the barrister (*avocat*) Simon Marion challenging the validity of a six-year royal privilege granting exclusive printing rights in an edition of Seneca's works, annotated by a humanist scholar, Marc-Antoine Muret (1526–85). Marion made his arguments on behalf of two Parisian printers who were seeking the freedom to print Muret's works. As university printers, they were probably hoping to print large numbers of cheap copies for students eager to absorb the new, humanistic learning drawn from antiquity.[50]

Marion's arguments for nullifying the privilege, based on the sovereign lordship that an author exercises over his creation, may have been persuasive to the *Parlement*, which did nullify the privilege, albeit without leaving an explanation for their decision. In any case, the enduring legacy of this judicial decision for the history of intellectual property law rests in Simon Marion's dramatic argument on

47 Franklin (ed.), *Bodin on Sovereignty*, I.8; Lee, "Bodin," 198–203. Meaning of "absolute" (*absolu*): Berman, *Law and Revolution II*, 43; Collins, *State in Early Modern France*, xiv–xxiv.

48 Lee, "Bodin," 203 (emphasis added).

49 Ibid., 203–7; *cf.* Arendt, *Imperialism*, 96, 123–5.

50 Simon Marion's plea on privileges (1586), translated by Andrew Counter, *Primary Sources*; Frédéric Rideau, "Commentary on Simon Marion's Plea on Privileges" (2008), *Primary Sources*.

behalf of authorial rights, an argument that drew explicit analogy between divine and human creators, and the sovereign powers of lordship flowing from creativity.[51]

In his 2008 commentary on Marion's argument, Frédéric Rideau notes the extent to which it echoes arguments by Bodin, who had also drawn on Seneca's writings to articulate legal boundaries and definitions for his new conception of state sovereignty. Those boundaries were articulated in the language of natural law, marked by the point at which the state's sovereignty infringed on property. The granting of privileges was within the sovereign's prerogative power but only where the privileges did not infringe on property. Where a privilege did infringe on property, it was invalid, and this was the legal basis upon which the two university printers were challenging the printing patent.[52]

Although the author in question (Muret) was dead, Simon Marion argued, in effect, that Muret had exercised a kind of property right in publishing, without any privileges attached, his edition of Seneca's works. He had, in other words, exercised his proprietary rights to render his creation free, a kind of early modern counterpart to modern "copy-left" movements, which use intellectual property rights to make creative and inventive products freely accessible. The grounding for the property rights was in the mutual "recognition" that all humans have, by "common instinct" (*commun instinct*), that a person is "lord and master" (*seigneur*) over that which he creates or invents.[53]

As God is lord of his creation, so a human author is lord over that which he has created.

> Such that by analogy, the author of a book is entirely its master (*maistre*), and as such may dispose of it freely: he may even keep it forever in his private hands, as one would a slave, or free it, granting it the liberty enjoyed by all; this may be accorded purely and simply, with no restriction of any kind, or with a reservation, by a kind of right of patronage, that no other person may print it before a certain time. Which is effectively a contract without a fixed name, mutually binding, since there is a fair obligation on both sides, the one not wishing to give to the public his personal property (*donner au public ce qui luy appartient en particulier*), unless the public grant him this prerogative (*prerogative*) in return.

Muret had exercised his lordly rights to make his creative work freely available, and therefore the six-year printing patent, granted by the king to another printer, was null and void. Here is a striking and early articulation of the argument, still made by lawyers today, that intellectual property rights represent a kind of tacit contract between creative individuals and the broader society, with mutual benefits and restrictions on both sides. But here also is a strong argument for authors' proprietary rights, grounded in creative lordship, analogous to that of God, and therefore

[51] Ibid.

[52] Rideau, "Commentary on Simon Marion's Plea," *Primary Sources*.

[53] Simon Marion's plea on privileges (1586), translated by Andrew Counter, 11.

protected by the same natural and contractual law that sets boundaries to the sovereign power of the king.[54]

Bodin's argument for state sovereignty was informed by a line of juristic scholarship drawing on a synthesis of Biblical and Roman law. In these arguments, Roman *imperium* was synthesized with Biblical conceptions of divine creativity and lordship. This creative synthesis could be taken in many directions, but, in seeking to understand the emergence of intellectual property, we are focusing primarily on two trajectories: (1) the elaboration of an increasingly impersonal conception of state sovereignty, which stands above a society of individuals, and which exercises conceptually limited but "absolute" public powers of lordship over that society; and (2) an elaboration of creative and inventive lordship, grounding proprietary rights in creative works by authors in natural law and a kind of contractual obligation between authors and the broader "society" of which they are part, the foundation for later articulations of "authorial right," and of moral rights that transcend economic considerations.

As we are seeing an increasingly abstract and "absolutist" conception of state sovereignty, in other words, we are seeing more absolute conceptions of personal rights, particularly in property and contract-based rights. We see this in Bodin's arguments about the limits on state sovereignty, and we see it in Simon Marion's arguments for an early version of authorial rights. We see it also in the Protestant "Reformation of Rights," which John Witte, Jr., has persuasively rooted in the Calvinist tradition, developed with particular clarity by Theodore Beza (1519–1605) and Johannes Althusius (1557–1638), a linkage of theological and legal reflection, with practical grounding in the experience of violence, that lent radical meanings to religious conceptions of human rights.[55]

At the core of Reformed conceptions of human rights, as Witte persuasively argues, is a basic concern for freedom of conscience. In the Protestant understanding, a person ultimately stands alone before God, and that person accordingly has an ultimate responsibility to understand the nature of their vocation, their calling to love and serve God with their whole heart, mind, and strength, to learn what this means for the ways they relate to their neighbors and themselves. In order to protect this sacred calling, a person must be free in their conscience to interpret the will of God, especially as this may be discerned from the Bible and church leadership, so that they can recognize what God's intentions mean for the ways they live and serve their neighbors. Compulsion at the level of personal conscience is therefore a kind of spiritual violence, preventing a person from performing their most sacred obligation and vocation. Protestant resistance theories and doctrines of "absolute"

54 Ibid., 12; *compare* Jean Calvin, *Institutes of the Christian Religion*, 2 Vols., edited by John T. McNeill, translated by Ford Lewis Battles (Louisville: Westminster John Knox Press, 1960), I.2.2 ("since you are his handiwork, you have been made over and bound to his command by right (*droit*) of creation").

55 John Witte, Jr., *The Reformation of Rights: Law, Religion, and Human Rights in Early Modern Calvinism* (Cambridge, UK: Cambridge University Press, 2007).

individual rights developed through theological and juristic reflections on the kinds of social boundaries necessary to protect this sacred sphere of individual conscience. We can see here, perhaps, a new zone of exclusivity, which sets boundaries around the mind and spirit of an individual human person, protecting their capacity to freely serve their God in fullest devotion.[56]

This protection for the freedom of individual conscience did not prevent reformers like Calvin from erecting strict forms of doctrinal and moral discipline, or even from decreeing death to heretics in extreme cases. Calvin's Geneva became a magisterial republican theocracy in which civic and religious authorities jointly exercised strict scrutiny over the behavior of citizens. And the progression of Calvin's own writings shows an increasing appreciation for the role of "positive law" (in church and state alike), as a vital social support for moral law and Christian conscience. Over time, however, the religious authority that had once been exercised by theologians like Calvin was absorbed into the civic authority of Reformation states, exercised by civilian magistrates. This transfer of ecclesiastical authority to civilian state powers was in some cases an explicit process of "de-sacramentalization, " as it certainly was for marriage in Protestant lands.[57]

Given the way in which marriage bonds have served, in western Christianity, as a kind of synecdoche for human social bonds more broadly, this is a deeply significant move, illustrating the ways in which sacramental bonds of obligation were intentionally shifted to spheres of civilian responsibility and discipline in the Protestant Reformation.

10.5 REACTIONS TO ROMAN LAW IN THE LUTHERAN REFORMATION

The heightened emphasis on individual conscience, which helped give rise to Protestant legitimations for resistance to governmental power, carried meaningful legacies from Martin Luther's (1483–1546) religious emphases on faith and scripture. In the Lutheran ideal, faith is an orientation of the entire conscious person to God, a transformation in personal motivation, which enables voluntary and joyful adherence to divinely commanded obligations. This faithful, personal orientation can only come as a gift of God, and it is imperfect because it coexists with sin, in human

56 Ibid, passim, esp. 2, 43–62, 74–5, 85–7, 106–34, 170–76; *cf.* Donald R. Kelley, *The Beginning of Ideology: Consciousness and Society in the French Reformation* (Cambridge, UK: Cambridge University Press, 1981), 53–87. This comes through with particular clarity in the "protest" issued by the dissenting minority of lords at the Diet of Speyer (1529), the dissent that gave "Protestantism" its name. Berman, *Law and Revolution II*, 49–52; Rev. B. J. Kidd, *Documents Illustrative of the Continental Reformation* (Oxford: Clarendon Press, 1911), 106–7.

57 Witte, Jr., *Reformation of Rights*, 39–80; also Berman, *Law and Revolution II*, 39–68; Robert Kingdon, Thomas A. Lambert, and Isabella M. Watt (eds.), translated by M. Wallace McDonald, *Registers of the Consistory of Geneva in the Time of Calvin, Vol. I: 1542–1544* (Grand Rapids, MI: Wm. B. Eerdmans, 2000); John Witte, Jr., *From Sacrament to Contract: Marriage, Religion, and Law in the Western Tradition*, 2nd ed. (Louisville: Westminster John Knox Press, 2012).

life. But it is something that we can cling to in hope and love. Living an existentially personal dialectic between despair and encouragement, we carry our Christian vocation into the world, performing our divinely given obligations in our daily activities and in our official duties.[58]

For Luther, the vitality of Christian orientation in faith was fatally compromised by Romanist jurisprudence, however, as seen with special monstrosity in indulgences. These grants of privilege from the pope had morphed over time into a method of fundraising for the church, one that Luther saw as preventing Christians from doing the difficult work involved in true repentance. Indulgences had transformed the spiritual journey of penitence into a commodity to be purchased, and they were preying on the ignorance and fear of the Christian laity. Roman-canon law was culpable in the indulgence controversy, because indulgences were supported by papal instruments of legal power (i.e., papal bulls), together with centralizing legal systems in France and the Holy Roman Empire, which supported the spiritual power of the church with military and political powers, organized with the help of Romanist jurisprudence.[59]

Prior to the fifteenth century, influences from Roman law in German-speaking lands had been diffuse and relatively informal. However, Roman law had formed an important basis for legal reformations in the Holy Roman Empire which occurred in the late fifteenth and early sixteenth centuries. These reformations, carried out at the local, regional, and imperial levels, strengthened the institutional influence of Roman law.[60]

This phenomenon of Roman law influence in Germany is known as the "Reception." Referring to the impact of the Reception on territorial German rulers of the sixteenth century, Joachim Whaley writes that "Roman law, with its clarity and authority, now seemed more attractive than ever to rulers and officials seeking to establish, at the regional and local level, the kind of rule of law that many believed at been achieved in the institutions of the Reich." Over the course of the sixteenth

58 John Dillenberger (ed.), *Martin Luther: Selections from His Writings* (New York: Anchor Books, 1962), xi–xxxiii.

59 Martin Luther, "Explanations of the Ninety-Five Theses, 1518," translated by Carl W. Folkemer, in *Luther's Works, Vol. 31: Career of the Reformer: I*, edited by Harold J. Grimm (Philadelphia: Fortress Press and Concordia Publishing House, 1957), 83–252; idem, "Why the Books of the Pope and His Disciples Were Burned, 1520," translated by Lewis W. Spitz, in Grimm (ed.), *Luther's Works, Vol. 31*, 381–95; idem, "To the Christian Nobility of the German Nation Concerning the Reform of the Christian Estate, 1520," translated by Charles M. Jacobs, revised by James Atkinson, in *Luther's Works, Vol. 44: The Christian in Society: I*, edited by James Atkinson (Philadelphia: Fortress Press and Concordia Publishing House, 1966), 202–4.

60 Berman, *Law and Revolution II*, 33, 35–6; Joachim Whaley, *Germany and the Holy Roman Empire, Vol. I: Maximilian I to the Peace of Westphalia, 1493–1648* (Oxford: Oxford University Press, 2012), 61–152; Franz Wieacker, A *History of Private Law in Europe*, translated by Tony Weir (Oxford: Clarendon Press, 1995), 32–67 (esp. 51–3), 84–90, 136–42; Peter H. Wilson, *Heart of Europe: A History of the Holy Roman Empire* (Cambridge, MA: Harvard University Press, 2016).

century, Roman law became a foundation for German law at all levels of administration, from the empire to the estates, princes, regional rulers, and cities.[61]

But there was, at the same time, a strong reaction. The Reformation was a rebellion against the legal power of Rome, nearly as much as it was a rebellion against the religious power of Rome. On December 10, 1520, Martin Luther and his supporters had performatively symbolized their break with the legal power of Rome by burning several editions of canon law, together with a papal bull of excommunication that had been issued in June against Luther. In a written defense of this symbolic act, published in December 1520, Luther elaborated thirty criticisms of canon law, all of which were rooted in his distinctive understanding of the Biblical Gospel.[62]

Roman-canon law did not disappear in Lutheran principalities and cities, however. Instead, it was reformulated and placed to a greater extent under the "will" of divinely ordained Protestant rulers. Philip Melanchthon (1497–1560), Luther's Wittenberg colleague and vocal defender, shared the scholastic view of Roman law as "written reason," elevating its principles to "beams of divine wisdom." His lectures on Roman law provided the basis for a new jurisprudence which synthesized Lutheran theology with Roman-canon law in a new way. This new Lutheran jurisprudence influenced, in turn, a younger generation of legal scholars who would develop and extend its application.[63]

In many ways, indeed, Lutheran theology was a theology of law. It should be recalled that Luther's original "calling" was to the law. He obtained a master's degree from the University of Erfurt and matriculated to the law faculty of that university in May 1505. He elected to study Roman civil law (rather than canon law), and he owned a copy of the *Corpus Iuris Civilis*. However, shortly after beginning his legal studies, Luther experienced a personal crisis, which led him to renounce the legal calling, embracing strict monasticism and entering the Order of Augustinian Hermits.[64]

One of Luther's biographers, Martin Brecht, persuasively argues that Luther's crisis was rooted in disillusionment with law. Luther found the uncertainty of law profoundly disappointing. Unlike theology, which Luther believed could be a demonstrative science, law is only dialectical, always subject to variation in application to concrete circumstances. This made it an ineffective resource for the

[61] Whaley, *Holy Roman Empire, Vol. I*, 492; Wieacker, *History of Private Law*, 71–167. The authority of academic jurists trained in Roman law was particularly strong in Germany, due to the institution of the *Aktenversendung*, the practice of referring difficult legal questions for resolution by a scholarly faculty of law. By the beginning of the sixteenth century, the practice had become widespread. Wieacker, *History of Private Law*, 136–42.

[62] Luther, "Why the Books of the Pope and His Disciples Were Burned," in Grimm (ed.), *Luther's Works, Vol. 31*, 381–95; Berman, *Law and Revolution II*, 45–6; Martin Brecht, *Martin Luther: His Road to Reformation, 1483–1521*, translated by James L. Schaaf (Minneapolis: Fortress Press, 1985), 423–6; Gerald Strauss, *Law, Resistance, and the State: The Opposition to Roman Law in Reformation Germany* (Princeton: Princeton University Press, 1986).

[63] Berman, *Law and Revolution II*, 71–99.

[64] Brecht, *Martin Luther*, 44–51.

Christian seeking a fixed source of righteousness and justice (*Rechtigkeit*). In the face of the Devil's assaults, the Christian's only hope was to trust faithfully in the righteousness of Christ, and to believe the Gospel's promise that, in so trusting and believing, the Christian would be reckoned (adjudicated) Righteous by God. Luther's doctrine of "Justification by Faith" is, after all, *forensic*, that is, legal.[65]

A fundamental theme in Lutheran theology is the relationship between Law and Gospel. The Law makes commands that we cannot obey, leading us in despair to the promises of the Gospel, which, if believed, enable Christ's righteousness to be attributed to us. Our deep gratitude for this divine gift (grace) causes us to fall in love with the mercy, goodness, and beauty of the divine giver, making it possible for us to love the divine commands, and to voluntarily wish to adhere to them. Inevitably we fall short of the divine standard, however, and we are driven to recognize, yet again, our sin. In repentance, we turn again to the scriptural word of the Gospel, seeking new levels of depth in the divine promise. This ever-repeating process of justification by faith is the source of ultimate freedom and unity in Christian community, for Luther. Since it is the fundamental source of righteousness for king and peasant alike, it eliminates all status differences in the spiritual realm, making us a "Priesthood of all Believers."[66]

However, this spiritual realm is limited to the "inward" dimension, the dimension of mind, spirit, and conscience. In their "outward" dimension, Christians are called to servitude, and to humble participation in status differences. These outward, behavioral requirements for Christian character do not make us righteous, but instead follow from our love of God, and our desire for reconciliation with God and neighbor. By bringing our bodies "into subjection" to our divinely inspired minds and hearts, we become able to serve others. As servants, however, we are called to submit ourselves to divinely appointed authorities and to hard work in our appointed vocations.[67]

> Christians should be subject to the governing authorities and be ready to do every good work, not that they shall in this way be justified, since they already are righteous through faith, but that in the liberty of the Spirit they shall by so doing serve others and the authorities themselves and obey their will freely and out of love .... Although tyrants do violence or injustice in making their demands, yet it will do no harm as long as they demand nothing contrary to God.[68]

In Luther, the will is a profoundly arbitrary and inscrutable force, particularly the will of God. And, because God's will is the source of all law, law itself is basically arbitrary and inscrutable. God's revealed law, as seen in the Bible, as well as the

65 Brecht, *Martin Luther*, 44–6.

66 Martin Luther, "The Freedom of a Christian, 1520" in Grimm (ed.), *Luther's Works, Vol.* 31, 329–77; Jerome B. Schneewind, *The Invention of Autonomy: A History of Modern Moral Philosophy* (New York: Cambridge University Press, 1998), 26–31.

67 Luther, "Freedom," 358–60, 364–5.

68 Luther, "Freedom," 369–70.

natural law that flows from God's creative will, are good and right because God made them so not because they participate in any kind of comprehensible quality or standard that makes them good and right. Since there is no comprehensible standard that makes divine and natural law "just," that justice – God's justice – is basically inscrutable to us, inaccessible to the human intellect.[69]

> For if his righteousness were such that it could be judged to be righteous in human standards, it would clearly not be divine and would in no way differ from human righteousness. But since he is the one true God, and is wholly incomprehensible and inaccessible to human reason, it is proper and indeed necessary that his righteousness should also be incomprehensible.

Strictly positive human law, in turn, owes its source to the often-arbitrary choices of human rulers, who govern according to God's inscrutable will.[70]

Natural law, for Luther, may be seen as the "positive," volitional law of God. And the principles of this divine, volitional law are fundamentally incomprehensible for us. In contrast, then, to the Thomistic tradition of natural law, which saw in the intellect a capacity to grasp the underlying principles of law, and in the "conscience" a capacity to apply those principles to concrete circumstances, Luther saw the application of law to facts as an act of faith, dependent fundamentally on divine grace. Conscience, for Luther, is a means through which divine revelation speaks to human souls, and it is a superior, as well as transformative, force in relation to human reason and will. Reason, in other words, is subordinate to inspiration and revelation in the application of law to facts.[71]

A crucially important source of law for the Lutheran philosophy of law is the Hebrew Bible, particularly the Decalogue ("Ten Commandments"). Luther's colleague Melanchthon, in fact, built on this Biblical foundation in developing a new method for organizing and systematizing law. Melanchthon's "topical method" was developed to systematize theology, as a whole, to articulate its fundamental categories and classify its truths as part of an overarching system. The foundation for Melanchthon's legal categories, which comprised part of his theological system, was the Decalogue.[72]

Jurists who were drawn to the Lutheran revolution, like Johannes Apel (1485–1536), extended Melanchthon's method, synthesizing Biblical law, Roman law, natural law, customary law, and "positive" law. The new topical method, combined with the new degree of comprehensiveness in synthesis, enabled a reformulation of legal categories. The law of things (*res*) became centrally focused on property and

69 Martin Luther, "The Bondage of the Will, 1525," in *Luther's Works, Vol. 33: Career of the Reformer III*, edited by Philip S. Watson (Minneapolis: Fortress Press, 1972), passim; Schneewind, *Invention of Autonomy*, 29–31.

70 Luther, "Bondage of the Will," 290.

71 Berman, *Law and Revolution II*, 75.

72 Berman, *Law and Revolution II*, 77–87, 111–13.

ownership, subordinating the law of "persons," while "obligations" became a new general category under which "actions" and "contracts" were subordinated.[73]

To reiterate, the Lutheran jurists did not reject Roman law. However, the theological and political transformations of the Lutheran Reformation created a space in which the interpretive social activity of jurists could draw on the Roman legal tradition in novel and newly comprehensive ways. The *Ordnungen* that they would draft on behalf of Lutheran princes drew inspiration from Melanchthon's topical method in fundamentally transforming entire areas of law, including property law and the law of personal status.[74]

10.6 REFORMING PROPERTY IN PRUSSIA

Legal reforms inspired by Lutheran jurisprudence and Roman law emphasized generality, conceptual clarity, and uniformity in property relationships. At a practical level, these reforms gradually contributed to changes in the legal relationships between nobles and peasants: feudal relationships, under which vassals held possessory rights (not ownership) through investiture by a lord, and in turn exercised lordship rights over their peasants, were transformed into lease arrangements. Under leasehold arrangements, complex combinations of personal services, jurisdictional privileges, and nonownership-based rights to use and profit from land were transformed into rental arrangements between a property owner and his tenant.[75]

But the changes were complex, and there was strong resistance, as we see in Brandenburg-Prussia.

Under Frederick William (the "Great Elector," 1640–88) and his successors, Prussia's rapid expansion as a military and political power had been vitally supported by a noble status group, the *Junkers*, who were both large-scale agricultural producers and members of the military officer class. The fact that they had originally settled their eastern lands as colonizers meant that their relations with the original Slavic inhabitants were structured as the hierarchical and mutually dependent relations of lord and serf (*colonus*). Over time, and especially in the wake of the Thirty Years' War, their significance in a highly militarized society enabled them to tighten their power over peasants working on their lands and to resist the liberalizing legal reforms being carried out elsewhere in Germany.[76]

73 Berman, *Law and Revolution II*, 113–30; Wieacker, *History of Private Law*, 117.

74 Berman, *Law and Revolution II*, 131–97.

75 Berman, *Law and Revolution II*, 166–74.

76 Christopher Clark, *Iron Kingdom: The Rise and Downfall of Prussia, 1600–1947* (Cambridge, MA: Harvard University Press, 2006), 38–66, 155–74; Guy Stanton Ford, *Stein and the Era of Reform in Prussia, 1807–1815* (Princeton: Princeton University Press, 1922); Hajo Holborn, *A History of Modern Germany, 1648–1840* (New York: Alfred A. Knopf, 1964); Friedrich Meinecke, *The Age of German Liberation, 1795–1815*, translated by Peter Paret and Helmuth Fischer, edited by Peter Paret (Berkeley: University of California Press, 1977).

Legally speaking, the *Junkers* had few (if any) formal constitutional powers. Prussian rulership was exercised through committees of ministers tied directly and personally to the king, and any formal recognition of a political role for Prussia's status-based groupings ("estates") was limited. However, the belief that Prussia's officer class should come from the nobility was a deeply entrenched tradition which carried significant weight. As Prussia's preeminent agricultural producers, and as the traditional suppliers of military officers in a militaristic state, the *Junkers* were therefore able to exert considerable informal pressures in retaining and intensifying their legal control over the peasants on their lands.[77]

However, Prussia's devastating defeat by Napoleon in 1806 – which was followed by an economically predatory period of occupation and reparation – altered the political dynamics considerably. An episode of debate and reflection on Prussia's constitutional structures began, and a window of opportunity was opened for wide-ranging reforms to be directed by liberalizing jurist-administrators, including the baron Heinrich vom Stein (1757–1831).[78]

This liberal period in Prussian politics lasted until the end of 1819, when Frederick William III symbolized his refusal to continue the discussion by dismissing William von Humboldt (1767–1835), together with several other reformers. A central question of the liberal period, one on which all specific proposals hung in one way or another, concerned the position of Prussia's legal estates. The *Junkers*, as Prussia's preeminent nobles, were the most vocal opponents of reforms that would eliminate the estates altogether. However, the *Junkers* were not the only Prussian estate. Proposals for constitutional structures that would include the estates in one way or another carried implications for peasants and burghers, as well.[79]

In 1672, the influential jurist Samuel Pufendorf (1632–94) had described corporate groups as "moral persons": persons united by a "moral tie" and defined collectively by the status and office that they occupy in common life. The belief that such "moral communities," including the estates, should continue to play a role in Prussia's constitutional society was widely shared, including by reformers like Stein.[80]

The sustained commitment to estate society (*Ständestaat*), even on the part of early nineteenth-century Prussian reformers, may be partly explained by the fact that Lutheran legal theology had retained the "three estates doctrine," albeit in a revised form. In the revised, Lutheran form, the family became a kind of foundational estate, "the source of the economy and the polity and the seed-bed of the Church." The clergy also remained an important estate, although, by virtue of the radical equality

77 Clark, *Iron Kingdom*, 155–74; Ford, *Era of Reform*, 163–98; Holborn, *Modern Germany*, 20, 59–63; Meinecke, *Age of Liberation*, 12–14, 37–43.

78 Ford, *Era of Reform*, 78–162; Daniel Lee, "The Legacy of Medieval Constitutionalism in the Philosophy of Right: Hegel and the Prussian Reform Movement," *History of Political Thought* 29 (4) (2008): 601–34; Meinecke, *Age of Liberation*, 44–101.

79 Clark, *Iron Kingdom*, 399–408; Lee, "Hegel and the Prussian Reform Movement," 627.

80 Samuel Pufendorf, *Of the Law of Nature and Nations, Eight Books*, 4th ed., translated by Basil Kennett (London: J. Walthoe et al., 1729), I.I.XII-XIII; Meinecke, *Age of Liberation*, 52.

of Luther's "priesthood of all believers," they were now a "civilian" estate of church officers (*kirchliche Beamten*), rather than a "spiritual" estate. For devout Lutherans, a legal concept of estates was closely linked to concepts of vocation and calling, a sense that we are called to serve in particular capacities, and that our conforming of ourselves to these callings is a demonstration of our loving faithfulness to divine will.[81]

The problem for reformers like Stein, who were committed to retaining some place for the estates, lay in the fact that the estates did not sit easily alongside the liberal forms of thought that inspired many of the reforms. The 1807 Edict of Emancipation, which eliminated the legal status of personal servitude, is a case in point.[82]

This Edict (§ 10) abolished all "servility-relationships" (*Untertänigkeits-Verhältniß*), and therefore eliminated the legal status of serfdom, regardless of how it was acquired, whether through birth, marriage, or contract. The Edict also established the basis for free exchange of property (§ 1) by eliminating any connection between possession of certain types of property and legal status. From this time forward, for example, nobles could own peasant lands without losing their noble status. Finally, the Edict (§ 2) established freedom of choice in occupational industry: nobles, without any loss of noble status, could work in bourgeois (*Bürger*) occupations. And peasants and bourgeois also became free to move between these two status groups.[83]

The Edict, in other words, retained the basic framework of estate society, maintaining the legal status groups of noble, bourgeois, and peasant. However, it transformed the property relations that had previously underpinned that estate society, eliminating both the restrictions and the protections those property relations had embodied. The fact, for example, that nobles were now free to acquire peasant properties without suffering a loss in legal status meant that peasants had become much more vulnerable to becoming mere wage laborers. *Junker* nobles, whose economic bargaining position was much stronger, could now simply buy up the lands that had previously been used for farming plots by their peasants.[84]

In the years following the 1807 Emancipation Edict, a number of additional edicts and regulations would limit its concrete effects, insofar as peasant liberation in east Prussia was concerned. However, the Edict did effectuate a significant change in the property relations between *Junker* lords and their peasant tenants. The *Junkers* substantially increased the size of their agricultural estates, taking over many of the peasant holdings in free ownership and ejecting the peasants from the soil that

81 Berman, *Law and Revolution II*, 177–8, 446.

82 Ford, *Era of Reform*, 199–220.

83 Edict vom 9 October 1807, in Dr. Jur. Schering (ed.), *Nachtrag zum Allgemeinen Landrecht für die Preussischen Staaten*, 2nd ed., Vol. II (Berlin: A. Nauck, 1876), Nr. 74, portions translated in Ford, *Era of Reform*, 203–5.

84 Ford, *Era of Reform*, 202–12; Meinecke, *Age of Liberation*, 80–6.

had been the source of their enslavement and protection. Some of these peasants remained on the estates as wage laborers, and many moved to growing cities.[85]

In 1810 and 1811, Prussia's guilds were also radically transformed. Guild membership became voluntary rather than compulsory, and guilds accordingly lost their monopoly control (*Zunftzwang*) over particular industries. Industrial techniques and craft knowledge could no longer be the property of guilds, pursuant to these reforms.[86]

A similar tension between liberal forms of thought and Prussian estate society can be seen in Prussia's first general patent regime. Toward the end of the reform period (in October 1815), the Prussian finance minister issued a Cabinet Order instituting a system of patents for new inventions and discoveries. This order created a framework for the granting of patents, to inventors or importers of inventions, so long as the inventors were bourgeois or voting members of a community (*Gemeinde*) forming part of the Prussian state (§1). Patent requests were to be registered with provincial governments, and then to be subjected to an examination by experts, in determining whether a patent should issue, and for how long (§3). Patent durations varied from six months to fifteen years under this patent regime (§4), which was reformed and incorporated into the Toll-Union (*Zollverein*) in 1842.[87]

Reformers like Stein, who wanted to retain the moral bonds of estate society while liberalizing agriculture and industry, seem to have believed that the estates could continue to play a role in the political sphere without playing a role in the economic and legal spheres. What the period of Prussian reform showed, however, is that the estates could not continue to function if their proprietary foundations were undermined. Those proprietary foundations were essentially rooted in the communal property structures of the medieval manor and guild. When these communal property structures were individualized, the estates were doomed.

10.7 INTELLECTUAL PROPERTY ANALOGUES IN ESTATE SOCIETY

The constitutional structure of estate society can be difficult to grasp, especially when we are used to more unitary theories of state–society relations. However, we can gain some insights, I think, from the doctrinal legal theorizing of Otto von Gierke (1841–1921). According to Gierke's jurisprudential understanding, "Germany" had come into legal existence as a complex conglomerate of overlapping, interrelated, status-based "fellowships" (*Genossenschaften*), combined with

85 Ford, *Era of Reform*, 213–20; Meinecke, *Age of Liberation*, 80–6.

86 Meinecke, *Age of Liberation*, 86–7.

87 Supreme Cabinet Order of September 27, 1815, in Dr. Jur. Schering (ed.), *Nachtrag zum Allgemeinen Landrecht für die Preussischen Staaten*, No. 153; idem, Agreement of September 21, 1842, between the governments bound in the Toll and Trade Union, regarding the issuance of patents for inventions, Nr. 495.

increasing state powers of sovereign "lordship" (*Herrschaft*), operating at multiple levels. In his massive history of "fellowship law" (*Genossenschaftsrecht*), as well as in his other works, Gierke sought to recover more indigenous, "Germanic" forms of social organization, and to show how these had been weakened over the course of Germanic history by the reception of Roman law.[88]

Gierke's communitarian ideal of legal "fellowship" drew on estate-based forms of social organization, which remained influential in his time. We see these concretely revealed in the Prussian General Law of the Land (*Allgemeines Landrecht*, hereafter the "General Code"), which was promulgated in 1794 but remained effective in parts of Prussia until 1900, when a new German Civil Code (*Bürgerliches Gesetzbuch*) went into effect. One scholar, Christopher Clark, has written of the Prussian General Code that "no single text" better captures the transitional character of Prussia in the late eighteenth century.[89]

Initiated in 1780, under Frederick II (1740–86) – "Frederick the Great," king of Prussia and elector of the Holy Roman Empire – and completed under his successor Frederick William II (1786–97), this code was championed and drafted by jurists anxious to bring order and cohesion to Prussian politics, economy, and society. They sought to accomplish this goal by drawing concepts and principles from the Roman law and natural law traditions together with particular legal traditions and "privileges" of Prussia's diverse estates: peasant farmers (*Bauern*), serfs (*Untertanen*), city residents (*Bürger*), craftsmen/manufacturers and guildsmen (*Handwerken und Zünften*), nobles (*Adel*), clerics and laymen affiliated with churches, schools, and universities, civil servants, military men, and the "servants" of the state itself. By codifying in extensive detail the general principles (*Grundsätze*) and specific rules to be applicable to different status-based groupings within Prussian society, the code articulated a vocational ideal for social relationships, a vision in which legal rights and obligations vary depending on legal status: an "estate society."[90]

In the Prussian General Code, the political community is conceptualized as a "civic association" (*bürgerliche Gesellschaft*). This civic association consists of a multitude of smaller associations and status groups (*Gesellschaften und Ständen*) that are "bound together through nature or law, or both together."

88 Otto von Gierke, *Community in Historical Perspective: A Translation of Selections from Das deutsche Genossenshaftsrecht (The German Law of Fellowship) by Otto von Gierke*, translated by Mary Fischer, edited by Antony Black (Cambridge, UK: Cambridge University Press, 1990); Otto von Gierke, *Associations and Law: The Classical and Early Christian States*, edited and translated by George Heiman (Toronto: University of Toronto Press, 1977); Otto von Gierke, *Political Theories of the Middle Age*, translated by Frederic William Maitland (Cambridge, UK: Cambridge University Press, 1913); John D. Lewis, *The Genossenschaft Theory of Otto von Gierke* (Madison: University of Wisconsin Studies in the Social Sciences and History, 1935).

89 Clark, *Iron Kingdom*, 281; Wieacker, *History of Private Law*, 263.

90 *Allgemeines Landrecht für die Preusischen Staaten*, im Auftrage des Justiz-Ministers, herausgegeben von Dr. Jur. Schering, 7 Bände (Berlin: A. Nauck, 1876–1881) (hereafter "ALR"), Part II; Van den Berg, *European Codification*, 67–82.

These include household associations (consisting of married persons, their children, and their servants) and the wider family structures comprising "clans" (*Stämme*).[91]

Beyond participating, as members (*Mitglieder*), in family-based fellowships, individuals belong to a status group and, very likely, to one or more associative and corporate groupings (e.g., a city or a village). A status group is comprised of persons who share – by virtue of birth, regulation, or occupation – the same rights in the political community. The members of a status group have, as individuals, certain rights and duties particular to their status group. Associations and corporate groupings also have certain rights and duties specific to their legal status, which their members participate in to various degrees and in various ways; these are determined partly internally and partly by virtue of their legally defined relationship to the government (*Obrigkeit*). Part II of the code elaborates these varying status-based, associative, and corporate rights and duties.[92]

The relevance of all this for intellectual property starts to become apparent when we observe that there is no provision within the code for "patents of invention" (*Erfindungspatenten*). The closest we come to this within the code is in a provision addressing the industrial monopolies of guilds (*Zunftzwang*). Here the code refers to craftsmen/manufacturers "who have obtained a particular privilege (*Privilegium*) from the state." These "Freemasters" (*Freimeister*) are exhorted to correctly observe the legal limits of their privileges.[93]

Through this provision, and its context within the code, we catch a glimpse into a world in which monopolies over the making, using, and selling of particular types of goods (i.e., the analog to a modern "patent") are possessed primarily by guilds. These guilds, in turn, are required to coexist with Freemasters who have obtained a special privilege from the state. The fact that certain of these privileges were issued to reward the invention, improvement, or importation of new industrial techniques can be inferred from annotations in later editions of the code, which reference the 1815 "Supreme Cabinet Order" governing the issuance of patents for industrial "discoveries."[94]

The *Zunftzwang* resulted from the obligation to join a guild in order to engage in a particular type of industrial activity (e.g., metalworking or linen weaving). Its effect was an exclusive, guild-based right to engage in an industrial activity, the consequence of which was an exclusive, guild-based right to make, use, or sell particular types of goods. The degree to which guilds were able to accomplish this craft-based social closure depended on the cities within which the guilds were formed. The

91 ALR, Part I, Title I, §§ 2–5.

92 ALR, Part I, Title I, §§6–8; Part II.

93 ALR, Part II, Title 8, §225.

94 Supreme Cabinet Order of September 27, 1815, regarding issuance and use of patents for inventions or improvements, in Dr. Jur. Schering (ed.), *Nachtrag zum Allgemeinen Landrecht für die Preussischen Staaten*, No. 153.

degree to which the cities were able to effectuate this social closure depended, in turn, on their relationships with regional and imperial overlords.[95]

This is a social world in which legal status remains highly significant. The opportunity to partake in certain kinds of activities (e.g., making, using, or selling certain kinds of goods; voting for civic magistrates; owning real property within the boundaries of a city or village community) is explicitly tied to a specific legal status, which in turn is explicitly tied to membership in overlapping corporate bodies that, as corporate bodies, have the authority to determine the conditions for membership and legal status.

In this social world, the closest analog to a patent for new inventions is the privilege granted to an individual enabling them to practice a particular industrial art – thus to make, use, or sell particular types of goods – which would otherwise be the exclusive right of a guild by virtue of the *Zunftzwang*. The language of property is not used with respect to such privileges. They exist solely by the "freely given gift" (grace) of the sovereign (*Oberhaupt*). These, like the prerogative rights of an English king, are a temporary allocation of property belonging to the sovereign: they are part of the sovereign's "regalia" (*Regalien*) or "magisterial right" (*Majestätsrecht*).[96]

The analog to copyright in the Prussian General Code is comparable to a status-based right, albeit closer to a modern copyright. Part I, Title 11 of the code addresses "the title to acquisition of ownership, which grounds itself in contracts between living persons." Section 7 of Chapter 8 addresses "printing contracts" (*Verlagsverträge*). The "printing right" (*Verlagsrecht*) delineated in this section of the code is said to "consist in the authority to copy a written work through printing, and exclusively to sell it at fairs, to booksellers, and the like." The right extends beyond written works to encompass maps, copper engravings, topographical drawings, and musical compositions.[97]

To be sure, a "right of authors" (*Recht des Verfassers*), which extends to their heirs, is mentioned in the code. However, this is only a "negative" right: the publisher cannot undertake a new edition of a written work without the contractual consent of the author. This right does not extend to reprints of the same edition: absent contractual provisions to the contrary, the publisher can continue reprinting the author's work, although he does have to pay the author a fee. The author has no rights (in the absence of a contract) with respect to "derivative works" (translations, commentaries, etc.). Furthermore, the right of the author to produce a new edition of his own work is limited by the right of the publisher to sell remaining copies of the

95 ALR, Part II, Title 8, §224; Mack Walker, *German Home Towns: Community, State, and General Estate, 1648–1871* (Ithaca: Cornell University Press, 1971), 73–107; Hugo C. M. Wendel, *The Evolution of Industrial Freedom in Prussia, 1845–1849* (New York: New York University Press, 1921), 1–16.

96 ALR, Part II, Title 13 et seq.; Rudolf Huebner, *A History of Germanic Private Law*, translated by Francis S. Philbrick (Boston: Little, Brown, and Company, 1918), 268–71.

97 ALR, Part I, Title 11, §§996–7.

prior edition. Finally, even the author's limited, "negative" right is eliminated if the initial conception for the work was the publisher's, rather than the author's.[98]

This is primarily a printers' right, albeit with some limited gestures in the direction of moral rights for authors. Therefore, it is primarily a right that belongs to persons in virtue of their occupational status as printer-publishers. Like the sections of the code that govern the activity of guilds, this section of the code governs the activity of printer-publishers, and in so doing articulates certain limited rights possessed by authors. The rights and obligations of authors, pursuant to the Prussian General Code, are inextricably linked to the status-based rights and obligations of printer-publishers.[99]

Arguments had certainly been made for authors' proprietary rights. Among the authors of such arguments were some of the most culturally influential philosophers of the late eighteenth century: Johann Gottlieb Fichte (1762–1814) and Immanuel Kant (1724–1804). Protests against the piracy of printers went all the way back to Martin Luther, and the French revolutionary embrace of literary property would certainly have been known to Prussian jurists and lawgivers. Nonetheless, Prussia struck a more conservative balance, seeking to reform, rather than eliminate, an estate-based legal framework for industrial and literary works.[100]

10.8 CONCLUSION

In the same momentous year (1774) that Louis XVI opened his reign, Johann Wolfgang von Goethe (1749–1832) published his *Sufferings of Young Werther* in Leipzig. The publisher was Weygand's Booksales (*Weygandische Buchhandlung*), an important publisher in the Holy Roman Empire. Together with Weimar, Leipzig had become a center for the "Storm and Pressure" (*Sturm und Drang*) of a newly emerging "German" literature. Goethe's *Werther*, along with Friedrich Schiller's *Robbers* (1781) and other publications of the *Sturm und Drang* writers, facilitated

98 ALR, Part I, Title 11, §§1011–22; Friedemann Kawohl, "Commentary on the Reprinting Provisions in the Prussian Statute Book (1794)," *Primary Sources*.

99 For a broader perspective on the German book trade, as seen from the perspective of a Berlin-based publisher, Friedrich Nicolai (1733–1811), see Pamela E. Selwyn, *Everyday Life in the German Book Trade: Friedrich Nicolai as Bookseller and Publisher in the Age of Enlightenment, 1750–1810* (University Park, Pennsylvania: The Pennsylvania State University Press, 2000).

100 Graham Mayeda, "Commentary on Fichte's 'The Illegality of the Unauthorised Reprinting of Books',: An Essay on Intellectual Property During the Age of Enlightenment," *University of Ottawa Law and Technology Journal* 5 (2008): 141–98; Immanuel Kant, "On the Wrongfulness of Unauthorized Publication of Books (1785), in *Immanuel Kant: Practical Philosophy*, edited and translated by Mary J. Gregor (New York: Cambridge University Press, 1996), 29–35; Martin Luther, "Warning to the Printers, Wittenberg (1545)," translated by Luis Sundkvist, *Primary Sources*.

Hegel was perhaps the first major philosopher to give intellectual property (*geistiges Eigentum*) a significant place in his philosophy of law. Georg Wilhelm Friedrich Hegel, *Elements of the Philosophy of Right*, edited by Allen W. Wood (Cambridge, UK: Cambridge University Press, 1991) §§43, 64, 68–9, 319; see also Frederick Beiser, *Hegel* (New York: Routledge, 2005); Allen W. Wood, *Hegel's Ethical Thought* (Cambridge, UK: Cambridge University Press, 1990).

something of singular importance: they gave expressive form to the restless impressions and emotions of a generation, enabling that generation to engage in a new type of self-conscious reflection and to consider what it might mean to be a "a modern German."[101]

But "Germany," as we know it, did not exist, and neither did German "patents," "copyrights," or "intellectual property." Indeed, the patronage and protection that Goethe and his fellow authors received depended very much on the personal relationships they maintained with printers and princely benefactors.[102]

Goethe's life provides valuable insight into the legal and institutional position of authors and printers within the socio-legal architecture of the late Holy Roman Empire. He grew up in Frankfurt, an imperial free city that had been an early center for the medieval book trade. He studied law in Strasbourg, another imperial free city (until its annexation by France in 1681), home to Johannes Gutenberg (c. 1400–68) before his return to Mainz, where the movable-type press was invented. Goethe's university years were spent in Leipzig, a thriving commercial city in the Electorate of Saxony, which overtook Frankfurt as a publication center in the post-Reformation period. His later years would be spent in Weimar, a city in the Duchy of Saxony from which authors were recruited and nurtured by ambitious printers. Together with many of his generation, Goethe had, as a child, looked north with expectant hope to Berlin (also becoming a center of publication and commerce), to Frederick the Great.[103]

By the end of Goethe's life, however, a categorical shift had occurred across Europe and North America. "Copyrights" (or "literary property" – exclusive rights to print copies of a literary work) and inventors' "patents" (exclusive rights to make, use, and sell a newly invented machine or process of manufacture) were spoken of, and thought of, as a type of property in Britain, France, and the United States. This categorical shift had not yet taken place across all German speaking lands, but a transition toward viewing copyrights and patents as property was occurring there, too. In Prussia, as we have seen, analogues to copyrights and patents were recognized in 1794 as printers' rights, guild monopolies, and privileged exceptions to guild monopolies.

In this chapter, we have seen how French and German jurists contributed meaning to orders of legal obligation, formulating concepts and principles intended

101 Viscount Goschen, *The Life and Times of Georg Joachim Goschen: Publisher and Printer of Leipzig, 1752–1828*, Vol. I (New York: G. P. Putnam's Sons, 1903), 1–3, 13–39; Terry Pinkard, *German Philosophy 1760–1860: The Legacy of Idealism* (Cambridge, UK: Cambridge University Press, 2002), 14.

102 Johann Wolfgang von Goethe, *From My Life: Poetry and Truth*, translated by Robert R. Heitner, edited by Thomas P. Saine and Jeffrey L. Sammons (Princeton: Princeton University Press, 1987), 382–4; Goschen, *Life and Times*, 40–55; Selwyn, *Friedrich Nicolai*, 299–374; Martha Woodmansee, "The Genius and the Copyright: Economic and Legal Conditions of the Emergence of the 'Author'," *Eighteenth-Century Studies* 17(4) (1984): 425–48.

103 von Goethe, *From My Life*, 46–8 and passim; Goschen, *Life and Times*, passim.

to guide the development of social bonds and boundaries, within new governing communities. In the case of Revolutionary France, the concepts and principles drew on liberal and national ideals, as well as Roman legal traditions. In the case of Prussia, there was a heroic effort to reform traditional concepts of "estate society," shaped over centuries by jurists interpreting Biblical and Roman law, reformed in Lutheran jurisprudence, drawing selectively on liberal ideals in constituting vocational groupings, and in conceptualizing ethical obligations involving property within these vocational groupings. In the wake of France's revolutionary earthquake, however, orders of obligation were being semantically reconstituted across continental Europe, with explicit recognition for property "rights" in products of human ingenuity, intellect (*Geist*), and authorship.

French jurisprudence played an especially significant role in the area of "moral rights." Unlike the Anglo-American tradition of copyright, which came to emphasize almost exclusively the economic (or "pecuniary") dimensions of copyright, the French tradition of literary property adopted the view that, beyond economic interests, authors and artists have a moral, personality-related interest in their artistic creations. This means that certain uses of their artistic works can be prohibited, even if there is no identifiable economic harm, and even if all their rights have been seemingly transferred (e.g., through an assignment).

France has played an important role on the global stage as a progenitor of moral rights, which were incorporated into the Berne Convention of 1886, and are now enshrined in a global intellectual property framework. However, in France, the concept of moral rights did not receive legislative recognition until 1957. In fact, the concept developed in its earliest form through judicial decisions, and it was maintained through these jurisprudential principles until 1886, when the Berne Convention gave it a treaty-based recognition.[104]

Arguably, indeed, the French tradition of moral rights – involving a more "absolutist" conception of authorial rights – goes back all the way to the Reformation era, as seen in an argument made before the *Parlement* of Paris in 1586.

In Chapter 1, I defined the process of semantic legal ordering as one in which *enduring legal meanings, received through legal traditions, exercise causal power in forming and solidifying our patterns of social activity and social relationships*. Throughout this book, the legal traditions exercising this causal power have been Roman and Biblical law, carried by generations of jurists who have referenced these legal traditions in their efforts to lend order, power, and peace to their governing communities. In the French Revolution, jurists began directing their semantic efforts toward an abstract, collective "nation," one that was being constituted and idealized in an anti-clerical break with the Christian church. In Prussia and Lutheran Germany, jurists sought a more "conservative" path, seeking to find ways of preserving the ideals of estate society, blessed by

[104] Sirvinskaite, "Copyright 'Europeanification'," 276.

Lutheran jurisprudence, with legal communities organized on the basis of status, while selectively incorporating more liberal ideals. In the previous chapter, we saw how these liberal ideals, themselves, drew on European traditions of Roman and Biblical law, reinterpreted to dramatic effect in the Protestant Reformation.

In the liberalism of John Locke, knowledge production was naturalized, and a legal framework of natural law, rooted in Roman law, was transformed into a foundation for claims to property rights in the products of human labor, independent of, and indeed superior to, legislation and political consent. In the French Revolution, this argument was transformed into a foundation for property rights in the products of human ingenuity, an idealization of human "genius" that was now coming to be seen as something entirely natural, and yet as something to be protected in the form of "moral rights," an entitlement claim that goes beyond economic compensation, toward recognizing and protecting a more "spiritual" bond that connects a creative human "maker" with her creation.

Products of the human spirit (*Geist*) can be appropriated just like any other natural object, and they can be made into the economic foundation for governing communities, but the rights of genius transcend the banal sphere of economic exchange. In the jurisprudence of French courts, and in the literature of German philosophers, natural law arguments for intellectual property became doctrinal foundations for a widening set of legal institutions, extending into protections for regional identification of commercial products, and ultimately to the mental associations that consumers make with mass-produced objects of commercial exchange. At the organizational level, these developments were facilitated by the development of the national state, which sprang suddenly into existence in France, and developed more fitfully out of the Holy Roman Empire.

In the Prussian General Code, we saw rights that are analogous to intellectual property, protecting printers and guilds as part of a broader framework for an estate-based order of obligation. In this type of order, people are born into status groups, and they are governed under a law that is specific to their status grouping. Seeing that intellectual property, as we know it, seems impossible in this type of order helps us recognize the extent to which modern intellectual property depends on an underlying logic of legal uniformity in the modern national state.

The semantic formality and substantive rationality underpinning modern intellectual property involve logics of legality and well-being that are meant to apply equally to everyone within the borders of a national state, at the very least to all citizens. The legal logics of estate society simply could not be made to fit with the newly radicalized natural rights which were supposed to collectively underpin certain basic and absolute rights of human beings, including rights in the products of their creative expression and inventive ingenuity.

As we will see in Chapter 12, Prussia's estate society did not endure. Treaty-based legal frameworks helped to create a German nation which began to recognize intellectual property rights according to legal frameworks created through positive law, particularly treaties. Seeing how intellectual property analogues look in an estate society, however, helps us to see the extent to which intellectual property, as we know it, is a property of a unitary nation-state, a property of nations.

In the next chapter, we will see how intellectual property licensing contributed to a national telecommunications network which now connects the world, underpinning a new development in the application of global intellectual property frameworks: artificial intelligence.

11

Instruments of Legal Power in the American Republic

Intellectual Property and Telecommunications

On November 10, 1879, two companies signed a momentous contract. The National Bell Telephone Company signed away all its rights to telegraph-related patents, transferring those rights to the Western Union Telegraph Company (including its wholly owned subsidiary the Gold and Stock Company, a provider of "ticker" and wire news services). In return, National Bell received all rights to telephone-related patents held by Western Union. From this day forward, telephone- and telegraph-related services would be cleanly divided between the two companies. And these companies would remain the dominant providers of telecommunications services into the second half of the twentieth century. Through this 1879 contract, the companies had settled a vicious battle for economic power, a battle waged through patent litigation and through famously aggressive stock market trading tactics. Viewed from the perspective of later developments, we can see in this contract the foundations for a national telecommunications industry, and for a phase of venture capitalism solidifying the fortunes of investment banking firms like J. P. Morgan.[1]

[1] A copy of this contract is available as part of a massive collection of exhibits (Exhibit 1360-C, Appendix 7) to the Federal Communications Commission's Special Investigation Docket No. 1, an investigation of the telephone industry in the United States, carried out as part of the FCC's establishment as a new regulatory agency in 1934. See FCC Annual Reports to Congress, 1935–39, available at www.fcc.gov/reports-research/reports (accessed July 31, 2019). The Final Report, issued to Congress in June 1939 on the basis of this investigation, is readily available in both print and electronic versions. Federal Communications Commission, *A Report on the Investigation of the Telephone Industry in the United States*, House Doc. No. 340 (1939) [hereafter 1939 *FCC Report*].

Summaries of the contract in its context may be found in another set of exhibits (2096F) to FCC Special Investigation Docket No. 1, which are electronically accessible as part of the Clay T. Whitehead archive from the Library of Congress, available at http://claytwhitehead.com/the_papers/ (accessed July 31, 2019), Boxes 61–2. See also the dissertation by Rosario Joseph Tosiello, *The Birth and Early Years of the Bell Telephone System, 1876–1880* (New York: Arno Press, 1979), 452–91.

For historical accounts focusing on the context for business strategies in the early telecommunications industry, see David Hochfelder, *The Telegraph in America, 1832–1920* (Baltimore: Johns Hopkins University Press, 2012); Paul Israel, *From Machine Shop to Industrial Laboratory: Telegraphy and the Changing Context of American Invention, 1830–1920* (Baltimore: Johns Hopkins University Press, 1992); George David Smith, *The Anatomy of a Business Strategy: Bell, Western Electric, and the Origins of the American Telephone Industry* (Baltimore: Johns Hopkins University Press, 1985).

Both Western Union and National Bell, along with their national networks in wire-based telegraph and telephone services, had been legally founded on patents and contractual licenses of those patents. Samuel Morse received the first electromagnetic telegraph patent in 1840. As we will see, this patent provided a foundation for the Magnetic Telegraph Company, which expanded its telegraph lines and operations through contractual licenses and assignments. Western Union, which had been founded on a competing telegraph patent – Royal House's "printing telegraph patent" of 1846 – also expanded through contractual organization and licensing practices, as well as acquisition of competitors, a process that culminated in the absorption of the Morse companies.[2]

By 1877, when the Bell Telephone Association was formed from Alexander Graham Bell's patents, nearly forty years of experience had been gained in telegraph-related patent acquisition and licensing practices aimed at national organization and control. A succession of Bell companies would draw on this experience to build, in the estimation of the Federal Communications Commission (FCC), "the largest aggregation of capital and resources that has ever been controlled by a single private company at any time in the history of business." Indeed, the FCC attributed the growth and success of the Bell System in "occupying almost the entire telephone field in the United States" primarily to patent acquisition and licensing practices.[3]

The nineteenth century has been labeled as an era of free contracts and laissez-faire liberalism. It was then that basic institutional patterns, which endure today, were established for the contractual licensing of intellectual property. The establishment of these institutional patterns depended on the fundamental assumption that contracts represent a reciprocal exchange of promises, which the state reinforces, reflecting a capacity on the part of individuals (and corporations) to voluntarily create rights and obligations. This, broadly speaking, is the "will theory" of contracts, a doctrinal perspective that enables the creation of voluntary obligations through the exercise of contractual free will by property-owning persons ("proprietors").[4]

[2] Samuel Morse's patent: "Improvement in the Mode of Communicating Information by Signals by the Application of Electro-Magnetism," US Patent No. 1,647 (1840). This was preceded by several other telegraph-related patents, the earliest of which dated back to 1800 (US Patent No. 305X, issued to J. Grout, Jr. on October 24, 1800). These earlier telegraphs, including that patented by Jonathan Grout in 1800, were "semaphore telegraphs," which relied on visual signals sent between tall poles. Robert Luther Thompson, *Wiring a Continent: The History of the Telegraph Industry in the United States, 1832–1866* (Princeton: Princeton University Press, 1947), 11–12 n.18; James D. Reid, *The Telegraph in America and Morse Memorial* (New York: John Polhemus Publishers, 1886), 1–6. Royal House's "printing telegraph patent," US Patent No. 4,464 (1846).

[3] Bell Patents: US Patent Nos. 161,739 (1875); 174,465 (1876); and 178,399 (1876); 1939 *FCC Report*, xxiii–xxiv; 213–46.

[4] P. S. Atiyah, *The Rise and Fall of Freedom of Contract* (Oxford: Clarendon Press, 1979); Lawrence M. Friedman, *A History of American Law*, 3rd ed. (New York: Simon & Schuster, 2005), 202–6; Morton J. Horwitz, *The Transformation of American Law: 1780–1860* (Cambridge, MA: Harvard University Press, 1977), 160 ff; Morton J. Horwitz, *The Transformation of American Law, 1870–1960: The Crisis of Legal Orthodoxy* (Oxford: Oxford University Press, 1992), 33–63.

In this chapter, I argue that the will theory of contracts enabled intellectual property to dramatically expand in the scale and scope of its impact on everyday social life. Contracts became instruments of legal power, which today form a vital part of intellectual property-related ties radiating throughout society, an infrastructure of state power that helps to constitute the modern nation-state system. I ground this argument in the empirical cases of Western Union and the American Telephone and Telegraph Company ("AT&T"), companies whose strategic use of patent licenses enabled the creation of a national (now global) telecommunications network.

11.1 THE WILL THEORY OF CONTRACTS

In 1871, newly appointed Harvard Law professor Christopher Columbus Langdell published a textbook for use in teaching contract law to American law students. The second edition of this textbook, published in 1879, concluded with a "Summary" of the contract "doctrines" that Langdell believed were revealed by the selected cases. This *Summary of the Law of Contracts* came to be seen as a treatise in its own right and was published separately in 1880.[5]

The opening paragraph of Langdell's *Summary* is significant. Under the heading "Acceptance," Langdell wrote:

> According to the popular apprehension of the term, a promise is the act of the promisor alone; but in truth it requires also an act of the promisee. Before any act by the promisee, the so-called promise is in law only an offer, *called by the Romans a pollicitation*. It is not until it is accepted that it becomes in law a promise. A promise is in this respect like a gift of property, which is commonly supposed be the act of the donor alone, but which requires the acceptance of the donee to pass the title to the property.[6]

With this opening, Langdell was stating that the fundamental basis for a legally binding contract is a promissory offer that is accepted. This may seem blindingly obvious, but, in fact, as Patrick Atiyah has shown, this way of thinking about contracts represented a new development for the Anglo-American common law tradition.[7]

During the first decade of the nineteenth century, French civilian conceptions of contract law had become influential in the United States, mediated in part by Robert Joseph Pothier's *Treatise on Obligations*. Pothier's treatise was first translated into

[5] Christopher Columbus Langdell, A *Summary of the Law of Contracts*, 2nd ed. (Boston: Little, Brown & Co., 1880; Steve Sheppard (ed.), *The History of Legal Education in the United States: Commentaries and Primary Sources* (Pasadena: Salem Press, Inc., 1999), 24–9; Steve Sheppard, "Casebooks, Commentaries, and Carmudgeons: An Introductory History of Law in the Lecture Hall," *Iowa Law Review* 82 (1997): 547–644, 596–605.

[6] Langdell, *Summary*, 1 (emphasis added).

[7] Atiyah, *Freedom of Contract*, passim; also Horwitz, *Transformation*, 1780–1860, 160–210.

English by a Marseillaise North Carolinian, Francoise-Xavier Martin, who would go on to serve for thirty-one years (1815–46) as a justice of the Louisiana Supreme Court. The popularity of Martin's translation was quickly supplanted, however, by William David Evans' translation, which was published first in London, and then in Philadelphia. In 1839, Luther Stearns Cushing, Harvard Law professor and Boston editor of a prominent legal periodical (*The American Jurist and Law Magazine*), pronounced Pothier's treatise to be a "standard work, without which even a moderately sized law-library would scarcely be considered complete."[8]

According to Patrick Atiyah, Pothier's treatise was "avidly seized upon" by English jurists because it supplied "general principles" of contract law, which could help in systematizing and developing the English common law. The general principles supplied by Pothier's treatise were Romanist principles of consensual contracts, as these had been reinterpreted for a unifying French nation. Pothier's emphasis on the abstract nature of contracts, as consensual agreements constituted by reciprocal promises, enabled English lawyers to begin formulating a generalized law of contracts that was viewed as operating uniformly, regardless of person, type of transaction, or subject matter.[9]

In America, Pothier's influence was also powerful and widespread. Between 1800 and 1870, Pothier's treatise on obligations was cited as an authority in 186 federal court opinions, 94 of which were Supreme Court opinions. Pothier was also cited extensively by the early American treatise writers. Joseph Story, for example, relied heavily on Pothier in his treatises, citing him with approval and relying on his definitions of basic legal concepts, such as partnership:

> Pothier says that partnership is a contract whereby two or more persons put, or contract to put, something in common to make a lawful profit in common, and reciprocally engage with each other to render an account thereof.[10]

In his widely read *Commentaries on the Constitution*, Story relied on Pothier's definition of a contract, in interpretively characterizing the US Constitution as a "compact."

[8] Robert Joseph Pothier, *A Treatise on Obligations Considered in a Moral and Legal View*, translated by Francois-Xavier Martin (New Bern, NC: Martin & Ogden, 1802), reprinted by the Lawbook Exchange with an introduction by Warren M. Billings (Union, N. J., 1999); Luther S. Cushing (trans.), *Treatise on the Contract of Sale by R. J. Pothier* (Boston: Charles C. Little and James Brown, 1839), v–vi. *The American Jurist and Law Magazine* was first published in 1829 and continued in publication until 1846 (from 1843 as *The American Law Magazine*), offering an invaluable window into Ante-Bellum US legal culture. Volume 1 opens with an 1821 address by Joseph Story to the Suffolk County Bar Association and contains a lengthy article on copyright ("Literary Property").

[9] Atiyah, *Freedom of Contract*, 351–2, 399–400.

[10] Joseph Story, *Commentaries on the Law of Partnership as a Branch of Commercial and Maritime Jurisprudence*, 7th ed. (Boston: Little, Brown, and Co., 1881) [1841], 2. Reliance on Pothier in US federal court opinions: Westlaw database search, conducted on June 29, 2020, results on file with author. For broader discussion of Pothier's foundational importance for US contract law, see Joseph M. Perillo, "Robert J. Pothier's Influence on the Common Law of Contract," *Texas Wesleyan Law Review* 11 (2005): 267–90.

> Pothier distinguishes between a contract and an agreement. An agreement, he says, is the consent of two or more persons to form some engagement . . .. An agreement, by which two parties reciprocally promise and engage, or one of them singly promises and engages to the other, to give some particular thing, or to do or abstain from some particular act, is a contract; by which he means such an agreement, as gives a party the right legally to demand its performance.[11]

Through Pothier, but also through independent study, Story came to greatly admire Roman law. In the preface to his treatise on partnership law, Story highly recommended the study of Roman law, pronouncing its principles to be "well adapted to the convenience and policy of commercial nations in all ages." Chancellor Kent, in his *Commentaries on American Law*, likewise extolled the Roman law for its clarity and brevity in defining and illustrating "the rights and duties flowing from personal contracts, express and implied, and under the infinite variety of shapes which they assume in the business and commerce of life."[12]

This American embrace of the Roman law tradition, as being well suited to a "commercial nation," signals a process of reception that went beyond Pothier and the law of contracts. Through incorporation of the "law of nations" into American law – especially mercantile and commercial law – the Roman law tradition was exercising a profound cultural influence.

According to Chancellor Kent, the United States became subject to the law of nations the moment she gained independence from Britain. This meant that in situations of international commerce, war, treaty-making, and so on, the United States was bound by this law of nations, or "international law." Congress had acknowledged subjection to this law in 1781, according to Kent. Even more fundamentally, this law of nations was part of the common law heritage from England.

> The English judges have frequently declared that the law of nations was part of the common law of England . . . and it is well settled that the common law of England, so far as it may be consistent with the constitutions of this country and remains unaltered by statute, is an essential part of American jurisprudence.[13]

As Kent was aware, the law of nations had been heavily influenced by Roman law. In his history of the law of nations, Kent cited the opening sections of Justinian's *Digest* and *Institutes*, noting that Justinian's codifiers had taken an important step toward the modern law of nations in equating the law that they applied between tribes with "the natural reason of mankind." Despite its imperfections,

> [t]he Roman law was destined to obtain the honorable distinction of becoming a national guide to future ages, and to be appealed to by modern tribunals and

[11] Joseph Story, *Commentaries on the Constitution of the United States*, 5th ed. by Melville M. Bigelow, Vol. I (Boston: Little, Brown, and Co., 1891) [1833], Book III, Ch. 3, § 323, 232 n.2.

[12] Story, *Law of Partnership*, ix; James Kent, *Commentaries on American Law*, 12th ed. by Oliver W. Holmes, Jr. (Boston: Little, Brown, and Co., 1873) [1826], 547.

[13] Kent, *Commentaries*, 1, n.(a).

writers, in cases in which usage and positive law are silent, as one authoritative evidence of the decisions of the law of nations.

Thus, according to Chancellor Kent, the Roman law tradition was part of American law, both through its impact on international law, and through its impact on common law.[14]

The importance of this Roman law influence, by means of international law, can be seen if we return, once again, to Langdell's treatise on contracts. Langdell cited two authorities for his pronouncement that a contract consists in a consensual agreement (i.e., an accepted offer). One of these authorities was Robert Joseph Pothier. The other was Hugo Grotius, an early seventeenth-century legal scholar from Holland, who is widely seen as a "founding father" of contemporary international law, and whose "modernizing" views on natural law decisively influenced Pothier.[15]

Langdell's citation was to Grotius' most famous book *On the Law (Rights) of War and Peace*, first published in 1625, while the wars over Christian politics were tearing Europe apart. Langdell cited Chapter 11 of Book II, a section of the treatise addressing the principles according to which promises create binding obligations. In Grotius' text, this was part of an extended account detailing the circumstances under which parties acquire rights under the principles of natural law, as supplemented by the law of nations and the positive (or "municipal") law of states. Grotius' purpose was to provide a basis for determining when rights had been violated, such that war was justified. In Langdell's text, however, Grotius' natural law framework became the foundation for basic principles of (commercial) contract law.[16]

Grotius' systemic presentation of natural law wove basic principles from the Roman law tradition together with Biblical, theological, and philosophical traditions. Although Grotius relied heavily on scholastic foundations, his system of natural law is nonetheless seen as a point of departure, pointing the way toward

14 Ibid., 7.

15 Langdell, *Summary*, 1. Hugo Grotius "among the founding fathers" of modern international law: C. G. Roelofsen, "Grotius and the International Politics of the Seventeenth Century," in *Hugo Grotius and International Relations*, edited by Hedley Bull, Benedict Kingsbury, and Adam Roberts (Oxford: Clarendon Press, 1990), 95; *cf.* Hedley Bull, "The Importance of Grotius in the Study of International Relations," in Bull, Kingsbury, and Adams (eds.), Hugo Grotius, 65–93. Influence of "Grotian" legal ideas on modern contract law, by way of Pothier: Atiyah, *Freedom of Contract*, 406. On the academic distinction between "modern" ("Protestant") natural law theory and the older, "metaphysical" ("neoscholastic") tradition, see Michael Seidler, "Pufendorf's Moral and Political Philosophy," *Stanford Encyclopedia of Philosophy* (2018), available at https://plato.stanford.edu/entries/pufendorf-moral/ (accessed June 30, 2020).

16 Langdell, *Summary*, 1; Stephen C. Neff (ed.), *Hugo Grotius on the Law of War and Peace* (Cambridge, UK: Cambridge University Press, 2012), xvii–xxi, 186–201 and passim; Richard Tuck (ed.), *The Rights of War and Peace* by Hugo Grotius, 3 Vols. (Indianapolis: Liberty Fund, 2005), 699–728. Grotius' stated purpose: Tuck (ed.), *Rights of War*, 71–132, 136.

modernizing principles of international law that emphasized the sovereign power of states, and the promissory will of contracting parties.[17]

Like his scholastic predecessors, Grotius emphasized the role of human reason in grasping basic principles of law that are rooted in divine order and human nature (sources of natural law), together with the historical evidence of common consent (a source for the law that is common to all nations, the *ius gentium*). On the other hand, in emphasizing the sovereign power of states to institute, through positive law, departures from natural law principles, and in emphasizing the role of will in instituting these legal departures, Grotius pointed forward to a legal future in which positive legality would subsume natural law, and will would overtake reason as the defining capacity for determining law. Ultimately, what is at stake here is the source of legal and moral obligation.[18]

Grotius equated positive law – law that is instituted by God or by humans – with voluntary law, law that originates in the will (*voluntas*). Likewise, the activities connected with acquiring and exercising both sovereign jurisdiction (*imperium*) and ownership (*dominium*) – closely related concepts for Grotius – are rooted in the will, which may be subjected to reason and therefore to principles of law. A legally recognized transfer of property or sovereign jurisdiction is an act of will, which is given an external appearance in words, or in another sign accessible to the senses. Likewise, a voluntary promise to transfer a right to another person, which is accompanied by an outward sign of this intention, gives rise to a legally enforceable obligation on the part of the promisor.[19]

For Grotius, then, legally enforceable obligations, particularly those involving the transfer of property, arise fundamentally from acts of will, governed by reason. This emphasis on will in relation to property was rooted in the Roman law tradition, going back to classical Roman law, particularly in the area of possession (*possessio*).

Roman law recognized and enforced rights to possession of property, which were distinct from full-scale ownership, on the one hand, and actual physical possession, on the other hand. Acquisition of legally protected possession required both a physical element – a bodily act of holding or taking (*corpus*) – and a mental element: the will to possess (*animus*). Continuation of the will to possess, even when physical possession was lost, ensured that a legal remedy for recovering the property would continue. On the other hand, loss of the will to possess was sufficient, by itself, to eliminate the legal right to possession.

[17] Atiyah, *Freedom of Contract*, 49, 63, 140–41; Heinrich A. Rommen, *The Natural Law: A Study in Legal and Social History and Philosophy* (Indianapolis: Liberty Fund, 1998), 62–96.

[18] Tuck (ed.), *Rights of War*, 85–7, 150–62, and passim; also Atiyah, *Freedom of Contract*, 140–1; Rommen, *Natural Law*, 4, 36, 51–8, 62–6; Russell Hittinger, "Introduction" to Rommen, *Natural Law*, xxv–xxxii.

[19] Tuck (ed.), *Rights of War*, 107, 111–12, 162–6, 420, 454–9, 566, 704–8, 848–9; Latin from William Whewell (ed.), *Hugonis Grotii, De Jure Belli et Pacis, Libri Tres* (Cambridge, UK: Cambridge University Press, 1853). "Contracts" are simply a subset of obligations involving the reciprocal exchange of promises. Ibid., 729–67.

> Again, for the loss of possession, the possessor's mental attitude must be considered; if you are on a piece of land and lose the will to possess it, you immediately cease to possess it. Hence, possession can be lost, though it cannot be acquired, by will alone.[20]

In the area of obligations, including contracts, emphasis on will was a postclassical development, the seeds of which are associated with the influence of Christian-Byzantine jurisprudence, particularly under Justinian. Despite initial shifts toward a focus on shared will (*consensus*) in later Roman contract law, obligations were nonetheless still predominantly seen as arising out of the legal status of persons, or the nature of their activities, not their particular intention as manifested in words. The transformative emphasis on will, expressed by words, as the basis for contractual obligation came only in the late sixteenth and early seventeenth centuries, in Protestant/modern natural law jurisprudence, with Hugo Grotius marking a turning point.[21]

The jurisprudence of Hugo Grotius, then, marks a shift toward modern natural and international law. In his famous treatise, emphasis on will in relation to both property and contracts is heightened and made the source of basic social obligations: obligations to respect property, and to keep contractual promises, operating simultaneously at levels that we would consider "public" and those we would consider "private." As we have seen, both directly and indirectly through French legal scholarship (Pothier), Grotius' basic framework became foundational for American contract law in the nineteenth century.

Grotius had developed his conceptual framework of legal and moral obligation within a social context in which the capacities of human will power had become a focus of intense theological attention. Grotius was born in 1583 into a rapidly changing Dutch society, a time when Reformed Protestant doctrine had contributed to a revolt against imperial Spain, and to increasing social divisions. During Grotius' youth, these divisions were reflected in a fierce theological dispute between advocates for strict interpretations of Calvinism and a friend of Grotius' family, Jacob Arminius (c. 1559–1609), whose name would come to stand for theological developments ("Arminianism") that many Protestants considered heretical.[22]

At the heart of these disputes were questions of obligation, authority, and divine will, and about human capacities to pursue a path of Christian repentance, faith, and

20 Alan Watson (ed.), *The Digest of Justinian* (Philadelphia: University of Philadelphia Press, 1985), 41.2.3; also W. W. Buckland, *A Text-Book of Roman Law: From Augustus to Justinian*, 3rd ed. Revised by Peter Stein (Cambridge, UK: Cambridge University Press, 1963), 199.

21 Reinhard Zimmerman, *The Law of Obligations: Roman Foundations of the Civilian Tradition* (Oxford: Oxford University Press, 1996), 544, 565, 624–5, 636, 656–69; also Atiyah, *Freedom of Contract*, 36–60, 140–41.

22 Carl Bangs, *Arminius: A Study in the Dutch Reformation*, 2nd ed. (Grand Rapids: Zondervan, 1985); Jonathan I. Israel, *The Dutch Republic: Its Rise, Greatness, and Fall, 1477–1806*, 2nd ed. (Oxford: Oxford University Press, 1998), 30–1, 74–398, 421–77, and passim; George Masselman, *The Cradle of Colonialism* (New Haven: Yale University Press, 1963).

righteous perseverance. According to strictly systematized, "high" Calvinist theology, divine will is reflected in a plan of "absolute predestination," in which God decreed, from eternity (before the time of creation and human sin), that some would be capable of faith, while others would not. According to this decree, some are given God's grace, a gift that heals their willing capacities, enabling them to repent and to be faithful to their divine calling. Likewise, according to this decree, God wills that some humans continue in a state of corrupted will, remaining incapable of repentance and faith, and consequently suffering the eternal tortures of damnation.[23]

Arminius' theology, on the other hand, offered a more optimistic picture of the divine plan. According to Arminius, God wills and effectuates only good for human beings, offering to everyone through his self-sacrifice a grace that makes the human will capable of faith. The sinful will is capable only of evil. However, a capacity for faith remains in human beings such that they can cooperate with grace and freely believe. Arminius did not dispute the doctrine of predestination, but he viewed it as operating differently than in the strictly formulated Calvinist framework.[24]

Arminius died in 1609. However, his theological teachings continued to provoke controversy. Moderate Calvinists, especially those connected with the Holland magistracy, supported Arminius' views, or argued that they should at least be tolerated. Prominent among such supporters was Johan van Oldenbarnevelt (1547–1619), a leading magistrate and family friend of Hugo Grotius. However, the radical Calvinists succeeded, in the 1619 Synod of Dort (Dordrecht), in having Arminius' views declared heretical. Shortly afterward, Oldenbarnevelt was executed for treason, and Grotius, because of his association with Oldenbarnevelt and Arminius, was committed to life imprisonment.[25]

Grotius escaped from prison in 1621 and began writing his famous treatise on the *Law of War and Peace* one year later, under the protection and support of Louis XIII of France (1610–40). Written in the context of this intense debate over divine and human will, by a lawyer and theologian associated closely with Arminianism, it is perhaps not surprising that the emphasis on will – in relation to sovereignty, property, and contracts – is heightened in Grotius' treatise. Developing an emphasis that was already present in the Roman and Biblical legal traditions, Grotius transformed it into an organizing principle that would become a staple of Protestant natural law traditions.[26]

[23] Bangs, *Arminius*, 64–70, arguing that this is Theodore Beza's (1519–1605) second-generation systematization of Calvin's teachings, not the more nuanced systematization of Calvin himself.

[24] Bangs, *Arminius*, 191–205, 209–19, 262–3, 269, 307–14, 332–55; background at ibid., 102, 138–50, 169–70; *cf.* Israel, *Dutch Republic*, 393–5.

[25] Bangs, *Arminius*, 176–85, 231, 273–75, 284–306, 330, 356–7; Israel, *Dutch Republic*, 421–77; Masselman, *Cradle of Colonialism*, 471–5 and passim; Neff (ed.), *Hugo Grotius*, xviii.

[26] Tuck (ed.), *Rights of War*, 90–91, 111–12, 124–5, 154, 162–4; also Knud Haakonssen, *Natural Law and Moral Philosophy: From Grotius to the Scottish Enlightenment* (Cambridge, UK: Cambridge University Press, 1996), 24–30 and passim; Neff (ed.), *Hugo Grotius*, xviii; Rommen, *Natural Law*, 64 and passim.

The emphasis on proprietary and contractual will in Grotius and Pothier may help to explain their appeal in nineteenth-century America. Methodism – an English import that drew heavily on Arminian theology – was one of the fastest-growing Christian denominations. At the same time, the emphasis on will resonated with American individualism and mercantile capitalism.[27]

Looking back on his legal education at Harvard, Roscoe Pound (1870–1964) wrote:

> A general will theory of the science of law – a general reduction of everything to the manifested individual will – got currency in the eighteenth and fore part of the nineteenth century. It was generally adhered to in doctrinal expositions of Anglo-American law until the present century, although the courts still held to many rules here and there which had come down from older modes of thought. In *Parsons on Contracts*, which went through nine editions from 1853–1904 and was the standard American textbook used by lawyers and courts for two generations, *the willed assumption of duties was put at the foundation of all law* .... When I was a law student in 1889 I read Pothier .... Reading of French treatises on natural law was part of the training of the well-read American lawyer from the eve of the American Revolution in the last third of the eighteenth century till the American Civil War.[28]

The will theory of contracts was popularized for American businessmen through legal manuals written especially for them. One popular manual was published by Theophilus Parsons, mentor to Christopher Columbus Langdell at Harvard, whom Pound identifies in the above quote as a standard authority. Parsons' *Laws of Business for Business Men* laid out basic principles of commercial and contract law, providing forms for a variety of legal transactions. The treatise was organized around a will theory of contracts: binding contracts are formed when a promissory offer is accepted, and they are interpreted based on the intention of the parties, as manifested in their precise words.[29]

Parsons also included forms for the assignment of patents and copyrights.[30]

11.2 PROPRIETARY VOLUNTARISM

The will theory of contracts offers an extraordinary legal power, to anyone, to create institutions, obligations, and rights: a private, lawmaking power, a power to make what Max Weber called "special law." However, this power ranges along a continuum, depending on the nature of the contract.[31]

[27] Mark A. Noll, *America's God: From Jonathan Edwards to Abraham Lincoln* (Oxford: Oxford University Press, 2002), 165–70, 330–64, and passim; also Bangs, *Arminius*, 192, 206–8.

[28] Roscoe Pound, "The Role of the Will in Law," *Harvard Law Review* 68(1) (1954): 1–19, 18–19 (emphasis added).

[29] Theophilus Parsons, *The Laws of Business for Business Men in All the States of the Union* (Boston: Little, Brown, and Co., 1857), 26–37.

[30] Parsons, *Laws of Business*, 433–54.

[31] Weber on the power to make "special law": Max Rheinstein (ed.), *Max Weber on Law in Economy and Society* (New York: Simon and Schuster, 1967), 125–9, 140–91; Max Weber, *Economy and Society*,

The power is strongest when it is exercised by a property owner over his property. As we have seen, the Roman law tradition placed great stress on the power of a property owner to dispose of his own property, according to the determinations of his will. This conception of a property owner as lord and master (*dominus*) over that which is his own, when joined to an expanded conception of contractual capacities to create private law agreements, meant that parties viewed as property owners under the law were capable of exercising very broad powers to create rights and obligations, impacting third parties, as well as themselves.

On the other hand, the power was weaker when it pertained merely to future activity (e.g., repayment of a debt). A basic principle of Roman law held that contractual obligations incurred between two parties were fundamentally personal, as between those two parties, and therefore not capable of giving rise to rights on the part of third parties. This *in personam* character of contractual obligations meant that, in most cases, they could not be assigned or otherwise transferred to third parties. This default rule limited the development of negotiable instruments, the forerunners to paper money and financial instruments like stocks and bonds.[32]

Rights and obligations that are nontransferable have much less potential for impact on third parties, and for the creation of special law. They cannot be accumulated through assignment and transfer to a single party, and they cannot be deployed as creatively and purposefully to structure institutions. As we will see, it was through very purposeful strategies of accumulation and partial licensing of intellectual property (particularly patents) that Western Union and AT&T built their telecommunications networks. These strategies would have been impossible if the rights and obligations connected with the intellectual property had been nontransferable.

Not all rights are transferable, even today. In America, many of the welfare state-related rights that T. H. Marshall called "social rights" are nontransferable. Social Security benefits, for example, are explicitly nontransferable by statute: "the right of any person to any future payment under this subchapter shall not be transferable or assignable, at law or in equity." Such transfer restrictions prevent objects from being "monetized" (sold in exchange for their assessed value), and therefore restrict the formation of market exchange in the objects. By prohibiting individuals from bargaining away certain rights, transfer restrictions limit the large-scale accumulation of rights that might, on the one hand, enable the purposeful exercise of economic power, while, on the other hand, eliminate a social safety net for vulnerable individuals.[33]

edited by Guenther Roth and Claus Wittich, 2d ed. (Berkeley: University of California Press, 2013), 683–6, 694–731.

32 Watson (ed.), *Digest*, 45.1.38.17; Zimmerman, *Law of Obligations*, 1–28, 58–60.

33 Thomas H. Marshall, "Citizenship and Social Class," in *Citizenship and Social Class*, edited by Thomas H. Marshall and Tom Bottomore (London: Pluto Press, 1992), Part I; 42 U.S.C. §407; William H. Simon, "Social-Republican Property," *UCLA Law Review* 38 (1992): 1335–1413, 1341–2.

The categorization of patents and copyrights as property, which we have seen in previous chapters, strongly contributed to their transferability, due to the Roman law tradition's emphasis on the powers of a property owner to exercise their will in relation to their property. However, the fact that this new category of property emerged alongside a will theory of contracts meant that large-scale accumulations could occur with even greater ease, and on a much broader scale. Purposeful transfers of intellectual property, according to strategies that were learned through a long sequence of trial and error, enabled a hitherto unprecedented accumulation of social power in the institutionalization of America's telecommunications network.

11.3 SEEING THE IMPACT OF CONTRACTS: THE MAGNETIC TELEGRAPH COMPANY AND THE O'REILLY CONTRACT

In 1929, an economic historian described organizations in the electronics industry as having "crystallized around patent rights." It is important to add, however, that the parties relied on licensing to effectuate their organizational "crystallization," and to develop into a national presence. Early patent licensing practices involved poorly drafted contracts, hampering organizational development. Western Union would build on much more systematic patent acquisition and licensing practices, becoming a much stronger national organization. The Bell System, likewise, would expand through systematic patent and trademark licensing practices, and would grow into a national organization that endured through the 1980s. To see how this happened, we must go back to the early nineteenth century, beginning with Samuel Morse and the telegraph.[34]

Before patenting his electromagnetic telegraph, Samuel Morse had experience with the patent system, having patented a fire engine pump with his brother, Sidney, in 1817. Working toward electromagnetic telegraphy in 1832, Morse found it necessary to bring in partners more experienced in electrochemistry and practical machinery: Leonard Gale and Alfred Vail. The fact that a patent was a significant goal of their collective work is first evident from September 1837, when Morse and Vail executed a partnership contract. Pursuant to this contract, Morse and Vail agreed to joint ownership of US patent rights, and Morse agreed to transfer a portion

[34] Victor S. Clark, *History of Manufactures in the United States*, Vol. II, 1860–1893 (New York: McGraw-Hill Book Company, 1929), 381. Given our contemporary perspectives, it might seem odd to treat the growth of the Bell System as an extension of the telegraph industry. However, once it is recalled that Alexander Graham Bell's inventions were seen initially as improvements in *telegraph* technology, this treatment may seem more natural. Good evidence for the fact that Bell's inventions were initially seen as improvements in telegraphy comes from the titles of Bell's patents: "Improvement in Transmitters and Receivers for Electric *Telegraphs*" (US Patent No. 161,739 (issued April 6, 1875)); "Improvement in *Telegraphy*" (US Patent No. 174,465 (issued March 7, 1876)); and "Improvement in Telephonic *Telegraph*-Receivers" (US Patent No. 178,399 (issued June 6, 1876)).

of his patent rights, if Vail incurred expenses in obtaining English and French patents.[35]

By early October 1837, Morse had filed a "caveat" with the US patent office in order to preserve his patent rights for one year while he worked to "perfect" a working model of the electromagnetic telegraph. The following year, 1838, Morse filed his patent application and entered into a much more detailed partnership agreement with Vail, Gale, and Francis Smith, chairman of the House Committee on Commerce. Pursuant to this contract, the partners divided their prospective domestic and foreign patent rights into 1/16 shares, allocating these shares based on their respective responsibilities for obtaining the patents.[36]

In May 1845, the Magnetic Telegraph Company was formed to control Morse's telegraph patent, and to construct and operate telegraph lines. The company was initially organized on the basis of a trust agreement: by contract, the patent "Proprietors" granted their patent rights to two trustees who were authorized to hold the patent in trust, and to exercise certain powers on behalf of the Proprietors and the other joint stock "Subscribers." Samuel Morse and another of his early partners, attorney Amos Kendall, had hoped that the US Congress would authorize the US government to develop the telegraph and purchase the patent. However, although Congress appropriated $30,000 to finance the construction of the first telegraph line between Washington, DC and Baltimore, most congressmen were uninterested in US government ownership or control of the telegraph. This meant that development of the telegraph depended on private initiative and investment.[37]

One month later (on June 13, 1845), the co-owners of Samuel Morse's telegraph patent (Morse, Leonard Gale, Alfred Vail, and Francis Smith) entered into a contract with Henry O'Reilly, an Irishman from Rochester, New York, who was to undertake a westward expansion of telegraph lines. Pursuant to this contract, the Morse patentees agreed to convey their patent rights to O'Reilly once he had procured funds to build lines of wire that would extend from Philadelphia ("or at such other convenient point" on a projected "great Seaboard Line") through Pittsburgh, and then onward to cities further west, including Cincinnati and St. Louis. Loosely drafted and poorly specified, this contract (the "O'Reilly

35 Reid, *Telegraph in America*, 33–4; Thompson, *Wiring a Continent*, 6, 10. I rely heavily on Thompson's book, which offers a detailed history of the telegraph industry, with extensive documentation and appended transcriptions of primary sources.

36 *O'Reilly* v. *Morse*, 56 U.S. 62, 75–6 (1853); Thompson, *Wiring a Continent*, 13–14. The caveat was an innovation of the 1836 Patent Act.

37 Hochfelder, *Telegraph in America*, 2; Israel, *Machine Shop to Industrial Laboratory*, 37–43; Thompson, *Wiring a Continent*, 16–29, 41–6. The agreement is transcribed in full in Thompson, *Wiring a Continent*, 447–51. Among the subscribers to this company was Ezra Cornell, whose work had been essential in developing the basic technology for the first telegraph lines. Reid, *Telegraph in America*, 102–4. Cornell's involvement in the telegraph business is described in his biography, "*True and Firm*": *Biography of Ezra Cornell* (New York: A. S. Barnes & Company, 1884), written by his son, Alonzo B. Cornell, who was himself a telegraph operator and, later, director of Western Union.

Contract") would provide the basis for a fragmented, materially shoddy, and deeply contested westward expansion of Morse telegraph lines.[38]

By failing to establish any conditions, other than time and access to funding, under which O'Reilly was to conduct his westward expansion, the contract created a very wide interpretive space within which O'Reilly could believe that he was acting in accordance with his obligations. On the other hand, by becoming "null and void," within six months, on the basis of ambiguous conditions, the contract enabled the Morse patentees to understandably believe, by the end of 1845, that the patent was being infringed by O'Reilly's activities. Although it was probably intended to enable flexibility, the ambiguous contract contributed to misunderstandings and disagreements between O'Reilly and the Morse patentees.[39]

Furthermore, because the O'Reilly Contract contained no specification with respect to the organizational form under which Henry O'Reilly should undertake his westward expansion, he was free to decide this for himself. Fatefully, O'Reilly decided to form a separate company for each route, envisioning a vast confederacy that would be loosely held together by a "Telegraph Association." O'Reilly's early partner, James Reid, regarded this decision as "the source of much mischief, and the cause of final extinction" for the O'Reilly companies.[40]

The conflict between the Morse patentees and the O'Reilly developers culminated in competition over development through the Ohio River Valley, a route that would connect Philadelphia (and the Atlantic seaboard) to Louisville, Kentucky, via Pittsburgh. During the 1840s, increasing uses of steam power in manufacturing, combined with the development of metal smelting industries, were coming together to transform Louisville – "situated directly on the great coal highway afforded by the Ohio River" – into a leading industrial city of the (then) American Southwest.[41]

As the first part of their plan to construct and operate a route to Louisville, the O'Reilly developers formed the Atlantic and Ohio Telegraph Company, opening a line from Philadelphia to Pittsburgh on December 26, 1846. Five days earlier (on December 21, 1846), the Morse patentees (led by Smith) had formed their own company – The Western Telegraph Company – to develop the route to Louisville.[42]

By 1847, the conflict between the Morse patentees and the O'Reilly developers had erupted into litigation. In early January, the Morse patentees applied for an injunction in federal court to prevent the O'Reilly developers from proceeding. The

38 Reid, *Telegraph in America*, 152–65; Thompson, *Wiring a Continent*, 39–40, 452–4.

39 Reid, *Telegraph in America*, 152–65; Thompson, *Wiring a Continent*, 80–9. The contract contained a provision specifying that it would become "null and void" within six months if O'Reilly had not constructed a line to Harrisburg from an unspecified eastern point of connection with the "Great Seaboard Line." Thompson, *Wiring a Continent*, 453.

40 Reid, *Telegraph in America*, 164–5; Thompson, *Wiring a Continent*, 73–5.

41 Victor Selden Clark, *History of Manufactures in the United States, 1607–1860* (Washington, DC: The Carnegie Institution of Washington, 1916), 331–2; Clark, *History of Manufactures*, Vol. II, 190–1.

42 Reid, *Telegraph in America*, 147–51, 163–78; Thompson, *Wiring a Continent*, 81, 89, 98–9. The first message to be sent along this line was a war dispatch to US President Polk, indicating the readiness of Mexican War troops to march from Pittsburgh.

basis for the application was breach of contract, and, in consequence, infringement of the Morse patent. The court refused to grant the injunction despite recognizing that injunctions are normally available to protect against patent infringement. Reasoning that the injunction was being sought to enforce the termination of the O'Reilly Contract, the court held that this would be an unwarranted extension of an equitable remedy. As in normal cases of a contract breach, the remedy should come through monetary damages rather than judicial interference. According to James Reid, this decision "gave great joy to Mr. O'Reilly and his friends," enabling completion of the line through Louisville, along with the organization of a new company – the Pittsburgh, Cincinnati and Louisville Telegraph Company – to operate the lines from Pittsburgh to Louisville.[43]

James Reid, superintendent of the Cincinnati-based company, recalled in his memoirs that the ultimate significance of the Ohio River Valley connection to Louisville was seen in its potential to connect the Eastern Seaboard to New Orleans. Having already been served with notice that his contract with the Morse patentees was terminated, Henry O'Reilly decided to form a new company – formally the Southwestern Telegraph Company, but, more popularly, the "People's Telegraph Company" – to develop telegraph lines extending from Louisville to New Orleans, via Nashville, with a westward extension to Memphis. In order to avoid patent litigation, two of O'Reilly's partners (Ed Barnes and Samuel Zook) constructed telegraph transmission machinery that they claimed as an independent invention, calling it the "Columbian Telegraph." At the same time, however, the Morse patentees were developing two separate lines – one along the Southeastern Seaboard and one running right alongside O'Reilly's route – to connect to New Orleans.[44]

On March 7, 1848, the People's Telegraph Company began operating its line to Nashville, Tennessee, using the Columbian Telegraph machinery. Shortly thereafter, the Morse patentees, acting through Amos Kendall, filed for an injunction, claiming that the Columbian Telegraph violated Morse's patent. At one level, this litigation brought victory for the Morse patentees: they obtained a Federal injunction (September 1848) against further use of the Morse telegraph by O'Reilly, and the US Supreme Court ultimately ruled that Samuel Morse was the first inventor of the electromagnetic telegraph. However, the Morse patentees' failure to adequately

[43] *Morse* v. *O'Reilly*, 17 F. Cas. 867, 870 (Circuit Court, E. D. Penn. 1847); Reid, *Telegraph in America*, 180–2. The line to Louisville was completed on December 29, 1847, and an operational office was opened on the same day.

[44] Reid, *Telegraph in America*, 197–8; Thompson, *Wiring a Continent*, 74, 139–65. The line connecting Washington, DC to New Orleans by way of the Carolinas, Georgia, Alabama, and Mississippi was completed in 1848. It was operated by the Washington and New Orleans Company, which licensed the Morse patent. According to James Reid, the licensing contract between the Morse patentees and the Washington and New Orleans Company was a model of clarity, due directly to lessons learned from the O'Reilly Contract. Reid, *Telegraph in America*, 144; Thompson, *Wiring a Continent*, 142–3.

provide for development of their telegraph through contract was, at a deeper level, more important.[45]

In parallel with his efforts to enjoin the Columbian Telegraph, Amos Kendall was also fighting a losing battle to eliminate potential competition from another telegraph machine – the "Electro-Chemical Telegraph" invented by the Scotsman, Alexander Bain. Bain had received an English patent for his invention in December 1846 and applied for a US patent in April 1848. The Commissioner of Patents, after reviewing the application, declared an interference with a pending application by Samuel Morse (filed in January 1848) and determined that Morse's application had priority. However, Bain successfully appealed this decision, obtaining a patent for his Electro-Chemical Telegraph the following year.[46]

In June 1849, Henry O'Reilly obtained judicial permission to reopen his Louisville line, swearing to install Bain's Electro-Chemical Telegraph in place of the Columbian Telegraph. By 1850, the line to New Orleans was open, operating with Bain telegraphs. At this point, the Morse patentees could only reassert their control over the lines to New Orleans by buying out the People's Telegraph Company. In 1853, a consolidated organization was formed, and the threat of the Bain telegraph was neutralized.[47]

The chaotic early development of the telegraph that followed in the wake of the O'Reilly Contract taught the parties involved a painful lesson: carefully considered and clearly specified contracts would be essential to further telegraph development. Henry O'Reilly had been defeated, but at great cost to the Morse patentees. And, in the wake of the ill-fated O'Reilly Contract there remained multiple, semi-independent telegraph companies that were continuing to expand westward. One of these companies – the Illinois and Mississippi Telegraph Company – was credited by James Reid with perfecting a contractual step that would prove vital in the westward expansion of the telegraph: railroad protection contracts.[48]

11.4 RAILROAD PROTECTION CONTRACTS AND WESTWARD EXPANSION

The value of alliance between telegraph and railroad companies became apparent with the completion of the lines to New Orleans, and in their extensions to nearby southern cities. Beginning in 1854, the newly consolidated New Orleans and Ohio Telegraph Company undertook a program of systematically rebuilding its lines,

45 *Morse* v. *O'Reilly*, 17 F.Cas. 871 (Circuit Court, District of Kentucky, 1848); *O'Reilly* v. *Morse*, 56 U.S. 62 (1853); Reid, *Telegraph in America*, 199.

46 US Patent No. 6837 (issued October 30, 1849); *Bain* v. *Morse*, 2 F.Cas. 394 (Circuit Court, District of Columbia, 1849); Arthur J. Stansbury, *Report of the Case of Alexander Bain, Appellant, v. Samuel F.B. Morse, Respondent* (Washington, DC: Gideon & Co., 1849), 4–5 and passim.

47 Israel, *Machine Shop to Industrial Laboratory*, 50; Reid, *Telegraph in America*, 203–9; Thompson, *Wiring a Continent*, 159 n.61, 162.

48 Reid, *Telegraph in America*, 144, 244.

running them along newly built railroad lines. The advantages of this arrangement for construction and maintenance of the telegraph lines were obvious. However, railroad companies were slow to see the advantages that telegraph technology could bring to them.[49]

According to James Reid, the credit for developing a contractual structure of benefit to both telegraph and railroad companies was due to John Dean Caton, Chief Justice of the Illinois Supreme Court. Judge Caton had become a director of Henry O'Reilly's newly formed Illinois and Mississippi Company almost by accident, encountering a meeting of potential stockholders in an Ottawa courthouse, agreeing to represent their interests, and playing a leadership role in the organizational meeting that created the company. In 1852, Judge Caton was elected president of the company, drawing on his legal expertise and position to obtain special legislation that would rescue the company from financial ruin. As president, Judge Caton dedicated himself to establishing contractual relationships with railroad companies, working out very precise terms for these contracts that enabled them to work for the advantage of both the railroads and the telegraph.[50]

Pursuant to the contracts developed by Judge Caton, railroads were given priority in sending telegraph messages and allowed to share in the profits from commercial messages. In return, the railroad companies contributed to the construction of telegraph lines along their railroad lines, monitored these lines, and staffed telegraph offices in their railroad stations. The railroads also committed to exclusive use of the company's telegraph machinery and services.[51]

The basic benefit obtained by the Telegraph Company under these contracts was protection, both for its physical infrastructure and for its patent. The contract protected the patent by extending its sphere of legal exclusivity: beyond the federal government's time-limited guarantee, the railroads added their own physical exclusivity and enforcement power to the legal exclusivity of the patent. For the railroads, the basic benefit was communicative: making use of the telegraph, the railroad companies could coordinate their activities much more effectively and precisely. In addition, both parties were able to split the profits from commercial telegraph business, which was beginning to be substantial.

At roughly the same time that Judge Caton was developing his railroad protection contracts, the company that would become Western Union was also contracting with railroads to build telegraph lines that would extend an existing line – connecting New York City with Buffalo and Cleveland – to Louisville, Kentucky. This company (the New York and Mississippi Valley Printing Telegraph Company) had been originally formed, in 1851, to incorporate a group of Rochester-based lawyers and businessmen led by Samuel Selden and Hiram Sibley. These men collectively owned and managed a third competitor to Morse's patent: the "printing telegraph" patent of

49 Reid, *Telegraph in America*, 209, 243–4; Thompson, *Wiring a Continent*, 203–16.

50 Reid, *Telegraph in America*, 238–40, 243–4; Thompson, *Wiring a Continent*, 130–5.

51 Reid, *Telegraph in America*, 209, 243–5; Thompson, *Wiring a Continent*, 212–14.

Royal E. House. The company was formed under New York's newly permissive framework for incorporation, which included a law authorizing the contractual "self-incorporation" of telegraph companies.[52]

In February 1854, the New York and Mississippi Valley Printing Telegraph Company executed the first stage in what would become a "career of conquest," entering into a contract with three railroad companies to extend its existing telegraph lines from Cleveland to Chicago. There were five parties to this contract: (1) the New York and Mississippi Valley Printing Telegraph Company, (2) the Trustees for the House patents, (3) the Cleveland and Toledo Railroad Company, (4) the Michigan Southern and Northern Indiana Railroad Companies, and (5) the New York State Printing Telegraph Company. Pursuant to this contract, the Trustees of the House patents granted exclusive rights to operate and use House's patented telegraph, in exchange for a commitment on the part of the railroad companies to construct the telegraph lines pursuant to detailed specifications, and to exclusively use House's patented telegraph along their railroad lines.[53]

Railroad protection contracts like this one provided the basis for Western Union's eventual dominance of the field of telegraphy. By 1881, approximately 800 such contracts were in place, extending the exclusivity of Western Union's patented telegraph technology well beyond the terms of the patents, and permitting a unity of organizational control over the telegraph industry that had been missing in the early days of the telegraph. In 1883, the infamous Jay Gould testified to the

52 US Patent No. 4,464 (issued April 18, 1846); Thompson, *Wiring a Continent*, 54, 264–74, 454–503. New York's 1846 Constitution (Article 8, Section 1) had enabled corporations to be formed "under general laws," specifying that corporations (other than municipal corporations) were no longer to be created through special legislation, as had been previously required. In 1848, New York enacted a general authorization for the incorporation of telegraph companies. Pursuant to this law, telegraph operators and investors would become a corporation once they had executed a "certificate" specifying the firm's name, the route of the telegraph lines, the capital stock and number of shares into which that stock was to be divided, the names and addresses of the stockholders, and the date upon which the corporation would terminate. Laws of the State of New York, 71st Session, Chapter 265 (April 12, 1848). This law was amended in 1851 to facilitate the extension of telegraph lines, and to enable the combination of telegraph companies. Laws of the State of New York, 74th Session, Chapter 98 (April 8, 1851). The law was amended again in 1853, specifying limits to the liability of shareholders and empowering telegraph companies to further extend and develop their lines. Laws of the State of New York, 76th Session, Chapter 471 (June 29, 1853). New York had provided a favorable legislative environment for telegraph development since 1845, when it enacted "the first general easement and protective telegraph act in the country." Thompson, *Wiring a Continent*, 67 n.46. See An Act to facilitate the construction of Morse's Electro-Magnetic Telegraph, Laws of the State of New York, 68th Session, Chapter 243 (May 13, 1845); see also Fred Freedland, "History of Holding Company Legislation in New York State," *Fordham Law Review* 24 (1955): 369–411; idem, "Merger and Consolidation of New York Business Corporations: History of Enabling Legislation, 1776–1956," *Fordham Law Review* 25 (1956): 672–701.

53 Thompson, *Wiring a Continent*, 275, 473–8, 482–91. Very precise and detailed specifications for the construction, which was to be overseen by the New York and Mississippi Valley Printing Telegraph Company, were laid out in the contract. Once the lines were built, they were to be staffed by Telegraph Company employees. Priority, within legal limits, was to be given to railroad company messages.

importance of these contracts before Congress, contending that they made competition in the field of telegraphy "perfectly impracticable." In conjunction with contracts of alliance between competing telegraph companies, these railroad protection contracts constituted the legal framework for the telegraph industry's "Era of Consolidation," which began in the mid-1850s and extended through the civil war.[54]

11.5 CONTRACTS OF ALLIANCE, GEOGRAPHIC EXCLUSIVITY, AND CONSOLIDATION

By 1866, the Magnetic Telegraph Company, the O'Reilly companies, and the Rochester-based New York and Mississippi Valley Printing Telegraph Company had all been absorbed into the powerful Western Union Corporation. From a single line connecting Washington, DC and Baltimore, the telegraph system had been expanded to connect all major American cities, and to connect North and South America with Europe. With the 1866 absorption of its two remaining major competitors (the American Telegraph Company and the United States Telegraph Company), Western Union became the dominant telegraph service provider in the United States, handling, according to a recent estimate, at least 80 percent of the nation's telegraph traffic. As "the first corporation to operate on a nationwide scale," Western Union built on aggressive patent acquisition and licensing practices to "web the world in a network of throbbing life."[55]

An important early step in Western Union's post–civil war ascendancy came in April 1854, with a contractual alliance between the House patent holders and two significant Morse patent holders: J. J. Speed, Jr. and J. H. Wade. In exchange for $50,000 in cash and promissory notes, Speed and Wade transferred to the New York and Mississippi Valley Printing Telegraph Company all their "rights and interests" in Morse's telegraph patents, including any future rights in renewed, reissued, or extended patents. As a result of this contract, the company claimed exclusive control of all telegraph patents in the states of Ohio, Indiana, Illinois, Michigan, Wisconsin, Iowa, and the Territory of Minnesota. However, as Ezra Cornell promptly protested, this claim was unfounded: outstanding "rights and interests" in the Morse patents for those states were still held by Cornell, Judge Caton, and the companies they directed.[56]

Final patent consolidation for western telegraph development came the next year, with the formation of the Western Union Telegraph Company out of the union of Cornell's Erie and Michigan Telegraph Company and the New York and Mississippi Valley Printing Telegraph Company. This consolidation was legally

54 Hochfelder, *Telegraph in America*, 39; Reid, *Telegraph in America*, 209, 243–7; Thompson, *Wiring a Continent*, 203–16.

55 Hochfelder, *Telegraph in America*, 3; Israel, *Machine Shop to Industrial Laboratory*, 2; Reid, *Telegraph in America*, 141, 534–5, 876; Thompson, *Wiring a Continent*, 328–30, 424–6.

56 Thompson, *Wiring a Continent*, 280–5, 493–7, Appendix 12.

effectuated by means of a consolidation agreement, which recognized a patent assignment. Pursuant to this contract, the entirety of the House and Morse patent rights for the States of Ohio, Indiana, Illinois, Michigan, Wisconsin, Iowa, and the Territory of Minnesota, together with the existing telegraph lines of both companies, became part of the property standing behind the "capital" of Western Union, the value of which was named at $500,000.[57]

Writing thirty years later, with the benefit of hindsight, James Reid pronounced the assignment of the Morse patent rights as "the most valuable item in the entire conveyance." Building on the strength of this consolidation, Western Union (in concert with Judge Caton and his Illinois and Mississippi Company) promptly began to enter into a series of protection agreements with railroads, extending Western Union's lines ever further westward and gradually acquiring (through lease or purchase) the remaining O'Reilly companies.[58]

In the meantime, however, a new player had entered the field, holding a new patent. On May 20, 1856, David E. Hughes of Louisville, Kentucky, had received a patent for an "Improvement in Telegraphs." Even before receiving his patent, Hughes had assigned all rights to its use in North America to Daniel Craig, entrepreneurial agent of the New York Associated Press ("NYAP"), in exchange for $100,000. On the same day (November 1, 1855), a new telegraph company was incorporated under New York's press-friendly telegraph law: the American Telegraph Company. The nominal capitalization of this company was $200,000, half the value of which was rooted in Hughes' patent, which Craig had assigned to his partners in the new company.[59]

With the entry of the American Telegraph Company into the field of competition, the dynamics of competition were fundamentally altered. Aside from the railroads, the press represented by far the most important consumer of telegraph services. The initial formation of the NYAP had come at the opening of the Mexican War (1846), when six New York daily papers (the *New York Journal of Commerce*, the *New York Courier and Enquirer*, the *New York Express*, the *New York Sun*, the *New York Herald*, and the *New York Tribune*) agreed to coordinate their efforts in obtaining and transmitting war news from the South, as well as European news

57 Reid, *Telegraph in America*, 280–1, 455–71; Thompson, *Wiring a Continent*, 279–85; 497–503, Appendix 13. Judge Caton's Illinois and Mississippi Telegraph Company together with two other telegraph companies controlled by Ezra Cornell (the Wisconsin State and Ohio, Indiana and Illinois companies) were recognized as continuing to exist as licensees of Cornell's Morse patent rights. The contract specified a noncompetition agreement with these companies (§8).

58 Reid, *Telegraph in America*, 174–5, 469, 472–81; Thompson, *Wiring a Continent*, 293–7.

59 US Patent No. 14,917 (1856); Menahem Blondheim, *News over the Wires: The Telegraph and the Flow of Public Information in America, 1844–1897* (Cambridge, MA: Harvard University Press, 1994), 107–8; Reid, *Telegraph in America*, 405–7; Thompson, *Wiring a Continent*, 303–5. New York's 1848 telegraph company incorporation law specified that telegraph companies were to transmit messages in the order they were received, but provided an exception for the public press, which was to be given priority in transmission. According to Menahem Blondheim, New York was the only state to provide for such an exception. Blondheim, *News over the Wires*, 85, 243 n.60.

coming off ships in the Eastern harbors, and to share the costs of telegraph transmissions in furtherance of these goals. Having grown into a dominant purchaser of telegraph services by 1855, the NYAP had pursued a policy of "divide and rule," patronizing competing telegraph companies on an equal basis. However, the formation of the American Telegraph Company by NYAP agent Daniel Craig (in conjunction with a group of New York merchants) represented a new development: henceforth, NYAP business would be given only to the American Company, in the East, and to Western Union in the West.[60]

Recognizing that the power dynamics of their industry had changed, the Morse patent holders proposed a meeting among the leading telegraph companies "for the purpose of devising a plan for harmonizing all interests and protecting existing lines." Side-stepping the Morse patent holders, the House and Bain patent holders entered into an alliance with the Hughes patent holders. This alliance was effectuated on August 10, 1857, through a "Six-Party Contract," which purported to partition the entirety of telegraph business within the United States among six contracting "nations": the American Telegraph Company; the Atlantic and Ohio Telegraph Company; the New York, Albany and Buffalo Telegraph Company; Western Union; the New Orleans and Ohio Telegraph Lessees; and the Illinois and Mississippi Telegraph Company.[61]

The basis for the Six-Party Contract was a license of the Hughes telegraph patent, the cost of which was shared by the contracting parties. Pursuant to Article III of the contract, the parties mutually agreed that each party would have exclusive ownership of the Hughes patent rights within the territorial boundaries set forth in the contract (also Article V). In addition, the parties agreed that each party would have "exclusive enjoyment of all telegraph business within the territory in which the patent right has been allotted" (Article IV, Section 2). In this way, the license of the Hughes patent became the basis for dividing the entire telegraph business regardless of which patent actually covered the technology in use. Adding strength to the territorial division of business, the Contract obligated the parties to prevent third-party competition, for example, through a refusal to sell patent rights or telegraph lines to third-party competitors.[62]

The Morse patentees reacted to this "perfidy" by forming their own alliance. Given their strength in the northeast and along the Atlantic Seaboard, the Morse patentees were able to hold out for two years against the Six Parties. Nevertheless, by early 1860, the combined forces of the North American Telegraph Association (the Six Parties plus the Montreal Telegraph Company) had persuaded the Morse patentees to give in, and to sell their patents. At the opening of the civil war,

60 Blondheim, *News over the Wires*, 47–67, 96–106; Hochfelder, *Telegraph in America*, 73–100; Reid, *Telegraph in America*, 191, 196; Thompson, *Wiring a Continent*, 47, 217–39. *The New York Times* joined the association when it emerged in 1851.

61 Thompson, *Wiring a Continent*, 311–30, Appendix 14.

62 Thompson, *Wiring a Continent*, 504–15.

therefore, the telegraph industry had been nationally organized and partitioned on the basis of patent licenses.[63]

Although competitive skirmishes – especially over fractious relations with the NYAP – did undermine the solidity of the North American Telegraph Association, it was ultimately the civil war itself that fatally weakened the American Telegraph Company, enabling Western Union to achieve final dominance. Stretching from North to South, the American Telegraph Company was severed in half by the war. Western Union, on the other hand, stretched from the northeast to the northwest and gained enormous strength from the wartime services it provided to the press and to the Union government. Western Union also controlled the Overland Telegraph Company, which – pursuant to US legislative privileges and subsidization – by October 1861 had completed a telegraph line connecting Chicago to San Francisco.[64]

From November 1861 to the close of the war in 1865, Western Union's general manager, Anson Stager, also served as the Union government's superintendent of Military Telegraphs. In this capacity, Stager oversaw the development of an "extensive government-owned-and-operated military telegraph system." While Stager was overseeing this expanding military telegraph system, his colleagues at Western Union were hard at work to acquire the other members of the North American Telegraph Association. By the close of the war, Western Union possessed approximately 44,000 miles of telegraph wire and over a thousand telegraph offices, vastly outdistancing its nearest rival, the American Telegraph Company.[65]

On June 12, 1866, the American Telegraph Company gave in, entering a merger agreement with Western Union. One month later, a secure cable was finally laid across the Atlantic Ocean, linking Europe and North America. Telegraph messages between Europe and the Americas began running on August 26, 1866. From its position of dominance, particularly in relation to the vital news link between Europe and the United States, Western Union could now compel a settlement between the NYAP and the Western Associated Press, which had been fighting one another for control of telegraphic news service. In 1867, the Associated Press emerged.[66]

In his Pulitzer Prize–winning history of nineteenth-century America, Daniel Walker Howe has pointed to the telegraphic "communications revolution" as an essential force behind America's transformational shift into the Reconstruction era. In Howe's estimation, the electric telegraph played a role of singular importance in drawing the United States together into a national economic entity and a political

63 Thompson, *Wiring a Continent*, 317, 320, 323–30. Part of the impetus for settlement was the upcoming expiration of Morse's patents, which was scheduled to occur in April 1860 and June 1861.

64 Thompson, *Wiring a Continent*, 335–42, 348–71, 373.

65 Reid, *Telegraph in America*, 483; Thompson, *Wiring a Continent*, 393, 407–8.

66 Hochfelder, *Telegraph in America*, 85; Thompson, *Wiring a Continent*, 424, 434.

community. As we have seen, patent licenses played a vital institutional role in linking together the telegraphic network that transmitted national news and financial data. As we have also seen, a considerable amount of experience was required before the contractual structure of these patent licenses began to serve their signatories effectively.[67]

Learning from the failures of early patent licensing efforts such as the O'Reilly Contract, Alexander Graham Bell's partner, Gardiner Hubbard, would insist on retaining complete control over Bell's telephone patents, laying the foundations for a national framework of "agency agreements" that set Bell on a trajectory toward national dominance of the telephone industry. Bell's framework of agency agreements comprised the institutional foundations for its dominant position and helped to constitute a model for franchising arrangements which have become ubiquitous in the modern economy.[68]

The foundations for McDonald's business model had been laid.

11.6 THE ALTERNATIVE TO CONTRACTUAL ALLIANCE: THE BELL TELEPHONE SYSTEM

It is important at this point to recall that the tele*phone* emerged out of sustained and widespread efforts to patent improvements on the tele*graph*. Alexander Graham Bell's early patents – even the patent claim that so controversially secured control over the marketing and sale of telephone technology to Bell and his partners – were conceived and described as improvements to the telegraph. Letters from Bell and his partners, as well as early AT&T records, support this conclusion; Bell and his partners even tried, unsuccessfully, to sell their invention to Western Union.[69]

David Hochfelder has spoken of the technological transition from telegraphy to telephony as a case of "industrial succession." With the hindsight of historical vision, it is possible to see (as Hochfelder does) Bell's telephone beginning to displace Western Union's telegraph at the moment when the two parties entered into their 1879 contract to partition the US market. According to Hochfelder, the drafters of this contract made two fundamental mistakes which enabled AT&T to continue competing with Western Union in the field of telegraphy, while monopolizing the emerging market for telephones. These contractual mistakes, combined with Western Union's technological complacency, helped to enable the telephone to

[67] Daniel Walker Howe, *What Hath God Wrought: The Transformation of America, 1815–1848* (Oxford: Oxford University Press, 2007), 1–4, 690–8.

[68] 1939 *FCC Report*, 18–20; Thomas S. Dicke, *Franchising in America: The Development of a Business Method, 1840–1980* (Chapel Hill: University of North Carolina Press, 1992).

[69] "Improvement in Transmitters and Receivers for Electric *Telegraphs*" (US Patent No. 161,739 (issued April 6, 1875)); "Improvement in *Telegraphy*" (US Patent No. 174,465 (issued March 7, 1876)); and "Improvement in Telephonic *Telegraph*-Receivers" (US Patent No. 178,399 (issued June 6, 1876)), Hochfelder, *Telegraph in America*, 138–75; Tosiello, *Bell Telephone System*, 4–17.

replace the telegraph, relegating Western Union to an increasingly marginal position in the telecommunications industry.[70]

The context for the 1879 contract between Western Union and Alexander Graham Bell's company (at the time, "National Bell") was a patent priority dispute between Bell and another inventor, Elisha Gray, along with a basic question about which company's patent portfolio was stronger. Scholars, patent lawyers, journalists, and technology enthusiasts continue to debate whether Bell should have received his telephone patent, especially in light of a very close race with Elisha Gray to establish priority of invention, coupled with evidence of Patent Office improprieties. However, a narrow focus on the priority dispute between Bell and Gray does not enable sufficient understanding of the role that patents played in the settlement between Western Union and National Bell.[71]

The basic technological problem to which the "harmonic" (or "acoustic") telegraph provided a solution was the need for greater capacity on telegraph wires. Thomas Edison had patented a "quadruplex" telegraph system in 1874 that enabled four messages to be sent at the same time along a telegraph wire, and had assigned this valuable patent to an upstart telegraph company formed by Jay Gould to compete with Western Union: the Atlantic and Pacific Telegraph Company.[72]

Within this context, pressure to invent alternative high-capacity telegraph technologies only increased, and people like Bell, Gray, Edison, and others began experimenting with methods to utilize a range of musical scales and pitches to simultaneously send multiple messages along a wire at different frequencies. The discovery that the sound of a human voice could be transformed into an electrical signal, conveyed along a telegraph wire, and transmitted as audible sound through a receiver was an outgrowth of these experiments. However, at the time, a higher-capacity telegraph was seen as a more important application of these technological developments.[73]

From 1875 to 1879, Western Union employed its former operator, Thomas Edison, to discover and patent as many methods of multiplex telegraphy as possible. Edison had already proved his value to Western Union's managers through his patents on a printing telegraph design, which contributed to the commercialization of the financial "ticker" by Western Union's subsidiary, the Gold and Stock Telegraph Company. In 1877, when Western Union decided to directly compete

70 Hochfelder, *Telegraph in America*, 138–75. These mistakes involved a failure to completely foreclose Bell from involvement in the telegraph industry, and a failure to secure royalties on transactions involving local exchanges.

71 Barton H. Baker, *The Gray Matter: The Forgotten Story of the Telephone* (St. Joseph, MI: Telepress, 2000); Seth Shulman, *The Telephone Gambit: Chasing Alexander Graham Bell's Secret* (New York: W. W. Norton, 2008); also Hochfelder, *Telegraph in America*, 138–75. Elisha Gray filed a "caveat" with the Patent Office on the same day that Bell's patent application was filed, and there is some question about which document was actually filed first.

72 Hochfelder, *Telegraph in America*, 140; Paul Israel, *Edison: A Life of Invention* (New York: John Wiley & Sons, 1998), 97–9; Israel, *Machine Shop to Industrial Laboratory*, 79–80, 97–102.

73 Israel, *Edison*, 131–2; Tosiello, *Bell Telephone System*, 4–17.

in the field of telephony, a new contract with Edison was drawn up to cover telephone-related inventions.[74]

During the period leading up to the November 1879 contract between Western Union and National Bell, Edison successfully applied for at least forty-five patents relating to multiplex telegraphy and telephony. Nearly all of these would have been assigned to Western Union pursuant to the company's contracts with Edison. In addition, Western Union acquired Elisha Gray's telephone patents, together with his inventive activity, through the purchase of Gray's Harmonic Telephone Company on November 17, 1877.[75]

Western Union was clearly approaching its negotiations with Bell from an aggressive patent position, employing Edison, Gray, and others to build up an arsenal of patents covering the entire field of harmonic and acoustic telegraphs, including the telephone. Indeed, since 1870, Western Union had pursued an explicit policy "to control all improvements which may present themselves and by the possession of which we can more surely control our business, perfect our system, extend its usefulness, and render it the most complete in the world." This involved a strategy of "covering the field" with patents, employing inventors like Edison and Gray to work closely with patent attorneys in patenting every conceivable permutation of a particular telegraph- or telephone-related technology.[76]

Compared to Western Union's arsenal of patents, Bell only possessed a handful. How was it, then, that a relatively new company with far fewer patents was able to negotiate a contract allocating to it the entire US market in telephone sales? Part of the answer to this question surely lies in the belief – shared by most of the major players – that the telephone was really only a sideshow, relative to the telegraph. From this perspective, Western Union was willing to renounce all of its market share in telephone production, distribution, and sales – in exchange for a 20 percent royalty payment – because it believed the sacrifice to be relatively minimal, relative to the benefit it secured in relation to a primary competitor for the exclusive production, distribution, and sales of telegraph technology.[77]

However, an equally important answer to this question rests upon Bell's relatively strong negotiating position, a strength that was rooted in two things: the breadth and

[74] Hochfelder, *Telegraph in America*, 105, 142; Israel, *Edison*, 49–65, 108–41.

[75] Israel, *Edison*, 129–41. For documentation relating to Edison's patent applications, see The Thomas A. Edison Papers Digital Edition, hosted by Rutgers University, available at http://edison.rutgers.edu/digital/ (accessed September 4, 2020).

[76] Israel, *Edison*, 53, 56, 67, 72, 78–80. The impact of this strategy on inventors like Thomas Edison has been noted by Edison's biographer, Paul Israel, who documents Edison's use of his notebooks to set boundaries around the extent to which his inventions would belong to his employer. On the first page of the notebook he used to record his inventions for the Gold & Stock Company, Edison explicitly "reserved" ownership to himself of "any ideas contained in this book which I do not see fit to give," said G & Stock Telegraph. In another notebook recording his inventions relating to a system of rapid telegraphy, Edison stated that a particular system was "Invented for myself exclusively, and not for any small brained capitalist." Ibid., 67.

[77] Hochfelder, *Telegraph in America*, 138–75, Tosiello, *Bell Telephone System*, 148.

perceived validity of Bell's telephone patent, and the contractual strategy that Bell had already begun employing in producing and distributing the telephone.

The claim that ultimately secured patent protection of telephone technology to Bell was claim number 5 in the March 1876 patent for an "Improvement in Telegraphy." This claim was for "the method of, and apparatus for, transmitting vocal or other sounds telegraphically . . . by causing electrical undulations, similar in form to the vibrations of the air" that constitute the sound of a human voice. Bell had mentioned this possible application of his basic invention – a new method of "multiple telegraphy" employing continuous, "vibratory or undulatory" electrical currents, rather than "intermittent or pulsatory" electrical currents – toward the end of his description, as something of an afterthought to the basic invention, which was essentially a higher-capacity telegraph system.[78]

Nevertheless, this claim was seen as covering the telephone, even by Western Union's patent attorneys. This one claim was therefore broad enough to provide a powerful counter to Western Union's arsenal of telephone-related patents. In 1888, the US Supreme Court determined that this claim covered the entire "art of transferring to or impressing upon a current of electricity the vibrations of air produced by the human voice in articulate speech, in a way that the speech will be carried to and received by a listener at a distance on the line of current."[79]

However, the broad scope of the patent was not sufficient, on its own, to enable National Bell to stand up to Western Union. Bell had also made an early and very explicit decision to maintain complete control of its patents in its licensing and distribution arrangements. Rather than selling its telephones to wholesalers or retail customers, Bell leased the telephones, retaining title to the instruments and collecting royalties for their use by customers. In creating a national system for distributing its telephones, and for setting up local exchanges, Bell offered exclusive licenses to regional "agents," who were permitted to retain a portion of the royalties on leased instruments, while being subjected to strong centralized control of their manufacturing and organizational decision-making. Eventually, AT&T acquired Elisha Gray's Western Electric Company, transforming it into a centralized manufacturer and developer of telephone-related exchange technology and instruments.[80]

This strategy of maintaining centralized control of patents through a clearly specified licensing policy is attributed to Bell's early partner and father-in-law, Gardiner Hubbard, who was a close observer of Western Union's rise to national power, and who had previously served as an attorney for a manufacturer of shoemaking machinery. The effect of Bell's broad patent, combined with its centrally

78 US Patent No. 174, 465 (1876).

79 The Telephone Cases, 126 U.S. 1 (1888); Hochfelder, *Telegraph in America*, 150–1.

80 William Chauncy Langdon, *The Early Corporate Development of the Telephone* (New York: AT&T, 1935), 10–13; Smith, *Anatomy of a Business Strategy*, passim; Tosiello, *Bell Telephone System*, 92–136.

controlled licensing and distribution policy, was to ensure that the telephone industry was firmly controlled by a single company from the very beginning.[81]

From 1879 to 1900, National Bell would undertake a series of corporate reorganizations, culminating in its organization under a publicly owned New York holding company, AT&T. During this period, extensive managerial attention was focused on formalizing and standardizing AT&T's exclusive licensing arrangements. In addition, an organizational infrastructure was established to enable continuous research and development. The explicit goal of this research and development program, as outlined in a letter to corporate president William H. Forbes, was to "apply for patents . . . to cover all that is patentable." During this period, AT&T also began to stamp its retail products with distinctive logos, and to protect these as its trademarks.[82]

In 1939, the Federal Communications Commission looked back on the period from 1879 to 1937 as the period during which the "Bell System" was established and consolidated. Crucial to the establishment of this System, in the FCC's view, were AT&T's patents, licensing arrangements, and the 1879 contract with Western Union, which gave AT&T control over all telephone-related patents, and the entire US market in telephone-related transactions and services. During the period leading up to the outbreak of World War II, AT&T focused on consolidating this system by acquiring majority shareholder interests in its licensees. This was accomplished through extensions of patent licensing terms in exchange for shares of stock.[83]

In order to provide further consolidation to its patent-acquisition activities, in 1924, AT&T incorporated Bell Laboratories to house Western Electric's engineering and patent departments. Among other things, this enabled exploitation and development of vacuum tube-related patents, which were acquired in the years leading up to World War I. These were of central importance to the development of "wireless" communications (radio) and to further development of telephony and telegraphy.[84]

11.7 CONCLUSION: INTELLECTUAL PROPERTY LICENSING IN THE INSTITUTIONALIZATION OF A TELECOMMUNICATIONS NETWORK

When the newly created Federal Communications Commission undertook its investigation of AT&T in the mid-1930s, nearly 100 years had passed since Samuel Morse applied for his first telegraph patent. Recognizing the importance of licenses in establishing an international network of wire-based telecommunications, Congress empowered the FCC to oversee "all contracts, agreements, or arrangements" between telecommunications carriers. Pursuant to the requirement that

81 Langdon, *Early Corporate Development*, 10–13; *cf.* Hochfelder, *Telegraph in America*, 138–80.

82 1939 *FCC Report*, 1–10; Tosiello, *Bell Telephone System*, 403 ff., 427–32 (quote at 430).

83 1939 *FCC Report*, 1–26, 147–246.

84 1939 *FCC Report*, 188–9.

regulated carriers register such contracts with the FCC, that agency was able to detail the extent to which contractual arrangements had helped to enable "the largest aggregation of capital and resources that has ever been controlled by a single private company at any time in the history of business."[85]

In this chapter, I have traced the development of the American telecommunications network through contractual licenses of intellectual property. The legal capacity to effectuate these contractual structures was premised, I have argued, on the proprietary voluntarism of nineteenth-century American law. Patent holders, as property owners, were viewed as being free to create forms of "special law," through a formalized exercise of the will, which had significant impacts on third parties, as well as the contracting parties themselves.

We can imagine counterfactual alternatives by considering the possibilities if intellectual property had been treated like Social Security benefits: as a nontransferable right. None of the contractual structures that have been discussed in this chapter would have been possible. All were premised on transfers of intellectual property through contractual licenses. In short, America's telecommunications network could not have developed, in the way that it did, if technology patents had not been treated as transferable property.

Intellectual property licenses became, in nineteenth-century America, instruments of legal power, enabling purposeful establishment of national economic control. A national telecommunications network was created which is today global.

In Chapter 2, I introduced the argument by Larissa Katz that property involves powers to "set the agenda for a resource," comparing this argument to Max Weber's conception of property, where property involves powers of disposition and control. Exclusivity is certainly an important aspect of property – one that I have argued is enabled by organized social closure, ultimately the organized social closure facilitated by powerful nation-states. We will return to this in the next chapter. But, in this chapter, we have seen how the powers of proprietary voluntarism enabled by the legal recognition of patents as property facilitated the exercise of tremendous social powers through the contractual structures created by intellectual property licenses.

We have also seen, however, that this did not happen automatically. It took nearly a century of learning in methods of organizational restraint and systematic licensing practices for contractual licenses of intellectual property to become the foundation for national strategies of economic power.

The wires laid by Western Union and AT&T, the cables laid under oceans between continents, the accumulated resources of myriad small companies, together with the savings invested by countless households and businesses, these were the foundation for today's telecommunications networks which connect billions of computers around the world, forming the basis of our modern internet. This is the materialistic infrastructure that makes our modern social networks, our

85 1939 *FCC Report*, xxiii; 1934 Communications Act § 211.

Facebooks and our Twitters, possible. Behind this materialistic infrastructure, I am emphasizing, is a legal and cultural infrastructure, one that bridges public and private spheres of social life.

In our modern telecommunications and social networks, the public sphere of the state is inextricably linked to the private sphere of property, contracts, corporations, and households. Intellectual property, as an infrastructure of state power, has facilitated this linkage: it has encouraged the technological innovations, corporate strategies, and the huge financial investments that enabled the wires to be laid down, and the voices and the images to be carried along those wires.

These dramatic innovations and corporate strategies did not just happen. They were actively encouraged by an infrastructure of state power, intellectual property, a legal institution formed by centuries of experience with instruments of legal power. And they were further facilitated through the intentional deployment of intellectual property by means of contractual licensing strategies as a basis for national organization.

These are the institutional foundations that make computer-based social networks like Facebook possible. But, of course, as we are seeing today, these social networks represent reserves of tremendous social energies that rumble and boil beneath a tenuously stable surface.

12

Legal Orders and Social Performance

Globalizing Intellectual Property

On June 27, 2018, *The New York Times* reported that Apple and Samsung had settled an epic court battle over smartphone technology. Spanning nearly a decade, this struggle over intellectual property rights in those handheld computers without which our daily lives now seem unthinkable had taken many twists and turns. At certain moments, the lawsuit dramatically revealed the ways in which intellectual property is now institutionalized within globally extended power networks. At the same time, the litigation threw a harsh spotlight on the extent to which, even under conditions of globalized industrial capitalism, nation-states remain fundamental.[1]

One of these revealing moments came in February 2014, in a legal decision by US district court judge Lucy Koh, called upon to adjudicate whether the second of two jury awards should be disregarded. Apple and Samsung had both made motions to set aside the jury's verdict, which awarded nearly $300 million in damages to Apple for patent infringement. Apple basically wanted more money, and Samsung thought there should be a completely new trial. One of Samsung's reasons for seeking a new trial responded to arguments made by Apple's attorneys in their closing statements to the jury.[2]

The trial, lasting about a week in November 2013, had been held in San Jose, that is, in Silicon Valley. Among many other arguments presented to the jury, Apple's attorneys had appealed to the jury's situational awareness. The controversial aspect of the closing statement, as set forth in Judge Koh's decision, went like this:

> We are extremely fortunate to live in what I'll call the Greater Bay Area. Not only is it beautiful, but we live in the center of one of the most vibrant economies in the world. Intel, Yahoo, Oracle, Facebook, eBay, and hundreds and hundreds of other companies, including Google, and including Apple, and these companies attract talented employees at every level. Even, we heard, Samsung has opened a research center here so that they can take advantage of the talent in this area.

[1] Jack Nicias, "Apple and Samsung End Smartphone Patent Wars," *The New York Times*, June 27, 2018.

[2] *Apple* v. *Samsung*, 2014 WL 549324 (N.D. Cal., February 7, 2014) (not reported in F. Supp. 2d).

> The companies provide jobs. They create technology that improves the way people work. And the company – and this economy – supports an education system that is second to none in the world. Berkeley, Stanford, San Jose State, U.S. [sic] Santa Cruz, even Santa Clara where I went to school.
>
> These educational institutions interact with this economy, interact with these companies and create a place that the whole world knows as Silicon Valley.
>
> But let's be equally clear about one thing. Our vibrant economy absolutely depends on fair competition. It depends on a patent system that encourages inventors to invent, it encourages investors to invest, and it encourages employers to hire.
>
> If we allow that system of law to decay, investors will not invest, people will not take risks, and our economy will disappear.
>
> When I was young, I used to watch television on televisions that were manufactured in the United States. Magnavox, Motorola, RCA. They were real companies. They were well known and they were famous. They were creators. They were inventors. They were like the Apple and Google today.
>
> But they didn't protect their intellectual property. They couldn't protect their ideas. And you all know the result. There are no American television manufacturers today.[3]

Everyone can hear the appeal to nationalistic economic hopes and fears ringing through Apple's closing statement to the jury.

The question Judge Koh had to decide was whether this closing statement appealed to ethnic prejudices and stereotypes in a way that should invalidate the jury's verdict and be judged a mistrial. Judge Koh was clearly troubled by the statements, noting in her decision that the transcript cannot fully capture aspects of the ethnic and national appeal inside the courtroom. These came through, apparently, in the rhetoric of the attorney's delivery, which included dramatic and significant pauses. It also came through in the composition of the crowded courtroom, where ethnic and national differences were highlighted in seating arrangements behind the attorneys for both sides. We are left to guess exactly what this means, but perhaps we should imagine a crowded courtroom in which people who look like South Koreans (whatever this means) sit behind Samsung's attorneys, while people who look like Americans (whatever this means) sit behind Apple's attorneys. Many of these people may have been employees of the two companies, as well as citizens of their respective nation-states, who were closely invested (materially and spiritually) in the outcome of the case.[4]

Judge Koh cited a law review article in her decision. The conclusion of the article, as cited, was that "foreign patent holder win rates" in US jury trials against US patent holders are dramatically lower than "domestic patent holder win rates" against foreign patent holders. In other words, US juries are overly friendly to US plaintiffs

[3] *Apple* v. *Samsung*, 2014 WL, 11.

[4] Ibid., 13

against non-US defendants. The point of comparison was with trials in which there is no jury, where a judge decides matters of fact and law, in which the win rate differences were nearly eliminated, according to the author of the study. Win rates were roughly 33 percent in trials decided by judges, regardless of whether the plaintiff was domestic or foreign. Judge Koh highlighted this study as evidence to support a broader concern about whether US juries can be truly fair in patent trials where a US company is pitted against a foreign company. The relevant legal standard for granting a mistrial required a showing that the jury had been motivated by passion and prejudice in rendering its verdict. Judge Koh did not believe this standard had been met, and she did not grant the mistrial. But she was clearly troubled by the implications of nationalistic economic interest which had been raised in her courtroom.[5]

The passions stirred in Apple's closing arguments were evidently national, but they did not appeal to hatred of South Koreans based on national stereotypes or ethnic slurs. Instead, they appealed to fears of national economic decline, and pride in economic power. And they did so by drawing on precisely the substantive rational logic that has been built into the legal institution of intellectual property. That logic, as we know, is as follows: strong protection of intellectual property encourages investment in innovation, which is the essential means for enabling the end that we all want: national economic growth. Without strong protection of intellectual property, the American economy will decline. We will be back in the troubling times of the 1970s, when televisions – and many other things – were no longer being manufactured by US companies. Placed in a unique position to prevent that, what responsible juror could easily say no?

The problem, of course, is that substantive commitments to the economic good of the national community are not supposed to be part of the basis for a jury's decision. The jury is supposed to decide strictly on the basis of the formal law, impartially applying the criteria for patent protection equally to both sides. Economic outcomes are supposed to be irrelevant. But they cannot be when part of our justification for the existence of the legal institution is itself premised on the purposive pursuit of economic power.

The smartphone wars waged over the past decade are now over. The parties retired, exhausted, settling for undisclosed amounts of money. Meanwhile, smartphones have taken over our lives, providing the technological foundation for legions of software applications, and for social and political manipulation on an epic scale.

What the smartphone wars reveal in one acute moment in late 2013, I believe, is a paradoxical and tragic conflict of priorities that is built into the legal institution of intellectual property, an institution that Americans have played an outsized role in establishing, and in spreading around the world. As the smartphone wars neatly

[5] Ibid., 13–16. The article cited by Judge Koh is Kimberly A. Moore, "Xenophobia in American Courts," *Northwestern University Law Review* 97 (2003): 1497–1550.

demonstrate, we live in a capitalistic world of globalized intellectual property law. But that law is firmly anchored in the nation-state system, is indeed built into the foundations of that system. As Michael Mann helps us to see, modern capitalism and nation-states have grown constitutionally entwined together. And intellectual property law has played a vital role in that constitutional entwining.[6]

Mann sees the contemporary, globalized world as one in which America has come to exercise imperial power, albeit an imperialism of a newly informal and indirect kind. US victory in the "Cold War" fight with the Soviet Union, combined with an extraordinary burst to US power in the wake of World War II, left the United States as the leading superpower in the concluding decades of the twentieth century. This placed the United States in a culturally dominant ("hegemonic") position, with respect to the rest of the world, with the implication that US social power dynamics – whether these are cultural, economic, or political/military – became uniquely "significant" for the rest of the world.[7]

Put differently, American efforts to find meaning and freedom in a national, governing community became globally influential, to an unprecedented extent, in the second half of the twentieth century. Mann describes the growth of a new kind of American citizenship, a new conception of belonging to the national community, "consumer citizenship," in which political and economic belonging are inextricably linked. To be a member of American national society means, according to this concept of belonging, not only having the capacity to participate in political life, but also the capacity to participate in myriad forms of economic abundance that are made possible by America's supersized economy. These forms of economic abundance prominently include new technological devices, such as smartphones, "with new models every year, plus ever-changing desirable logos on everything." The forms of economic abundance also include homeownership, a form of proprietary belonging and inter-generational wealth transmission that has become iconic for the well-lived life in America. Making this possible on an unprecedented scale has required massive levels of mortgage-backed lending, enabled by highly complex financial instruments and contractual exchanges of debt obligations between banks, all controlled by inadequately understood computer systems. Failures in human, social, and legal capacities to regulate these complex systems helped drive the world into recession in the first decade of the twenty-first century.[8]

Because Mann tends to lump law in with ideology and/or politics, he ignores the contributions of intellectual property to the dynamics of consumer citizenship. This is unfortunate, because an awareness of the dynamics through which intellectual property has emerged and expanded can help a great deal in our understanding of consumer citizenship. The longing for economic and political belonging, which we

6 Mann, *Sources Vols 1–4*.

7 Mann, *Sources, Vol. 4*, 37.

8 Mann, *Sources, Vol. 4*, 46, 322–60; also Lynn A. Stout, "Derivatives and the Legal Origin of the 2008 Credit Crisis," *Harvard Business Law Review* 1 (2011): 1–38.

see in consumer citizenship, is a mirror image of the quest for economic and political power, which has become fundamental to the substantive logic of intellectual property law. Through global treaties, and treaty-based trading regimes, this substantive (materialist) logic has spread around the world, helping to constitute the nation-state system.

In this final chapter, I link the globalization of intellectual property law to the American story of consumer citizenship. I draw the link by focusing on the role of American jurists, as increasingly specialized apologists for intellectual property protections in globalized and transnational economies. Ironically, American jurists have played a significant role in building an infrastructure of state power that now extends around the world, constraining our own democratic and humanistic capacities, at the same time that we have effectively constrained others to embrace our value-commitments.

We have contributed to an infrastructure of state power that now links all nation-states of the world, drawing in the enormous social energies of new economic powers like India and China. We have done this through the World Trade Organization (WTO), which offers a framework for exerting law-changing pressures on other nation-states, and that, in conjunction with the World Intellectual Property Organization (WIPO), institutionalizes a globalized order for the protection of intellectual property rights. In the case of China, specifically, we are perhaps only now realizing that a genuine recognition of Chinese contributions to the world of globalized law, culture, and trade will challenge some of our most basic assumptions about how these should be and what they mean.

The United States has made China's protection of intellectual property central to our recognition of China as a legitimate trading partner. US pressure on China to recognize intellectual property principles was applied through WTO dispute settlement processes between 2007 and 2010, with a focus on Chinese implementation of copyright and trademark protections. Other forms of "soft pressure" have also been brought to bear on China, including a unique degree of involvement by US lawyers and judges, in dialog with Chinese lawyers and judges, who have overseen the establishment of Chinese courts and administrative processes involved in the implementation of intellectual property-related protections.[9]

US lawyers involved in these discussions have expressed profound admiration for the rapidity and sophistication with which China has embraced intellectual property protections, and has institutionally implemented those protections, including through a court system modeled to some extent on the US federal court system, with

[9] WTO Dispute Settlement (DS) 362: www.wto.org/english/tratop_e/dispu_e/cases_e/ds362_e.htm (accessed September 3, 2020); Mark Cohen and David Kappos, "China as an IP Stakeholder," China IPR Blog entry dated June 2, 2012, available at https://chinaipr.com/2012/06/02/china-as-an-ip-stakeholder/#more-402 (accessed September 6, 2020); also David Kappos and Mark Cohen, "Director's Forum: A Blog from the USPTO's Leadership: China as an IP Stakeholder," USPTO Blog entry dated June 1, 2012, available at www.uspto.gov/blog/director/entry/china_as_an_ip_stakeholder (accessed September 6, 2020).

its specialized court (the US Court of Appeals for the Federal Circuit) exercising appellate review in patent litigation. In January 2020, the United States and China were able to reach agreement on a range of intellectual property-related principles, announced with great fanfare in the Phase One Trade Agreement, opening a window of possibility for resolution of broader trade-related tensions between the United States and China.[10]

But lawyers and law professors who have declared their admiration for China's intellectual property system have also acknowledged the intractability of the present trade-related tensions, arguing that these run deeper than anything a treaty on intellectual property protections can resolve. Several legal scholars have used the phrase "techno-nationalism" to describe our current moment, highlighting parallels with the protectionist economic principles of mercantilism, which organized geopolitical competition in the early modern period of European history. The basic problem, according to these scholars, comes in the fact that cutting-edge technological inventions being developed today often have an inbuilt duality in their possible applications: they can be used to design consumer products, or they can enhance the geopolitical power of nation-states. Increasingly, they do both at the same time.[11]

From self-driving motor vehicles to algorithmically intelligent social networks, the cutting-edge technologies of today can be used to develop new commercial products, *and* they can be used to develop devices with direct implications for military and political power. Especially in the case of computer-implemented inventions, which span an ever-increasing range of consumer devices and underpin so many aspects of social connectivity, it is difficult to draw a distinction between cultural, economic, military, and political implications. In other words, we are living in a moment – one perhaps analogous to the historical moment in which nuclear power was being developed – when technological innovation has very direct implications for geopolitical power between the most powerful of nation-states. In such a moment, institutions like intellectual property become part of a broader, existential struggle for power, which is much harder to resolve through diplomatic agreement on legal principles.

10 Hon. David Kappos, Former Director USPTO, Partner – Cravath, remarks dated July 15, 2020, "The Future of IP and Tech Collaboration in China," event hosted by the Berkeley Center for Law & Technology: China Law, Trade and IP 2020, www.law.berkeley.edu/research/bclt/bcltevents/trade-tech-china/ (accessed September 6, 2020). Phase One Trade Agreement: https://ustr.gov/phase-one (accessed September 6, 2020).

11 Alex Capri, "Semiconductors at the Heart of the US-China Tech War," Hinrich Foundation White Paper, available at www.hinrichfoundation.com/research/wp/tech/semiconductors-at-the-heart-of-the-us-china-tech-war/ (accessed September 6, 2020); Mark Wu, "The 'China, Inc.' Challenge to Global Trade Governance," *Harvard International Law Journal* 57(2) (2016): 261–324; Mark Wu, remarks dated July 15, 2020, "The Future of IP and Tech Collaboration in China," event hosted by the Berkeley Center for Law & Technology: China Law, Trade and IP 2020, www.law.berkeley.edu/research/bclt/bcltevents/trade-tech-china/ (accessed September 6, 2020).

:onically, intellectual property-related treaties have been vitally important in contributing to the legal architecture that has facilitated these geopolitical dynamics. Because these treaties are part of broader, treaty-based frameworks for multilateral global cooperation, however, institutional processes for discussion and dispute resolution have been available to help prevent conflicts from escalating. But those mechanisms are increasingly challenged by China's rapid movement into a position of economic dominance, leaving us in a treacherous situation where "techno-nationalism" is less constrained.[12]

Hinting at connections between techno-nationalism and consumer citizenship, I will briefly sketch the developmental process by which the treaty-based legal architecture for globalized intellectual property law has been created, viewing treaties as instruments of legal power, which are legally analogous to contracts. In viewing treaties as instruments of legal power, I focus on the ways in which they mobilize, perform, and memorialize relationships of social power, on a global scale, constituting a form of symbolic social action, oriented toward orders of obligation. In seeking the meaningful conceptions of law that inform these performances of legality from the US side, I focus especially on a jurisprudential narrative that I think holds special appeal for lawyers involved in the drafting and governmental implementation of intellectual property-related treaties. This jurisprudential narrative is self-consciously "progressive," a narrative that appeals to lawyers trained in common law systems, who see wisdom and goodness in an incremental, thoughtful adaptation of legal doctrines to constant technological innovation, through court-based jurisprudence. This model, while appealing, ignores very real constraints on the power of courts to engage in traditional forms of common law reasoning, especially at the federal level, where the important decisions about US intellectual property law are made.

Surveying the globalized world of intellectual property law in 2020, it is tempting to conclude that a technocratic logic – particularly in patent law – has outstripped the capacity of common law courts to devise meaningful boundaries. I worry that the courts are now mocked – even the US Supreme Court – when they make the attempt to set meaningful boundaries to patent eligibility, especially in a moment when some are arguing that artificial intelligence has developed the capacity to invent autonomously. I do not reach a final conclusion about whether these concerns are appropriate, because I honestly do not know. I invite the reader to think with me rather than trying to arrive at a conclusion that would be premature.

But I do believe there is cause for grave concern.

The dynamics of power politics do seem to be exceeding our jurisprudential capacities for meaningful interpretation of legal obligations, rooted in legal traditions, and I am afraid that we are now in a race with China for technological supremacy, a race in which the legal system that best promotes innovation wins.

12 Wu, "'China Inc.' Challenge," 269–95, 300–8; Wu, remarks dated July 15, 2020.

Efforts to constrain the incentives for innovation, in the name of alternative value-commitments, seem increasingly like national suicide from the standpoint of power politics. Such a situation is extremely dangerous, because it is one in which very well-meaning people might see no alternative but to embrace the naked pursuit of power, at the cost of all value-commitments, even while, perhaps, believing that they are doing so in an effort to protect the capacity for national determination in value-commitments.

12.1 GLOBALIZED INTELLECTUAL PROPERTY LAW

Intellectual property law today is part of a global, treaty-based order. The WTO oversees an international intellectual property law framework defined in the Agreement on Trade-Related Aspects of Intellectual Property Rights ("TRIPS"). Through the WTO–TRIPS legal framework, intellectual property has become part of the overarching, international, institutional system governing global trade relations. This organization coordinating legal, political, military, and economic powers receives important support from WIPO, an organ of the United Nations established in 1967, which currently administers twenty-six intellectual property treaties and serves as a coordinator for global intellectual property-related policy discussion and implementation.[13]

Currently, the WTO has 164 member states, joined recently by Afghanistan (2016) and the Russian Federation (2012). The vast majority of the world's nation-states are either members or observers (on their way to becoming members). India and South Africa became members in 1995, China in 2001, the Kingdom of Saudi Arabia in 2005, Vietnam in 2007, Montenegro in 2012, and Yemen in 2014. Under TRIPS, all member states participating in the WTO system are required to implement specified, substantive provisions for the protection of intellectual property. These "minimum standards of protection" were originally required to be implemented in phases: by January 1996 for developed countries, by January 1999 for developing countries, and by January 2005 for "Least-Developed Countries." For Least-Developed Countries, however, the requirement to implement minimum standards of protection has been extended to July 2021, unless the country has first passed out of Least-Developed Country status.[14]

Under WTO–TRIPS, in other words, virtually the whole world is governed under intellectual property law principles, subject to grace periods for the poorest of

[13] TRIPS: Annex (1C) to the 1994 Marrakesh Treaty establishing the WTO, as amended January 23, 2017, available at www.wto.org/english/docs_e/legal_e/31bis_trips_01_e.htm (accessed August 5, 2020). WIPO: www.wipo.int/portal/en/index.html (accessed August 5, 2020).

[14] WTO member states: www.wto.org/english/thewto_e/whatis_e/tif_e/org6_e.htm (accessed August 5, 2020). Implementation of minimum standards for Least-Developed Countries: Council for TRIPS, Extension of the Transition Period under Article 66.1 for Least-Developed Country Members, IP/C/64, June 11, 2013, available for download at www.wto.org/english/tratop_e/trips_e/ldc_e.htm (accessed August 5, 2020).

developing countries. Furthermore, all WTO member states, regardless of development status, are required to follow the TRIPS principles of national treatment and most-favored nation status with respect to intellectual property, treating the nationals of other member states the same as their own nationals and extending to all member state nationals any additional intellectual property rights that are extended to particular countries through treaties.[15]

Both WIPO and the WTO are successors to older multilateral treaty arrangements. The WTO is the successor to the General Agreement on Tariffs and Trade (GATT), a multilateral trading framework created in the wake of World War II. Unlike GATT, however, the WTO has been constituted by the 1994 Marrakesh treaty to be an organization with legal personality, that is, an organizational entity that exists independently from the signatory nation-states. Moreover, the WTO encompasses a substantive dispute-resolution framework while also specifying member state rights and responsibilities for implementing sanctioning measures where there is failure to comply with dispute settlement decisions. This combination of dispute-resolution and sanctioning powers has enabled WTO member states to exert meaningful pressure, compelling one another to bring domestic law and enforcement into line with evolving interpretations of TRIPS minimum standards.[16]

WIPO was created in 1967 to administer international unions, created in 1883 and 1886 to ensure international protection of patents, industrial designs (trademarks), and copyrights. As a reformed organizational apparatus for administering the Paris Union (created by the 1883 Paris Convention for the Protection of Industrial Property) and the Berne Union (created by the 1886 Berne Convention for the Protection of Literary and Artistic Works), WIPO is the successor to the United International Bureaux for the Protection of Intellectual Property (known as "BIRPI"), which was created in 1893 to administer both the Paris and the Berne Union. The convention establishing the World Intellectual Property Organization – signed in Stockholm on July 14, 1967, and amended in September 1979 – established WIPO as a member state-led international organization, absorbing BIRPI and assuming responsibility for the Madrid Agreement for the Repression of False or Deceptive Indications of Source on Goods, a multilateral treaty framework from 1891, which protects trademarks and related rights through an international registration system. In 1974, WIPO became a specialized agency of the United Nations, with the purpose of promoting intellectual property throughout the world.[17]

15 General principles of national treatment and most-favored nation status: www.wto.org/english/tratop_e/trips_e/intel2_e.htm#generalprovisions (accessed August 5, 2020).

16 WTO legal personality: Marrakesh Agreement Establishing the World Trade Organization Art. VIII (1), available at www.wto.org/english/docs_e/legal_e/04-wto_e.htm (accessed August 5, 2020). WTO dispute resolution regime: www.wto.org/english/tratop_e/dispu_e/dispu_e.htm (accessed August 5, 2020).

17 Background to WIPO in intellectual property-related unions created by multilateral treaties: www.wipo.int/about-wipo/en/history.html (accessed August 5, 2020).

12.2 LAW-CHANGING PRESSURE THROUGH THE WTO

An early example of the law-changing pressure that can be brought to bear on a member state through the WTO can be seen in the case of *India – Patent Protection for Pharmaceutical and Agricultural Chemical Products*. This was the first TRIPS-related dispute resolution process to be conducted within the WTO, and it established important principles for guidance in resolving future TRIPS-related disputes.[18]

The dispute pertained to obligations on the part of developing countries, like India, to establish transitional arrangements for patent protection of pharmaceutical products and agricultural chemicals. The dispute resolution process was initiated by the United States based on the argument that "India's legal regime appears to be inconsistent with the obligations of the TRIPS Agreement." The European Communities (now the European Union) sided with the United States, supporting US arguments and reserving third-party rights. The European Communities also filed a separate but similar complaint in 1998.[19]

The final decision of the WTO Dispute Settlement Body was that India had indeed failed to implement domestic laws adhering to its obligations under the TRIPS agreement. Although the United States lost a significant argument about the interpretation of TRIPS, the United States did successfully trigger a change in India's domestic law through the WTO Dispute Settlement process.[20]

In March 1999, under the pressure of potential trade sanctions, India's Parliament enacted an amendment to its 1970 Patents Act, implementing a filing system and exclusive marketing rights for pharmaceutical products and agricultural chemicals, to operate during the transitional period prior to full implementation of patent protections. In 2005, India implemented a complete framework of substantive patent

[18] WTO Dispute Settlement (DS) 50: www.wto.org/english/tratop_e/dispu_e/cases_e/ds50_e.htm (accessed August 5, 2020). Appellate Body Report dated December 19, 1997, WT/DS50/AB/R, available at www.wto.org/english/tratop_e/dispu_e/cases_e/ds50_e.htm (accessed August 5, 2020), 11: "The dispute that gives rise to this case represents the first time the TRIPS Agreement has been submitted to the scrutiny of the WTO dispute settlement system."

[19] TRIPS Art. 70.8, available at www.wto.org/english/docs_e/legal_e/31bis_trips_01_e.htm (accessed September 6, 2020); US Request for the Establishment of a Dispute Resolution Panel, WT/DS50/4, November 8, 1996; Note by the Secretariat, WT/DS50/5, February 5, 1997; WTO Appellate Body Report, WT/DS50/AB/R, December 19, 1997. European Communities complaint: WT/DS79, available at www.wto.org/english/tratop_e/dispu_e/cases_e/ds79_e.htm (accessed September 6, 2020).

[20] India-Patent Protection, WTO Appellate Body Report, WT/DS50/AB/R, December 19, 1997, available at www.wto.org/english/tratop_e/dispu_e/cases_e/ds50_e.htm (accessed Sept. 6, 2020). The United States had argued that the "legitimate expectations" of WTO–TRIPS Member States *and private parties* (such as pharmaceutical companies) should shape the interpretation of obligations under the TRIPS agreement. The Dispute Resolution Panel that initially decided the case accepted the US argument, but the Appellate Body overruled this determination, holding that it was based on a mistaken conflation of analytically separate interpretive principles, rooted in the GATT framework and carried over into WTO–TRIPS.

protection for pharmaceutical products and agricultural chemicals, in keeping with its obligations as a WTO–TRIPS Member State.[21]

The use of the WTO–TRIPS Dispute Settlement process to exert law-changing pressure has by no means been limited to developing countries. Developed countries and regional bodies like the EU also exert law-changing pressure upon one another in this way. For example, the EU has used this process to trigger changes in US trademark law. And the United States has used this process to trigger changes in Canadian patent law.[22]

The creation of an international body with effective power to legitimately punish trade violations, including those relating to intellectual property, was a central objective coming out of the GATT's Uruguay Round of Multilateral Trade Negotiations (1986–94). With the creation of the WTO–TRIPS framework, a transnational legal body has been established which oversees the coordination of national intellectual property frameworks and facilitates the sanctioning of deviations from global standards. In combination, therefore, WTO–TRIPS and WIPO constitute a transnational, global, intellectual property order.[23]

The creation of this global order of obligation would not have been possible in the absence of important legal foundations. In particular, the "will theory" of contracts, which we explored in the previous chapter, played a foundational role in enabling the purposeful creation of global institutions through treaties. As national states acquired legal personality, exercising their proprietary will in the global arena, they could benefit from the same proprietary voluntarism that enabled individuals to create legal institutions through their contractual exchanges of property. Treaties, in

21 Patents (Amendment) Act of 1999, The Gazette of India, Extraordinary, Ministry of Law, Justice, and Company Affairs, March 26, 1999, available at WIPOLEX, Member Profile for India, https://wipolex.wipo.int/en/legislation/details/7622 (accessed September 6, 2020); Patents (Amendment) Act, 2005 (Act No. 15 of 2005), available at WIPOLEX, Member Profile for India, https://wipolex.wipo.int/en/legislation/details/2407 (accessed September 6, 2020). Notably, however, in its 2005 patent law, India included a patentability exclusion for "the mere discovery of a new form of a known substance which does not result in the enhancement of the known efficacy of that substance" (India Patents Act of 1970, as amended, Section 3(d), available at WIPOLEX, Member Profile for India, https://wipolex.wipo.int/en/legislation/details/13104 (accessed September 6, 2020)). On April 1, 2013, India's Supreme Court held that this provision represented a legally valid limitation on patentability under India's patent law, which operated in conjunction with TRIPS-compliant standards of "Invention" to establish a higher inventive bar for pharmaceutical products under Indian patent law. The Court determined that these legal provisions represent a legally valid protection for India's generic drug manufacturing business, a business that provides life-saving drugs at relatively low cost to many developing and least-developed countries around the world (see *Novartis* v. *Union of India*, Supreme Court of India, April 2013).

22 United States – Section 211 Omnibus Appropriations Act of 1998, WT/DS176/AB/R, available at www.wto.org/english/tratop_e/dispu_e/cases_e/ds176_e.htm (accessed September 6, 2020); Canada – Term of Patent Protection, WT/DS170/AB/R, available at www.wto.org/english/tratop_e/dispu_e/cases_e/ds170_e.htm (accessed September 6, 2020).

23 Marrakesh Declaration of April 15, 1994, as reprinted in *World Trade Organization, The Legal Texts: The Results of the Uruguay Round of Multilateral Trade Negotiations* (Cambridge, UK: Cambridge University Press, 1999) also Christopher May, *The World Intellectual Property Organization: Resurgence and the Development Agenda* (London: Routledge, 2007); Amrita Narlikar, *The World Trade Organization: A Very Short Introduction* (Oxford: Oxford University Press, 2005).

other words, are also instruments of legal power, which function between nation-states on an explicit analogy with contracts between property owners.

12.3 TREATIES AS NATIONAL CONTRACTS

Historical accounts commonly point to the year 1873 as an important turning point in the movement toward our modern, globalized intellectual property order. Refusals on the part of American inventors to attend a World Exposition in Vienna, due to their fears about ineffective protections for their intellectual property, prompted a series of international congresses and conferences, which ultimately led to the Paris and Berne Unions. However, it is important to recognize that the lobbying for an effective international regime for the protection of intellectual property which erupted around the 1873 Vienna Exposition depended on cultural ideals and economic interests connected to older treaty-based frameworks, which had already established international frameworks for the protection of intellectual property.[24]

These cultural ideals have their roots in the Congress of Vienna (1814–15), a collective effort to establish order in Europe, in the wake of the Napoleanic Wars. Underpinning that collective effort was the will theory of contracts, applied to treaties between nations. To see the impact of that theory, for intellectual property law, it is necessary to recognize the extent to which intellectual property regimes remained nationally bounded, with protections focused primarily on domestic citizens and residents, even toward the end of the nineteenth century. This is clear in the case of US copyright law.

Until 1891, in fact, America's copyright statutes explicitly limited copyright protection to American citizens and residents. Prominent British authors, such as Charles Dickens (1812–70), repeatedly sought to awaken their American neighbors to the injustice of such legislation. Some American authors agreed that a world in which popular English literature could be pirated and published so cheaply was a world in which the monetary value of their own works might be precarious. However, Congress remained unmoved. Despite repeated legislative efforts, bills always died in committee, or were voted down.[25]

In 1853, it had looked like things might change. In that year, the American Secretary of State, Edward Everett, signed a treaty with the United Kingdom on behalf of President Fillmore. This treaty, if ratified, would have created a system of "national treatment" for copyrights between the United Kingdom and the United States: UK authors would have been entitled to the same copyrights as Americans in

24 May, *World Intellectual Property Organization*, 15–23.

25 Stuart Ray Givens, "The American Struggle for an International Copyright Law," MA Thesis, Stanford University, 1949; also B. Zorina Khan, *The Democratization of Invention: Patents and Copyrights in American Economic Development, 1790–1920* (New York: Cambridge University Press, 2005), 258–87.

America, and American authors would have been entitled to the same copyrights as Britons in the United Kingdom. However, the treaty was not ratified in the Senate.[26]

In 1854, the British Ambassador to the United States, John Crampton, raised a question about the constitutional effect of the treaty relative to US domestic law. Assuming it was ratified, would the treaty alone be sufficient to secure national treatment for UK citizens, or would a US statute to amend the copyright law be required? The US Attorney General, Caleb Cushing (1853–57), gave his opinion that, pursuant to Article VI of the US Constitution (the "Supremacy Clause"), the treaty alone would be sufficient to amend US copyright law, such that the principle of reciprocal national treatment would be established. What is interesting about Cushing's opinion is the way he describes the legal nature and operation of the treaty (which he calls a "convention").

> The convention *being a contract between the two nations*, duly entered into and ratified by the President of the United States, by and with the advice and consent of the Senate, it thereby is a law of the United States, without any further action by the Government of the United States.[27]

In just the way that contracts create effective legal bonds between private parties, Cushing says, treaties create legal bonds between sovereign nation-states. Under Article VI of the US Constitution, according to Cushing's interpretation, these contractual legal bonds become operative as domestic law.

12.4 IN THE NEW LAW OF NATIONS

The concept of treaties as legal contracts between nation-states received forceful explication by jurists of the "natural law" school, interpreting the Roman law tradition. Among the most influential of these natural law scholars was Hugo Grotius, whom we met in the previous chapter.

Grotius viewed treaties as contracts made by order of the sovereign. Such contracts, like their private counterparts, create enforceable rights and obligations so long as they are made voluntarily and involve reciprocal promises. Failure to conform to the obligations incurred through any contract, including a treaty, constitutes an injury to the other party, giving rise to a right of reparation, which, in the case of sovereign states acting in relation to one another, means a lawful "public" war.[28]

Grotius elaborated this legal theory of treaties as part of a general framework of natural and international law (*ius gentium*). Writing during Europe's terrible wars

[26] Givens, "American Struggle," 28–9; British-American Copyright Convention Draft, Washington (1853), available at Primary Sources on Copyright (1450–1900), edited by Lionel Bently and M. Kretschmer, www.copyrighthistory.org (hereafter *Primary Sources*).

[27] *Official Opinions of the Attorneys General of the United States*, Vol. VI, edited by C. C. Andrews (Washington, DC: Robert Farnham, 1856), 292–3 (emphasis added).

[28] Richard Tuck (ed.), *The Rights of War and Peace* by Hugo Grotius, 3 Vols. (Indianapolis: Liberty Fund, 2005), II.I, II.XV.

over politicized religion, Grotius had relied extensively on the Roman law tradition to articulate a comprehensive framework of international order, law based on common consent among nations, rooted in sovereign legal actors who would behave toward one another in a manner analogous to Roman property owners. The resulting body of law was to govern the mutual relations among states, or rulers of states, in their conduct of war, their peaceful interaction, and their alliances.[29]

Grotius' international order was, fundamentally, a law-governed arrangement of relations among sovereign entities. Sovereignty, for Grotius, is the "moral faculty" of governing a state which is not subject to the legal control of another. A moral faculty – a legal capacity to create enforceable "right" (*ius*) – is the qualitative attribute of a person which enables that person to take legal actions, that is, to have or do something lawfully. This "civil power" of sovereignty, just like any other intangible object – such as an easement or right of way over land – is an object of property, which may be possessed in full ownership, or in something less than full ownership, and which may be transferred, depending on how it is possessed. And, just like any other object of property, it may be possessed by a single individual (as in a monarchy) or by a group of people in common (as in a republic).[30]

The state is a public association, which is the "common subject" of sovereignty. The possessor of sovereignty on behalf of the state, on the other hand, is the "special subject" of sovereignty. The state is conceived as a kind of corporate body that may be composed of one or more peoples, and that may also combine with other states to form a confederate "system."[31]

The overall conception of interaction between states is one of law-abiding autonomy, punctuated by occasional cooperation and limited partnership. Grotius' primary goal was to establish a framework that would impose legal restrictions on the initiation and conduct of war. While he was seeking to articulate legal constraints on the exercise of war, he clearly did not envision anything like a permanent organization standing over sovereign states and placing legal limits on their behavior. From his perspective, the moment such an entity comes into existence, sovereignty would cease to reside in the states and would instead reside in the organization standing above them. The commercial and military alliances that he envisioned were much more limited and temporary.

Significantly, the language that Grotius used to describe commercial and military alliances between sovereign states, which arise out of their contractual agreements, was that of partnership (*societas*), not incorporation. In the chapter addressing contracts in general, Grotius noted that contracts can create partnerships (*societates*), whereby certain actions or things become common property (*res*) held jointly between partners for their common advantage (*utilitas*). In his chapter on treaties – that is, on contracts between sovereigns of states – Grotius noted that such treaties

[29] Ibid, *Preliminary Discourse*, I, XVIII, XXIX, XLI.
[30] Ibid., I.I.IV-V; I.III.VI-VII; I.III.VIII, XI.
[31] Ibid., I.III.VII; II.V.XVII, XXIII.

can be used to create partnerships (*societates*) between states, either for the sake of commerce or for the sake of war.[32]

There is one exceptional instance in which Grotius used language of incorporation (*universitas*) in characterizing the relationships between states. This is in the *Prolegomena*, where he was echoing Aristotle and Cicero in discussing basic principles of human sociability that underlie natural law. Grotius introduced a distinction between laws that arise purely from human, social nature (natural law), and laws that derive from the exercise of human will. The exercise of will, whether through unanimous agreement or through imposition and acquiescence, is the source of positive, domestic ("municipal") law, as well as the "volitional law of nations." And, just as the exercise of will for the sake of creating domestic law "has in view the advantage (*utilitas*) of that state," so also the exercise of will for the sake of creating international law has in view an advantage. In the latter case, however, the advantage (*utilitas*) in view is not that of one state "Body," but of "all in general."[33]

Grotius did not say what he meant by his universalist, corporate language (*universitas*). Available translations do not highlight Grotius' use of corporate language, emphasizing instead his universalism. However, it is possible that Grotius has in mind the nebulous, quasi-corporate concept of "Christendom." Henry Kissinger believed that the "concept of world order," tied to the symbolism of Christendom (with its associated "medieval aspiration to universality"), held into the seventeenth century, when it was replaced by the "Balance of Power" system.[34]

Grotius appears, in any case, to envision a larger whole of cooperating states, working to define interests that serve the whole, rather than one particular state. Laws created between states, including those that establish enduring alliances and partnerships, should serve those broader, holistic interests, rather than a particular state's interests. Nevertheless, actual treaty structures are viewed as creating nothing more than partnerships, and certainly nothing like an incorporated entity standing over the contracting parties.

As we saw in the previous chapter, Grotius was a transitional figure in the natural law tradition. In emphasizing the role of will in effectuating international arrangements, particularly in portraying treaties as consensual contracts between property-owning states, Grotius contributed to a new legal understanding of the international order. According to this legal understanding, sovereigns of states are closely analogous to Roman property owners. Like ancient Romans lords, these sovereigns (whether they be a king or a "people") acquire ownership of landed territories through the method of physical possession, coupled with an externally symbolized will to possess (*occupatio*). The landed territory of a state, in other words, is quite literally the property of the sovereign, subject to the sovereign's disposition by

32 Ibid., II.XII.IV; II.XV.VI.

33 Ibid, *Preliminary Discourse*, XVIII; compare II.XV.XII.

34 Henry Kissinger, *Diplomacy* (New York: Simon & Schuster, 1994), 56.

contract, at least to the extent that it is not otherwise controlled by operation of succession and inheritance.[35]

Through their consensual contracts, the sovereigns of states may transfer property between themselves, and they may voluntarily create partnerships in which their property is shared jointly for the benefit of all the partners. These contractual structures are created through an exercise of sovereign will, and, once created, they bind sovereign states to their maintenance. Violations of the contractual promises underlying the contractual structures constitute a just cause for war.

This vision of an international order, which received an early modern, Protestant articulation in the person of Hugo Grotius, and which is so clearly rooted in the Roman law tradition, is a vision of national property: a vision of independent sovereign states as bearers of the capacity to purposefully create rights and obligations, rooted in their property, through a formalized exercise of the will, and thereby to create contractual structures that operate between themselves, while also inevitably impacting states that are not party to their agreements.[36]

Two hundred years later, this vision endured, providing a foundation for American conceptions of the international order, as seen in James Kent's *Commentaries on American Law*:

> There can be no doubt that the power competent to bind the nation by treaty may alienate the public domain and property by treaty. If a nation has conferred upon its executive department, without reserve, the right of treating and contracting with other states, it is considered as having invested it with all the power necessary to make a contract. That department is the organ of the nation, and the alienations by it are valid, because they are done by the reputed will of the nation.[37]

National states, like Roman lords, acquire ownership of property through occupation of territory, and they can transfer their property through instruments of legal power, treaties, which are legally understood as a type of contract.

12.5 THE WESTPHALIAN SYSTEM

As the Swedish ambassador to France during the Thirty Years' War, in a period (1634–45) when French–Swedish alliance helped to shape the course of the war, Grotius concretely impacted the interstate relations of the Westphalian system (1648). That system embraced the *cuius regio, eius religio* framework of the Augsburg Settlement (1555), with two important exceptions: principles of state sovereignty were significantly emphasized and enhanced, and Reformed

[35] Tuck (ed.), *Rights of War and Peace*, II.II.IV.

[36] Stephen C. Neff (ed.), *Hugo Grotius on the Law of War and Peace* (Cambridge, UK: Cambridge University Press, 2012), xxvi.

[37] James Kent, *Commentaries on American Law*, 12th ed. by Oliver W. Holmes, Jr. (Boston: Little, Brown, and Co., 1873) [1826], 167.

(Calvinist) Christianity was officially recognized as a legitimate confessional commitment for Christian sovereigns, alongside Catholicism and Lutheranism.[38]

The Westphalian emphasis on state sovereignty was of particularly dramatic import for the Holy Roman Empire. The treaties of Münster and Osnabrück, which formalized the Westphalian settlement, both contained articles affirming all "rights, prerogatives, liberties, privileges" and territorial powers of the electors, princes, and states of the Holy Roman Empire. In addition, however, each of these electors, princes, and states was explicitly granted the power to conclude alliances and execute treaties as an independent entity. Despite the proviso that such treaties and alliances were not to be made against the empire, these articles recognized an essential mark of sovereignty, the power to independently conduct foreign policy, now located in over 300 political entities within the empire.[39]

At the same time, moreover, the Westphalian system implicated the ultimate demise of Christendom, with corresponding implications for the international order. Beyond their official recognition of Christian denominational fragmentation, the treaties excluded any possibility that the pope's objections would carry legal force. Accordingly, the objections of Pope Innocent X (1644–55) were ignored. With the demise of Christendom, the sense of a sacramental or spiritual communal purpose, operating as an effective check on individual state interests, declined in favor of *raison d'etat* ("reason of state") calculation in the Balance of Power system.[40]

In the absence of an overarching organizational order, however loose, legal conceptions of proprietary will contributed to instability in the Balance of Power system. The will, as Hannah Arendt has argued, is a human capacity "to bring about something new and hence to 'change the world'." As such, it can be a profoundly unruly force which, when unchecked by reasoning and principled judgment, produces extreme instability and unpredictability.[41]

The Balance of Power System, premised as it was on the exercise of proprietary will by sovereign states in pursuit of their *raison d'etat* interests, offered only the conflict of national and sovereign wills as a security against this destabilizing force. According to the diplomatic historian Paul Schroeder, such a balancing system can only work when guiding principles and goals of *raison d'etat* are identifiable and comprehensible between international actors. As long as international actors are

38 R. Warden Lee, "Grotius: The Last Phase, 1635–45," *Transactions of the Grotius Society* 31 (1945): 193–215; Die Westfälischen Friedensverträge vom 24. Oktober 1648. Texte und Übersetzungen (Acta Pacis Westphalicae. Supplementa electronica, 1), available at www.pax-westphalica.de/ (accessed September 6, 2020).

39 Instrumentum Pacis Osnabrugensis (IPO, Treaty of Osnabrück), available in English translation (1713), at www.pax-westphalica.de/ipmipo/pdf/o_1732en-treatys.pdf (accessed September 6, 2020), Art. 8, §§ 1–2; Instrumentum Pacis Monasteriensis (IPM, Treaty of Münster), available in English translation (1710), at www.pax-westphalica.de/ipmipo/pdf/m_1710en-treatys.pdf (accessed September 6, 2020), Arts. LXIV-LXV; Kissinger, *Diplomacy*, 65.

40 IPO, Treaty of Osnabrück, Art. 5 §1; Hajo Holborn, *A History of Modern Germany, 1648–1840* (New York: Alfred A. Knopf, 1964), 4; Kissinger, *Diplomacy*, 56 ff.

41 Hannah Arendt, *The Life of the Mind* (San Diego: Harcourt, 1978), 7.

able to see a meaningful pattern in the actions taken by another international actor, they can comprehend this pattern in terms of guiding principles and goals of *raison d'etat* action that are being pursued by the other, make their own calculations accordingly, and operate as effective counterweights to the will of the other. Under these conditions, a "balance" of powers is theoretically possible.[42]

However, a meaningful and comprehensible pattern of *raison d'etat* action is conditional upon guiding principles and goals that are discernable in the decisions of international actors. Where no such principles and goals are effective, there is only the emptiness of a demand that others stay out of the way, that the sovereign will be left free to pursue an entirely spontaneous course of action. In Schroeder's view, this was precisely the threat that Napoleon posed to European stability. According to Schroeder:

> Napoleon's great service to European international politics was to be a very efficient scourge of God. He convinced European princes and statesmen that an alternative to eighteenth century politics had to be found because playing the old game with him was intolerable . . .. And so they had to end this game of poker and invent a new post-1815 game of contract bridge. Napoleon contributed nothing positive to this outcome. Nevertheless, lawless to the end, a law unto himself, he drove Europe into a new system of international politics bounded by law.[43]

This new system emerged out of the Congress of Vienna, a series of diplomatic meetings and agreements among the European powers, in which, among many other points of attention, principles of intellectual property protection received international recognition.

12.6 COPYRIGHT TREATIES IN THE CONCERT OF EUROPE

In the wake of the Napoleanic wars and the formal elimination of the Holy Roman Empire (1806), a diplomatic system was established at the Congress of Vienna which held firm until the Crimean War of 1854, and which continued to structure international diplomacy until the closing decades of the nineteenth century. This diplomatic system is often referred to as the "Concert of Europe," or, alternatively, the "Metternich System."[44]

From a legal perspective, the creation of the Concert of Europe was embodied in a number of treaties, which were bundled together as appendices, summarized in a "General Treaty" of June 9, 1815. Fundamentally, the General Treaty created an institutional framework for "Great Power" consultation and cooperation. The bulk of the treaty aimed to accomplish this by resolving territorial conflicts between the

[42] Paul W. Schroeder, *Systems, Stability, and Statecraft: Essays on the International History of Modern Europe*, edited by David Wetzel, Robert Jervis, and Jack S. Levy (New York: Palgrave Macmillan, 2004).

[43] Schroeder, *Systems*, 33.

[44] Kissinger, *Diplomacy*, 78–102.

Great Powers. In very much the same way that a modern title to real property would do, the treaty articulated new territorial boundaries for the states of Europe, declaring each title owner, together with its "heirs and assigns," as possessor of "full sovereignty and property" in the delineated territories. In the words of Edward Hertslet, librarian of the English Foreign Office from 1842 to 1896, the General Treaty "settled the Territorial Arrangements of Europe," and thereby laid a foundation for the "Title Deeds of the European Family."[45]

For Germany, the Congress of Vienna was especially significant in creating a constitutional substitute for the Holy Roman Empire. The General Treaty, together with Annex IX, created the legal framework for a "perpetual, Germanic Confederation" composed of Prussia, Austria, Bavaria, Saxony, Hanover, Württemberg, Baden, Hesse-Cassel, Hesse-Darmstadt, four remaining free cities (Lübeck, Frankfort, Bremen, and Hamburg), and a number of smaller principalities. Article XIII of the Annexed Federative Treaty established basic rights that would be possessed by the individual "subjects" of the confederated states. National treatment in property taxes was in principle established together with a right to emigrate from one state to another within the confederation. And, finally, Article XVIII(d) of this federative treaty declared that the newly created Diet (Parliament) for the confederation would, upon its first meeting, "adopt such measures as may secure authors and editors against the piracy of their works."[46]

This treaty-based commitment to copyright principles was prompted by an 1815 petition from six German book publishers: one from Württemberg (Stuttgart) and five from Saxony (Leipzig and Weimar). The publishers drew by analogy on treaty-based commitments to a regulatory framework for the free navigation of rivers, arguing that:

> [T]he task of the blessed Congress at Vienna is to facilitate communication between the various peoples so that they cease to look upon each other as strangers. This facilitation, this bringing [of peoples] closer together, by freeing Europe's navigable rivers, can equally be encouraged by safeguarding rights of ownership .... The question is whether it will continue to be tolerated that a citizen of a German state should be able to appropriate the rightfully acquired property of a citizen in another German state.[47]

In short, the publishers wanted "a law, valid throughout all Germany, against the reprinting of books." Such a law could only come from the German Confederation, and the publishers were hopeful that the federative treaty provision would help them to secure it.[48]

45 Edward Hertslet (ed.), *The Map of Europe by Treaty*, Vol. I (London: Butterworths, 1875), v.
46 Hertslet (ed.), *Map of Europe*, 200–77.
47 Annotated Publishers' Petition to the Congress of Vienna (1815), translated by Luis Sundkvist, *Primary Sources*.
48 Ibid.

During the late eighteenth century, the southwestern German states of Baden and Württemberg had become centers of unauthorized book publishing, much to the frustration of publishers based in Saxony. In the wake of French occupation, however, Baden had enacted a Civil Code modeled on that of France, with additional provisions that explicitly recognized literary property. This left Württemberg as a remaining center of republication, which Saxony's publishers obviously hoped could be eliminated through a law of the German Confederation.[49]

Although it took much longer than they hoped, the publishers got their law in 1837. On November 9 of that year, the Confederation Diet passed a directive, articulating principles for the protection of literary and artistic works throughout the confederation. According to these principles, authors of literary and artistic works held a "property" in such works from the moment of their creation and publication, which was subject to inheritance and transfer, for a period of at least ten years. Although individual German states had some flexibility in determining the form through which to implement these principles, they were required to include certain penalties and prohibitions, and they were accountable to the Confederation Diet to show how they had implemented the principles. Pursuant to this confederation directive, Württemberg enacted a copyright act the following year.[50]

Prussia, meanwhile, had observed the effectiveness of treaties in establishing legal institutions and had grown frustrated in waiting for the Confederation Diet to act. In 1827, Frederick William III issued a Supreme Cabinet Order authorizing negotiations with other German states for the purpose of establishing reciprocal ("national") treatment in the area of copyright protection. Between 1827 and 1829, Prussia executed thirty of these bilateral treaties, establishing reciprocal copyright arrangements with nearly all of the larger German states – including Hanover, Saxony, Bavaria, Baden, and Württemberg – with the exception of Austria. According to Friedemann Kawohl, these treaties effectively established the minimum standards for copyright protection throughout the German Confederation.[51]

In 1840, Austria and Sardinia built on this momentum to establish a literary and artistic property framework for operation between northern Italy and Austria. In their bilateral treaty, Austria and Sardinia agreed to "guarantee writers and artists the lifetime right of ownership to those works of theirs which appear in either of both of

49 Baden Civil Code, Karlsruhe (1809), § 577d, translated by Luis Sundkvist, *Primary Sources*; Friedemann Kawohl, "Commentary on the Copyright Provisions in the Baden Statute Book of 1809," *Primary Sources*.

50 Directive for reciprocal copyright protection within the German Confederation, Berlin (1837), translated by Luis Sundkvist, *Primary Sources*; Friedemann Kawohl, "Commentary on the Resolution on Reciprocal Copyright Protection within the German Confederation, Berlin (1837)," *Primary Sources*.

51 Treaties on reciprocal protection between Prussia and various German States, Berlin (1827), translated by Luis Sundkvist, *Primary Sources*; Friedemann Kawohl, "Commentary on Reciprocal Protection between Prussia and Various German States (1827)," *Primary Sources*.

these States," and to secure the rights to their heirs, for a fixed period of time. As the Kingdom of Sardinia only included regions in northern Italy, Article 27 of the treaty contemplated inviting other Italian governments to accede to its provisions.[52]

In 1846, Prussia and Britain followed suit, executing a convention for the establishment of international copyright. This convention established a regime of reciprocal ("national") treatment between Prussia and Britain, which would apply to works of "literature and fine art." As a result of this agreement, British authors would receive the same protections in Prussia as Prussian authors, and vice versa.[53]

Because Prussia had recently enacted a new copyright law, which set an international standard for protection of "ownership" (*Eigentum*) in "works of science and art," Britain was pressured to "modernize" its copyright law as part of the diplomatic negotiations leading up to the signing of the 1846 Convention. The result was the British Copyright Act of 1842, which provided Britain's first statutory definition of copyrights as "personal property," and brought together all the varied strands of copyright-related case law and legislation that had developed since 1774. This followed Britain's International Copyright Act of 1838, which had provided a statutory basis for recognizing the copyrights of foreign authors.[54]

By the mid-1840s, then, copyright had already become a multinational institution which was founded on a web of treaty-based frameworks and rooted in the Concert of Europe System. During the 1850s, the Concert of Europe System broke down, and the framework of treaties rooted in it became insecure. However, the experience provided by nearly two decades of copyright treaties, together with a host of other international institutions created under the Concert of Europe System, had persuaded many parties that effective international institutions for the protection of intellectual property could be created this way.

12.7 INTERNATIONAL PATENT AND TRADEMARK PROTECTION

By 1872, then, intellectual property was already relatively established as an international institution. We can see the impacts of this on American popular consciousness, in the pages of *Scientific American*, a widely read American periodical, which, after 1847, was published by a dominant firm of US patent attorneys, Munn & Co. International news of relevance to intellectual property law, especially patent law,

52 Bilateral Treaty between Austria and Sardinia, Vienna (1840), translated by Luis Sundkvist, *Primary Sources*.

53 Bilateral Treaty between Prussia and Britain (1846), *Primary Sources*; Friedmann Kawohl, "Commentary on Bilateral Treaty between Prussia and Britain (1846)," *Primary Sources*.

54 Prussian Copyright Act, Berlin (1837), translated by Friedemann Kawohl, *Primary Sources*; International Copyright Act, London (1838), *Primary Sources*; Ronan Deazley, "Commentary on International Copyright Act 1838," *Primary Sources*; Copyright Act, London (1842), *Primary Sources*; Ronan Deazley, "Commentary on Copyright Amendment Act," *Primary Sources*; Brad Sherman and Lionel Bently, *The Making of Modern Intellectual Property Law* (Cambridge, UK: Cambridge University Press, 1999), 111–18.

regularly featured in *Scientific American* articles, as did descriptions of domestic and foreign patents. However, the complexity of a system rooted in multiple, free-standing treaty arrangements nonetheless lent force to American inventors' fears that their inventions were not adequately protected for display at the worldwide Vienna Exhibition.[55]

In the wake of American recalcitrance over this exhibition, the Paris and Berne Unions were created to administer a framework of international treaties for the protection of patents, copyrights, and, later, trademarks. In the area of trademarks, the French pressed especially hard to ensure international uniformity. In 1869, a treaty was executed between France and the United States regarding trademarks. After the US Supreme Court struck down, as unconstitutional, federal trademark statutes anchored in the Intellectual Property Clause, France exerted considerable pressure on the United States to enact new federal legislation, which it did under new authorization in the Commerce Clause.[56]

Even after the Paris and Berne Conventions were signed, bilateral treaties continued to be executed between states. However, through the Paris and Berne Conventions, together with the periodic negotiations taking place between states under their purview, intellectual property had been given an international, institutional structure, which became an independent organizational structure, in the second half of the twentieth century, through the WTO.

The fateful impacts of this globalizing framework of intellectual property law on multinational corporations can be seen in the annual reports of a corporation chartered in New York: International Business Machines (IBM). IBM, like Western Union and AT&T, was built on intellectual property, especially patents. However, IBM was also international from its very beginnings. IBM was a successor to the Tabulating Machine Company of Herman Hollerith, which, through licensing arrangements, had spun off international partnerships with British and German associates. As a result of these international foundations, international patents constituted a portion of the materially significant line item for patents on IBM's balance sheets into the 1940s.[57]

The creation of a global order of obligation, for intellectual property, structured on the basis of international treaties, was enabled by the proprietary voluntarism underpinning international legal relations, rooted deeply in Roman law. This

55 *Scientific American*, 1845–1909, Internet Archive: https://archive.org/details/scientific-american-1845–1909 (accessed September 7, 2020); also Jean Lipman, *Rufus Porter: Yankee Pioneer* (New York: Clarkson N. Potter, 1968); idem, *Rufus Porter: Rediscovered* (New York: The Hudson River Museum, 1980); Paul Israel, *Edison: A Life of Invention* (New York: John Wiley & Sons, 1998), 68.

56 In re Trademark Cases, 100 U.S. 82 (1879); Convention between the United States of America and France Concerning Trademarks, 16 Stat. 771 (1869); also Paul Duguid, "French Connections: The International Propagation of Trademarks in the Nineteenth Century," *Enterprise & Society* 10(1) (2009): 3–37.

57 Emerson W. Pugh, *Building IBM: Shaping an Industry and Its Technology* (Cambridge, MA: MIT Press, 1995).

proprietary voluntarism recognized states as property-owning subjects, treating their diplomatic agreements as contracts, that is, as formalized exercises of proprietary will that consensually created free-standing legal bonds and institutional structures. In the WTO, that proprietary voluntarism has today extended so far as to enable the creation of an organizational entity with legal personality which coordinates a globalized trading regime, including intellectual property protections, for nearly all nation-states around the world.

12.8 "ONE HUNDRED YEARS OF SOLICITUDE": AMERICA'S JURISPRUDENTIAL NARRATIVE OF PROGRESS

Throughout this book, I have periodically highlighted the role of jurisprudential narratives in contributing meaning to orders of obligation and legality. For lawyers trained in common law traditions, a jurisprudential narrative that has been especially meaningful is one that emphasizes the wisdom of courts in synthesizing strands of legal tradition, responding to technological and economic changes. We can see a version of this in an "end of the century" article published by Robert Merges, a prominent and influential US scholar of intellectual property law.[58]

Drawing on the magical-realist novel by Gabriel García Márquez, *One Hundred Years of Solitude*, Merges has labeled the twentieth century an era of "solicitude," as regards intellectual property in the United States. By this, Merges means that the twentieth century was a period in which US jurists displayed a characteristic attitude toward intellectual property and its legal protections: "interest or concern, with a hint of anxiety or fearfulness, a feeling that something is not quite right." This is ironic, of course, because American judges, lawmakers, and jurists had expended enormous efforts over the course of the twentieth century, in tinkering with the legal frameworks, seeking to get everything exactly right. In his article, Merges provides a helpful overview of such efforts, an overview that offers important insights into the twentieth century's "spirit" of globalized intellectual property law, as seen from a US legal perspective.[59]

An evident set of background viewpoints gives order and organization to Merges' narrative, a juristic worldview anchored in classical ideals of lawyers in the Anglo-American common law tradition. Merges idealizes incremental, thoughtful, adaptive changes as legal responses to technological and economic developments. The capacity of common law courts to wisely adapt principles of law to changing social conditions is one argument for their idealization as the "least dangerous branch" of government. And it is their incremental adaptiveness that has often been cited by

[58] Robert P. Merges, "One Hundred Years of Solicitude: Intellectual Property Law, 1900–2000," *California Law Review* 88 (2000): 2187–240.

[59] Merges, "One Hundred Years of Solicitude," 2189; Gabriel García Márquez, *One Hundred Years of Solitude*, translated by Gregory Rabassa (New York: HarperCollins, 1991).

those who argue for the superiority of common law-based approaches to law, relative to civilian approaches.[60]

Although Merges sees possibilities for thoughtful responsiveness in Congressional legislation, he likewise sees a strong propensity in Congress toward narrow responses to interest-specific (and possibly even firm-specific) priorities in lawmaking, responses to pressures from wealthy and powerful voices, and thus a failure to adequately ensure that the legal system wisely supports economic progress. "Progressivism" is the criterion for good and wise adaptations to technological change, according to Merges, and possibilities for such progressivism are constrained by legislative "rent-seeking," as seen in the lobbying for industry-specific responses to technological change.[61]

As Merges portrays the historical development, the twentieth century dawned with a legal framework that was progressive, in his sense. The law had been sufficiently adaptive and flexible to continually encourage, while adapting to, ongoing technological innovation. In the copyright arena, this was exemplified in judicial decisions extending legislative protections to cover moving pictures and film, invented by Thomas Edison. Even though the technology for moving pictures was new, progressive jurisprudence brought it within the broad description of the photographic art, enabling it to be covered by legislation drafted at a time when the technology for moving pictures did not exist. A judicial decision, in other words, drew creatively on principles defining photography – reproduction of images enabled through the action of light – and reasoned that, while the detailed means and mechanisms of the technology for moving pictures might be new, the overall technological process was sufficiently analogous to be covered by legislation protecting copyrights in photographs.[62]

At the beginning of the twentieth century, moreover, a consolidated legislative and administrative framework for patent, trademark, and copyright law mostly worked well, although the US Supreme Court had complicated things in 1879 by holding that trademarks could not be based on the Constitution's Intellectual Property Clause. In 1881, trademark legislation limited to international commerce was enacted under the Commerce Clause. A fuller framework for trademark protection, one that extended to interstate commerce within the United States, came in 1905, affording much-needed protection for national brands.[63]

60 Alexander M. Bickel, *The Least Dangerous Branch: The Supreme Court at the Bar of Politics*, 2nd ed. (New Haven: Yale University Press, 1986).

61 Merges, "One Hundred Years of Solicitude," 2192–8.

62 *Edison* v. *Lubin*, 122 F. 240 (3rd Cir. 1903); Merges, "One Hundred Years of Solicitude," 2192–3. The legislation at issue here was an 1865 act which had amended the legislative framework for US copyright law, dating from 1831. The 1831 legislative framework had, in turn, repealed and replaced the US Congress' first copyright act of 1790. 1 Stat. 124 (1790); 4 Stat. 436 (1831); 13 Stat. 540 (1865).

63 Merges, "One Hundred Years of Solicitude," 2206–10. Legislative consolidation; 16 Stat. 198 (1870); Trade-Mark Cases, 100 U.S. 82 (1879); 21 Stat. 502 (1881); 33 Stat. 724 (1905).

The first half of the twentieth century, according to Merges, was a period in which US courts and legislatures responded progressively to technological and economic changes. Trademark law was further adapted to facilitate the protection of national brands, and patent law was adjusted to the new realities of large-scale corporate research and development, a world in which individual geniuses are swamped by well-staffed and well-funded R&D (research and development) offices. Part of the legislative adaptation that this entailed facilitated, in turn, a "quiet administrative revolution," a restructuring of the US Patent Office to offer greater levels of expertise in the examination of patent applications.[64]

The dynamics of progressive adaptation changed, however, in the second half of the twentieth century. For Merges, the shift is marked primarily by new and disruptive technological changes, particularly the development of computing devices and the internet. Merges barely hints, however, at the extent to which development of these technologies was linked to existential struggles for national power, playing out during World War II and continuing into the Cold War.[65]

While Merges idealizes the capacity of common law courts to wisely and reasonably adapt to technological developments, he fails to acknowledge the extent to which this has been limited in the second half of the twentieth century, and especially for federal courts. A Supreme Court decision that is sometimes cited in this regard is *Erie Railroad Company* v. *Tompkins*, a 1938 opinion authored by Justice Brandeis, which was gradually extended in its implications over the course of the twentieth century. In this opinion, which narrowly applied to federal cases premised on "diversity jurisdiction," that is, litigation between residents of different US states, Justice Brandeis declared that "[t]here is no federal general common law." Hailed as a victory for legal positivism, this case restricted the jurisdictional power of federal courts in cases where state law is at issue: federal courts must apply state law, rather than substituting their own independent line of common law reasoning. However, the case has sometimes been read more broadly, as establishing limits on the capacities of federal courts to engage in common law reasoning, even where federal law is at issue.[66]

In intellectual property law cases, federal courts are often limited to statutory interpretation, and this, together with the general shift toward positive legality in contemporary jurisprudence, has contributed to interpretive developments that Peter Menell has labeled "textualism." Essentially the court seeks to tie a line of jurisprudential reasoning, say about patent eligibility, to the narrow meaning of a statutory text, and in so doing restricts its own broader capacities to articulate legal meanings and boundaries, drawing on previous jurisprudence and on its powers to

64 Merges, "One Hundred Years of Solicitude," 2215–17.

65 Ibid., 2200–5, 2213–15, 2233–40; Johnny Ryan, *A History of the Internet and the Digital Future* (London: Reaktion Books, 2010).

66 *Erie R. Co.* v. *Tompkins*, 304 U.S. 64, 78 (1938); Louise Weinberg, "A General Theory of Governance: Due Process and Lawmaking Power," *William and Mary Law Review* 54 (2013): 1057–121.

directly interpret the constitution's Intellectual Property Clause. This basically means that courts are not free – or at least they do not see themselves as being free – to exercise the wise and reasonable jurisprudence that Merges idealizes as the "progressivism" of common law. Given the fact that federal judges are unelected government officers serving for lifetime terms, that lack of jurisprudential freedom may seem to be a victory for democracy, but it also means that federal jurisprudence is tightly constrained to follow the logic of Congressional legislation and executive decision-making in treaty-based frameworks and administration, lacking the capacity to independently exercise judicial reasoning and thereby to provide meaningful reasons for judicial decisions.[67]

This becomes especially perilous for the Supreme Court when it endeavors to set limits on tendencies toward economic protectionism in intellectual property jurisprudence, something that the Court has tried to do in recent years. The incomprehensibility of recent patentability jurisprudence – decisions surrounding questions about what kinds of inventions can be patented – is arguably an instance of this. The Court is trying to set limits, while limiting itself to textualist foundations in ways that sow confusion. The failure to adequately set meaningful limits on the patent eligibility for social dimensions of human beings, as seen in business method patents and social networking patents, has been one result.[68]

The dangerous situation that this exacerbates can now be seen in the race to patent artificial intelligence which is currently playing out between the United States and China, among other technologically competitive nations.

12.9 THE CHALLENGE OF ARTIFICIAL INTELLIGENCE

On January 31, 2019, WIPO announced the release of a flagship study, utilizing patent data to reveal significant trends in the development of artificial intelligence. This report was intended to provoke discussion within and between WIPO member states over policies with respect to the expansion of artificial intelligence. That discussion is moving forward under the WIPO Secretariat, with public discussion sessions held in 2019 and 2020 (virtually).[69]

The implications of artificial intelligence for economies and societies around the world are dramatic, as is the rate of increase in patenting activity. The level of

67 Peter S. Menell, "Forty Years of Wondering in the Wilderness and No Closer to the Promised Land: *Bilski's* Superficial Textualism and the Missed Opportunity to Return Patent Law to Its Technological Mooring," *Stanford Law Review* 63 (2011): 1289–314.

68 Laura R. Ford, "Patenting the Social: Alice, Abstraction, and Functionalism in Software Patent Claims," *Cardozo Public Law, Policy and Ethics Journal* 14 (2016): 259–342, available at https://papers.ssrn.com/sol3/papers.cfm?abstract_id=2802750 (accessed July 1, 2019); *cf.* Menell, "Forty Years of Wandering," 1299–314.

69 WIPO and AI Policy: www.wipo.int/about-ip/en/artificial_intelligence/policy.html (accessed September 2, 2020). WIPO's announcement (January 31, 2019): www.wipo.int/pressroom/en/articles/2019/article_0001.html (accessed September 2, 2020).

urgency for policy-makers has been markedly enhanced, moreover, with the December 2019 announcement that "AI-implemented inventions" have now developed the capacity to invent and create "autonomously," such that the AI inventions themselves can now be credited with patent-eligible inventiveness. If the claims turn out to be true – and they are highly debatable – artificially intelligent machines (computer-implemented algorithms and inferential "machine learning" from large data sets) have now developed the capacity for creativity, sufficient to meet basic patent law requirements for technical inventiveness.[70]

The possibilities for artificially intelligent inventions (and other forms of creative expression by artificial intelligence) are attention-grabbing, in their own right, but there are also important geopolitical implications that come through clearly in the race to patent artificial intelligence. As the WIPO report reveals, this is a race that is, to some extent, playing out between the United States and China, one that helps us understand the broader trade disputes between these two nations.

China is a global leader in patenting activity for artificial intelligence, a position that is fully in keeping with the national priority that China has given to intellectual property protection over the past two decades. Far from being a systematic violator of intellectual property rights, as is perhaps the mistaken impression for many Americans, China is currently positioning herself as a strong protector of intellectual property, embracing intellectual property at the very highest political and military levels, as a central element in the Chinese nation's strategic plans for economic development.[71]

China National Intellectual Property Administration (CNIPA) is the state-level administrative organization overseeing the implementation of intellectual property-related protections. The CNIPA website includes extensive materials in English, indicating an obvious intention to communicate China's commitment to intellectual property protections to an English-speaking audience. Even before joining the WTO, and with rapidly developing sophistication, China has been performing an intention to recognize and protect intellectual property.[72]

As of May 2020, that performance has extended to the deepest possible level, for a civilian legal system, in the announcement of a new Chinese civil code, one that embeds protections for intellectual property at a foundational level analogous to the US constitution. Unlike France, China has made intellectual property part of the bedrock architecture for a civilian legal system, one modeled with strong doses of pragmatism on a combination of US institutions and European historical experience, but one that will nonetheless ultimately be rooted at the level of meaning in

70 "WIPO Technology Trends 2019 – Artificial Intelligence," available at www.wipo.int/tech_trends/en/artificial_intelligence (accessed September 2, 2020). AI implemented inventions: Ryan Abbott, "The Artificial Inventor Project," WIPO Magazine (December 2019), available at www.wipo.int/wipo_magazine/en/2019/06/article_0002.html (accessed September 2, 2020).

71 Commissioner's Message, CNIPA Commissioner Shen Changyu, http://english.cnipa.gov.cn/aboutsipo/index.htm (accessed September 7, 2020).

72 Ibid.

Chinese cultural frameworks, including traditions of Confucianism and Buddhism that remain culturally significant, even when they are unacknowledged in a formally communist state.[73]

In Chapter 2, I described performances as a kind of social action, action that demonstrates an intentional commitment to orders of obligation. In subsequent chapters I have written about these performances using the language of "legality," highlighting the ways in which contemporary western modes of legality (positive and natural legality) have developed through the nationalization and secularization of Roman-Christian modes. The medievalist Geoffrey Koziol has emphasized the extent to which performances are political and cultural, displays of commitment that are oriented toward orders of meaning and that enact an intentionality to make a difference in a current array of social and political possibilities. Jeffrey Alexander has also emphasized the cultural and political importance of social performances, in constituting both public sphere and civil society. Returning to Hannah Arendt's conception of culture, as briefly surveyed in Chapter 2, we can see performances of legality as a type of social action that is demonstrative of legal value-commitments, of faithfulness to legal values and ideals, which become embodied in intellectual and artistic artifacts, things that we make and create through words and technical craftsmanship. Our globalized legal order placing intellectual property protections at the center of inter-national legal value-commitments is, in a way, a type of historically-created artifact, one that our governments cultivate and care for, in their geo-political negotiations, conflicts, and ongoing relationships.[74]

We can see the trade dynamics between the United States and China in this light, both narrowly in the rituals surrounding the Phase One treaty agreement of January 15, 2020, and more broadly in the ways these nations are warily circling one another, alternately displaying their commitments to national power, to legality, and to culturally informed orders of obligation. China's committed embrace of intellectual property protections, performed repeatedly and dramatically over the past decade, culminating in comprehensive overhaul of China's national legal system, demonstrates and memorializes a recognition that intellectual property is a vital infrastructure for national state power. And all these performances, of course, because they are memorialized and recorded in legal documents, will leave vital legacies for the future, a future in which intellectual property will undoubtedly continue to play an essential part in strategies for cultural, economic, military, and political power.

73 "Civil Code of the People's Republic of China," NPC Observer, available at https://npcobserver.com/legislation/civil-code/ (accessed September 7, 2020); Mark Cohen, "An Unwelcome Addition and a Welcome Subtraction in the Technology Transfer Provisions of the New Civil Code," China IPR Blog entry dated June 1, 2020, available at https://chinaipr.com/2020/06/01/an-unwelcome-addition-and-a-welcome-subtraction-in-the-technology-transfer-provisions-of-the-new-civil-code/ (accessed September 7, 2020).

74 Geoffrey Koziol, *The Politics of Memory and Identity in Carolingian Royal Diplomas: The West Frankish Kingdom (840–987)* (Turnhout, Belgium: Brepols Publishers, 2012).

12.10 LOVE AND DANGER IN GLOBALIZED ORDERS OF OBLIGATION

We are living in a frightening moment of human history, when the scale of social power wielded by national and corporate leaders surpasses comprehension, and when the pace of innovation has accelerated to a degree that threatens to exceed our meaning-seeking capacities, both in jurisprudence and in our daily lives. In such moments, I believe that we can find comfort and wisdom in historical experience, because we can see that our forebears have also faced unprecedented and frightening circumstances that are closely analogous. While the contemporary circumstances are certainly new, the challenges involved are not, and we can learn important lessons from the past, both by recognizing mistakes and by taking courage in the extraordinary capacities – for love, creativity, and fidelity – that we have, as human beings.

The challenge, I think, is to respond, not with fear and anger, but with openness and a genuine desire to learn. We can seek to understand the cultural traditions that have contributed such extraordinary capacities, on the part of new and growing nations like China and India, to bring new, national orders of obligation into the world. We can seek to understand the ways that law is meaningful, within these national orders of obligation, and in the ways that people understand their social ties. In doing so, we will undoubtedly see aspects of legal meaning that are entwined with religious meaning, together with concepts of communal belonging, that are beautiful, wise, and good. In recognizing the beauty, wisdom, and goodness, we will perhaps experience what Krister Stendahl (1921–2008) reportedly called "holy envy": the experience of seeing something, in another cultural tradition, that we "admire and wish might find greater scope" in our own.[75]

Only time can tell whether, and to what extent, cultural differences in the orders of obligation that give meaning to intellectual property-related legal traditions in the United States and China, for example, will matter decisively at an empirical level. Similar questions are also involved in comparative studies with Europe, Japan, and India, as intellectual property institutions have developed there. What all these national and international legal traditions have in common, however, is an anchoring in Roman law traditions, which have certainly influenced the civil law countries of Europe, but which have also exercised a deep influence in common law countries, like England and the United States, together with a host of civilian national states around the world. Through international treaties, premised on Roman law foundations, Roman legal traditions are now part of the basic architecture for global legal relationships between nations, facilitating the kind of law-changing pressure that has contributed to the embrace of intellectual property around the world.

[75] John F. Hobbins, "Krister Stehndahl's Three Rules of Religious Understanding," *Ancient Hebrew Poetry*, May 7, 2010, available at https://ancienthebrewpoetry.typepad.com/ancient_hebrew_poetry/2010/05/krister-stendahls-three-rules-of-religious-understanding.html (accessed September 7, 2020).

This book has been premised on the belief that culture and religious traditions matter deeply for the way that law works in giving order and meaning to our daily social lives. The very emergence of intellectual property, as a legal institution with roots in the Christianization of Roman law traditions, I have argued, is evidence for this. As countries with legal traditions rooted in Hinduism, Buddhism, Confucianism, and Islam have embraced intellectual property protections, we will see how cultural differences in orders of obligation matter at a more granular level in the application of legal principles. And we will, I hope and expect, see things that we love in these orders of obligation, things that can inform our efforts to rediscover the meaning in our own jurisprudential traditions.

In the area of computer-implemented inventions, however, which have now encroached into all dimensions of our social and personal lives, I strongly believe that we need clearer, categorical limits on patent eligibility, which would set firm boundaries on the extent to which property claims are allowed to reach into the social dimensions of human life. So far, the scholarship on intersections between human rights and intellectual property norms has not, to my knowledge, focused much attention on patent eligibility for computer-implemented inventions. Other concerns, particularly for developing countries, doubtless seem more pressing, and map more neatly onto the existing frameworks for human right law. Nonetheless, I believe there are real and pressing reasons for concern with computer-implemented inventions directed toward the management of social interaction between human beings, especially given the difficulties that the Supreme Court has faced in its efforts to articulate limitations on patent eligibility.[76]

I worry that we are allowing our race for economic and political power to trump our commitments to basic humanistic concerns, together with our commitments to a flourishing civil society, which are deeply embedded in our constitutional tradition. With the rise of artificial intelligence, fueled by massive databases from social networks like Facebook, the possibilities for exercise of social power by nongovernmental entities, under the cover of property, are truly alarming.[77]

A tragic and paradoxical possibility for globalized intellectual property law, which seems to loom menacingly on the horizon, is that it will continue to depend on strong national states while at the same time appropriating (often for short-term, economic profit) the very cultural sources that have historically empowered those states, for better and for worse. The globalized expansion of intellectual property law, which has coincided with the growth of computer-based telecommunication networks, means that we may be losing our capacities to form social ties outside the dominions of Silicon Valley moguls, globalized investment funds, and transnational technocrats, whose claims to lordly ownership now extend to the very

76 For a more extended discussion, see Ford, "Patenting the Social," passim; Laurence R. Helfer and Graeme W. Austin, *Human Rights and Intellectual Property: Mapping the Global Interface* (New York: Cambridge University Press, 2011).

77 Ford, "Patenting the Social," 316–42.

methods and computerized means by which we seek to carry out our daily social interactions and communications.

It is through these computer-based social networks that we now exercise many aspects of citizenship. And that means that our basic concepts of belonging, our sense that we are part of a governing community, are terribly vulnerable to manipulation and control, under the cover of property. The consumer citizenship that Michael Mann describes is older, of course, than the Amazons and Facebooks of the world, but it is part of a commercial world that has been built through national branding, in a national society increasingly structured around economic consumption.

Intellectual property fuels the innovation and creativity that offer ever-expanding possibilities for our consumption. And it is our consumption of these ever-expanding, creative products that keeps our economy afloat. But our need for rootedness in stable and meaningful governing communities runs deeper than our economy-sustaining consumption.

If that need is too long ignored, we will become lethal to ourselves and others, without even meaning to. Indeed, we already are.

12.11 CONCLUSION

Today, intellectual property is part of a globalized system of nation-states which are regularly pressured to adhere to rules for economic trade, struggling for mastery with one another through transnational bodies like the WTO. Sometimes, however, trade-related arguments over intellectual property escape the bounds of institutional frameworks, breaking out into aggressive announcements sent by means of a globalized telecommunications network that has itself been built on a foundation of intellectual property. We see this starkly in the crude "diplomacy by Tweet" of a sitting US president, but it is also evident in news reports highlighting tariff-related threats exchanged between national leaders.

China and the United States are not the only parties involved. Literally the whole world is involved, and many developing countries want to ensure that, whatever principles the economic power houses manage to agree upon, they also establish terms for global trade that enable developing countries to grow their own economies.

Nonetheless, even as the multilateral processes of dialog and dispute resolution seem to be increasingly challenged in the WTO, and as political leaders express doubts about the possibilities for further agreement in bilateral negotiations between the United States and China, China is moving forward with strategic plans for national economic growth, centered upon protection for intellectual property. And, with fewer and clearer limitations on patent eligibility for computer-implemented inventions, relative to the United States, China is racing ahead with patented innovations on artificial intelligence.

Our only hope in such a situation, I think, is to reach deeply into the cultural traditions that have given meaning to our present-day legal systems while at the same time turning, in a spirit of open-minded learning, to the cultural traditions that give meaning to legal systems in other nations around the world. The possibility of "holy envy," as reportedly articulated by the Lutheran theologian Krister Stendahl, is one in which love for the beauty, goodness, and wisdom to be found in other cultural traditions need not threaten our commitment to the beauty, goodness, and wisdom to be found in our own cultural traditions.[78]

Finding something that we can love and care for together, in a spirit of mutual learning, might just help us to avoid rising aggression in fear and mutual recrimination. My fervent hope is that such a spirit of mutual learning can enable us, working together, to articulate principled limits on the appropriation, through intellectual property claims, of social dimensions of human beings, limits that are meaningful from the perspective of ancient cultural traditions, which, after all, have been learning from one another for a very long time.

[78] Hobbins, "Krister Stehndahl's Three Rules of Religious Understanding," *Ancient Hebrew Poetry*.

Conclusion

The Intellectual Property of Nations

As happened in many other cases, this prerogative of the king came to be regarded as the right of the subject.

– Frederic William Maitland[1]

With the discussion of intellectual property protections for artificial intelligence, a discussion that is especially urgent in connection with the claim that artificially intelligent devices now possess the power to "autonomously" invent and create, we have reached the end of a long story, a story that leads from a world united under the power of ancient Rome to the globalized world of our present day.

Powers to invent and create are today being "automated" and appropriated, in the form of computer-implemented inventions, organized through telecommunications networks which facilitate and govern in all the ways that we interact on a daily basis, giving order and direction to the ways we engage in commercial interaction, political action, and even our religious rituals. The conviction underlying this lengthy book is that we need to have an intuitive grasp of the full story of intellectual property, in its sociological and religious dimensions, in order to be prepared to take an evaluative stance on its place in our contemporary world.

I have sought to tell a story about how intellectual property emerged, and about how it has been built into the foundations of our modern nation-state system. As a matter of factual understanding, this story involves geopolitical dynamics in the national development of social capacities to cooperate and compete, drawing vast populations into the struggles for power between nation-states. Michael Mann's analysis of the role that organized social power has played in the development toward a globalized infrastructure of state power coordinating networks of people linked together through cultural, economic, military, and political ties offers, I think, a valuable framework in order to grasp these broader, geopolitical dynamics. My effort, however, has primarily been to understand the role that legal and religious

1 F. W. Maitland, *The Constitutional History of England* (Cambridge, UK: Cambridge University Press, 1908), 271.

traditions have played, working together across time, in contributing to these networks of social power, focusing on the development of intellectual property law as an intrinsic part of the broader developments toward a nation-state system rendered fiercely dynamic in modern capitalism.

With the accelerating efforts to patent artificial intelligence which are playing out right now in a struggle for geopolitical power between the United States and China (among other nations), the time has come, I think, to take an evaluative stance. Whenever we have to make such determinations – to make judgments – orders of obligation become fundamental, not only for understanding, but also for political action.

Social theory and social science are informed by our value-commitments, but it is also the case that, in crossing a line from understanding to action, we cross from what can be known, with probabilistic degrees of (un)certainty, into the realm of existential questions, and leaps of faith. There are no universal rules to determine what we do here, only traditions carried forward from the past which offer principles, models, and paradigms, images with which we try to work as we try to think together about who we want to be in the world, and perhaps about who we want to be like, as we figure out who we will be in the world. We cross, to summarize, from knowledge to judgment, where character and tradition become vitally important to the ways that we act in the world, as well as the ways that we understand what our action means.

Narratives, significantly, contribute to knowledge, to understanding, and to judgment. Knowing how someone has come to be the person that they are helps us to know them in a deeper way, and it also helps us to make better judgments about them, for example, about whether we can rely on them. Narratives about social institutions and organizations, similarly, can help us to gain experiential knowledge about the character of those institutions and organizations, to see how they are likely to contribute to future patterns of social behavior, and therefore to make evaluative judgments about the extent to which they should be endorsed and supported.

The institution of intellectual property, as I have narrated its lengthy emergence, has been a related outgrowth of longer and deeper causes, to which I have often devoted greater attention. Indeed, patient and charitable readers, who have followed this lengthy story to its end, would be amply forgiven if they have, at times, felt a sense of frustration, for in some ways, surely, intellectual property has seemed epiphenomenal, in the story I have told. I have treated intellectual property as an almost incidental sign and signal, bearing witness to the character of governing communities that have constituted themselves in recognizing it, and then elevated it into an organizing principle for a global order of inter-national, social power.

Geistiges Eigentum, Spiritual Ownership. This is a somewhat literalistic rendering of the German phrase for intellectual property, and there is something profoundly revealing in the phrase. Through the legal institution of intellectual property, nation-states around the world claim ownership over materially embodied, creative ideas, temporarily allocating that ownership to relatively small groups of people so that the ideas might be controlled in ways that are advantageous, benefitting nation-states in their competitive struggles with one another.

In the modern nation-state system, intellectual property is part of a highly impersonal order of social power, one that links public and private spheres of social life, with very deep effects in everyday experience, while yet being fragmented into nodes and links that we name under a wide variety of headings: economy, society, state, government, politics, military, religion, and emancipatory fight for social justice. Copyrights, patents, trademarks, and trade secrets radiate through all of these, with potent concentration in the computers we incessantly use, and in the telecommunications networks that link those computers together in a globalized network. What we have in intellectual property, and in the nation-state system with which it is globally entwined, is an impersonal order of social power, a structure of lordship in which human lords exercise power impersonally, increasingly through computer-based social networks.

At the core of intellectual property, as a legal institution, is prerogative power, which was a medieval development of ancient *imperium* – the power to give commands that were binding in virtue of a hierarchical relationship between the giver of the command and the recipient. In the Middle Ages, prerogative power was increasingly defined through law, and the definitions increasingly emphasized proprietary dimensions in the prerogative power. With the rise of national sovereignty, as seen in the rise of parliaments and national legislative bodies around the world, the property of monarchs became the property of subjects. The process happened with peculiar clarity in Britain because the prerogative power had developed there in extremity and precocity, and in ways that emphasized formal definition through law at an early stage.

In the western historical experience, as seen again with peculiar clarity in Britain, Roman imperial law has been mediated by the Christian church. The positive and natural law of western modernity is marked by a feudal transformation, which is a name for the historical period in which Roman imperial structures were gradually Christianized, while the Christian church was gradually Romanized. Reformation and Renaissance are names that we give to historical periods in which efforts were made to render Christian commitments deeper, and to break with legal forms that were increasingly seen as being both false and harmful. In the sixteenth and seventeenth centuries, repeated cycles of reform led to definitive splits between secular and spiritual legal structures, and to the early formation of national churches. The birth of European nation-states is inextricably tied to these developments, as is the emergence of intellectual property: a new type of legal property that recognizes the appropriation of creative products of the human mind.

Our nation-state system – which is now a world system – has been constituted through the gradual but nonetheless intentional creation of intellectual property, an infrastructure of state power that functions by encouraging technological innovation and literary/artistic production, on a massive scale.

Intellectual property emerged as part of the modern nation-state system and has contributed to the foundations of the nation-state system. What is it, though, that makes for this magnetic connection – what Max Weber, drawing on Goethe, might have called an "elective affinity" – between the nation-state system and intellectual property? *Why* did intellectual property emerge as part of the modern nation-state?

The nation-state, I have asserted, is a project of the will, a project that rests hopes for a future of well-being on national, economic growth, fueled by innovation and creativity. I have presented two lines of development leading to the formation of this project. The first line of development, rooted theoretically in Max Weber's ideal types of legitimate rulership, views the modern nation-state as an order of obligation, one that is oriented toward a characteristically modern type of faith, a faith in legality. The second line of development, rooted in Weber's legal sociology, traces the development of intellectual property as an infrastructure of state power, as an accretion of legal rationalities, both formal and substantive, that have developed around ancient practices involving legal documents, which I have discussed as instruments of legal power.

The modern nation-state system, powered partly by intellectual property law, is fundamentally an order of obligation, an organization of vast social networks, in which legal instruments with ancient roots performatively link people and organizations together with their national polities into a joint project of economic expansion. The social formation story that I have told in tracing the development of this system is one in which Roman law and Biblical law were drawn together under the organizational authority of bishops and kings to support a very modern, and very strange, adaptation of Abrahamic faith traditions, an adaptation in which faith is placed in legality and hope is placed in innovation. A characteristic set of anxieties accompanies this modern faith tradition, one that we explored in the previous chapter – anxieties that our nation will fall behind in the race for innovation, and will lose its fragile position of dominance in a global order of power.

Two cultural revolutions have been fundamental – "earthquakes" in the metaphorical imagery I have used – to the story that I have told. The first of these came in the Christianization of empire, and in the imperialization of Christianity. The second came in the liberalization of Christianity, and in the Christianization of liberalism. In this second movement, as seen perhaps most explicitly in the sermons of John Tillotson, national prosperity became a sign of God's favor, something that we should consciously seek to promote, through our legal structures and in our moral lives.

This is an articulate and conscious blueprint for a national project, one that the American Revolution embedded into the US constitutional structure, and that the French Revolution radicalized. Intellectual property is an integral part of that nation-state project. Through legal frameworks of intellectual property, granting lordly powers over products of the human mind, we seek to fuel the powers of genius, and we work to make our national states powerful.

The power that we see in our national economies, militaries, and politics, I have argued, is ultimately social – the power that comes from our human capacity to obligate ourselves to one another, to our local and national communities, to our faith in legality, and to our God or gods. In obligating ourselves to one another, in communities of various kinds, we build structures of power which can be deployed for a variety of purposes, both good and evil. Instruments of legal power – like medieval diplomas, contracts, modern patents, and modern treaties – enact and memorialize our performative intentions to bind ourselves to one another and to our national governments. In doing so, however, they also perform an intentionality to bind and exclude others.

Here, I think, is a fundamental tragedy that we see in intellectual property, which is really a tragedy of our nation-state project, of the role that law plays in that project, and of the social nature of property. The tragedy is also a kind of paradox, seen in the fact that nation-states and national legal systems are both inclusive and exclusive, they bind together some and they exclude others. And, as Hannah Arendt has shown so powerfully in her studies of totalitarianism, nation-states have become necessary for recognition of foundational human rights, indeed for the exercise of very basic human capacities. Nation-states are, in other words, a source of human liberation and terrible suffering, at the same time.

The "feudal transformation" of the European Middle Ages was important, in our tragic story, because it marked a moment when powers of social obligation, mobilized through instruments of legal power, began to be intentionally deployed for purposes of systematic wealth accumulation. Traditional blueprints for the wielding of power and authority began to be replaced by newly intentional and voluntaristic patterns. The first developments were seen in new monastic orders within the church and in feudal bonds between aristocratic warriors, connecting them to one another and to landed territory. These bonds of promissory fidelity were sacralized through oaths and vows, and through instruments of legal power, like charters and diplomas.

Zones of exclusivity, in the feudal worlds of northwestern Europe, were initially about powers of jurisdiction – powers to say what the law is. But the exercise of these powers was a service for which people were compelled to pay, and it generated revenue. A good steward of these revenues was charged with the responsibility to reinvest them, and sometimes these reinvestments were used to fund technological infrastructures, even innovative ones. An example that we saw in Chapter 7 was the windmill. Gradually, lords and kings recognized that zones of exclusivity, like the traditional ones for jurisdictional powers, could be created around innovative activities, as a way of channeling and controlling those innovations for the benefit of king and kingdom, or for the republic, as in Venice and the fledgling United States. In the light of these new experiences and dawning realizations, old Roman law precedents and Biblical texts began to be read in new ways, conjoined with local customary norms and political priorities. The western legal traditions of common law and civil law were outgrowths of these new readings.

I have presented these developments, ideal-typically, as an accretion of rationalities, both formal and substantive, around instruments of legal power-granting privileges to favored subjects. The earliest roots of such instruments, I have argued, are to be found in Persian and Hellenistic documents, which were developed by Roman jurists into imperial instruments of legal power. Christianity emerged as a faith tradition within this context, with conceptions of law strongly marked by the character of Roman imperial law, together with Biblical law. In the synthesis of Roman and Biblical legal traditions, instruments of legal power were adapted in ways that began to favor economic expansion. This was not at first intentional, but the economic benefits eventually became apparent, particularly to English and French kings, in their repeated struggles for power. In French and English privileges, granted through letters patent to enable jurisdictional powers and market exclusivity, we see early precursors to modern intellectual property, which did support economic expansion and technological innovation, albeit probably initially as an unintended consequence.

In this story, as I have told it, the instruments of legal power came first. I have drawn on a theoretical approach to such instruments articulated by Geoffrey Koziol, a diplomatist and scholar of medieval legal documents. I have found in Koziol's work a rich conception of the ways that legal documents matter, first and foremost because of the ways that they connect us to each other. In Koziol's language, these legal documents are performative, in the sense that they enact the social realities they purport to prescribe. In Koziol's view, this social enactment is more important than the behaviors prescribed, at least in the immediate context of the social relationships being affected and effectuated. But Koziol goes further than this because he also focuses attention on the memorializing functions that instruments of legal power can have, memorials that extend not only to the maintenance and governance of social relationships, but also to the identities that are expressed and memorialized in instruments of legal power.

Instruments of legal power, from this perspective, are forms of social action, in a Weberian sense. They are a type of social action that is oriented to others and invested with meaning. They are, moreover, oriented to orders of obligation that help to define the form that they take and the meaning that they have. But, because they take place through writings that are recorded and copied, they also become a cultural object and memorial which can be taken up into jurisprudential narratives, thereby becoming part of a much larger story. In both the performances and the jurisprudential narratives, moreover, the orders of obligation to which they are oriented are reinforced and then carried forward in the form of legal traditions.

Instruments of legal power have been transmitted to us through jurisprudential narratives and related doctrinal traditions, through stories that theorize the instruments, offering a way of seeing their purpose and their meaning. This purpose and meaning is what ultimately guides the social process I have called semantic legal ordering. To put this another way, it is the stories that provide a background of meaning enabling an ever-ongoing process of (re)defining legal concepts and principles.

The feudal transformation in western Europe was important in the overall story of western law because it marked a moment in which Biblical legal traditions emphasizing covenantal relationships became paradigmatic in two ways. First, covenantal relations became the ideal for social and political relations, not only in the relationship between a lord and his vassal, but also between a man and his wife. In the intimate sphere of sexuality, in the loyalty between warriors, and in the relationship between subjects, their lords, and their king, Christian virtues of faith, hope, and love became the orienting values in a spiritually organizing ideal. This cultural ideal was backed by very real powers, not only by the physical powers of the sword, but also by spiritual powers of excommunication. Relations of obligation and violent power became inflected with Christian communitarian ideals and conceptions of ultimate obligation to a divine, covenantal partner. This stabilized and empowered emerging forms of governing community in Europe.

At the same time, however, the covenantal conception of relations had the potential to be revolutionary in placing limits on the social power of lords and kings alike. The archetypal moment for this, in the legal traditions of the English-speaking world, came in the year 1215, a moment when, with the benefit of hindsight, we can see kings and popes becoming bound by the "rule of law," a law that governs the wielders of social power and their subjects alike.

Patents are the oldest of the four basic forms of intellectual property, and these grow out of the "letters patent" of the British Empire. It is more accurate to say, however, that they represent a formalizing limitation of British letters patent – a set of formal legal boundaries on the ways in which British monarchs could use their letters patent. This limitation turns out to be very important, because it is part of a broader movement in the formalization of law, one that stretches forward from the "feudal transformation." Formal rationality in law, as it has developed since the feudal transformation, involves semantic boundaries and covenantal understandings of the social world. These are the legacies of feudalism that stand at the very core of our modern nation-state project, and it is this often-invisible core that a long-term perspective on the emergence of intellectual property can help to uncover.

The US Supreme Court recently characterized a patent as a "public franchise." The Court offered very little reflection on the meaning of this, and bloggers have poked fun, but this book reflects the conviction that there is a very deep truth in the Court's characterization. The franchise is a legal instrument of power that stretches back to late antiquity, a Frankish adaptation of Roman imperial letters. Historically speaking, it is quite literally true that intellectual property is an instrument of empire.

But we must immediately qualify this to see what it means. Empire is, for us, a bad word. For the Romans, it was not. *Imperium* was the power to issue legal commands that were backed with the threat of violent force. It could be an instrument of peace, offering the security of "law and order," and it was closely associated with the *pax Romana*, which was greatly valued and gratefully accepted by many throughout long stretches of Roman history. The *imperium* of the Romans was embraced as the *bannum* of the Carolingians, and, in the regions of France where collapse of Carolingian imperial power meant a rise in localized brutality and violence, the *bannum* was something that could be a source of security. It was also something that came in the form of a legal grant, a franchise, given in the form of a royal charter. It was a beneficent gift because, as much as it might be a source of social peace, it was also a source of economic revenue and power.

In the feudal transformation, traditional legal customs involving discretionary grants of privilege were reinterpreted as binding promises on both sides: a foundation of modern contract law and the "proprietary voluntarism" that it ushered into the world. This reinterpretation marked one of those "track-laying" moments of history – one that Weber identified with a break from traditionalism in the Protestant Reformation.

This breaking moment came, in part, because European clerics were reading their Bibles differently. Here is an important place where the social process I have called semantic legal ordering made a very real difference in history. A new historical literalism came into Biblical interpretation, contributing to new conceptions of law and legal practice. The final revolutionary effects of this Biblical reading played out over a very long time, and a complex series of radical moments in the Protestant Reformation were defining, especially in establishing a national foundation for law-giving, as for legal positivism more broadly. Nonetheless, the new forms of Biblical interpretation stretch much further back into the Middle Ages, giving legal foundations to the earlier radical movements in earth-shattering conflicts with popes and kings: the urban communes, mendicant orders, early universities, and the early foundations of the English Parliament.

Biblical scholars sometimes discuss the overarching shift as a transition from "Alexandrian" modes of Biblical interpretation to "Antiochene." This language transports us back into the world of the eastern Mediterranean, with a reminder that some of the deepest cultural legacies for our modern world have come from the northeastern tip of Africa and the northwestern tip of Asia: from the Hellenistic cities of Alexandria and Antioch.

Europe was once the wild and backward west of the world, and the Americas were not yet an inkling for Eurasian sophisticates. It was in this cosmopolitan world, connected into a single world through the Mediterranean and the new legal powers of Rome, that the foundations were laid for our ultramodern legal institutions, including intellectual property law.

What was it about this cosmopolitan world that made it so historically powerful? In Michael Mann's language, it was the birth of a new set of ideologies that each linked themselves, albeit in different ways, to the covenantal faith of Abraham: Judaism, Christianity, and Islam. These religious traditions, in different ways, each carried legacies from Greek, Roman, Phoenician, and Persian religion, even as they added something distinctive and new in their legal and prophetic scriptures. In focusing on the "leading edge of power" in the west, however, Mann focuses on Christianity, which was socially powerful because it was transcendently intensive and extensive.

WHY TRANSCENDENTLY INTENSIVE?

Here I believe we must return to Max Weber, who adds something vital to Mann's account. In his *Economic Ethics of the World Religions*, Weber focused on the salvation-logics of religious traditions in explaining how they could have what Mann calls "track-laying power." In Christianity, the salvation-logic is a narrative of "redemption" – paying a debt or a ransom-price – and this is a salvation-logic that depends for its validity and power on the validity and power of Mosaic law. It was only because they believed the Mosaic law to be still valid – because they believed that God kept his promises – that the early Christians, like Paul, believed the sacrificial death of a man named Jesus to be ultimately meaningful. Christian acceptance of this redemption meant their acceptance by God, and their incorporation into a religious community, which was part of an overarching, providential plan for human beings, Jew and Gentile, male and female, slave and free, together.

This narrative, according to Mann, spoke powerfully to an age of Roman unification, an age in which questions of identity had become problems to be solved. Christianity offered a new, vocational identity – one to which we are called by God, a call that we can either accept or reject, rather than one ascribed from birth in an ethnic or national grouping – to the Greco-Roman world, and this became part of a salvation-logic about living well in relation to a transcendently loving, good and wise God, one that has spoken powerfully to the human condition in the form of sacred, written scriptures.

Salvation-logics are important, in Weberian sociology, because they provide orders of meaning toward which people orient themselves, in their everyday activity, and particularly in their economic activity. It is this profound linkage between religion and economic activity that is so characteristic of Weberian insight into contemporary social dynamics. As human beings, we are meaning-seeking creatures, according to Weber, and in seeking meaning, we follow the salvation-logics of religious, ethical, political, aesthetic, or experiential meaning systems, which have been rationalized over long stretches of human history by culture-carrying intellectuals. Their track-laying ideas have helped to establish the channels along which everyday economic and political interests propel human behavior. And among these track-laying ideas are religiously inflected conceptions of law, traceable to covenantal and Biblical conceptions of law, as well as Roman imperial law, which today form part of the deep background to modern conceptions of property and contracts.

In the wake of the Protestant Reformation and with the rise of positivism and empiricism in philosophy and science, the sacramental and covenantal senses of law have been pushed deeper and deeper down into an unrecognized and unacknowledged aspect of the way that we relate to "law and order." Our relationship to law is deeply religious, but we have lost our recognition of this fact. We trust in law to solve our social problems, while we use it mainly as a weapon of force rather than as a teaching about how to live.

But this itself is a deeply and ambivalently Christian way of relating to law. The apostle Paul, who regarded himself as the bearer of a special mission to non-Jewish Christian converts, used the metaphor of a pedagogue in explaining the role of law (*nomos*). Law teaches us by disciplining and terrifying us. Only in this way can we be brought to a recognition of our limitation, frailty, and ultimate vulnerability to the negating, corruptive power of sin. The function of law is primarily punitive, in this rhetorical presentation, which was significant to the understanding of early modern Reformers, like Martin Luther.

In Chapter 1, I argued that law is meaningful and powerful because of its history. Through this book, I have endeavored to show that, for long stretches of human history, and around the world, law has been much more than a technocratic method of administration. In the world of eastern Mediterranean antiquity, people related to law as a repository of wisdom and as a means of social governance. But it was a means of social governance *because* it was a repository of wisdom. The wisdom it contained was a wisdom about how to live well, about how to relate to each other in our political and social groupings, and about how to relate to – to cultivate and care for – our gods. This basic conception of law has been carried forward in the Abrahamic faith traditions, and it was retained in Christianity until the time of the Protestant Reformation. But with the experience of politicized violence unleashed through the Protestant Reformation, law became nationalized, naturalized, and liberalized. A newly positivistic conception of public law, rooted in Roman law-based conceptions of imperial sovereignty, contributed to new legal bonds between nation-states, covenantal promises to keep the peace for the sake of wealth generation if not for justice and righteousness, since it now seemed impossible to reach agreement about what these mean.

In the modern, liberal nation-state, the conviction that state and church should be separated has meant that law becomes, almost inevitably, a rationalizing tool of the state, in service of economic power. We seem to have lost the sense that it can be, or should be, anything else.

And yet, at the same time, law works as a carrier for the salvation-narratives of modernity. We see this with intellectual property, which carries the conviction that innovation and creativity can save us. In incentivizing innovation and creativity, as in preventing "consumer confusion," intellectual property makes our national communities more prosperous, enabling the mass consumption that fuels our national economy and making us better off. This is a salvation-logic, pure and simple. What differentiates it from recognizably religious salvation-narratives is simply the fact that it is this-worldly rather than other-worldly.

Salvation-narratives and logics, for Weber, offer solutions to the problem of human suffering, and they can come in either this-worldly or other-worldly forms. Our secular project of national world-building is a project of human salvation no less than the projects of Jean Calvin in Geneva or St. Paul in Corinth.

Many people comment on the tone of vicious anger that has lately entered US politics. We are perhaps waking up to the fact (which we have always really known) that the nation-state cannot save us. That is a terrifying recognition, and it is no wonder that the response of many is one of furious anger. Perhaps, rather than condemning that anger, we can try to understand it. In doing so, perhaps we can also move toward a more realistic understanding of the nation-state, and of the role that law plays in the nation-state project.

The nation-state cannot save us, but it can be a stabilizing home base, helping us to live at peace with each other and to offer basic forms of sustenance and protection to one another. The same is true of private property, just so long as we do not elevate it into a transcendent principle.

Property, including intellectual property, can play an important role in our political communities, but this means it should be negotiated and discussed as part of our democratic processes. It should be a subject of compromise and mutual learning, not a transcendent absolute. Studying the development of intellectual property can be almost therapeutic in enabling us to see just how immanent the ideology of private property in products of the human mind has actually been. The possibility was contemplated already in the time of Cicero, and property-like claims to creative products were made well before Cicero.

Modern intellectual property, I have argued, is legal institution, one that works distinctively through instruments of legal power, one that helps to link people together into social networks, associations, and communities. It is an instrument of legal power that connects people in a specific kind of way, creating zones of exclusivity around products of intellectual creativity and innovation, while at the same time solidifying a relationship of dependency on the modern state. As a bureaucratically administered nation-state, this modern state is itself a kind of community – a governing community – one that draws us into a shared project of national wealth in a hoped-for future, and that guarantees the zones of exclusivity around innovative and creative activities with tremendous social power.

In recognizing and guaranteeing the existence of intellectual property, as a legal institution, the state encourages the innovative and creative activities that we believe are the linchpin of our economic and political success. We have designed the modern nation-state to be a generator of innovation because we believe it makes us wealthy and powerful, and historical evidence does provide support for this belief.

Intellectual property did emerge very early in the nation-states that have become globally powerful, and it was intentionally constituted as part of the foundational legal infrastructure in those nation-states. Other nation-states that have since joined the global arena of national competition and cooperation have been compelled – legally, politically, and economically – to contend with intellectual property as part of their own projects in national state-building.

In clinging to our hopes for national wealth and power, however, we are giving tremendous and dangerous amounts of social power to technology companies, like Facebook, and to global franchises, like McDonald's. And we are, arguably, destroying ourselves and our governing communities in the process.

There is nothing that compels us to continue in this direction, other than power politics, international treaties, national laws, and national salvation-logics. But we do not need to accept these as they are. We can reach into their deeper meanings in an effort to reform and transform them.

History teaches us that developmental trajectories can be turned in new directions. But none of us alone can accomplish this. Only by working together toward a new conception of our national projects in a world constituted by national states will we be able to protect ourselves against a dehumanizing logic of ever-expanding economic growth. Recognition of human creativity and inventive capacities should surely be part of any alternative legal frameworks that we might build.

But intellectual property, in any of its current forms, cannot be considered sacred by anyone whose worldview is informed by Biblical law. As I have tried to show, worldviews informed by Biblical law extend much more widely than we might initially recognize, but for many of my fellow Americans, the Bible is in any case an avowed rule of life. To those Americans, I plead as an insider, as someone who also sees ultimate significance in Biblical law, as affirmed and interpreted in the life, death, and resurrection of Jesus of Nazareth. To them I ask, rhetorically: can the treatment of any form of property as sacred, except where it is recognized as a gift from God, be anything other than idolatry?

Speaking to all readers of this book, regardless of worldview, I can only plead that we think afresh about the extent to which we often prioritize economic growth above all else, in our policy-making discussions, and the degree to which we treat intellectual property as an inevitable part of our nation-state system. As computers take over all aspects of our social lives, we should question anew intellectual property protections for software-implemented inventions, especially where the details of the software programming are not actually disclosed, as is often the case with software-related patent claims.

The conversation being enabled right now through the World Intellectual Property Organization, concerning intellectual property protections for artificial intelligence, is an important one, and it is one that I hope many more people will join.

Intellectual property is playing a vitally important role in contemporary forms of social power, whether these are cultural, economic, military, or political. In democratically constituted nation-states, and in a nationally constituted world system, we need urgently to think together about this.

I hope that this book will be helpful in inviting more people to join the discussion and debate.

Index

CPSIA information can be obtained
at www.ICGtesting.com
Printed in the USA
LVHW010829190821
695649LV00001B/104

9 781107 198975